NCERT

SOLUTIONS

PHYSICS

CLASS 12th

NCERT
SOLUTIONS

PHYSICS

CLASS 12th

by
Nidhi Goel

arihant

ARIHANT PRAKASHAN, MEERUT

ARIHANT PRAKASHAN, MEERUT

All rights reserved

卐 Administrative & Production Offices

Corporate Office: 'Ramchhaya' 4577/15, Agarwal Road, Darya Ganj, New Delhi -110002
Tele: 011- 47630600, 43518550; Fax: 011- 23280316

Head Office: Kalindi, TP Nagar, Meerut (UP) - 250002
Tele: 0121-2401479, 2512970, 4004199; Fax: 0121-2401648

All disputes subject to Meerut (UP) jurisdiction only.

卐 Sales & Support Offices

Agra, Ahmedabad, Bengaluru, Bhubaneswar, Bareilly, Chennai, Delhi, Guwahati, Haldwani Hyderabad, Jaipur, Jalandhar, Jhansi, Kolkata, Kota, Lucknow, Meerut, Nagpur & Pune

卐 ISBN 978-93-5141-611-1

卐 Price : ₹ 145
Typeset by Arihant DTP Unit at Meerut

PRINTED & BOUND BY
ARIHANT PUBLICATIONS (I) LTD. (PRESS UNIT)

For further information about the products from Arihant
log on to **www.arihantbooks.com** or email to **info@arihantbooks.com**

Preface

Feeling the immense importance and value of NCERT books, we are presenting this book, having the NCERT Exercises Solutions.

For the overall benefit of the students we have made this book unique in such a way that it presents not only solutions but also detailed explanations. Through these detailed and through explanations, students can learn the concepts which will enhance their thinking and learning abilities.

We have introduced some **Additional Features** with the solutions which are given below :

Thinking Process ( ) Before giving solutions to questions we have discussed the points that tell how to approach to solve a problem. Here we have tried to cover all those loopholes which may lead to confusion. All formulae and hints are discussed in full detail.

Note We have provided notes also to solutions in which special points are mentioned which are of great value for the students.

This book also covers Solutions to selected problems of **NCERT Exemplar Problems.**

With the hope that this book will be of great help to the students, we wish great success to our readers.

Nidhi Goel

Contents

Chapter 1

Electric Charges and Fields

Important Results

1. Quantisation principle $q = \pm\, ne$, where n is the number of electrons.

2. Coulomb's law $F_{\text{vac}} = \dfrac{1}{4\pi\varepsilon_0} \cdot \dfrac{q_1 q_2}{r^2}$; $F_{\text{med}} = \dfrac{1}{4\pi\varepsilon_0\, K} \cdot \dfrac{q_1 q_2}{r^2}$

3. **Superposition principle** Resultant force on a point charge due to a number of point charges. :
$$\mathbf{F}_0 = \mathbf{F}_{01} + \mathbf{F}_{02} + \mathbf{F}_{03} + \ldots + \mathbf{F}_{0n}$$

4. Electric field $E = \dfrac{1}{4\pi\varepsilon_0}\dfrac{q}{r^2}, \ \mathbf{F} = q_0\,\mathbf{E}$

5. **Superposition principle** Resultant electric field on a point due to a number of point charges
$$\mathbf{E}_0 = \mathbf{E}_{01} + \mathbf{E}_{02} + \mathbf{E}_{03} + \ldots + \mathbf{E}_{0n}$$

6. Dipole moment $\mathbf{p} = q \times 2\mathbf{a}$
Its direction is from negative charge towards positive charge.

7. Electric field intensity on axial line of dipole
$$\mathbf{E}_{\text{axial}} = \dfrac{1}{4\pi\varepsilon_0} \cdot \dfrac{2\,pr}{(r^2 - a^2)^2}$$

8. Electric field intensity on equitorial line of dipole
$$\mathbf{E}_{\text{eq}} = \dfrac{1}{4\pi\varepsilon_0} \cdot \dfrac{\mathbf{p}}{(r^2 + a^2)^{3/2}}$$

9. Electric field intensity at any point due to a short dipole
$$\mathbf{E} = \dfrac{1}{4\pi\varepsilon_0}\, \mathbf{p}\, \sqrt{3\cos^2\theta + 1}$$

10. Torque on dipole $\tau = \mathbf{p} \times \mathbf{E}$ or $\tau = pE\sin\theta$

11. Potential energy of dipole in electric field $U = -\,\mathbf{p}.\mathbf{E}$

12. Gauss's theorem $\phi_E = \oint \mathbf{E}\cdot d\mathbf{S} = E\, dS \cos\theta = \dfrac{q}{\varepsilon_0}$

13. Electric field intensity due to a line charge $E = \dfrac{\lambda}{2\pi\varepsilon_0 r}$

14. Electric field intensity due to a thin infinite plane sheet of charge

$$E = \dfrac{\sigma}{2\varepsilon_0}$$

15. Electric field intensity due to a thick sheet $E = \dfrac{\sigma}{\varepsilon_0}$

16. Electric field intensity at a point on the surface or outside a charged spherical shell.

$$E = \dfrac{1}{4\pi\varepsilon_0}\dfrac{Q}{r^2}$$

where, $r = R$ on the surface.

17. Electric field intensity at a point inside a charged solid non-conducting sphere

$$E = \dfrac{\rho r}{3\varepsilon}$$

where, $\rho = $ charge density per volume and $r = $ radius

18. Electric field intensity inside a charged spherical shell

$$E = 0$$

Exercises

Question 1.   What is the force between two small charged spheres having charges of 2×10^{-7} C and 3×10^{-7} C placed 30 cm apart in air?

Solution   Let us consider two charges q_1 and q_2. According to the question, $q_1 = 2 \times 10^{-7}$C, $q_2 = 3 \times 10^{-7}$C

Distance between q_1 and q_2, $d = 30$ cm $= 0.3$ m

Using Coulomb's law, the force between two charges is given by

$$F = \dfrac{1}{4\pi\varepsilon_0} \cdot \dfrac{q_1 q_2}{d^2}$$

(The charges are placed in air, so we have neglected dielectric constant k, became in air $k = 1$)

Putting the values of $\dfrac{1}{4\pi\varepsilon_0}$, q_1, q_2 and d, we get

$$F = \dfrac{9 \times 10^9 \times 2 \times 10^{-7} \times 3 \times 10^{-7}}{0.3 \times 0.3} = \dfrac{9 \times 2 \times 3 \times 10^{-5}}{3 \times 3 \times 10^{-2}} = 6 \times 10^{-3} \text{ N}$$

As the two charges q_1 and q_2 both are positive in nature. So, they repel each other as like charges repel each other.

Question 2. The electrostatic force on a small sphere of charge $0.4\,\mu C$ due to another small sphere of charge $-0.8\,\mu C$ in air is 0.2 N.

(a) What is the distance between the two spheres?

(b) What is the force on the second sphere due to the first?

Solution Let us consider two charges q_1 and q_2. According to the question, $q_1 = 0.4\,\mu C$, $q_2 = -0.8\,\mu C$

Let the distance between two charges be r. Force on charge q_1 $(0.4\,\mu C)$ due to another charge q_2 $(-0.8\,\mu C)$ is

$$F = 0.2 \text{ N}.$$

(a) We have to find the value of r. Using Coulomb's law, the force between two charges is

$$F = \frac{1}{4\pi\varepsilon_0} \cdot \frac{q_1 q_2}{r^2}$$

Putting the values of F, $\dfrac{1}{4\pi\varepsilon_0}$, q_1 and q_2, we get

$$0.2 = 9 \times 10^9 \times \frac{0.4 \times 10^{-6} \times 0.8 \times 10^{-6}}{r^2}$$

$$r^2 = 16 \times 9 \times 10^{-4}$$

$$r = 4 \times 3 \times 10^{-2}$$

$$r = 12 \times 10^{-2} \text{ m}$$

$$r = 12 \text{ cm}$$

Here, the charge q_2 is negative in nature and q_1 is positive in nature. So, the force between q_1 and q_2 will be attractive in nature as unlike charges attract each other.

(b) The force of attraction on the second sphere due to the first sphere as the force between the two charges *i.e.*, 0.2 N. The electrostatic force between two charges is interactive force that means force on q_1 due to q_2 is same as force on q_2 due to q_1 is same. Electrostatic force between two changes obeys the Newton's third law of action-reaction law.

Question 3. Check that the ratio $ke^2/G\,m_e m_p$ is dimensionless. Look up a table of physical constants and determine the value of this ratio. What does the ratio signify?

Solution In the ratio $\dfrac{ke^2}{Gm_e m_p}$, $k = 4\pi\varepsilon_0$ (constant)

where, G = gravitational constant

m_e = mass of an electron

m = mass of a proton

From Coulomb's law

$$F = k\,\frac{q_1 q_2}{r^2} \;\Rightarrow\; k = \frac{F r^2}{q_1 q_2} \quad \text{or} \quad k = \frac{F r^2}{q^2}$$

The dimensions of $k = \left(\dfrac{1}{4\pi\varepsilon_0}\right) = \dfrac{[\text{MLT}^{-2}][\text{L}^2]}{[\text{AT}]\,[\text{AT}]} = [\text{ML}^3\text{T}^{-4}\text{A}^{-2}]$

The dimensions of e (electronic charge) $= [\text{AT}]$

The dimensions of G (universal gravitational constant)

$$= \frac{[\text{MLT}^{-2}]\,[\text{L}^2]}{[\text{M}^2]} = [\text{M}^{-1}\text{L}^3\text{T}^{-2}]$$

The dimensions of m_e or m_p (mass of electron or mass of proton) $= [\text{M}]$

The dimensions of $\dfrac{ke^2}{G\,m_e m_p} = \dfrac{[\text{ML}^3\text{T}^{-4}\text{A}^{-2}]\,[\text{A}^2\text{T}^2]}{[\text{M}^{-1}\text{L}^3\text{T}^{-2}]\,[\text{M}^2]} = [\text{M}^0\text{L}^0\text{T}^0]$

Thus, the given ratio is dimensionless.

The value of $k = \left(\dfrac{1}{4\pi\varepsilon_0}\right) = 9 \times 10^9 \;\text{N-m}^2/\text{C}^2$

The value of e (charge of an electron) $= 1.6 \times 10^{-19}\,\text{C}$

The value of G (universal gravitational constant) $= 6.67 \times 10^{-11}\,\text{N-m}^2/\text{kg}^2$

The value of m_e (mass of electron) $= 9.1 \times 10^{-31}\,\text{kg}$

The value of m_p (mass of proton) $= 1.67 \times 10^{-27}\,\text{kg}$

The value of $\dfrac{ke^2}{G\,m_e m_p} = \dfrac{9 \times 10^9 \times (1.6 \times 10^{-19})^2}{6.67 \times 10^{-11} \times 9.1 \times 10^{-31} \times 1.67 \times 10^{-27}}$

$$= 2.29 \times 10^{39}$$

The ratio signifies that the ratio of electrostatic force to the gravitational force is 2.29×10^{39}. This means the electrostatic force between an electron and a proton is 2.29×10^{39} times the gravitational force between an electron and a proton.

Question 4. (a) Explain the meaning of the statement 'electric charge of a body is quantized'.

(b) Why can one ignore quantization of electric charge when dealing with macroscopic, *i.e.*, large scale charges?

Solution

(a) The electric charge of a body is quantized means that the charge on a body can occur in some particular values only. Charge on any body is the integral multiple of charge on an electron because the charge of an electron is the elementary charge in nature. The charge on any body can be expressed by the formula

$$q = \pm\, ne$$

where, n = number of electrons transferred

and e = charge on one electron.

The cause of quantization is that only integral number of electrons can be transferred from one body to other.

(b) We can ignore the quantization of electric charge when dealing with macroscopic charges because the charge on one electron is 1.6×10^{-19} C in magnitude, which is very small as compared to the large scale change.

Question 5. When a glass rod is rubbed with a silk cloth, charges appear on both. A similar phenomenon is observed with many other pairs of bodies. Explain how this observation is consistent with the law of conservation of charge.

Solution According to the law of conservation of charge, "charge can neither be created nor be destroyed but can be transferred from one body to another body".

Before rubbing the two bodies they both are neutral *i.e.*, the total charge of the system is zero. When the glass rod is rubbed with a silk cloth, the charge appears on both glass rod and the silk cloth. Some electrons from glass rod are transferred to silk cloth hence glass rod attains positive charge (due to loss of electrons) and silk cloth attains same negative charge (due to gain of electrons).

Again the total charge of the system is zero, *i.e.*, the charge before rubbing is same as the charge after rubbing. This is consistent with the law of conservation of charge. Here, we can also say that changes can be created only inequal and unlike pairs.

Question 6. Four point charges $q_A = 2\,\mu$C, $q_B = -5\,\mu$C, $q_C = 2\,\mu$C, and $q_D = -5\,\mu$C are located at the corners of a square $ABCD$ of side 10 cm. What is the force on a charge of $1\,\mu$C placed at the centre of the square?

Charge placed at the centre is in the influence field of four charges located at the corners of the square. Therefore, we can find force acting on charge placed at the centre using superposition principle. Use the law of vectors to find the net resultant force because force is a vector quantity.

Solution Let the centre of the square is at O. The charge placed on the centre is $1\,\mu$C.

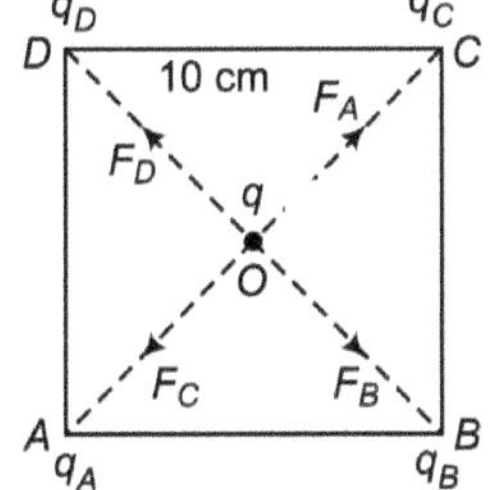

$$AB = BC = CD = DA = 10 \text{ cm}$$
$$AC = \sqrt{2} \times 10 = 10\sqrt{2} \text{ cm}$$
$$AC = BD = 10\sqrt{2} \text{ cm}$$
$$AO = BO = CO = DO = \frac{10\sqrt{2}}{2} = 5\sqrt{2} \text{ cm}$$

Let the force on charge 1μC due to q_A is F_A which away from both charges q_A and q (because both charges are positive in nature, so will repel each other).

The force on charge $1\mu C$ due to q_C is F_C which away from both q_C and q (as they both are positive in nature, so will repel each other).

The force on charge $1\mu C$ due to q_B is F_B which is towards q_B (because q_B is negatively charged and q is positively charged, so will attract each other).

The force on charge $1\mu C$ due to q_D is F_D which is towards q_D (because q_D is negatively charged and q is positively charged, so will attract each other).

Force between q and q_A

$$F_A = \frac{1}{4\pi\varepsilon_0}\cdot\frac{qq_A}{(OA)^2} = \frac{9\times10^9\times1\times10^{-6}\times2\times10^{-6}}{(5\sqrt{2}\times10^{-2})^2} = \frac{9\times2\times10^{-3}}{25\times2\times10^{-4}}$$

$$F_A = \frac{90}{25} = \frac{18}{5} = 3.6\ \text{N} \qquad\qquad \text{(direction towards } O \text{ to } C)$$

Force between q and q_C

$$F_C = \frac{1}{4\pi\varepsilon_0}\cdot\frac{qq_C}{(OC)^2} = \frac{9\times19^9\times1\times10^{-6}\times2\times10^{-6}}{(5\sqrt{2}\times10^{-2})^2} = \frac{9\times2\times10^{-3}}{25\times2\times10^{-4}}$$

$$F_C = \frac{90}{25} = \frac{18}{5} = 3.6\ \text{N} \qquad\qquad \text{(direction towards } O \text{ to } A)$$

Here, we observe that F_A and F_C are of same magnitude and opposite in direction. So, the resultant force of F_A and F_C is zero.

Force between q and q_B

$$F_B = \frac{1}{4\pi\varepsilon_0}\cdot\frac{qq_B}{(OB)^2} = \frac{9\times10^9\times1\times10^{-6}\times2\times10^{-6}}{(5\sqrt{2}\times10^{-2})^2} = 3.6\ \text{N}$$

$$\text{(direction towards } O \text{ to } B)$$

Force between q and q_D

$$F_D = \frac{1}{4\pi\varepsilon_0}\cdot\frac{qq_D}{(OD)^2} = \frac{9\times10^9\times1\times10^{-6}\times2\times10^{-6}}{(5\sqrt{2}\times10^{-2})^2} = 3.6\ \text{N}$$

$$\text{(direction towards } O \text{ to } D)$$

Here, we observe that F_B and F_D are of same magnitude and opposite in direction. So, the resultant force of F_D and F_B is zero.

Thus, the net resultant force on $1\mu C$ (placed at O) is zero as all the forces balances each other.

Question 7.   **(a) An electrostatic field line is a continuous curve. That is, a field line cannot have sudden breaks. Why not?**

    (b) Explain why two field lines never cross each other at any point?

Solution

    (a) An electrostatic field line represents the actual path travelled by a unit positive charge in an electric field. If the line have sudden breaks it means the unit positive test charge jumps from one place to another which is not possible. It also means that electric field becomes zero suddenly at the breaks which is not possible. So, the field line cannot have any sudden breaks.

(b) If two field lines cross each other, then we can draw two tangents at the point of intersection which indicates that (as tangent drawn at any point on electric line of force gives the direction of electric field at that point) there are two directions of electric field at a particular point, which is not possible at the same instant. Thus, two field lines never cross each other at any point.

Question 8.   Two point charges $q_A = 3\,\mu C$ and $q_B = -3\,\mu C$ are located 20 cm apart in vacuum.

(a) What is the electric field at the mid-point O of the line AB joining the two charges?

(b) If a negative test charge of magnitude $1.5 \times 10^{-9} C$ is placed at this point, what is the force experienced by the test charge?

(a) First of all calculate the electric fields at mid-point due to both charges and then find the resultant electric field by vector addition.

(b) Force on a charge in an electric field is $F = qE$.

Solution   (a) $AB = 20\,cm$

$$AO = OB = 10\,cm = 0.1\,m$$

$$q_A = 3\,\mu C = 3 \times 10^{-6} C,$$

$$q_B = -3\,\mu C = -3 \times 10^{-6} C$$

The electric field at a point due to a charge q is $E = \dfrac{1}{4\pi\varepsilon_0} \cdot \dfrac{q}{r^2}$

where, r is the distance between charge and the point.

Electric field due to q_A at O is E_A.

$$E_A = \frac{1}{4\pi\varepsilon_0} \cdot \frac{q_A}{(AO)^2}$$

$$E_A = \frac{9 \times 10^9 \times 3 \times 10^{-6}}{(0.1)^2} = \frac{27 \times 10^3}{0.1 \times 0.1} = 2.7 \times 10^{-6}\ \text{N/C}$$

The direction of E_A is A to O i.e., towards O or towards OB as the electric field is always directed away from positive charge.

Electric field due to q_B at O is E_B.

$$E_B = \frac{1}{4\pi\varepsilon_0} \cdot \frac{q_B}{(OB)^2}$$

$$E_B = \frac{9 \times 10^9 \times 3 \times 10^{-6}}{(0.1)^2} = \frac{27 \times 10^3}{0.1 \times 0.1} = 2.7 \times 10^6\ \text{N/C}$$

The direction of E_B is O to B i.e., towards O or towards OB as the electric field is always directed towards the negative charge.

Now, we see that both E_A and E_B are in same direction. So, the resultant electric field at O is E. Hence,

$$E = E_A + E_B = 2.7 \times 10^6 + 2.7 \times 10^6 = 5.4 \times 10^6 \text{ N/C}$$

The direction of E (resultant electric field) will be from O to B or towards B.

(b) Let us consider, the charge q is placed at the mid-point O. According to the question,

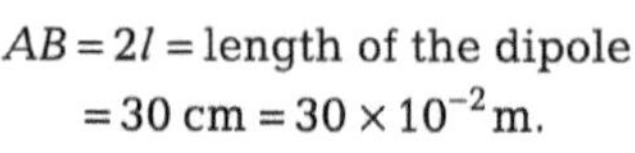

$$q = -1.5 \times 10^{-9} \text{C}$$

By the basic definition of electric field,

$$E = \frac{F}{q}$$

or $F = qE$, where, E is the net electric field at point O.

$$F = -1.5 \times 10^{-9} \times 5.4 \times 10^6 = -8.1 \times 10^{-3} \text{N}$$

The direction of force is opposite to the direction of field because the charge q is negatively charged. Thus, the direction of force is from O to A.

Question 9. A system has two charges $q_A = 2.5 \times 10^{-7} \text{C}$ and $q_B = -2.5 \times 10^{-7} \text{C}$ located at points A (0, 0, –15 cm) and B (0, 0, +15 cm), respectively. What are the total charge and electric dipole moment of the system?

Solution Given A (0, 0, –15 cm) and B (0, 0, 15 cm)

$$q_A = 2.5 \times 10^{-7} \text{C}$$

$$q_B = -2.5 \times 10^{-7} \text{C}$$

The distance between A and B is the length of dipole (because q_A and q_B are same in magnitude and opposite in nature, so they form a dipole).

$$AB = 2l = \text{length of the dipole}$$

$$= 30 \text{ cm} = 30 \times 10^{-2} \text{m}.$$

The total charge q on the dipole is

$$q = q_A + q_B = 2.5 \times 10^{-7} - 2.5 \times 10^{-7} \text{C} = 0$$

The electric dipole moment $p = $ Any charge $\times$ Length of the dipole

$$p = q_A \times 2l = 2.5 \times 10^{-7} \times 30 \times 10^{-2}$$

$$p = 7.5 \times 10^{-8} \text{C-m}$$

The direction of the dipole moment is always from negative charge to positive charge that is along B to A.

Question 10. An electric dipole with dipole moment 4×10^{-9} C-m is aligned at $30°$ with the direction of a uniform electric field of magnitude 5×10^4 N/C. Calculate the magnitude of the torque acting on the dipole.

Solution   Given, dipole moment $p = 4 \times 10^{-9}$ C-m

Electric field $E = 5 \times 10^4$ N/C

θ = Angle between electric field and the dipole moment = $30°$

Torque applied on a dipole in the electric field

$$\tau = \mathbf{p} \times \mathbf{E} = pE \sin \theta$$

or $$\tau = 4 \times 10^{-9} \times 5 \times 10^4 \sin 30° = \frac{20 \times 10^{-5}}{2} = 10^{-4} \text{N-m}$$

The direction of torque is perpendicular to both electric field and dipole moment.

Question 11. A polythene piece rubbed with wool is found to have a negative charge of 3×10^{-7}C.

(a) Estimate the number of electrons transferred (from which to which)?

(b) Is there a transfer of mass from wool to polythene?

> The charge on a body in terms of number of electrons loss or gained by it is given $q = \pm ne$. If electrons are lost then charge obtained will be positive and if electrons are gained then charge obtained will be negative. We should also keep in mind that a material particle always has some mass.

Solution   Given, charge on polythene $= -3 \times 10^{-7}$C

(a) The charge on an object is given by $q = \pm ne$

The number of electrons transferred $n = \dfrac{\text{Total charge } (q)}{\text{Charge of electron } (e)}$

$$n = \frac{-3 \times 10^{-7}}{-1.6 \times 10^{-19}} = 1.875 \times 10^{12}$$

Thus, the number of electrons transferred is 1.875×10^{12}. Electrons will be transferred from wool to polythene because polythene attains the negative charge that means it gains the electrons.

(b) As the electrons are transferred from wool to polythene, the mass is also transferred because along with the charge each electron will also carry its mass.

The number of electrons transferred $= 1.875 \times 10^{12}$

The mass of one electron $= 9.1 \times 10^{-3}$ kg

Mass transferred from wool to polythene

$$= \text{Number of electrons} \times \text{Mass of one electron}$$
$$= 1.875 \times 10^{12} \times 9.1 \times 10^{-31} = 1.8 \times 10^{-18} \text{ kg}$$

Thus, 1.8×10^{-18} kg mass is transferred from wool to polythene.

Question 12. (a) Two insulated charged copper spheres A and B have their centres separated by a distance of 50 cm. What is the mutual force of electrostatic repulsion if the charge on each is 6.5×10^{-7} C? The radii of A and B are negligible compared to the distance of separation.

(b) What is the force of repulsion if each sphere is charged double the above amount and the distance between them is halved?

Solution (a) Let us consider, the charge on sphere A is q_A and on sphere B is q_B. According to the question,

$$q_A = 6.5 \times 10^{-7} \text{C}$$

$$q_B = 6.5 \times 10^{-7} \text{C}$$

$r =$ distance between A and B $= 50$ cm $= 50 \times 10^{-2}$ m

From the Coulomb's law, the force between the two spheres is

$$F = \frac{1}{4\pi\varepsilon_0} \cdot \frac{q_A q_B}{r^2} = \frac{9 \times 10^9 \times 6.5 \times 10^{-7} \times 6.5 \times 10^{-7}}{(50 \times 10^{-2})^2}$$

$$= \frac{9 \times 6.5 \times 6.5 \times 10^{-5}}{50 \times 50 \times 10^{-4}} = 1.521 \times 10^{-2} \text{ N}$$

Thus, the force between A and B is 1.521×10^{-2} N, this force is repulsive in nature because the charges are similar (positive) in nature.

(b) According to the question, if the charge is doubled

$$q_A' = 2q_A \quad \text{and} \quad q_B' = 2q_B$$

Distance between them is halved *i.e.*, $r' = \dfrac{r}{2}$

Now, the force between the two spheres is

$$F' = \frac{1}{4\pi\varepsilon_0} \cdot \frac{q_A' q_B'}{r'} = \frac{1}{4\pi\varepsilon_0} \frac{(2\,q_A)(2\,q_B)}{(r/2)^2} = \frac{1}{4\pi\varepsilon_0} \cdot \frac{4q_A q_B}{r^2/4}$$

$$= 16\,\frac{1}{4\pi\varepsilon_0}\,\frac{q_A q_B}{r^2} = 16\,F = 16 \times 1.521 \times 10^{-2} = 0.24 \text{ N}$$

This force is also repulsive in nature because both the charges are similar (positive) in nature.

Question 13. Suppose the spheres A and B in Q. 12 have identical sizes. A third sphere of the same size but uncharged is brought in contact with the first, then brought in contact with the second, and finally removed from both. What is the new force of repulsion between A and B?

It is based on the distribution of charges when the two identical bodies come into contact, charge is distributed equally on identical bodies.

Solution Now, the sphere C comes in contact with A, the charges will be divided equally on both spheres as they have same mass and size.

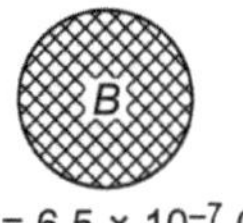

Now, charge on A is

$$q_A' = \frac{q_A + q_C}{2} = \frac{6.5 \times 10^{-7} + 0}{2}$$

$$q_A' = 3.25 \times 10^{-7}\text{C}$$

Now, the charge on C will also be $3.25 \times 10^{-7}\text{C}$

$$\therefore \qquad q_C' = 3.25 \times 10^{-7}\text{C}$$

Now, the sphere C comes in contact with B, the charges are shared again.

Now, charge on B is $q_B' = \dfrac{q_B + q_C'}{2} = \dfrac{6.5 \times 10^{-7} + 3.25 \times 10^{-7}}{2}$

$$q_B' = 4.875 \times 10^{-7}\text{C}$$

Finally, the charge on C is $q_C' = 4.875 \times 10^{-7}$ C

Finally, the charge on A is $q_A' = 3.25 \times 10^{-7}\text{C}$

The charge on B is $q_B' = 4.875 \times 10^{-7}\text{C}$

From the Coulomb's law, the force between two spheres is

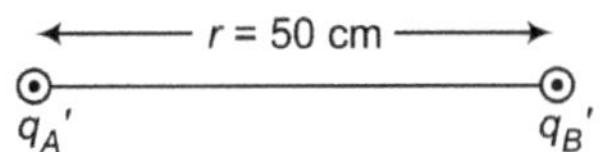

$$F = \frac{1}{4\pi\varepsilon_0} \cdot \frac{q_A' \cdot q_B'}{r^2}$$

$$= \frac{9 \times 10^9 \times 3.25 \times 10^{-7} \times 4.875 \times 10^{-7}}{(50 \times 10^{-2})^2}$$

$$= \frac{9 \times 3.25 \times 4.875 \times 10^{-5}}{50 \times 50 \times 10^{-4}}$$

$$= 5.7 \times 10^{-3}\,\text{N}$$

This force will be repulsive in nature because both spheres have like charges.

Question 14. The given figure shows tracks of three charged particles in a uniform electrostatic field. Give the signs of the three charges. Which particle has the highest charge to mass ratio?

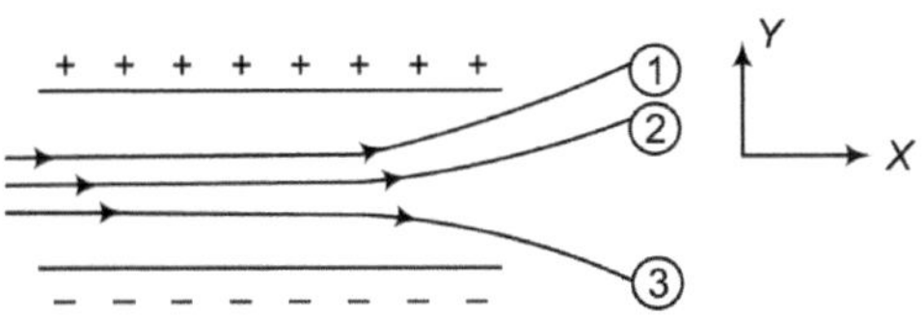

Solution We know that a positively charged particle is attracted towards the negatively charged plate and a negatively charged particle is attracted towards the positively charged plate.

Here, particle 1 and particle 2 are attracted towards positive plate that means particle 1 and particle 2 are negatively charged. Particle 3 is attracted towards negatively charged plate so it is positively charged.

As the deflection in the path of a charged particle is directly proportional to the charge/mass ratio.

$$y \propto \frac{q}{m}$$

Here, the deflection in particle 3 is maximum, so the charge to mass ratio of particle 3 is maximum.

Question 15. Consider a uniform electric field $E = 3 \times 10^3 \hat{i}$ N/C.

   (a) What is the flux of this field through a square of 10 cm on a side whose plane is parallel to the *Y-Z* plane?

   (b) What is the flux through the same square if the normal to its plane makes a 60° angle with the *X*-axis?

Solution Electric field $\mathbf{E} = 3 \times 10^3 \hat{i}$ N/C, *i.e.*, electric field is directed towards X-axis (due to involvement of $\hat{i}$).

  (a) As the surface is in Y-Z plane, so the area vector (normal to the square) is along X-axis.

$$\text{Area } S = 10 \times 10 = 100 \text{ cm}^2 = 10^{-2} \text{ m}^2$$

Area vector $\mathbf{S} = 10^{-2} \hat{i} \text{ m}^2$

Using the formula of electric flux

$$\phi = \mathbf{E} \cdot \mathbf{S} = ES \cos \theta$$
$$= ES \qquad [\because \text{ angle between } \mathbf{E} \text{ and } \mathbf{S} \text{ is } 0°]$$
$$\phi = 3 \times 10^3 \times 10^{-2} = 30 \text{ N-m}^2/\text{C}$$

  (b) Now, the area vector makes an angle of 60° with X-axis.

$$\mathbf{E} = 3 \times 10^3 \hat{i} \text{ N/C}$$
$$\mathbf{S} = 100 \text{ cm}^2 = 10^{-2} \text{ m}^2, \ \theta = 60°$$

Using the formula of electric flux $\phi = \mathbf{E} \cdot \mathbf{S}$

$$\phi = ES \cos \theta = 3 \times 10^3 \times 10^{-2} \cos 60° = 3 \times 10 \times \frac{1}{2} = 15 \text{ N-m}^2/\text{C}$$

Note *Remember that the direction of area vector is always perpendicular to the area of a face.*

Question 16. What is the net flux of the uniform electric field of Q.15 through a cube of side 20 cm oriented so that its faces are parallel to the coordinate planes?

Solution As we know that the number of lines entering in the cube is the same as that the number of lines leaving the cube. So, no flux is remained on the cube and hence, the net flux over the cube is zero.

Question 17. Careful measurement of the electric field at the surface of a black box indicates that the net outward flux through the surface of the box is 8.0×10^3 N-m^2/C.

    (a) What is the net charge inside the box?

    (b) If the net outward flux through the surface of the box were zero, could you conclude that there were no charges inside the box? Why or why not?

Here we have to find the net electric charge inside a box and we have the total outward flux through it, so we have to apply Gauss's theorem.

Solution Using the concept of Gauss's theorem,

(a) Given, Net outward flux $\phi = 8.0 \times 10^3$ N-m^2/C

    We know that

$$\text{Net flux } \phi = \frac{\text{Charge}}{\varepsilon_0} = \frac{q}{\varepsilon_0} \Rightarrow q = \varepsilon_0 \phi = 8.854 \times 10^{-12} \times 10^3$$

    From Gauss's theorem $q = 0.07 \times 10^{-6}$ C $= 0.07\,\mu$C

    The flux is outward hence the charge is positive in nature.

(b) Net outward flux $= 0$

    Then, we can conclude that the net charge inside the box is zero, *i.e.*, the box may have either zero charge or have equal amount of positive and negative charges. It means we cannot conclude that there is no charge inside the box.

Question 18. A point charge $+10\,\mu$C is at a distance 5 cm directly above the centre of a square of side 10 cm, as shown in figure. What is the magnitude of the electric flux through the square?

(Hint : Think of the square as one face of a cube with edge 10 cm.)

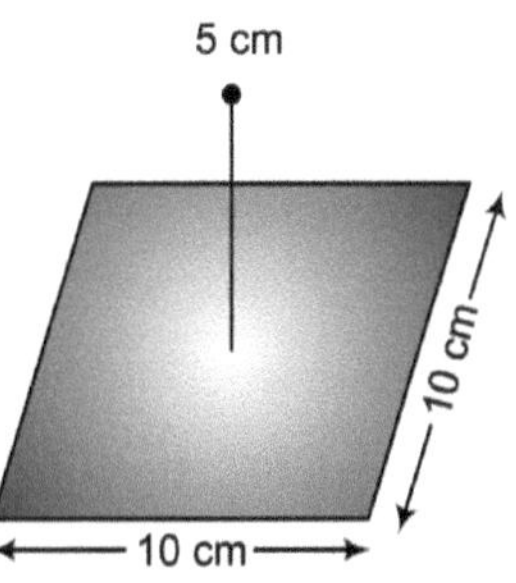

Electric flux linked with a surface can be calculated using Gauss's theorem, according to which total electric flux linked with a closed surface is $\dfrac{q}{\varepsilon_0}$.

Solution Now, we imagine an enclosed cubical surface and the given square be one side of this cubical surface. Let the charge q is placed at the centre of cube. Now, the figure looks like

The total flux enclosed through the cube is

$$\phi = \frac{q}{\varepsilon_0} \qquad \ldots(i)$$

[According to Gauss's theorem]

Here, $q = 10\,\mu$C

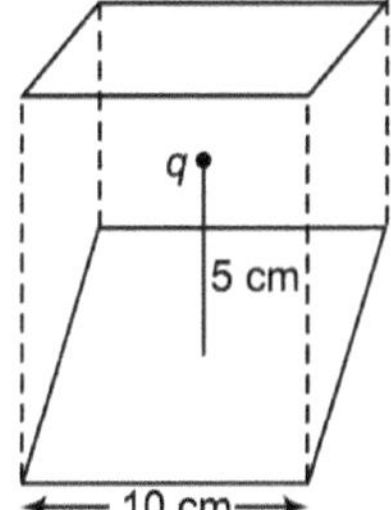

The flux enclosed by one face *i.e.,* square is 1/6 of total flux (because the cube has six square shaped faces), so
The flux linked with each square

$$\phi' = \frac{\phi}{6} = \frac{1}{6} \cdot \frac{q}{\varepsilon_0} \qquad \text{[From Eq. (i)]}$$

$$\phi' = \frac{1}{6} \times \frac{10 \times 10^{-6}}{8.854 \times 10^{-12}}$$

$$= 1.88 \times 10^5 \text{ N-m}^2/\text{C}$$

Thus, the flux linked with the square is 1.88×10^5 N-m^2/C.

Question 19. A point charge of $2.0\,\mu$C is at the centre of a cubic Gaussian surface 9.0 cm on edge. What is the net electric flux through the surface?

 Electric flux linked with a surface can be calculated using Gauss's theorem according to which total electric flux linked with a closed surface is given by $\phi = \dfrac{q}{\varepsilon_0}$.

Solution   Let us consider a charge q is placed at the centre of a cubic Gaussian surface. As per the question, $q = 2\,\mu\text{C} = 2 \times 10^{-6}\,\text{C}$

Length of edge $= 9$ cm

According to Gauss's theorem, the net electric flux (ϕ) through the surface is

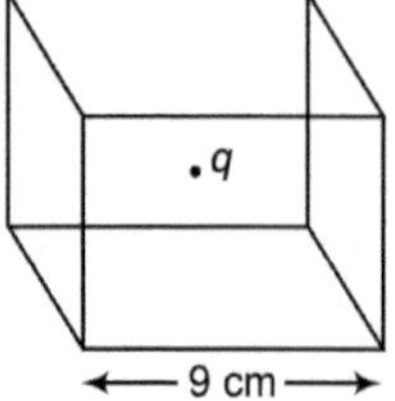

$$\phi = \frac{q}{\varepsilon_0} = \frac{2 \times 10^{-6}}{8.854 \times 10^{-12}}$$

$$= 2.26 \times 10^5 \text{ N-m}^2/\text{C}$$

Thus, the net electric flux through the surface is 2.26×10^5 N-m^2/C.

Question 20. A point charge causes an electric flux of -1.0×10^3 N-m^2/C to pass through a spherical Gaussian surface of 10.0 cm radius centred on the charge.

  (a) If the radius of the Gaussian surface were doubled, how much flux would pass through the surface?

  (b) What is the value of the point charge?

Solution

  (a) As we know the electric flux passing through any surface is independent of the radius of Gaussian surface, so if the radius of Gaussian surface were doubled, the electric flux linked with the surface remains same $\left(\phi = \dfrac{q}{\varepsilon_0}\right)$. It depends only on charge.

(b) $\phi = -1.0 \times 10^3$ N-m^2/C

Radius $= 10.0$ cm

Using Gauss's theorem,

The flux linked $\phi = \dfrac{q}{\varepsilon_0}$

$$q = \phi\varepsilon_0 = -1.0 \times 10^3 \times 8.854 \times 10^{-12} = -8.85 \times 10^{-9} \text{ C}$$

Thus, the value of point charge is -8.85×10^{-9} C.

Question 21. A conducting sphere of radius 10 cm has an unknown charge. If the electric field 20 cm from the centre of the sphere is 1.5×10^3 N/C and points radially inwards, what is the net charge on the sphere?

Solution   Let the value of unknown charge be q.

Electric field at 20 cm away $E = 1.5 \times 10^3$ N/C   (radially inwards)

From the formula, electrid field

$$E = \frac{1}{4\pi\varepsilon_0} \cdot \frac{q}{r^2} \qquad\qquad (r = \text{distance})$$

$$1.5 \times 10^3 = \frac{9 \times 10^9 \times q}{(20 \times 10^{-2})^2}$$

$$q = \frac{1.5 \times 10^3 \times 20 \times 20 \times 10^{-4}}{9 \times 10^9} = 6.67 \times 10^{-9} \text{ C}$$

As, the electric field is radially inwards which shows that the nature of unknown charge q is negative.

Question 22. A uniformly charged conducting sphere of 2.4 m diameter has a surface charge density of 80.0 μC/m^2.

(a) Find the charge on the sphere.

(b) What is the total electric flux leaving the surface of the sphere?

Solution   Given, diameter of sphere $= 2.4$ m

Radius of sphere $r = \dfrac{2.4}{2} = 1.2$ m

Surface charge density $\sigma = 80\,\mu$C/m^2

$$= 80 \times 10^{-6} \text{C/m}^2$$

(a) Surface charge density $= \dfrac{\text{Charge}}{\text{Surface area}}$

$$\sigma = \frac{q}{4\pi r^2}$$

$$q = \sigma \times 4\pi r^2 = 80 \times 10^{-6} \times 4 \times 3.14 \times 1.2 \times 1.2$$

$$q = 1.4 \times 10^{-3} \text{C}$$

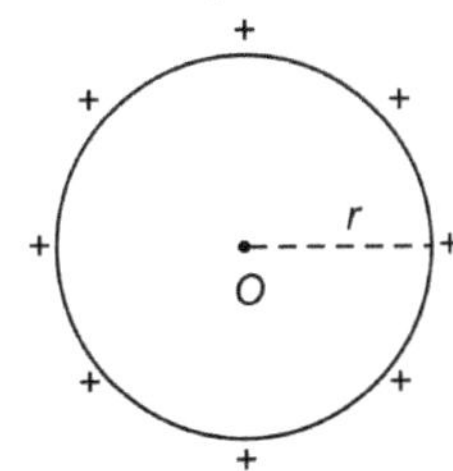

(b) Total flux $= \phi$

Using Gauss's theorem,

Total flux leaving the surface $\phi = \dfrac{\text{Total charge}}{\varepsilon_0}$

$$\phi = \frac{q}{\varepsilon_0} = \frac{1.45 \times 10^{-3}}{8.854 \times 10^{-12}}$$

$$\phi = 1.6 \times 10^{8} \ \text{N-m}^2/\text{C}$$

Thus, the flux leaving the surface of sphere is 1.6×10^{8} N-m^2/C.

Question 23. An infinite line charge produces a field of 9×10^{4} N/C at a distance of 2 cm. Calculate the linear charge density.

 To find the linear charge density, use the formula of electric field due to infinite linear charge distribution.

Solution   Let λ be the linear charge density.

Given, distance $r = 2$ cm $= 2 \times 10^{-2}$ m

Electric field $E = 9 \times 10^{4}$ N/C.

Using the formula of electric field due to an infinite line charge.

Electric field due to infinite line charge, $E = \dfrac{\lambda}{2\pi\varepsilon_0 r}$

Dividing and multiplying by 2 to get $\dfrac{1}{4\pi\varepsilon_0}$ because, we have

the value of $\dfrac{1}{4\pi\varepsilon_0}$.

$$E = \frac{2}{2} \times \frac{\lambda}{2\pi\varepsilon_0 \, r} = \frac{2\lambda}{4\pi\varepsilon_0 \, r}$$

Putting the values, we get

$$9 \times 10^{4} = \frac{2 \times 9 \times 10^{9} \times \lambda}{2 \times 10^{-2}}$$

$$\lambda = \frac{9 \times 10^{4} \times 2 \times 10^{-2}}{2 \times 9 \times 10^{9}} = 10^{-7} \ \text{C/m}$$

Thus, the linear charge density is 10^{-7} C/m.

Question 24. Two large, thin metal plates are parallel and closed to each other. On their inner faces, the plates have surface charge densities of opposite signs and of magnitude 17.0×10^{-22} C/m^2. What is E

(a) in the outer region of the first plate?

(b) in the outer region of the second plate?

(c) between the plates?

Solution There are two plates A and B having surface charge densities $\sigma_A = 1.70 \times 10^{-22}$ C/m^2 on A and $\sigma_B = -17.0 \times 10^{-22}$ C/m^2 on B respectively.

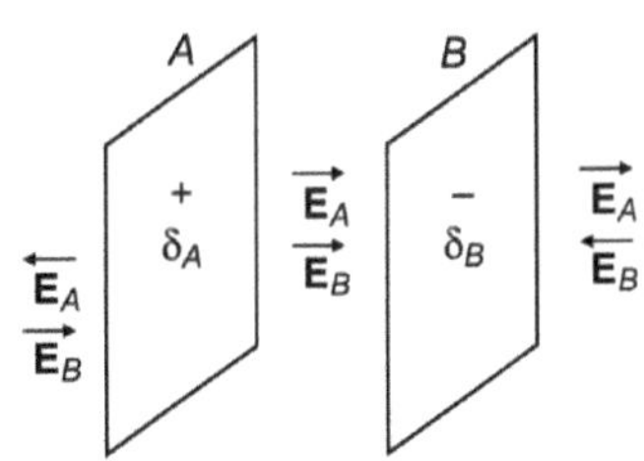

There are three regions—
Region I is the outer region of first plate.
Region II is the region between the plates.
Region III is the outer region of the second plate.

(a) According to Gauss's theorem, if the plates have same surface charge density but having opposite signs, then the electric field in region I is zero.

$$\mathbf{E_I} = \mathbf{E}_A + \mathbf{E}_B = \frac{\sigma}{2\varepsilon_0} + \left(-\frac{\sigma}{2\varepsilon_0}\right) = 0$$

(b) Similarly, the electric field in region III is also zero.

$$\mathbf{E_{III}} = \mathbf{E}_A + \mathbf{E}_B = \frac{\sigma}{2\varepsilon_0} + \left(-\frac{\sigma}{2\varepsilon_0}\right) = 0$$

(c) In region II, the electric field

$$\mathbf{E_{II}} = \mathbf{E}_A + \mathbf{E}_B = \frac{\sigma}{2\varepsilon_0} + \frac{\sigma}{2\varepsilon_0}$$

$$= \frac{\sigma}{\varepsilon_0} = \frac{\sigma_A \text{ or } \sigma_B}{\varepsilon_0} = \frac{17.0 \times 10^{-22}}{8.85 \times 10^{-12}}$$

$$E = 1.92 \times 10^{-10} \text{ N/C}$$

Additional Exercises

Question 25. An oil drop of 12 excess electrons is held stationary under a constant electric field of 2.55×10^4 N/C in Millikan's oil drop experiment. The density of the oil is 1.26 g/cm^3. Estimate the radius of the drop. ($g = 9.81$ m/s^2; $e = 1.60 \times 10^{-19}$ C).

 Here, oil drop is held stationary under electric field that means the weight of the drop is balanced by the electrostatic force applied on it.

Solution Given, the number of excess electrons $n = 12$

Electric field $E = 2.55 \times 10^4$ N/C

Density of oil $(\rho) = 1.26$ g/cm$^3 = 1.26 \times 10^3$ kg/m^3

Electronic charge $e = 1.6 \times 10^{-19}$ C

$$g = 9.81 \text{ m/s}^2$$

Let the radius of drop be r.

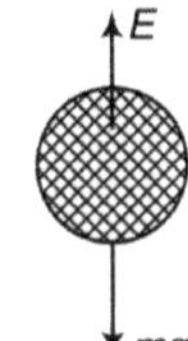

The electrostatic force on drop $= qE = neE$ $[\because q = ne]$

The gravitational force on the drop $= mg$ [where, $m =$ mass of the drop]

$$= \text{Volume} \times \text{Density} \times g$$

$$(\because \text{mass} = \text{volume} \times \text{density})$$

$$= \frac{4}{3}\pi r^3 \times \rho \times g$$

As the drop is held stationary. So, the net force on the drop is zero.

$\therefore$ Electrostatic force = Gravitational force

$$neE = \frac{4}{3}\pi r^3 \rho g$$

$$r^3 = \frac{3neE}{4\pi\rho g} = \frac{3 \times 12 \times 1.6 \times 10^{-19} \times 2.55 \times 10^4}{4 \times 3.14 \times 1.26 \times 10^3 \times 9.8}$$

$$r^3 = 0.94 \times 10^{-18}$$

$$r = (0.94 \times 10^{-18})^{1/3} = 9.81 \times 10^{-7} \text{ m}$$

Thus, the radius of the drop is 9.81×10^{-7} m.

Question 26. Which among the curves shown in figures cannot possibly represent electrostatic field lines?

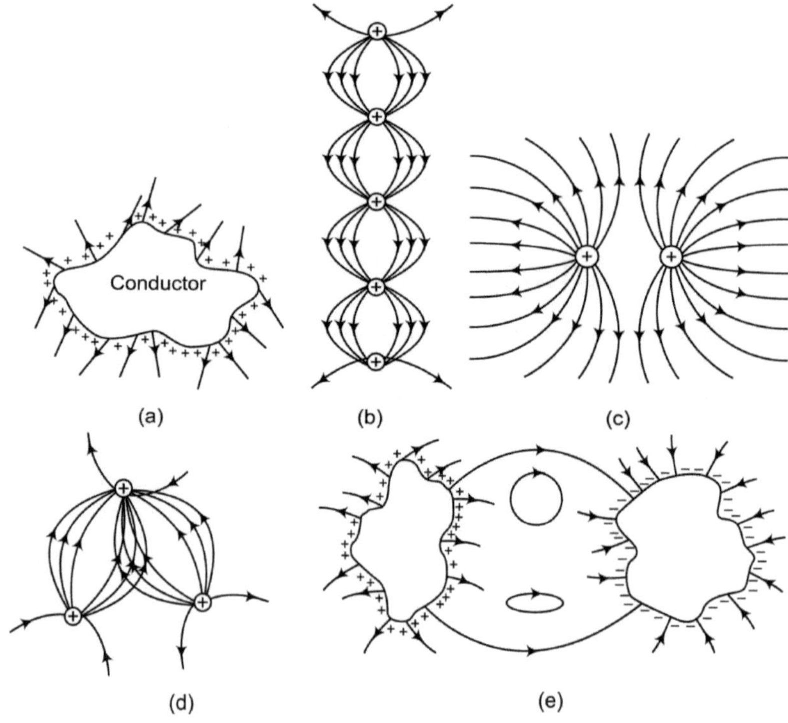

 It is based on the properties of electric field lines.

Solution

(a) According to the properties of electric lines of force, the lines should be always perpendicular to the surface of a conductor as they starts or they ends. Here, some of the lines are not perpendicular to the surface, thus it cannot represent the electrostatic field lines.

(b) According to the property of electrostatic field lines, they never start from negative charge, here some of the lines start from negative charge. So, it cannot represent the electrostatic field lines.

(c) As the property of electric field lines that they start outwards from positive charge. Hence, it represents the electrostatic field lines.

(d) By the property of electric field lines, two electric field lines never intersect each other. Here, two lines intersect so it does not represent the electric field lines.

(e) By the property of electric field lines that they are not in the form of closed loops. Here, the lines form closed loop, so it does not represent the electric field lines.

Question 27. In a certain region of space, electric field is along the Z-direction throughout. The magnitude of electric field is, however not constant but increases uniformly along the positive Z-direction, at the rate of 10^5 N/C-m. What are the force and torque experienced by a system having a total dipole moment equal to 10^{-7} C-m in the negative Z-direction?

Solution The electric field increases in positive Z-direction,

$$\frac{dE}{dZ} = 10^5 \text{ N/C-m}$$

The direction of dipole moment is in the negative Z-direction, so the negative charge q is placed at A and positive charge q is placed at B as the direction of dipole moment is from negative charge to positive charge.

$$p_Z = -10^{-7} \text{ C-m}$$

The negative sign shows its direction in negative Z-axis.

According to the basic definition of electric field,

$$F = q \cdot dE$$

Now, multiplying and dividing by dZ,

$$F = q \cdot \frac{dE}{dZ} \cdot dZ = q \cdot dZ \cdot \frac{dE}{dZ}$$

qdZ = dipole moment p_Z, as the length of the dipole is dZ.

$$\therefore \qquad F = p_Z \cdot \frac{dE}{dZ} = -10^{-7} \times 10^5 = -10^{-2} \text{ N}$$

The direction of electric field (increasing) is in positive Z-axis and the direction of dipole moment is in negative Z-axis, that means the angle between electric field and dipole moment is 180°.

So, $\qquad\qquad$ Torque $= p \times E \times \sin\theta$ (θ angle between p and E)

$$\tau = pE \sin 180°$$

$$\tau = 0 \qquad\qquad\qquad (\sin 180° = 0)$$

Thus, the force is -10^{-2} N and the torque is 0.

Question 28. (a) A conductor A with a cavity as shown in Fig. (a) is given a charge Q. Show that the entire charge must appear on the outer surface of the conductor.

(b) Another conductor B with charge q is inserted into the cavity keeping B insulated from A. Show that the total charge on the outside surface of A is $Q + q$ [Fig. (b)].

(c) A sensitive instrument is to be shielded from the strong electrostatic field in its environment. Suggest a possible way.

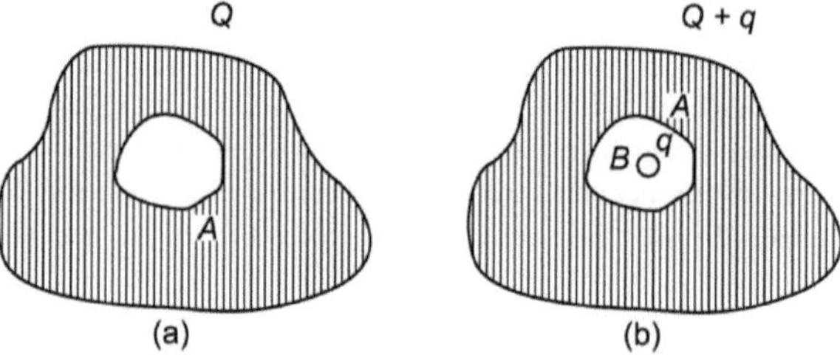

Solution

(a) As we know the property of conductor that the net electric field inside a charged conductor is zero, *i.e.*, $\mathbf{E} = 0$.

Now let us choose a Gaussian surface lying completely inside the conductor enclosing the cavity. So, from Gauss's theorem

$$\oint \mathbf{E} \cdot d\mathbf{S} = \frac{q}{\varepsilon_0}$$

As $\mathbf{E} = 0$

$$\frac{q}{\varepsilon_0} = 0$$

$$q = 0$$

That means the charge inside the cavity is zero. Thus, the entire charge Q on the conductor must appear on the outer surface of the conductor.

(b) As the conductor B carrying a charge $+q$ inserted in the cavity, the charge $-q$ is induced on the metal surface of the cavity and then charge $+q$ induced on the outside surface of the conductor A. Initially the outer surface of A has a charge Q and now it has a charge $+q$ induced, so the total charge on the outer surface of A is $Q + q$.

(c) To protect any sensitive instrument from electrostatic field, the sensitive instrument must be put in the metallic cover. This is known as electrostatic shielding.

Question 29. A hollow charged conductor has a tiny hole cut into its surface. Show that the electric field in the hole is $\left(\dfrac{\sigma}{2\varepsilon_0}\right)\hat{n}$, where $\hat{n}$ is the unit vector in the outward normal direction and σ is the surface charge density near the hole.

 Electric field due to hollow charge sphere (continuous charge distribution) can be calculated using Gauss theorem.

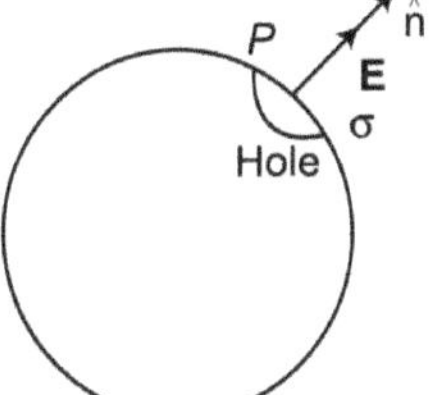

Solution Surface charge density near the hole $= \sigma$

Unit vector $= \hat{n}$ (normal directed outwards)

Let P be the point on the hole. The electric field at point P closed to the surface of conductor, according to Gauss's theorem,

$$\oint \mathbf{E}.\,d\mathbf{S} = \frac{q}{\varepsilon_0}$$

where, q is the charge near the hole.

$$E\,dS\cos\theta = \frac{\sigma dS}{\varepsilon_0}$$

$$\left(\because \sigma = q/dS \therefore q = \sigma dS \text{ where, } dS = \text{area}\right)$$

$\because$ Angle between electric field and area vector is $0°$.

$$\therefore \qquad E\,dS = \frac{\sigma\,dS}{\varepsilon_0}$$

$$E = \frac{\sigma}{\varepsilon_0}$$

$$\mathbf{E} = \frac{\sigma}{\varepsilon_0}\,\hat{\mathbf{n}}$$

This electric field is due to the filled up hole and the field due to the rest of the charged conductor. The two fields inside the conductor are equal and opposite. So, there is no electric field inside the conductor. Outside the conductor, the electric fields are equal and are in the same direction.

So, the electric field at P due to each part $= \dfrac{1}{2}\mathbf{E} = \dfrac{\sigma}{2\varepsilon_0}\,\hat{\mathbf{n}}$

Question 30. Obtain the formula for the electric field due to a long thin wire of uniform linear charge density λ without using Gauss's law.

[Hint : Use Coulomb's law directly and evaluate the necessary integral.]

Solution Let us consider a long thin wire of linear charge density λ. We have to find the resultant electric field due to this wire at point P.

Let $\qquad\qquad\qquad\qquad PC = r$

Now, consider a very small element of length dx at a distance x from C.

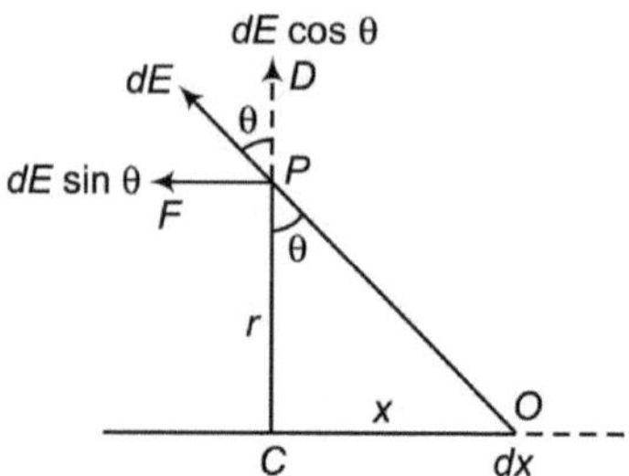

The charge on this elementary portion of length dx

$$q = \lambda\, dx \qquad \ldots(i)$$

Electric field intensity at point P due to the elementary portion

$$dE = \frac{1}{4\pi\varepsilon_0} \cdot \frac{q}{(OP)^2} = \frac{1}{4\pi\varepsilon_0} \cdot \frac{\lambda dx}{(OP)^2} \qquad \text{[From Eq. (i)]}$$

Now, in $\Delta\, PCO$

$$(PO)^2 = (PC)^2 + (CO)^2$$

$$(OP)^2 = r^2 + x^2$$

$$\therefore \qquad dE = \frac{1}{4\pi\varepsilon_0} \cdot \frac{\lambda dx}{(x^2 + r^2)} \qquad \ldots(ii)$$

Now, resolve the components of dE.

The component $dE \cos\theta$ is along PD and the component $dE \sin\theta$ is along PF.

Here, there are so many elementary portion, so all the $dE \sin\theta$ components balance each other. The resultant electric field at P is due to only $dE \cos\theta$ components.

The resultant electric field due to elementary component

$$dE' = dE \cos\theta$$

$$dE' = \frac{1}{4\pi\varepsilon_0} \cdot \frac{\lambda dx}{(x^2 + r^2)} \cos\theta \qquad \ldots(iii)$$

$$\text{[From Eq. (ii)]}$$

In ΔOCP, $\qquad \tan\theta = \dfrac{x}{r}$

$$x = r \tan\theta$$

Differentiating with respect to θ, we get

$$dx = r \sec^2\theta\, d\theta$$

Putting in Eq. (iii), we get

$$dE' = \frac{1}{4\pi\varepsilon_0} \cdot \frac{\lambda \cdot r \sec^2\theta d\theta \cos\theta}{(r^2 + r^2 \tan^2\theta)}$$

$$dE' = \frac{1}{4\pi\varepsilon_0} \cdot \frac{\lambda \cdot r \sec^2\theta d\theta \cos\theta}{r^2 \sec^2\theta}$$

$$dE' = \frac{1}{4\pi\varepsilon_0} \cdot \frac{\lambda}{r} \cos\theta \, d\theta$$

As the wire is of infinite length, so integrate within the limits $-\dfrac{\pi}{2}$ to $+\dfrac{\pi}{2}$, we get

$$E' = \int dE' = \frac{1}{4\pi\varepsilon_0} \cdot \frac{\lambda}{r} \int_{-\pi/2}^{\pi/2} \cos\theta \, d\theta$$

$$E' = \frac{1}{4\pi\varepsilon_0} \cdot \frac{\lambda}{r} [\sin\theta]_{-\pi/2}^{\pi/2} = \frac{1}{4\pi\varepsilon_0} \cdot \frac{\lambda}{r} \left[\sin\frac{\pi}{2} - \sin\left(-\frac{\pi}{2}\right)\right]$$

$$E' = \frac{1}{4\pi\varepsilon_0} \cdot \frac{\lambda}{r} [1 + 1]$$

$$E' = \frac{2\lambda}{4\pi\varepsilon_0 \, r}$$

$$E' = \frac{\lambda}{2\pi\varepsilon_0 r}$$

Question 31. It is now believed that protons and neutrons (which constitute nuclei of ordinary matter) are themselves built out of more elementary units called quarks. A proton and a neutron consist of three quarks each. Two types of quarks, the so called 'up' quark (denoted by u) of charge $+\left(\dfrac{2}{3}\right) e$ and the 'down' quark (denoted by d) of charge $\left(-\dfrac{1}{3}\right) e$, together with electrons build up ordinary matter. (Quarks of other types have also been found which give rise to different unusual varieties of matter). Suggest a possible quark composition of a proton and neutron.

Solution   For the protons, the charge on it is $+ e$.

Let the number of up quarks are a, then the number of down quarks are $(3 - a)$ as the total number of quarks are 3.

So, $a \times$ up quark charge $+ (3 - a)$ down quark charge $= + e$

$$a \times \frac{2}{3} e + (3 - a)\left(-\frac{e}{3}\right) = e$$

$$\frac{2ae}{3} - \frac{(3 - a)e}{3} = e$$

$$2a - 3 + a = 3$$

$$3a = 6$$

$$a = 2$$

Thus, in the proton there are two up quarks and one down quark.

$\therefore$ Possible quark composition for proton $= uud$

For the neutron, the charge on neutron is 0.

Let the number of up quarks are b and the number of down quarks are $3 - b$.

So, $b \times$ up quark charge + $(3 - b)$ down quark charge $= 0$

$$b\left(\frac{2e}{3}\right) + (3 - b)\left(-\frac{e}{3}\right) = 0$$

$$2b - 3 + b = 0$$

$$3b = 3$$

$$\Rightarrow \qquad\qquad b = 1$$

Thus, in neutron, there are one up quark and two down quarks.

$\therefore$ Possible quark composition for neutrons $= udd$

Question 32. (a) Consider an arbitrary electrostatic field configuration. A small test charge is placed at a null point (*i.e.*, where, $E = 0$) of the configuration. Show that the equilibrium of the test charge is necessarily unstable.

   (b) Verify this result for the simple configuration of two charges of the same magnitude and sign placed a certain distance apart.

Solution

 (a) Let us consider that initially the test charge is in the stable equilibrium. When the test charge is displaced from the null point (where, $E = 0$) in any direction, it must experience a restoring force towards the null point.

   This means that there is a net inward flux through a closed surface around the null point. According to the Gauss's theorem, the net electric flux through a surface net enclosing any charge must be zero. Hence, the equilibrium is not stable.

 (b) The middle point of the line joining two like charges is a null point. If we displace a test charge slightly along the line, the restoring force try to bring the test charge back to the centre.

   If we displace the test charge normal to the line, the net force on the test charge takes it further away from the null point. Hence, the equilibrium is not stable.

Question 33. A particle of mass m and charge $(-q)$ enters the region between the two charged plates initially moving along X-axis with speed v_x (like particle 1 in figure.). The length of plate is L and a uniform electric field E is maintained between the plates. Show that the vertical deflection of the particle at the far edge of the plate is $qEL^2 / (2mv_x^2)$.

Compare this motion with motion of a projectile in gravitational field.

In this question, we have to discuss the motion of particle under the effect of electrostatic field as the electric field is uniform, so the force on the particle will be contant, hence we can use euqation of uniformally accelerated motion.

Solution   Mass of particle $= m$

Charge on particle $= -q$

Speed of particle $= v_x$

Length of plates $= L$

Electric field between the plates $= E$ (from positive plate to negative plate).

Let the deflection in the path of charge $-q$ is Y, because the force acting in $+Y$ axis direction. The direction of force is from negative plate to positive plate because the charge is negative in nature.

Let us discuss the motion in Y axis direction

Initial velocity $u = 0$

Acceleration $a = \dfrac{F}{m} = \dfrac{+qE}{m}$

Deflection $y = ?$

$$\text{Time} = \dfrac{\text{Distance}}{\text{Velocity}} = \dfrac{L}{v_x}$$

Using second equation of motion,

$$s = ut + \frac{1}{2}at^2$$

Putting the values,

$$y = 0 + \frac{1}{2} \times \left(+ \frac{qE}{m} \right) \cdot \frac{L^2}{v_x^2}$$

$$y = \frac{qEL^2}{2mv_x^2}$$

In the case of projectile motion $y = \dfrac{1}{2}gt^2$. Thus, it is exactly similar to the projectile motion in the gravitational field.

Question 34.   Suppose that the particle in Q. 33 is an electron projected with velocity $v_x = 2.0 \times 10^6$ m/s. If E between the plates separated by 0.5 cm is 9.1×10^2 N/C, where will the electron strike the upper plate? ($|e| = 1.6 \times 10^{-19}$ C, $m_e = 9.1 \times 10^{-31}$ kg.)

Solution   Given, $v_x = 2 \times 10^6$ m/s

$$E = 9.1 \times 10^2 \text{ N/C}$$

$$q = e = 1.6 \times 10^{-19} \text{ C}$$

$$m_e = 9.1 \times 10^{-31} \text{ kg}$$

$$d = 0.5 \text{ cm} = 0.5 \times 10^{-2} \text{ m} = 5 \times 10^{-3} \text{ m}$$

The electron will strike the upper plate at its other end at $x = L$ as it get deflected.

$$y = \frac{d}{2} = \frac{5 \times 10^{-3}}{2} = 2.5 \times 10^{-3} \text{ m}$$

Using

$$y = \frac{qEL^2}{2mv_x^2}$$

$$L = \sqrt{\frac{2mv_x^2 \cdot y}{qE}} = \sqrt{\frac{2my}{qE}} \cdot v_x$$

$$L = \sqrt{\frac{2 \times 9.1 \times 10^{-31} \times 2.5 \times 10^{-3}}{1.6 \times 10^{-19} \times 9.1 \times 10^2}} \times 2 \times 10^6$$

$$L = 1.12 \times 10^{-2} \text{ m}$$

$$= 1.12 \text{ cm}$$

Selected NCERT Exemplar Problems

Question 1.   An arbitrary surface encloses a dipole. What is the electric flux through this surface?

Solution   If any arbitrary surface encloses a dipole, the net charge is zero because the total charge on the dipole is zero (dipole consists of two equal and opposite charges). According to the formula for electric field,

$$E = \frac{1}{4\pi\varepsilon_0} \cdot \frac{q}{r^2}$$

where, q is the charge and r is the distance from the charge. Here, charge $q = 0$

$\Rightarrow$ $\qquad\qquad\qquad\qquad\qquad E = 0$

Electric flux $\qquad\qquad\qquad\qquad \Delta\phi = E \cdot \Delta S$

$$\Delta\phi = 0$$

Question 2.   The dimensions of an atom are of the order of an Angstrom. Thus, there must be large electric fields between the protons and electrons. Why, then is the electrostatic field inside a conductor zero?

Solution   The electrostatic field inside a conductor is zero because the electrostatic field is only due to the excess charge. As we know that any atom is electrically neutral *i.e.*, there is no excess charge on the atom. If charge is zero, then according to the formula

$$E = \frac{1}{4\pi\varepsilon_0} \cdot \frac{q}{r^2} , \qquad\qquad\qquad \text{as } q = 0, E = 0$$

where, q is the charge of an atom and r is the distance of any point from charge q.

Question 3.   Sketch the electric field lines for a uniformly charged hollow cylinder shown in figure.

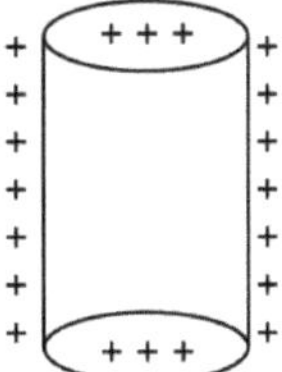

Solution   Here, the hollow cylinder is positively charged. We know that the electric lines of force appear to come out from the conductor. Thus, the lines of force for a uniformly positive charged hollow cylinder is shown in figure.

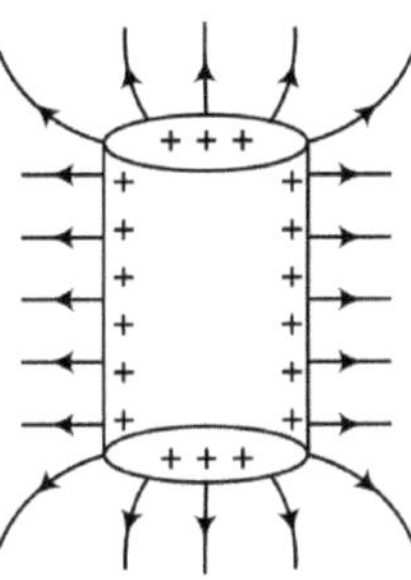

Question 4.   A paisa coin is made up of Al-Mg alloy and weighs 0.75 g. It has a square shape and its diagonal measures 17 mm. It is electrically neutral and contains equal amounts of positive and negative charges. Treating the paisa coins made up of only Al, find the magnitude of equal number of positive and negative charges. What conclusion do you draw from this magnitude?

Solution   According to the question, the coin is treated to be made by Al.

Weight of coin $(w) = 0.75$ g

Length of diagonal of square shaped coin $= 17$ mm

Atomic mass of Al $= 27$ g

Atomic number of Al $= 13$

As we know that the number of atoms in one molar mass of substance are 6.023×10^{23} (Avogadro's number).

i.e.,   27 g of Al contains 6.023×10^{23} atoms

$$1\text{ g of Al contains } \frac{6.023 \times 10^{23}}{27} \text{ atoms}$$

$$0.75\text{ g of Al contains } \frac{6.023 \times 10^{23}}{27} \times 0.75 = 1.67 \times 10^{22} \text{ atoms}$$

One atom of Al contains 13 electrons and 13 protons

1.67×10^{22} atoms of Al contains $13 \times 1.67 \times 10^{22} = 21.71 \times 10^{22}$ electrons

So, number of protons $= 21.71 \times 10^{22}$

The charge on one electron $= 1.6 \times 10^{-19}$ C

$\therefore$ Charge on 21.71×10^{22} electrons

$$= 1.6 \times 10^{-19} \times 21.71 \times 10^{22} = 34.736 \times 10^{3} \text{ C}$$

Thus, the amount of positive or negative charge on the coin

$$= 34.736 \times 10^{3} \text{C or } 34.73 \text{ kC}$$

From the above calculation, we can conclude that this is the very large amounts of charge. Thus, all the atoms contain a very large amount of positive and negative charges.

Question 5. Consider a sphere of radius R with charge density distribution
$$\rho(r) = kr \text{ for } r \leq R \text{ N/L} = 0 \text{ for } r > R$$

(a) Find the electric field at all points r.

(b) Suppose the total charge on the sphere is $2e$, where e is the electron charge. Where can two protons be embedded so that the force on each of them is zero? Assume that the introduction of the proton does not alter the negative charge distribution.

Solution   (a) Let there be a sphere of radius R.

Case I   Let we consider that $r < R$.

The electric field is radial in nature. Now for the points $r < R$, there is a Gaussian surface.

According to the Gauss's theorem,

$$\oint E.\,dS = \frac{1}{\varepsilon_0} \int_V \rho \,.\, dV \qquad ...(i)$$

where, ρ is the charge density and dV be the small volume.

As we know that the volume of sphere of radius r is

$$V = \frac{4}{3}\pi r^3$$

Differentiating with respect to r on both the sides,

$$dV = \frac{4}{3} \cdot \pi \cdot 3r^2 \, dr = 4\pi r^2 \, dr \qquad ...(ii)$$

Putting the value of dV in Eq. (i), we get

$$\oint E \cdot dS = \frac{1}{\varepsilon_0} \int \rho \cdot 4\pi r^2 \, dr \qquad \rho = kr \text{ for } r < R$$

$$E \oint dS = \frac{1}{\varepsilon_0} \cdot 4\pi \int kr \cdot r^2 \, dr$$

$$E.4\pi r^2 = \frac{1}{\varepsilon_0} \cdot 4\pi k \int_0^r r^3 \, dr = \frac{4\pi k}{\varepsilon_0} \left. \frac{r^4}{4} \right|_0^r$$

$$E.4\pi r^2 = \frac{4\pi k r^4}{4\,\varepsilon_0}$$

$$E = \frac{kr^4}{4\,\varepsilon_0 r^2}$$

$$E = \frac{1}{4\varepsilon_0} kr^2$$

The vector form of the electric field is

$$\mathbf{E} = \frac{1}{4\varepsilon_0} \cdot kr^2 \hat{\mathbf{r}}$$

Case II If $r = R$, that means we have to find the electric field at the surface of sphere. According to Gauss's theorem,

$$\oint_S \mathbf{E} \cdot d\mathbf{S} = \frac{1}{\varepsilon_0} \int_V \rho \, dV$$

Here, the direction of $\mathbf{E}$ and $d\mathbf{S}$ is same.

$$\oint E \cdot dS \cdot \cos 0° = \frac{1}{\varepsilon_0} \int kr \cdot 4\pi r^2 \, dr \qquad \text{[From Eq. (ii)]}$$

$$E \cdot 4\pi R^2 = \frac{k \cdot 4\pi}{\varepsilon_0} \int_0^R r^3 \, dr = \frac{4\pi k}{\varepsilon_0} \cdot \left. \frac{r^4}{4} \right|_0^R$$

$$E \cdot 4\pi R^2 = \frac{4\pi k \cdot R^4}{\varepsilon_0 \, 4}$$

$$E = \frac{1 \cdot k}{4\varepsilon_0} \cdot R^2$$

The vector form of the electric field is

$$\mathbf{E} = \frac{1}{4\varepsilon_0} \cdot kR^2 \hat{\mathbf{R}}$$

Case III If $r > R$, that means we have to find the electric field outside the sphere. According to Gauss's theorem,

$$\oint_S \mathbf{E} \cdot d\mathbf{S} = \frac{1}{\varepsilon_0} \cdot \int_V \rho \, dV \qquad \text{[From Eq. (ii)]}$$

$$E \oint dS = \frac{1}{\varepsilon_0} \cdot \int kr \cdot 4\pi r^2 \, dr \qquad (\because \mathbf{E} \,||\, d\mathbf{S})$$

$$E \cdot 4\pi r^2 = \frac{1}{\varepsilon_0} \cdot k 4\pi \int_0^R r^3 \, dr$$

$$E \cdot r^2 = \frac{k}{\varepsilon_0} \cdot \left. \frac{r^2}{4} \right|_0^R$$

$$E = \frac{1}{4\varepsilon_0} \cdot k \cdot \frac{R^4}{r^2}$$

The vector form of the electric field is

$$\mathbf{E} = \frac{1}{4\varepsilon_0} \cdot k \cdot \frac{R^4}{r^2} \cdot \hat{\mathbf{r}}$$

(b) To get the force on protons zero, the two protons must be embedded on the opposite sides of the centre along the diameter of the sphere. Let the distance of each proton from the centre O is r. The position of two protons are at P_1 and P_2.

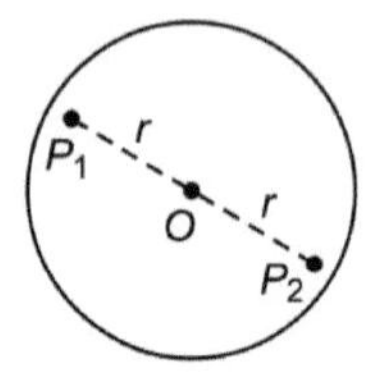

According to the question,

$$\int_V \rho \, dV = 2e$$

$$\int_0^R kr.4\pi r^2 \, dr = 2e \qquad \text{[From Eq. (ii)]}$$

$$k.4\pi. \int_0^R r^3 \, dr = 2e$$

$$4\pi k. \frac{R^4}{4} = 2e$$

$$k = \frac{2e}{\pi R^4} \qquad \qquad \dots \text{(iii)}$$

The forces on proton 1 (*i.e.*, P_1). The force is attractive in nature.

$$\mathbf{F}_a = -e\,\mathbf{E} = -e \cdot \frac{1}{4\varepsilon_0} kr^2 \hat{\mathbf{r}} \quad \text{(From the result of case I)}$$

$$\mathbf{F}_a = -\frac{e}{4\varepsilon_0} \cdot \frac{2e}{4R^4} \cdot r^2 \hat{\mathbf{r}} \qquad \text{[From Eq. (iii)]}$$

$$\mathbf{F}_a = \frac{-2e^2}{4\pi\varepsilon_0.R^4} \cdot r^2 \hat{\mathbf{r}} \qquad \qquad \dots \text{(iv)}$$

The repulsion force between P_1 and P_2 placed at a distance $2r$ is

$$\mathbf{F}_b = \frac{1}{4\pi\varepsilon_0} \cdot \frac{e.e}{(2r)^2} \hat{\mathbf{r}} \qquad \text{(By using the Coulomb's law)}$$

$$\mathbf{F}_b = \frac{1}{4\pi\varepsilon_0} \cdot \frac{e^2}{4r^2} \hat{\mathbf{r}} \qquad \qquad \dots \text{(v)}$$

The net force is $\mathbf{F} = \mathbf{F}_a + \mathbf{F}_b$

$$\mathbf{F} = \frac{-2e^2}{4\pi\varepsilon_0.R^4} r^2 \hat{\mathbf{r}} + \frac{1}{4\pi\varepsilon_0} \frac{e^2}{4r^2} \cdot \hat{\mathbf{r}}$$

$$\text{[From Eqs. (iv) and (v)]}$$

According to the question, this net force is zero. Hence,

$$\left(\frac{-2e^2}{4\pi\varepsilon_0 R^4} r^2 + \frac{1}{4\pi\varepsilon_0} \cdot \frac{e^2}{4r^2} \right) \hat{\mathbf{r}} = 0$$

$$\frac{2e^2 r^2}{4\pi\varepsilon_0.R^4} = \frac{1}{4\pi\varepsilon_0} \cdot \frac{e^2}{4r^2}$$

$$8r^4 = R^4$$

$$r = \frac{R}{8^{1/4}}$$

Thus, the distance of each proton from the centre is $\dfrac{R}{8^{1/4}}$.

Question 6. Two fixed identical conducting plates (α and β), each of surface area S are charged to $-Q$ and q, respectively, where $Q > q > 0$. A third identical plate (γ), free to move is located on the other side of the plate having charge q at a distance d. This third plate is released and collides with the plate β. Assume the collision is elastic and the time of collision is sufficient to redistribute charge amongst β and γ.
   (a) Find the electric field acting on the plate γ before collision.
   (b) Find the charge on β and γ after the collision.
   (c) Find the velocity of the plate γ after collision and at a distance d from the plate β.

Solution (a) Here, the condition is before collision.

The electric field at any point due to a thin sheet of charge Q,

$$E = \frac{Q}{2\varepsilon_0 . A}$$

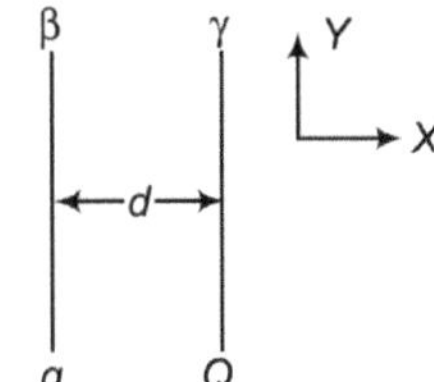

So, the electric field at the plate γ due to the plate α is

$$\mathbf{E}_1 = \frac{-Q}{2\varepsilon_0 . S} \cdot \hat{\mathbf{X}}$$

where, S be the area of plates and the direction of field is along $-X$ axis.

The electric field at the plate γ due to the plate β is

$$\mathbf{E}_2 = \frac{q}{2\varepsilon_0 S} \cdot \hat{\mathbf{X}}$$

where, S be the area of plates and the direction of electric field is in X-axis.

The net electric field on the plate γ due to both the plates

$$\mathbf{E} = \mathbf{E}_1 + \mathbf{E}_2$$
$$= -\frac{Q}{2\varepsilon_0 S} \cdot \hat{\mathbf{X}} + \frac{q}{2\varepsilon_0 S} \hat{\mathbf{X}}$$
$$\mathbf{E} = -\frac{(Q - q)\,\hat{\mathbf{X}}}{2\varepsilon_0 S}$$

Thus, the electric field acting on plate γ before collision is $-\dfrac{(Q - q)}{2\varepsilon_0 S}\,\hat{\mathbf{X}}$, the direction of electric field is along $-X$ axis.

(b) Now, there is collision between plates β and γ. As the two plates collide each other they both have same common potential. Let the charge on β is q_1 and on γ is $- q_2$. Let there is a point O where the electric field must be zero.

The electric field at O due to plate α is

$$\mathbf{E}_1 = \frac{-Q}{2\varepsilon_0 S}\, \hat{\mathbf{X}}$$

Electric field at O due to plate β is

$$\mathbf{E}_2 = \frac{+ q_1}{2\varepsilon_0 S}\, \hat{\mathbf{X}}$$

Electric field at O due to plate γ is

$$\mathbf{E}_3 = \frac{- q_2}{2\varepsilon_0 S}\, \hat{\mathbf{X}}$$

The net electric field at O is

$$\mathbf{E} = \mathbf{E}_1 + \mathbf{E}_2 + \mathbf{E}_3 = 0 \quad \text{(According to the question)}$$

$$-\frac{Q}{2\varepsilon_0 S}\hat{\mathbf{X}} + \frac{q_1}{2\varepsilon_0 S}\hat{\mathbf{X}} - \frac{q_2}{2\varepsilon_0 S}\hat{\mathbf{X}} = 0$$

$$q_1 - q_2 = Q \qquad \qquad \ldots\text{(ii)}$$

As there is no loss of charge on collision,

$$Q + q = q_1 + q_2$$

On solving Eqs. (i) and (ii), we get

$$q_1 = (Q + q/2) = \text{charge on plate } \beta$$
$$q_2 = (q/2) = \text{ charge on plate } \gamma$$

(c) After collision, at a distance d from plate β, let the velocity of plate γ be v.

After the collision, electric field at plate γ is

$$E_2 = \frac{-Q}{2\varepsilon_0 S} + \frac{(Q + q/2)}{2\varepsilon_0 S} = \frac{q/2}{2\varepsilon_0 S} \text{ to the right.}$$

Just before collision, electric field at plate γ is $E_1 = \dfrac{Q - q}{2\varepsilon_0 S}$

If, F_1 is force on plate γ before collision, then $F_1 = E_1 Q = \dfrac{(Q - q)\, Q}{2\varepsilon_0 S}$

Similarly, force F_2 on plate γ after collision, $F_2 = E_2\, \dfrac{q}{2} = \dfrac{(q/2)^2}{2\varepsilon_0 S}$

Total work done by the electric field in round trip movement of plate γ

$$W = (F_1 + F_2)\, d = \frac{[(Q - q)\, Q + (q/2)^2]\, d}{2\varepsilon_0 S} = \frac{(Q - q/2)^2\, d}{2\varepsilon_0 S}$$

If m is mass of plate γ, the Kinetic Energy (KE) gained by plate $\gamma = \dfrac{1}{2} mv^2$

According to work energy principle, $\dfrac{1}{2} mv^2 = W = \dfrac{(Q - q/2)^2 d}{2\varepsilon_0 S}$

$$v = (Q - q/2)\left(\dfrac{d}{m\varepsilon_0 S}\right)^{1/2}$$

Question 7. Two charges $-q$ each are fixed separated by distance $2d$. A third charge q of mass m placed at the mid-point is displaced slightly by $x\,(x \ll d)$ perpendicular to the line joining the two fixed charged as shown in figure.

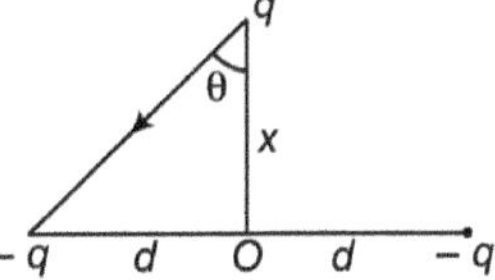

Show that q will perform simple harmonic oscillation of time period.

$$T = \left[\dfrac{8\pi^3 \varepsilon_0 m d^3}{q^2}\right]^{1/2}$$

Use the condition of simple harmonic oscillation, that means if the force on any particle is directly proportional to negative of displacement, the motion executed by the particle is simple harmonic oscillation.

Solution The force between $-q$ and q placed at A and C respectively is F_1.

$$F_1 = \dfrac{1}{4\pi\varepsilon_0} \cdot \dfrac{qq}{(AC)^2}$$

$$F_1 = \dfrac{1}{4\pi\varepsilon_0} \cdot \dfrac{q^2}{(d^2 + x^2)} \qquad \text{(along } C \text{ to } A) \quad \ldots(i)$$

$$AC = \sqrt{d^2 + x^2} = BC \quad \text{(By Pythagoras theorem)}$$

The force between $-q$ and q placed at B and C respectively is F_2.

$$\therefore \qquad F_2 = \dfrac{1}{4\pi\varepsilon_0} \cdot \dfrac{qq}{(BC)^2} = \dfrac{1}{4\pi\varepsilon_0} \cdot \dfrac{q^2}{d^2 + x^2} \qquad \ldots(ii)$$

Now, resolve the components of F_1 and F_2.

Forces along C to O is $F_1 \cos \theta$ and $F_2 \cos \theta$, they both are in the same direction. Forces along perpendicular to CO is $F_1 \sin \theta$ and $F_2 \sin \theta$, these components are opposite to each other and the values of F_1 and F_2 are same. So, they balance each other.

So, net force on q is

$$F = F_1 \cos \theta + F_2 \cos \theta$$

$$F = 2F_1 \cos \theta = 2 \cdot \frac{1}{4\pi\varepsilon_0} \cdot \frac{q^2}{(d^2 + x^2)} \cdot \cos \theta \qquad (\because F_1 = F_2)$$

In $\triangle ACO$,

$$\cos \theta = \frac{x}{\sqrt{d^2 + x^2}}$$

$$F = \frac{1}{4\pi\varepsilon_0} \cdot \frac{2q^2}{(d^2 + x^2)^{3/2}} \, x$$

This force is attractive in nature, so

$$F = -\frac{1}{4\pi\varepsilon_0} \cdot \frac{2q^2 \cdot x}{(d^2 + x^2)^{3/2}}$$

According to question, $x \ll d$, so neglect x^2 as compared to d^2.

$$F = -\frac{1}{4\pi\varepsilon_0} \cdot \frac{2q^2}{d^3} \cdot x \qquad \qquad \ldots\text{(iii)}$$

Here,

$$F \propto -x \text{ or } F = -\omega^2 x, \qquad \qquad \ldots\text{(iv)}$$

So, the motion is simple harmonic, where ω is the angular frequency.

By comparing Eqs. (iii) and (iv), we get

$$\omega = \sqrt{\frac{2q^2}{4\pi\varepsilon_0 d^3 m}} = \sqrt{\frac{2q^2}{4\pi\varepsilon_0 d^3 m}} = \sqrt{\frac{k \text{ (Spring factor)}}{m \text{ (Inertia factor)}}}$$

$$\omega = \frac{2\pi}{T} = \sqrt{\frac{2q^2}{4\pi\varepsilon_0 d^3 m}}$$

where, T is the time period of the charged particle of mass m.

$$T = \left(\frac{8\pi^3 \varepsilon_0 m d^3}{q^2}\right)^{1/2}$$

Chapter 2

Electrostatic Potential and Capacitance

Important Results

1. Electrostatic potential at a distance r from charge q,
$$V = \frac{1}{4\pi\varepsilon_0} \cdot \frac{q}{r} \quad \text{(volt)}$$

2. Electrostatic potential difference,
$$V_B - V_A = \frac{1}{4\pi\varepsilon_0} \cdot q_0 \left[\frac{1}{r_B} - \frac{1}{r_A} \right] = \frac{W_{AB}}{q_0}$$

3. Electrostatic potential at a point due to a group of N charges,
$$V = \frac{1}{4\pi\varepsilon_0} \sum_{i=1}^{n} \frac{q_i}{r_i}$$

4. Relation between electric field and potential gradient is
$$E = -\frac{\partial V}{\partial r} \quad \text{or} \quad E_x = -\frac{\partial V}{\partial x}, \; E_y = -\frac{\partial V}{\partial y}, \; E_z = -\frac{\partial V}{\partial z}$$

5. Electrostatic potential energy of a system of two point charges,
$$U = \frac{1}{4\pi\varepsilon_0} \cdot \frac{q_1 q_2}{r}$$

(Put values of charges with their signs)

6. Electrostatic potential energy of a system of n point charges,
$$U = \frac{1}{4\pi\varepsilon_0} \cdot \sum_{\substack{i=1, \\ j=2}}^{n} \frac{q_j\, q_i}{r_{ji}}$$

7. Electrostatic potential due to an electric dipole at axial point,
$$V = \frac{1}{4\pi\varepsilon_0} \cdot \frac{p}{r^2}$$
(where p = dipole moment)

8. Electrostatic potential due to an electric dipole at equatorial point,
$$V = 0$$

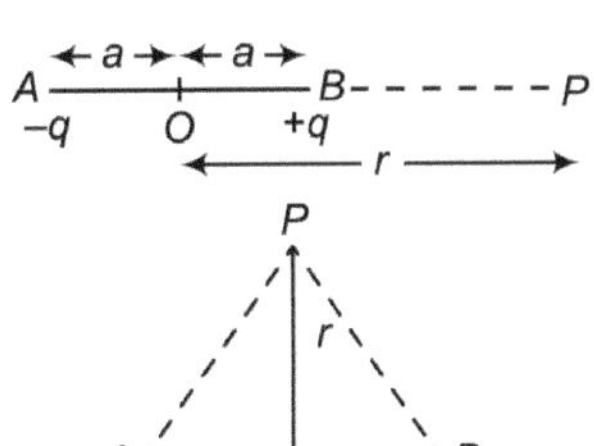

9. Electrostatic potential due to an electric dipole at any arbitrary point, $\quad V = \dfrac{1}{4\pi\varepsilon_0} \cdot \dfrac{\mathbf{p}.\hat{\mathbf{r}}}{r^2}$

10. Capacity $C = \dfrac{q}{V}$

11. Capacitance of a spherical conductor
$$C = 4\pi\varepsilon_0 r \qquad\qquad (r = \text{radius})$$

12. Capacitance of a parallel plate capacitor with air as dielectric
$$C = \dfrac{\varepsilon_0 A}{d}$$
(where $A =$ area of plates and $d =$ distance between plates)

13. Capacity of a parallel plate capacitor with insulating medium as dielectric
$$C = \dfrac{K\varepsilon_0 A}{d} \qquad\qquad (K = \text{dielectric constant})$$

14. Series combination of capacitances
$$\dfrac{1}{C_s} = \dfrac{1}{C_1} + \dfrac{1}{C_2} + \dfrac{1}{C_3} + \dots$$

15. Parallel combination of capacitances
$$C_p = C_1 + C_2 + C_3 + \dots$$

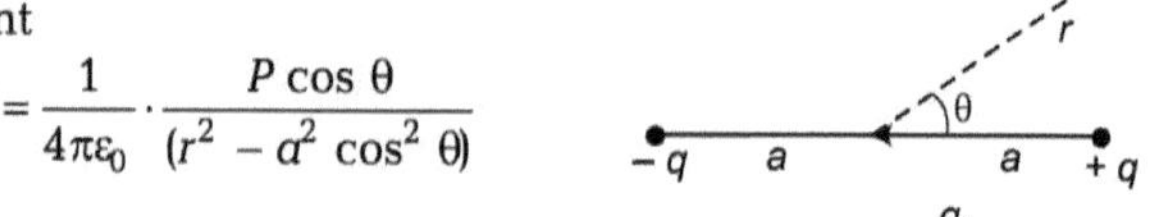

16. Energy stored in a capacitor
$$E = \dfrac{1}{2}QV = \dfrac{1}{2}\dfrac{Q^2}{C} = \dfrac{1}{2}CV^2$$

17. Common potential $V = \dfrac{C_1 V_1 + C_2 V_2}{C_1 + C_2}$

18. Loss of energy on sharing charges
$$E_1 - E_2 = \dfrac{C_1 C_2 (V_1 - V_2)^2}{2(C_1 + C_2)}$$

19. Electric potential due to a dipole at any arbitrary point
$$V = \dfrac{1}{4\pi\varepsilon_0} \cdot \dfrac{P\cos\theta}{(r^2 - a^2\cos^2\theta)}$$

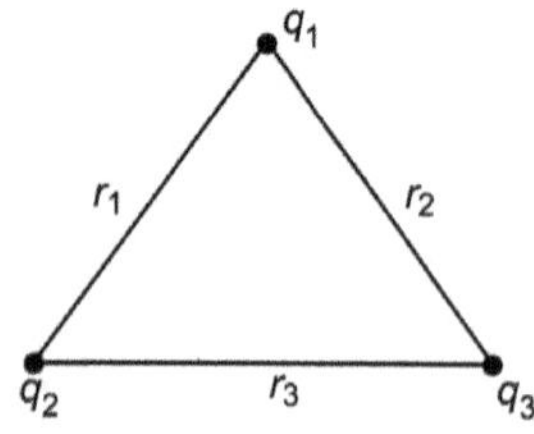

20. Potential energy of a system of three charges
$$U = \dfrac{1}{4\pi\varepsilon_0}\left[\dfrac{q_1 q_2}{r_1} + \dfrac{q_1 q_3}{r_2} + \dfrac{q_2 q_3}{r_3}\right]$$

Exercises

Question 1.   Two charges 5×10^{-8} C and -3×10^{-8} C are located 16 cm apart. At what point(s) on the line joining the two charges is the electric potential zero? Take the potential at infinity to be zero.

It is based on the potential due to two charges remember that the potential is a scalar quantity so put the value of charge with sign.

Solution Let the potential be zero at point C at a distance x from point B. Let us consider two charges q_1 and q_2. According to the question,

$$q_1 = 5 \times 10^{-8} \text{ C}, \, q_2 = -3 \times 10^{-8} \text{ C}, \, AB = 16 \text{ cm} = 16 \times 10^{-2} \text{ m}$$

The potential at point C due to charge q_1

$$V_A = \frac{1}{4\pi\varepsilon_0} \cdot \frac{q_1}{AC} = \frac{9 \times 10^9 \times 5 \times 10^{-8}}{(16 - x) \times 10^{-2}} \qquad \ldots \text{(i)}$$

The potential at point C due to charge q_2

$$V_B = \frac{1}{4\pi\varepsilon_0} \cdot \frac{q_2}{BC} = \frac{-9 \times 10^9 \times 3 \times 10^{-8}}{x \times 10^{-2}} \qquad \ldots \text{(ii)}$$

Now the net potential at point C is zero *i.e.*, $V_A + V_B = 0$
Putting the values from Eqs. (i) and (ii), we get

$$\frac{9 \times 10^9 \times 5 \times 10^{-8}}{(16 - x) \times 10^{-2}} + \left(\frac{-9 \times 10^9 \times 3 \times 10^{-8}}{x \times 10^{-2}} \right) = 0$$

$$\frac{5}{16 - x} - \frac{3}{x} = 0$$

or $\qquad\qquad\qquad 5x - 3(16 - x) = 0$

or $\qquad\qquad\qquad 5x - 48 + 3x = 0$

or $\qquad\qquad\qquad\qquad 8x = 48$

or $\qquad\qquad\qquad\qquad x = 6 \text{ cm}$

Thus, the electric potential is zero at the distance of 6 cm from $q_2 \, (= -3 \times 10^{-8} \text{ C})$.

Question 2.   A regular hexagon of side 10 cm has a charge $5\,\mu$C at each of its vertices. Calculate the potential at the centre of the hexagon.

It is based on the potential due to n number of charges and total potential is equal to the sum of potential produced by individual charges.

Solution $ABCDEF$ is a regular hexagon of side 10 cm each. At each corner the charge $q = 5\mu$C is placed. O is the centre of the hexagon.

Given, $AB = BC = CD = DE = EF = FA = 10 \text{ cm}$

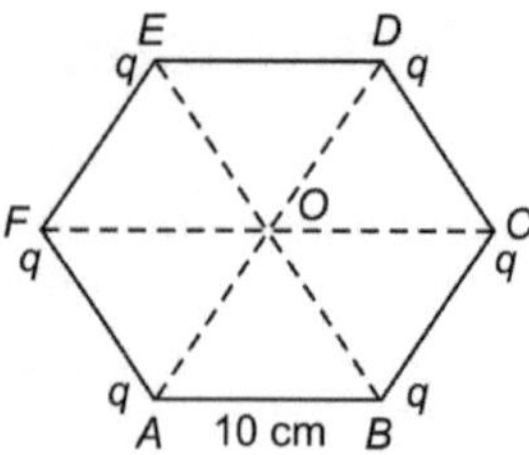

As the hexagon has six equilateral triangles, so the distance of centre O from every vertex is 10 cm.

i.e., $\qquad OA = OB = OC = OD = OE = OF = 10$ cm

Potential at point O = Sum of potential at centre O due to individual point charges.

$\therefore \qquad V_O = V_A + V_B + V_C + V_D + V_E + V_F$

$$V_O = \frac{1}{4\pi\varepsilon_0} \cdot \left[\frac{q}{OA} + \frac{q}{OB} + \frac{q}{OC} + \frac{q}{OD} + \frac{q}{OE} + \frac{q}{OF}\right]$$

$$\left(\because V = \frac{1}{4\pi\varepsilon_0} \cdot \frac{q}{r}\right)$$

Putting the values,

$$V_O = 9 \times 10^9 \left[\frac{5 \times 10^{-6}}{10 \times 10^{-2}} + \frac{5 \times 10^{-6}}{10 \times 10^{-2}} + \frac{5 \times 10^{-6}}{10 \times 10^{-2}} + \frac{5 \times 10^{-6}}{10 \times 10^{-2}} \right.$$

$$\left. + \frac{5 \times 10^{-6}}{10 \times 10^{-2}} + \frac{5 \times 10^{-6}}{10 \times 10^{-2}}\right]$$

or $\qquad V_O = 9 \times 10^9 \times \dfrac{6 \times 10^{-6} \times 5}{10 \times 10^{-2}}$

or $\qquad V_O = 27 \times 10^4$

$\qquad V_O = 2.7 \times 10^6$ V

Question 3.   Two charges $2\,\mu C$ and $-2\,\mu C$ are placed at points A and B; 6 cm apart.

    (a) Identify an equipotential surface of the system.

    (b) What is the direction of the electric field at every point on this surface?

Solution   (a) Equipotential surface means the surface where potential remains same at each point.

Here, this is the system of two equal and opposite charges.

$\therefore$ The potential at C

$$V = \frac{1}{4\pi\varepsilon_0}\left[\frac{2 \times 10^6}{0.03} + \frac{(-2 \times 10^{-6})}{0.03}\right] = 0$$

So, the potential is zero at each point on the line which passes through the mid-point of AB and perpendicular to it. So, a plane passing through the mid-point C of AB is an equipotential surface.

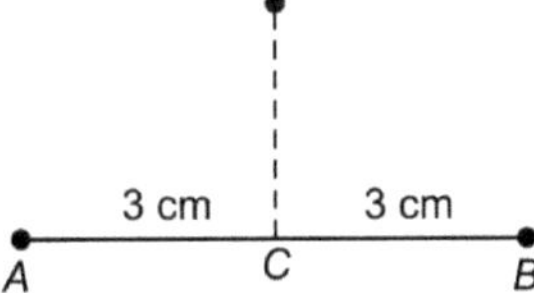

(b) According to the formula $\mathbf{E}.dr = dV$, the value of $dV = 0$ at each point of equipotential surface.

$$\therefore \qquad \mathbf{E}.dr = 0$$

So, the angle between electric field vector and distance vector will be 90°. Thus, the electric field is always normal to the plane passing through AB.

Question 4. A spherical conductor of radius 12 cm has a charge of 1.6×10^{-7} C distributed uniformly on its surface. What is the electric field

(a) inside the sphere?

(b) just outside the sphere?

(c) at a point 18 cm from the centre of the sphere?

 Charge uniformly distributed over a spherical conductor behaves as total charge is present at its centre.

Solution   Radius of spherical conductor $(r) = 12$ cm $= 0.12$ m and charge on conductor $(q) = 1.6 \times 10^{-7}$ C.

(a) According to the property of electric field, inside the conductor it is zero. So, the electric field inside the spherical sphere is zero.

(b) For a point just outside the sphere i.e., for a point lying on the surface of the sphere, the charge may be supposed to be cancentrated on the centre of the sphere by using the formula of electric field.

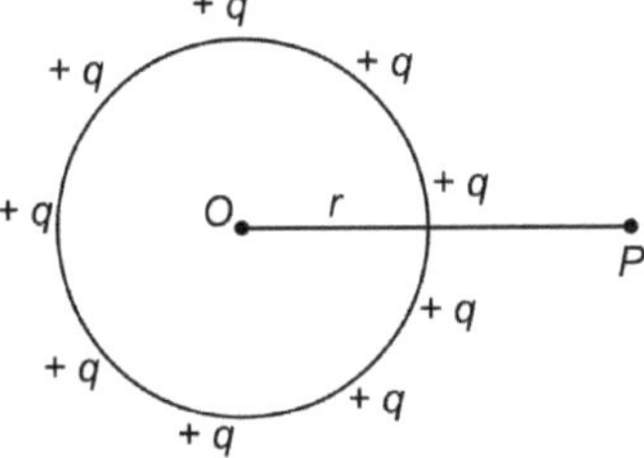

$$E = \frac{1}{4\pi\varepsilon_0} \cdot \frac{q}{r^2} = \frac{9 \times 10^9 \times 1.6 \times 10^{-7}}{0.12 \times 0.12} = 1 \times 10^5 \text{ N/C}$$

(c) Now, we have to find the electric field at point P, where $OP = 18$ cm $= 0.18$ m

Using the formula of electric field

$$E = \frac{1}{4\pi\varepsilon_0} \cdot \frac{q}{(OP)^2} = \frac{9 \times 10^9 \times 1.6 \times 10^{-7}}{0.18 \times 0.18} = 4.4 \times 10^4 \text{ N/C}$$

Question 5. A parallel plate capacitor with air between the plates has a capacitance of 8 pF ($1\ pF = 10^{-12}$ F). What will be the capacitance, if the distance between the plates is reduced by half and the space between them is filled with a substance of dielectric constant 6?

Solution Let initially the distance between the plates be d and air be filled between the plates. Now, the capacitance is C_0.

$$C_0 = 8\ pF = 8 \times 10^{-12}\ F$$

Using the formula of capacitance of a parallel plate capacitor, we get

$$C_0 = \frac{\varepsilon_0 A}{d}$$

(where A is the area of plates and d is the distance between two plates)

$$8 \times 10^{-12} = \frac{\varepsilon_0 A}{d} \qquad \ldots(i)$$

Now, the distance between the plates is reduced to half, $d' = \dfrac{d}{2}$ and the space between the plates is filled with a dielectric of dielectric constant 6. Now, let the new capacitance be C. In this condition area remains same.

$$\therefore \qquad C = \frac{K\varepsilon_0 A}{d'}$$

(where K is the dielectric constant)

$$C = 6.\frac{\varepsilon_0 A}{d} \cdot 2$$

or $$C = 12 \times 8 \times 10^{-12} \qquad \text{[From Eq. (i)]}$$

or $$C = 96 \times 10^{-12}\ F = 96\ pF$$

The capacitance becomes 96 pF.

Question 6. Three capacitors each of capacitance 9 pF are connected in series.

    (a) What is the total capacitance of the combination?

    (b) What is the potential difference across each capacitor, if the combination is connected to a 120 V supply?

 Use the formula of equivalent capacitance when two or more capacitors are connected in series and remember that charges at the plates of each capacitor in series remain same.

Solution There are three capacitors each of capacitance 9 pF.

$$\therefore \qquad C_1 = C_2 = C_3 = 9\ pF$$

and   voltage $V = 120\ V$

(a) The total capacitance in series combination

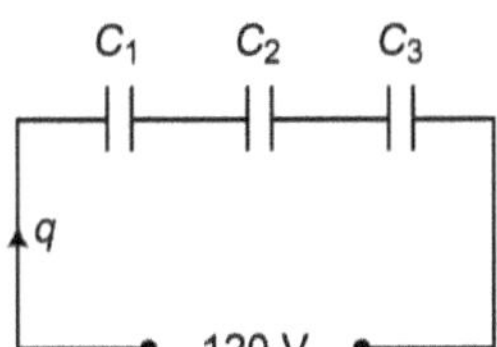

$$\frac{1}{C_s} = \frac{1}{C_1} + \frac{1}{C_2} + \frac{1}{C_3} = \frac{1}{9} + \frac{1}{9} + \frac{1}{9}$$

$$\frac{1}{C_s} = \frac{3}{9} \quad \Rightarrow \quad C_s = 3 \text{ pF}$$

(b) Let the charge across the system be q and potentials across C_1, C_2 and C_3 be V_1, V_2 and V_3 respectively.

Charge $q = C_s \cdot V = 3 \times 120 = 360$ pC

Potential difference across C_1, $(V_1) = \dfrac{q}{C_1} = \dfrac{360}{9} = 40$ V

Potential difference across C_2, $(V_2) = \dfrac{q}{C_2} = \dfrac{360}{9} = 40$ V

Potential difference across C_3, $(V_3) = \dfrac{q}{C_3} = \dfrac{360}{9} = 40$ V

Thus, the potential difference across each capacitor is 40 V.

Question 7. Three capacitors of capacitances 2 pF, 3 pF and 4 pF are connected in parallel.

  (a) What is the total capacitance of the combination?

  (b) Determine the charge on each capacitor, if the combination is connected to a 100 V supply.

 Use the formula of equivalent capacitance when two or more capacitors are connected in parallel and remember that potential difference across the plates of each capacitor remains same in parallel.

Solution   Given, $C_1 = 2$ pF, $C_2 = 3$ pF and $C_3 = 4$ pF

(a) The total capacitance of the parallel combination is given by

$$C_p = C_1 + C_2 + C_3 = 2 + 3 + 4 = 9 \text{ pF}.$$

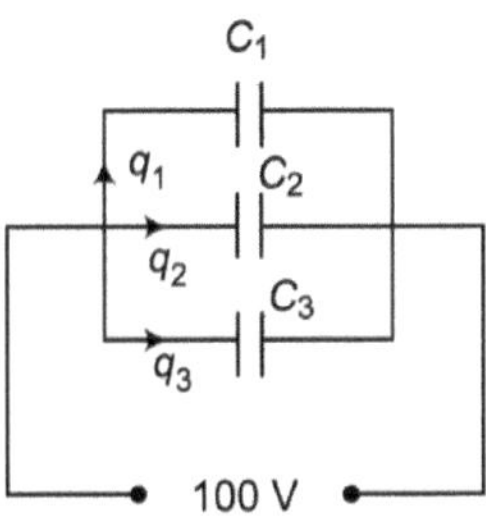

(b) Let the charges on the capacitors C_1, C_2 and C_3 be q_1, q_2 and q_3 respectively. The potential difference across each of the capacitors is same as 100 V.

Charge q_1 at $C_1 = C_1 V = 2 \times 100 = 200$ pC

Charge q_2 at $C_2 = C_2 V = 3 \times 100 = 300$ pC

Charge q_3 at $C_3 = C_3 V = 4 \times 100 = 400$ pC

Question 8. In a parallel plate capacitor with air between the plates, each plate has an area of 6×10^{-3} m^2 and the distance between the plates is 3 mm. Calculate the capacitance of the capacitor. If this capacitor is connected to a 100 V supply, what is the charge on each plate of the capacitor?

 It is a straight question to calculate the capacitance of a parallel plate capacitor. Here we are provide area of plates (A), distance between plates (d), capacitance $C = \dfrac{\varepsilon_0 A}{d}$.

Solution Area of plates $(A) = 6 \times 10^{-3}\,\text{m}^2$

Distance between plates $(d) = 3\ \text{mm} = 3 \times 10^{-3}\ \text{m}$

and potential $V = 100\ \text{V}$

Capacitance of a parallel plate capacitor

$$C = \frac{\varepsilon_0 A}{d} = \frac{8.854 \times 10^{-12} \times 6 \times 10^{-3}}{3 \times 10^{-3}}$$

$$C = 1.77 \times 10^{-11}\ \text{F}$$

When the capacitor is connected to a 100 V supply, charge on each plate of the capacitor $q = CV = 1.77 \times 10^{-11} \times 100$

$$q = 1.77 \times 10^{-9}\ \text{C}$$

Question 9.   Explain what would happen, if in the capacitor given in Q.8, a 3 mm thick mica sheet (of dielectric constant = 6) were inserted between the plates,

(a) while the voltage supply remained connected?

(b) after the supply was disconnected?

 Whenever a dielectric is placed in between the plates of a parallel plate capacitor, then its capacitance increases (it becomes K times the capacitance when there is air in between the plates, where K = dielectric constant).

Solution

(a) As we insert a mica sheet of dielectric constant $K = 6$ between the plates and the voltage supply remained connected.

As we know that the capacitance is directly proportional to the dielectric constant.

$$C \propto K$$

So, as we insert the dielectric the new capacitance becomes

$$C' = CK = 6 \times 1.77 \times 10^{-11} = 1.062 \times 10^{-10}\ \text{F}$$

Now, we see that the capacitance increases, so the charge will also increase.

Charge q' on the capacitor $= C'V = 1.062 \times 10^{-10} \times 100$

or $\qquad\qquad q' = 1.062 \times 10^{-8}\ \text{C}$

(b) When the voltage supply was disconnected, charge of the capacitor remains the same.

New capacitance after inserting the dielectric

$$C' = 1.062 \times 10^{-10}\ \text{F}$$

The potential difference across the plates of the capacitor

$$V' = \frac{q}{C'} = \frac{1.77 \times 10^{-9}}{1.062 \times 10^{-10}} = 16.67 \, V$$

Note *When the battery remains connected, the capacity of the capacitor and charge stored is changed.*
When the battery disconnected, charge remains same but capacitance and potential are changed.

Question 10. A 12 pF capacitor is connected to a 50 V battery. How much electrostatic energy is stored in the capacitor?

Solution Given, voltage connected across the capacitor $V = 50 \, V$ and Capacitance of the capacitor $C = 12 \, pF = 12 \times 10^{-12} \, F$

Energy stored in the capacitor

$$E = \frac{1}{2}CV^2 = \frac{1}{2} \times 12 \times 10^{-12} \times 50 \times 50 = 1.5 \times 10^{-8} \, J$$

Question 11. A 600 pF capacitor is charged by a 200 V supply. Then, it is disconnected from the supply and is connected to another uncharged 600 pF capacitor. How much electrostatic energy is lost in the process?

 When one charged and another uncharged capacitor connected, the energy is transferred from charged capacitor to another uncharged capacitor. In this process, there is a loss in energy in the form of heat in connecting wire.

Solution Given, capacitance of capacitor $C_1 = 600 \, pF = 600 \times 10^{-12} \, F$ and supply voltage $V_1 = 200 \, V$

$$C_2 = 600 \, pF = 600 \times 10^{-12} \, F \text{ and } V_2 = 0$$

$$\text{Loss in energy } (E) = \frac{C_1 C_2 (V_1 - V_2)^2}{2 (C_1 + C_2)}$$

$$E = \frac{600 \times 10^{-12} \times 600 \times 10^{-12} (200 - 0)^2}{2 (600 + 600) \times 10^{-12}}$$

$$= 6 \times 10^{-6} \, J$$

Thus, the 6×10^{-6} J amount of electrostatic energy is lost in the sharing of charges.

Additional Exercises

Question 12. A charge of 8 mC is located at the origin. Calculate the work done in taking a small charge of -2×10^{-9} C from a point $P(0, 0, 3)$ (in cm) to a point $Q\,(0, 4, 0)$ (in cm), *via* a point $R\,(0, 6, 9)$ (in cm).

Solution Charge at origin O is $q_O = 8 \, mC = 8 \times 10^{-3} C$

Charge q_P at point $P = -2 \times 10^{-9}$ C

Distance $OP = r_P = 3$ cm $= 0.03$ m

Distance $OQ = r_Q = 4$ cm $= 0.04$ m

Work done in bringing the charge q_P from P to Q

$= q_P \times$ Potential difference between P and Q

$W_{PQ} = q_P (V_Q - V_P)$

$$= -2 \times 10^{-9} \left(\frac{1}{4\pi\varepsilon_0} \cdot \frac{q_O}{OQ} - \frac{1}{4\pi\varepsilon_0} \cdot \frac{q_O}{OP} \right)$$

$$W_{pq} = -2 \times 10^{-9} \left(\frac{9 \times 10^9 \times 8 \times 10^{-3}}{0.04} - \frac{9 \times 10^9 \times 8 \times 10^{-3}}{0.03} \right)$$

$$= -2 \times 10^{-9} \times 9 \times 10^9 \times 8 \times 10^{-3} \left(\frac{1}{0.04} - \frac{1}{0.03} \right)$$

$$= -18 \times 8 \times 10^{-3} \left(-\frac{0.01}{0.0012} \right) = \frac{18 \times 8 \times 10^{-3} \times 0.01}{0.0012} = 1.2 \text{ J}$$

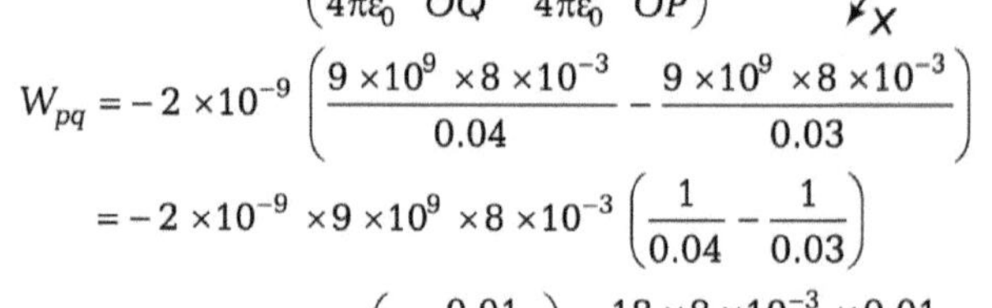

Thus the work done in bringing the charge of -2×10^{-9} C from P to Q is 1.2 J.

Question 13. A cube of side b has a charge q at each of its vertices. Determine the potential and electric field due to this charge array at the centre of the cube.

 Here, we have to find the electric potential and electric field due to multiple charges, so we have to apply superposition principle to calculate net electric field and potential.

Solution Let there is a cube of side b and its centre is O. The charge q is placed at each of the corners. Side of the cube $= b$

Length of the main diagonal of the cube

$$= \sqrt{b^2 + b^2 + b^2} = \sqrt{3}\,b$$

Distance of centre O from each of the vertices is r.

$$r = \frac{b\sqrt{3}}{2} \qquad \qquad \ldots(i)$$

Potential at point O due to one charge is $V = \dfrac{1}{4\pi\varepsilon_0} \cdot \dfrac{q}{r}$

Potential at point O due to all charges placed at the vertices of the cube

$$V' = 8V = \frac{8 \times 1 \times q}{4\pi\varepsilon_0 \cdot r} = \frac{8q \times 2}{4\pi\varepsilon_0 \cdot b\sqrt{3}} \qquad \text{[From Eq. (i)]}$$

$$= \frac{4q}{\sqrt{3}\pi\varepsilon_0 b}$$

The electric field due to one vertex is balanced by the electric field due to the opposite vertex because all charges are positive in nature. Thus, the resultant electric field at the centre O of the cube is zero.

Question 14. Two tiny spheres carrying charges $1.5\ \mu C$ and $2.5\ \mu C$ are located 30 cm apart. Find the potential and electric field

    (a) at the mid-point of the line joining the two charges and

    (b) at a point 10 cm from this mid-point in a plane normal to the line and passing through the mid-point.

 Use the concept of total potential and vector addition for electric field *i.e.*, resultant potential at mid-point is equal to the algebraic sum of potentials produced by both spheres and resultant electric field is equal to the vector sum of fields produced by both spheres.

Solution   Charge at point A is

$$q_1 = 1.5\ \mu C = 1.5 \times 10^{-6}\ C$$

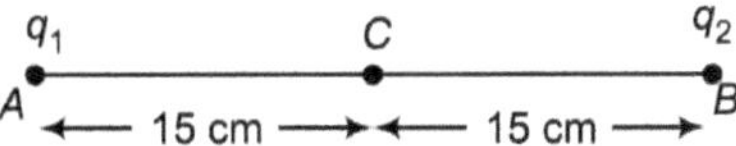

Charge at point B is

$$q_2 = 2.5\ \mu C = 2.5 \times 10^{-6}\ C$$

(a)   Distance between points A and B

$$AB = 30\ cm = 0.3\ cm$$

Let point C be the mid-point of AB.

$\therefore$ $AC = CB = 0.15\ m$

Potential at point C

V_C = Potential due to charge q_1 + Potential due to charge q_2

$$V_C = \frac{1}{4\pi\varepsilon_0}\cdot\frac{q_1}{AC} + \frac{1}{4\pi\varepsilon_0}\cdot\frac{q_2}{CB}$$

$$= 9\times10^9 \left[\frac{1.5\times10^{-6}}{0.15} + \frac{2.5\times10^{-6}}{0.15}\right]$$

$$= \frac{9\times10^9 \times 10^{-6}}{0.15}\ [1.5 + 2.5]$$

$$= \frac{9\times10^3}{0.15}\times4 = 2.4\times10^5\ V$$

Electric field due to charge q_1 at point $C = E_A$

$$E_A = \frac{1}{4\pi\varepsilon_0}\cdot\frac{q_1}{AC}$$

$$= \frac{9\times10^9 \times 1.5 \times 10^{-6}}{(0.15)^2}$$

$$= \frac{9\times10^3 \times 1.5}{(0.15)^2}$$

Electric field due to charge q_2 at point $C = E_B$

$$E_B = \frac{1}{4\pi\varepsilon_0} \cdot \frac{q_1}{BC} = \frac{9\times10^9 \times 2.5\times10^{-6}}{(0.15)^2} = \frac{9\times10^3 \times 2.5}{(0.15)^2}$$

The direction of E_A is along C to B and the direction of E_B is along C to A. Here the magnitude of E_B is more than E_A.

Thus, the resultant electric field

$$E = E_B - E_A = \frac{9\times10^3 \times 2.5}{(0.15)^2} - \frac{9\times10^3 \times 1.5}{(0.15)^2}$$

$$= \frac{9\times10^3}{(0.15)^2}(2.5-1.5) = \frac{9\times10^3 \times 1}{0.15\times0.15}$$

$$= 4\times10^5 \text{ N/C towards } C \text{ to } A$$

(b) The distance from point P to point A is equal to the distance from point P to point B.

$(BC = AC = 15 \text{ cm} = 0.15 \text{ cm}, PC = 10 \text{ cm} = 0.1 \text{ m})$

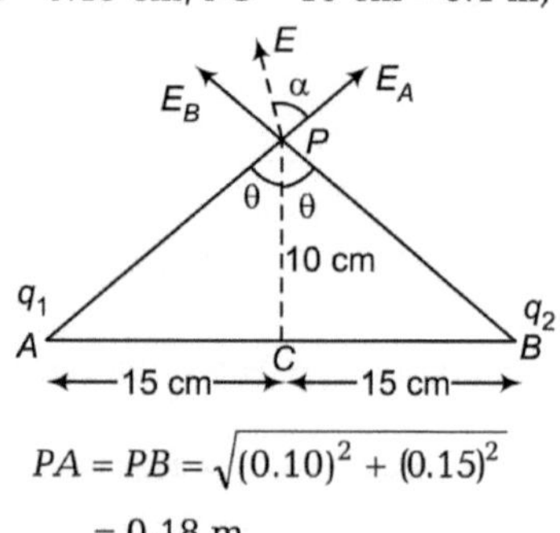

$$\therefore \qquad PA = PB = \sqrt{(0.10)^2 + (0.15)^2}$$

$$= 0.18 \text{ m}$$

Potential at point P

V_P = Potential at point P due to charge q_1

+ Potential at point P due to charge q_2

$$V_P = \frac{1}{4\pi\varepsilon_0} \cdot \frac{q_1}{PA} + \frac{1}{4\pi\varepsilon_0} \cdot \frac{q_2}{PB} = 9\times10^9 \left[\frac{1.5\times10^{-6}}{0.18} + \frac{2.5\times10^{-6}}{0.18} \right]$$

$$= \frac{9\times10^9}{0.18}\times10^{-6} \times 4 = 2\times10^5 \text{ V}$$

To find the resultant electric field at point P, we have to find the value of angle θ because electric field is a vector quantity.

In $\triangle APC$, $\qquad \cos\theta = \frac{0.10}{0.18} = \frac{5}{9}$

$$\cos 2\theta = 2\cos^2\theta - 1 = 2\left(\frac{5}{9}\right)^2 - 1 = \frac{-31}{81}$$

$$\therefore \qquad \sin 2\theta = \sqrt{1 - \cos^2 2\theta} = \sqrt{1 - \left(\frac{-31}{81}\right)^2} = 0.9239$$

Electric field at point P due to charge q_1 is E_A.

$$E_A = \frac{1}{4\pi\varepsilon_0} \cdot \frac{q_1}{(PA)^2} = \frac{9 \times 10^9 \times 1.5 \times 10^{-6}}{(0.18)^2} = 0.42 \times 10^6 \text{ N/C}$$

Electric field at point P due to charge q_2 is E_B.

$$E_B = \frac{1}{4\pi\varepsilon_0} \cdot \frac{q_2}{(PB)^2} = \frac{9 \times 10^9 \times 2.5 \times 10^{-6}}{(0.18)^2} = 0.69 \times 10^6 \text{ N/C}$$

The angle between E_A and E_B is $28°$, therefore the resultant electric field at point P due to charges q_1 and q_2 is given by

$$E = \sqrt{E_A^2 + E_B^2 + 2E_A \cdot E_B \cos 2\theta}$$

$$= \sqrt{(0.42 \times 10^6)^2 + (0.69 \times 10^6)^2 + 2(0.42 \times 10^6)(0.69 \times 10^6) \times \left(-\frac{31}{81}\right)}$$

$$= 6.58 \times 10^5 \text{ N/C}$$

Let the angle subtended between the resultant electric field E and E_A be α.

$$\therefore \qquad \tan \alpha = \frac{E_B \sin 2\theta}{E_A + E_B \cos 2\theta} = \frac{0.69 \times 10^6 \times 0.9239}{0.42 \times 10^6 + 0.69 \times 10^6 \left(-\frac{31}{81}\right)}$$

$$\tan \alpha = 4.08$$

$$\alpha = \tan^{-1}(4.08)$$

Thus, the resultant electric field E makes an angle $\tan^{-1}(4.08)$ from E_A.

Question 15. A spherical conducting shell of inner radius r_1 and outer radius r_2 has a charge Q.

(a) A charge q is placed at the centre of the shell. What is the surface charge density on the inner and outer surfaces of the shell?

(b) Is the electric field inside a cavity (with no charge) zero, even if the shell is not spherical but has any irregular shape? Explain.

Solution

(a) The charge $+Q$ resides on the outer surface of the shell. As the charge q is placed at the centre of the shell, there is charge $-q$ induced on the inner surface and a charge $+q$ is induced on the outer surface of the shell. Thus, the total charge on the inner surface of the shell is $-q$ and on the outer surface of the shell is $(Q + q)$.

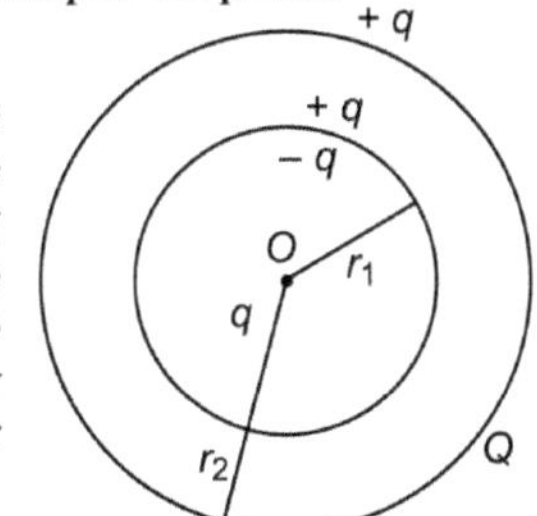

The surface charge density on the inner surface

$$\sigma_1 = -\frac{q}{4\pi r_1^2}$$

The surface charge density on the outer surface

$$\sigma_2 = \frac{Q + q}{4\pi r_2^2}$$

(b) Yes, the electric field inside a cavity is zero, if the shape of the shell is not spherical. If we take a closed- loop which is inside the cavity along a field line and the rest outside it, the net work done by the field in carrying a test charge over the closed-loop will not be zero. So, the electric field inside a cavity with no charge is always zero.

Question 16. (a) Show that the normal component of electrostatic field has a discontinuity from one side of a charged surface to another given by

$$(\mathbf{E}_2 - \mathbf{E}_1) \cdot \hat{n} = \frac{\sigma}{\varepsilon_0}$$

where, n̂ is a unit vector normal to the surface at a point and σ is the surface charge density at that point. (The direction of n̂ is from side 1 to side 2.) Hence, show that just outside a conductor, the electric field is σ n̂/ε₀.

(b) Show that the tangential component of electrostatic field is continuous from one side of a charged surface to another.
[Hint: For (a), use Gauss's law. For (b), use the fact that work done by electrostatic field on a closed-loop is zero.]

Solution

(a) Let *AB* be a charged surface having two sides as marked in the figure. A cylinder enclosing a small area Δ*S* of the charged surface is the Gaussian surface.

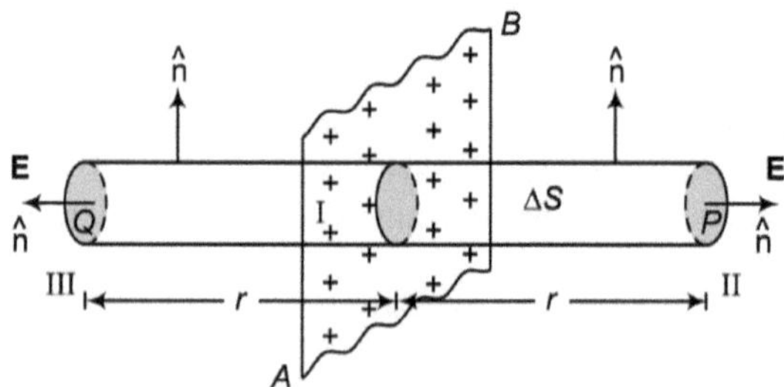

∴ According to Gauss's theorem, total flux linked with the surface

$$\oint_S \mathbf{A} \cdot d\mathbf{S} = \oint_I \mathbf{A} \cdot d\mathbf{S} + \oint_{II} \mathbf{A} \cdot d\mathbf{S} + \oint_{III} \mathbf{A} \cdot d\mathbf{S}$$

$$= \frac{\sigma \Delta S}{\varepsilon_0}$$

or $$\oint_{II} \mathbf{A_1} \cdot d\mathbf{S} + \oint_{III} \mathbf{E}_q \cdot d\mathbf{S} = \frac{\sigma \Delta S}{\varepsilon_0} \qquad \because \oint_S \mathbf{A} \cdot d\mathbf{S} = 0$$

$$\text{as } \theta = 90° \quad \therefore \cos 90° = 0$$

or $$\mathbf{E}_1 \cdot \Delta S \hat{\mathbf{n}}_1 + \mathbf{E}_2 \cdot \Delta S \hat{\mathbf{n}}_1 = \frac{\sigma}{\varepsilon_0} \Delta S$$

where $\mathbf{E}_1 + \mathbf{E}_2$ are the electric fields through circular cross-sections of cylinder at II and III respectively.

or $$\mathbf{E}_1 \cdot \hat{\mathbf{n}}_1 + \mathbf{E}_2 \cdot \hat{\mathbf{n}}_2 = \frac{\sigma}{\varepsilon_0}$$

or $$\mathbf{E}_1 \cdot (-\hat{\mathbf{n}}_2) + \mathbf{E}_2 \cdot \hat{\mathbf{n}}_2 = \frac{\sigma}{\varepsilon_0} \qquad (\because \hat{\mathbf{n}}_1 = -\hat{\mathbf{n}}_2)$$

or $$(\mathbf{E}_2 - \mathbf{E}_1) \cdot \hat{\mathbf{n}}_2 = \frac{\sigma}{\varepsilon_0}$$

or $$(\mathbf{E}_2 - \mathbf{E}_1) \cdot \hat{\mathbf{n}} = \frac{\sigma}{\varepsilon_0} \qquad \ldots(i)$$

$$(\because \hat{\mathbf{n}}_2 = \hat{\mathbf{n}} = \text{unit vector from side 1 to side 2.})$$

Hence proved.

It is clear from the figure that $\mathbf{E}_1$ lies inside the conductor. Also we know that the electric field inside the conductor is zero.

$\therefore$ $$\mathbf{E}_1 = 1$$

Thus from Eq. (i),

$$\mathbf{E}_2 \cdot \hat{\mathbf{n}} = \frac{\sigma}{\varepsilon_0}$$

or $$(\mathbf{E}_2 \cdot \hat{\mathbf{n}}) \cdot \hat{\mathbf{n}} = \frac{\sigma}{\varepsilon_0} \hat{\mathbf{n}}$$

or $$\mathbf{E}_2 = \frac{\sigma}{\varepsilon_0} \hat{\mathbf{n}} \qquad (\because \hat{\mathbf{n}} \cdot \hat{\mathbf{n}} = 1)$$

or electric field just outside the conductor $= \dfrac{\sigma}{\varepsilon_0} \hat{\mathbf{n}}$

Hence proved.

(b) The tangential component of electrostatic field is continuous from one side of a charged surface to another, we use that the work done by electrostatic field on a closed-loop is zero.

Let ABA be a charged surface in the field of a point charge q lying at origin.

Let $\mathbf{r}_A$ and $\mathbf{r}_B$ be its positive vectors at points A and B respectively.

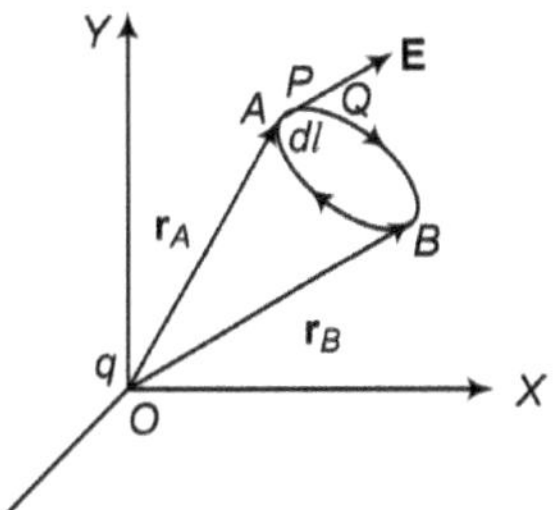

Let $\mathbf{E}$ be the electric field at point P, thus $E \cos \theta$ is the tangential component of electric field $\mathbf{E}$.

$$\therefore \qquad \mathbf{E}\cdot d\mathbf{l} = Edl\cdot\cos\theta = (E\cos\theta)\,dl.$$

To prove that $E\cos\theta$ is continuous from one to another side of the charge surface, we have to find the value of $\oint_{\text{AaBba}} \mathbf{E}\cdot d\mathbf{l}$. If it comes to be zero then we can say that tangential component of $\mathbf{E}$ is continuous.

$$\therefore \qquad \int_A^B \mathbf{E}\cdot d\mathbf{l} = \frac{1}{4\pi\varepsilon_0}\,q\cdot\left(\frac{1}{r_A} - \frac{1}{r_B}\right)$$

$$\text{and} \qquad \int_B^A \mathbf{E}\cdot d\mathbf{l} = \frac{1}{4\pi\varepsilon_0}\,q\cdot\left(\frac{1}{r_B} - \frac{1}{r_A}\right)$$

$$\therefore \qquad \oint_{\text{AaBbA}} \mathbf{E}\cdot d\mathbf{l} = \int_A^B \mathbf{E}\cdot d\mathbf{l} + \int_B^A \mathbf{E}\cdot d\mathbf{l}$$

$$= \frac{1}{4\pi\varepsilon_0}\cdot q\cdot\left(\frac{1}{r_A} - \frac{1}{r_B} + \frac{1}{r_B} - \frac{1}{r_A}\right)$$

$$= 0$$

Hence proved.

Question 17. A long charged cylinder of linear charged density λ is surrounded by a hollow co-axial conducting cylinder. What is the electric field in the space between the two cylinders?

Here we use the concept of Gauss's theorem. According to which the electric flux through a closed surface is $\dfrac{1}{\varepsilon_0}$ times the total charge enclosed by that surface.

Solution   Let there be a long charged cylinder A of linear charge density λ, length l and radius a. Now, one more hollow co-axial cylinder B of same length l and radius b surrounds the cylinder A ($b > a$).

The charge on cylinder A, $q = \lambda l$

Total charge = Linear charge density $\times$ Length

This charge spreads uniformly on A and a charge $-q$ is induced on B. Let $\mathbf{E}$ be the electric field produced in the space between the two cylinders. Consider a Gaussian cylindrical surface of radius r between the two given cylinders.

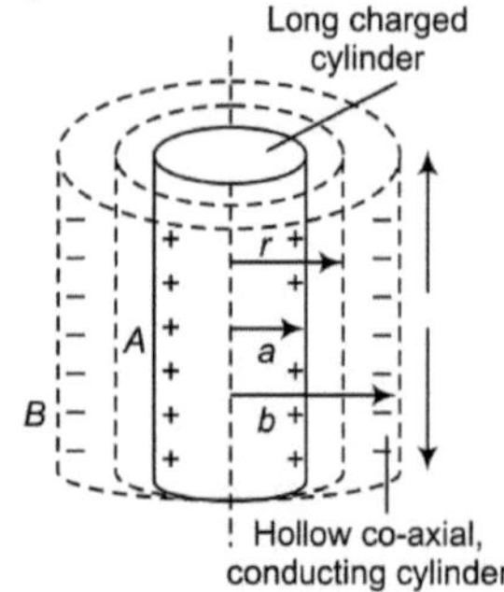

Electric flux linked with the Gaussian surface

$$\phi_E = \int \mathbf{E}\cdot d\mathbf{S} = \int E\cdot dS\cos 0° = E\int dS = E\times 2\pi rl$$

[As angle between the direction of electric field and area vector is zero]
According to Gauss's theorem,

$$\phi_E = E\times 2\pi rl = \frac{q}{\varepsilon_0}$$

$$E \times 2\pi r l = \frac{\lambda l}{\varepsilon_0}$$

$$E = \frac{\lambda}{2\pi\varepsilon_0 r}$$

Question 18. In a hydrogen atom, the electron and proton are bound at a distance of about 0.53 Å.

(a) Estimate the potential energy of the system in eV, taking the zero of the potential energy at infinite separation of the electron from proton.

(b) What is the minimum work required to free the electron, given that its kinetic energy in the orbit is half the magnitude of potential energy obtained in (a)?

(c) What are the answers to (a) and (b) above if the zero of potential energy is taken at 1.06 Å separation?

 The potential energy of any object at any point is equal to the difference in its potential energy at infinity and at that point. Work done is equal to the total energy of the system.

Solution Charge on electron, $q_e = -1.6 \times 10^{-19}$ C

and charge on proton, $q_p = 1.6 \times 10^{-19}$ C

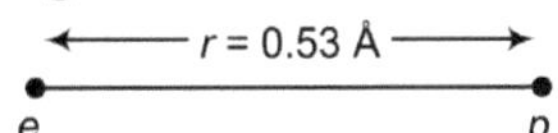

(a) Potential energy of the system
= Potential energy at infinity
$\qquad$ – Potential energy at a distance or 0.53 Å

$$= 0 - \frac{1}{4\pi\varepsilon_0} \cdot \frac{q_e q_p}{r}$$

$$= 0 - \frac{9 \times 10^9 \times 1.6 \times 10^{-19} \times (-1.6) \times 10^{-19}}{0.53 \times 10^{-10}}$$

$$= 43.47 \times 10^{-19} \text{ J} \qquad\qquad (\because 1 \text{ eV} = 1.6 \times 10^{-19} \text{ J})$$

$$= \frac{43.47 \times 10^{-19}}{1.6 \times 10^{-19}} = -27.16 \text{ eV}$$

(b) The kinetic energy $= -\dfrac{1}{2} \times$ Potential energy

$$= -\frac{1}{2} \times 27.16 = 13.58 \text{ eV}$$

Total energy $= \text{KE} + \text{PE} = 13.58 - 27.16 = -13.58$ eV

Thus, work done required to free the electron is 13.58 eV.

(c) Potential energy at separation of 1.06 Å

$$= \frac{1}{4\pi\varepsilon_0} \cdot \frac{q_e q_p}{1.06 \times 10^{-10}}$$

$$= \frac{-9 \times 10^9 \times 1.6 \times 10^{-19} \times (-1.6) \times 10^{-19}}{1.06 \times 10^{-10}}$$

$$= -21.73 \times 10^{-19} \text{ J}$$

$$= -\frac{21.73 \times 10^{-19}}{1.6 \times 10^{-19}} = -13.58 \text{ eV}$$

Thus, the potential energy of the system at 1.06 Å is

$$= \text{PE at distance } 1.06 \text{ Å} - \text{PE at distance } 0.53 \text{ Å}$$

$$= -13.58 - (-27.16) = 13.58 \text{ eV}$$

Thus, on shifting the zero of potential energy, work required to free electron remains same and it is equal to 13.58 eV.

Question 19. If one of the two electrons of an H_2 molecule is removed, we get a hydrogen molecular ion H_2^{2+}. In the ground state of an H_2^+, the two protons are separated by roughly 1.5 Å and the electron is roughly 1 Å from each proton. Determine the potential energy of the system. Specify your choice of the zero of potential energy.

 Use the total potential energy formula of system of charges and consider that the potential energy of the system at infinity is zero.

Solution   There are two protons P_1 and P_2 with an electron e.

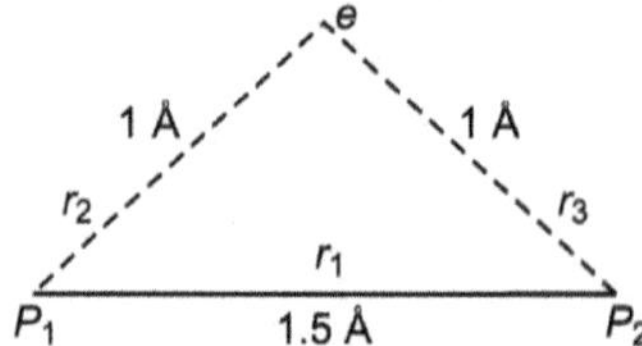

Distance between two protons $r_1 = 1.5$ Å $= 1.5 \times 10^{-10}$ m

Distance between proton P_1 and e is $r_2 = 1$ Å $= 1 \times 10^{-10}$ m

Distance between proton P_2 and e is $r_3 = 1$ Å $= 1 \times 10^{-10}$ m

The total potential energy of the system

$$U = \frac{1}{4\pi\varepsilon_0} \cdot \left[\frac{q_{P_1} \cdot q_{P_2}}{r_1} + \frac{q_{P_1} \cdot q_e}{r_2} + \frac{q_{P_2} \cdot q_e}{r_3} \right]$$

Given, $q_{P_1} = q_{P_2} = 1.6 \times 10^{-19}$ C and $q_e = -1.6 \times 10^{-19}$ C

Putting these values, we get

$$U = 9 \times 10^9 \left[\frac{1.6 \times 10^{-19} \times 1.6 \times 10^{-19}}{1.5 \times 10^{-10}} + \frac{(1.6 \times 10^{-19}) \times (-1.6 \times 10^{-19})}{10^{-10}} \right.$$

$$\left. + \frac{1.6 \times 10^{-19} \times (-1.6 \times 10^{-19})}{10^{-10}} \right]$$

$$U = \frac{9 \times 10^9 \times 1.6 \times 1.6 \times 10^{-38}}{10^{-10}} \left[\frac{1}{1.5} - 1 - 1\right]$$

$$= -30.78 \times 10^{-19} \text{ J}$$

or

$$U = \frac{-30.78 \times 10^{-19}}{1.6 \times 10^{-19}} = -19.2 \text{ eV}$$

Here, we use that the potential energy at infinity is zero.

Question 20. Two charged conducting spheres of radii a and b are connected to each other by a wire. What is the ratio of electric fields at the surfaces of the two spheres? Use the result obtained to explain why charge density on the sharp and pointed ends of a conductor is higher than on its flatter portions.

Solution As the two conducting spheres are connected to each other by a wire, the charge always flows from higher potential to lower potential till both have same potential.

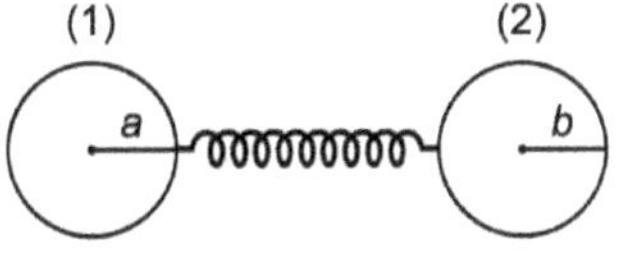

Capacitance of sphere (1), $\qquad C_1 = 4\pi\varepsilon_0\, a$

Capacitance of sphere (2), $\qquad C_2 = 4\pi\varepsilon_0\, b$

Charge Q_1 on C_1, $\qquad\qquad Q_1 = C_1 V$ ...(i)

Charge Q_2 on C_2, $\qquad\qquad Q_2 = C_2 V$ ...(ii)

where, V is the same potential on both the spheres.

$\therefore \qquad\qquad \dfrac{Q_1}{Q_2} = \dfrac{C_1}{C_2}$ [From Eqs. (i) and (ii)]

Putting the values of C_1 and C_2, we get

$$\frac{Q_1}{Q_2} = \frac{4\pi\varepsilon_0 a}{4\pi\varepsilon_0 b} = \frac{a}{b}$$

$$\frac{Q_1}{Q_2} = \frac{a}{b} \qquad\qquad \text{...(iii)}$$

Charge density on sphere (1), $\sigma_1 = \dfrac{\text{Charge}}{\text{Surface area}}$

$$\sigma_1 = \frac{Q_1}{4\pi a^2}$$

Charge density on sphere (2), $\sigma_2 = \dfrac{\text{Charge}}{\text{Surface area}}$

$$\sigma_2 = \frac{Q_2}{4\pi b^2}$$

$\therefore \qquad \dfrac{\sigma_1}{\sigma_2} = \dfrac{b^2}{a^2} \cdot \dfrac{Q_1}{Q_2} = \dfrac{b^2}{a^2} \cdot \dfrac{a}{b}$ [From Eq. (iii)]

or
$$\frac{\sigma_1}{\sigma_2} = \frac{b}{a} \qquad \text{(iv)}$$

The ratio of electric field on both spheres
$$\frac{E_1}{E_2} = \frac{\sigma_1}{\sigma_2} = \frac{b}{a} \qquad \text{[From Eq. (iv)]}$$

As, charge density is inversely proportional to radius.
Thus, for flatter portions, the radius is more and at pointed ends radius is less, thus the charge density is more at pointed or sharp ends.

Question 21. Two charges $- q$ and $+ q$ are located at points $(0, 0, - a)$ and $(0, 0, a)$ respectively.

    (a) What is the electrostatic potential at the points $(0, 0, z)$ and $(x, y, 0)$?

    (b) Obtain the dependence of potential on the distance r of a point from the origin when $r/a >> 1$.

    (c) How much work is done in moving a small test charge from the point $(5, 0, 0)$ to $(- 7, 0, 0)$ along the X-axis? Does the answer change, if the path of the test charge between the same points is not along the X-axis?

Use the formula of electric potential due to an electric dipole at any arbitrary point.

Solution   Here two charges placed at Z-axis at position $(0, 0, - a)$ and $(0, 0, a)$. They form a dipole of length $2a$.

Let the coordinates of C is $(0, 0, z)$ and of D is $(x, y, 0)$.

    (a) Potential at $(0, 0, z)$ is V.

$$V = \text{Potential at } C \text{ due to } A$$
$$+ \text{ Potential at } C \text{ due to } B$$
$$V = V_A + V_B = \frac{1}{4\pi\varepsilon_0} \cdot \frac{(- q)}{AC} + \frac{1}{4\pi\varepsilon_0} \cdot \frac{q}{BC}$$

$$= \frac{1}{4\pi\varepsilon_0} \left[\frac{-q}{AO + OC} + \frac{q}{OC - BO} \right]$$

$$= \frac{q}{4\pi\varepsilon_0} \left[\frac{-1}{z + a} + \frac{1}{z - a} \right] = \frac{q}{4\pi\varepsilon_0} \left[\frac{-z + a + z + a}{z^2 - a^2} \right]$$

$$= \frac{q \cdot 2a}{4\pi\varepsilon_0 \cdot (z^2 - a^2)} \qquad \text{(where, } q \cdot 2a = p \text{ dipole moment)}$$

$$= \frac{p}{4\pi\varepsilon_0 (z^2 - a^2)}$$

The point $(x, y, 0)$ is perpendicular to Z-axis and we know that the potential due to a dipole on the equatorial line of dipole is zero.
So, the potential due to dipole at $(x, y, 0)$ will be zero.

(b) The formula for the potential due to an electric dipole at any arbitrary point is

$$V = \frac{1}{4\pi\varepsilon_0} \cdot \frac{p\cos\theta}{(r^2 - a^2\cos^2\theta)}$$

As according to question, if $r >> a$, neglect a^2 as compared to r^2, then electric potential

$$V = \frac{p\cos\theta}{4\pi\varepsilon_0 . r^2}$$

or $$V \propto \frac{1}{r^2}$$

(c) The work done = Product of charge and potential difference between potential at $(5, 0, 0)$ due to $-q$ and $+q$

$$\text{Potential } V_1 = \frac{1}{4\pi\varepsilon_0} \cdot \frac{(-q)}{\sqrt{(5-0)^2 + (0-a)^2}} + \frac{1}{4\pi\varepsilon_0} \cdot \frac{q}{\sqrt{(5-0)^2 + (a-0)^2}}$$

$$= \frac{-q}{4\pi\varepsilon_0 \sqrt{a^2 + 25}} + \frac{q}{4\pi\varepsilon_0 \sqrt{a^2 + 25}} = 0$$

Potential at $(-7, 0, 0)$ due to $-q$ and $+q$ is

$$V_2 = \frac{1}{4\pi\varepsilon_0} \cdot \frac{(-q)}{\sqrt{(-7-0)^2 + a^2}} + \frac{1}{4\pi\varepsilon_0} \cdot \frac{q}{\sqrt{(-7-0)^2 + a^2}} = 0$$

$\therefore$ Work done $= q\,(V_2 - V_1) = q \times 0 = 0$

Here, work done is independent of path so if the path changes between the two points on x-axis, work is always zero.

Question 22. Given figure shows a charge array known as an electric quadrupole. For a point on the axis of the quadrupole, obtain the dependence of potential on r for $r/a >> 1$ and contrast your results with that due to an electric dipole and an electric monopole (*i.e.*, a single charge).

A quadrupole is considered always a system of three charges q, $-2q$ and q.

Solution Given, $AC = 2a$, $BP = r$

$AP = r + a$ and $PC = r - a$

The potential at P is V.

$$V = \text{Potential at } P \text{ due to } A + \text{Potential at } P \text{ due to } B + \text{Potential at } P \text{ due to } C$$

$$V = \frac{1}{4\pi\varepsilon_0}\left[\frac{q}{AP} - \frac{2q}{BP} + \frac{q}{CP}\right] = \frac{1}{4\pi\varepsilon_0} \cdot q\left[\frac{1}{r+a} - \frac{2}{r} + \frac{1}{r-a}\right]$$

$$= \frac{q}{4\pi\varepsilon_0}\left[\frac{r(r-a)-2(r+a)(r-a)+r(r+a)}{r(r+a)(r-a)}\right]$$

$$= \frac{q}{4\pi\varepsilon_0}\left[\frac{r^2-ra-2r^2+2a^2+r^2+ra}{r(r^2-a^2)}\right]$$

$$= \frac{q.2a^2}{4\pi\varepsilon_0\, r(r^2-a^2)} = \frac{q.2a^2}{4\pi\varepsilon_0.r.r^2\left(1-\dfrac{a^2}{r^2}\right)}$$

If $\dfrac{r}{a} >> 1$, $a << r$

According to the question,

$$V = \frac{q\cdot 2a^2}{4\pi\varepsilon_0.r^3} \implies V \propto \frac{1}{r^3}$$

As, we know that electric potential at a point on axial line due to an electric dipole, $V \propto \dfrac{1}{r^2}$.

In case of electric monopole $V \propto \dfrac{1}{r}$.

Then, we canclude that for larger r, the electric potential due to a quadrupole is inversely proportional to the cube of the distance r while due to an electric dipole it is inversely proportional to the square of r and inversely proportional to the distance r for a monopole.

Question 23. An electrical technician requires a capacitance of $2\,\mu F$ in a circuit across a potential difference of 1 kV. A large number of $1\,\mu F$ capacitors are available to him each of which can withstand a potential difference of not more than 400 V. Suggest a possible arrangement that requires the minimum number of capacitors.

Solution   The required capacitance $C = 2\,\mu F$

Potential difference
$$V = 1\,kV = 1000\,V$$

Capacitance of each capacitor $C_1 = 1\mu F$ and it can withstand a potential difference of $V_1 = 400$ V

Let the n capacitors are connected in series and there are m rows of such capacitors.

As the potential difference across each row is 1000 V.

So, the potential difference across each capacitor $= \dfrac{1000}{n}$

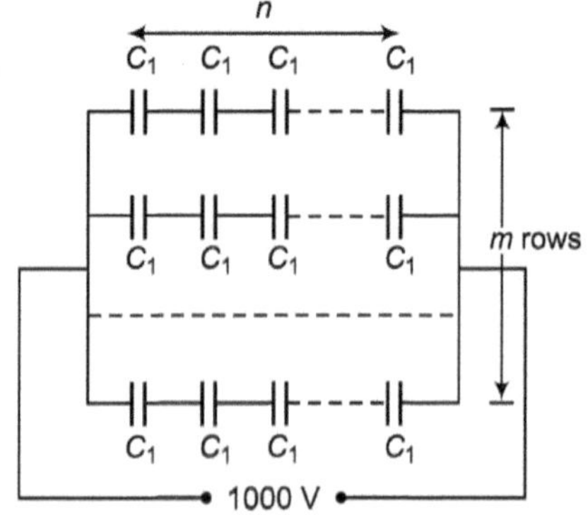

Minimum number of capacitors that must be connected in series in a row are —

$$\frac{1000}{n} = 400$$

$$n = 2.5$$

Here n is the number of capacitors, so it should be a whole number. If we take $n = 2$, then potential difference across each capacitor is 500 V. Here according to question a capacitor can bear only 400 V, so they burst. We take the value of $n = 3$.

So, the capacitance of each row (in series)

$$\frac{1}{C'} = \frac{1}{1} + \frac{1}{1} + \frac{1}{1} = \frac{3}{1}$$

$$\Rightarrow \qquad C' = \frac{1}{3}$$

The total capacitance of m rows is $m \times \dfrac{1}{3} = \dfrac{m}{3}$

According to question, the total capacitance required is $2\,\mu F$. So,

$$\frac{m}{3} = 2$$

$$m = 6$$

Thus, the total number of capacitor $= m \times n = 3 \times 6 = 18$ So, 1 μF capacitors are connected that of 6 rows having 3 capacitors in each row.

Question 24. What is the area of the plates of a 2 F parallel plate capacitor, given that the separation between the plates is 0.5 cm? [You will realise from your answer why ordinary capacitors are in the range of μF or less. However, electrolytic capacitors do have a much larger capacitance (0.1 F) because of very minute separation between the conductors.]

Solution   Given, capacitance $C = 2\,F$

and separation between plates $d = 0.5\,cm = 0.5 \times 10^{-2}\,m$

Capacitance of a parallel plate capacitor

$$C = \frac{\varepsilon_0 A}{d}$$

or

$$A = \frac{Cd}{\varepsilon_0} = \frac{2 \times 0.5 \times 10^{-2}}{8.854 \times 10^{-12}}$$

$$= 1.13 \times 10^9\,m^2$$

$$= 1130\,km^2$$

This area is very large, so it is not possible that the capacitance of a capacitor is too large as 2 F. So, the capacitance of any capacitor should be of range of $2\,\mu F$.

Question 25. Obtain the equivalent capacitance of the network in given figure. For a 300 V supply, determine the charge and voltage across each capacitor.

Use the formula of series and parallel combinations of resistances and remember that in parallel combination, the potential difference across each capacitor is same.

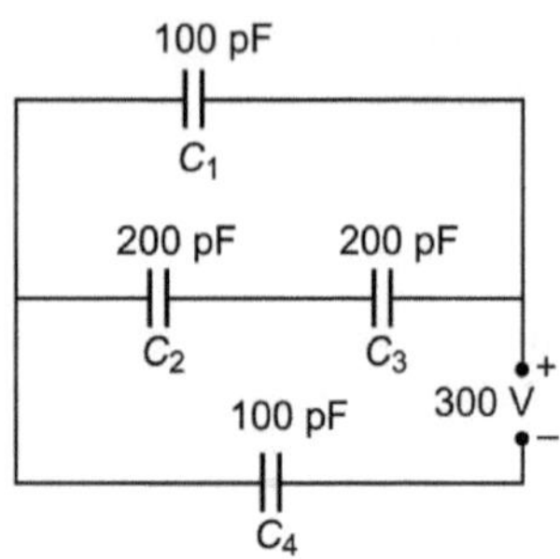

Solution We can resolve the circuit as shown in figure.

Let the charge passing through the circuit be q. Let the charge through C_2 and C_3 be q_1 and through C_1 be q_2.

Let the potential across C_4 be V_1. Potential difference across C_1 is V_2, C_2 is V_3 and C_3 is V_4.

Here, C_2 and C_3 are in series,

$$\frac{1}{C'} = \frac{1}{C_2} + \frac{1}{C_3} = \frac{1}{200} + \frac{1}{200} = \frac{1}{100}$$

$$C' = 100 \text{ pF}$$

Now, C' and C_1 are in parallel

$\therefore$ $$C'' = C' + C_1 = 100 + 100 = 200 \text{ pF}$$

Now, C'' and C_4 are in series

$\therefore$ $$\frac{1}{C} = \frac{1}{C''} + \frac{1}{C_4} = \frac{1}{200} + \frac{1}{100} = \frac{3}{200}$$

$$C = \frac{200}{3} \text{ pF} = 66.7 \times 10^{-12} \text{ F}$$

Total charge on the combination

$$q = CV = \frac{200}{3} \times 300 = 20000 \text{ pC}$$

$$= 20000 \times 10^{-12} = 2 \times 10^{-8} \text{ C}$$

$$V_1 = \frac{q}{C_4} = \frac{2 \times 10^{-8}}{100 \times 10^{-12}} = 200 \text{ V}$$

and $$V_2 = V - V_1 = 300 - 200 = 100 \text{ V}$$

Charge $q_2 = C_1 V_2 = 100 \times 10^{-12} \times 100 = 10^{-8} \text{ C}$

and charge $q_1 = q - q_2 = 2 \times 10^{-8} - 10^{-8} = 10^{-8} \text{ C}$

$$V_3 = \frac{q_1}{C_2} = \frac{10^{-8}}{200 \times 10^{-12}} = 50 \text{ V}$$

and
$$V_4 = \frac{q_1}{C_3} = \frac{10^{-8}}{200 \times 10^{-12}} = 50 \text{ V}$$

Thus, the equivalent capacitance of the network is 66.7×10^{-12} F.

Charge on C_1 is $q_2 = 10^{-8}$ C ;   Charge on C_2 and C_3 is $q_1 = 10^{-8}$ C

Charge on C_4 is $q = 2 \times 10^{-8}$ C

Potential difference on C_1 is $V_2 = 100$ V

Potential difference on C_2 is $V_3 = 50$ V

Potential difference on C_3 is $V_4 = 50$ V

Potential difference on C_4 is $V_1 = 200$ V

Question 26. The plates of a parallel plate capacitor have an area of 90 cm^2 each and are separated by 2.5 mm. The capacitor is charged by connecting it to a 400 V supply.

(a) How much electrostatic energy is stored by the capacitor?

(b) View this energy as stored in the electrostatic field between the plates and obtain the energy per unit volume u. Hence, arrive at a relation between u and the magnitude of electric field E between the plates.

Solution   Area of plates $A = 90$ cm$^2 = 90 \times 10^{-4}$ m^2

Distance between plates $d = 2.5$ mm $= 2.5 \times 10^{-3}$ m

and potential difference across capacitor $V = 400$ V

(a) Electrostatic energy

$$U = \frac{1}{2} CV^2$$

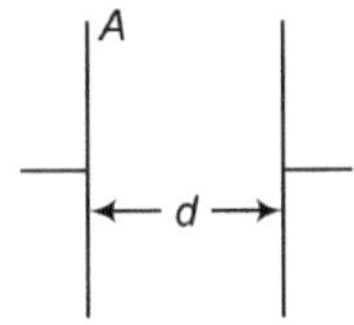

where, C is the capacitance of the capacitor. Capacitance of a parallel plate capacitor

$$C = \frac{\varepsilon_0 A}{d} = \frac{8.854 \times 10^{-12} \times 90 \times 10^{-4}}{2.5 \times 10^{-3}}$$

$\therefore$
$$U = \frac{1}{2} CV^2 = \frac{1}{2} \times \frac{8.854 \times 10^{-12} \times 90 \times 10^{-4}}{2.5 \times 10^{-3}} \times 400 \times 400$$

$$= 2.55 \times 10^{-6} \text{ J}$$

(b) Volume of the capacitor $= A \times d = 90 \times 10^{-4} \times 2.5 \times 10^{-3}$

$$= 2.25 \times 10^{-5} \text{ m}^3$$

Energy stored per unit volume = Energy/Volume

$$= \frac{2.55 \times 10^{-6}}{2.25 \times 10^{-5}} = 0.113 \text{ J/m}^3$$

$$u = \frac{\text{Energy}}{\text{Volume}} = \frac{1}{2} \frac{CV^2}{A \times d} = \frac{1}{2} \cdot \frac{\varepsilon_0 A}{dA} \cdot \frac{V^2}{d}$$

$$u = \frac{1}{2} \cdot \left(\frac{V}{d}\right)^2 \varepsilon_0 = \frac{1}{2} \varepsilon_0 E^2 \qquad \left(\because \frac{V}{d} = \text{Electric field}\right)$$

$$u = \frac{1}{2} \varepsilon_0 E^2$$

Question 27. A $4\,\mu$F capacitor is charged by a 200 V supply. Then, it is disconnected from the supply and is connected to another uncharged $2\,\mu$F capacitor. How much electrostatic energy of the first capacitor is lost in the form of heat and electromagnetic radiation?

Solution   Let us consider two capacitors C_1 and C_2. According to the question, $C_1 = 4\,\mu$F, $C_2 = 2\,\mu$F, $V_1 = 200$ V and $V_2 = 0$

$$\text{Loss in energy} = \frac{1}{2} \frac{C_1 C_2 \,(V_1 - V_2)^2}{(C_1 + C_2)} = \frac{1}{2} \times \frac{4 \times 2 \times 10^{-12} \,(200 - 0)^2}{(4 + 2) \times 10^{-6}} = \frac{8}{3} \times 10^{-2}$$

$$\text{Loss in energy} = 2.67 \times 10^{-2} \text{ J}$$

This loss in energy is equal to the energy dissipated in the form of heat and electromagnetic radiation.

Question 28. Show that the force on each plate of a parallel plate capacitor has a magnitude equal to $\frac{1}{2}\,QE$, where Q is the charge on the capacitor and E is the magnitude of electric field between the plates. Explain the origin of the factor 1/2.

 Here, we can use the concept that the work done in displacing the plates against the force is equal to the increase in energy of the capacitor.

Solution   Let the distance between the plates be increased by a very small distance Δx. The force on each plate is F.

The amount of work done in increasing the separation by Δx

$$= \text{Force} \times \text{Increased distance}$$

$$= F.\Delta x \qquad \qquad \ldots\text{(i)}$$

Increase in volume of capacitor = Area of plates $\times$ Increased distance

$$= A.\Delta x$$

$$u = \text{Energy density} = \frac{\text{Energy}}{\text{Volume}}$$

$$\text{Energy} = u \times \text{Volume} = u \cdot A \cdot \Delta x \qquad \qquad \ldots\text{(ii)}$$

As $\text{Energy} = \text{Work done}$

$$F \cdot \Delta x = u \cdot A \cdot \Delta x \qquad \qquad \text{[From Eqs. (i) and (ii)]}$$

$$= u \cdot A$$

$$= \frac{1}{2} \varepsilon_0 E^2 \cdot A \qquad \qquad \left(\because \ u = \frac{1}{2} \varepsilon_0 E^2 \text{ and } E = \frac{V}{d}\right)$$

$$= \frac{1}{2}\varepsilon_0 \cdot \frac{V^2}{d^2} \cdot A$$

$$= \left(\frac{\varepsilon_0 A}{d} \cdot V\right) \frac{V}{d} \times \frac{1}{2} \qquad \left(\because C = \frac{\varepsilon_0 A}{d}, CV = q\right)$$

$$= \frac{1}{2} \cdot E \cdot C \cdot V = \frac{1}{2}QE$$

The factor of $\frac{1}{2}$ in the force can be explained by the fact that the field is zero inside the conductor and outside the conductor, field is E. So, the average value of the field $i.e., \frac{E}{2}$ contributes to the force against which the plates are moved.

Question 29. A spherical capacitor consists of two concentric spherical conductors, held in position by suitable insulating supports (see bolow figure). Show that the capacitance of a spherical capacitor is given by

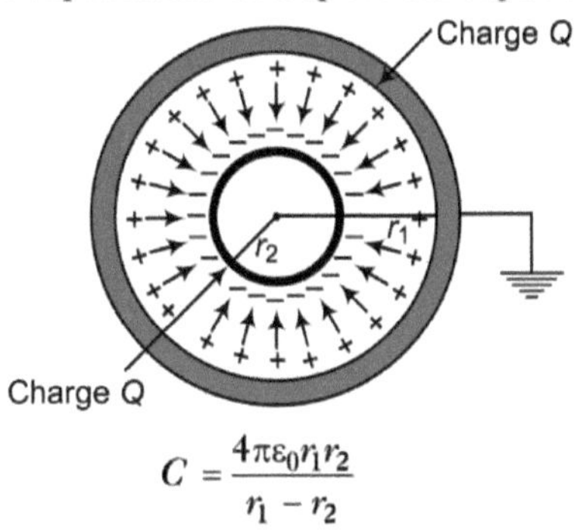

$$C = \frac{4\pi\varepsilon_0 r_1 r_2}{r_1 - r_2}$$

where, r_1 and r_2 are the radii of outer and inner spheres, respectively.

Solution From the figure, it is clear that $+ Q$ charge spreads uniformly on inner surface of outer sphere of radius r_1. Due to which induced charge $- R$ spreads uniformly on the outer surface of inner sphere of radius r_2. Due to electrostatic shielding $E = 0$ for $r < r_2$ as there is no field inside the conductor and $E = 0$ for $r > r_1$ as outer surface of outer sphere is earthed.

Charge on outer spherical conductor $= + Q$

Charge on inner spherical conductor $= - Q$

Potential at outer spherical conductor $V_1 = \dfrac{1}{4\pi\varepsilon_0} \cdot \dfrac{Q}{r_1}$

Potential at inner spherical conductor $V_2 = -\dfrac{1}{4\pi\varepsilon_0} \cdot \dfrac{Q}{r_2}$

$\therefore$ The potential difference between two spheres $V = V_2 - V_1$

$$V = \frac{1}{4\pi\varepsilon_0} \cdot \frac{Q}{r_2} - \frac{1}{4\pi\varepsilon_0} \cdot \frac{Q}{r_1} = \frac{Q}{4\pi\varepsilon_0}\left[\frac{1}{r_2} - \frac{1}{r_1}\right]$$

$$V = \frac{Q}{4\pi\varepsilon_0}\left[\frac{r_1 - r_2}{r_1 r_2}\right]$$

Capacitance of the spherical capacitor $C = \dfrac{Q}{V} = \dfrac{Q4\pi\varepsilon_0 r_1 r_2}{Q(r_1 - r_2)}$

$$= \frac{4\pi\varepsilon_0 r_1 r_2}{r_1 - r_2}$$

Question 30. A spherical capacitor has an inner sphere of radius 12 cm and an outer sphere of radius 13 cm. The outer sphere is earthed and the inner sphere is given a charge of 2.5 µC. The space between the concentric spheres is filled with a liquid of dielectric constant 32.

(a) Determine the capacitance of the capacitor.

(b) What is the potential of the inner sphere?

(c) Compare the capacitance of this capacitor with that of an isolated sphere of radius 12 cm. Explain why the latter is much smaller.

 Use the formula for the capacitance of a spherical capacitor.

Solution   Radius of inner sphere $r_1 = 12$ cm

Radius of outer sphere $r_2 = 13$ cm

and charge on inner sphere $q = 2.5$ µC

The dielectric constant $K = 32$

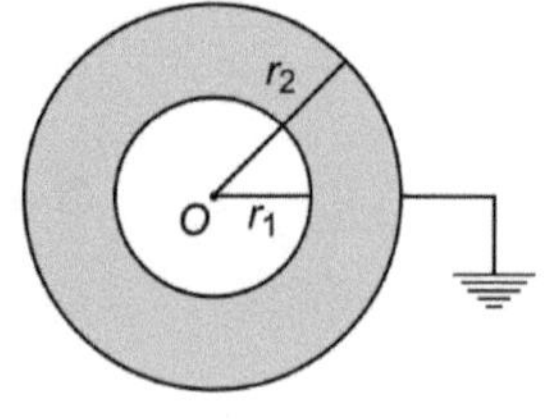

(a) Capacitance of a spherical capacitor

$$C = \frac{4\pi\varepsilon_0 K r_1 r_2}{r_1 - r_2} = \frac{1}{9\times 10^9}\cdot\frac{32\times 12\times 13\times 10^{-4}}{(13-12)\times 10^{-2}}$$

$$C = 5.5\times 10^{-9}\ \text{F}$$

(b) Electric potential of inner sphere

$$V = \frac{q}{C} = \frac{2.5\times 10^{-6}}{5.5\times 10^{-9}} = 4.5\times 10^2\ \text{V}$$

(c) Capacitance of an isolated sphere of radius $r = 12$ cm

$$C = 4\pi\varepsilon_0 r = \frac{1}{9\times 10^9}\times 12\times 10^{-2}$$

$$= 1.33\times 10^{-11}\ \text{F}$$

The capacitance of an isolated sphere is much smaller as compared to the spherical capacitor because as the outer sphere is earthed. The potential difference decreases and hence the capacitance increases.

Question 31. Answer the following problems carefully:

(a) Two large conducting spheres carrying charges Q_1 and Q_2 are brought close to each other. Is the magnitude of electrostatic force between them exactly given by $Q_1 Q_2 / 4\pi\varepsilon_0 r^2$, where r is the distance between their centres?

(b) If Coulomb's law involved $1/r^3$ dependence (instead of $1/r^2$), would Gauss's law be still true?

(c) A small test charge is released at rest at a point in an electrostatic field configuration. Will it travel along the field line passing through that point?

(d) What is the work done by the field of a nucleus in a complete circular orbit of the electron? What if the orbit is elliptical?

(e) We know that electric field is discontinuous across the surface of a charged conductor. Is electric potential also discontinuous there?

(f) What meaning would you give to the capacitance of a single conductor?

(g) Guess a possible reason why water has a much greater dielectric constant ($= 80$) than say, mica ($= 6$).

Solution

(a) As the two large conducting spheres carrying charges Q_1 and Q_2 are brought close to each other, the charge distribution is not uniform and the electrostatic force which is given by $\dfrac{Q_1 Q_2}{4\pi\varepsilon_0 r^2}$ is not valid. It is valid for only uniform charge distribution.

(b) No, Gauss's law cannot be true. It is true only if the Coulomb's law involved $\dfrac{1}{r^2}$ dependence.

(c) If the electric field lines are straight, then the direction of acceleration on the test charge is same as that of electric field and test charge move along the field lines.

If the electric field lines are curved, then the direction of acceleration charge at each point and the test charge do not move along the field lines.

(d) As we know that the electrostatic force is conservative in nature, *i.e.*, the work done is independent of path travelled. Hence, if the path is circular or elliptical, then always the work done is zero.

(e) No, the electric potential is always continuous, if the electric field is discontinuous.

(f) If there is a single conductor that means the second conductor is placed at infinity.

(g) Water has greater dielectric constant than mica because the shape of water molecule is unsymmetrical and it has a permanent dipole moment.

Question 32. A cylindrical capacitor has two co-axial cylinders of length 15 cm and radii 1.5 cm and 1.4 cm. The outer cylinder is earthed and the inner cylinder is given a charge of 3.5 μC. Determine the capacitance of the system and the potential of the inner cylinder. Neglect end effects (*i.e.*, bending of field lines at the ends).

 Use the formula of the capacitance of a cylindrical capacitor *i.e.*,

$$C = \frac{2\pi\varepsilon_0 l}{\log_e\left(\dfrac{b}{a}\right)}$$

where l = length, a = radius of inner cylinder, b = radius of outer cylinder.

Solution   Length of the capacitor $l = 15$ cm

Radius of inner cylinder $a = 1.4$ cm
Radius of outer cylinder $b = 1.5$ cm
Charge $q = 3.5\,\mu C = 3.5 \times 10^{-6}$ C
The capacitance of the cylindrical capacitor

$$C = \frac{2\pi\varepsilon_0 l}{\log_e\left(\dfrac{b}{a}\right)}$$

$$= \frac{2 \times 3.14 \times 8.85 \times 10^{-12} \times 15 \times 10^{-2}}{2.303 \log_{10}\left(\dfrac{1.5 \times 10^{-2}}{1.4 \times 10^{-2}}\right)}$$

$$= \frac{2 \times 3.14 \times 8.85 \times 10^{-12} \times 15 \times 10^{-2}}{2.303\,[\log 1.5 - \log 1.4]} = 1.2 \times 10^{-10} \text{ F}$$

$$\text{Potential } V = \frac{q}{C} = \frac{3.5 \times 10^{-6}}{1.2 \times 10^{-10}} = 2.9 \times 10^4 \text{ V}$$

Question 33. A parallel plate capacitor is to be designed with a voltage rating 1 kV, using a material of dielectric constant 3 and dielectric strength about 10^7 V/m. (Dielectric strength is the maximum electric field a material can tolerate without breakdown *i.e.*, without starting to conduct electricity through partial ionization.) For safety, we should like the field never to exceed, say 10% of the dielectric strength. What minimum area of the plates is required to have a capacitance of 50 pF?

 Use the concept of dielectric strength *i.e.*, the maximum electric field a material can tolerate without breakdown.

Solution   Voltage $V = 1$ kV $= 1000$ V

Dielectric constant $K = 3$
and dielectric strength $= 10^7$ V/m
Here, the electric field should be 10% of the dielectric strength due to safety reasons.

$$E = 10\% \text{ of dielectric strength} = \frac{10}{100} \times 10^7 = 10^6 \text{ V/m}$$

$$C = 50 \text{ pF} = 50 \times 10^{-12} \text{ F}$$

$$\text{Electric field } E = \frac{V}{d} \quad \Rightarrow \quad d = \frac{V}{E} = \frac{1000}{10^6} = 10^{-3} \text{ m}$$

$$\text{Capacitance } C = \frac{K\varepsilon_0 A}{d} \quad \Rightarrow \quad A = \frac{Cd}{\varepsilon_0 K} = \frac{50 \times 10^{-12} \times 10^{-3}}{8.854 \times 10^{-12} \times 3}$$

$$A = 1.9 \times 10^{-3} \text{ m}^2$$

Question 34. Describe schematically the equipotential surfaces corresponding to

    (a) a constant electric field in the Z-direction,

    (b) a field that uniformly increases in magnitude but remains in a constant (say, Z) direction,

    (c) a single positive charge at the origin and

    (d) a uniform grid consisting of long equally spaced parallel charged wires in a plane.

 Use the concept that the equipotential surface is always normal to the direction of electric field.

Solution

    (a) As the constant electric field in the Z-axis direction, the equipotential surfaces are normal to the field, *i.e.*, in X-Y plane. The equipotential surfaces are equidistant from each other.

    (b) As the electric field increases in the direction of Z-axis, the equipotential surface is normal to Z-axis *i.e.*, in X-Y plane and they become closer and closer as the field increases.

    (c) As a single positive charge placed at origin, the equipotential surfaces are concentric circles with origin at centre.

    (d) The shape of equipotential surfaces changes periodically and they are distant from each other. They are parallel to grid itself.

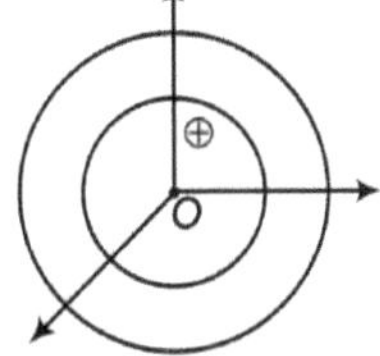

Question 35. In a Van de Graff type generator, a spherical metal shell is to be a 15×10^6 V electrode. The dielectric strength of the gas surrounding the electrode is 5×10^7 V/m. What is the minimum radius of the spherical shell required? (You will learn from this exercise why one

cannot build an electrostatic generator using a very small shell which requires a small charge to acquire a high potential.)

Solution   Given, $V = 15 \times 10^6$ V and dielectric strength $= 5 \times 10^7$ V/m

As we know that the electric field is 10% of dielectric strength.

Safer value of electric field $E = 10\%$ of dielectric strength

$$= \frac{10}{100} \times 5 \times 10^7$$

$$E = 5 \times 10^6 \text{ V/m}$$

$\because$
$$E = \frac{V}{r}$$

$\therefore$
$$r = \frac{V}{E} = \frac{15 \times 10^6}{5 \times 10^6} = 3 \text{ m}$$

The minimum radius of the spherical shell required is 3 m.

Question 36. A small sphere of radius r_1 and charge q_1 is enclosed by a spherical shell of radius r_2 and charge q_2. Show that if q_1 is positive, charge will necessarily flow from the sphere to the shell (when the two are connected by a wire) no matter what the charge q_2 on the shell is.

Solution   As we know that the charge always resides on the outer surface of shell, they are connecting by a wire. So, the charge surely flows from the sphere to shell. It is independent to the sign of q_2.

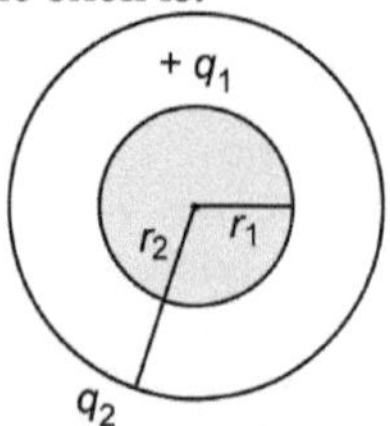

Question 37. Answer the following:

    (a) The top of the atmosphere is at about 400 kV with respect to the surface of the earth, corresponding to an electric field that decreases with altitude. Near the surface of the earth, the field is about 100 V/m. Then why do we not get an electric shock as we step out of our house into the open? (Assume the house to be a steel cage so there is no field inside.)

    (b) A man fixes outside his house one evening a 2 m high insulating slab carrying on its top a large aluminium sheet of area 1 m^2. Will he get an electric shock, if he touches the metal sheet next morning?

    (c) The discharging current in the atmosphere due to the small conductivity of air is known to be 1800 A on an average over the globe. Then why does the atmosphere not discharge itself completely in due course and become electrically neutral? In other words, what keeps the atmosphere charged?

    (d) What are the forms of energy into which the electrical energy of the atmosphere is dissipated during a lightning?

       (Hint: The earth has an electric field of about 100 V/m at its surface in the downward direction, corresponding to a surface charge density $= -10^{-9}$ C/m^2. Due to the slight conductivity of the atmosphere upto about 50 km (beyond which it is good conductor), about $+1800$ C is pumped every second into the earth as a whole. However, the earth, does not get discharged since thunderstorms and lightning occurring continually all over the globe pump an equal amount of negative charge on the earth.)

Solution

(a) As our body and the earth both are conducting in nature, so our body and earth form an equipotential surface. As we goes out into the open air from our house, the original equipotential surfaces of open air charge keeping our body and ground at the same potential. So, we do not get any shock. As our house is a steel cage *i.e.,*it is protected by electric field or there is electrostatic shielding for our house.

(b) Yes, the man gets an electric shock, if he touches the metal sheet next morning because the atmospheric currents charge the sheet and thus its potential raises and we get a shock.

(c) The atmosphere does not discharge itself completely in due course because our atmosphere is charged by thunderstorms and also discharge due to the small conductivity of air.

(d) The electrical energy of the atmosphere is dissipated during a lightning in the form of heat, sound and light energy.

Selected NCERT Exemplar Problems

Question 1. Calculate the potential energy of a point charge $-q$ placed along the axis due to a charge $+Q$ uniformly distributed along a ring of radius R. Sketch potential energy as a function of axial distance z from the centre of the ring. Looking at graph, can you see what would happen if $-q$ is displaced slightly from the centre of the ring (along the axis)?

 Use the concept to find the potential at any point due to a very small charge called elementary charge and then integrate it within proper limits.

Solution Let there be a ring of radius R and centre point O. The charge $+Q$ is spread uniformly on the length of the ring. The charge $-q$ is placed at a point P. The distance of point P from O is z. Le us consider an elementary length portion $AB = dl$.

Let the charge on this elementary portion be dq.

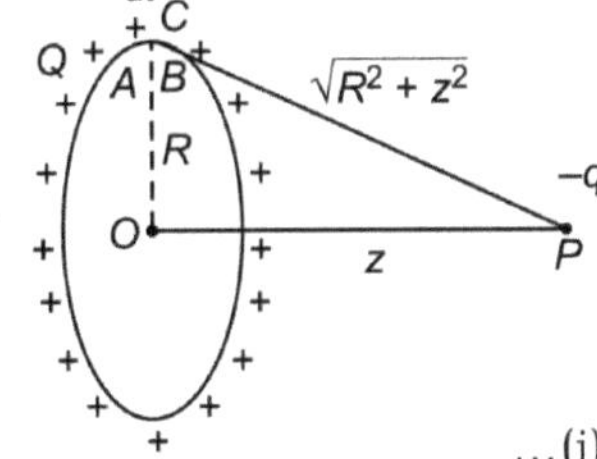

$$dq = \frac{Q}{2\pi R} \cdot dl \qquad \ldots(i)$$

(where, $2\pi R$ is the total length of the ring.)

The potential at point P due to the small element dl is

$$dV = \frac{1}{4\pi\varepsilon_0} \cdot \frac{dq}{CP} \qquad \left(CP = \sqrt{R^2 + z^2}\right)$$

(According to Pythagoras theorem)

$$= \frac{1}{4\pi\varepsilon_0} \cdot \frac{Qdl}{2\pi R \sqrt{(R^2 + z^2)}}$$

On integrating,

$$\int dV = \frac{1}{4\pi\varepsilon_0} \cdot \frac{Q}{2\pi R} \sqrt{R^2 + z^2} \int_0^{2\pi R} dl$$

$$V = \frac{1}{4\pi\varepsilon_0} \cdot \frac{Q}{2\pi R} \cdot \frac{2\pi R}{\sqrt{R^2 + z^2}}$$

$$= \frac{1}{4\pi\varepsilon_0} \cdot \frac{Q}{\sqrt{R^2 + z^2}} \qquad \qquad \text{...(i)}$$

The potential energy at P due to this charged ring and small charge $-q$ is

$$U = -q.V = -\frac{1}{4\pi\varepsilon_0} \cdot \frac{Qq}{\sqrt{R^2 + z^2}} \qquad \text{[From Eq. (i)]}$$

$$= -\frac{1}{4\pi\varepsilon_0 R} \frac{Qq}{\sqrt{1 + \dfrac{z^2}{R^2}}}$$

As we plot the graph between z and U. We get the adjoint graph if $z = 0$, the U is maximum.

As we displace the charge $-q$ from point P it performs oscillations. We cannot conclude more by looking the graph.

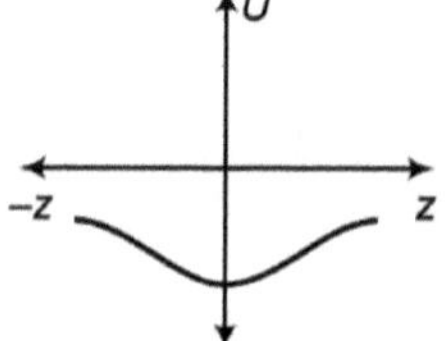

Question 2.   Find the equation of equipotentials for an infinite cylinder of radius r_0, carrying charge of linear density λ.

Solution   There is an infinite cylinder of radius r_0 and having linear charge density λ. Assume a Gaussian surface of radius r and length l.

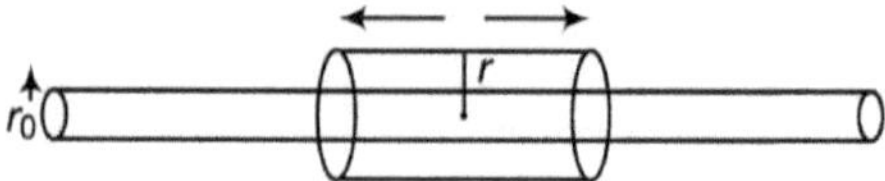

According of Gauss's theorem,

$$\oint \mathbf{E} \cdot d\mathbf{S} = \frac{q}{\varepsilon_0}$$

$$\oint E \cdot dS = \frac{\lambda l}{\varepsilon_0} \qquad (\because q = \lambda l)$$

$$(\because \text{Angle between } \mathbf{E} \text{ and } dS \text{ is zero.})$$

$$E \int dS = E \cdot 2\pi r l = \frac{\lambda l}{\varepsilon_0}$$

[where $(2\pi r l)$ is area of the curved surface of the cylinder.]

$$E = \frac{\lambda}{2\pi\varepsilon_0 r} \qquad \ldots(i)$$

If the radius is r_0, we find the potential difference at distance r from the line consider the electric field. According to the formula of potential gradient,

$$V_{(r)} - V_{(r_0)} = -\int_{r_0}^{r} \mathbf{E}. \, d\mathbf{r}$$

$$V_{(r)} - V_{(r_0)} = -\int_{r_0}^{r} \frac{\lambda}{2\pi\varepsilon_0 r} \cdot dr$$

$$(\text{angle between } \mathbf{E} \text{ and } d\mathbf{r} \text{ is zero.})$$

$$= -\frac{\lambda}{2\pi\varepsilon_0} \int_{r_0}^{r} \frac{dr}{r} = -\frac{\lambda}{2\pi\varepsilon_0} \cdot [\log_e r]_{r_0}^{r}$$

$$= -\frac{\lambda}{2\pi\varepsilon_0} [\log_e r - \log_e r_0]$$

$$= \frac{\lambda}{2\pi\varepsilon_0} [\log_e r_0 - \log_e r]$$

$$= \frac{\lambda}{2\pi\varepsilon_0} \cdot \log \frac{r_0}{r}$$

$$\log_e \frac{r_0}{r} = \frac{2\pi\varepsilon_0}{\lambda} [V_{(r)} - V_{(r_0)}]$$

$$\log_e \frac{r}{r_0} = -\frac{2\pi\varepsilon_0}{\lambda} [V_{(r)} - V_{(r_0)}]$$

$$\frac{r}{r_0} = e^{-\frac{2\pi\varepsilon_0}{\lambda}} [V_{(r)} - V_{(r_0)}]$$

$$r = r_0 e^{-\frac{2\pi\varepsilon_0}{\lambda}} [V_{(r)} - V_{(r_0)}]$$

This is the equation of required equipotential surfaces.

Question 3. Two point charges of magnitude $+q$ and $-q$ are placed at $\left(-\dfrac{d}{2}, 0, 0\right)$ and $\left(\dfrac{d}{2}, 0, 0\right)$ respectively. Find the equation of the equipotential surface where the potential is zero.

Solution Let the charges $+q$ be placed at point $A\left(-\dfrac{d}{2}, 0, 0\right)$ and $-q$ be placed at point $B\left(\dfrac{d}{2}, 0, 0\right)$ and the electric potential be zero at point P.

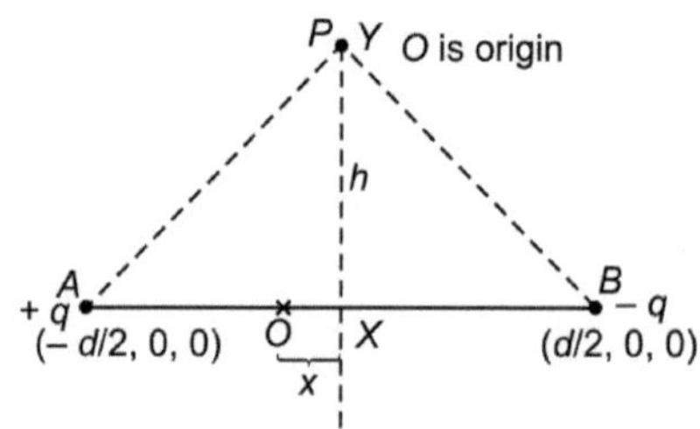

$$OP = h, \ OX = x$$

$$AP = \sqrt{(AX)^2 + (OP)^2} = \sqrt{\left(x + \frac{d}{2}\right)^2 + h^2} = \sqrt{h^2 + \left(x + \frac{d}{2}\right)^2}$$

$$BP = \sqrt{(OP)^2 + (BX)^2} = \sqrt{h^2 + \left(\frac{d}{2} - x\right)^2}$$

Potential at point P due to charge $(+q)$ is V_A.
By using the formula of potential at a point P due to a charge

$$V = \frac{1}{4\pi\varepsilon_0} \cdot \frac{q}{r}$$

$$V_A = \frac{1}{4\pi\varepsilon_0} \cdot \frac{q}{AP} = \frac{1}{4\pi\varepsilon_0} \cdot \frac{q}{\sqrt{h^2 + \left(x + \frac{d}{2}\right)^2}} \qquad \ldots\text{(i)}$$

Potential at point P due to charge $-q$ is V_B.

$$V_B = \frac{1}{4\pi\varepsilon_0} \cdot \frac{(-q)}{BP} = -\frac{1}{4\pi\varepsilon_0} \cdot \frac{q}{\sqrt{h^2 + \left(\frac{d}{2} - x\right)^2}} \qquad \ldots\text{(ii)}$$

Total potential at point P,

$$V = V_A + V_B$$

$$\therefore \quad V = \frac{1}{4\pi\varepsilon_0} \cdot \frac{q}{\sqrt{h^2 + \left(x + \dfrac{d}{2}\right)^2}} - \frac{1}{4\pi\varepsilon_0} \cdot \frac{q}{\sqrt{h^2 + \left(\dfrac{d}{2} - x\right)^2}}$$

According to the question, potential $V = 0$

$$\therefore \quad \frac{1}{4\pi\varepsilon_0} \cdot q \left[\frac{1}{\sqrt{h^2 + \left(x + \dfrac{d}{2}\right)^2}} - \frac{1}{\sqrt{h^2 + \left(\dfrac{d}{2} - x\right)^2}} \right] = 0$$

$$h^2 + \left(x + \frac{d}{2}\right)^2 = h^2 + \left(\frac{d}{2} - x\right)^2$$

$$x^2 + \frac{d^2}{4} + xd = x^2 + \frac{d^2}{4} - xd$$

$$2xd = 0$$

$$x = 0$$

Thus, the equation of the equipotential surface is $x = 0$.

(*i.e.*, we can say that the equipotential surface lies in Y-axis only).

Question 4. A parallel plate capacitor is filled by a dielectric whose relative permittivity varies with the applied voltage (V) as $E = \alpha V$ where $\alpha = 2\,\text{V}^{-1}$. A similar capacitor with no dielectric is charged to $V_0 = 78$ V. Then, it is connected to the uncharged capacitor with the dielectric. Find the final voltage on the capacitors.

Solution Let the final voltage be U and C be the capacitance of the capacitor without the dielectric, then the charge on the capacitor

$$Q_1 = CV \qquad \qquad \text{...(i)}$$

There is capacitor with dielectric, then its capacitance is εC (as $C \propto K$ dielectric constant).

The charge on the capacitor is

$$Q_2 = \varepsilon\, CV \qquad \qquad (\text{Given, } E = \alpha\, U)$$

$$Q_2 = \alpha\, CV^2 \qquad \qquad \text{...(ii)}$$

The charge on the capacitor initially

$$Q_0 = CV_0 \qquad \qquad \text{...(iii)}$$

$$(\text{where, } U_0 = 78 \text{ V})$$

According to the law of charge conservation,

Charge before connecting $=$ Total charge after connecting

$$Q_0 = Q_1 + Q_2$$

Putting the values of Q_0, Q_1 and Q_2 from Eqs. (i), (ii) and (iii), we get

$$CU_0 = CU + \alpha\, CU^2$$

or $$\alpha\, CU^2 + CU - CU_0 = 0$$

or $$\alpha\, U^2 + U - U_0 = 0$$

It is a quadratic equation, we solve it by formula

$$U = \frac{-1 \pm \sqrt{1 + 4\,\alpha\, U_0}}{2\alpha} \quad [\text{Given, } \alpha = 2V^{-1},\ U_0 = 78\,V]$$

$$= \frac{-1 \pm \sqrt{1 + 4\,(2)\,78}}{2 \times 2} = \frac{-1 \pm \sqrt{625}}{4}$$

As potential is positive on charge. So,

$$U = \frac{-1 + \sqrt{625}}{4} = \frac{-1 + 25}{4} = 6\,V$$

Thus, the voltage on the capacitor is 6 V.

Question 5.   A capacitor is made of two circular plates of radius R each, separated by a distance $d << R$. The capacitor is connected to a constant voltage. A thin conducting disc of radius $r << R$ and thickness $t << r$ is placed at a centre of the bottom plate. Find the minimum voltage required to lift the disc, if the mass of the disc is m.

Solution   There are two circular plates of radius R and they are separated by a distance d.

They are connected to a voltage V.

Radius of small disc $= r$

Thickness of disc $= t$

Mass of the disc $= m$

As the disc of radius r is in touch with the bottom plate of radius R, the entire plate becomes an equipotential surface.

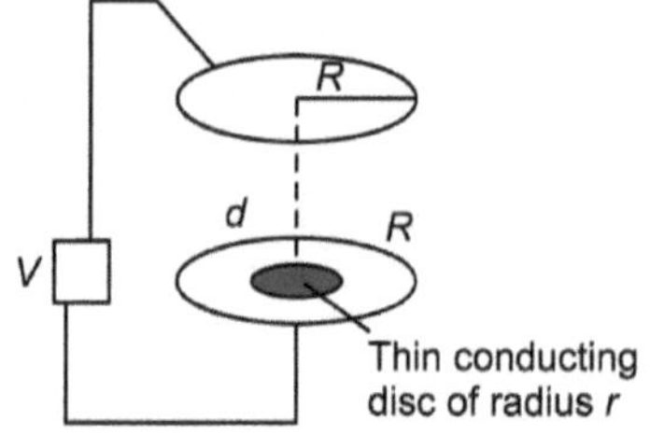

Let the amount of charge transferred to the disc be q'.

$$\text{The electric field on the disc} = \frac{\text{Potential Difference}}{\text{Distance}} = \frac{V}{d} \qquad \ldots(i)$$

$$\text{Charge } q' = \text{Capacitance} \times \text{Voltage}$$

$$q = CV = \varepsilon_0 \frac{A}{d} \cdot V$$

$$= \frac{\varepsilon_0 \pi r^2}{d} \cdot V \qquad \ldots(ii)$$

(where, A is area of disc of radius r and distance between plates is d.)

Force on the disc F = Charge × Electric field

$$= q' \times \frac{V}{d}$$

$$= \varepsilon_0 \frac{\pi r^2 V}{d} \cdot \frac{V}{d} \qquad \text{[From Eq. (ii)]}$$

$$\therefore \qquad F = \varepsilon_0 \pi r^2 \frac{V^2}{d^2} \qquad \qquad \ldots \text{(iii)}$$

If the disc is lifted up, then its weight is balanced by the electrostatic force.

$$mg = F$$

$$mg = \varepsilon_0 \pi r^2 \frac{V^2}{d^2} \qquad \text{[From Eq. (iii)]}$$

$$V^2 = \frac{mg \, d^2}{\varepsilon_0 \pi r^2}$$

$$V = \sqrt{\frac{mgd^2}{\varepsilon_0 \pi r^2}}$$

Thus, the minimum voltage required to lift the disc is $\sqrt{\dfrac{mgd^2}{\varepsilon_0 \pi r^2}}$.

Question 6.   Two metal spheres, one of radius R and the other of radius $2R$, both have same surface charge density σ. They are brought in contact and separated. What will be new surface charge densities on them?

Use the concept of conservation of charge and also use the concept that potential remains same when two metal spheres are brought in contact.

Solution   Radius of sphere $A = R$

Surface charge density on sphere $A = \sigma$

Radius of sphere $B = 2R$

Surface charge density on sphere $B = \sigma$

Before contact, the charge on sphere A is

$$Q_1 = \text{Surface charge density} \times \text{Surface area}$$

$$= \sigma \cdot 4\pi R^2 \qquad \qquad \ldots \text{(i)}$$

Before contact, the charge on sphere B is

$$Q_2 = \text{Surface charge density} \times \text{Surface area}$$

$$Q_2 = \sigma \cdot 4\pi (2R)^2 = \sigma \cdot 16\pi R^2 \qquad \qquad \ldots \text{(ii)}$$

Let after the contact, the charge on A is Q_1' and the charge on B is Q_2'. According to the conservation of charge, the charge before contact is equal to charge after contact.

$$Q_1' + Q_2' = Q_1 + Q_2$$

Putting the values of Q_1 and Q_2 from Eqs. (i) and (ii), we get

$$Q_1' + Q_2' = 4\pi R^2 \sigma + 16\pi R^2 \sigma = 20\pi R^2 \sigma \qquad \ldots\text{(iii)}$$

As they are in contact. So, they have same potential.

Potential on sphere A is $V_A = \dfrac{1}{4\pi\varepsilon_0} \cdot \dfrac{Q_1'}{R}$

Potential on sphere B is $V_B = \dfrac{1}{4\pi\varepsilon_0} \cdot \dfrac{Q_2'}{2R}$

So,

$$V_A = V_B$$

$$\frac{1}{4\pi\varepsilon_0} \cdot \frac{Q_1'}{R} = \frac{1}{4\pi\varepsilon_0} \cdot \frac{Q_2'}{2R}$$

$$\frac{Q_1'}{R} = \frac{Q_2'}{2R}$$

$$2Q_1' = Q_2'$$

Putting the value of Q_2' in Eq. (iii), we get

$$Q_1' + 2Q_1' = 20\,\pi R^2 \sigma$$

$$3Q_1' = 20\,\pi R^2 \sigma$$

$$Q_1' = \frac{20}{3}\,\pi R^2 \sigma$$

and

$$Q_2' = \frac{40}{3}\,\pi R^2 \sigma$$

Let the new charge densities be σ_1 and σ_2.

$$\sigma_1 = \frac{Q_1'}{4\pi R^2} = \frac{20\,\pi\,R^2 \sigma}{3\cdot 4\,\pi\,R^2} = \frac{5}{3}\,\sigma$$

$$\sigma_2 = \frac{Q_2'}{4\pi\,(2R)^2} = \frac{40\,\pi\,R^2 \sigma}{3\times 4\,\pi\times 4\,R^2} = \frac{40\,\sigma}{16\times 3}$$

$$\sigma_2 = \frac{10\,\sigma}{4\times 3} = \frac{5}{6}\,\sigma$$

Thus, the surface charge densities on spheres after contacting are $\dfrac{5}{3}\sigma$ and $\dfrac{5}{6}\sigma$.

Question 7. In the circuit shown in figure, initially K_1 is closed K_2 is opened. What are the charges on each capacitors. Then, K_1 was opened and K_2 was closed (order is important), what will be the charge on each capacitor now? (Given $C = 1\mu F$)

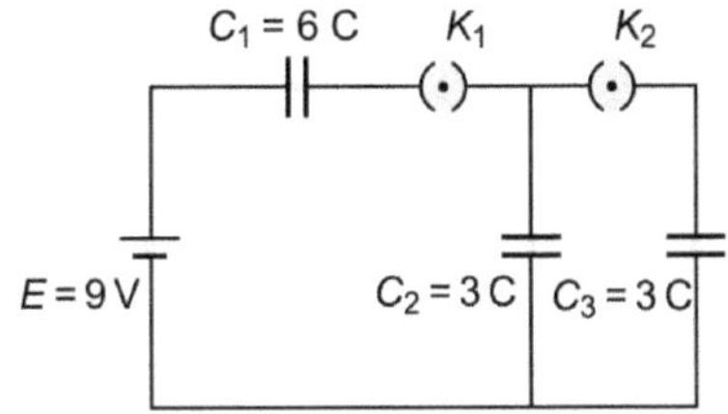

Solution Let us discuss the first case that K_1 is closed and K_2 is opened.

In this situation the capacitors C_1 and C_2 are in series.

Total capacitance

$$\frac{1}{C_s} = \frac{1}{C_1} + \frac{1}{C_2} = \frac{1}{6C} + \frac{1}{3C} = \frac{1+2}{6C} = \frac{3}{6C} = \frac{1}{2}C$$

$$C_s = 2C = 2 \times 1 = 2\mu F \qquad (\because \text{Given } C = 1\mu F)$$

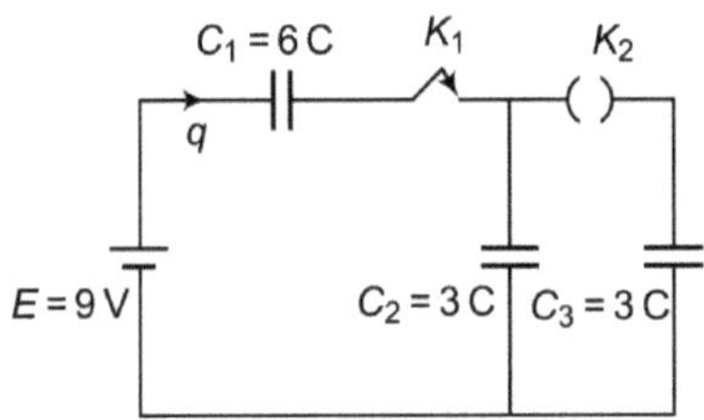

Charge in the circuit is q.

$$q = C_s \cdot E = 2 \times 10^{-6} \times 9 = 18 \times 10^{-6} \text{ C}$$

Thus, charge on C_1 is $18\mu C$, on C_2 is $18\mu C$ and on C_3 is zero.

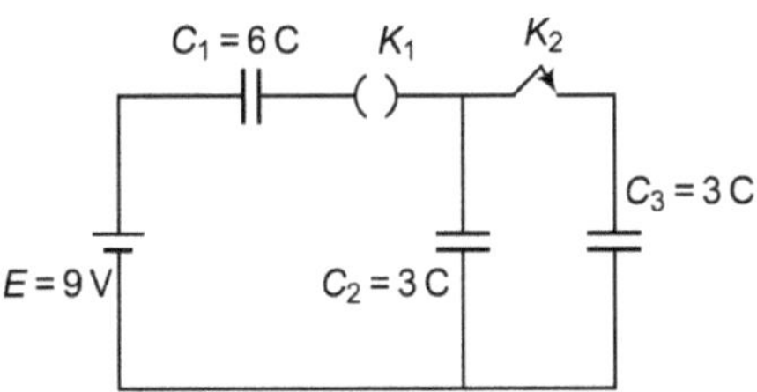

In second case, K_1 is opened and K_2 is closed.

C_2 and C_3 are in parallel.

Total capacity, $C_s = 3 + 3 = 6\,C$

Total charge, $q = C_s \cdot E = 6 \times 9 = 54\,\mu F$

Thus, charge on C_2 is $54\,\mu F$ and C_3 is $54\,\mu F$ and on C_1 is zero.

Question 8.   Two charges $-q$ each are separated by distance $2d$. A third charge $+q$ is kept at mid-point O. Find the potential energy of $+q$ as a function of small distance x from O due to $-q$ charges. Sketch potential energy *versus* x and convince yourself that the charge at origin O is in an unstable equilibrium.

 For unstable equilibrium, the double derivative of the potential energy should be zero *i.e.,* $\dfrac{d^2V}{dx^2} = 0$.

Solution   Let the charge $+q$ be displaced upto X, where OX is x.

$$OX = x$$
$$AO = OB = d$$

The potential energy due to charges $-q$ and q placed at points A and X is

$$U_1 = \frac{1}{4\pi\varepsilon_0} \times \frac{(-q)\,(q)}{Ax} \qquad \left(U = \frac{1}{4\pi\varepsilon_0}\cdot\frac{q_1 q_2}{r} \right)$$

$$= \frac{1}{4\pi\varepsilon_0}\frac{(-q^2)}{(d-x)} \qquad \qquad \ldots(i)$$

The potential energy due to charges $-q$ and q placed at points B and X is

$$U_2 = \frac{1}{4\pi\varepsilon_0}\cdot\frac{(-q)\,(q)}{BX}$$

$$= \frac{1}{4\pi\varepsilon_0}\cdot\frac{(-q)^2}{(d+x)} \qquad \qquad \ldots(ii)$$

The total potential energy $U = U_1 + U_2$

$$U = \frac{1}{4\pi\varepsilon_0}\cdot(-q^2)\left(\frac{1}{d-x} + \frac{1}{d+x} \right)$$

[From Eqs. (i) and (ii)]

$$= \frac{1}{4\pi\varepsilon_0}\frac{(-q^2)\,(2d)}{(d^2 - x^2)} \qquad \qquad \ldots(iii)$$

The potential energy for small displacement $x <\!<\! d$.
So, neglect small distance x as compared to distance d.

$$U_0 = \frac{1}{4\pi\varepsilon_0}\cdot\frac{(-q)\cdot 2d}{d^2}$$

$$U_0 = -\frac{1}{4\pi\varepsilon_0}\frac{2q^2}{d}$$

Thus, the potential energy for small distance is

$$U_0 = \frac{-1}{4\pi\varepsilon_0} \cdot \frac{2q^2}{d}$$

Now, we check the equilibrium, differentiate Eq. (iii) w.r.t. x,

$$\frac{dU}{dx} = \frac{1}{4\pi\varepsilon_0} \cdot 2\,(-q)^2\,d\left[\frac{0-(-2x)}{(d^2-x^2)^2}\right]$$

or

$$\frac{dU}{dx} = \frac{-2q^2 d}{4\pi\varepsilon_0} \cdot \frac{(2x)}{(d^2-x^2)^2}$$

Now, at $x=0$, $\dfrac{dU}{dx}=0$, so we find the second derivative of potential energy.

$$\frac{d^2U}{dx^2} = \frac{-4q^2 d}{4\pi\varepsilon_0} \cdot \left[\frac{(d^2-x^2)^2\cdot 2 - 2x \times 2\,(d^2-x^2)\,(-2x)}{(d^2-x^2)^4}\right]$$

$$\frac{d^2U}{dx^2} = -\frac{4q^2 d}{4\pi\varepsilon_0}\,(d^2-x^2)\left[\frac{2\,(d^2-x^2)+8x}{(d^2-x^2)^4}\right]$$

For $x=0$,

$$\frac{d^2U}{dx^2} = \text{'--ve' value}$$

So, the equilibrium is unstable.

Chapter 3

Current Electricity

Important Results

1. Electric current $I = \dfrac{q}{t} = \dfrac{h\rho}{t}$

2. Current density $\mathbf{J} = \dfrac{I}{\mathbf{A}}$

3. Drift velocity of electrons
$$v_d = \frac{eE\tau}{m} = \frac{ve\tau}{ml}$$

4. Mobility of free electrons $\mu = \dfrac{v_d}{E} = \dfrac{e\tau}{m}$

5. Relation between drift velocity and free electrons, $v_d = \dfrac{I}{Ane}$

6. Ohm's law $\dfrac{V}{I} = R = \dfrac{ml}{Ane^2\tau} = $ constant

   where, R is called electrical resistance.

7. Resistivity or specific resistance
$$\rho = \frac{RA}{l} = \frac{m}{ne^2\tau}$$

8. In series combination of resistors,
$$R = R_1 + R_2 + R_3$$
   and total potential drop $V = V_1 + V_2 + V_3$.

9. In parallel combination of resistors,
$$\frac{1}{R} = \frac{1}{R_1} + \frac{1}{R_2} + \frac{1}{R_3}$$

   Total current drawn $I = I_1 + I_2 + I_3$

10. Temperature dependence of resistance
$$R_t = T_0\,(1 + \alpha t)$$
   and
$$\alpha = \frac{R_2 - R_1}{R_1(t_2 - t_1)}$$

11. Emf of a cell $E = V + Ir$

   and $\quad I = \dfrac{E}{(R + r)}\quad$ and $\quad r = \left(\dfrac{E}{V} - 1\right) R$

12. Joule's law of heating
$$W = I^2 Rt = VIt = \frac{V^2}{R} t \text{ joule}$$

13. Power dissipated
$$P = \frac{W}{t} = I^2 R = VI = \frac{V^2}{R} \text{ watt}$$

14. Conductance $G = \dfrac{1}{\text{Electrical resistance } (R)}$

15. Conductivity $\sigma = \dfrac{1}{\text{Resistivity } (\rho)}$

16. Kirchhoff's laws
    (i) Junction law $\Sigma I = 0$;   (ii) Loop law $\Sigma V = 0$

17. Wheatstone bridge $\dfrac{P}{Q} = \dfrac{R}{S}$

18. **Meter bridge**   Unknown resistance
$$(S) = \left(\frac{100 - l}{l}\right) R$$

19. **Potentiometer**   Potential gradient $(K) = \dfrac{V}{l}$

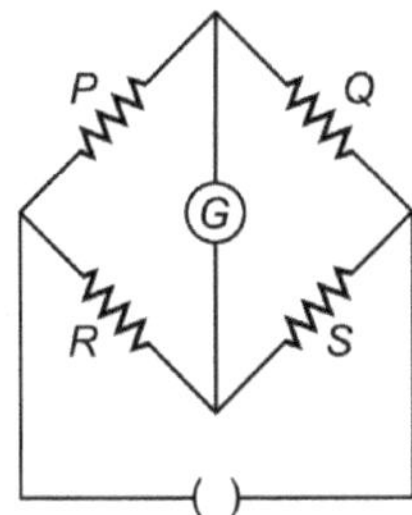

Exercises

Question 1.   The storage battery of a car has an emf of 12 V. If the internal resistance of the battery is 0.4 Ω, what is the maximum current that can be drawn from the battery?

To find the maximum current, use the concept that the current is maximum, if the external load resistance is zero.

Solution   Given, emf $E = 12$ V, internal resistance $r = 0.4\,\Omega$

∴ Current drawn from the battery $I = \dfrac{E}{R + r}$

In case of maximum current, $R = 0$

∴
$$I_{\max} = \frac{E}{r}$$
$$= \frac{12}{0.4} = 30 \text{ A}$$

Question 2.   A battery of emf 10 V and internal resistance 3Ω is connected to a resistor. If the current in the circuit is 0.5 A, what is the resistance of the resistor? What is the terminal voltage of the battery when the circuit is closed?

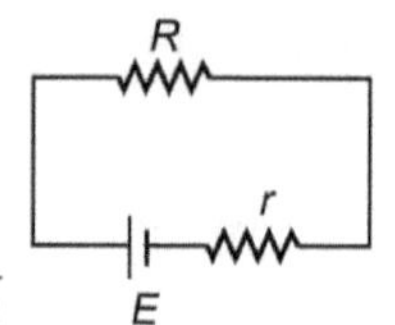

Solution   Given, emf of battery, $E = 10$ V

Internal resistance, $r = 3\ \Omega$

Current in circuit, $I = 0.5$ A

The current in the circuit $= \dfrac{\text{emf}}{\text{Total resistance of the circuit}}$

$$I = \dfrac{E}{R + r}$$

$\therefore$ $0.5 = \dfrac{10}{R + 3}$

or $R + 3 = 20$

$$R = 17\ \Omega$$

When the circuit is closed, the terminal voltage

$$V = E - Ir = 10 - 0.5 \times 3 = 10 - 1.5 = 8.5\ \text{V}$$

Thus, the resistance in the circuit is 17 Ω and terminal voltage of the battery when the circuit is closed, is 8.5 V.

Question 3.   (a) Three resistors 1 Ω, 2 Ω and 3 Ω are combined in series. What is the total resistance of the combination?

  (b) If the combination is connected to a battery of emf 12 V and negligible internal resistance, obtain the potential drop across each resistor.

 Use the formula of series combination of resistances. In series combination, current in each resistor is same but potential drop is different in different resistors.

Solution   (a) $R_1 = 1\,\Omega$, $R_2 = 2\,\Omega$ and $R_3 = 3\,\Omega$

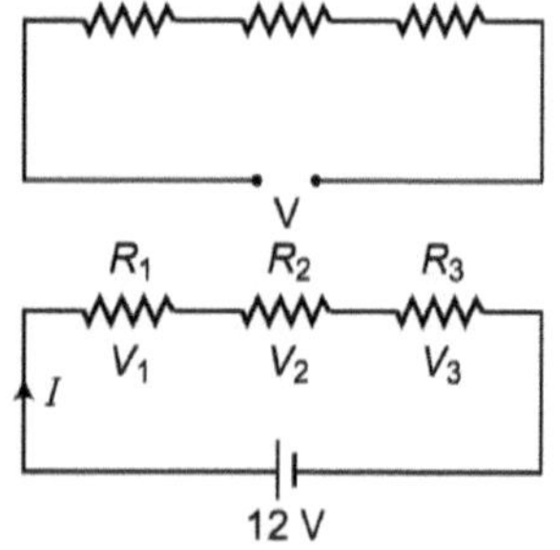

Resultant resistance in series

$$R_S = R_1 + R_2 + R_3$$
$$R_S = 1 + 2 + 3 = 6\,\Omega$$

(b) The potential drop across each resistor is different when two or more resistances are connected in series combination.

Let V_1, V_2 and V_3 be the potential drops across resistances R_1, R_2 and R_3 respectively and the current flowing through the circuit is I.

$\therefore$ $I = \dfrac{V}{R_S} = \dfrac{12}{6} = 2$ A

Current is same through each resistor as they are in series.

Potential drop across resistance R_1, $V_1 = IR_1 = 2 \times 1 = 2$ V

Potential drop across resistance R_2, $V_2 = IR_2 = 2 \times 2 = 4$ V

Potential drop across resistance R_3, $V_3 = IR_3 = 2 \times 3 = 6$ V

Thus, the potential drop across resistance $1\,\Omega$ is 2V, resistance $2\,\Omega$ is 4 V and resistance $3\,\Omega$ is 6 V.

Question 4. (a) Three resistors $2\,\Omega$, $4\,\Omega$ and $5\,\Omega$ are combined in parallel. What is the total resistance of the combination?

(b) If the combination is connected to a battery of emf **20 V** and negligible internal resistance, determine the current through each resistor and the total current drawn from the battery.

Use the formula of parallel combination of resistances. In parallel combination, the current flowing through each resistor is different but potential drop across each resistore remains same.

Solution Given, $R_1 = 2\,\Omega$, $R_2 = 4\,\Omega$ and $R_3 = 5\,\Omega$

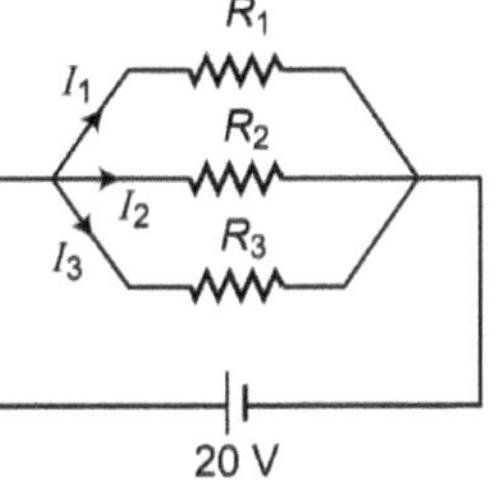

(a) Resultant resistance in parallel

$$\frac{1}{R_P} = \frac{1}{R_1} + \frac{1}{R_2} + \frac{1}{R_3} = \frac{1}{2} + \frac{1}{4} + \frac{1}{5}$$

$$\frac{1}{R_P} = \frac{10 + 5 + 4}{20} = \frac{19}{20}$$

$$R_P = \frac{20}{19}\,\Omega$$

(b) In case of parallel combination, the current flowing through each resistance is different, let I_1, I_2 and I_3 and the potential drop across each resistor is same as the applied potential difference $V = 20$ V

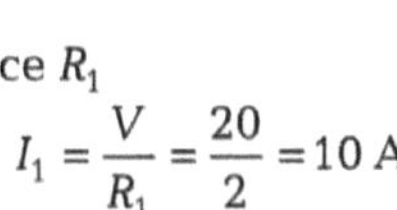

Current through resistance R_1

$$I_1 = \frac{V}{R_1} = \frac{20}{2} = 10\ \text{A}$$

Current through resistance R_2

$$I_2 = \frac{V}{R_2} = \frac{20}{4} = 5\ \text{A}$$

Current through resistance R_3

$$I_3 = \frac{V}{R_3} = \frac{20}{5} = 4\ \text{A}$$

Total current drawn $I = I_1 + I_2 + I_3$

$$= 10 + 5 + 4 = 19\ \text{A}$$

Thus, the current flowing through $2\,\Omega$ is 10 A, $4\,\Omega$ is 5 A and $5\,\Omega$ is 4 A. Total current drawn from the battery $I = I_1 + I_2 + I_3$

$$= 10 + 5 + 4$$

$$= 19\ \text{A}$$

Question 5. At room temperature (27.0°C) the resistance of a heating element is $100\,\Omega$. What is the temperature of the element, if the resistance is found to be $117\,\Omega$, given that the temperature coefficient of the material of the resistor is $1.70 \times 10^{-4}/°C$.

 Use the concept that the resistance of a heating element increases with increase in temperature.

Solution Given, the resistance of heating element at temperature 27 °C

$$= R_{27} = 100\,\Omega$$

Resistance of heating element at temperature $t°C = R_t = 117\,\Omega$

Temperature coefficient of resistance $\alpha = 1.70 \times 10^{-4}/°C$

Temperature coefficient of resistance

$$\alpha = \frac{R_t - R_{27}}{R_{27}\,(t - 27)}$$

$$1.70 \times 10^{-4} = \frac{117 - 100}{100\,(t - 27)}$$

or

$$t - 27 = \frac{17}{100 \times 1.70 \times 10^{-4}}$$

or

$$t = 1000 + 27 = 1027\,°C$$

Thus, the temperature of element is 1027 °C when its resistance is 117 Ω.

Question 6. A negligible small current is passed through a wire of length 15 m and uniform cross-section $6.0 \times 10^{-7}\,m^2$ and its resistance is measured to be 5.0 Ω. What is the resistivity of the material at the temperature of the experiment?

Solution Given, area of cross-section of wire $(A) = 6.0 \times 10^{-7}\,m^2$

Length of the wire $l = 15$ m

Resistance of wire $R = 5\,\Omega$

Let the resistivity of the material be ρ.

Resistance of wire $R = \rho\dfrac{l}{A}$

or

$$\rho = \frac{RA}{l} = \frac{5 \times 6.0 \times 10^{-7}}{15} = 2 \times 10^{-7}\,\Omega\text{-m}$$

Thus, the resistivity of the material at the temperature of the experiment is $2 \times 10^{-7}\,\Omega$-m.

Question 7. A silver wire has a resistance of 2.1 Ω at 27.5 °C and a resistance of 2.7 Ω at 100 °C. Determine the temperature coefficient of resistivity of silver.

Solution Given, resistance of silver wire at 27.5 °C $= R_{27.5} = 2.1\,\Omega$

Resistance of silver wire at 100 °C $= R_{100} = 2.7\,\Omega$

Let the temperature coefficient of silver be α.

$$\alpha = \frac{R_{t_2} - R_{t_1}}{R_1 (t_2 - t_1)}$$

$$\alpha = \frac{R_{100} - R_{27.5}}{R_{27.5} (100 - 27.5)}$$

$$= \frac{2.7 - 2.1}{2.1 \times 72.5}$$

$$\alpha = 0.0039/\,^\circ C$$

Thus, the temperature coefficient of resistivity of silver is $0.0039/\,^\circ C$.

Question 8.　A heating element using nichrome connected to a **230 V** supply draws an initial current of **3.2 A** which settles after a few seconds to a steady value of **2.8 A**. What is the steady temperature of the heating element, if the room temperature is **27.0°C?** Temperature coefficient of resistance of nichrome averaged over the temperature range involved is $1.70 \times 10^{-4}\,^\circ C^{-1}$.

Solution　Given, potential difference $= 230$ V

Initially current at $27^\circ C = I_{27^\circ C} = 3.2$ A

Finally current at $t^\circ C = I_{t^\circ C} = 2.8$ A

Room temperature $= 27^\circ C$

Temperature coefficient of resistance

$$\alpha = 1.70 \times 10^{-4}/\,^\circ C$$

Resistance at $27\,^\circ C$, $\quad R_{27^\circ C} = \dfrac{V}{I_{27^\circ C}} = \dfrac{230}{3.2} = \dfrac{2300}{32}\,\Omega$

Resistance at $t^\circ C$, $\quad R_{t^\circ C} = \dfrac{V}{I_{t^\circ C}} = \dfrac{230}{2.8} = \dfrac{2300}{28}\,\Omega$

Temperature of coefficient of resistance

$$\alpha = \frac{R_t - R_{27}}{R_{27} (t - 27)}$$

$$\Rightarrow \quad 1.7 \times 10^{-4} = \frac{\dfrac{2300}{28} - \dfrac{2300}{32}}{\dfrac{2300}{32} (t - 32)}$$

or $\quad\quad t - 27 = \dfrac{82.143 - 71.875}{71.875 \times 1.7 \times 10^{-4}} = 840.347$

or $\quad\quad\quad\quad t = 840.3 + 27$

$$= 867.3\,^\circ C$$

Thus, the steady temperature of heating element is $867.3\,^\circ C$.

Question 9. Determine the current in each branch of the network shown in given figure.

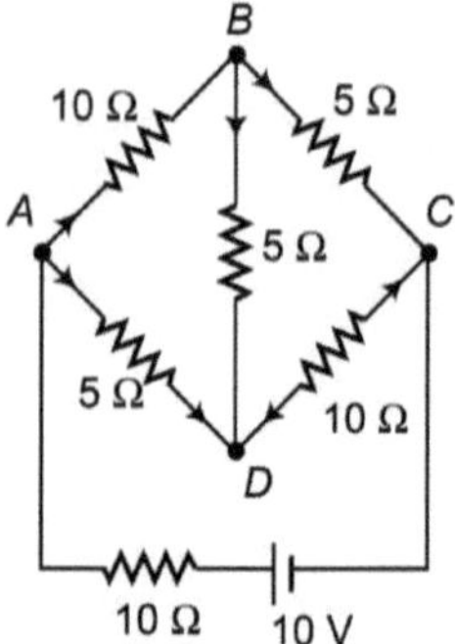

 Here, the given circuit is closed having two closed loops, so to calculate the current in the circuit we have to apply Kirchhoff's laws.

Solution From Kirchhoff's Ist law, *i.e.*, loop law,

$$\Sigma V = \Sigma IR$$

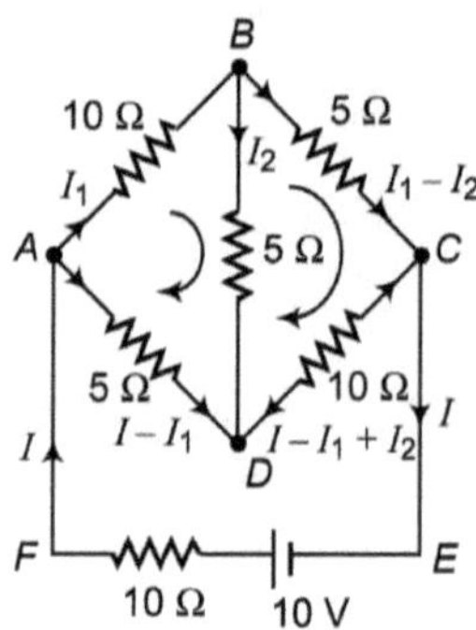

In loop *ABDA* Distributing the current

$$10I_1 + 5I_2 - 5(I - I_1) = 0$$
$$2I_1 + I_2 - I + I_1 = 0$$
$$3I_1 + I_2 = I \qquad \ldots(i)$$

In loop *BCDB*

$$5(I_1 - I_2) - 10(I - I_1 + I_2) - 5I_2 = 0$$
$$I_1 - I_2 - 2I + 2I_1 - 2I_2 - I_2 = 0$$
$$3I_1 - 4I_2 = 2I \qquad \ldots(ii)$$

By solving the Eq. (i) and Eq. (ii), we get

$$I_1 = \frac{2I}{5} \text{ and } I_2 = -\frac{I}{5} \qquad \ldots(iii)$$

In loop *ABCEFA*

$$10 = 10I + 10I_1 + 5\,(I_1 - I_2)$$
$$2 = 2I + 3I_1 - I_2 \qquad \qquad \text{...(iv)}$$

Putting the values of I_1 and I_2 from Eq. (iii) in Eq. (iv), we get

$$2 = 2I + 3\left(\frac{2I}{5}\right) - \left(-\frac{I}{5}\right)$$

or
$$2 = \frac{17}{5}I$$

or
$$I = \frac{10}{17}\ \text{A}$$

Current in branch *AB*,
$$I_1 = \frac{2}{5} \times \frac{10}{7} = \frac{4}{17}\ \text{A}$$

and
$$I_2 = -\frac{I}{5} = -\frac{2}{17}\ \text{A}$$

Current in branch *AB* is $I_1 = \dfrac{4}{17}\ \text{A}$

Current in branch *BC* is $I_1 - I_2 = \dfrac{4}{17} - \left(-\dfrac{2}{17}\right) = \dfrac{6}{17}\ \text{A}$

Current in branch *AD* is $I - I_1 = \dfrac{10}{17} - \dfrac{4}{17} = \dfrac{6}{17}\ \text{A}$

Current in branch *DC* is $(I - I_1) + I_2 = \dfrac{6}{17} + \left(-\dfrac{2}{17}\right) = \dfrac{4}{17}\ \text{A}$

Question 10. (a) In a meter bridge, the balance point is found to be at 39.5 cm from the end A, when the resistor Y is of 12.5 Ω. Determine the resistance of X. Why are the connections between resistors in a Wheatstone or meter bridge made of thick copper strips?

(b) Determine the balance point of the bridge above, if X and Y are interchanged.

(c) What happens, if the galvanometer and cell are interchanged at the balance point of the bridge? Would the galvanometer show any current?

Use the concept of balanced Wheatstone bridge as meter bridge works on the principle of a balanced Wheatstone bridge.

Solution (a) Balance point from end A,
$$l = 39.5\ \text{cm}$$

Resistance of resistor $Y = 12.5\ \Omega$

Resistance of resistor $X = ?$

According to the condition of balanced Wheatstone bridge

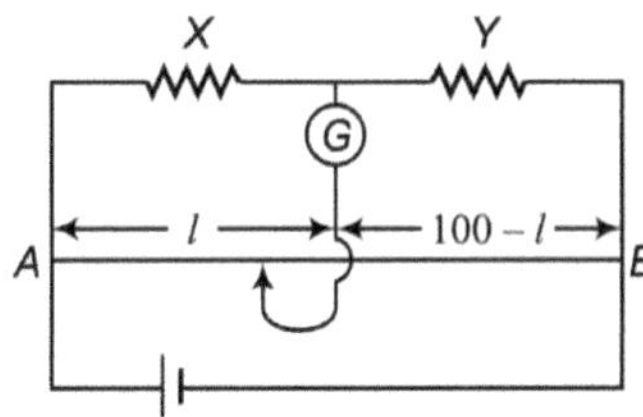

$$\frac{X}{Y} = \frac{l}{100 - l}$$

$$X = \frac{l}{100 - l} \cdot Y$$

$$X = \frac{39.5 \times 12.5}{100 - 39.5} = 8.16 \ \Omega$$

The resistance of resistor X is $8.16 \ \Omega$.

In meter bridge, the resistance at the connections is not taken in the consideration that's why the connections between resistors in a Wheatstone bridge or meter bridge made of thick copper strips because more is the thickness, lesser be the resistance $\left(\text{as } R \propto \dfrac{1}{A} \right)$, so due to thick copper stripes, the resistance at the connections becomes minimum.

(b) If X and Y are interchanged, then the balance length will also interchanged. Thus, the balance length becomes

$$100 - 39.5 = 60.5 \text{ cm}$$

(c) If the galvanometer and cell are interchanged at the balance point of the bridge, the balance point is not obtained. The galvanometer shows no deflection.

Question 11. A storage battery of emf 8.0 V and internal resistance 0.5 Ω is being charged by a 120 V DC supply using a series resistor of 15.5 Ω. What is the terminal voltage of the battery during charging? What is the purpose of having a series resistor in the charging circuit?

 Use the formula of terminal potential difference in charging a cell.

Solution   Emf of the battery $e = 8$ V, emf of DC supply $V = 120$ V

Since, the battery is bring changed, so effective emf in the circuit

$$E = V - e = 120 - 8 = 112 \text{ V}$$

Current in circuit,

$$I = \frac{\text{Effective emf}}{\text{Total resistance}} = \frac{E}{r + R}$$

$$= \frac{112}{0.5 + 15.5}$$

$$= \frac{112}{16} = 7 \text{ A}$$

The battery of 8 V is being charged by 120 V, so the terminal potential across battery of 8 V will be greater than its emf

Terminal potential difference $V = E + Ir = 8 + 7 \, (0.5) = 11.5$ V

The purpose of the series resistance is to control the current drawn from the external supply, other the current in the circuit will be very high.

Question 12. In a potentiometer arrangement, a cell of emf 1.25 V gives a balance point at 35.0 cm length of the wire. If the cell is replaced by another cell and the balance point shifts to 63.0 cm, what is the emf of the second cell?

 Use the concept of potential gradient as in case of potentiameter it remains constant *i.e.,* $\dfrac{E_1}{l_1} = \dfrac{E_2}{l_2}$.

Solution Given, $E_1 = 1.25$ V, $l_1 = 35$ cm and $l_2 = 63$ cm

As we know that in case of potentiometer, the potential gradient remains constant.

i.e.,
$$E \propto l$$

$\therefore$
$$\frac{E_1}{E_2} = \frac{l_1}{l_2}$$

$$\frac{1.25}{E} = \frac{35}{63}$$

or
$$E = \frac{1.25 \times 63}{35} = 2.25 \text{ V}$$

Thus, the emf of the second cell is 2.25 V.

Question 13. The number density of free electrons in a copper conductor estimated at 8.5×10^{28} m^{-3}. How long does an electron take to drift from one end of a wire 3.0 m long to its other end? The area of cross-section of the wire is 2.0×10^{-6} m^2 and it is carrying a current of 3.0 A.

 To find the time for the electrons to drift from one end to other, we have to calculate the drift velocity of the electrons first.

Solution Given, number density of electrons $n = 8.5 \times 10^{28}/\text{m}^3$

Length of wire $l = 3$ m

Area of cross-section of wire $A = 2 \times 10^{-6} \text{m}^2$

Current $I = 3$ A and charge on electron $e = 1.6 \times 10^{-19}$ C

Time taken by electron to drift from one end to another of the wire,
$$t = \frac{\text{Length of the wire}}{\text{Drift velocity}} = \frac{l}{v_d} \qquad \ldots(\text{i})$$

Using the relation,
$$I = ne\, A\, v_d$$

or
$$v_d = \frac{I}{ne\, A} \qquad \ldots(\text{ii})$$

Putting the value in Eq. (ii) from Eq. (i),
$$t = \frac{l\, ne\, A}{I} = \frac{3 \times 8.5 \times 10^{28} \times 1.6 \times 10^{-19} \times 2 \times 10^{-6}}{3}$$

or
$$t = 2.72 \times 10^4 \text{ s} = 7 \text{ h } 33 \text{ min}$$

Thus, the time taken by an electron to drift from one end to another end is 7 h 33 min.

Additional Exercises

Question 14. The earth's surface has a negative surface charge density of 10^{-9} C/m^2. The potential difference of 400 kV between the top of the atmosphere and the surface results (due to the low conductivity of the lower atmosphere) in a current of only 1800 A over the entire globe. If there were no mechanism of sustaining atmospheric electric field, how much time (roughly) would be required to neutralise the earth's surface? (This never happens in practice because there is a mechanism to replenish electric charges, namely the continual thunderstorms and lightning in different parts of the globe. Radius of earth = 6.37×10^6 m)

Solution   Given, radius of earth $R = 6.37 \times 10^6$ m

Negative surface charge density $\sigma = 10^{-9}$ C/m^2

Potential difference $V = 400$ kV $= 400 \times 10^3$ V

Current on the globe $I = 1800$ A

Surface area of earth $A = 4\pi R^2 = 4 \times 3.14 \times (6.37 \times 10^6)^2$

$$= 509.64 \times 10^{12} \text{ m}^2$$

Charge on earth surface $Q = $ Area of earth surface

$$\times \text{ Surface charge density}$$

$$Q = A\sigma = 509.64 \times 10^{12} \times 10^{-9}$$

$$= 509.64 \times 10^3 \text{ C}$$

We know that $\qquad\qquad Q = It$

$\therefore$ Time required to neutralize earth's surface

$$t = \frac{Q}{I} = \frac{509.64 \times 10^3}{1800}$$

$$t = 283.1 \text{ s or } t = 4 \text{ min } 43 \text{ s}$$

Thus, the time required to neutralize the earth's surface is 283.1 s.

Question 15. (a) Six lead-acid type of secondary cells each of emf 2.0 V and internal resistance 0.015 Ω are joined in series to provide a supply to a resistance of 8.5 Ω. What are the current drawn from the supply and its terminal voltage?

  (b) A secondary cell after long use has an emf of 1.9 V and a large internal resistance of 380 Ω. What maximum current can be drawn from the cell? Could the cell drive the starting motor of a car?

The question is based on the grouping of cells, so we have to use the formula for equivalent emf and internal resistance for the group of the cells.

Solution (a) Six cells are joined in series shown in figure.

Emf of each cells $E = 2$ V

Total emf of circuit $= n \times E = 6 \times 2$

$$= 12 \text{ V}$$

Number of cells $\quad n = 6$

Internal resistance of each cell $r = 0.015 \; \Omega$

Total internal resistance $= n \times r = 6 \times 0.015 = 0.09 \; \Omega$

External load $R = 8.5 \; \Omega$

Current in the circuit

$$I = \frac{nE}{nr + R} = \frac{12}{0.09 + 8.5} = 1.4 \text{ A}$$

The terminal voltage of battery $V = IR = 1.4 \times 8.5 = 11.9$ V

(b) Emf of cell $E = 1.9$ V

Internal resistance of cell $r = 380 \; \Omega$

Maximum current can be drawn from the cell, if there is zero external resistance. Therefore,

$$I_{max} = \frac{E}{r} = \frac{1.9}{380} = 0.005 \text{ A}$$

Now, we see that the maximum current drawn from the cell is very low, thus the cell cannot be used to drive the starting motor of a car as the current required for this purpose is approximately 100 A for few records.

Question 16. Two wires of equal lengths, one of aluminum and the other of copper have the same resistance. Which of the two wires is lighter? Hence, explain why aluminium wires are preferred for overhead power cables?
$(\rho_{Al} = 2.63 \times 10^{-8} \; \Omega\text{-m}, \rho_{Cu} = 1.72 \times 10^{-8} \; \Omega\text{-m}$. Relative density of Al = 2.7 of Cu = 8.9.)

Solution Parameters for aluminum are as follows :

Length $l_{Al} = l$, density $d_{Al} = 2.7$ and area $A_{Al} = A_1$

Parameters for copper are as follows :

Length $l_{Cu} = l$, density $d_{Cu} = 8.9$ and area $A_{Cu} = A_2$

Let the resistivity of aluminum is ρ_{Al} and the resistivity of copper is ρ_{Cu}.

Using the relation $R = \rho \dfrac{l}{A}$

Resistance of aluminium wire

$$R_{Al} = \rho_{Al} \cdot \frac{l_{Al}}{A_{Al}} = \frac{2.63 \times 15^{-8} \times l}{A_1} \qquad \ldots \text{(i)}$$

Mass of aluminium wire $m_{Al} = A_{Al} \times l_{Al} \times d_{Al} = A_1 \times l \times 2.7 \qquad \ldots \text{(ii)}$

Resistance of copper wire

$$R_{Cu} = \rho_{Cu} \times \frac{l_{Cu}}{A_{Cu}} = \frac{1.72 \times 10^{-8} \times l}{A_2} \qquad \ldots\text{(iii)}$$

Mass of copper wire

$$m_{Cu} = A_{Cu} \times l_{Cu} \times d_{Cu} = A_2 \times l \times 8.9 \qquad \ldots\text{(iv)}$$

According to the question, the resistance of aluminium wire is same the resistance of copper wire.

i.e.,
$$R_{Al} = R_{Cu}$$
$$\frac{2.63 \times 10^{-8} \times l}{A_1} = \frac{1.72 \times 10^{-8} \times l}{A_2}$$

[From Eqs. (i) and (iii)]

or
$$\frac{A_1}{A_2} = \frac{2.63}{1.72} \qquad \ldots\text{(v)}$$

From Eqs. (ii) and (iv), we get

$$\frac{m_{Al}}{m_{Cu}} = \frac{A_1 \times l \times 2.7}{A_2 \times l \times 8.9}$$

$$\frac{m_{Al}}{m_{Cu}} = \frac{2.63 \times 2.7}{1.72 \times 8.9} \qquad \text{[From Eq. (v)]}$$

or
$$\frac{m_{Cu}}{m_{Al}} = 2.16$$

Here, we conclude that the copper wires are 2.16 times heavier than aluminium. Now, we see that for equal lengths and resistances, aluminium wire is lighter than copper wire, so aluminium wire due to its lesser mass is used for overhead power cables. Because a heavy cable may break or drown due to its higher mass or weight.

Question 17. What conclusion can you draw from the following observations on a resistor made of alloy manganin?

Current (in A)	Voltage (in V)	Current (in A)	Voltage (in V)
0.2	3.94	3.0	59.2
0.4	7.87	4.0	78.8
0.6	11.8	5.0	98.6
0.8	15.7	6.0	118.5
1.0	19.7	7.0	138.2
2.0	39.4	8.0	158.0

 In these types of questions, first of all calculate the ratio of voltage and current on the basis of which we will be able to draw any conclusion like it follows Ohm's law or not etc.

Solution

Current (in A)	Voltage (in V)	Ratio (V/I)	Current (in A)	Voltage (in V)	Voltage (in V)
0.2	3.94	19.7	3.0	59.2	59.2
0.4	7.87	19.675	4.0	78.8	78.8
0.6	11.8	19.66	5.0	98.6	98.6
0.8	15.7	19.625	6.0	718.5	118.5
1.0	19.7	19.7	7.0	138.2	138.2
2.0	39.4	19.7	8.0	158.0	158.0

As the ratio of voltage and current for different reading is same. So, Ohm's law is valid for manganin.

The resistance of alloys (manganin here) does not depend on temperature as their temperature coefficient of resistance is negligibly small. So, the resistance and resistivity of manganin is independent of temperature.

Question 18. Answer the following questions :

(a) A steady current flows in a metallic conductor of non-uniform cross-section. Which of these quantities is constant along the conductor : current, current density, electric field and drift speed?

(b) Is Ohm's law universally applicable for all conducting elements? If not, give examples of elements which do not obey Ohm's law.

(c) A low voltage supply from which one needs high currents must have very low internal resistance. Why?

(d) A High Tension (HT) supply of (say) 6 kV must have a very large internal resistance. Why?

Solution (a) Current does not depend on area of conductor, so current remains constant. Current density is inversely proportional to area of cross-section, $\left(J \propto \dfrac{1}{A} \right)$, electric field and drift speed also depend on area $\left(E \propto \dfrac{1}{A} \text{ and } v_d \propto \dfrac{1}{A} \right)$. So, current density, electric field and drift speed do not remain constant as area changes.

(b) No, Ohm's law is not universally applicable for all conducting elements. Vacuum tubes, semiconductors, diodes, transistors, thermistors and electrolytes are the examples of elements which do not obey Ohm's law.

(c) For very high current, the internal resistance should be low by according to the formula $I_{max} = \dfrac{V}{r}$, as lesser be the value of r (internal resistance) more is the current.

(d) A high tension supply must have a very large internal resistance because if the circuit is shorted the internal resistance is not large enough than current drawn will exceed the safe limit and will cause the damages.

Question 19. Choose the correct alternative.

(a) Alloys of metals usually have (greater/less) resistivity than that of their constituent metals.

(b) Alloys usually have much (lower/higher) temperature coefficients of resistance than pure metals.

(c) The resistivity of the alloy manganin is nearly (independent of/increases) rapidly with increase of temperature.

(d) The resistivity of a typical insulator (*e.g.*, amber) is greater than that of a metal by a factor of the order of $(10^{22}/10^{23})$.

Solution (a) The resistivity of alloys of metals usually have **greater** resistivity than that of their constituent metals.

(b) Alloys usually have much **lower** temperature coefficients of resistance than pure metals.

(c) The resistivity of the alloy manganin is nearly **independent of** increase of temperature because the coefficient of resistance is very low and its resistivity is quite large.

(d) The resistivity of a typical insulator (mica and amber) is greater than that of a metal by a factor of the order of 10^{22}. Because insulator has maximum resistivity in comparison to metals and alloys.

Question 20. (a) Given, n resistors each of resistance R, how will you combine them to get the (i) maximum (ii) minimum effective resistance? What is the ratio of the maximum to minimum resistance?

(b) Given the resistances of $1\,\Omega$, $2\,\Omega$ and $3\,\Omega$, how will we combine them to get an equivalent resistance of (i) $(11/3)\,\Omega$, (ii) $(11/5)\,\Omega$, (iii) $6\,\Omega$ and (iv) $(6/11)\,\Omega$?

(c) Determine the equivalent resistance of networks shown in given figure.

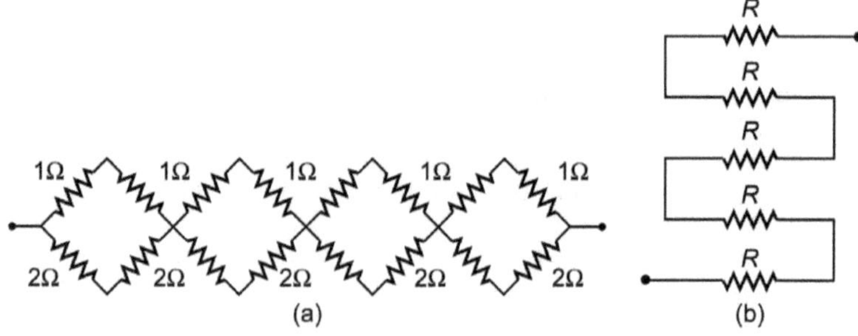

Solution (a) To get the maximum effective resistance, we connect the n resistors in series combination.

$$R_{\max} = R + R + \ldots + n \text{ times} = nR \qquad \ldots(\text{i})$$

To get the minimum effective resistance, we connect the n resistors in parallel combination.

$$\frac{1}{R_{min}} = \frac{1}{R} + \frac{1}{R} + \ldots + n \text{ times} = \frac{n}{R}$$

$$R_{min} = \frac{R}{n} \qquad \ldots(ii)$$

Ratio of maximum to minimum resistance

$$= \frac{R_{max}}{R_{min}} = \frac{nR.n}{R} \qquad \text{[From Eqs. (i) and (ii)]}$$

$$= n^2$$

Thus, the ratio of maximum to minimum resistance, is n^2.

(b) Given, $R_1 = 1\,\Omega$, $R_2 = 2\,\Omega$ and $R_3 = 3\,\Omega$

(i) To get the equivalent resistance as $\frac{11}{3}\,\Omega$, we join them as shown.

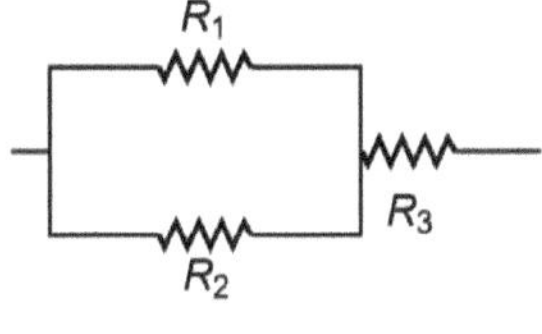

Here, R_1 and R_2 in parallel, $i.e.$,

$$\frac{1}{R_P} = \frac{1}{R_1} + \frac{1}{R_2} = 1 + \frac{1}{2} = \frac{3}{2}$$

$$R_P = \frac{2}{3}\,\Omega$$

Now, R_P and R_3 are in series. So, resultant resistance

$$R = R_P + R_3 = 3 + \frac{2}{3} = \frac{11}{3}\,\Omega$$

(ii) To get the equivalent resistance as $\frac{11}{5}\,\Omega$, we join them as shown.

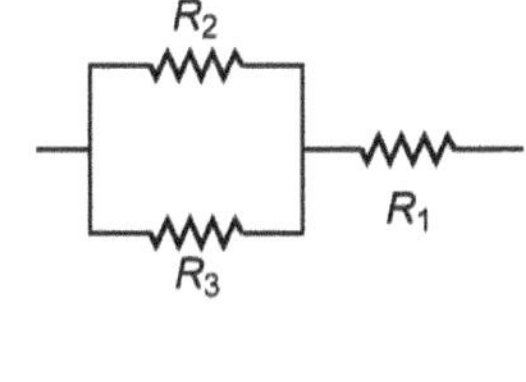

Here, R_2 and R_3 are in parallel, $i.e.$,

$$\frac{1}{R_P} = \frac{1}{R_2} + \frac{1}{R_3} = \frac{1}{2} + \frac{1}{3} = \frac{3+2}{6} = \frac{5}{6}$$

$$R_P = \frac{6}{5}\,\Omega$$

Now, R_P and R_1 are in series. So resultant resistance

$$R = R_P + R_1 = \frac{6}{5} + 1 = \frac{11}{5}\,\Omega$$

(iii) To get the equivalent resistance as $6\,\Omega$, we join them in series as shown.

Resultant resistance

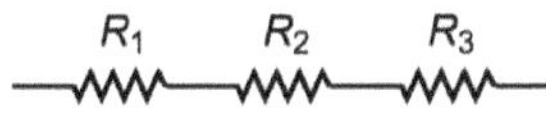

$$R_S = R_1 + R_2 + R_3 = 1 + 2 + 3 = 6\,\Omega$$

(iv) To get the equivalent resistance as $\dfrac{6}{11}$ Ω, we get join them as shown *i.e.*, in parallel.

$$\frac{1}{R_P} = \frac{1}{1} + \frac{1}{2} + \frac{1}{3} = \frac{6+3+2}{6} = \frac{11}{6}$$

Resultant resistance $R_P = \dfrac{6}{11}\ \Omega$

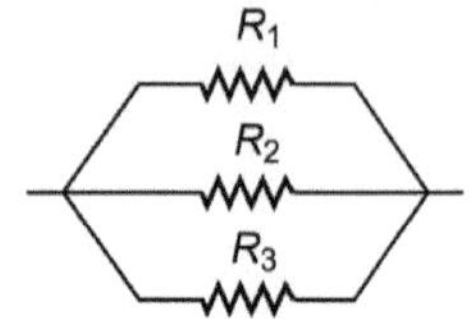

(c) We take one section of Fig. (a).
Here, $1\,\Omega$ and $1\,\Omega$ are in series.

$\therefore$ $\qquad\qquad R_S = 1 + 1 = 2\,\Omega$

and $2\,\Omega$ and $2\,\Omega$ are in series.

$\therefore$ $\qquad\qquad R'_S = 2 + 2 = 4\,\Omega$

Now, R_S and R'_S in parallel,

$$\frac{1}{R'} = \frac{1}{R_S} + \frac{1}{R'_S} = \frac{1}{2} + \frac{1}{4} = \frac{2+1}{4} = \frac{3}{4}$$

$\therefore$ Resultant resistance, $\qquad\qquad R' = \dfrac{4}{3}\ \Omega$

There are four such sections in the Fig. (a) which are connected in series. So, equivalent resistance of Fig. (a)

$$R = 4R' = 4 \times \frac{4}{3} = \frac{16}{3}\ \Omega$$

or $\qquad\qquad\qquad\qquad R = 5.33\ \Omega$

In the Fig. (b), all resistances are connected in series, so the equivalent resistance

$$R' = R + R + R + R + R = 5\,R$$

Question 21. Determine the current drawn from a 12 V supply with internal resistance 0.5 Ω by the infinite network shown in given figure. Each resistor has 1 Ω resistance.

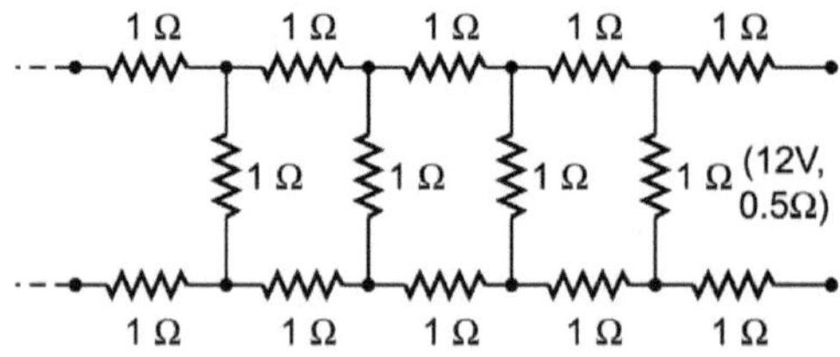

Solution   Let the effective resistance of the network is x. If one part of the network has resistance $(1\,\Omega, 1\,\Omega, 1\,\Omega)$ is separated as shown, the effective resistance remains x (as it is infinitely network). Here, x and $1\,\Omega$ are in parallel.

$$\frac{1}{R_p} = \frac{1}{x} + \frac{1}{1} = \frac{1+x}{x}$$

$$R_p = \frac{x}{1+x}$$

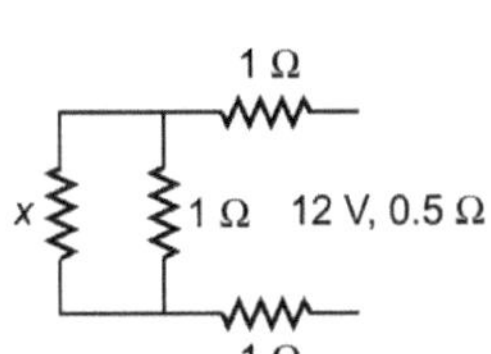

Now, resistances R_p, $1\,\Omega$ and $1\,\Omega$ are in series. So, the resultant resistance

$$R = R_p + 1 + 1 = \frac{x}{1+x} + 1 + 1 = \frac{x}{1+x} + 2 \qquad \dots(i)$$

In case of infinite resistances, the value of R remains x.

$$\therefore \qquad x = \frac{x}{1+x} + 2$$

$$x\,(x+1) = x + 2 + 2x$$

$$x^2 - 2x - 2 = 0$$

$$x = \frac{-(-2) \pm \sqrt{4+8}}{2}$$

$$= \frac{2 \pm \sqrt{12}}{2} = 1 \pm \sqrt{3}$$

The value of resistance cannot be negative. So, the resistance of network

$$x = 1 + \sqrt{3} = 1 + 1.732$$

$$x = 2.732\,\Omega$$

Total resistance of the circuit $= 2.732 + 0.5 = 3.232\,\Omega$

Current drawn from the supply,

$$I = \frac{V}{3.232} = \frac{12}{3.232} = 3.72\text{ A}$$

Question 22. Figure shows a potentiometer with a cell of 2.0 V and internal resistance 0.40 Ω maintaining a potential drop across the resistor wire AB. A standard cell which maintains a constant emf of 1.02 V (for very moderate currents upto a few mA) gives a balance point at 67.3 cm length of the wire. To ensure very low currents drawn from the standard cell, a very high resistance of 600 kΩ is put in series with it, which is shorted close to the balance point. The standard cell is then replaced by a cell of unknown emf ε and the balance point found similarly, turns out to be at 82.3 cm length of the wire.

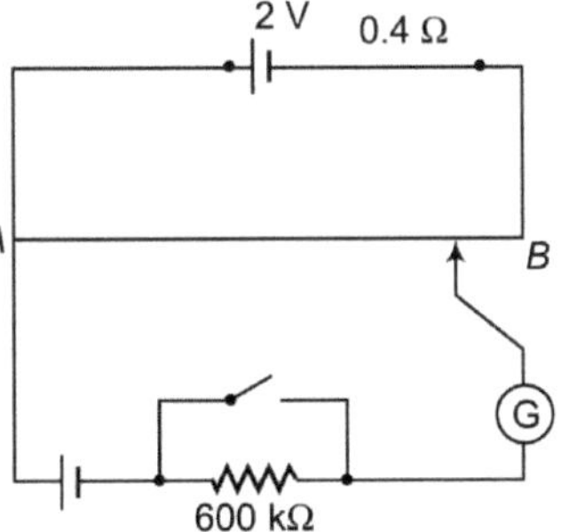

(a) What is the value of ε?

(b) What purpose does the high resistance of 600 kΩ have?

(c) Is the balance point affected by this high resistance?

(d) Is the balance point affected by the internal resistance of the driver cell?

(e) Would the method work in the above situation, if the driver cell of the potentiometer had an emf of 1.0 V instead of 2.0 V?

(f) Would the circuit work well for determining an extremely small emf, say of the order of a few mV (such as the typical emf of a thermocouple)? If not, how will you modify the circuit?

Solution   (a) Here, $E_1 = 1.02$ V, $l_1 = 67.3$ cm, $E_2 = E = ?$ and $l_2 = 82.3$ cm

$$E \propto l$$

$$\therefore \quad \frac{E_1}{E_2} = \frac{l_1}{l_2}$$

$$\Rightarrow \quad \frac{1.02}{E} = \frac{67.3}{82.3}$$

or

$$E = \frac{1.02 \times 82.3}{67.3} = 1.247 \text{ V}$$

Emf of cell $E = 1.247$ V

(b) The use of very high resistance of 600 kΩ is to allow a very small current through the galvanometer when it is too far from the balance point.

(c) No, the balance point is not affected by high resistance of 600 kΩ.

(d) No, the balance point is not affected by the internal resistance of the driver cell.

(e) If the emf of driver cell is less than the driver cell, the method cannot work.

(f) No, the circuit does not work well for determining an extremely small emf of millivolt because in this situation, the balance point is very near to end A. To modify, we use high resistance in series with the cell. This decreases the current in the potential wire. So, the potential gradient decreases.

Question 23. Figure shows a potentiometer circuit for comparison of two resistances. The balance point with a standard resistor $R = 10.0\ \Omega$ is found to be 58.3 cm, while that with the unknown resistance X is 68.5 cm. Determine the value of X. What might you do if you failed to find a balance point with the given cell of emf ε ?

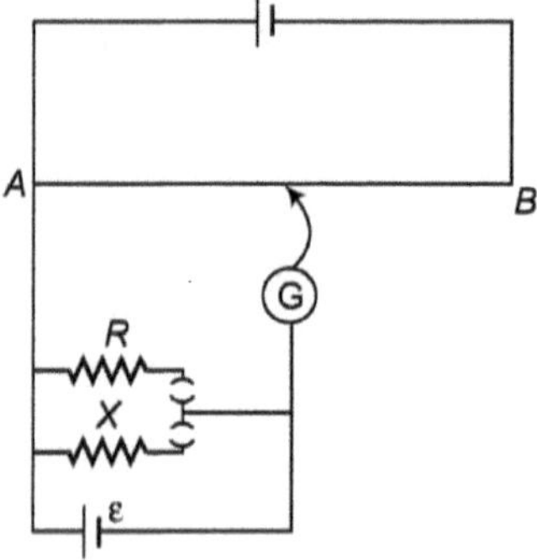

Solution Here, $l_1 = 58.3$ cm, $l_2 = 68.5$ cm, $R = 10\ \Omega$, $X = ?$

Let I be the current in the potentiometer wire and E_1 and E_2 be the potential drops across R and X respectively.
Then,

$$\frac{E_2}{E_1} = \frac{IX}{IR} = \frac{X}{R}$$

or

$$X = \frac{E_2}{E_1} \cdot R \qquad \qquad \ldots(i)$$

According to the principle of potentiometer,

$$\frac{E_2}{E_1} = \frac{l_2}{l_1}$$

From Eq. (i), we get

$$X = \frac{l_2}{l_1} \cdot R = \frac{68.5}{58.3} \times 10 = 11.75 \ \Omega$$

If we failed to find a balance point with the given cell of emf E, it means the potential drop across R or X is greater than the potential drop across potentiometer wire. It may be possible that voltage across driver cell is less than that of emf ε.

Question 24. Figure shows a 2.0 V potentiometer used for the determination of internal resistance of a 1.5 V cell. The balance point of the cell in open-circuit is 76.3 cm. When a resistor of 9.5 Ω is used in the external circuit of the cell, the balance point shifts to 64.8 cm length of the potentiometer wire. Determine the internal resistance of the cell.

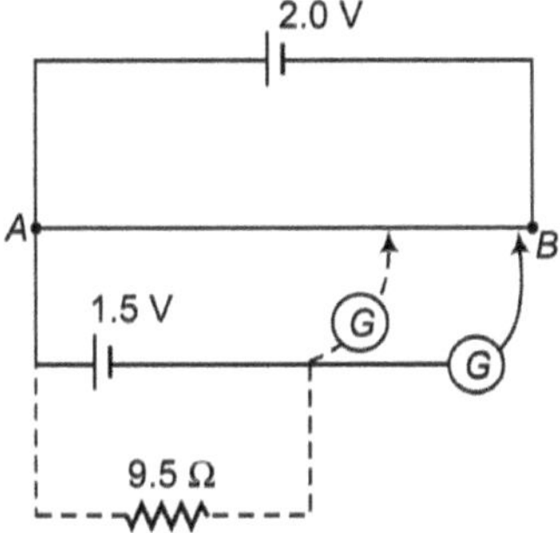

Solution Here, balancing length when cell is in open-circuit,

$$l_1 = 76.3 \text{ cm}$$

Balancing length when cell is in closed-circuit,

$$l_2 = 64.8 \text{ cm}$$

and resistance $R = 9.5 \ \Omega$

The internal resistance of the cell is given by

$$r = \left(\frac{l_1}{l_2} - 1 \right) R$$

$$= \left(\frac{76.3}{64.8} - 1 \right) \times 9.5 = 1.68 \ \Omega$$

The internal resistance of the cell is 1.68 Ω.

Selected NCERT Exemplar Problems

Question 1.   The relaxation time τ is nearly independent of applied E field whereas it changes significantly with temperature T, first fact is (in part) responsible for Ohm's law whereas the second fact leads to variation of P with temperature. Elaborate why?

Solution   The relaxation time depends on the velocity of electrons or ions. As we know that an application of electric field, it affects the velocities of electrons as they move in particular direction. But on the application of electric field, the speed of electrons differ by 1 mm/s which is very small and thus it is an insignificant effect. As we change the temperature T, the velocity of electrons changes by large amount as 100 m/s. Thus, it is an significant effect that relaxation time changes with change in temperature.

Question 2. AB is a potentiometer wire (see figure). If the value of R is increased, in which direction will the balance point J shift?

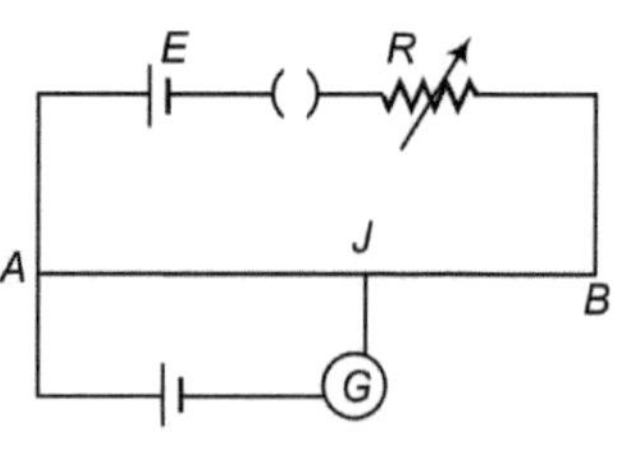

Solution   As the value of R increased, the current flowing in the circuit will decrease. And the potential gradient *i.e.*, potential drop per unit length also decreases so that the balance length will increase. Thus, J will shift towards B.

Question 3.   Two cells of voltages 10 V and 2 V and internal resistances 10 Ω and 5 Ω respectively, are connected in parallel with the positive end of 10 V battery connected to negative pole of 2 V battery (see figure). Find the effective voltage and effective resistance of the combination.

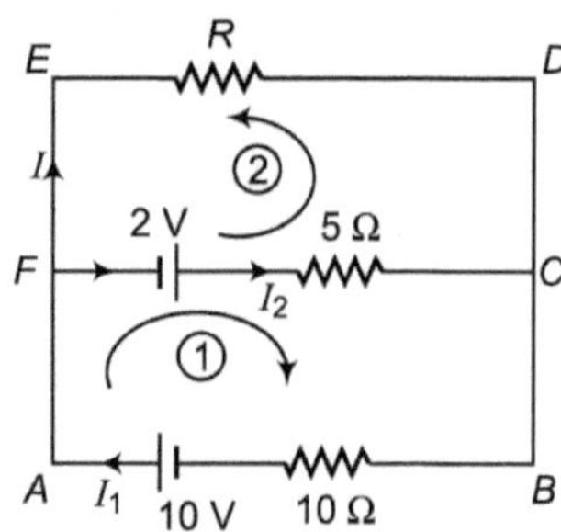

 Use Kirchhoff's Ist law ($\Sigma I = 0$) and IInd law ($\Sigma E = \Sigma IR$).

Solution   Use the Kirchhoff's Ist law, *i.e.*, junction law at point F.

$$\Sigma I = 0$$
$$I_1 = I_2 + I \qquad \qquad \text{...(i)}$$

Use Kirchhoff's second law in mesh **AFCBA**

$$\Sigma E = \Sigma iR$$
$$10 + 2 = 10\,I_1 + 5\,I_2$$
$$12 = 10\,I_1 + 5\,I_2 \qquad \qquad \text{...(ii)}$$

Use Kirchhoff's second law in mesh **CDEFC**

$$\Sigma E = \Sigma IR$$
$$2 = 5\,I_2 - IR \qquad \qquad \text{...(iii)}$$

From Eq. (i), we get $\qquad\qquad I_2 = I_1 - I$

Putting in Eq. (ii), we get $\qquad 12 = 10\,I_1 + 5\,(I_1 - I) = 15\,I_1 - 5\,I$

$$\frac{12 + 5I}{15} = I_1$$

Putting in Eq. (i), we get $\qquad I_2 = I_1 - I = \frac{12 + 5I}{15} - I = \frac{12 - 10I}{15}$

Putting the value of I_2 in Eq. (iii), we get

$$2 = 5\left(\frac{12 - 10I}{15}\right) - I\,R$$

$$2 = \frac{12 - 10I}{3} - I\,R = \frac{12 - 10I - 3\,IR}{3}$$

$$2 = 4 - \left(\frac{10 + 3R}{3}\right) I$$

$$\left(\frac{10}{3} + R\right) I = 2 \qquad\qquad\qquad\qquad \text{...(iv)}$$

Now, comparing it with $V_{\text{eff}} = (R + R_{\text{eff}})\,I$

$$V_{\text{eff}} = 2 \text{ V}$$

$$R_{\text{eff}} = \frac{10}{3}\ \Omega$$

The circuit becomes

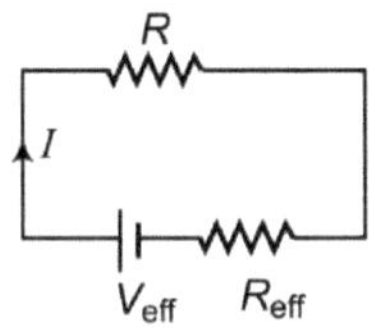

Question 4. (a) Consider circuit in given figure. How much energy is absorbed by electrons from the initial state of no current (ignore thermal motion) to the state of drift velocity?

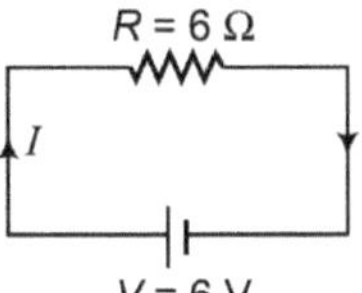

  (b) Electrons give up energy at the rate of RI^2 per second to the thermal energy. What time scale would one associate with energy in problem (a)?

Given, $n = $ number of electrons per volume $= 10^{29}/\text{m}^3$, length of circuit $= 10$ cm, cross-section $A = 1\,\text{mm}^2$.

Solution   (a) Given, $V = 6$ V, $R = 6\ \Omega$, $A = 1 \times 10^{-6}\,\text{m}^2$

$\qquad\qquad$ and $l = 10$ cm $= 0.1$ m

The current in the circuit, $I = \dfrac{V}{R} = \dfrac{6}{6} = 1$ A

Use the relation $I = ne\,A\,v_d$

Drift velocity of electrons,

$$v_d = \frac{I}{neA} = \frac{1}{10^{29} \times 1.6 \times 10^{-19} \times 1 \times 10^{-6}} = \frac{1}{1.6} \times 10^{-4} \text{ m/s}$$

The energy of electrons, $(KE) = \frac{1}{2} mv^2$

$$= \frac{1}{2} \times m_e \times v_d^2 \times \text{Volume} \times \text{Number of electrons per volume}$$

$$= \frac{1}{2} \times 9.1 \times 10^{-31} \times \left(\frac{10^{-4}}{1.6}\right)^2 \times A \times l \times n$$

$$[\because \text{Mass of electron } m_e = 9.1 \times 10^{-31}]$$

$$= \frac{9.1 \times 10^{-39}}{2 \times 1.6 \times 1.6} \times 10^{-6} \times 0.1 \times 10^{29} = 2 \times 10^{-17} \text{ J}$$

(b) Energy loss in the circuit $= I^2 R = 1^2 \times 6 = 6 \text{ J/s}$

All of the KE of electrons lost

$$= \frac{\text{Total KE}}{\text{Energy loss per second}}$$

$$= \frac{2 \times 10^{-17}}{6} = 3.33 \times 10^{-18} \text{ s}$$

Chapter 4

Moving Charges and Magnetism

Important Results

1. The total force F experienced by charge (q) when it is moving with velocity v in the presence of electric field $\mathbf{E}$ and magnetic field $\mathbf{B}$

$$\mathbf{F} = q\,(v \times \mathbf{B} + \mathbf{E})$$

   This is called **Lorentz force**.

2. Force experienced by a current carrying conductor having current I and length l, when placed in a magnetic field B is

$$\mathbf{F} = I\,l \times \mathbf{B} = Ilb \sin \theta$$

3. The frequency of a charged particle (q) when it enters perpendicular to magnetic field B and it attains a circular path is

$$v = \frac{qB}{2\pi m}$$

   where, m is the mass of charged particle. This is called **cyclotron frequency.**

4. **The Biot-Savart law** The magnetic field dB due to an element of length dl carrying a current I at a point P at a distance r from the conductor is

$$d\mathbf{B} = \frac{\mu_0}{4\pi} \frac{Idl \times \mathbf{r}}{r^3}$$

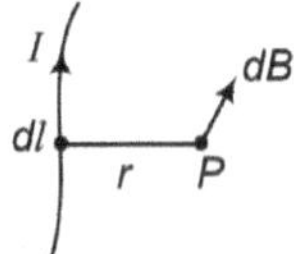

   The direction of magnetic field is given by Fleming left hand rule.

5. The magnetic field intensity at a point due to a straight conductor carrying current I is

$$B = \frac{\mu_0}{4\pi} \frac{I}{a} [\sin \phi_1 + \sin \phi_2]$$

6. Magnetic field strength at a distance a due to an infinitely long conductor carrying conductor is

$$B = \frac{\mu_0}{4\pi} \cdot \frac{2I}{a}$$

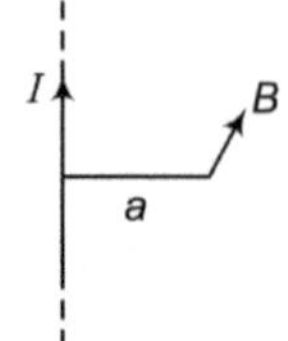

7. Magnetic field strength due to a circular coil of radius r carrying current I at a distance x on its axis from the centre of the coil is

$$B = \frac{\mu_0}{4\pi} \cdot \frac{2\,I\,A}{(r^2 + x^2)^{3/2}}$$

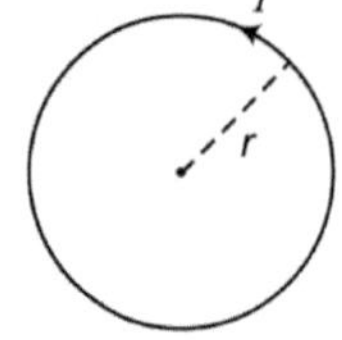

where $A = \pi r^2$ is the area of the coil.

If there are n number of turns in the coil, the magnetic field

$$B = \frac{\mu_0}{4\pi} \cdot \frac{2\,I\,A\,n}{(r^2 + x^2)^{3/2}}$$

8. Magnetic field strength at the centre of the circular coil having radius r and current I is

$$B = \frac{\mu_0}{4\pi} \cdot \frac{2\,I}{r}$$

If there are n number of turns in the coil, the magnetic field

$$B = \frac{\mu_0}{4\pi} \cdot \frac{2In}{r}$$

9. Magnetic field strength at the centre of an arc of radius r subtending an angle θ. Carrying current I is

$$B = \frac{\mu_0}{4\pi} \cdot \frac{I}{r}\,\theta$$

10. **Ampere's circuital law** $\oint \mathbf{B}.\,dl = \mu_0 I$, where B is the magnetic field induction at a point on the closed path and I is the current in the closed path.

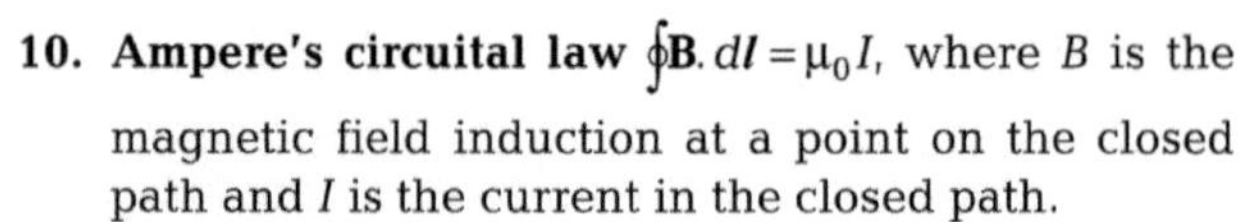

11. The magnetic field induction B inside a long solenoid carrying current I is given by

$$B = \mu_0 nI$$

where, n is the number of turns per unit length.

The magnetic field induction at the ends of solenoid is given by

$$B = \frac{\mu_0 nI}{2}$$

12. The magnetic field induction B at a point inside the toroid carrying current I is given by
$$B = \mu_0 n I$$
where, n is number of turns per unit length.

13. The magnetic field induction outside the toroid is zero.

14. Magnetic moment $\mathbf{M} = N I \mathbf{A}$
where, A is the area and I is the current.

15. The magnetic moment of an electron moving around the nucleus is given by
$$= \frac{e}{2m} l$$
where, l is the magnitude of angular momentum.

The smallest value of μ is called the Bohr magneton is given by
$$\mu_B = 9.27 \times 10^{-24} \text{ J/T}$$

16. Torque on a current loop $\tau = \mathbf{M} \times \mathbf{B} = N I \mathbf{AB}$
where, M is the magnetic moment.

17. Force between the two parallel currents carrying conductors
$$F = \frac{\mu_0}{4\pi} \cdot \frac{2 I_1 I_2}{r}$$

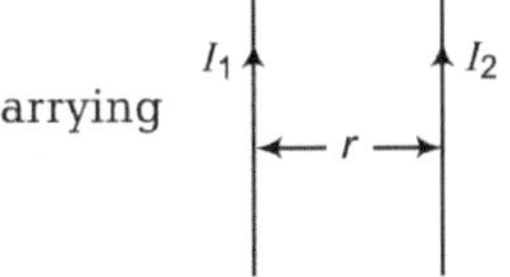

If the direction of flow of current is same, then they repel each other.
If the direction of flow of current is opposite, they attract each other.

18. Current sensitivity $= \dfrac{\theta}{I} = \dfrac{NAB}{k}$

where, k is the spring constant.

19. Voltage sensitivity $= \dfrac{\theta}{V} = \dfrac{\theta}{IR} = \dfrac{SI}{R} = \dfrac{NAB}{kR}$

where, k is the spring constant.

Exercises

Question 1. A circular coil of wire consisting of 100 turns, each of radius 8.0 cm carries a current of 0.40 A. What is the magnitude of the magnetic field B at the centre of the coil?

Solution Here, $n = 100$, $r = 8 \text{ cm} = 8 \times 10^{-2}$ m

and $I = 0.40$ A

The magnetic field B at the centre

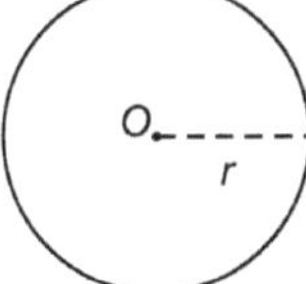

$$B = \frac{\mu_0}{4\pi} \cdot \frac{2\pi I n}{r} = \frac{10^{-7} \times 2 \times 3.14 \times 0.4 \times 100}{8 \times 10^{-2}}$$

$$= 3.1 \times 10^{-4} \text{ T}$$

The direction of magnetic field depends on the direction of current if the direction of current is anticlockwise. According to Maxwell's right hand rule, the direction of magnetic field at the centre of coil will be perpendicular outwards to the plane of paper.

Question 2. A long straight wire carries a current of 35 A. What is the magnitude of the field B at a point 20 cm away from the wire?

 Use the formula for magnetic field produced by a current carrying infinite long wire. Here the length of the wire is not given so we can consider it of infinite length.

Solution Here, we have to find the magnetic field at point P.

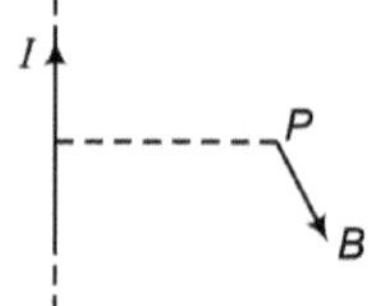

$$I = 35 \text{ A and } r = 20 \text{ cm} = 0.2 \text{ m}$$

The wire is long and it is considered as an infinite length wire. The magnetic field

$$B = \frac{\mu_0}{4\pi} \cdot \frac{2I}{r} = \frac{10^{-7} \times 2 \times 35}{0.2} = 3.5 \times 10^{-5} \text{ T}$$

The direction of magnetic field is given by Maxwell's right hand rule. If current is upward, magnetic field at P is perpendicular inwards to the plane of paper.

Question 3. A long straight wire in the horizontal plane carries a current of 50 A in north to south direction. Give the magnitude and direction of B at a point 2.5 m east of the wire.

 As the length of wire is not mentioned in the question, so use the formula to find the magnetic field at a point due to infinite length wire.

Solution Here, the point P is in the east direction from the wire which is placed in north-south direction and in the horizontal plane.

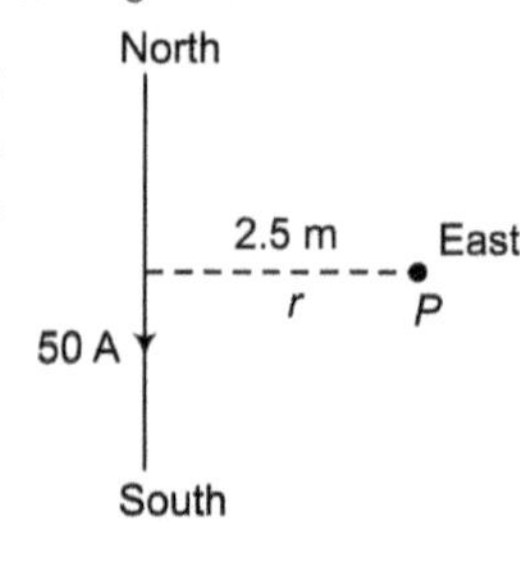

Given, $I = 50$ A and $r = 2.5$ m

The magnitude of magnetic field

$$B = \frac{\mu_0}{4\pi} \cdot \frac{2I}{r} = 10^{-7} \cdot \frac{2 \times 50}{2.5}$$

$$= 4 \times 10^{-6} \text{ T}$$

The direction of magnetic field at point P is given by Maxwell's right hand rule. The current flows from north to south, *i.e.*, downwards, then the direction of magnetic field at P is perpendicularly outwards to the plane of paper.

Question 4. A horizontal overhead power line carries a current of 90 A in east to west direction. What are the magnitude and direction of the magnetic field due to the current 1.5 m below the line?

 The overhead power line is considered as an infinite length wire so use the formula to find the magnetic field at a point due to infinite length wire.

Solution Given, $I = 90$ A and $r = 1.5$ m

Here, point P is below the power line, where we have to find the magnetic field and its direction. The magnitude of magnetic field

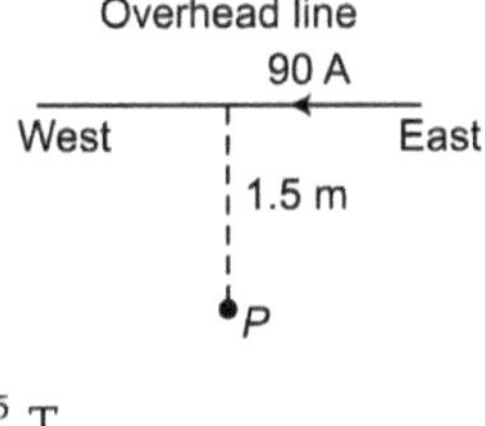

$$B = \frac{\mu_0}{4\pi} \cdot \frac{2I}{r}$$

$$= \frac{10^{-7} \times 2 \times 90}{1.5} = 1.2 \times 10^{-5} \text{ T}$$

The direction of magnetic field is given by Maxwell's right hand rule. So, the direction of magnetic field at point P due to the flowing current is perpendicularly outwards to the plane of paper.

Question 5. What is the magnitude of magnetic force per unit length on a wire carrying a current of 8 A and making an angle of 30° with the direction of a uniform magnetic field of 0.15 T?

Solution According to the question, $I = 8$ A, $\theta = 30°$, $B = 0.15$ T, $l = 1$ m

The magnitude of magnetic force

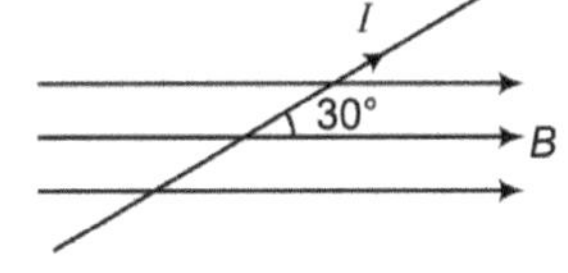

$$\mathbf{F} = I\,(\mathbf{l} \times \mathbf{B}) = I\,l\,B \sin\theta$$

$$= 8 \times 1 \times 0.15 \times \sin 30°$$

$$= \frac{8 \times 0.15}{2} = 0.6 \text{ N/m}$$

The direction of force is perpendicular to both the direction of magnetic field and the direction of flow of current both, $[\because F = I(I \times B)$ i.e., force is a cross product of two vector quantities so it will be perpendicular to both of these]. Here, the direction of force is perpendicularly inwards to the plane of paper (according to the given diagram) by using right hand palm rule.

Question 6. A 3.0 cm wire carrying a current of 10 A is placed inside a solenoid perpendicular to its axis. The magnetic field inside the solenoid is given to be 0.27 T. What is the magnetic force on the wire?

Solution Here, the angle between the magnetic field and the direction of flow of current is 90°. Because the magnetic field due to a solenoid is along the axis of the solenoid and the wire is placed perpendicular to the axis.

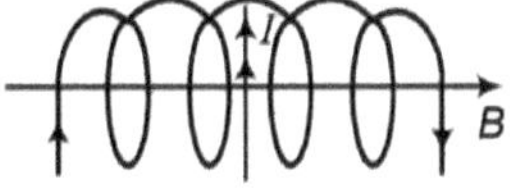

Given, $l = 3$ cm $= 3 \times 10^{-2}$ m, $I = 10$ A, $B = 0.2$ T,

The magnitude of magnetic force on the wire

$$F = I\,l\,B \sin 90° = 10 \times 3 \times 10^{-2} \times 0.27 \times \sin 90° = 8.1 \times 10^{-2} \text{ N}$$

According to right hand palm rule, the direction of magnetic force is perpendicular to plane of paper inwards.

Question 7.   Two long and parallel straight wires A and B carrying currents of 8.0 A and 5.0 A in the same direction are separated by a distance of 4.0 cm. Estimate the force on a 10 cm section of wire A?

Solution Given, $I_1 = 8$ A, $I_2 = 5$ A and $r = 4$ cm $= 0.04$ m

Force per unit length on two parallel wire carrying current

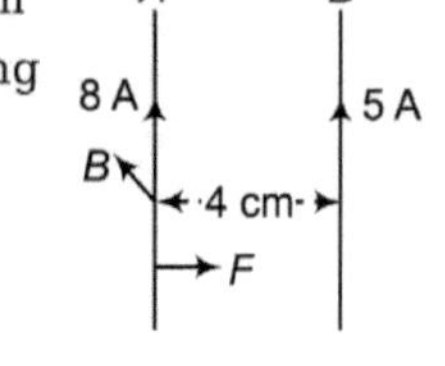

$$F = \frac{\mu_0}{4\pi} \cdot \frac{2I_1 \cdot I_2}{r}$$

$$= \frac{10^{-7} \times 2 \times 8 \times 5}{0.04} = 2 \times 10^{-4} \text{ N}$$

The force on A of length 10 cm is $F' = F \times 0.1$ $\qquad$ ($\because$ 1m = 100 cm)

$\Rightarrow$ $\qquad\qquad\qquad F' = 2 \times 10^{-4} \times 0.1$

$$= 2 \times 10^{-5} \text{ N}$$

Using Maxwell's right hand rule the direction of magnetic field due to B on A is perpendicularly outwards to the plane of paper.

According to Fleming's left hand rule, the direction of force is towards B and the nature of force is attractive.

Question 8.   A closely wound solenoid 80 cm long has 5 layers of windings of 400 turns each. The diameter of the solenoid is 1.8 cm. If the current carried is 8.0 A, estimate the magnitude of B inside the solenoid near its centre.

Solution The length of solenoid, $l = 80$ cm $= 0.8$ m

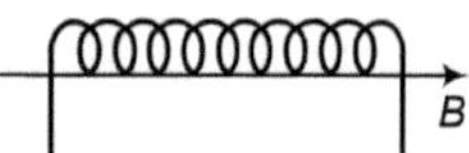

Number of layers $= 5$

Number of turns per layer $= 400$

Diameter of solenoid $= 1.8$ cm

Current in solenoid $I = 8$ A

$\therefore$ The total number of turns $N = 400 \times 5 = 2000$

and number of turns/length, $n = \dfrac{2000}{0.8} = 2500$

The magnitude of magnetic field inside the solenoid

$$B = \mu_0 nI = 4 \times 3.14 \times 10^{-7} \times 2500 \times 8$$

$$= 2.5 \times 10^{-2} \text{ T}$$

The direction of magnetic field is along the axis of solenoid.

Question 9.   A square coil of side 10 cm consists of 20 turns and carries a current of 12 A. The coil is suspended vertically and the normal to the plane of the coil makes an angle of 30° with the direction of a uniform horizontal magnetic field of magnitude 0.80 T. What is the magnitude of torque experienced by the coil?

Solution Given, side of square coil $= 10$ cm $= 0.1$ m

Number of turns $(n) = 20$

Current in square coil $I = 12$ A

Angle made by coil $\theta = 30°$

Magnetic field $B = 0.80$ T

The magnitude of torque experienced by the coil

$$\tau = NI\,AB \sin\theta$$
$$= 20 \times 12 \times (10 \times 10^{-2})^2 \times 0.80 \times \sin 30°$$
$$\tau = 2.4 \times 0.80 \sin 30° = \frac{2.4 \times 0.80}{2} = 0.96 \text{ N-m}$$

Question 10. Two moving coil meters M_1 and M_2 having the following particulars :

$R_1 = 10\ \Omega$, $N_1 = 30$, $A_1 = 3.6 \times 10^{-3}$ m^2, $B_1 = 0.25$ T

$R_2 = 14\ \Omega$, $N_2 = 42$, $A_2 = 1.8 \times 10^{-3}$ m^2, $B_2 = 0.50$ T

(The spring constants are identical for the two meters).

Determine the ratio of (a) current sensitivity and (b) voltage sensitivity of M_2 and M_1.

 Use the formula for current sensitivity and voltage sensitivity.

$$I_s \text{ (current sensitivity)} = \frac{nBA}{k}$$

$$V_s \text{ (voltage sensitivity)} = \frac{nBA}{kR}$$

where, n be the number of turns in the coil, B be the magnetic field, A be the area of cross-section of the coil, R be the resistance and k is the spring constant.

Solution Given, $R_1 = 10\ \Omega$, $n_1 = 30$, $A_1 = 3.6 \times 10^{-3}$ m^2, $B_1 = 0.25$ T

$R_2 = 14\ \Omega$, $n_2 = 42$, $A_2 = 1.8 \times 10^{-3}$ m^2, $B_2 = 0.50$ T

$k_1 = k_2$ (spring constants are same)

(a) Using the formula of current sensitivity,

$$I = \frac{NAB}{k}$$

$$\therefore \quad \frac{I_{S_2}}{I_{S_1}} = \frac{n_2 B_2 A_2 . k_1}{n_1 B_1 A_1 k_2} = \frac{42 \times 0.50 \times 1.8 \times 10^{-3}}{30 \times 0.25 \times 3.6 \times 10^{-3}} = 1.4$$

(b) Using the formula of voltage sensitivity,

$$V = \frac{NAB}{kR}$$

$$\therefore \quad \frac{V_{s_2}}{V_{s_1}} = \frac{n_2 B_2 A_2 . k_1 R_1}{k_2 . R_2 . n_1 B_1 A_1}$$

$$= \frac{42 \times 0.50 \times 1.8 \times 10^{-3} \times k \times 10}{k \times 14 \times 30 \times 0.25 \times 3.6 \times 10^{-3}} = 1$$

Question 11. In a chamber, a uniform magnetic field of 6.5 G $(1\text{G} = 10^{-4}\text{ T})$ is maintained. An electron is shot into the field with a speed of 4.8×10^{6} m/s normal to the field explain why the path of the electron is a circle. Determine the radius of the circular orbit. ($e = 1.6 \times 10^{-19}$ C, $m_e = 9.1 \times 10^{-31}$ kg)

 As the charge particle enters perpendicularly in a uniform magnetic field, it acquires a circular path as the required centripetal force is provided by the magnetic force acting on the charged particle.

Solution   Given, magnetic field
$$B = 6.5\text{ G} = 6.5 \times 10^{-4}\text{ T}$$

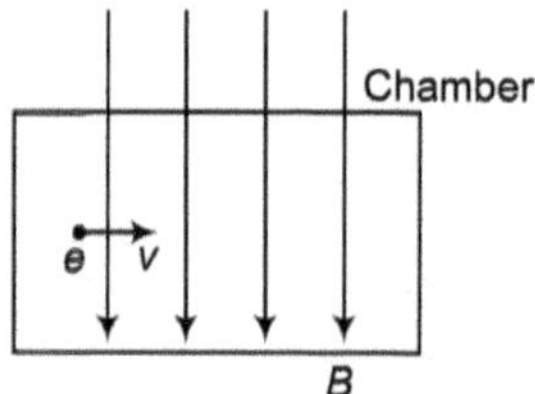

Charge $e = -1.6 \times 10^{-19}$ C

Speed of electron $v = 4.8 \times 10^{6}$ m/s

Mass of electron $m_e = 9.1 \times 10^{-31}$ kg

Angle between magnetic field and electron
$\theta = 90°$

The force on the charge particle entering in the magnetic field
$$\mathbf{F} = q\,(\mathbf{v} \times \mathbf{B}) = e(\mathbf{v} \times \mathbf{b})$$

According the right hand palm rule, the direction of force is perpendicular to both velocity and magnetic field.

So, the force will only change the direction of motion without changing the magnitude of velocity. So, the electron attains a circular path and the necessary centripetal force is provided by the magnetic force.

$$\therefore \qquad e\,(\mathbf{v} \times \mathbf{B}) = \frac{mv^2}{r}$$

$$\text{or} \qquad e\,v\,B\sin 90^0 = \frac{mv^2}{r}$$

$$\text{or} \qquad r = \frac{mv}{eB \times 1} = \frac{9.1 \times 10^{-31} \times 4.8 \times 10^{6}}{1.6 \times 10^{-19} \times 6.5 \;\; 10^{-4}}$$

$$= 4.2 \times 10^{-2}\text{ m}$$

$$= 4.2\text{ cm}$$

Question 12. In Q. 11. obtain the frequency of revolution of the electron in its circular orbit. Does the answer depend on the speed of the electron? Explain.

Solution   Given, $\qquad B = 6.5\text{ G} = 6.5 \times 10^{-4}\text{ T}$

$$v = 4.8 \times 10^{6}\text{ m/s}, \; e = 1.6 \times 10^{-19}\text{ C}$$

and $\qquad m_e = 9.1 \times 10^{-31}$ kg

We know that when an electron (charged particle) moves on a circular path in unifrom magnetic field, then the required centripetal force is provided by the magnetic force on it.

$$\frac{mv^2}{r} = qvB \quad \Rightarrow \quad \frac{mv}{r} = qB$$

If angular velocity of electron is ω, then

$$v = r\omega$$

$$\therefore \quad \frac{m\,(r\omega)}{r} = qB$$

$$\omega = \frac{qB}{m}$$

(if frequency of revolution is n then $\omega = 2\pi n$)

$$\therefore \quad 2\pi n = \frac{qB}{m} \quad \Rightarrow \quad n = \frac{qB}{2\pi m}$$

Frequency of revolution of electron in the orbit

$$\nu = \frac{Bq}{2\pi m} = \frac{Be}{2\pi m_e} = \frac{6.5 \times 10^{-4} \times 1.6 \times 10^{-19}}{2 \times 3.14 \times 9.1 \times 10^{-31}} \qquad (\because \text{For electron } q = e)$$

$$= 18.18 \times 10^6 \text{ Hz}$$

Here, we observe that the frequency of electron is independent to the velocity.

Question 13. (a) A circular coil of 30 turns and radius 8.0 cm carrying a current of 6.0 A is suspended vertically in a uniform horizontal magnetic field of magnitude 1.0 T. The field lines make an angle of 60° with the normal of the coil. Calculate the magnitude of the counter torque that must be applied to prevent the coil from turning.
(b) Would your answer change, if the circular coil in (a) were replaced by a planar coil of some irregular shape that encloses the same area? (All other particulars are also unaltered)

Solution (a) Given, number of turns $n = 30$, radius $(r) = 8$ cm $= 0.08$ m

Current in the coil $I = 6$ A

Magnetic field $B = 1.0$ T

Angle made by field with the normal of the coil, $\theta = 60°$

Magnitude of torque acting on the current
carrying coil due to the magnetic field

$$\tau = nIAB \sin \theta$$

$$= 30 \times 6 \times \pi\,(0.08)^2 \times 1 \times \sin 60°$$

$$= 30 \times 6 \times 3.14 \times 0.08 \times 0.08 \times \sqrt{\frac{3}{2}}$$

$$= 3.133 \text{ N-m}$$

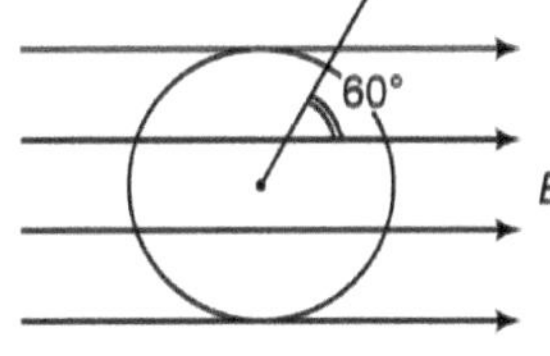

(b) From the formula, it is clear that the torque on the loop does not depend on the shape if area remains constant. So, the torque remains constant (become all other particulars are unaltered).

Additional Exercises

Question 14. Two concentric circular coils x and y of radii 16 cm and 10 cm, respectively lie in the same vertical plane containing the north to south direction. Coil x has 20 turns and carries a current of 16 A; coil y has 25 turns and carries a current of 18 A. The sense of the current in x is anticlockwise and clockwise in y, for an observer looking at the coils facing west. Find the magnitude and direction of the net magnetic field due to the coils at their centre.

 Here, we have to find the net magnetic field due to two coils. So, first of all find the magnetic fields due to individual coil and find the net field is the law of vector addition, as magnetic field is a vector quantity.

Solution   **For coil x**

Radius of coil, $r_x = 16$ cm $= 0.16$ m

Number of turns $n_x = 20$

Current in the coil, $I_x = 16$ A (anticlockwise)

For coil y Radius of coil, $r_y = 10$ cm $= 0.1$ m

Number of turns $n_y = 25$

Current in the coil $I_y = 18$ A (clockwise)

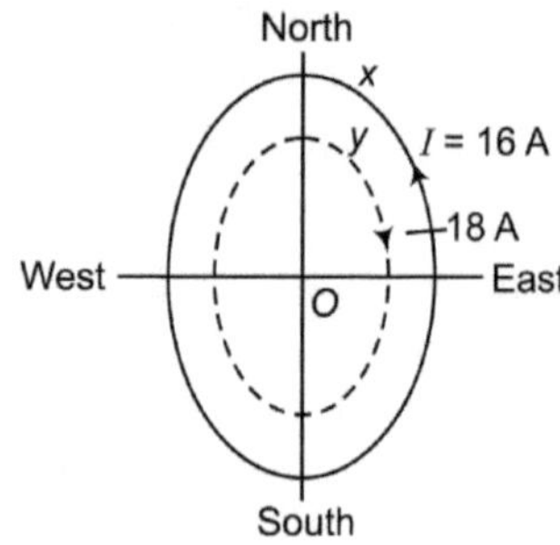

The magnitude of the magnetic field at the centre of coil x,

$$B_x = \frac{\mu_0}{4\pi} \cdot \frac{2I_x \pi n_x}{r_x} = \frac{10^{-7} \times 2 \times 16 \times 3.14 \times 20}{0.16} \text{ T}$$

$$= 4\pi \times 10^{-4} \text{ T}$$

The direction of magnetic field due to the coil x at centre O is towards right *i.e.*, east, according to Maxwell's right hand rule.

The magnitude of the magnetic field at the centre of coil y,

$$B_y = \frac{\mu_0}{4\pi} \cdot \frac{2\pi I_y n_y}{r_y} = \frac{10^{-7} \times 2 \times \pi \times 18 \times 25}{0.1} = 9\pi \times 10^{-4} \text{ T}$$

The direction of magnetic field due to coil y at centre O is towards left, *i.e.*, west, according to Maxwell's left hand rule.

Here, the magnitude of B_y is greater than B_x, so the resultant magnetic field will be in the direction of B_y, *i.e.*, left (west).

Net magnetic field at the centre $B = B_y - B_x = (9\pi - 4\pi)10^{-4} = 5\pi \times 10^{-4}$

$$(\because B_y \text{ and } B_x \text{ are opposite to each other})$$

$$= 1.6 \times 10^{-3} \text{ T} \text{ (towards west)}$$

Question 15. A magnetic field of 100 G $(1G = 10^{-4}$ T$)$ is required which is uniform in a region of linear dimension about 10 cm and area of cross-section about 10^{-3}m^2. The maximum current carrying capacity of a given coil of wire is 15 A and the number of turns per unit length that can be wound round a core is at most 1000 turns/m. Suggest same appropriate design particulars of a solenoid for the required purpose. Assume the core is not ferromagnetic.

Solution Magnetic field $B = 100\,G = 100 \times 10^{-4}\,T = 10^{-2}\,T$

Maximum current $I = 15\,A$, $n = 1000/m$

To design the solenoid, let we find the product of current and number of turns in the solenoid.

The magnitude of magnetic field $B = \mu_0 nI$

$$\text{or} \qquad nI = \frac{B}{\mu_0} = \frac{10^{-2}}{4 \times 3.14 \times 10^{-7}}$$

$$\Rightarrow \qquad nI = 7961 \approx 8000$$

Here, the product of nI is 8000 so,

current $I = 8\,A$

and number of turns $n = 1000$

The other design is $I = 10\,A$ and $n = 800/m$. This is the most appropriate design as the requirement.

Question 16. For a circular coil of radius R and N turns carrying current I, the magnitude of the magnetic field at a point on its axis at a distance x from its centre is given by

$$B = \frac{\mu_0 I R^2 N}{2(x^2 + R^2)^{3/2}}$$

(a) Show that this reduces to the familiar result for field at the centre of the coil.

(b) Consider two parallel co-axial circular coils of equal radius R and number of turns N, carrying equal currents in the same direction and separated by a distance R. Show that the field on the axis around the mid-point between the coils is uniform over a distance that is small as compared to R, and is given by

$$B = 0.72 \frac{\mu_0 NI}{R} \text{ (approximately)}$$

[Such an arrangement to produce a nearly uniform magnetic field over a small region is known as Helmholtz coils]

Solution (a) Given, magnetic field at distance x

$$B = \frac{\mu_0 NIR^2}{2(x^2 + R^2)^{3/2}}$$

To get the magnetic field at the centre of coil, we put $x = 0$ (distance x from the centre of coil at its axis)

$\therefore$ The magnetic field at the centre $\quad B = \dfrac{\mu_0 IR^2 N}{2R^3}$

$$B = \frac{\mu_0 I \, N}{2R}$$

This result is same as the magnetic field due to current loop at its centre.

(b) Radius of two parallel co-axial coil $= R$, number of turns $= N$ and current $= I$ (same direction)

Let the mid-points between the coils is at point O and P be the point around the mid-point O.

Suppose, the distance between $OP = d$ which is very less than R $(d \ll R)$.

For the coil A, $\qquad O_A P = \dfrac{R}{2} + d$

The magnetic field at point P due to coil A

$$B_A = \frac{\mu_0}{4\pi} \cdot \frac{2\pi n I R^2}{(O_A P^2 + R^2)^{3/2}}$$

$$= \frac{\mu_0}{2} \cdot \frac{NI.\,R^2}{\left\{ \left(\dfrac{R}{2} + d\right)^2 + R^2 \right\}^{3/2}} = \frac{\mu_0 N I R^2}{2\left[\dfrac{R^2}{4} + d^2 + Rd + R^2 \right]^{3/2}}$$

As according to the question $d \ll R$, so neglect term d^2.

$$B_A = \frac{\mu_0 N I R^2}{2\left[\dfrac{5R^2}{4} + Rd \right]^{3/2}} = \frac{\mu_0 N I R^2}{2 \times \left(\dfrac{5R^2}{4} \right)^{3/2} \left[1 + \dfrac{R \times d \times 4}{5R^2} \right]^{3/2}}$$

$$= \frac{\mu_0 N I R^2 \left(1 + \dfrac{4d}{5R} \right)^{-3/2}}{2 \left(\dfrac{5R^2}{4} \right)^{3/2}} \qquad \dots (i)$$

The direction of B_A is along PO_B according to the Maxwell's right hand rule.

For the coil B, $\qquad O_B P = \left(\dfrac{R}{2} - d \right)$

The magnetic field at point P due to coil B

$$B_B = \frac{\mu_0}{4\pi} \cdot \frac{2\pi N I R^2}{(O_B P^2 + R^2)^{3/2}} = \frac{\mu_0}{2} \cdot \frac{2 N I R^2}{\left[\left(\dfrac{R}{2} - d \right)^2 + R^2 \right]^{3/2}}$$

$$= \frac{\mu_0 NIR^2}{2\left[\dfrac{R^2}{4} + d^2 - Rd + R^2\right]^{3/2}}$$

$$= \frac{\mu_0 nIR^2\left(1 - \dfrac{4d}{5R}\right)^{-3/2}}{2\left[\dfrac{5R^2}{4}\right]^{3/2}} \qquad \text{[Neglect term } d^2]$$

The direction of magnetic field B_B is towards PO_B.

So, the resultant magnetic field at P due to coil A and coil B is

$$B = B_A + B_B = \frac{\mu_0 \cdot NIR^2}{2\left(\dfrac{5R^2}{4}\right)^{3/2}}\left[\left(1 + \frac{4d}{5R}\right)^{-3/2} + \left(1 - \frac{4d}{5R}\right)^{-3/2}\right]$$

Now, use binomial theorem and neglect higher powers as $d \ll R$.

$$B = \frac{\mu_0 NIR^2}{2\left(\dfrac{5R^2}{4}\right)^{3/2}}\left[1 - \frac{3}{2} \times \frac{4d}{5R} + 1 + \frac{3}{2} \times \frac{4d}{5R}\right]$$

$$= \frac{\mu_0 NIR^2 \cdot 4^{3/2}}{2 \times R^3 \times 5^{3/2}} \times 2 \ = \ \frac{\mu_0 NI}{2R}\left(\frac{4}{5}\right)^{3/2} \times 2$$

$$= \left(\frac{4}{5}\right)^{3/2} \cdot \frac{\mu_0 NI2}{2R} = \frac{2\mu_0 NI}{(5)^{3/2} 2R}(4)^{3/2}$$

$$= 0.72 \cdot \frac{\mu_0 NI}{R}$$

Question 17. A toroid has a core (non-ferromagnetic) of inner radius 2.5 cm and outer radius 26 cm, around, which 3500 turns of a wire are wound. If the current in the wire is 11A, what is the magnetic field (a) outside the toroid, (b) inside the core of the toroid, and (c) in the empty space surrounded by the toroid.

The toroid is considered as the infinite long solenoid. so, find the length of the toroid so, you can find the number of turns per unit length and apply the formula of solenoid to calculate the magnetic field.

Solution

(a) For outside the toroid, the magnetic field is zero, because the magnetic field due to toroid is only inside it and along the length of toroid.

(b) Inner radius of toroid, $r_1 = 25$ cm $= 0.25$ m

Outer radius of toroid, $r_2 = 26$ cm $= 0.26$ m

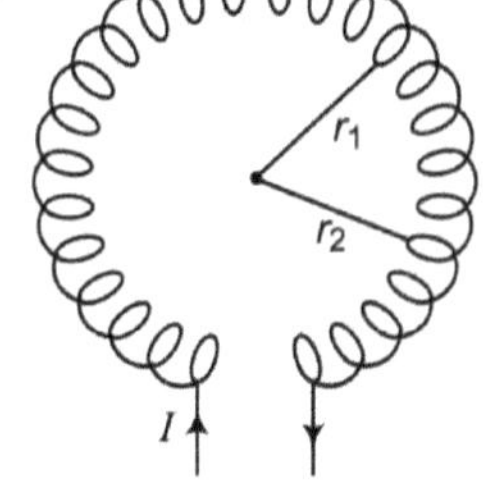

Number of turns, $N = 3500$

Current in the wire, $I = 11\,A$

The mean radius of the toroid $r = \left(\dfrac{r_1 + r_2}{2}\right) = \dfrac{2}{2}\,(0.25 + 0.26) = 0.51$

$\therefore$ Length of the toroid $= 2\pi r = 2\pi \times 0.51$

The magnetic field strength due to toroid is $\quad B = \mu_0 n I$

where n is number of turns per unit length;

$$n = \frac{N}{l}$$

$$B = 4\pi \times 10^{-7} \times \frac{3500}{\pi \times 0.51} \times 11 = 3.02 \times 10^{-2}\ T$$

(c) The magnetic field in the empty space surrounded by the toroid is also zero, because the magnetic field due to a toroid is only along its length.

Question 18. Answer the following questions :

    (a) A magnetic field that varies in magnitude from point to point but has a constant direction (east to west) is set up in a chamber. A charged particle enters the chamber and travels undeflected along a straight path with constant speed. What can you say about the initial velocity of the particle?

    (b) A charged particle enters an environment of a strong and non-uniform magnetic field varying from point to point both in magnitude and direction, and comes out of it following a complicated trajectory would its final speed equal the initial speed, if it suffered no collisions with the environment?

    (c) An electron travelling west to east enters a chamber having a uniform electrostatic field in north to south direction. Specify the direction in which a uniform magnetic field should be set up to prevent the electron from deflecting its straight line path.

Solution

    (a) The magnetic field is in constant direction from east to west. According to the question, a charged particle travels undeflected along a straight path with constant speed. It is only possible, if the magnetic force experienced by the charged particle is zero.

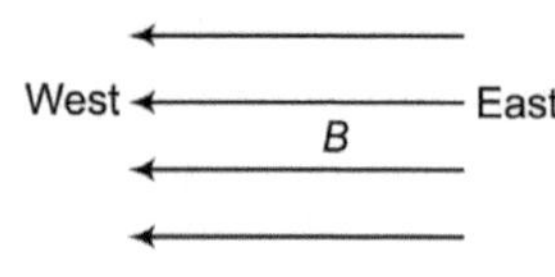

The magnitude of magnetic force on a moving charged particle in a magnetic field is given by $F = qv\,B \sin\theta$. (where θ is the angle between v and B). Here $F = 0$, if and only if $\sin\theta = 0$ (as $v \neq 0$, $q \neq 0$, $B \neq 0$). This indicates the angle between the velocity and magnetic field is $0°$ or $180°$.

Thus, the charged particle moves parallel or antiparallel to the magnetic field **B**.

(b) Yes, the final speed be equal to its initial speed as the magnetic force acting on the charged particle only changes the direction of velocity of charged particle but cannot change the magnitude of velocity of charged particle.

(c) As the electric field is from North to south, that means the plate in north is positive and in south is negative. Thus, the electrons (negatively charged) attract towards the positive plate that means move towards north. If we want that there is no deflection in the path of electron the magnetic force should be in south direction.

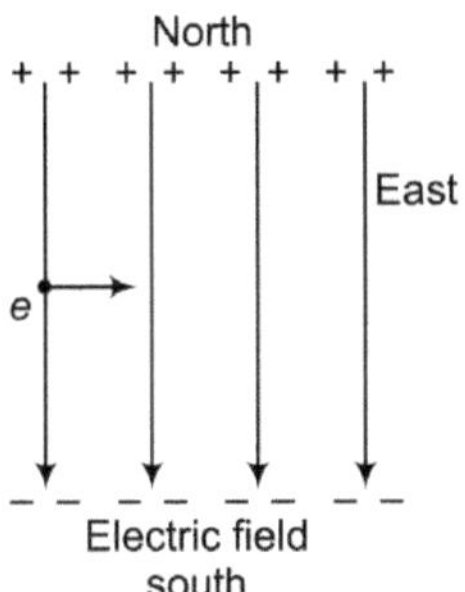

By $\mathbf{F} = -e\,(\mathbf{v} \times \mathbf{B})$, the direction of velocity is west to east, the direction of force is towards south, by using the Fleming's left hand rule, the direction of magnetic field ($\mathbf{B}$) is perpendicularly inwards to the plane of paper.

Question 19. An electron emitted by a heated cathode and accelerated through a potential difference of 2.0 kV, enters a region with uniform magnetic field of 0.15 T. Determine the trajectory of the electron, if the field (a) is transverse to its initial velocity, (b) makes an angle of 30° with the initial velocity.

The electrostatic energy obtained by the electron due to the applied potential difference gives the kinetic energy to it, so we can equate these two.

Solution Given, potential difference, $V = 2\ \text{kV} = 2000\ \text{V}$

Charge on electron, $e = 1.6 \times 10^{-19}\ \text{C}$

Mass of electron, $m_e = 9.1 \times 10^{-31}\ \text{kg}$

The electron is accelerated due to the applied potential difference which gives the kinetic energy to the electron. Let v be the velocity of electron.

$$\therefore \qquad eV = \frac{1}{2}\,m_e v^2$$

$$1.6 \times 10^{-19} \times 2000 = \frac{1}{2} \times 9.1 \times 10^{-31}\, v^2$$

or

$$v^2 = \frac{1.6 \times 10^{-19} \times 2000 \times 2}{9.1 \times 10^{-31}}$$

or

$$v = \frac{8 \times 10^7}{3}\ \text{m/s} = 2.7 \times 10^7\ \text{m/s}$$

(a) Magnetic field $B = 0.15\ \text{T}$, the direction of field is transverse to the initial velocity of the electron.

Here, the magnetic force $F = Bev$ and the direction of force is perpendicular to the magnetic field (by right hand palm rule), the electron moves on a circular path. The magnetic force provides the centripetal force to the electron.

$$\therefore \qquad Bev = \frac{mv^2}{r}$$

where, r is the radius of circular path.

$$\therefore \qquad r = \frac{mv}{Be}$$

$$= \frac{9.1 \times 10^{-31} \times 8 \times 10^7}{3 \times 0.15 \times 1.6 \times 10^{-19}}$$

$$= 10^{-3} \text{ m} = 1 \text{ mm}$$

(b) As the electron enters in the magnetic field at an angle 30° to the field.

Here, the vertical component of velocity is v_1 and the horizontal component of velocity is v_2.

$$v_1 = v \sin 30° = \frac{8 \times 10^7 \times 1}{3 \times 2} = \frac{4 \times 10^7}{3} \text{ m/s}$$

$$v_2 = v \cos 30° = \frac{8 \times 10^7 \times \sqrt{3}}{3 \times 2} = \frac{4\sqrt{3} \times 10^7}{3} \text{ m/s}$$

There is no force acting on the particle, due to the horizontal component of velocity as $\mathbf{v}_2$ is parallel to $\mathbf{B}$ and $\mathbf{F} = q\,(\mathbf{v}_2 \times \mathbf{B})$ is zero. The force on the electron is only due to the vertical component of the velocity *i.e.*, v_1.

$$\mathbf{F} = e\,(\mathbf{v}_1 \times \mathbf{B}) = ev_1 B \sin 90°$$

This force gives the centripetal force to the electron.

$$i.e., \qquad ev_1 B = \frac{mv_1^2}{r'}$$

$$= \frac{mv_1}{eB} = \frac{9.1 \times 10^{-31} \times 4 \times 10^7}{3 \times 1.6 \times 10^{-19} \times 0.15}$$

$$r' = 0.5 \times 10^{-3} \text{ m} = 0.5 \text{ mm}$$

Question 20. A magnetic field using Helmholtz coils (described in Q. 16) is uniform in a small region and has a magnitude of 0.75 T. In the same region, a uniform electrostatic field is maintained in a direction normal to the common axis of the coils. A narrow beam of (single species) charged particles all accelerated through 15 kV enters this region in a direction perpendicular to both the axis of the coils and the electrostatic field. If the beam remains undeflected when the electrostatic field is 9×10^{-5} V/m make a simple guess as to what the beam contains. Why is the answer not unique?

Solution Given, the magnitude of magnetic field $B = 0.75$ T,

$$\text{Potential difference, } V = 15 \text{ kV} = 15 \times 10^3 \text{ V}$$

$$\text{Electric field, } E = 9 \times 10^{-5} \text{ V/m}$$

Let q be the charge and m be the mass of the particles and the velocity acquired by the particles is v as they are accelerated by potential difference of 15 kV.

The energy due to the potential difference gives the kinetic energy to the particle.

$$\therefore \qquad qV = \frac{1}{2} mv^2 \qquad \text{...(i)}$$

As the charge particle is not deflected as magnetic and electric field apply. That means the force due to the magnetic force is balanced by the force due to electric field.

$$q\mathbf{E} = q\,(\mathbf{v} \times \mathbf{B})$$

or

$$qE = q\,v\,B$$

or

$$v = \frac{E}{B}$$

Putting this value in Eq. (i), we get

$$\frac{1}{2} m \left(\frac{E}{B}\right)^2 = eV$$

or

$$\frac{e}{m} = \frac{E^2}{2vB^2} = \frac{(9 \times 10^5)^2}{2 \times 15000 \times (0.75)^2} = 4.8 \times 10^7 \text{ C/kg}$$

The value of e/m corresponds to the deuterons, so the particles are deuteron ions. The value of e/m also corresponds to He^{++} and Li^{+++}. So, the particles may be deuteron, He^{++} or Li^{+++}.

Question 21. A straight horizontal conducting rod of length 0.45 m and mass 60 g is suspended by two vertical wires at its ends. A current of 5.0A is set up in the rod through the wires.

  (a) What magnetic field should be set up normal to the conductor in order that the tension in the wires is zero?
  (b) What will be the total tension in the wires if the direction of current is reversed keeping the magnetic field same as before? (Ignore the mass of wires) $g = 9.8$ m/s^2.

Solution Length of conducting rod, $l = 0.45$ m

Mass of conducting rod, $m = 60$ g $= 60 \times 10^{-3}$ kg

Current $I = 5$ A

  (a) Let the magnetic field applied be B so that the magnetic force is balanced by the weight of the wire and so tension in the wire becomes zero.

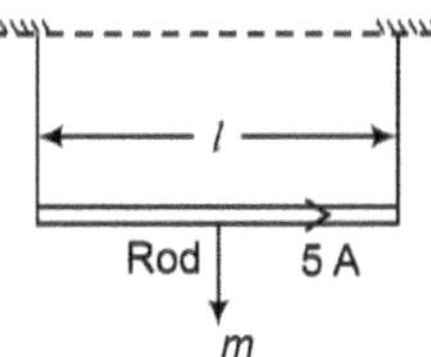

i.e., Magnetic force = Weight of conducting rod

$$I\,(l \times B) = mg \qquad \text{(The angle between } l \text{ and } B \text{ is } 90^\circ\text{)}$$

$$IlB \sin 90^\circ = mg$$

$$B = \frac{mg}{I\,l} = \frac{60 \times 10^{-3} \times 9.8}{5 \times 0.45} \qquad (\because \sin 90^\circ = 1)$$

$$= 0.26 \text{ T}$$

(b) As the direction of magnetic field is reversed, the magnetic force and the weight of the rod both act downwards. Hence, the tension in the wires

$$T = BI\,l + mg$$

$$= (0.26 \times 5 \times 0.45) + (60 + 10^{-3} \times 9.8)$$

$$= 1.176 \text{ N}$$

Question 22. The wires which connect the battery of an automobile to its starting motor carry a current of 300 A (for a short time). What is the force per unit length between the wires, if they are 70 cm long and 1.5 cm apart? Is the force attractive or repulsive?

Solution   Currents of both wires, $I_1 = I_2 = 300$ A

Distance between the wires, $r = 1.5$ cm $= 1.5 \times 10^{-2}$ m

Length of wire, $l = 70$ cm

Force per unit length, $F = \dfrac{\mu_0}{4\pi} \cdot \dfrac{2 I_1 I_2}{r} = \dfrac{10^{-7} \times 2 \times 300 \times 300}{1.5 \times 10^{-2}}$

$$= 0.12 \text{ N/m}$$

The currents in the wires are opposite to each other because they are connected with a battery. So, the force is repulsive in nature.

Question 23. A uniform magnetic field of 1.5 T exists in a cylindrical region of radius 10.0 cm, its direction parallel to the axis along east to west. A wire carrying current of 7.0 A in the north to south direction passes through this region. What is the magnitude and direction of the force on the wire if,

  (a) the wire intersect the axis?

  (b) the wire is turned from **N-S** to northeast-northwest direction?

  (c) the wire in the **N-S** direction is lowered from the axis by a distance of 6.0 cm?

Solution   (a) Uniform magnetic field, $B = 1.5$ T

Radius $= 10.0$ cm $= 0.1$ m

Current in the wire $I = 7.0$ A

The magnitude of force on the wire

$$\mathbf{F} = I\,(l \times \mathbf{B})$$

$$= IlB \sin 90^\circ$$

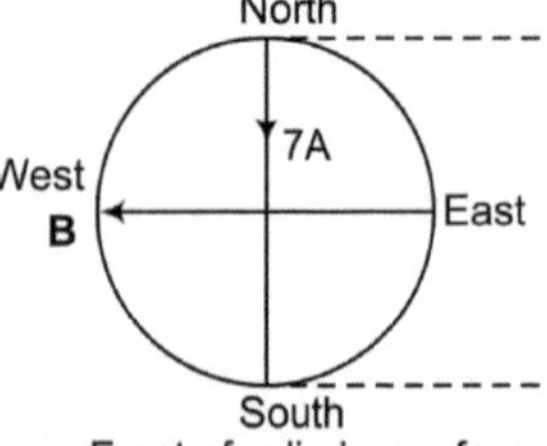

(Angle between I and **B** is 90° and the length of wire is equal to the diameter of the cylindrical region.)

∴ Force on the wire, $F = I \times 2r \times B = 7 \times 2 \times 0.1 \times 1.5 = 2.1$ N

According to Fleming's left hand rule, the direction of force is vertically inwards to the plane of paper.

$\Rightarrow \qquad\qquad\qquad F = 2.1$ N

(b) Now, we take the component of length of wire. The horizontal component experiences no force as B is parallel to length.

The vertical component

$\qquad y =$ Diameter of the cylinder

So force $\quad F = I\,l\,B \sin 90°$

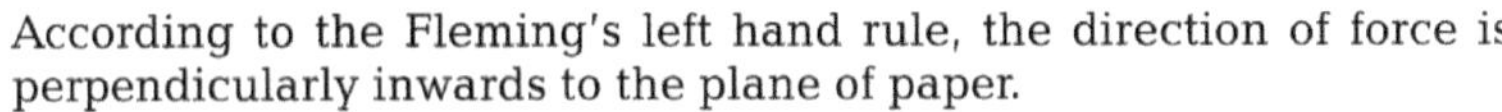

$\qquad\qquad = 7 \times 0.1 \times 1.5 \times 2 \times 1 = 2.1$ N

According to the Fleming's left hand rule, the direction of force is perpendicularly inwards to the plane of paper.

(c) Let the wire is shifted by 6 cm and the position of wire is CD.

$\qquad\qquad\qquad OE = 6$ cm

$\qquad\qquad\qquad OD = 10$ cm

$\qquad\qquad\qquad DE = EC = x$

In $\Delta ODE,\qquad OD^2 = OE^2 + DE^2$

$\qquad\qquad\qquad 100 = 36 + DE^2$

$\qquad\qquad\qquad DE^2 = 64$

or $\qquad\qquad\qquad DE = 8$ cm

$\qquad\qquad l = CD = 2DE = 16$ cm $= 0.16$ m

Magnitude of force $F' = I\,(l \times \mathbf{B}) = 7\,(0.16 \times 1.5 \times \sin 90°)$

$\qquad\qquad\qquad = 1.68$ N

According to Fleming's left hand rule, the direction of force is vertically downwards to the paper.

Question 24. A uniform magnetic field of 3000 G is established along the positive Z-direction. A rectangular loop of sides 10 cm and 5 cm carries a current of 12 A. What is the torque on the loop in the different cases shown in figures. What is the force in each case? Which case corresponds to state equilibrium?

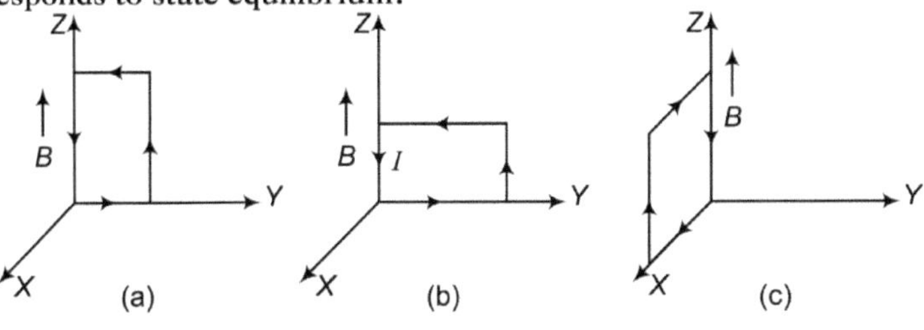

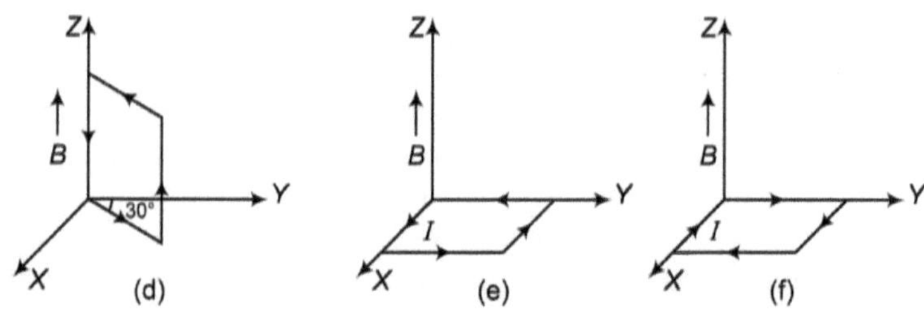

Solution   Given, uniform magnetic field along Z-axis,

$$B = 3000 \text{ G} = 3000 \times 10^{-4} = 0.3 \text{ T}$$

Area of rectangular loop, $A = 10 \times 5 = 50 \text{ cm}^2 = 50 \times 10^{-4} \text{ m}^2$

Current on the loop, $I = 12$ A

Torque on the loop, $\tau = I \, \mathbf{A} \times \mathbf{B}$.

(a) $\mathbf{B} = 0.3 \, \mathbf{k} \text{ T}$ (magnetic field is in Z-direction)

              $\mathbf{A} = 50 \times 10^{-4} \, \mathbf{i} \text{ m}^2$ (area vector is in X-direction)

     and $I = 12$ A

     Torque, $\tau = 12 \, (50 \times 10^{-4} \, \mathbf{i} \times 0.3 \, \mathbf{k})$

$$= -1.80 \times 10^{-2} \, \mathbf{j} \text{ N-m}$$

The direction of torque is along negative Y-direction.

(b) $\mathbf{B} = 0.3 \, \mathbf{k} \text{ T}, \ \mathbf{A} = 50 \times 10^{-4} \, \mathbf{i} \text{ m}^2 \text{ and } I = 12$ A

     Torque, $\tau = I \, (\mathbf{A} \times \mathbf{B}) = 12 \times 50 \times 10^{-4} \, \mathbf{i} \times 0.3 \, \mathbf{k}$

$$= -1.80 \times 10^{-2} \, \mathbf{j} \text{ N-m}$$

The torque is in negative Y-axis direction.

(c) $\mathbf{B} = 0.3 \, \mathbf{k} \text{ T}, \ \mathbf{A} = 50 \times 10^{-4} \, (-\mathbf{j}) \text{ m}^2 \text{ and } I = 12$ A

     Torque, $\tau = 12 \, (-50 \times 10^{-4} \, \mathbf{j} \times 0.3 \, \mathbf{k})$

$$= -1.80 \times 10^{-2} \, \mathbf{i} \text{ N-m}$$

Torque is in negative X-axis direction.

(d) $\mathbf{B} = 0.3 \, \mathbf{k} \text{ T}, \ \mathbf{A} = 50 \times 10^{-4} \text{ m}^2 \text{ and } I = 12$ A

Here, area vector is in *XY*-plane which is perpendicular to Z-axis.

$\therefore$ Torque, $\tau = 12 \times 50 \times 10^{-4} \times 0.3 = 1.80 \times 10^{-2}$ N-m

The direction of torque is $(90° + 30°)$ from negative x-axis or we can say that $360° - 120° = 240°$ from positive X-axis.

(e) $\mathbf{B} = 0.3 \, \mathbf{k} \text{ T}, \ \mathbf{A} = 50 \times 10^{-4} \, \mathbf{k} \text{ m}^2 \text{ and } I = 12$ A

     Torque, $\tau = 12 \, (50 \times 10^{-4} \, \mathbf{k} \times 0.3 \mathbf{k}) = 0$

(f) $\mathbf{B} = 0.3 \, \mathbf{k} \text{ T}, \ \mathbf{A} = -50 \times 10^{-4} \, \mathbf{k} \text{ m}^2 \text{ and } I = 12$ A

     Torque, $\tau = 12 \, (-50 \times 10^{-4} \, \mathbf{k} \times 0.3 \, \mathbf{k}) = 0$

Question 25. A circular coil of 20 turns and radius 10 cm is placed in a uniform magnetic field of 0.10 T normal to the plane of the coil. If the current in the coil is 5.0 A, what is the (a) total torque on the coil, (b) total force on the coil, (c) average force on each electron in the coil due to the magnetic field?
(The coil is made of copper wire of cross-sectional area 10^{-5} m^2 and the free electron density in copper is given to be about $10^{29}/\text{m}^3$).

Solution   Given, number of turns $n = 20$

Radius of circular coil $r = 10$ cm $= 0.1$ m

Magnitude of magnetic field $B = 0.1$ T

The angle between the area vector and magnetic field is $0°$.

$\Rightarrow$ $\qquad\qquad\qquad\qquad\qquad\qquad\qquad \theta = 0°$

Current in the coil $I = 5.0$ A

(a) Torque on the coil $\tau = nIAB \sin \theta$
$$= 20 \times 5 \times \pi \,(0.1)^2 \times 0.1 \times \sin 0° = 0 \quad [\because \sin 0° = 0]$$

(b) The forces on the planar loop are in pairs *i.e.,* the forces on two opposite sides are equal and opposite to each other and on the other two opposite sides, it is same. Thus, the total force on the coil is zero. ($\because$ $\mathbf{F}_1 = -\,\mathbf{F}_2$ and $\mathbf{F}_3 = -\,\mathbf{F}_4$)

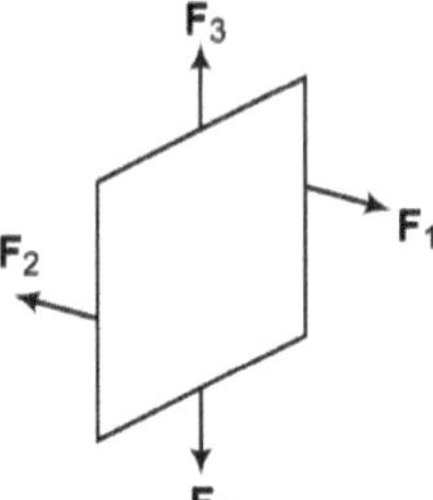

(c) Number density of electrons $N = 10^{29}/\text{m}^3$.

Area of cross-section of copper wire,
$$A = 10^{-5}\,\text{m}^2.$$

The magnitude of magnetic force $\mathbf{F} = e\,(\mathbf{v}_d \times \mathbf{B})$

$\because$ $\qquad\qquad\qquad\qquad\qquad I = neAv_d$

$\therefore$ $\qquad\qquad\qquad\qquad\qquad v_d = \dfrac{I}{neAI}$

$\Rightarrow$ $\qquad\qquad\qquad\qquad F = e \cdot \dfrac{I}{NeA} \cdot B \sin 90°$

$$= \dfrac{0.1 \times 5}{10^{-5} \times 10^{29}}\,\text{N}$$

$$= 5 \times 10^{-25}$$

Question 26. A solenoid 60 cm long and of radius 4.0 cm has 3 layers of winding of 300 turns each. A 2.0 cm long wire of mass 2.5 g lies inside the solenoid (near its centre) normal to its axis, both the wire and the axis of the solenoid are in the horizontal plane. The wire is connected through two leads parallel to the axis of the solenoid to an external battery which supplies a current of 6.0 A in the wire. What value of current (with appropriate sense of circulation) in the windings of the solenoid can support the weight of the wire? ($g = 9.8$ m/s^2)

Solution **For solenoid,**

Given, length $l = 60$ cm, radius $= 4$ cm

Number of layers $= 3$

Number of turns in each layer $= 300$

For wire, Given, length $l_w = 2$ cm

Mass $m = 2.5$ g, current $I_w = 6$ A

Let I be the current passing through the solenoid, the magnetic field due to the solenoid

$$B = \mu_o nI \qquad \left(n = \frac{\text{Number of turns}}{\text{Length}} = \frac{300 \times 3}{0.6} \right)$$

$$= 4\pi \times 10^{-7} \times \frac{300 \times 3}{0.6} \times I \qquad \ldots(i)$$

Force on the wire, $F = I_w (l_w \times \mathbf{B}) I_w (l_w B \sin \theta)$ (Angle between l_w and B is $90°$)

This force balances by the weight of wire $= mg$

$\therefore$
$$I_w l_w \sin 90° = mg$$

$$6 \times 0.02 \times \frac{4\pi \times 10^{-7} \times 300 \times 3}{0.6} I = 2.5 \times 10^{-3} \times 9.8 \quad \text{[from Eq, (i)]}$$

$$\text{Current } I = \frac{2.5 \times 10^{-3} \times 9.8 \times 0.6}{108 \times 4\pi \times 10^{-7}}$$

$$= 108.36 \text{ A}$$

Question 27. A galvanometer coil has a resistance of 12 Ω and the meter shows full scale deflection for a current of 3 mA. How will you convert the meter into a voltmeter of range 0 to 18 V?

Solution Given, resistance of galvanometer coil

$$G = 12 \, \Omega$$

Current in galvanometer $I_g = 3$ mA $= 3 \times 10^{-3}$ A

and potential difference $V = 18$ V

We can convert the galvanometer into voltmeter by using a large resistance R in series. The resistance can be calculated using the fomrula $R = \dfrac{V}{I_g} - G$

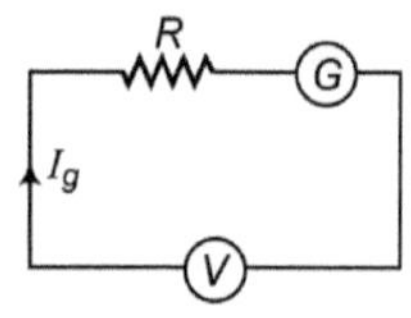

$$R = \frac{18}{3 \times 10^{-3}} - 12 = 5988 \, \Omega$$

This resistance ($R = 5988 \, \Omega$) is connected in series with the galvanometer. The resistance is connected in series become we have to increase the resistance of the galvanometer, so that almost no current flows through it and it gives the exect value of potential difference.

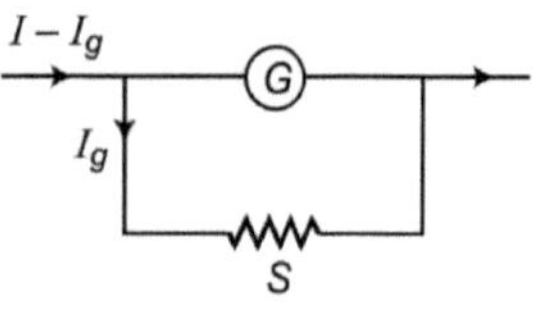

Question 28. A galvanometer coil has a resistance of $15\,\Omega$ and the meter shows full scale deflection for a current of 4 mA. How will you convert the meter into an ammeter of range 0 to 6 A?

Solution Given, Resistance of galvanometer coil $G = 15\,\Omega$

Current in galvanometer $I_g = 4 \times 10^{-3}$ A ; Current range $I = 6$ A

By connecting a small resistance S called shunt in parallel to the galvanometer it is converted into ammeter.

The required resistance (shunt) can be calculated by the formula

$$\text{Shunt } S = \frac{I_g \cdot G}{I - I_g} = \frac{4 \times 10^{-3} \times 15}{6 - 4 \times 10^{-3}} = 0.01\,\Omega$$

This resistance $(S = 0.01\,\Omega)$ is connected in parallel with the galvanometer. The small resistance is connected in parallel, become we have to decrease the resistance of the galvanometer, so that most of the current passes through it and it gives the exact value of the current.

Selected NCERT Exemplar Problems

Question 1. Show that a force that does no work must be a velocity dependent force.

Solution As we know that work $dW = \mathbf{F}.\,d\mathbf{l}$ $(\because d\mathbf{l} = \mathbf{v}dt)$

$$dW = \mathbf{F}.\mathbf{v}\,dt$$

According to question $dW = 0$,

$$\therefore \qquad\qquad \mathbf{F}.\mathbf{v} = 0$$

Here, force depends on the velocity from the above condition, the angle between $\mathbf{F}$ and $\mathbf{v}$ is 90°. If $\mathbf{v}$ changes its direction with $\mathbf{F}$, then $\mathbf{F}$ should also change so that the above condition remains satisfied.

Question 2. Two long wires carrying currents I_1 and I_2 are arranged as shown in figure. One carrying current I_1 is along the X-axis. The other carrying current I_2 is along a line parallel to Y-axis, given by $x = 0$ and $z = d$. Find the force exerted at point O_2 because of the wire along the X-axis.

Solution Here, first we have to find the direction of magnetic field at point O_2 due to the wire carrying current I_1. Use Maxwell's right hand grip rule, the direction of magnetic field at point O_2 due to current I_1 is along Y-axis.

Here, the wire at point O_2 is placed along Y-axis. Now, by the formula

$$\mathbf{F} = I_2\,(\mathbf{l} \times \mathbf{B})$$

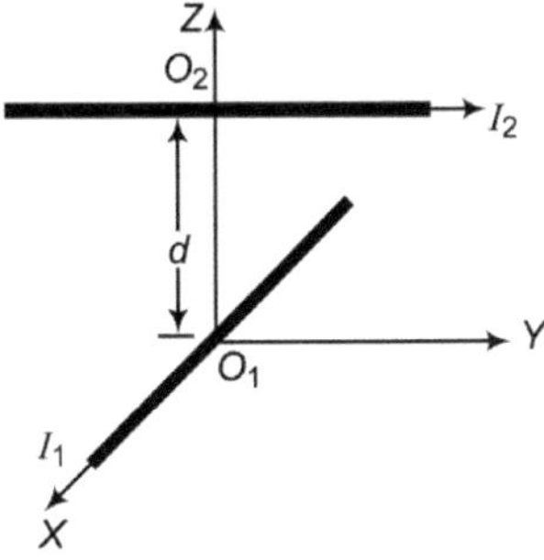

(Angle between I and $\mathbf{B}$ is $0°$ both are in Y-axis)

$$\therefore \qquad\qquad \mathbf{F} = IlB \sin 0° = 0$$

So, the force exerted at point O_2 because of wire along X-axis is zero.

Question 3. A multirange voltmeter can be constructed by using a galvanometer circuit as shown in figure. We want to construct a voltmeter that can measure 2 V, 20 V and 200 V using galvanometer of resistance 10 Ω and that produces maximum deflection for current of 1mA. Find R_1, R_2 and R_3 that have to be used.

Solution Resistance of galvanometer $G = 10\ \Omega$

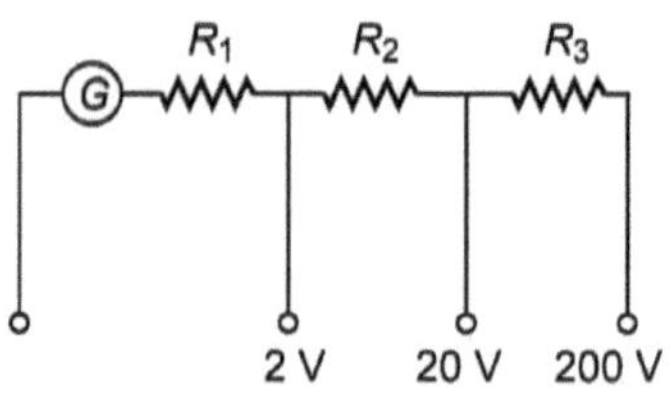

Deflection for current $I_G = 1\,\text{mA} = 10^{-3}$ A

For 2 V range, $\qquad I_G (G + R_1) = 2$

$$G + R_1 = \frac{2}{I_G} = \frac{2}{10^{-3}} = 2000$$

Resistance $R_1 = 2000 - 10 = 1990\ \Omega$

For 20 V range, $\ I_G (G + R_1 + R_2) = 20$

$$G + R_1 + R_2 = \frac{20}{I_G} = \frac{20}{10^{-3}} = 20000$$

Resistance $R_2 = 20000 - 10 - 1990 = 18000\ \Omega$

For 200 V range $I_G (G + R_1 + R_2 + R_3) = 200$

$$G + R_1 + R_2 + R_3 = \frac{200}{I_G} = \frac{200}{10^{-3}} = 200000$$

$$R_3 = 200000 - 10 - 1990 - 18000$$

Resistance $R_3 = 180000\ \Omega$

Question 4. A long straight wire carrying current of 25 A rests on a table shown in figure. Another wire PQ of length 1m, mass 2.5 g carries the same current but in the opposite direction. The wire PQ is free to slide up and down. To what height will PQ rise?

Solution Mass of wire

$$PQ\ (m) = 2.5\ \text{g} = 2.5 \times 10^{-3}\ \text{kg}$$

Length of wire $PQ\ (l) = 1\,\text{m}$

Current in wire PQ and $AC\ (I) = 25$ A

Let the wire PQ rises upto a height h.

The magnetic field on wire PQ due to wire AC is B.

By using the formula of magnetic field due to an infinite length of wire

$$B = \frac{\mu_0}{4\pi} \cdot \frac{2I}{r} = \frac{\mu_0}{4\pi} \times \frac{2 \times 25}{h}$$

$$= \frac{10^{-7} \times 50}{h} = \frac{50 \times 10^{-7}}{h} \qquad\qquad \dots\text{(i)}$$

The direction of magnetic field B on wire PQ is perpendicularly inwards to the plane of paper (by using Maxwell's right hand rule).

Force on wire $PQ \qquad F = I \, (\mathbf{l} \times \mathbf{B})$ (Angle between $\mathbf{l}$ and $\mathbf{B}$ is 90°)

$$F = I \, lB \sin 90°$$

$$= 25 \times 1 \times \frac{50 \times 10^{-7}}{h} \times 1 \quad \text{[By using Eq. (i)]}$$

$$\Rightarrow \qquad F = \frac{1250 \times 10^{-7}}{h} \qquad \qquad \dots \text{(ii)}$$

The wire will left, if the weight of the wire is balanced by force due to wire AC.

i.e.,
$$F = mg$$

$$\frac{1250 \times 10^{-7}}{h} = 2.5 \times 10^{-3} \times 9.8 \qquad \text{[By Eq. (ii)]}$$

$$h = \frac{1250 \times 10^{-7}}{2.5 \times 9.8 \times 10^{-3}} = 51.02 \times 10^{-4} \text{ m}$$

$$= 51.02 \times 10^{-2} \text{ cm} = 0.51 \text{ cm}$$

Thus, the PQ will rise upto a height of 0.51 cm.

Question 5. A 100 turn rectangular coil $ABCD$ (in XY-plane) is hung from one arm of a balance (shown in figure). A mass 500 g is added to the other arm to balance the weight of the coil. A current of 4.9 A passes through the coil and a constant magnetic field of 0.2 T acting inward (in XZ-plane) is switched On such that only arm CD of length 1 cm lies in the field. How much additional mass m must be added to regain the balance?

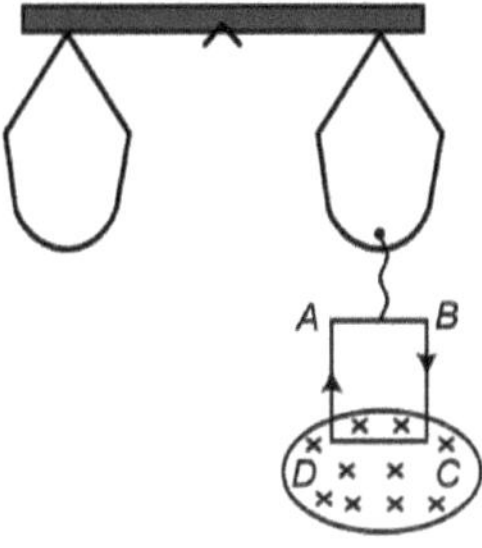

Solution When no current passes through the coil

The balance should be balanced, if the weight in both the pans is same.

Let the mass of coil $= M$

Mass added other arm $= 500 \text{ g} = 500 \times 10^{-3} \text{ kg}$

Mass of coil = Mass in other arm (for balancing)

$$Mg = 500 \times 10^{-3} \text{ kg}$$

$$M = 0.5 \text{ kg}$$

When the current is switched On,

Current $I = 4.9$ A

Magnetic field $B = 0.2$ T $\qquad$ (XZ-plane)

Length of arm $CD = 1$ cm

Mass added to balance $= m$

Let F be the force due to magnetic field.

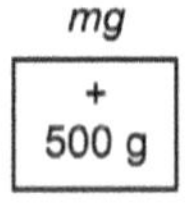

Mass of coil + force due to magnetic field.

The direction of magnetic field is inward in XZ-plane, the length vector is in left, so by using the Fleming's left hand rule, the direction of force is downwards in the plane of paper.

$$\mathbf{F} = I\,(\boldsymbol{l} \times \mathbf{B}) = 4.9\,(0.01 \times 0.2 \sin 90°)$$
$$F = 4.9 \times 0.01 \times 0.2 \qquad\qquad \ldots(i)$$

For balancing,   Mass of coil $\times g+$ Force due to magnetic field

$$= 500 \times 10^{-3}\, g + m \times g$$
$$0.5 \times 9.8 + 4.9 \times 0.01 \times 0.2 = 500 \times 10^{-3} \times 9.8 + m \times 9.8$$
$$9.8\,(0.5 + 0.001) = 9.8\,(0.5 + m) \qquad\qquad \text{[From Eq.(i)]}$$
$$m = 0.001 \text{ kg} = 1\,\text{g}$$

Thus, 1 g mass must be added to regain the balance.

Question 6. A uniform conducting wire of length 12 *a* and resistance *R* is wound up as a current carrying coil in the shape of (a) an equilateral triangle of side *a*, (b) a square of side *a* and (c) a regular hexagon of sides *a*. The coil is connected to a voltage source V_0. Find the magnetic moment of the coils in each case.

Solution   (a) Let number of turns is *n* and the current is *I*.

Resistance of wire = *R*

$\because$ Perimeter of triangle $= 12\,a$

$\therefore$ $\text{Side} = \dfrac{12\,a}{3} = 4a$

Area of equilateral triangle $= \dfrac{\sqrt{3}}{4}\,(\text{Side})^2 = \dfrac{\sqrt{3}}{4}\,(4a)^2 = 4\sqrt{3}\,a^2$

Magnetic moment M of triangle = Number of turns $\times$ Current $\times$ Area
$$= nIA = n \times I \times 4\sqrt{3}\,a^2 = 4\sqrt{3}\,Ia^2 n$$

(b) $\because$ Perimeter of square $= 12\,a$

$\therefore$ $\text{Side} = \dfrac{12\,a}{4} = 3a$

Area of square $= (\text{Side})^2 = (3a)^2 = 9a^2$

Magnetic moment M of square $= nIA = nI \times 9a^2 = 9nIa^2$

(c) $\because$ Perimeter of hexagon $= 12a$

$\therefore$ $\text{Side} = \dfrac{12a}{6} = 2a$

Area of hexagon

$$= 6 \times \text{Area of equilateral triangle of side } 2a$$
$$= 6 \times \dfrac{\sqrt{3}}{4}\,(2a)^2 = \dfrac{6\sqrt{3}}{4} \cdot 4a^2 = 6\sqrt{3}a^2$$

Magnetic moment M of hexagon $= nIA = nI \times 6\sqrt{3}a^2 = 6\sqrt{3}\,Ia^2 n$

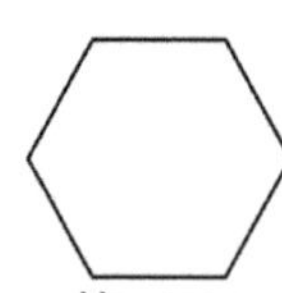

Chapter 5

Magnetism and Matter

Important Results

1. The magnetic moment of a bar magnet of pole strength m and of length $2l$ is given by

$$\mathbf{M} = m \times 2l$$

2. The force between the two poles of a magnet of pole strength m_1, m_2 and separated by r is given by

$$F = \frac{\mu_0}{4\pi} \cdot \frac{m_1 m_2}{r^2}$$

3. Magnetic field strength at a point on axial line of a bar magnet is given by

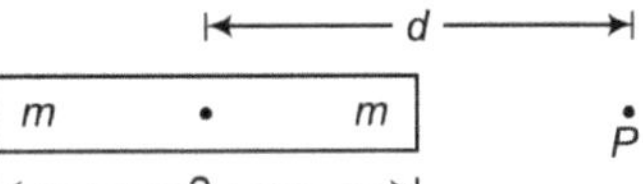

$$B_{\text{axial}} = \frac{\mu_0}{4\pi} \cdot \frac{2Md}{(d^2 - l^2)}$$

when $l \ll d$, $\qquad B_{\text{axial}} = \frac{\mu_0}{4\pi} \cdot \frac{2M}{d^3}$

where, d is the distance from the centre of magnet and $2l$ be the length of the magnet. M is the dipole moment.

4. Magnetic field strength at a point on equitorial line of a bar magnet is given by

$$B_{\text{eq}} = \frac{\mu_0}{4\pi} \cdot \frac{M}{(d^2 + l^2)^{3/2}}$$

when $l \ll d$, $\qquad B_{\text{eq}} = \frac{\mu_0}{4\pi} \cdot \frac{M}{d^3}$

where, d is the distance from the centre of the magnet and $2l$ be the length of magnet. M is the dipole moment.

5. The magnetic moment of a current loop is given by

$$\mathbf{M} = N I \mathbf{A}$$

where, N = number of turns, I = current, $\mathbf{A}$ = area vector.

6. When a bar magnet of dipole moment **M** is placed in a uniform magnetic field **B**, then
   (i) force on the magnet is zero.
   (ii) torque on the magnet

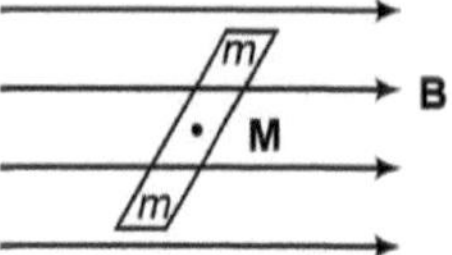

$$\tau = \mathbf{M} \times \mathbf{B}$$

   (iii) potential energy $U = -\mathbf{M} \cdot \mathbf{B} = -MB\,(\cos\theta_2 - \cos\theta_1)$

7. There are three quantities which are needed to specify the magnetic field of the earth on its surface
   (i) The horizontal component.
   (ii) The magnetic declination.
   (iii) The magnetic dip.
   These elements are called the earth's magnetic field.

8. The magnetic declination θ is the angle between the magnetic meridian and geographic meridian.

9. Horizontal component of earth's magnetic field

$$H = R\cos\delta$$

   Vertical component of earth's magnetic field

$$V = R\sin\delta$$

   where, δ is the angle of dip.

10. The angle of dip δ is given by $\tan\delta = \dfrac{V}{H}$

11. Gauss's law in magnetism states that the net magnetic flux through any closed surface is zero.

$$\int_S \mathbf{B}.\,d\mathbf{S} = 0$$

12. A material placed in an external magnetic field B_0. The magnetic intensity is defined as $\mathbf{H} = \dfrac{\mathbf{B}}{\mu_0}$

13. The magnetization **I** of the material is its dipole moment per unit volume, the magnetic field **B** in the material is

$$\mathbf{B} = \mu_0\,(\mathbf{H} + \mathbf{I})$$

14. For a material $\mathbf{I} = \chi\,\mathbf{H}$ and $\mathbf{B} = \mu\,\mathbf{H}$, where χ is called the magnetic susceptibility of the material. The relation between three quantities—the magnetic susceptibility χ, the relative magnetic permeability μ_r and the magnetic permeability μ is given by

$$\mu = \mu_0\mu_r,\ \mu_r = 1 + \chi$$

15. Magnetic materials are classified as, diamagnetic, paramagnetic and ferromagnetic.
    For diamagnetic $\rightarrow$ χ is negative and small.
    For paramagnetic $\rightarrow$ χ is positive and small.
    For ferromagnetic $\rightarrow$ χ is large and they are characterized by non-linear relation between **B** and **H**, they show the property of hysteresis.

Exercises

Question 1. Answer the following questions regarding earth's magnetism

(a) A vector needs three quantities for its specification. Name the three independent quantities conventionally used to specify the earth's magnetic field.

(b) The angle of dip at a location in southern India is about $18°$. Would you expect a greater or smaller dip angle in Britain?

(c) If you made a map of magnetic field lines at Melbourne in Australia, would the lines seem to go into the ground or come out of the ground?

(d) In which direction would a compass free to move in the vertical plane point to, if located right on the geomagnetic north or south pole?

(e) The earth's field, it is claimed, roughly approximates the field due to a dipole of magnetic moment 8×10^{22} J/T located at its centre. Check the order of magnitude of this number in some way.

(f) Geologists claim that besides the main magnetic N-S poles, there are several local poles on the earth's surface oriented in different directions. How is such a thing possible at all?

Solution

(a) The three independent quantities required to specify the earth's magnetic field are as follows.

Magnetic declination, angle of dip and horizontal component of earth's magnetic field, they are called the magnetic elements of earth.

(b) We can expect a greater value of angle of dip in Britain because Britain is located close to north pole. The value of angle of dip in Britain is about $70°$.

(c) Melbourne is situated in southern hemisphere. At southern hemisphere, the north pole of earth's magnetic field lies. So, the magnetic field lines seem to come out of the ground as magnetic lines of force emerges from North pole and enter in south pole.

(d) As we know that at the poles, the earth's magnetic field is exactly vertical. The compass needle is always free to rotate in horizontal plane only so at the poles it may point out in any direction.

(e) Dipole of magnetic moment $M = 8 \times 10^{22}$ J/T.

Now, we calculate the magnetic field intensity at magnetic equator of earth. We consider that at a point on equatorial line of short magnetic dipole for which distance $d = R$ (radius of earth).

Radius of earth $\quad R = 6400 \text{ km} = 6.4 \times 10^{6}$ m

Magnetic field $\quad B = \dfrac{\mu_0}{4\pi} \cdot \dfrac{M}{d^3} = 10^{-7} \times \dfrac{8 \times 10^{22}}{(6.4 \times 10^{6})^3}$

$\qquad\qquad\qquad = 0.31 \times 10^{-4} \text{ T} = 0.31 \text{ G}$

This value is same as that of earth's magnetic field.

(f) The earth's magnetic field is only due to the dipole field. As there are several local N-S poles may exist oriented in different directions, so they may nullify the effect of each other. These local N-S poles may occur due to the deposition of magnetized minerals.

Question 2.   Answer the following questions :

  (a) The earth's magnetic field varies from point to point in space.
    Does it also change with time? If so, on what time scale does it change appreciably?

  (b) The earth's core is known to contain iron. Yet geologists do not regard this as a source of the earth's magnetism. Why?

  (c) The charged currents in the outer conducting regions of the earth's core are thought to be responsible for earth's magnetism.
    What might be the 'battery' (*i.e.*, the source of energy) to sustain these currents?

  (d) The earth may have even reversed the direction of its field several times during its history of 4 to 5 billion yr. How can geologists know about the earth's field in such distant past?

  (e) The earth's field departs from its dipole shape substantially at large distances (greater than about 30000 km). What agencies may be responsible for this distortion?

  (f) Interstellar space has an extremely weak magnetic field of the order of 10^{-12} T. Can such a weak field be of any significant consequence? Explain.

    [Note   Q. 2 is meant mainly to arouse your curiosity. Answers to some questions above are tentative or unknown. Brief answers wherever possible are given at the end. For details, you should consult a good text on geomagnetism.]

Solution

  (a) Yes, the earth's magnetic field varies from point to point in space and it also changes with time. It may change daily, annually or secularly with period of order of about 1000 yr. It may change irregularly during magnetic storms etc. The time scale for appreciable change is about few hundred years.

  (b) The earth's core contains iron but in the molten state. The molten iron is not ferromagnetic material in nature thus, it cannot be treated as a source of earth's magnetism.

  (c) The source of energy to sustain these currents may be the radioactive material in the interior of the earth.

  (d) During the solidification of certain rocks, it is recorded that the field was very weak. The analysis of there rocks may give the history of direction of field.

  (e) The responsible reason for this distortion may be the motion of ions in the earth's ionosphere. The earth's magnetic field may get modified by the field due to the motion of ions in earth's atmosphere.

(f) As we know that when a charged particle moves in a magnetic field, it moves along a circular path.

The necessary centripetal force is provided by the magnetic force.

i.e.,
$$B\,ev = \frac{mv^2}{r}$$

or
$$r = \frac{mv}{Be}$$

As B is less, r is more. So, in the interstellar space they move in a circular path of a large radius. Thus, the deflection in their paths becomes negligible.

Question 3. A short bar magnet placed with its axis at 30° with a uniform external magnetic field of 0.25 T experiences a torque of magnitude equal to 4.5×10^{-2} J. What is the magnitude of magnetic moment of the magnet?

 To find the magnitude of magnetic moment of the magnet, use the concept of torque acting on magnetic dipole when placed in a magnetic field.

Solution   Given, uniform magnetic field
$$B = 0.25 \text{ T}$$

The magnitude of torque $\tau = 4.5 \times 10^{-2}$ J

Angle between magnetic moment and magnetic field $\theta = 30°$

Torque experienced on a magnet placed in external magnetic field

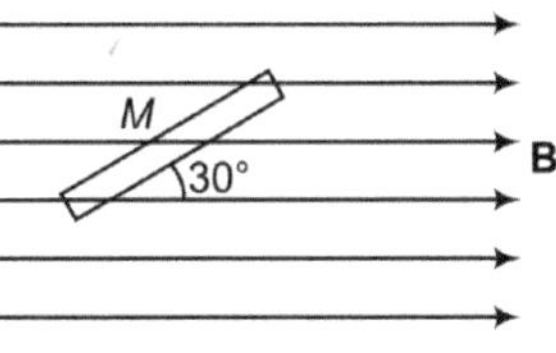

$$\tau = \mathbf{M} \times \mathbf{B}$$
$$\tau = MB \sin\theta \qquad (\because \mathbf{A} \times \mathbf{B} = AB \sin\theta)$$
$$4.5 \times 10^{-2} = M \times 0.25 \times \sin 30°$$
$$M = \frac{4.5 \times 10^{-2}}{0.25 \times \sin 30°}$$
$$= \frac{4.5 \times 10^{-2} \times 2}{0.25 \times 1} \qquad \left(\because \sin 30° = \frac{1}{2}\right)$$
$$= 0.36 \text{ J/T}$$

Thus, the magnitude of magnetic moment of the magnet is 0.36 J/T.

Question 4. A short bar magnet of magnetic moment $m = 0.32$ J/T is placed in a uniform magnetic field of 0.15 T. If the bar is free to rotate in the plane of the field, which orientation would correspond to its (a) stable and (b) unstable equilibrium? What is the potential energy of the magnet in each case?

Solution   Given, magnetic moment of magnet $m = 0.32$ J/T

The magnitude of magnetic field $B = 0.15$ T

(a) For stable equilibrium, the angle between magnetic moment (**m**) and magnetic field (**B**) is $\theta = 0°$

($\because$ In this position, it will be in a direction parallel to magnetic field thus no torque will act on it.)

$\because$ The potential energy of the magnet

$$U = - \mathbf{m} \cdot \mathbf{B}$$
$$= - mB \cos \theta \qquad (\because \mathbf{A} \cdot \mathbf{B} = AB \cos \theta)$$
$$= - 0.32 \times 0.15 \cos 0°$$
$$= - 4.8 \times 10^{-2} \text{ J}$$

Thus, for the stable equilibrium the potential energy is -4.8×10^{-2} J .

(b) For the unstable equilibrium, the angle between the magnetic moment and magnetic field is 180°. ($\because$ In this position it will be in a direction perpendicular to magnetic field thus maximum torque will act on it.)

$$\theta = 180°$$

Potential energy of the magnet

$$U = - mB \cos 180°$$
$$= - 0.32 \times 0.15 \, (-1) = 4.8 \times 10^{-2} \text{ J}$$

Thus, for the unstable equilibrium the potential energy is 4.8×10^{-2} J.

Question 5. A closely wound solenoid of 800 turns and area of cross-section 2.5×10^{-4} m^2 carries a current of 3.0 A. Explain the sense in which the solenoid acts like a bar magnet. What is its associated magnetic moment?

Solution   Given, number of turns $n = 800$

Area of cross-section of solenoid $A = 2.5 \times 10^{-4}$ m^2

Current through solenoid $I = 3$ A

As a current passes through a solenoid, a magnetic field is produced. By the use of Maxwell's right hand grip rule, the magnetic field is along the axis of the solenoid. Using the formula of magnetic moment.

$$\mathbf{M} = n I \mathbf{A}$$
$$M = n I \, A$$
$$= 800 \times 3 \times 2.5 \times 10^{-4}$$
$$= 0.6 \text{ J/T along the axis of the solenoid}$$

Question 6. If the solenoid in Q. 5 is free to turn about the vertical direction and a uniform horizontal magnetic field of 0.25 T is applied, what is the magnitude of torque on the solenoid when its axis makes an angle of 30° with the direction of applied field?

Solution   Given, magnetic field $B = 0.25$ T

Angle between magnetic moment and the magnetic field $\theta = 30°$

From the Q. 5, we get

Magnetic moment $M = 0.6$ J/T

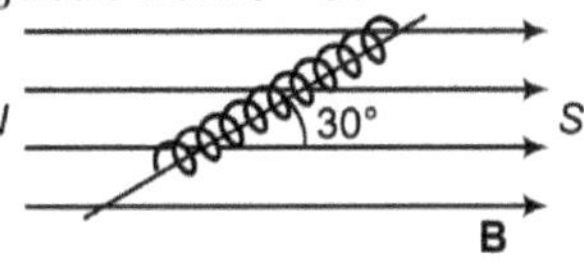

Torque acting on the solenoid when it is placed at an angle θ with the magnetic field.

$$\tau = MB \sin \theta = 0.6 \times 0.25 \sin 30°$$

$$= 0.6 \times 0.25 \times \frac{1}{2}$$

$$= 0.075 \text{ N-m}$$

Thus, the magnitude of torque on the solenoid is 0.075 N-m.

Question 7.   A bar magnet of magnetic moment 1.5 J/T lies aligned with the direction of a uniform magnetic field of 0.22 T.

(a) What is the amount of work required by an external torque to turn the magnet so as to align its magnetic moment: (i) normal to the field direction, (ii) opposite to the field direction?

(b) What is the torque on the magnet in cases (i) and (ii)?

Solution   Given, magnetic moment of magnet

$$M = 1.5 \text{ J/T}$$

Uniform magnetic field $B = 0.22$ T

(a)   (i) Angle $\theta_1 = 0°$ ($\because$ The magnet lies aligned in the direction of field)
and $\theta_2 = 90°$ ($\because$ The magnet is to be aligned normal to the field direction)

Work done in rotating the magnet from angle θ_1 to angle θ_2

$$W = - MB (\cos \theta_2 - \cos \theta_1)$$

$$= - 1.5 \times 0.22 (\cos 90° - \cos 0°)$$

$$= 0.33 \text{ J}$$

(ii) Angle $\theta_1 = 0°$ and $\theta_2 = 180°$ ($\because$ Magnet is to be aligned opposite to the direction of field)

Work done $= - MB (\cos \theta_2 - \cos \theta_1)$

$$= - 1.5 \times 0.22 (\cos 180° - \cos 0°) = 0.66 \text{ J}$$

(b)   Using the formula of torque,

$$\tau = MB \sin \theta$$

(i) $\theta = 90°$ (when magnetic moment normal to the field)

$$\tau = 1.5 \times 0.22 \sin 90° = 0.33 \text{ N-m}$$

(ii) $\theta = 180°$ (when magnetic moment opposite to the field)

$$\tau = 1.5 \times 0.22 \sin 180° = 0$$

Question 8. A closely wound solenoid of 2000 turns and area of cross-section 1.6×10^{-4} m^2, carrying a current of 4.0 A, is suspended through its centre allowing it to turn in a horizontal plane.

(a) What is the magnetic moment associated with the solenoid?

(b) What are the force and torque on the solenoid, if a uniform horizontal magnetic field of 7.5×10^{-2} T is set up at an angle of 30° with the axis of the solenoid?

Solution   Given, number of turns $n = 2000$

Area of cross-section $A = 1.6 \times 10^{-4}$ m^2

Current $I = 4$ A

(a) Magnetic moment associated with solenoid
$$M = nIA = 2000 \times 4 \times 1.6 \times 10^{-4} = 1.28 \text{ J/T}$$

(b) The force (net) on the solenoid is zero, because two equal and opposite forces (on each of its poles) one acting, but their lines of action are parallel so they form a couple thus a torque (no force) is applied on it.

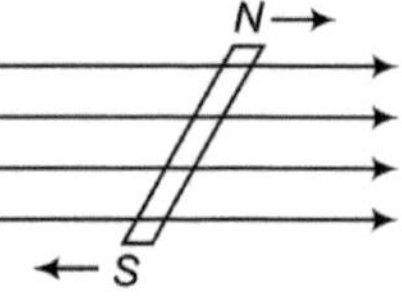

Torque on the solenoid $\tau = MB \sin \theta$ (given $\theta = 30°$)

$$= 1.28 \times 7.5 \times 10^{-2} \sin 30°$$

$$= 1.28 \times 7.5 \times 10^{-2} \times \frac{1}{2}$$

$$= 4.8 \times 10^{-2} \text{ N-m}$$

Question 9. A circular coil of 16 turns and radius 10 cm carrying a current of 0.75 A rests with its plane normal to an external field of magnitude 5.0×10^{-2} T. The coil is free to turn about an axis in its plane perpendicular to the field direction. When the coil is turned slightly and released, it oscillates about its stable equilibrium with a frequency of 2.0/s. What is the moment of inertia of the coil about its axis of rotation?

Solution   Given, number of turns of circular coil $n = 16$

Radius of circular coil $r = 10$ cm $= 0.1$ m

Current $I = 0.75$ A

Magnetic field $B = 5.0 \times 10^{-2}$ T

Frequency $f = 2/$s

Magnetic moment of the coil, $M = nIA = 16 \times 0.75 \times \pi\,(0.1)^2$

$$= 16 \times 0.75 \times 3.14 \times 0.1 \times 0.1$$

$$= 0.377 \text{ J/T}$$

Frequency of oscillation of the coil

$$f = \frac{1}{2\pi} \sqrt{\frac{M \times B}{I}}$$

where I = Moment of inertia of the coil.

Squaring on both the sides, we get

$$f^2 = \frac{1}{4\pi^2} \cdot \frac{MB}{I}$$

$$\Rightarrow \qquad I = \frac{MB}{4\pi^2 f^2} = \frac{0.377 \times 5 \times 10^{-2}}{4 \times 3.14 \times 3.14 \times 2 \times 2}$$

$$= 1.2 \times 10^{-4} \text{ kg-m}^2$$

Thus, the moment of inertia of the coil is 1.2×10^{-4} kg-m^2.

Question 10. A magnetic needle free to rotate in a vertical plane parallel to the magnetic meridian has its north tip pointing down at $22°$ with the horizontal. The horizontal component of the earth's magnetic field at the place is known to be 0.35 G. Determine the magnitude of the earth's magnetic field at the place.

Solution Given, angle of dip $\delta = 22°$

Horizontal component of the earth's magnetic field $H = 0.35$ G

Let the magnitude of the earth's magnetic field at the place is R.

Using the formula, $\qquad H = R \cos \delta$

or $\qquad R = \dfrac{H}{\cos \delta} = \dfrac{0.35}{\cos 22°} = \dfrac{0.35}{0.9272} = 0.38$ G

Thus, the value of the earth's magnetic field at that place is 0.38 G.

Question 11. At a certain location in Africa, a compass points $12°$ west of the geographic north. The north tip of the magnetic needle of a dip circle placed in the plane of magnetic meridian points $60°$ above the horizontal. The horizontal component of the earth's field is measured to be 0.16 G. Specify the direction and magnitude of the earth's field at the location.

Solution Given, angle of declination

$$\theta = 12° \text{ west}$$

Angle of dip $\delta = 60°$

Horizontal component of earth's magnetic field

$$H = 0.16 \text{ G}$$

Let the magnitude of earth's magnetic field at that place is R.

Using the formula, $H = R \cos \delta$

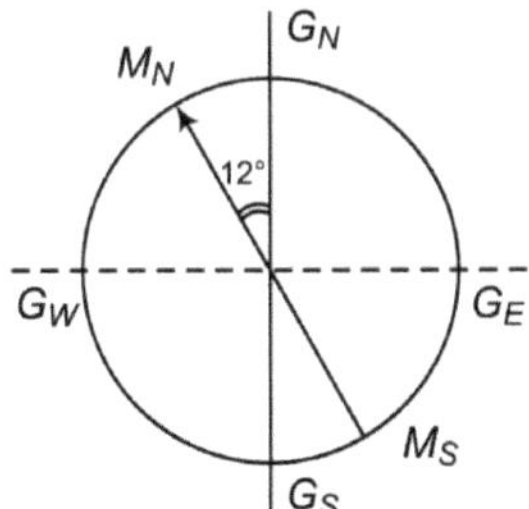

or
$$R = \frac{H}{\cos \delta} = \frac{0.16}{\cos 60°} = \frac{0.16 \times 2}{1}$$

$$= 0.32 \text{ G} = 0.32 \times 10^{-4} \text{ T}$$

The earth's magnetic field lies in a vertical plane 12° west of geographical meridian at an angle 60° above the horizontal.

Question 12. A short bar magnet has a magnetic moment of 0.48 J/T. Give the direction and magnitude of the magnetic field produced by the magnet at a distance of 10 cm from the centre of the magnet on (a) the axis, (b) the equatorial lines (normal bisector) of the magnet.

 Here we have to find out the magnetic field at a point on the axial line and on the equatorial line. So use the formula of magnetic field due to a bar magnet at its axial and equatorial position.

Solution   Given, magnetic moment of bar magnet $M = 0.48$ J/T

Distance from the centre of magnet $d = 10$ cm $= 0.1$ m

(a) When the point lies on the axial line. Magnetic field at point P

$$B = \frac{\mu_0}{4\pi} \cdot \frac{2M}{d^3}$$

$$= \frac{10^{-7} \times 2 \times 0.48}{(0.1)^3} = 0.96 \times 10^{-4} \text{ T}$$

The direction of magnetic field is along the direction of magnetic moment. We know that the direction of magnetic moment is from S to N pole. Thus, the direction of magnetic field is from S to N pole of the magnet.

(b) Use the formula of magnetic field due to a short bar magnet on its equatorial line.

$\therefore$ Magnetic field at point P

$$B = \frac{\mu_0}{4\pi} \cdot \frac{M}{d^3}$$

$$= 10^{-7} \times \frac{0.48}{(0.1)^3} = 0.48 \times 10^{-4} \text{ T}$$

The direction of magnetic field on equitorial line is opposite to the direction of magnetic moment. So, the direction of magnetic field is from N to S pole of the magnet.

Question 13. A short bar magnet placed in a horizontal plane has its axis aligned along the magnetic north-south direction. Null points are found on the axis of the magnet at 14 cm from the centre of the magnet. The earth's magnetic field at the place is 0.36 G and the angle of dip is zero. What is the total magnetic field on the normal bisector of the magnet at the same distance as the null-point (*i.e.*, 14 cm) from the centre of the magnet? (At null points, field due to a magnet is equal and opposite to the horizontal component of earth's magnetic field.)

Solution Distance of the null point from the centre of magnet
$$d = 14 \text{ cm} = 0.14 \text{ m}$$

The earth's magnetic field where the angle of dip is zero, is the horizontal component of earth's magnetic field.

i.e., $H = 0.36$ G

Initially, the null points are on the axis of the magnet. We use the formula of magnetic field on axial line (consider that the magnet is short in length).

$$B_1 = \frac{\mu_0}{4\pi} \cdot \frac{2m}{d^3}$$

This magnetic field is equal to the horizontal component of earth's magnetic field.

i.e., $$B_1 = \frac{\mu_0}{4\pi} \cdot \frac{2m}{d^3} = H \qquad \ldots(i)$$

On the equitorial line of magnet at same distance (d) magnetic field due to the magnet

$$B_2 = \frac{\mu_0}{4\pi} \cdot \frac{m}{d^3} = \frac{B_1}{2} = \frac{H}{2} \qquad \ldots(ii)$$

The total magnetic field on equitorial line at this point (as given in question)

$$B = B_2 + H = \frac{H}{2} + H$$

$$= \frac{3}{2}H = \frac{3}{2} \times 0.36$$

$$= 0.54 \text{ G}$$

The direction of magnetic field is in the direction of earth's field.

Question 14. If the bar magnet in Q. 13 is turned around by 180°, where will the new null points be located?

Solution When the bar magnet is turned by 180°, then the null points are obtained on the equitorial line.

So, magnetic field on the equitorial line at distance d' is

$$B' = \frac{\mu_0}{4\pi} \cdot \frac{m}{d'^3}$$

This magnetic field is equal to the horizontal component of earth's magnetic field

$$B' = \frac{\mu_0}{4\pi} \cdot \frac{m}{d'^3} = H \qquad \ldots(i)$$

From the Q. 13,

Magnetic field $$B_1 = \frac{\mu_0}{4\pi} \cdot \frac{2m}{d^3} = H \qquad \ldots(ii)$$

From Eqs. (i) and (ii), we get

$$\frac{\mu_0}{4\pi} \cdot \frac{m}{d'^3} = \frac{\mu_0}{4\pi} \cdot \frac{2m}{d^3}$$

or

$$\frac{1}{d'^3} = \frac{2}{d^3}$$

or

$$d'^3 = \frac{d^3}{2} = \frac{(14)^3}{2} \qquad\qquad (d = 14 \text{ cm})$$

or

$$d' = \frac{14}{(2)^{1/3}} = 11.1 \text{ cm}$$

Thus, the null points are located on the equitorial line at a distance of 11.1 cm.

Question 15. A short bar magnet of magnetic moment 5.25×10^{-2} J/T is placed with its axis perpendicular to the earth's field direction. At what distance from the centre of the magnet, the resultant field is inclined at 45° with earth's field on (a) its normal bisector and (b) its axis. Magnitude of the earth's field at the place is given to be 0.42 G. Ignore the length of the magnet in comparison to the distances involved.

Solution   Given, magnetic moment $m = 5.25 \times 10^{-2}$ J/T

Let the resultant magnetic field is B_{net}. It makes an angle of 45° with B_e.

$$\therefore \qquad\qquad B_e = 0.42 \text{ G} = 0.42 \times 10^{-4} \text{ T}$$

(a) **At normal bisector**

Let r is the distance between axial line and point P.

The magnetic field at point P, due to a short magnet

$$B = \frac{\mu_0}{4\pi} \cdot \frac{m}{r^3} \qquad ...(i)$$

The direction of B is along PA, *i.e.*, along N pole to S pole.

According to the vector analysis,

$$\tan 45° = \frac{B \sin 90°}{B \cos 90° + B_e}$$

$$1 = \frac{B}{B_e}$$

or

$$B = B_e$$

$$0.42 \times 10^{-4} = \frac{\mu_0}{4\pi} \cdot \frac{m}{r^3}$$

$$0.42 \times 10^{-4} = \frac{10^{-7} \times 5.25 \times 10^{-2}}{r^3}$$

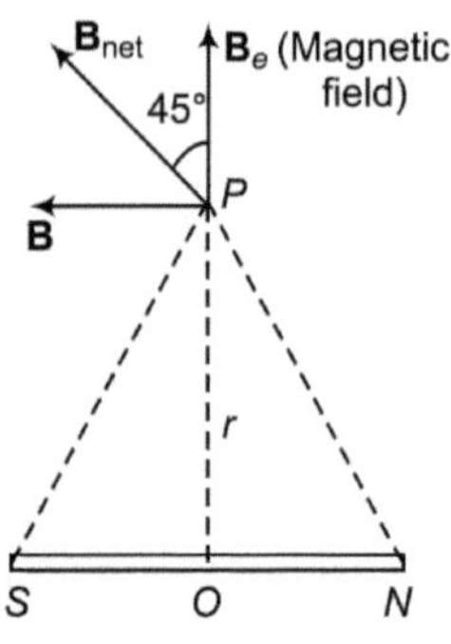

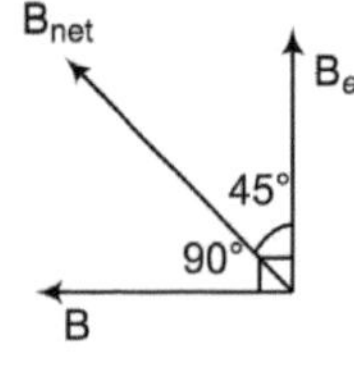

$$r^3 = \frac{5.25 \times 10^{-9}}{0.42 \times 10^{-4}} = 12.5 \times 10^{-5}$$

$$r = 0.05 \text{ m}$$

or $$r = 5 \text{ cm}$$

(b) When point lies on axial line

Let the resultant magnetic field B_{net} makes an angle $45°$ from B_e. The magnetic field on the axial line of the magnet at a distance of r from the centre of magnet

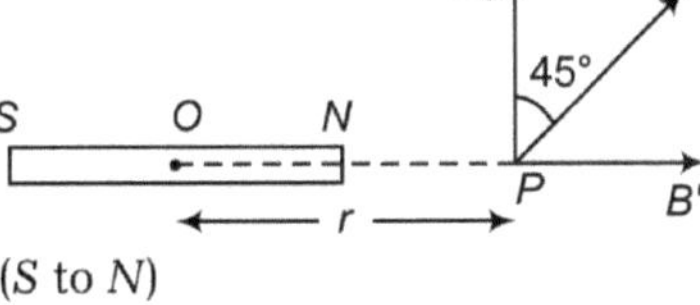

$$B' = \frac{\mu_0}{4\pi} \cdot \frac{2m}{r^3} \qquad (S \text{ to } N)$$

Direction of magnetic field is from S to N.

According to the vector analysis,

$$\tan 45° = \frac{B' \sin 90°}{B' \cos 90° + B_e}$$

$$1 = \frac{B'}{B_e}$$

or $$B_e = B'$$

$$0.42 \times 10^{-4} = \frac{\mu_0}{4\pi} \times \frac{2m}{r^3}$$

or $$0.42 \times 10^{-4} = \frac{10^{-7} \times 2 \times 5.25 \times 10^{-2}}{r^3}$$

$$r^3 = \frac{10^{-9} \times 2 \times 5.25}{0.42 \times 10^{-4}} = 2.5 \times 10^{-5}$$

$$r = 0.063 \text{ m} \quad \text{or} \quad 6.3 \text{ cm}$$

Additional Exercises

Question 16. Answer the following questions:

(a) Why does a paramagnetic sample display greater magnetization (for the same magnetizing field) when cooled?

(b) Why is diamagnetism, in contrast, almost independent of temperature?

(c) If a toroid uses bismuth for its core, will the field in the core be (slightly) greater or (slightly) less than when the core is empty?

(d) Is the permeability of a ferromagnetic material independent of the magnetic field? If not, is it more for lower or higher fields?

   (e) Magnetic field lines are always nearly normal to the surface of a ferromagnet at every point. (This fact is analogous to the static electric field lines being normal to the surface of a conductor at every point.) Why?
   (f) Would the maximum possible magnetization of a paramagnetic sample be of the same order of magnitude as the magnetization of a ferromagnet?

Solution   (a) A paramagnetic sample displays greater magnetisation when cooled because at the lower temperatures, the tendency to disrupt the alignment of magnetic dipoles decreases due to the reduced random thermal motion of atoms or molecules.
   (b) In a sample of diamagnetic substance, each molecule is not a magnetic dipole itself. So, the random thermal motion of the molecules does not affect the magnetism of the sample. Thus, the diamagnetism is almost independent of temperature.
   (c) Bismuth is a diamagnetic element, so the magnetic field in the core will be slightly less than when the core is empty, because the diamagnetic substances are feebly magnetized in the opposite direction of magnetic field.
   (d) No, the permeability of a ferromagnetic material is not independent of the magnetic fields. By observing the hysteresis curve, the value of permeability is greater for lower fields.
   (e) The magnetic field lines are always nearly normal to the surface of a ferromagnetic at every point because the value of permeability for ferromagnetic substance is always greater than 1 ($\mu \gg 1$). It is based on the conditions of B and H at the interface of two media in the hysteresis curve.
   (f) Yes, the maximum possible magnetization of a paramagnetic sample will be of the same order of magnitude as the magnetization of a ferromagnet. The condition of saturation requires very high magnetizing fields which cannot be achieved.

Question 17. Answer the following questions :
   (a) Explain qualitatively on the basis of domain picture the irreversibility in the magnetisation curve of a ferromagnet.
   (b) The hysteresis loop of a soft iron piece has a much smaller area than that of a carbon steel piece. If the material is to go through repeated cycles of magnetization, which piece will dissipate greater heat energy?
   (c) 'A system displaying a hysteresis loop such as a ferromagnet, is a device for storing memory?' Explain the meaning of this statement.
   (d) What kind of ferromagnetic material is used for coating magnetic tapes in a cassette player or for building 'memory stores' in a modern computer?
   (e) A certain region of space is to be shielded from magnetic fields. Suggest a method.

Solution (a) To explain qualitatively the domain picture of the irreversibility in the magnetization curve of a ferromagnet, we draw the hysteresis curve for ferromagnetic substance.

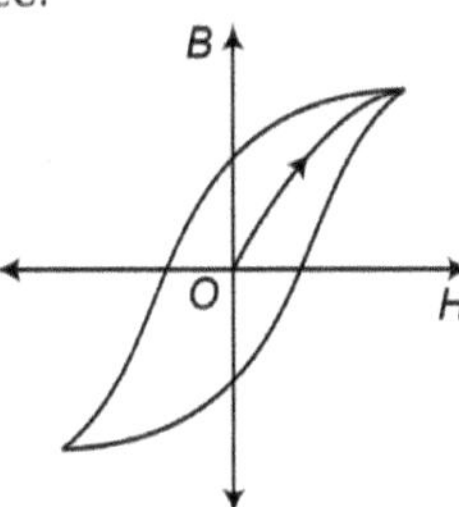

We can observe that the magnetization persists even when the external field is removed. This gives the idea of irreversibility of a ferromagnet.

(b) As we know that in hysteresis curve, the energy dissipated per cycle is directly proportional to the area of hysteresis loop. So, as according to the question, the area of hysteresis loop is more for carbon steel, thus carbon steel piece will dissipate greater heat energy.

(c) The magnetisation of a ferromagnet depends not only on the magnetizing field, but also on the history of magnetization (*i.e.,* how many times it already magnetized in the past). Thus, the value of magnetization of a specimen is a record of memory of the cycles of magnetization it has undergone. The system displaying such a hysteresis loop can thus act as a device for storing memory.

(d) The ferromagnetic materials which are used for coating magnetic tapes in a cassette player or for building memory stores in the modern computer are ferrites. The most commonly ferrites used are $MnFe_2O_4, FeFe_2O_4, CoFe_2O_4, NiFe_2O_4$ etc.

(e) To shield any space from magnetic field, surround the space with soft iron ring. As the magnetic field lines will be drawn into the ring, the enclosed region will become free of magnetic field.

Question 18. A long straight horizontal cable carries a current of **2.5 A** in the direction $10°$ south of west to $10°$ north of east. The magnetic meridian of the place happens to be $10°$ west of the geographic meridian. The earth's magnetic field at the location is 0.33 G and the angle of dip is zero. Locate the line of neutral points (ignore the thickness of the cable). (At neutral points, magnetic field due to a current-carrying cable is equal and opposite to the horizontal component of earth's magnetic field.)

Solution Given, current in the cable

$$I = 2.5 \text{ A}$$

Magnetic meridian $M_N M_S$ is $10°$ west of geographical meridian $G_N G_S$ earth's magnetic field $R = 0.33$ G

$$= 0.33 \times 10^{-4} \text{ T}$$

Angle of dip $\delta = 0°$

The neutral point is the point where the magnetic field due to the current

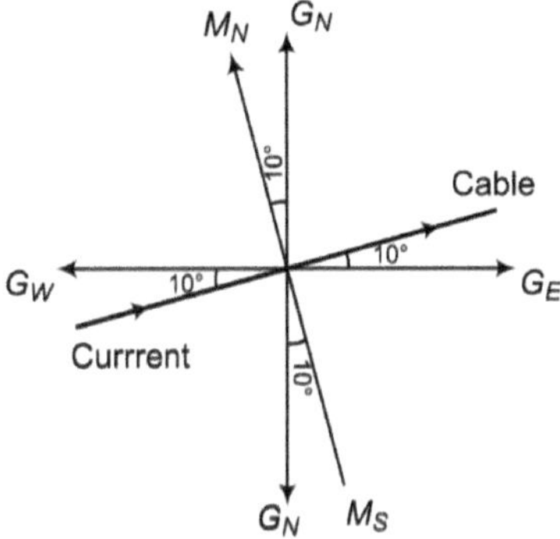

carrying cable is equal to the horizontal component of earth's magnetic field.

Horizontal component of earth's magnetic field

$$H = R \cos \delta = 0.33 \times 10^{-4} \cos 0° = 0.33 \times 10^{-4} \text{ T}$$

Using the formula of magnetic field at distance r due to an infinite long current carrying conductor

$$B = \frac{\mu_0}{4\pi} \cdot \frac{2I}{r} \qquad \qquad \text{...(ii)}$$

At neutral points, $\qquad\qquad H = B$

$$0.33 \times 10^{-4} = \frac{\mu_0}{4\pi} \cdot \frac{2I}{r}$$

$$0.33 \times 10^{-4} = \frac{10^{-7} \times 2 \times 2.5}{r}$$

or $\qquad\qquad$
$$r = \frac{5 \times 10^{-7}}{0.33 \times 10^{-4}}$$

or $\qquad\qquad$
$$r = 1.5 \times 10^{-2} \text{ m}$$

$$= 1.5 \text{ cm}$$

Thus, the line of neutral points is at a distance of 1.5 cm from the cable.

Question 19. A telephone cable at a place has four long straight horizontal wires carrying a current of 1.0 A in the same direction east to west. The earth's magnetic field at the place is 0.39 G and the angle of dip is 35°. The magnetic declination is nearly zero. What are the resultant magnetic fields at points 4.0 cm above and below the cable?

Solution   Given, number of wires $n = 4$

Current of horizontal wire $I = 1\,\text{A}$ (east to west)

Earth's magnetic field $R = 0.39\,\text{G} = 0.39 \times 10^{-4}$ T

Angle of dip $\delta = 35°$

Magnetic declination $\theta = 0°$

Distance from the cable $r = 4\,\text{cm} = 0.04$ m

Magnetic field due to four long wires at P is B.

Use the formula of magnetic field due to an infinitely long current carrying wire.

i.e., $\qquad\qquad$
$$B' = \frac{\mu_0}{4\pi} \cdot \frac{2I}{r}$$

So, the magnetic field produced by four long wires at a distance of 4 cm,

$$B = 4 \times \frac{\mu_0}{4\pi} \cdot \frac{2I}{r}$$

$$= \frac{4 \times 10^{-7} \times 2 \times 1}{4 \times 10^{-2}} = 2 \times 10^{-5} \text{ T} \qquad \text{...(i)}$$

According to the Maxwell's right hand grip rule, the direction of magnetic field B is perpendicularly outwards to the plane of paper. Horizontal component of earth's magnetic field

$$H = R\cos\delta = 0.39 \times 10^{-4} \times \cos 35°$$

$$= 3.19 \times 10^{-5}\ T$$

Vertical component of earth's magnetic field

$$V = R\sin\delta = 0.39 \times 10^{-4}\ \sin 35°$$

$$= 0.39 \times 10^{-4} \times 0.5736$$

$$= 2.2 \times 10^{-5}\ T$$

Now at point P, the horizontal component of earth's magnetic field is H'.

$$H' = H - B$$

(Because direction of B is opposite to H)

$$H' = 3.19 \times 10^{-5} - 2 \times 10^{-5} \qquad \text{[From Eq. (i)]}$$

$$= 1.19 \times 10^{-5}\ T$$

The resultant magnetic field at point P,

$$R' = \sqrt{H'^2 + V^2} = \sqrt{(1.19 \times 10^{-5})^2 + (2.2 \times 10^{-5})^2}$$

$$R' = 2.5 \times 10^{-5}\ T$$

Thus, the resultant magnetic field at point 4 cm below the cable is 2.5×10^{-5} T.

Now at point Q, the magnetic field due to cables

$$B_1 = 4 \times \frac{\mu_0}{4\pi} \times \frac{2I}{r} = \frac{4 \times 10^{-7} \times 2 \times 1}{0.04} = 2 \times 10^{-5}\ T$$

The direction of B_1 at Q is vertically inwards to the plane of paper. Thus, the horizontal components of earth's magnetic field

$$H_1 = H + B_1 \qquad \text{(Direction of } B_1 \text{ and } H \text{ is same)}$$

$$H_1 = 3.19 \times 10^{-5} + 2 \times 10^{-5}$$

$$= 5.19 \times 10^{-5}\ T$$

The resultant magnetic field at point Q,

$$R'' = \sqrt{H_1^2 + V^2} = \sqrt{(5.19 \times 10^{-5})^2 + (2.2 \times 10^{-5})^2}$$

$$= 5.54 \times 10^{-5}\ T$$

Thus, the resultant magnetic field at point 4 cm above the cable is 5.54×10^{-5} T.

Question 20. A compass needle free to turn in a horizontal plane is placed at the centre of circular coil of 30 turns and radius 12 cm. The coil is in a vertical plane making an angle of 45° with the magnetic meridian. When the current in the coil is 0.35 A, the needle points west to east.

(a) Determine the horizontal component of the earth's magnetic field at the location.

(b) The current in the coil is reversed and the coil is rotated about its vertical axis by an angle of 90° in the anticlockwise sense looking from above. Predict the direction of the needle. Take the magnetic declination at the places to be zero.

Solution　Given, number of turns in the coil $n = 30$

Current in the coil　$I = 0.35$ A

Radius of circular coil $= 12$ cm $= 0.12$ m

(a) Let N-S be the line of magnetic meridian, the coil is placed at an angle of 45° with the magnetic meridian. C_1 and C_2 be the plane of coil. The needle points west to east. The magnetic field produced due to the coil is B. The direction of B is along the axis of coil *i.e.*, it makes an angle of 45° with east. The needle points west to east only if the direction of magnetic field B is at 45° from east.

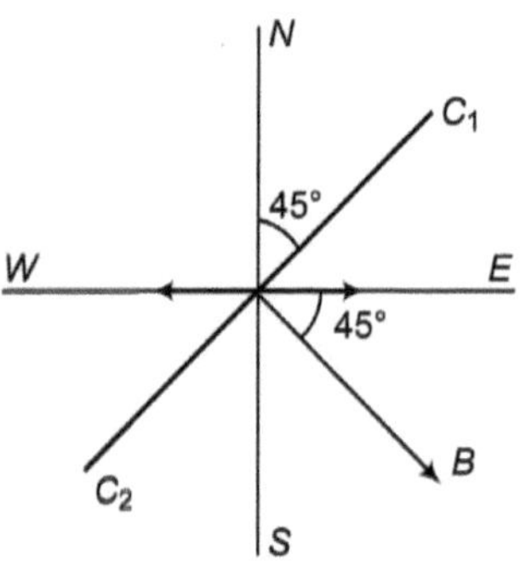

Use the formula, magnetic field produced by a current carrying coil

$$B = \frac{\mu_0}{4\pi} \cdot \frac{2\pi I}{r} = \frac{10^{-7} \times 2 \times 3.14 \times 0.35 \times 30}{0.12}$$

$$= 1.83 \times 10^{-6} \times 30 = 5.49 \times 10^{-5} \text{ T}$$

The horizontal component of magnetic field

$$H = B \sin 45° = 5.49 \times 10^{-5} \times \frac{1}{\sqrt{2}}$$

$$= 3.9 \times 10^{-5} \text{ T}$$

(b) As the direction of current in the coil is reversed and the coil is turned by 90° anticlockwise, the direction of needle will reverse *i.e.*, it points from east to west.

Question 21. A magnetic dipole is under the influence of two magnetic fields. The angle between the field directions is 60° and one of the fields has a magnitude of 1.2×10^{-2} T. If the dipole comes to stable equilibrium at an angle of 15° with this field, what is the magnitude of the other field?

Solution Let one of the magnetic fields is B_1 and other is B_2. Angle between B_1 and B_2 is $60°$.

Given, $\qquad\qquad\qquad B_1 = 1.2 \times 10^{-2}$ T

Dipole is in equilibrium at an angle $15°$ from B_1 or $60° - 15° = 45°$ from B_2

Torque on dipole due to magnetic field B_1,

$$\tau_1 = M \times B_1 \sin 15° \qquad\qquad \ldots(i)$$

where, M is the magnetic moment.

Torque on dipole due to magnetic field B_2

$$\tau_2 = M \times B_2 \sin 45° \qquad\qquad \ldots(ii)$$

As dipole is in the equilibrium, then

$$\tau_1 = \tau_2$$

$$M \times B_1 \sin 15° = M \times B_2 \sin 45°$$

[From Eqs. (i) and (ii)]

$$\frac{1.2 \times 10^{-2} \times \sin 15°}{\sin 45°} = B_2$$

$$B_2 = \frac{1.2 \times 10^{-2} \times 0.2588}{0.7071} = 4.4 \times 10^{-3} \text{ T}$$

Thus, the magnitude of the other field is 4.4×10^{-3} T.

Question 22. A monoenergetic (18 keV) electron beam initially in the horizontal direction is subjected to a horizontal magnetic field of 0.4 G normal to the initial direction. Estimate the up or down deflection of the beam over a distance of 30 cm ($m_e = 9.11 \times 10^{-19}$ C).

[Note : Data in this exercise are so chosen that the answer will give you an idea of the effect of earth's magnetic field on the motion of the electron beam from the electron gun to the screen in a TV set.]

 Use the concept that if a charged particle enters in a magnetic field normally, it attains a circular path as magnetic force acts normal to the direction of motion and provides required centripetal force.

Solution Given, energy of electron $E = 18$ keV

$$= 18 \times 10^3 \times 1.6 \times 10^{-19} \text{ J} \quad (\because 1 \text{ eV} = 1.6 \times 10^{-19} \text{ J})$$

$$= 18 \times 1.6 \times 10^{-16} \text{ J}$$

Let velocity of electron be v.

Magnetic field $B = 0.4$ G $= 0.4 \times 10^{-4}$ T

Distance $= 30$ cm $= 0.3$ m

Mass of electron $m_e = 9.1 \times 10^{-19}$ kg

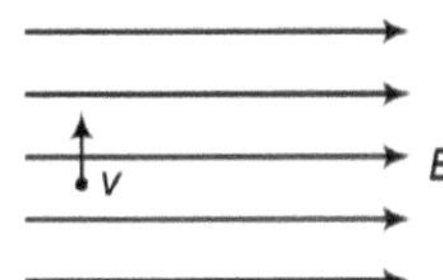

Energy of electron $E = \dfrac{1}{2}mv^2$

$\therefore \qquad 18 \times 1.6 \times 10^{-16} = \dfrac{1}{2} \times 9.1 \times 10^{-31}\, v^2$

or $\qquad\qquad\qquad\qquad v = 0.795 \times 10^8$ m/s

Let the electron beam deflects along a circular path of radius r.

The magnetic force applied on the electron provides the centripetal force.

$$e\,v\,B = \dfrac{mv^2}{r} \qquad (\text{By } \mathbf{F} = q\,(\mathbf{v} \times \mathbf{B}),\ \text{angle between } \mathbf{v} \times \mathbf{B} \text{ is } 90°)$$

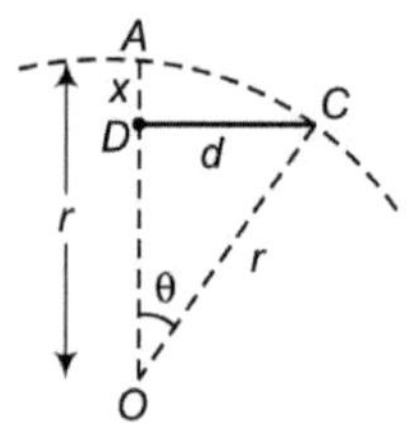

$$OA = r = OC,\ DC = d = 30 \text{ cm}$$

or $\qquad r = \dfrac{mv}{Be} = \dfrac{9.1 \times 10^{-31} \times 0.795 \times 10^8}{0.4 \times 10^{-4} \times 1.6 \times 10^{-19}} = 11.3 \text{ m}$

Let the deflection is $AD = x$

From $\triangle\, DCO$, $\qquad \sin\theta = \dfrac{DC}{OC} = \dfrac{d}{r} = \dfrac{0.3}{11.3}$

$$\theta = 1.521°$$

and $\qquad\qquad\qquad \cos\theta = \dfrac{OD}{OC} = \dfrac{OD}{r}$

or $\qquad\qquad\qquad OD = r \cos\theta$

Deflection at the end of the path

$$AD = x = AO - OD = r - r\cos\theta = r\,(1 - \cos\theta)$$

or $\qquad x = 11.3\,(1 - \cos 1.521°) = 0.0039 \text{ m}$

$$= 3.9 \text{ mm}$$

or $\qquad\qquad\qquad\qquad x \approx 4 \text{ mm}$

Thus, the up or down deflection of the beam is approximately 4 mm.

Question 23. A sample of paramagnetic salt contains 2.0×10^{24} atomic dipoles each of dipole moment 1.5×10^{-23} J/T. The sample is placed under a homogeneous magnetic field of 0.64 T and cooled to a temperature of 4.2 K. The degree of magnetic saturation achieved is equal to 15%. What is the total dipole moment of the sample for a magnetic field of 0.98 T and a temperature of 2.8 K? (Assume Curie's law).

Solution Given, number of atomic dipoles $n = 2 \times 10^{24}$

Dipole moment of each dipole $= 1.5 \times 10^{-23}$ J/T

Degree of magnetic saturation $= 15\%$

Homogeneous magnetic field $B_1 = 0.64$ T

Initial temperature $T_1 = 4.2$ K

Final magnetic field $B_2 = 0.98$ T

Final temperature $T_2 = 2.8$ K

The degree of magnetic saturation $= 15\%$

Dipole moment of sample M

$\qquad$ = Number of dipoles $\times$ Dipole moment of each dipole

$\qquad = 2 \times 10^{24} \times 1.5 \times 10^{-23} = 3 \times 10 = 30$

At saturation, the effective dipole moment $M_1 = 15\%$ of M

$$M_1 = \frac{15}{100} \times 30 = 4.5 \text{ J/T}$$

According to Curie law, $\qquad \chi_m = \dfrac{C}{T} = \dfrac{I}{H}$

$$I \propto M \text{ and } H \propto B$$

So, $\qquad\qquad\qquad \dfrac{C}{T} = \dfrac{M}{B}$

(where, M is magentic moment and B is magnetic field)

or $\qquad\qquad\qquad M \propto \dfrac{B \cdot C}{T}$

$\therefore \qquad\qquad\qquad \dfrac{M_1}{M_2} = \dfrac{B_1}{T_1} \cdot \dfrac{T_2}{B_2}$

or $\qquad M_2 = \dfrac{B_2 T_1}{B_1 T_2} \times M_1 = \dfrac{0.98 \times 4.2 \times 4.5}{0.64 \times 2.8}$

$$M_2 = 10.335 \text{ J/T}$$

Thus, the dipole moment of the sample at 2.8 K is 10.335 J/T.

Question 24. A Rowland ring of mean radius 15 cm has 3500 turns of wire wound on a ferromagnetic core of relative permeability 800. What is the magnetic field B in the core for a magnetizing current of 1.2 A?

Solution Given, radius of Rowland ring $r = 15$ cm $= 0.15$ m

Number of turns $N = 3500$

Relative permeability of ferromagnetic core

$$\mu_r = 800$$

Current $\qquad\qquad\qquad I = 1.2$ A

Magnetic field due to the toriod

$$B = \mu_0 nI \qquad \left(\because n = \frac{\text{Number of turns}}{\text{Length}} \right)$$

$$B = \mu_0 \mu_r \frac{N}{2\pi r} . I \qquad (\because \text{ Length of toriod} = 2\pi r)$$

$$= 4 \times 3.14 \times 10^{-7} \times 800 \times \frac{3500 \times 1.2}{2 \times 3.14 \times 0.15}$$

$$= 4.48 \text{ T}$$

Question 25. The magnetic moment vectors μ_s and μ_l associated with the intrinsic spin angular momentum s and orbital angular momentum l respectively, of an electron are predicted by quantum theory (and verified experimentally to a high accuracy) to be given by $\mu_s = -(e/m)\,s$, $\mu_l = -(e/2m)\,l$. Which of these relations is in accordance with the result expected classically? Outline the derivation of the classical result.

Solution Out of two relations given, only μ_l is in the accordance of classical physics.

$$\mu_l = -\left(\frac{e}{2m}\right) l \qquad \qquad \dots\text{(i)}$$

Magnetic moment $\mu_l = I \times \text{Area} = \left(\dfrac{\text{Charge}}{\text{Time}}\right) \pi r^2$

or

$$\mu_l = \left(-\frac{e}{T}\right) \pi r^2 \qquad \qquad \dots\text{(ii)}$$

Angular momentum $\qquad l = mvr = m\left(\dfrac{2\pi r}{T}\right) r \qquad \qquad \dots\text{(iii)}$

Dividing Eq. (ii) by Eq. (iii), we get

$$\therefore \qquad \frac{\mu_l}{l} = \frac{-e\,\pi\,r^2 \cdot T}{T \cdot m\,(2\pi r)\,r}$$

or

$$\frac{\mu_l}{l} = -\frac{e}{2m}$$

$$\mu_l = -\frac{e}{2m}\, l$$

Here, observe that μ_l and l are antiparallel to each other.

Selected NCERT Exemplar Problems

Question 1. A proton has spin and magnetic moment just like an electron. Why then its effect is neglected in magnetism of materials?

Solution As we know that the magnetic moment of electron or proton is inversely proportional to the mass of electron or proton respectively.

Magnetic moment of electron $\quad \mu_e \propto \dfrac{1}{m_e} \quad$ where, m_e = mass of electron

Magnetic moment of proton $\quad \mu_p \propto \dfrac{1}{m_p} \quad$ where, m_p = mass of proton

$$\dfrac{\mu_e}{\mu_p} = \dfrac{m_p}{m_e} \qquad \qquad \dots\text{(i)}$$

As we know that, $m_e << m_p$, so

$$\dfrac{m_p}{m_e} >> 1$$

$$\Rightarrow \qquad \dfrac{\mu_e}{\mu_p} >> 1$$

$$\mu_e >> \mu_p$$

Thus, as the value of magnetic moment of electron is much more as compared to magnetic moment of proton so, the effect of proton is neglected.

Question 2. A bar magnet of magnetic moment m and moment of inertia I (about centre, perpendicular to length) is cut into two equal pieces, perpendicular to length. Let T be the period of oscillations of the original magnet about an axis through the mid-point, perpendicular to length, in a magnetic field B. What would be the similar period T' for each piece?

Solution Moment of inertia $I_1 = I$

Time period $T_1 = T$

Magnetic field = B, mass of magnet = x

As the magnet cut into two pieces, mass of each

piece $= \dfrac{x}{2}$

Initial moment of inertia, $I = \dfrac{1}{12} \times$ mass $\times$ (length)^2

$$I = \dfrac{1}{12} \times x \times l^2 \quad \text{where, } l = \text{length of magnet} \dots\text{(i)}$$

Moment of inertia of half piece, $I' = \dfrac{1}{12} \times \dfrac{x}{2} \left(\dfrac{l}{2}\right)^2 = \dfrac{1}{12} \times \dfrac{xl^2}{2 \times 4} \qquad \dots\text{(ii)}$

The magnetic moment of half-piece, $m' = \dfrac{m}{2}$

Using the formula of time period,

$$T = 2\pi \sqrt{\dfrac{I}{mB}}$$

$$\dfrac{T}{T'} = \sqrt{\dfrac{I\,m'\,B}{I'\,mB}} = \sqrt{\dfrac{I}{I'} \cdot \dfrac{m'}{m}}$$

$$\dfrac{T}{T'} = \sqrt{\dfrac{xl^2 \times 12 \times 4 \times 2}{12 \times xl^2}} \times \dfrac{m}{2 \cdot m} = \sqrt{2 \times 2}$$

$$T' = \dfrac{T}{2}$$

The new time period of each piece is $\dfrac{T}{2}$.

Question 3. Assume the dipole model for earth's magnetic field **B** which is given by B_V = Vertical component of magnetic field $= \dfrac{\mu_0}{4\pi} \dfrac{2m \cos \theta}{r^3}$

B_H = Horizontal component of magnetic field $= \dfrac{\mu_0}{4\pi} \dfrac{\sin \theta\, m}{r^3}$

$\theta = 90°-$ latitude as measured from magnetic equator.

Find loci of points for which (a) |**B**| is minimum; (b) dip angle is zero; and (c) dip angle is $\pm$ 45°.

Solution   (a) $B_V = \dfrac{\mu_0}{4\pi} \dfrac{2m \cos \theta}{r^3}$ ...(i)

$$B_H = \dfrac{\mu_0}{4\pi} \dfrac{\sin \theta\, m}{r^3} \qquad \text{...(ii)}$$

Squaring both the equations and adding, we get

$$B_V^2 + B_H^2 = \left(\dfrac{\mu_0}{4\pi}\right)^2 \dfrac{m^2}{r^6} [4 \cos^2 \theta + \sin^2 \theta]$$

$$B = \sqrt{B_V^2 + B_H^2} = \dfrac{\mu_0}{4\pi} \dfrac{m}{r^3} [3\cos^2 \theta + 1]^{1/2} \qquad \text{...(iii)}$$

From Eq. (iii), the value of **B** is minimum, if $\cos \theta = \dfrac{\pi}{2}$

$\theta = \dfrac{\pi}{2}$. Thus, the magnetic equator is the locus.

(b) Angle of dip, $\tan \delta = \dfrac{B_V}{B_H} = \dfrac{\dfrac{\mu_0}{4\pi} \cdot \dfrac{2m \cos \theta}{r^3}}{\dfrac{\mu_0}{4\pi} \cdot \dfrac{\sin \theta \cdot m}{r^3}} = 2 \cot \theta$ ...(iv)

$$\tan \delta = 2 \cot \theta$$

For dip angle is zero *i.e.*, $\qquad \delta = 0$

$$\cot \theta = 0$$

$$\theta = \frac{\pi}{2}$$

It means that locus is again magnetic equator.

(c) $\qquad\qquad \tan \delta = \dfrac{B_V}{B_H}$

Angle of dip *i.e.*, $\delta = \pm\, 45$

$$\frac{B_V}{B_H} = \tan\,(\pm\,45°)$$

$$\frac{B_V}{B_H} = 1$$

$$2 \cot \theta = 1 \qquad\qquad\qquad \text{[From Eq. (iv)]}$$

$$\cot \theta = \frac{1}{2}$$

$$\tan \theta = 2 \quad \Rightarrow \quad \theta = \tan^{-1} 2$$

Thus, $\theta = \tan^{-1} (2)$ is the locus.

Question 4. Consider the plane S formed by the dipole axis and the axis of earth. Let P be point on the magnetic equator and in S. Let Q be the point of intersection of the geographical and magnetic equators. Obtain the declination and dip angles at P and Q.

Solution P is in the plane S, needle is in north, so the declination is zero.

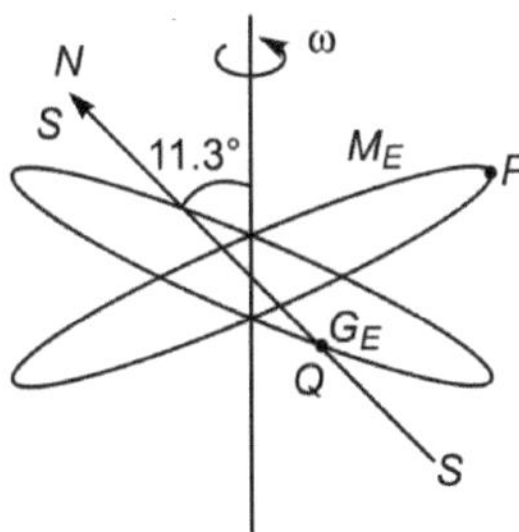

P is also on the magnetic equator, so the angle of dip = 0, because the value of angle of dip at equator is zero. Q is also on the magnetic equator, thus the angle of dip is zero.

As earth tilted on its axis by 11.3°, thus the declination at Q is 11.3°.

Question 5. There are two current carrying planar coils made each from identical wires of length L. C_1 is circular coil (radius R) and C_2 is square (side a). They are so constructed that they have same frequency of oscillation when they are placed in the same uniform magnetic field B and carry the same current. Find a in terms of R.

Solution

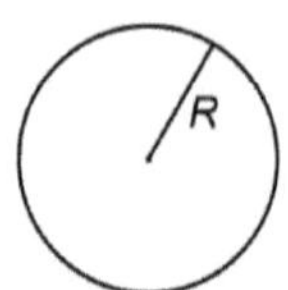

C_1 = circular
coil of radius R,
length L, number of
turns per unit length
$$n_1 = \frac{L}{2\pi R}$$

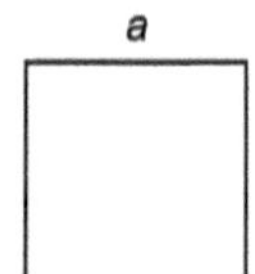

C_2 = square of side a
and perimeter L,
number of turns per unit length
$$n_2 = \frac{L}{4a}$$

Magnetic moment of $C_1 \Rightarrow m_1 = n_1 I A_1$

Magnetic moment of $C_2 \Rightarrow m_2 = n_2 I A_2$

$$m_1 = \frac{L \cdot I \cdot \pi R^2}{2\pi R} \quad , \quad m_2 = \frac{L}{4a} \cdot I \cdot a^2$$

$$m_1 = \frac{LIR}{2} \qquad \ldots\text{(i)} \quad , \quad m_2 = \frac{LIa}{4} \qquad \ldots\text{(ii)}$$

Moment of inertia of $C_1 \Rightarrow I_1 = \frac{MR^2}{2} \qquad \ldots\text{(iii)}$

Moment of inertia of $C_2 \Rightarrow I_2 = \frac{Ma^2}{12} \qquad \ldots\text{(iv)}$

Frequency of $C_1 \Rightarrow \qquad f_1 = 2\pi \sqrt{\frac{I_1}{m_1 B}}$

Frequency of $C_2 \Rightarrow \qquad f_2 = 2\pi \sqrt{\frac{I_2}{m_2 B}}$

According to question, $\qquad f_1 = f_2$

$$2\pi \sqrt{\frac{I_1}{m_1 B}} = 2\pi \sqrt{\frac{I_2}{m_2 B}}$$

$$\frac{I_1}{m_1} = \frac{I_2}{m_2} \quad \text{or} \quad \frac{m_2}{m_1} = \frac{I_2}{I_1}$$

Plugging the values by Eqs. (i), (ii), (iii) and (iv)

$$\frac{LIa \cdot 2}{4 \times LIR} = \frac{Ma^2 \cdot 2}{12 \cdot MR^2}$$

$$\frac{a}{2R} = \frac{a^2}{6R^2}$$

$$3R = a$$

Thus, the value of a is $3R$.

Chapter 6

Electromagnetic Induction

Important Results

1. The magnetic flux through any surface of area **A** placed in magnetic field **B** is given by

$$\phi = \mathbf{B} \cdot \mathbf{A} = BA \cos \theta$$

where, θ is the angle between magnetic field and area vector.

2. According to the Faraday's law of electromagnetic induction, the induced emf is given by

$$e = -\frac{d\phi}{dt}$$

or

$$= -\frac{Nd\phi}{dt}$$

where, N be the number of turns.

3. Lenz's law states that the polarity of the induced emf is such that it tends to produce a current which opposes the change in magnetic flux that produces it.

4. The motion emf in a rod of length l, placed normally in a uniform magnetic field B and moving with velocity v is

$$e = Bvl$$

5. The self inductance of a coil is given by, $\phi = LI$

where, L is coefficient of self inductance.

6. Induced emf $e = -\dfrac{L\, dI}{dt}$

where, L is coefficient of self inductance.

7. Induced emf $e = -M\dfrac{dI}{dt}$

where, M is coefficient of mutual inductance.

8. For a long solenoid, the self induction coefficient is

$$L = \mu_0 \frac{N^2 A}{l}$$

where, N is the total number of turns.

9. Mutual inductance for two co-axial solenoids of same length

$$M = \frac{\mu_0 N_1 N_2 A}{l}$$

where, N_1 and N_2 are total number of turns of the two solenoids. A is the area of cross-section of each coil.

10. In an AC generator, the induced emf produced is given by

$$\varepsilon = NB\,A\,(2\pi f)\sin 2\pi f\, t$$

where, f is the frequency.

11. (i) Inductance of coils in series is given by

$$L = L_1 + L_2 + L_3 + \dots$$

(ii) Inductance of coils in parallel is given by

$$\frac{1}{L} = \frac{1}{L_1} + \frac{1}{L_2} + \frac{1}{L_3} + \dots.$$

12. If two coils of inductances L_1 and L_2 are coupled together, then mutual inductance is given by

$$M = K\sqrt{L_2 L_2}$$

where, K is called coupling constant.

13. Energy stored in a coil of inductance L is given by

$$U = \frac{1}{2}LI^2$$

Exercises

Question 1. Predict the direction of induced current in the situations described by the following figures :

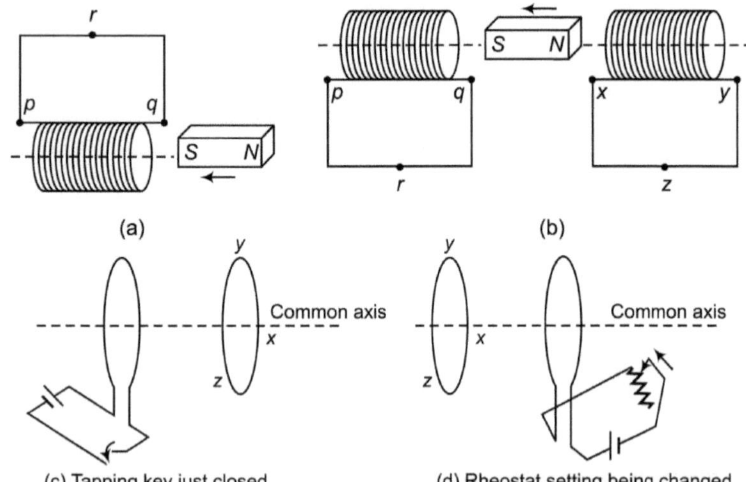

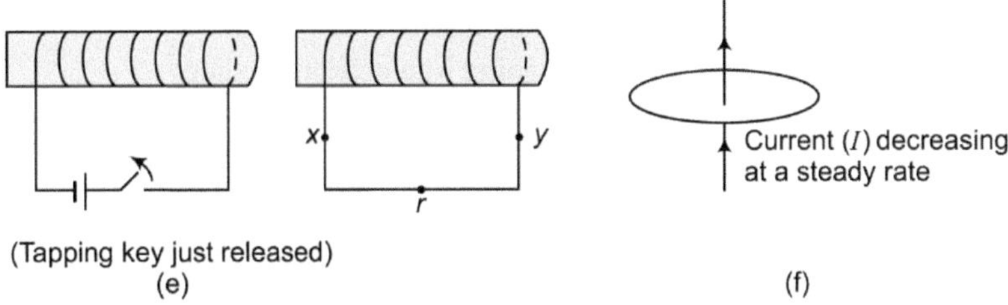

(Tapping key just released)
(e)

(f)

 According to Lenz's law, the direction of induced current is always in such a way that it opposes the cause due to which it is produced.

Solution. (a) Here, south pole is moving towards the coil, so according to Lenz's law this end becomes S-pole (To oppose the motion of south pole by repelling it). Hence, the direction of current is clockwise (by using clock rule) and the current flows from p to q.

(b) In coil p-q, at end $q \Rightarrow S$-pole is moving towards end q, so it behaves like a south pole (by Lenz's law). The direction of current is clockwise (by *clock rule*), *i.e.*, from p to q. North pole is moving away so this end will behave like South pole (To oppose its away motion by attracting it). In coil x-y, S-pole is induced (by Lenz's law) and the direction of current is clockwise *i.e.*, x to y.

(c) As the tapping key is just closed, the current in coil increases. So, the magnetic flux and field increases. According to Maxwell's right hand grip rule, the direction of magnetic field is leftwards. Thus, the direction of induced current in the neighbouring coil is such that it try to decrease the field, thus the direction of field in the neighbouring coil should be rightwards, *i.e.*, according to Maxwell's right hand rule the direction of induced current is anticlockwise, *i.e.*, xyz.

(d) As the rheostat setting is changed, the current is changed. The direction of field due to the coil is leftwards according to Maxwell's right hand grip rule. The direction of induced current in the left coil is such that the magnetic field produced by it in rightwards, thus the direction of current in left coil is anticlockwise *i.e.*, from zyx.

(e) As the key is just released, the current which is flowing anticlockwise goes on decreasing. Thus, the induced current developed in such a sense the magnetic field due to left coil increases (which is towards right). So, the magnetic field due to the right coil should also towards right and hence the induced current is in anticlockwise, *i.e.*, x to yx-direction.

(f) The magnetic field lines due to the current carrying wire are in the plane of the loop. Hence, no induced current is produced in the loop (because no flux lines crosses the area of loop).

Question 2. Use Lenz's law to determine the direction of induced current in the situations described by figure.

(a) A wire of irregular shape turning into a circular shape;

(b) A circular loop being deformed into a narrow straight wire.

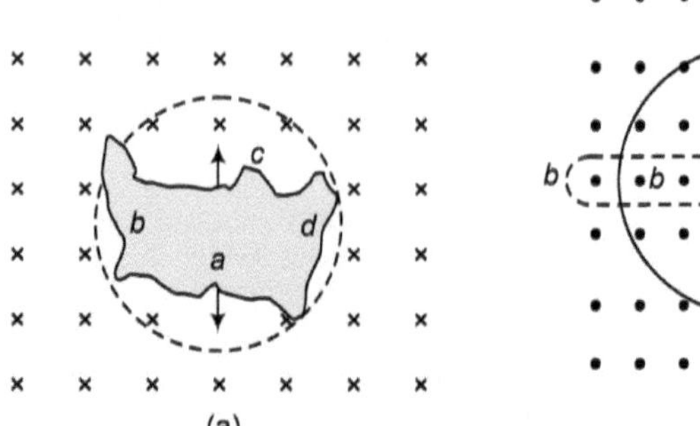

(a)   (b)

Solution. (a) Here, the direction of magnetic field is perpendicularly inwards to the plane of paper. If a wire of irregular shape turns into a circular shape then its area increases ($\because$ The circular loop has greater area than the loop of irregular shape.) so that the magnetic flux linked also increases. Now, the induced current is produced in a direction such that it decreases the magnetic field [*i.e.*, the current will flow in such a direction so that the wire forming the loop is pulled inward in all directions (to decrease the area)], *i.e.*, current is in anticlockwise direction, *i.e.*, *adcba*.

(b) When a circular loop deforms into a narrow straight wire, the magnetic flux linked with it also decreases. The current induced due to change in flux will flow in such a direction that it will oppose the decrease in magnetic flux so it will flow anticlockwise, *i.e.*, along $a'd'c'b'a'$, due to which the magnetic field produced will be out of the plane of paper.

Question 3. A long solenoid with 15 turns per cm has a small loop of area 2.0 cm^2 placed inside the solenoid normal to its axis. If the current carried by the solenoid changes steadily from 2.0 A to 4.0 A in 0.1 s, what is the induced emf in the loop while the current is changing?

Solution. Given, number of turns $n = 15$ per cm $= 1500$ per metre

Area of small loop $A = 2$ cm^2 $= 2 \times 10^{-4}$ m^2

Change in current $\dfrac{dI}{dt} = \dfrac{4-2}{0.1} = \dfrac{2}{0.1} = 20$ A/s

Let e be the induced emf,

According to Faraday's law,

$$e = \frac{d\phi}{dt} = \frac{d}{dt}(BA) \qquad\qquad (\because \phi = BA)$$

or
$$e = A\frac{dB}{dt} = A\frac{d}{dt}(\mu_0 n I)$$

($\because$ Magnetic field inside the solenoid $B = \mu_0\, nI$)

or
$$e = A\,\mu_0 n\,\frac{dI}{dt}$$
$$e = 2 \times 10^{-4} \times 4 \times 3.14 \times 10^{-7} \times 1500 \times 20$$

$$(\because\ \mu_0 = 4\pi \times 10^{-7})$$

$$e = 7.5 \times 10^{6}\ \text{V}$$

Thus, the induced emf in the loop is 7.5×10^{6} V.

Question 4. A rectangular wire loop of sides 8 cm and 2 cm with a small cut is moving out of a region of uniform magnetic field of magnitude 0.3 T directed normal to the loop. What is the emf developed across the cut if the velocity of the loop is 1 cm/s in a direction normal to the (a) longer side, (b) shorter side of the loop? For how long does the induced voltage last in each case?

 Use the concept of motional emf as wire loop is moving normal to the magnetic field.

Solution. Given, length of the loop

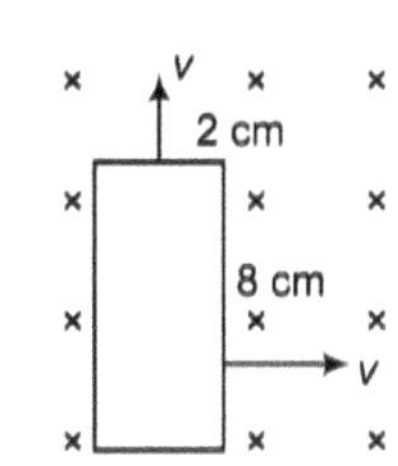

$$l = 8\ \text{cm} = 8 \times 10^{-2}\ \text{m}$$

Width of the loop $b = 2\ \text{cm} = 2 \times 10^{-2}\ \text{m}$

Velocity of the loop $= 1\ \text{cm/s} = 0.01\ \text{m/s}$

Magnitude of magnetic field $B = 0.3$ T

(a) **When velocity is normal to the longer side** ($l = 8\ \text{cm} = 8 \times 10^{-2}$ m)

In this case, motional emf
$$e = Blv = 0.3 \times 8 \times 10^{-2} \times 0.01 = 2.4 \times 10^{-4}\ \text{V}$$

$$\text{Time} = \frac{\text{Distance}}{\text{Velocity}} = \frac{\text{Shorter side (width)}}{\text{Velocity}}$$

$$t = \frac{2 \times 10^{-2}}{0.01} = 2\ \text{s}$$

(b) **When velocity is normal to the shorter side.** ($l = 2\ \text{cm} = 2 \times 10^{-2}$ m)

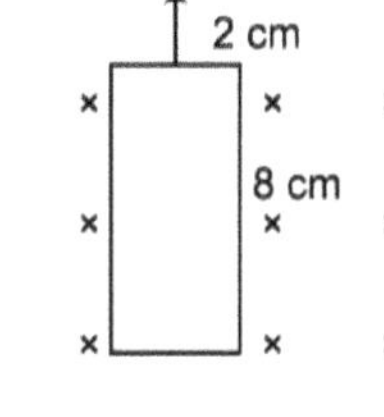

In this case, the developed emf
$$e = Blv = 0.3 \times 2 \times 10^{-2} \times 0.01$$
$$e = 0.6 \times 10^{-4}\ \text{V}$$

$$\text{Time} = \frac{\text{Longer side (length)}}{\text{Velocity}} = \frac{8 \times 10^{-2}}{0.01}$$

$$t = 8\ \text{s}$$

Question 5. A 1.0 m long metallic rod is rotated with an angular frequency of 400 rad/s about an axis normal to the rod passing through its one end. The other end of the rod is in contact with a circular metallic ring. A constant and uniform magnetic field of 0.5 T parallel to the axis exists everywhere. Calculate the emf developed between the centre and the ring.

Solution. Length of rod $l = 1$ m

Angular frequency of rod $\omega = 400$ rad/s

Magnetic field $B = 0.5$ T

The linear velocity of fixed end $= 0$

The linear velocity of other end $= l\omega$ $(\because v = r\omega)$

Average linear velocity $v = \dfrac{0 + l\omega}{2} = \dfrac{l\omega}{2}$ ...(i)

By using the formula of motional emf,

$$e = Bvl = \frac{Bl\omega}{2} \cdot l \qquad \text{[from Eq. (i)]}$$

$$e = \frac{0.5 \times 1 \times 400 \times 1}{2}$$

$$e = 100 \text{ V}$$

Thus, the emf developed between the centre and ring is 100 V.

Question 6. A circular coil of radius 8.0 cm and 20 turns is rotated about its vertical diameter with an angular speed of 50 rad/s in a uniform horizontal magnetic field of magnitude 3.0×10^{-2} T. Obtain the maximum and average emf induced in the coil. If the coil forms a closed-loop of resistance 10 Ω, calculate the maximum value of current in the coil. Calculate the average power loss due to Joule heating. Where does this power come from?

Solution. Given, radius of coil $= 8$ cm $= 0.08$ m

Number of turns $= 20$

Resistance of closed-loop $= 10 \ \Omega$

Angular speed $\omega = 50$ rad/s

Magnitude of magnetic field $B = 3 \times 10^{-2}$ T

Induced emf produced in the coil $e = NBA\omega \sin \omega t$

For maximum emf, $\sin \omega t = 1$

$\therefore$ Maximum emf $e_0 = NBA\omega = 20 \times 3 \times 10^{-2} \times 3.14 \ (0.08)^2 \times 50$

$$e_0 = 0.603 \text{ V}$$

Maximum current in the coil $I_0 = \dfrac{e_0}{R} = \dfrac{0.603}{10} = 0.0603$ A

Average induced emf

$$e_{av} = \frac{1}{T} \int_0^{2\pi} e \, dt = \frac{1}{T} \int_0^{2\pi} NBA\omega \sin \omega t \, dt$$

$$e_{av} = \frac{1}{T} \cdot NAB\omega \left[\frac{\cos \omega t}{\omega} \right]_0^{2\pi}$$

$$= \frac{NBA}{T} [\cos 2\pi - \cos 0°]$$

$$e_{av} = \frac{NBA}{T} [1-1] = 0$$

For full cycle average emf, $e_{av} = 0$

Average power loss due to heating

$$= \frac{E_0 I_0}{2} = \frac{0.603 \times 0.0603}{2} = 0.018 \text{ W}$$

The source of power dissipated as heat in the coil is the external rotar. The current induced in the coil causes a torque which opposes the rotation of the coil, so the external agent rotar counter this torque to keep the coil rotating uniformly.

Question 7. A horizontal straight wire 10 m long extending from east to west is falling with a speed of 5.0 m/s, at right angles to the horizontal component of the earth's magnetic field, 0.30×10^{-4} Wb/m^2.

(a) What is the instantaneous value of the emf induced in the wire?

(b) What is the direction of the emf ?

(c) Which end of the wire is at the higher electrical potential?

Solution. Given, velocity of straight wire $= 5$ m/s

Magnetic field of straight wire,

$$B = 0.30 \times 10^{-4} \text{ Wb/m}^2$$

Length of wire $l = 10$ m

(a) Emf induced in the wire $e = Blv \sin \theta$

Here, $\theta = 90°$

$\therefore$ $\quad\quad\quad\quad\quad\quad\quad \sin \theta = 1$

($\because$ Wire is falling at right angle to earth's horizontal magnetic field component.)

$$= 0.3 \times 10^{-4} \times 10 \times 5 = 1.5 \times 10^{-3} \text{ V}$$

(b) According to the Fleming's right hand rule, the force is downward, then the direction of induced emf will be from west to east.

(c) As the direction of induced emf or current is from west to east, the west end of the wire is at higher potential. ($\because$ Current always flows from a point at higher potential to a point at lower potential.)

Question 8. Current in a circuit falls from 5.0 A to 0.0 A in 0.1 s. If an average emf of 200 V induced, give an estimate of the self-inductance of the circuit.

Solution. Change in current, $dI = 5 - 0 = 5$ A

Time taken in current change $dt = 0.1$ s

Induced average emf $\qquad\qquad e_{av} = 200$ V

Induced emf in the circuit $\qquad e = L\dfrac{dI}{dt}$

$$200 = L\left(\dfrac{5}{0.1}\right) \quad \text{or} \quad L = \dfrac{200}{50} = 4 \text{ H}$$

Question 9. A pair of adjacent coils has a mutual inductance of 1.5 H. If the current in one coil changes from 0 to 20 A in 0.5 s, what is the change of flux linkage with the other coil?

Solution. Given, mutual inductance of coil

$$M = 1.5 \text{ H}$$

Current change in coil $dI = 20 - 0 = 20$ A

Time taken in change $dt = 0.5$ s

Induced emf in the coil $e = M\dfrac{dI}{dt} = \dfrac{d\phi}{dt}$

or $\qquad\qquad\qquad\qquad d\phi = M.\,dI = 1.5 \times 20$

$$d\phi = 30 \text{ Wb}$$

Thus, the change of flux linkage is 30 Wb.

Question 10. A jet plane is travelling towards west at a speed of 1800 km/h. What is the voltage difference developed between the ends of the wing having a span of 25 m, if the earth's magnetic field at the location has a magnitude of 5×10^{-4} T and the dip angle is 30°.

Solution. Speed of jet plane $v = 1800$ km/h $= 1800 \times \dfrac{5}{18} = 500$ m/s

l = Distance between the ends of the wings = 25 m

The magnitude of magnetic field $B = 5 \times 10^{-4}$ T

Angle of dip $\delta = 30°$

Use the formula of motional emf,

$$e = B_V vl$$

$$e = B \sin \delta \, vl$$

(where, B_V = vertical component of the earth's magnetic field.

$\therefore \qquad B_V = B \sin \delta$)

$$e = 5 \times 10^{-4} \sin 30° \times 500 \times 25 = 3.1 \text{ V}$$

Thus, the voltage difference developed between the ends is 3.1 V.

Additional Exercises

Question 11. Suppose the loop in Q. 4 is stationary but the current feeding the electromagnet that produces the magnetic field is gradually reduced so that the field decreases from its initial value of 0.3 T at the rate of 0.02 T/s. If the cut is joined and the loop has a resistance of 1.6 Ω, how much power is dissipated by the loop as heat? What is the source of this power?

Solution.   Area of loop $= 8 \times 2 = 16 \text{ cm}^2 = 16 \times 10^{-4} \text{ m}^2$ (in Q. 4)

Rate of change of magnetic field $\dfrac{dB}{dt} = 0.02$ T/s

Resistance of loop $R = 1.6 \ \Omega$

Induced emf of loop $e = \dfrac{d\phi}{dt} = \dfrac{d}{dt} = \dfrac{d}{dt}(BA)$ $(\because \phi = BA)$

$$e = A\frac{dB}{dt}$$

$$e = 16 \times 10^{-4} \times 0.02 = 0.32 \times 10^{-4} \text{ V}$$

Induced current in the loop

$$I = \frac{e}{R} = \frac{0.32 \times 10^{-4}}{1.6} = 0.2 \times 10^{-4} \text{ A}$$

Power of source as heat

$$P = I^2 R = (0.2 \times 10^{-4})^2 \times 1.6 = 6.4 \times 10^{-10} \text{ W}$$

$$P = 6.4 \times 10^{-10} \text{ W}$$

The agency which changing the magnetic field with time is the source of this power.

Question 12. A square loop of side 12 cm with its sides parallel to X and Y-axes is moved with a velocity of 8 cm/s in the positive X-direction in an environment containing a magnetic field in the positive Z-direction. The field is neither uniform in space nor constant in time. It has a gradient of 10^{-3} T/cm along the negative X-direction (that is it increases by 10^{-3} T c/m as one moves in the negative X-direction) and it is decreasing in time at the rate of 10^{-3} T/s. Determine the direction and magnitude of the induced current in the loop if its resistance is 4.50 mΩ.

Solution.   Given, side of loop $a = 12$ cm

$\therefore$ Area of loop $A = a^2 = (12)^2 = 144 \text{ cm}^2 = 144 \times 10^{-4} \text{ m}^2$

$(\because$ Area of square $= (\text{side})^2)$

Velocity $v = 8$ cm/s $= 8 \times 10^{-2}$ m/s   (X-axis)

Rate of change of magnetic field with distance

$$\frac{dB}{dx} = 10^{-3} \text{ T/cm} \qquad (-X\text{-axis})$$

Rate of change of magnetic field with time

$$\frac{dB}{dt} = 10^{-3} \text{ T/s}$$

Resistance of the loop $R = 4.5 \text{ m}\,\Omega = 4.5 \times 10^{-3}\ \Omega$

Rate of change of magnetic flux with respect to time

$$\frac{d\phi}{dt} = \frac{d(BA)}{dt} = \left(\frac{dB}{dt}\right)A$$

$$= 10^{-3} \times 144 \times 10^{-4}$$

$$= 1.44 \times 10^{-5} \text{ Wb/s} \qquad (\because \phi = BA)$$

Rate of change of magnetic flux due to the motion of loop

$$\frac{d\phi}{dt} = \frac{dB}{dx}\cdot A \cdot \frac{dx}{dt} = 10^{-3} \times 144 \times 10^{-4} \times 8 \quad \left(\because \frac{dx}{dt} = \text{velocity}\right)$$

$$= 11.52 \times 10^{-5} \text{ Wb/s}$$

Both of the effects cause a decrease in magnetic flux along the positive Z-direction.

Total induced emf in the loop $e = 1.44 \times 10^{-5} + 11.52 \times 10^{-5}$

$$e = 12.96 \times 10^{-5} \text{ V}$$

Induced current in the loop $= \dfrac{e}{R} = \dfrac{12.96 \times 10^{-5}}{4.5 \times 10^{-3}} = 2.88 \times 10^{-2}$ A

The direction of induced current in such as to increase the flux through the loop along positive Z-direction.

Question 13. It is desired to measure the magnitude of field between the poles of a powerful loud speaker magnet. A small flat search coil of area 2 cm^2 with **25** closely wound turns, is positioned normal to the field direction and then quickly snatched out of the field region. Equivalently, one can give it a quick **90°** turn to bring its plane parallel to the field direction. The total charge flown in the coil (measured by a ballistic galvanometer connected to coil) is 7.5 mC. The combined resistance of the coil and the galvanometer is 0.50 Ω. Estimate the field strength of magnet.

Solution. Area of coil $A = 2 \text{ cm}^2 = 2 \times 10^{-4} \text{ m}^2$

Number of turns $N = 25$

Total charge in the coil $Q = 7.5 \text{ mC} = 7.5 \times 10^{-3} \text{ C}$ $\qquad$ $(1 \text{ mC} = 10^{-3} \text{ C})$

Resistance of coil $R = 0.5 \, \Omega$

When the coil is removed from the field, the flux (final) is zero. $\phi_f = 0$.
Induced current in the coil

$$I = \frac{e}{R} = -\frac{Nd\phi/dt}{R} \qquad \left(\because e = -N\frac{d\phi}{dt} \right)$$

$$I \, dt = -\frac{N}{R} \cdot d\phi$$

Charge in the coil $Q = \int I \, dt = \int_{\phi_i}^{\phi_f} -\frac{N}{R} \, d\phi = -\frac{N}{R}(\phi_f - \phi_i)$

$$Q = \frac{N}{R}(\phi_i - \phi_f) = \frac{N}{R}\phi_i \qquad (\because \phi_f = 0)$$

$$Q = \frac{N}{R}(BA) \qquad (\because \phi_i = BA)$$

Magnetic field in the coil

$$B = \frac{QR}{NA} = \frac{7.5 \times 10^{-3} \times 0.5}{25 \times 2 \times 10^{-4}} = 0.75 \text{ T}$$

Thus, the strength of magnetic field is 0.75 T.

Question 14. Figure shows a metal rod PQ resting on the smooth rails AB and positioned between the poles of a permanent magnet. The rails, the rod and the magnetic field are in three mutual perpendicular directions. A galvanometer G connects the rails through a switch K. Length of the rod = 15 cm, B = 0.50 T, resistance of the closed loop containing the rod = 9.0 mΩ. Assume the field to be uniform.

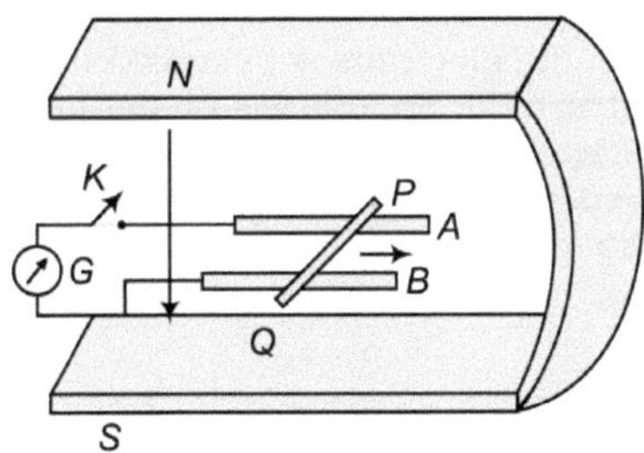

(a) Suppose K is open and the rod is moved with a speed of **12** cm/s in the direction shown. Give the polarity and magnitude of the induced emf.

(b) Is there an excess charge built up at the ends of the rods when K is open? What happend if K is closed?

(c) With K open and the rod moving uniformly, there is no net force on the electrons in the rod PQ even though they do experience magnetic force due to the motion of the rod. Explain.

(d) What is the retarding force on the rod when K is closed?

(e) How much power is required (by an external agent) to keep the rod moving at the same speed ($=12$ cm/s) when K is closed? How much power is required when K is open?

(f) How much power is dissipated as heat in the closed circuit? What is the source of this power?

(g) What is the induced emf in the moving rod if the magnetic field is parallel to the rails instead of being perpendicular?

Solution.   Given, length of rod $\quad l = 15$ cm $= 15 \times 10^{-2}$ m

Magnetic field $\quad B = 0.50$ T,

Resistance of the closed-loop containing the rod
$$R = 9 \text{ m}\Omega = 9 \times 10^{-3}\ \Omega$$

Velocity of rod $v = 12$ cm/s $= 12 \times 10^{-2}$ m/s

(a) The magnitude of the motional emf
$$e = Bvl = 0.50 \times 12 \times 10^{-2} \times 15 \times 10^{-2}$$
$$e = 9 \times 10^{-3} \text{ V}.$$

According to the Fleming's left hand rule, the direction of Lorentz force $[\mathbf{F} = -e\,(\mathbf{v} \times \mathbf{B})]$ on electrons in PQ is from P to Q. So, P would acquire positive charge and Q would acquire negative charge.

(b) Yes, an excess positive charge develops at P and the same amount of negative charge develops at Q as the key is open. When the key K is closed, the induced current flows and maintains the excess charge.

(c) When key is open, there is no net force on the electrons because the presence of excess change at P and Q sets up an electric field and magnetic force on the electrons is balanced by force on them due to force by the electric field. So, there is no net force on the rod.

(d) When the key K is closed, current flow in the loop and the current carrying wire experience a retarding force in the magnetic field. which is given by
$$\text{Force} = BIl = B \cdot \frac{e}{R}\, l = \frac{0.5 \times 9 \times 10^{-3} \times 15 \times 10^{-2}}{9 \times 10^{-3}} = 7.5 \times 10^{-2} \text{ N}$$

(e) To keep the rod moving at the same speed the required power
$$= \text{Retarding force} \times \text{Velocity}$$

$$= 7.5 \times 10^{-2} \times 12 \times 10^{-2}$$

$$= 9 \times 10^{-3} \text{ W}$$

(f) Power dissipated in closed circuit due to flow to current

$$= I^2 R = \left(\frac{e}{R}\right)^2 \times R = \frac{e^2}{R} = \frac{(9 \times 10^{-3})^2}{9 \times 10^{-3}}$$

$$= 9 \times 10^{-3} \text{ W}$$

The source of this power is the external agent.

(g) When the field is parallel to length of rails $\theta = 0°$. Induced emf $= e = Bvl \sin \theta = 0$ ($\because \sin 0° = 0$). In this situation, the moving rod will not cut the field lines so that flux change is zero and hence induced emf is zero.

Question 15. An air-cored solenoid with length 30 cm, area of cross-section 25 cm^2 and number of turns 500, carries a current of 2.5 A. The current is suddenly switched off in a brief time of 10^{-3} s. How much is the average back emf induced across the ends of the open switch in the circuit? Ignore the variation in magnetic field near the ends of the solenoid.

Solution. Given, length of solenoid $l = 30$ cm $= 30 \times 10^{-2}$ m

Area of cross-section $\quad A = 25$ cm$^2 = 25 \times 10^{-4}$ m^2

Number of turns $N = 500$

Current $I_1 = 2.5$ A, $I_2 = 0$

Brief time $dt = 10^{-3}$ s

Induced emf in the solenoid

$$e = \frac{d\phi}{dt} = \frac{d}{dt}(BA) \qquad\qquad (\because \phi = BA)$$

Magnetic field induction B at a point well inside the long solenoid carrying current I is

$$B = \mu_0 n I \text{ (where } n = \text{Number of turns per unit length } = \frac{N}{l}\text{)}$$

$$e = NA\frac{dB}{dt} = A\frac{d}{dt}\left(\mu_0 \frac{N}{l}I\right) = A\frac{\mu_0 N}{l}\cdot\frac{dI}{dt}$$

$$e = 500 \times 25 \times 10^{-4} \times 4 \times 3.14 \times 10^{-7} \times \frac{500}{30 \times 10^{-2}} \times \frac{2.5}{10^{-3}}$$

$$e = 6.5 \text{ V}$$

Question 16. (a) Obtain an expression for the mutual inductance between a long straight wire and a square loop of side a as shown in figure.

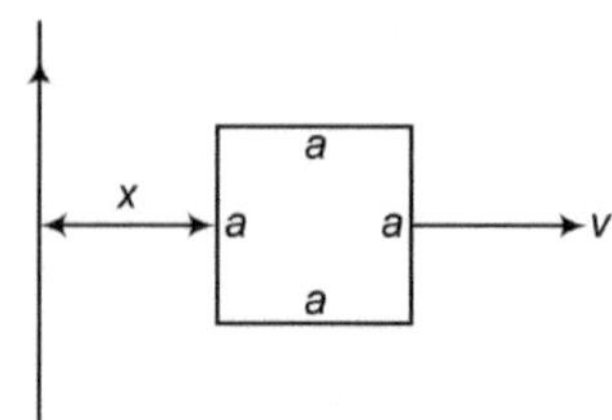

(b) Now, assume that the straight wire carries a current of 50 A and the loop is moved to the right with a constant velocity $v = 10$ m/s. Calculate the induced emf in the loop at the instant when $x = 0.2$ m.

Take $a = 0.1$ m and assume that the loop has a large resistance.

 Use the concept of elementary portion and then integrate to find the total value of magnetic flux linked.

Solution. (a) Let us assume that an elementary strip of width dx at a distance x from the wire carrying current I. Side of square $= a$.

The magnetic field due to current carrying wire at a distance x from the wire is

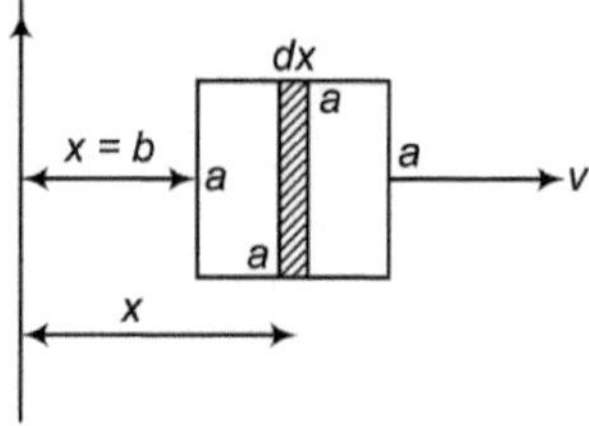

$$B = \frac{\mu_0}{4\pi} \cdot \frac{2I}{x} \qquad \ldots(i)$$

(Using the formula of magnetic field due to an infinitely long wire $B = \frac{\mu_0}{4\pi} \cdot \frac{2I}{x}$)

Small amount of magnetic flux associated with the strip

$$d\phi = B.\,dA = \frac{\mu_0}{4\pi} \cdot \frac{2I}{x} \cdot a\,dx$$

$[\because dA = \text{area of strip} = a\,dx \text{ from Eq. (i)}]$

$$d\phi = \frac{\mu_0}{4\pi} \cdot \frac{Ia}{x} \cdot dx$$

Integrate within proper limits, we get

$$\phi = \frac{\mu_0}{4\pi} \cdot Ia \int_x^{(x+a)} \frac{1}{x}\,dx = \frac{\mu_0}{4\pi} \cdot Ia\,[\ln x]_x^{x+a}$$

$$\phi = \frac{\mu_0}{4\pi} \cdot Ia\,[\ln(x+a) - \ln(x)] = \frac{\mu_0 Ia}{2\pi} \ln\left(\frac{x+a}{x}\right)$$

$$\phi = \frac{\mu_0 Ia}{2\pi} \ln\left(\frac{a}{x} + 1\right) \qquad \ldots(ii)$$

As we know that $\phi = MI$ $\ldots(iii)$

where, M is mutual inductance.

From Eqs. (ii) and (iii), we get

$$MI = \frac{\mu_0 Ia}{2\pi} \ln\left(\frac{a}{x} + 1\right)$$

$$M = \frac{\mu_0 a}{2\pi} \log_e\left(\frac{a}{x} + 1\right)$$

This is the mutual inductance between wire and square loop.

(b) Given, current $\qquad I = 50\,\text{A}$

Velocity $\qquad v = 10\,\text{m/s}$

$\qquad x = 0.2\,\text{m and } a = 0.1\,\text{m}$

Induce emf $\qquad e = -\dfrac{d\phi}{dt} = -\dfrac{d}{dt}\left[I\dfrac{\mu_0 a}{2\pi}\log_e\left(\dfrac{a+x}{x}\right)\right]$

$$= -\frac{\mu_0 aI}{2\pi}\frac{d}{dt}[\log(x+a) - \log x]$$

$$= -\frac{\mu_0 aI}{2\pi}\left[\frac{1}{(x+a)}\frac{d}{dt}(x+a) - \frac{1}{x}\frac{d}{dt}(x)\right]$$

$$= -\frac{\mu_0 aI}{2\pi}\left[\frac{1}{(x+a)}\frac{dx}{dt} - \frac{1}{x}\frac{dx}{dt}\right] \qquad \left[\because \frac{dx}{dt} = v\right]$$

$$= -\frac{\mu_0 aI}{2\pi}\left[\frac{v}{(x+a)} - \frac{v}{x}\right]$$

$$e = \frac{\mu_0}{2\pi}\cdot\frac{a^2 Iv}{x(a+x)}$$

$$e = \frac{4\pi \times 10^{-7}}{2\pi} \times \frac{(0.1)^2 \times (50) \times (10)}{0.2 \times (0.1 + 0.2)}$$

$$= \frac{2 \times 10^{-7} \times 50 \times 10^{-2} \times 10}{0.2 \times 0.3}$$

$$= 1.67 \times 10^{-5}\,\text{V}$$

Question 17. A line charge λ per unit length is lodged uniformly onto the rim of a wheel of mass M and radius R. The wheel has light non-conducting spokes and is free to rotate without friction about its axis (shown in figure). A uniform magnetic field extends over a circular region within the rim. It is given by, $B = -B_0\,\hat{k}$ $(r \leq a; a < R)$

$\qquad\qquad = 0$ (otherwise)

What is the angular velocity of the wheel after the field is suddenly switched off ?

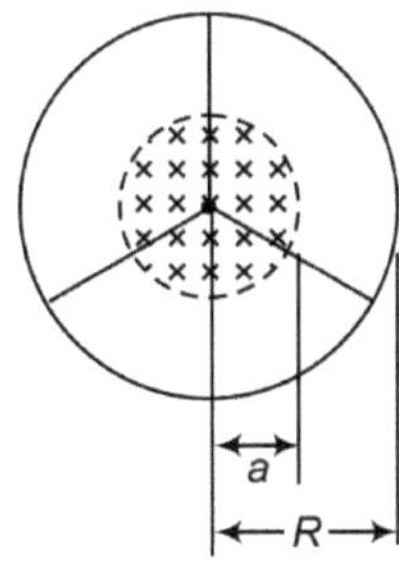

Solution. Given, linear charge density $\lambda = \dfrac{\text{Total charge}}{\text{Length}} = \dfrac{Q}{2\pi R}$ ...(i)

$$\text{Radius of rim} = R$$

$$\text{Mass of rim} = m$$

Magnetic field extends over a circular region

$$\mathbf{B} = -B_0\hat{\mathbf{k}} \ (r \le a, a < R)$$

$$= 0 \quad \text{(otherwise)}$$

Let the angular velocity of the wheel be ω, then

Induced emf $$e = -\frac{d\phi}{dt}$$

Thus, a relation between electric field and rate of charge of flux can be established

$$e = -\int \mathbf{E}.\,dl = -\frac{d\phi}{dt}$$

$\mathbf{E}$ exist along circumference of radius a due to change in magnetic flux

$$e\int dl = -\frac{d}{dt}(\pi a^2 B)$$

$$E \times 2\pi a = -\pi a^2 \frac{dB}{dt}$$

$$E = -\frac{a}{2}\frac{dB}{dt}$$

Force on charge $F = QE = (2\pi a \times \lambda)\left(-\dfrac{a}{2}\dfrac{dB}{dt}\right) = -\pi a^2 \lambda \dfrac{dB}{dt}$

But force $$(F) = \frac{dp}{dt} = \frac{d\,(mv)}{dt} = m\frac{dv}{dt}$$

$\therefore$ $$m\frac{dv}{dt} = -\pi\,a^2\lambda\,\frac{dB}{dt}$$

$$mR\,(d\omega) = -\pi a^2\lambda\,\frac{dB}{dt} \qquad\qquad (\because v = R\omega)$$

$$d\omega = -\frac{\pi a^2\lambda}{mR}\,dB$$

Integrating both sides

$$\omega = -\frac{\pi a^2\lambda B}{mR}$$

As direction of angular velocity is along axis

$$\omega = -\frac{\lambda a^2 \pi}{mR}\,Bv$$

Selected NCERT Exemplar Problems

Question 1. A magnetic field in a certain region is given by $B = B_0 \cos(\omega t)\hat{k}$ and a coil of radius a with resistance R is placed in the X-Y plane with its centre at the origin in the magnetic field (see figure). Find the magnitude and the direction of the current at $(a,0,0)$ at $t = \pi/2\omega$, $t = \pi/\omega$ and $t = 3\pi/2\omega$.

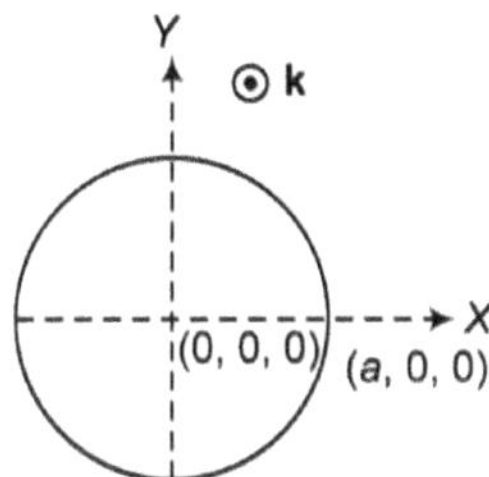

Solution. A magnetic field in a certain region is given by

$$\mathbf{B} = B_0 \cos \omega t \; \hat{k}$$

Given, a = radius of coil, R = resistance.

The flux through the ring is

$$\phi = BA = B_0 A \cos \omega t \qquad (\because A = \pi a^2)$$

$$\phi = B_0 \pi a^2 \cos \omega t$$

$$\text{Induced emf } e = -\frac{d\phi}{dt} = -B_0 \pi a^2 \frac{d}{dt}(\cos \omega t)$$

$$e = + B\pi a^2 \omega \sin \omega t$$

$\therefore$ Induced current

$$I = \frac{e}{R} = \frac{B\pi a^2 \omega \sin \omega t}{R}$$

At time $t = \pi/2\omega$, current

$$I = \frac{B\pi a^2 \omega \sin \omega \cdot \dfrac{\pi}{2\omega}}{R}$$

$$I = \frac{B\pi a^2 \omega}{R} \quad \text{along } \hat{j}$$

At $t = \dfrac{\pi}{\omega}$, current

$$I = \frac{B\pi a^2 \omega \sin \omega \cdot \dfrac{\pi}{\omega}}{R}$$

$$I = 0$$

Again, Current at $t = 3\pi/2\omega$, $I = B\pi a^2 \omega \sin \omega \cdot \dfrac{3\pi}{2\omega}$

$$I = \frac{B\pi a^2 \omega}{R} \quad \text{along } (-\hat{j})$$

Question 2. Find the current in the wire for the configuration shown in figure. Wire PQ has negligible resistance, B the magnetic field is coming out of the paper. θ is a fixed angle made by PQ travelling smoothly over two conducting parallel wires separated by a distance d.

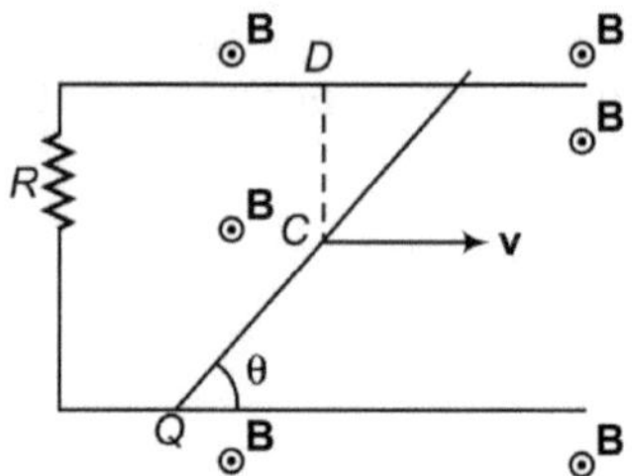

Solution. The motional electric field along $CD = \mathbf{v} \times \mathbf{B} = vB \sin 90° = vB$

Electromagnetic force along $PQ = $ (length PQ) $\times$ (field along PQ)

$$e = \frac{d}{\cos \theta} \times vB \cos \theta$$

$$= vBd$$

So, current in the wire $I = \dfrac{e}{R} = \dfrac{dvB}{R}$, it is independent of q.

Question 3. A magnetic field $B = B_0 \sin(\omega t)\, \hat{k}$ covers a large region, where a wire AB slides smoothly over two parallel conductors separated by a distance d (see figure). The wires are in the X-Y plane. The wire AB (of length d) has resistance R and the parallel wires have negligible resistance. If AB is moving with velocity v, what is the current in the circuit? What is the force needed to keep the wire moving at constant velocity?

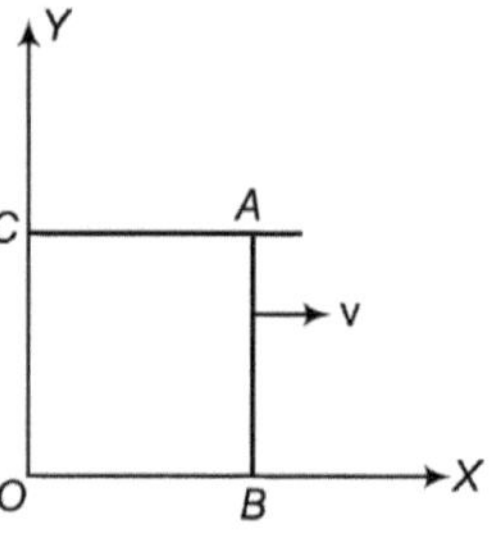

Solution. Given, magnetic field $\mathbf{B} = B_0 \sin \omega t\, \hat{k}$

$AB = d$ and resistance $= R$

Let us assume that the parallel wires are $y = 0$ and $y = d$.

At $t = 0$, wire AB has $x = 0$ and moves with a velocity $v\,\hat{i}$.

At time t, the position of AB wire is at $x = v \times t$

$$\text{Motional emf} = Bvd(-j) = B_0 (\sin \omega t)v \cdot d(-j)$$

Electromagnetic force due to the change in field along $OBAC$

$$= -B_0 \omega \cos \omega t \cdot x \cdot d$$

$$\text{Total emf} = -B_0 d[\omega \times \cos \omega t + v \sin \omega t]$$

Along $OBAC$, current in clockwise direction $= \dfrac{\text{Total emf}}{\text{Resistance}}$

$$\text{Current } I = \frac{B_0 d}{R} \, (\omega x \cos \omega t + v \sin \omega t)$$

Force needed to keep the wire moving at the constant velocity $F = IlB$

$$F = \frac{B_0 d}{R} \, (\omega x \cos \omega t + v \sin \omega t) \times d \cdot B_0 \sin \omega t$$

or

$$F = \frac{B_0^2 d^2}{r} \, [\omega x \cos \omega t + v \sin \omega t] \sin \omega t$$

Question 4. Consider an infinitely long wire carrying a current $I(t)$ with $\dfrac{dI}{dt} = \lambda = \text{constant}$. Find the current produced in the rectangular loop of wire $ABCD$ if its resistance is R (see figure).

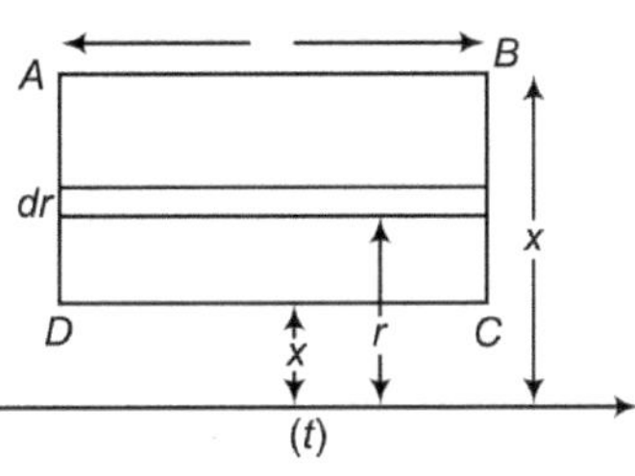

Solution. At the distance r, the magnetic field is

$$\mathbf{B} = \frac{\mu_0 I}{2\pi r} \quad \text{(perpendicularly outwards from the plane of paper)}$$

The magnetic flux through the

$$d\phi = BdA = B \cdot l \cdot dr \qquad [\because \text{ Area} = \text{Length} \times \text{Breadth}]$$

or

$$d\phi = Bldr = \frac{\mu_0 I}{2\pi r} \, l \cdot dr$$

On integrating

$$\phi = \int_{x_0}^{x} \frac{\mu_0 Il}{2\pi r} \cdot dr = \frac{\mu_0 Il}{2\pi} \int_{x_0}^{x} \frac{dr}{r}$$

$$\phi = \frac{\mu_0 I}{2\pi} \cdot l \, [\log_e r]_{x_0}^{x} = \frac{\mu_0 Il}{2\pi} \log_e \left(\frac{x}{x_0} \right)$$

Induced emf

$$e = \frac{d\phi}{dt} = \frac{d}{dt} \left(\frac{\mu_0 Il}{2\pi} \log_e \frac{x}{x_0} \right)$$

The current produced in the rectangular loop of wire $ABCD$

$$I = \frac{e}{R} = \frac{\mu_0 l}{2\pi R} \log_e \left(\frac{x}{x_0} \right) \frac{dI}{dt}$$

$$I = \frac{\mu_0 l\lambda}{2\pi R} \log_e \frac{x}{x_0} \qquad \left[\because \frac{dI}{dt} = \lambda \right]$$

Question 5. A magnetic field B is confined to a region $r \le a$ and points out of the paper (the Z-axis), $r = 0$ being the centre of the circular region. A charged ring (charge $= Q$) of radius b, $b > a$ and mass m lies in the X-Y plane with its centre at the origin. The ring is free to rotate and is at rest. The magnetic field is brought to zero in time Δt. Find the angular velocity ω of the ring after the field vanishes.

Solution. Let E be the electric field and the length of ring is $2\pi b$.

The emf $= E \times 2\pi b$ $\hspace{3cm}$ ...(i)

The induced emf $= \dfrac{d\phi}{dt} = \dfrac{d}{dt} BA = \dfrac{B \cdot \pi a^2}{dt}$ $\hspace{2cm}$ ...(ii)

From Eqs. (i) and (ii), we get

$$E \times 2\pi b = \dfrac{B\pi a^2}{dt}$$

$$E = \dfrac{Ba^2}{2b \cdot dt} \hspace{2cm} ...(iii)$$

$$\text{Torque} = \text{Force} \times \text{Perpendicular distance}$$

$$= QE \times b = \dfrac{Q \cdot Ba^2}{2b \cdot dt} \cdot b = \dfrac{QBa^2}{2dt}$$

If dL be the change in angular momentum

$$\dfrac{dL}{dt} = \text{torque} = \dfrac{Q \cdot Ba^2}{2 \cdot dt} \quad \text{or} \quad dL = \dfrac{QBa^2}{2}$$

Initial angular momentum $= 0$

and final angular momentum $= mb^2\omega = \dfrac{QBa^2}{2}$

The angular velocity ω of the ring $\quad \omega = \dfrac{QBa^2}{2mb^2}$

Question 6. A metallic ring of mass m and radius l (ring being horizontal) is falling under gravity in a region having a magnetic field. If Z is the vertical direction, the z-component of magnetic field is $\mathbf{B}_z = B_0 (1 + \lambda z)$. If R is the resistance of the ring and if the ring falls with a velocity v. Find the energy lost in the resistance. If the ring has reached a constant velocity, use the conservation of energy to determine v in terms of m, B, λ and acceleration due to gravity g.

Solution. Given, mass of ring $= m$

$$\text{Radius of ring} = l$$

The Z-component of magnetic field $\mathbf{B}_z = B_0 (1 + \lambda z)$

R is the resistance of the ring and v is the velocity. Rate of change in flux

$$\dfrac{d\phi}{dt} = \dfrac{d}{dt} (BA)$$

$$\dfrac{d\phi}{dt} = \dfrac{dB}{dt} \cdot A = \pi l^2 \dfrac{d}{dt} B_0 (1 + \lambda z) = \pi l^2 \cdot B_0 \lambda \dfrac{dz}{dt} \hspace{1.5cm} ...(i)$$

$$[\because \text{Area } A = \pi r^2]$$

We know that, the rate of change in flux

$$\dfrac{d\phi}{dt} = e = IR \hspace{3cm} ...(ii)$$

From Eqs. (i) and (ii), we get

$$IR = \pi l^2 \cdot B_0 \lambda \frac{dz}{dt}$$

$$I = \frac{\pi l^2 B_0 \lambda}{R} \cdot v \qquad \left[\because \frac{dz}{dt} = v \right]$$

$$\text{Energy lost/s} = I^2 R = \frac{(\pi l^2 B_0 \lambda)^2 v^2}{R}$$

This is equal to rate of change in potential energy

i.e.,
$$mg \frac{dz}{dt} = mgv = \frac{(\pi l^2 \lambda B_0)^2 v^2}{R}$$

$$\text{Velocity of the ring } v = \frac{mgR}{(\pi l^2 \lambda B_0)^2}$$

Question 7. A long solenoid S has n turns per metre, with diameter a. At the centre of this coil we place a smaller coil of N turns and diameter b (where, $b < a$). If the current in the solenoid increases linearly with time, what is the induced emf appearing in the smaller coil? Plot graph showing nature of variation in emf, if current varies as a function of $mt^2 + C$.

Solution. Given, diameter of solenoid is d, number of turns per length is n.
Magnetic field due to a solenoid $\mathbf{B} = \mu_0 n I$
Magnetic field in smaller coil $\phi = NBA$ (where, $A = \pi b^2$)
Induced emf appearing in the smaller coil

$$e = -\frac{d\phi}{dt} = -\frac{d}{dt}(NBA) = -N \cdot \pi b^2 \frac{dB}{dt} = -N \pi b^2 \frac{d}{dt}(\mu_0 n I)$$

or
$$e = -N \pi b^2 \mu_0 n \frac{dI}{dt}$$

or
$$e = -N \pi b^2 \mu_0 \frac{nd}{dt}(mt^2 + C) \qquad [\because I = mt^2 + C \, (dI = mt^2 + C)]$$

$$e = -\mu_0 N n \pi b^2 \cdot 2mt$$

The negative sign shows that the opposite nature of induced emf by Lenz's law.
Variation of emf (e) with time (t)

$$e = -\mu_0 N n \pi t b^2 \cdot 2mt$$

or
$$e \propto t$$

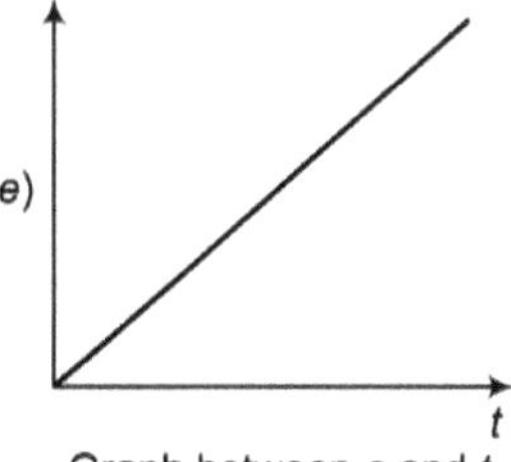

Graph between e and t

Chapter 7

Alternating Current

Important Results

1. The alternating voltage $V = V_0 \sin \omega t$ applied to a resistor R drives a current $I = I_0 \sin \omega t$, where $I_0 = \dfrac{V_0}{R}$. The current is in the phase with applied voltage.

2. The mean value of voltage and current for half cycle is given by
$$V_m = \frac{2V_0}{\pi} = 0.637 \, V_0$$
$$I_m = \frac{2I_0}{\pi} = 0.637 \, I_0$$

3. The mean value of voltage and current for complete cycle is zero.

4. The virtual value or rms value of voltage and current flowing in the circuit is given by (for complete cycle)
$$V_{\mathrm{rms}} = \frac{V_0}{\sqrt{2}} = 0.707 \, V_0$$
$$I_{\mathrm{rms}} = \frac{I_0}{\sqrt{2}} = 0.707 \, I_0$$

5. For a pure resistance circuit-the applied voltage
$V = V_0 \sin \omega t$

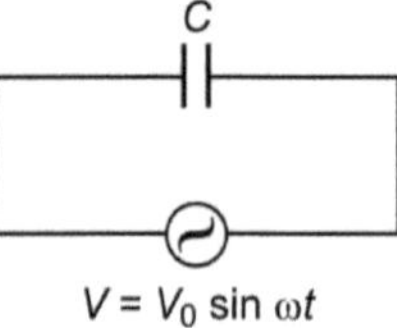

Current $I = I_0 \sin \omega t$

Resistance of AC circuit $= R$

Phase change is zero.

6. For a pure conductive circuit (containing capacitor only),
Applied voltage $V = V_0 \sin \omega t$

Current $I = I_0 \sin (\omega t + 90°)$

Capacitive reactance $X_C = \dfrac{1}{\omega C} = \dfrac{1}{2\pi f C}$

$$I_{\mathrm{rms}} = \frac{E_{\mathrm{rms}}}{X_C}$$

Average power consumed $= E_{\mathrm{rms}} \cdot I_{\mathrm{rms}} \cos 90° = 0$

Current leads the applied voltage by 90°.

7. For a pure inductive circuit,

Applied voltage $V = V_0 \sin \omega t$

Current $I = I_0 \sin (\omega t - 90°)$

Inductive reactance $X_L = \omega L = 2\pi f L$

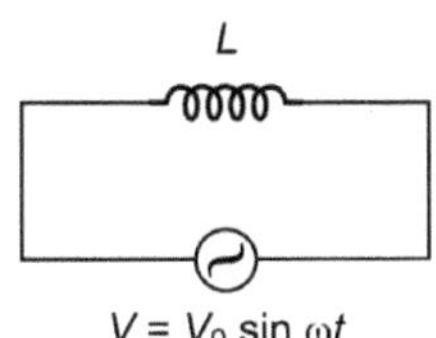

$$I_{rms} = \frac{E_{rms}}{X_L}$$

Average power consumed $= E_{rms} \cdot I_{rms} \cos 90° = 0$

Current lags behind the applied voltage by 90°.

8. For a series *LCR* circuit,

Applied voltage $V = V_0 \sin \omega t$

Current $I = I_0 \sin (\omega t + \phi)$

where, ϕ is the phase difference between current and voltage.

Impedance of circuit

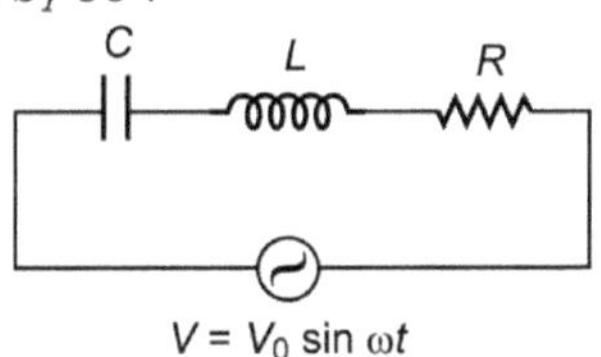

$$Z = \sqrt{R^2 + (X_L - X_C)^2}$$

$$\phi = \tan^{-1}\left(\frac{X_L - X_C}{R}\right)$$

$$\begin{bmatrix} X_L = \omega L \\ X_C = \dfrac{1}{\omega C} \end{bmatrix}$$

$$I_{rms} = \frac{E_{rms}}{Z} = \frac{E_{rms}}{\sqrt{R^2 + (X_L - X_C)^2}}$$

Average power consumed $P = I_{rms} \cdot V_{rms} \cdot \cos \phi$

(i) In case of AC circuit containing R and L

$$Z = \sqrt{R^2 + X_L^2}$$

(ii) In case of AC circuit containing R and C

$$Z = \sqrt{R^2 + X_C^2}$$

(iii) In case of AC circuit containing L and C, $Z = X_L - X_C$

9. In the condition of resonance in *LCR* circuit, the resonant frequency

$$\omega_0 = \frac{1}{\sqrt{LC}}$$

Quality factor $Q = \dfrac{\omega_0 L}{R} = \dfrac{1}{\omega_0 CR}$

10. In case of transformer, if there is no energy loss

$$\frac{V_S}{V_P} = \frac{N_S}{N_P} = K \text{ (transformation ratio)}$$

V_S = number of turns in secondary coil
V_P = number of turns in primary coil
N_S = number of turns in secondary coil
N_P = number of turns in primary coil

If $V_S > V_P$ or $N_S > N_P \rightarrow$ step up transformer

$\qquad N_S < N_P \rightarrow$ step down transformer

Efficiency of a transformer is given by $\eta = \dfrac{V_S - I_S}{V_P I_P}$

Exercises

Question 1. A $100\,\Omega$ resistor is connected to a **220 V, 50 Hz** AC supply.
  (a) What is the rms value of current in the circuit?
  (b) What is the net power consumed over a full cycle?

Solution   Given, resistance $R = 100\,\Omega$

$$V_{\text{rms}} = 220\text{ V}$$

(whenever a supply value is given, it means it is rms value)

$$\text{Frequency } f = 50\text{ Hz}$$

(a) Current in the circuit

$$I_{\text{rms}} = \frac{V_{\text{rms}}}{R} = \frac{220}{100} = 2.2\text{ A}$$

(b) Net power consumed in full cycle

$$P = V_{\text{rms}} \times I_{\text{rms}}$$
$$= 220 \times 2.2 = 484\text{ W}$$

Question 2. (a) The peak voltage of an AC supply is 300 V. What is the rms voltage?
  (b) The rms value of current in an AC circuit is 10 A. What is the peak current?

Use relation between peak value and rms value of voltage/current.

$$V_{\text{rms}} = \frac{V_0}{\sqrt{2}} \text{ and } I_{\text{rms}} = \frac{I_0}{\sqrt{2}}$$

Solution   (a) Given, peak value of voltage $V_0 = 300$ V

The rms value of current $I_{\text{rms}} = 10$ A
The rms value of voltage

$$V_{\text{rms}} = \frac{V_0}{\sqrt{2}} = \frac{300}{\sqrt{2}} = 212.1\text{ V}$$

(b) Using the formula, $I_{rms} = \dfrac{I_0}{\sqrt{2}}$

The peak value of current

$$I_0 = \sqrt{2}\, I_{rms} = \sqrt{2} \times 10 = 14.14 \text{ A}$$

Question 3.   A 44 mH inductor is connected to 220 V, 50 Hz AC supply. Determine the rms value of the current in the circuit.

Solution   Given, inductance $L = 44 \text{ mH} = 44 \times 10^{-3}$ H

$$V_{rms} = 220 \text{ V}$$

Frequency of inductor $f = 50$ Hz

Inductive reactance $X_L = 2\pi f L$

$$= 2 \times 3.14 \times 50 \times 44 \times 10^{-3}$$

$$= 13.83 \,\Omega$$

The rms value of current in the circuit

$$I_{rms} = \frac{V_{rms}}{X_L} = \frac{220}{13.83} = 15.9 \text{ A}$$

Question 4.   A 60 µF capacitor is connected to a 110 V, 60 Hz AC supply. Determine the rms value of the current in the circuit.

Solution   Given, capacitance of the capacitor $C = 60 \,\mu\text{F} = 60 \times 10^{-6}$ F

$$V_{rms} = 110 \text{ V}$$

Frequency of AC supply $f = 60$ Hz

Capacitive reactance $X_C = \dfrac{1}{2\pi f C} = \dfrac{1}{2 \times 3.14 \times 60 \times 60 \times 10^{-6}} = 44.23 \,\Omega$

The rms value of the current in the circuit

$$V_{rms} = \frac{V_{rms}}{X_C}$$

$$= \frac{110}{44.23} = 2.49 \text{ A}$$

Question 5.   In Q. 3 and 4, what is the net power absorbed by each circuit over a complete cycle? Explain your answer.

Solution   **In Q. 3** Average power $P = V_{rms}\, I_{rms} \cos \phi$

As we know that the phase difference between current and voltage in case of inductor is 90°.

$$P = V_{rms}\, I_{rms} \cos 90° = 0$$

In Q. 4 Average power $P = V_{rms} \cdot I_{rms} \cos \phi$

We know that the phase difference between current and voltage in case of capacitor is 90°.

$$P = V_{rms} I_{rms} \cos 90° = 0$$

Question 6. Obtain the resonant frequency ω of a series LCR circuit with $L = 2.0$ H, $C = 32$ μF and $R = 10$ Ω. What is the Q-value of this circuit?

Solution   Given, $L = 2$ H, $C = 32$ μF, $R = 10 \, \Omega$

Resonant angular frequency

$$\omega_r = \frac{1}{\sqrt{LC}} = \frac{1}{\sqrt{2 \times 32 \times 10^{-6}}} = 125 \text{ rad/s}$$

Q-factor of this circuit,

$$Q = \frac{1}{R}\sqrt{\frac{L}{C}} = \frac{1}{10}\sqrt{\frac{2}{32 \times 10^{-5}}} = \frac{10^3}{40} = 25$$

Question 7. A charged 30 μF capacitor is connected to a 27 mH inductor. What is the angular frequency of free oscillations of the circuit?

Solution   Capacitance of capacitor $C = 30$ μF $= 30 \times 10^{-6}$ F

Inductance $L = 27$ mH $= 27 \times 10^{-3}$ H

For free oscillations, the angular frequency should be resonant frequency.

Resonant angular frequency of oscillation of the circuit

$$\omega_r = \frac{1}{\sqrt{LC}}$$

$$= \frac{1}{\sqrt{27 \times 10^{-3} \times 30 \times 10^{-6}}} = \frac{10^4}{9}$$

$$= 1.1 \times 10^3 \text{ rad/s}$$

Question 8. Suppose the initial charge on the capacitor in Q. 7 is 6 mC. What is the total energy stored in the circuit initially? What is the total energy at later time?

Solution   Given, charge on the capacitor

$$Q = 6 \text{ mC} = 6 \times 10^{-3} \text{ C}$$

$$C = 30 \, \mu\text{F} \qquad\qquad\qquad \text{(given in Q. 7)}$$

$$= 30 \times 10^{-6} \text{ F}$$

Energy stored in the circuit

$$E = \frac{Q^2}{2C} = \frac{(6 \times 10^{-3})^2}{2 \times 30 \times 10^{-2}}$$

$$= \frac{36}{60} = 0.6 \text{ J}$$

After some time, the energy is shared between C and L, but the total energy remains constant. So, we assume that there is no loss of energy.

Question 9. A series LCR circuit with $R = 20\ \Omega$, $L = 1.5$ H and $C = 35$ μF is connected to a variable frequency 200 V AC supply. When the frequency of the supply equals the natural frequency of the circuit, what is the average power transferred to the circuit in one complete cycle?

Solution Given, resistance $R = 20\ \Omega$, inductance $L = 1.5$ H, capacitance $C = 35\ \mu\text{F} = 35 \times 10^{-6}$ F and voltage $V_{rms} = 200$ V

When the frequency of the supply equal to the natural frequency of the circuit, this is the condition of resonance. At the condition of resonance,

Impedance $Z = R = 20\ \Omega$

The rms value of current in the circuit

$$I_{rms} = \frac{V_{rms}}{Z} = \frac{200}{20} = 10 \text{ A}$$

$$\phi = 0° \qquad\qquad \text{(for resonance)}$$

Power transferred to the circuit in one complete cycle

$$P = I_{rms} \cdot V_{rms} \cos \phi = 10 \times 200 \times \cos 0° = 2000 \text{ W}$$

$$= 2 \text{ kW}$$

Question 10. A radio can tune over the frequency range of a portion of MW broadcast band: (800 kHz to 1200 kHz). If its LC circuit has an effective inductance of 200 μH, what must be the range of its variable capacitor?

[Hint For tuning, the natural frequency *i.e.*, the frequency of free oscillations of the LC circuit should be equal to the frequency of the radiowave.]

Solution Given, minimum frequency $f_1 = 800$ kHz $= 8 \times 10^5$ Hz

$$\text{Inductance } L = 200\ \mu\text{H} = 200 \times 10^{-6} \text{ H} = 2 \times 10^{-4} \text{ H}$$

$$\text{Maximum frequency } f_2 = 1200 \text{ kHz} = 12 \times 10^5 \text{ Hz}$$

For tuning, the natural frequency is equal to the frequency of oscillations that means it is the case of resonance.

$$\text{Frequency of oscillations } f = \frac{1}{2\pi \sqrt{LC}}$$

For capacitance C_1, $\qquad f_1 = \dfrac{1}{2\pi \sqrt{LC_1}}$

$$C_1 = \frac{1}{4\pi^2 f_1^2 L} = \frac{1}{4 \times 3.14 \times 3.14 \times (8 \times 10^5)^2 \times 2 \times 10^{-4}}$$

$$= 197.7 \times 10^{-12} \text{ F}$$

$$= 197.7 \text{ pF}$$

For capacitance C_2, $\quad f_2 = \dfrac{1}{2\pi\sqrt{LC_2}}$

$$C_2 = \dfrac{1}{4\pi^2 f_2^2 L} = \dfrac{1}{4 \times 3.14 \times 3.14 \times (12 \times 10^5)^2 \times 2 \times 10^{-4}}$$

$$= 87.8 \times 10^{-12} \text{ F}$$

$$= 87.8 \text{ pF}$$

Thus, the range of capacitor is 87.8 pF to 197.7 pF.

Question 11. Figure shows a series LCR circuit connected to a variable frequency 230 V source.

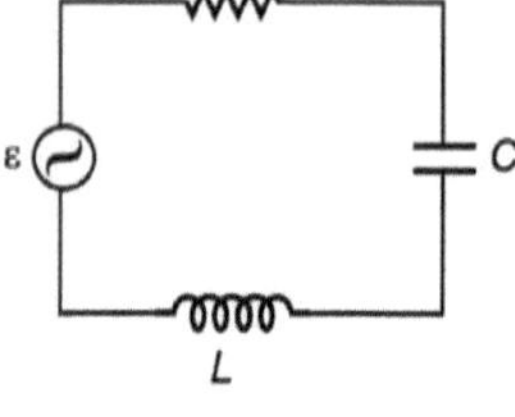

$$L = 5.0 \text{ H}, C = 80 \text{ }\mu\text{F}, R = 40 \text{ }\Omega.$$

(a) Determine the source frequency which drives the circuit in resonance.

(b) Obtain the impedance of the circuit and the amplitude of current at the resonating frequency.

(c) Determine the rms potential drops across the three elements of the circuit. Show that the potential drop across the LC combination is zero at the resonating frequency.

Solution Given, the rms value of voltage $\quad V_{rms} = 230$ V

$$\text{Inductance} \quad L = 5\,\text{H}$$

$$\text{Capacitance } C = 80 \text{ }\mu\text{F} = 80 \times 10^{-6}\,\text{F}$$

$$\text{Resistance} \quad R = 40 \text{ }\Omega$$

(a) For resonance frequency of circuit

$$\omega_r = \dfrac{1}{\sqrt{LC}} = \dfrac{1}{\sqrt{5 \times 80 \times 10^{-6}}} = 50 \text{ rad/s}$$

Source frequency at resonance, then

$$v_0 = \dfrac{\omega_0}{2\pi} = \dfrac{50}{2 \times 3.14}$$

$$= 7.76 \text{ Hz}$$

(b) At the resonant frequency, $\quad X_L = X_C$

So, impedance of the circuit $\quad Z = R$

$\therefore \qquad\qquad\qquad$ Impedance $Z = 40 \text{ }\Omega$

The rms value of current in the circuit

$$I_{rms} = \dfrac{V_{rms}}{Z} = \dfrac{230}{40} = 5.75 \text{ A}$$

Amplitude of current $I_0 = I_{rms}\sqrt{2}$

$$= 5.75 \times \sqrt{2} = 8.13 \text{ A}$$

(c) The rms potential drop across L,

$$V_L = I_{rms} \times X_L = I_{rms} \times \omega_r L$$
$$= 5.75 \times 50 \times 5 = 1437.5 \text{ V}$$

The rms potential drop across R

$$V_R = I_{rms} R = 5.75 \times 40 = 230 \text{ V}$$

The rms potential drop across C,

$$V_C = I_{rms} \times X_C = I_{rms} \times \frac{1}{\omega_r C}$$

$$= 5.75 \times \frac{1}{50 \times 80 \times 10^{-6}}$$

$$= 1437.5 \text{ V}$$

Potential drop across LC combinations

$$= I_{rms} (X_L - X_C)$$
$$= I_{rms} (X_L - X_L) = 0 \quad (\because X_L = X_C \text{ in resonance})$$

Additional Exercises

Question 12. An LC circuit contains a 20 mH inductor and a 50 μF capacitor with an initial charge of 10 mC. The resistance of the circuit is negligible.
Let the instant the circuit is closed be $t = 0$.

(a) What is the total energy stored initially? Is it conserved during LC oscillations?
(b) What is the natural frequency of the circuit?
(c) At what time is the energy stored
   (i) completely electrical (*i.e.*, stored in the capacitor)?
   (ii) completely magnetic (*i.e.*, stored in the inductor)?
(d) At what times is the total energy shared equally between the inductor and the capacitor?
(e) If a resistor is inserted in the circuit, how much energy is eventually dissipated as heat?

Solution   Given, inductance $L = 20 \text{ mH} = 20 \times 10^{-3} \text{ H}$

Capacitance of capacitor $C = 50 \mu\text{F} = 50 \times 10^{-6} \text{ F}$

Initial charge on the capacitor, $Q_i = 10 \text{ mC} = 10 \times 10^{-3} \text{ C}$

(a) The total energy stored across the capacitor initially,

$$E = \frac{q^2}{2C}$$

$$\therefore \qquad E_i = \frac{Q_i^2}{2C} = \frac{(10 \times 10^{-3})^2}{2 \times 50 \times 10^{-6}} = \frac{10^{-4}}{10^{-4}}$$

or $\qquad\qquad\qquad\qquad E_i = 1\,\text{J}$

Yes, this energy is conserved during LC oscillations.

(b) To get the natural frequency or resonant frequency,

$$f_r = \frac{1}{2\pi\sqrt{LC}} = \frac{1}{2 \times 3.14 \times \sqrt{20 \times 10^{-3} \times 50 \times 10^{-6}}}$$

$$= \frac{7 \times 10^3}{44} = 159.2\,\text{Hz}$$

The natural frequency of the circuit

$$\omega = 2\pi v = 2\pi \times 159.2$$

$$= 999.78 \approx 1000 = 10^3 \text{ rad/s}$$

(c) (i) Let at any instant, the energy stored is completely electrical.
The charge on the capacitor $Q = Q_0 \cos \omega t$

$$Q = Q_0 \cos \frac{2\pi}{T}.t \qquad\qquad\qquad ...(i)$$

Q is maximum as it is equal to Q_0, only if

$$\therefore \qquad \cos \frac{2\pi}{T} t = \pm 1 = \cos n\pi \text{ or } t = \frac{nT}{2}, \qquad \text{where } n = 0, 1, 2, 3, \ldots$$

$$\therefore \qquad\qquad t = 0, \frac{T}{2}, T, \frac{3T}{2}, \ldots$$

Thus, the energy stored is completely electrical (energy stored in capacitor) at $t = 0, \dfrac{T}{2}, T, \dfrac{3T}{2}, \ldots$

(ii) Let at any instant, the energy stored is completely magnetic as when the electrical energy across the capacitor is zero.

$$q = 0$$

$$Q = Q_0 \cos \frac{2\pi t}{T} = 0 \qquad\qquad\qquad [\text{from Eq.(i)}]$$

$$\therefore \qquad \cos \frac{2\pi}{T} t = 0 = \cos \frac{n\pi}{2} \text{ or } t = \frac{nT}{4}, \qquad \text{where } n = 0, 1, 2, 3, \ldots$$

It happens if $t = \dfrac{T}{4}, \dfrac{3T}{4}, \dfrac{5T}{4}, \ldots$

Thus, the energy stored is completely magnetic (energy stored in an inductor) at $t = \dfrac{T}{4}, \dfrac{3T}{4}, \dfrac{5T}{4}, \ldots$

(d) Equal sharing of energy between inductor and capacitor means the energy stored in capacitor $= \dfrac{1}{2} \times \text{Maximum energy}$

$$\frac{Q^2}{2C} = \frac{1}{2} \cdot \frac{Q_0^2}{2C}$$

$$Q = \frac{Q_0}{\sqrt{2}} \qquad\qquad \ldots(ii)$$

From
$$Q = Q_0 \cos \omega t = Q_0 \cos \frac{2\pi}{T} \cdot t$$

$$\frac{Q_0}{\sqrt{2}} = Q_0 \cos \frac{2\pi t}{T} \qquad\qquad \text{[from Eq. (ii)]}$$

$$\frac{1}{\sqrt{2}} = \cos \frac{2\pi t}{T}$$

or
$$\cos (2n + 1) \frac{\pi}{4} = \cos \frac{2\pi t}{T}$$

$$\frac{(2n + 1)\,\pi}{4} = \frac{2\pi t}{T}$$

$$t = \frac{T}{8}(2n + 1) \qquad\qquad (n = 0, 1, 2, 3, \ldots)$$

Hence, the energy will be shared half on capacitor and half on inductor,

$$t = \frac{T}{8}, \frac{3T}{8}, \frac{5T}{8}, \ldots$$

(e) As a resistor is inserted in the circuit, all of the energy loss during heating. Energy loss $=1$ J. The oscillations becomes damped and becomes disappear after sometime as the total energy loss in the form of heat.

Question 13. A coil of inductance 0.50 H and resistance $100\ \Omega$ is connected to a 240 V, 50 Hz AC supply.

    (a) What is the maximum current in the coil?

    (b) What is the time lag between the voltage maximum and the current maximum?

Solution   Given, inductance $L = 0.50$ H

Resistance $R = 100\ \Omega$

The rms value of voltage $V_{rms} = 240$ V, $f = 50$ Hz

    (a) Impedance of circuit

$$Z = \sqrt{R^2 + X_L^2} = \sqrt{R^2 + (2\pi f L)^2}$$

$$= \sqrt{(100)^2 + (2 \times 3.14 \times 50 \times 0.50)^2}$$

$$= 186.14\ \Omega$$

The rms value of current $I_{rms} = \dfrac{V_{rms}}{Z} = \dfrac{240}{186.14} = 1.29$ A

The maximum value of current in the circuit

$$I_0 = \sqrt{2}\, I_{rms} = 1.414 \times 1.29 = 1.824 \text{ A}$$

(b) Using the formula of time lag,

$$t = \frac{\phi}{\omega}$$

$$\tan \phi = \frac{X_L}{R} = \frac{\omega L}{R} = \frac{2\pi f L}{R} = \frac{2 \times 3.14 \times 50 \times 0.50}{100}$$

$$\phi = \tan^{-1}(1.571) = 57.5°$$

$$= \frac{57.5}{180}\, \pi \text{ rad}$$

$$\text{Time lag } t = \frac{\phi}{\omega} = \frac{57.5\,\pi}{180 \times 2\pi f}$$

$$= \frac{57.5}{180 \times 2 \times 50}$$

$$= 3.19 \times 10^{-3} \text{ s}$$

Thus, the time lag between the voltage maximum and the current maximum is 3.19×10^{-3} s.

Question 14. Obtain the answers (a) to (b) in Q. 13, if the circuit is connected to a high frequency supply (240 V, 10 kHz). Hence, explain the statement that at very high frequency, an inductor in a circuit nearly amounts to an open circuit. How does an inductor behave in a DC circuit after the steady state?

Solution   Given, frequency $f = 10$ kHz $= 10^4$ Hz

The rms value of voltage $V_{rms} = 240$ V

From Q. 13

Resistance $R = 100\,\Omega$

Inductance $L = 0.5$ H

Inductance $Z = \sqrt{R^2 + X_L^2} = \sqrt{R^2 + (2\pi f L)^2}$

$$= \sqrt{(100)^2 + (2 \times 3.14 \times 10^4 \times 0.5)^2} = 31400.15\,\Omega$$

The rms value of current

$$I_{rms} = \frac{V_{rms}}{Z} = \frac{240}{31400.15} = 0.00764 \text{ A}$$

Maximum value of current

$$I_0 = \sqrt{2}\, I_{rms} = 1.414 \times 0.00764 = 0.01080 \text{ A}$$

and $\qquad\qquad \tan \phi = \dfrac{X_L}{R} = \dfrac{2 \times \pi \times 10000 \times 0.5}{100}$

$$\tan \phi = 100\,\pi \qquad\qquad \text{(very large)}$$

On comparison, we find that at low frequencies $I_0 = 1.82$ A and at high frequencies, $I_0 = 0.0108$ A. That means at very high frequencies, inductor offer very large resistances or we can say that it nearly behaves open circuit.

In case of DC circuit, after a steady state $\omega = 0$.

Thus, $X_L = \omega L = 0$. Hence, L acts like a pure conductor of negligible inductive reactance.

Question 15. A 100 μF capacitor in series with a 40 Ω resistance is connected to a 110 V, 60 Hz supply.

    (a) What is the maximum current in the circuit?

    (b) What is the time lag between the current maximum and the voltage maximum?

Solution   Given, capacitance of capacitor $C = 100\ \mu F = 100 \times 10^{-6}$ F

Resistance $R = 40\ \Omega$

The rms value of voltage $V_{rms} = 110$ V

Frequency $f = 60$ Hz

  (a) Impedance $Z = \sqrt{R^2 + X_C^2} = \sqrt{R^2 + \left(\dfrac{1}{2\pi f C}\right)^2}$

$$= \sqrt{(40)^2 + \left(\dfrac{1}{2 \times 3.14 \times 60 \times 10^{-6} \times 100}\right)^2}$$

$$= \sqrt{1600 + 704.33} = 48\ \Omega$$

The rms value of current

$$I_{rms} = \frac{V_{rms}}{Z} = \frac{110}{48}$$

The maximum current in the circuit

$$I_0 = \sqrt{2} I_{rms} = 1.414 \times \frac{110}{48} = 3.24\ \text{A}$$

  (b) Time lag $(t) = \dfrac{\phi}{\omega}$

$$\tan \phi = \frac{X_C}{R} = \frac{1}{2\pi f C R} = \frac{1}{2 \times 3.14 \times 60 \times 10^{-4} \times 40}$$

$$\phi = \tan^{-1}(0.6628) = 33.5° = \frac{33.5\ \pi}{180}$$

$$\text{Time lag} = \frac{33.5\ \pi}{180 \times 2\pi \times 60} = 1.55 \times 10^{-3}\ \text{s}$$

Thus, the time lag between voltage maximum and current maximum is 1.55×10^{-3} s.

Question 16. Obtain the answers to (a) and (b) in Q. 15, if the circuit is connected to a 110 V, 12 kHz supply. Hence, explain the statement that a capacitor is a conductor at very high frequencies. Compare this behaviour with that of a capacitor in a DC circuit after the steady state.

Solution Given, the rms value of voltage, $V_{rms} = 110\,\text{V}$

The frequency of capacitor $f = 12\,\text{kHz} = 12000\,\text{Hz}$

Capacitance of capacitor $C = 10^{-4}\,\text{F}$

Resistance $R = 40\,\Omega$

Capacitive reactance $X_C = \dfrac{1}{2\pi f C} = \dfrac{1}{2 \times 3.14 \times 12000 \times 10^{-4}} = 0.133\,\Omega$

The rms value of current

$$I_{rms} = \frac{V_{rms}}{\sqrt{X_C^2 + R^2}} = \frac{110}{\sqrt{(40)^2 + (0.133)^2}} = 2.75\,\text{A}$$

The maximum value of current, $I_0 = \sqrt{2}\,I_{rms} = 1.414 \times 2.75 = 3.9\,\text{A}$

Here, the value of X_C is very small, so term containing C is negligible.

$$\tan\phi = \frac{1}{\omega C R} = \frac{1}{2 \times 3.14 \times 12000 \times 10^{-4} \times 40} = \frac{1}{96\,\pi}$$

It is very very small.
So, at high frequency ϕ tends to zero.
By comparison, at very high frequency, the resistance due to capacitor is negligible and hence, it works like a pure conductor of negligible capacitive reactance.
In DC circuits, $\omega = 0$ (at steady state)

$$X_C = \frac{1}{\omega C} = \infty$$

So, it behaves like an open circuit.

Question 17. Keeping the source frequency equal to the resonating frequency of the series LCR circuit, if the three elements, L, C and R are arranged in parallel, show that the total current in the parallel LCR circuit is minimum at this frequency. Obtain the current rms value in each branch of the circuit for the elements and source specified in Q. 11 for this frequency.

Solution As they are connected in the parallel combination

$$\frac{1}{Z} = \frac{1}{R} + \left(\frac{1}{X_L} - \frac{1}{X_C}\right)$$

As the reactance $(X_C - X_L)$ is perpendicular to the ohmic resistance R, therefore we can write as

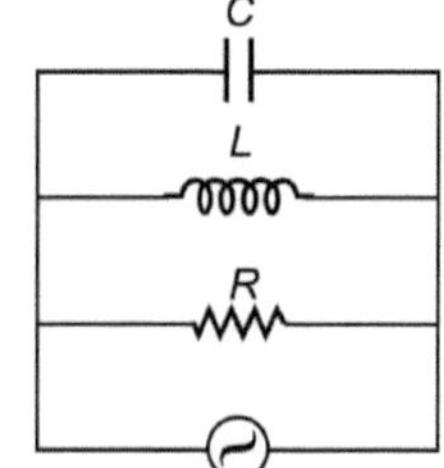

$$\frac{1}{Z} = \sqrt{\frac{1}{R^2} + \left(\frac{1}{X_L} - \frac{1}{X_C}\right)^2} = \sqrt{\frac{1}{R^2} + \left(\frac{1}{\omega L} - \omega C\right)^2}$$

At resonance, $\qquad \omega = \omega_r = \dfrac{1}{\sqrt{LC}}$

That means $\dfrac{1}{Z} = $ minimum

and thus $Z = $ maximum. As Z is maximum, current will be minimum.
Current through inductor

$$I_{rms_L} = \frac{V_{rms}}{X_L} = \frac{230}{50 \times 5} \qquad \text{(In Q. 11)}$$

$$I_{rms_L} = \frac{230}{250} = 0.92 \text{ A}$$

Current through capacitor

$$I_{rms_C} = \frac{V_{rms}}{X_C} = \frac{V_{rms} \times \omega C}{1}$$

$$= 230 \times 50 \times 80 \times 10^{-6}$$

$$= 0.92 \text{ A}$$

Current through resistor

$$I_{rms_R} = \frac{I_{rms}}{R} = \frac{230}{40} = 5.75 \text{ A}$$

As we observe that the current through inductor and capacitor are equal but they are at $180°$ phase difference. So, they cancel each other.
So, the total current $= I_{rms} = $ current through resistor $= 5.75$ A

Question 18. A circuit containing a 80 mH inductor and a 60 µF capacitor in series is connected to a 230 V, 50 Hz supply. The resistance of the circuit is negligible.

    (a) Obtain the current amplitude and rms values.
    (b) Obtain the rms values of potential drops across each element.
    (c) What is the average power transferred to the inductor?
    (d) What is the average power transferred to the capacitor?
    (e) What is the total average power absorbed by the circuit? ['Average' implies 'averaged over one cycle'.]

Solution Given, inductance $L = 80$ mH $= 80 \times 10^{-3}$ H

Capacitance of capacitor $C = 60$ µF $= 60 \times 10^{-6}$ F

The rms value of voltage $V_{rms} = 230$ V

$\qquad\qquad$ Frequency $f = 50$ Hz

$\qquad\qquad$ Resistance $R = 0$

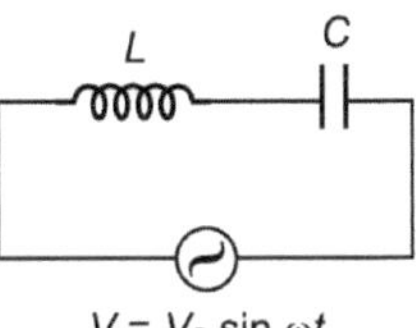

(a) Impedance of circuit

$$Z = \sqrt{R^2 + (X_L - X_C)^2}$$

$$= \sqrt{0 + \left(2\pi fL - \frac{1}{2\pi fC}\right)^2}$$

$$= \left(2\pi fL - \frac{1}{2\pi fC}\right)$$

$$= \sqrt{\left(2 \times 3.14 \times 50 \times 80 \times 10^{-3} - \frac{1}{2 \times 3.14 \times 50 \times 60 \times 10^{-6}}\right)^2}$$

$$= 25.12 - 53.07 = -27.95 \;\Omega$$

As $Z < 0$, means $X_L < X_C$, emf lags by current by $\dfrac{\pi}{2}$.

The rms value of current

$$I_{rms} = \frac{V_{rms}}{Z} = \frac{230}{27.95} = 8.29 \text{ A}$$

The maximum value of current

$$I_0 = \sqrt{2}I_{rms} = 1.414 \times 8.29 = 11.64 \text{ A}$$

(b) Potential drop across L

$$V_{rms_L} = I_{rms} \times X_L = 8.29 \times 2 \times 3.14 \times 50 \times 80 \times 10^{-3}$$

$$= 208.25 \text{ V}$$

Potential drop across C

$$V_{rms_C} = I_{rms} \times X_C = 8.29 \times \frac{1}{2 \times 3.14 \times 50 \times 60 \times 10^{-6}}$$

$$= 440.02 \text{ V}$$

Since, potential drop across L and C are $180°$ out of phase. So, V_L and V_C are subtracted to the applied rms voltage.

$\therefore$ Applied rms voltage $= V_C - V_L$

$$= 440 - 208.25 = 231.75 \text{ V}$$

(c) Average power transferred to the inductor

$$P = I_{rms}.V_{rms}.\cos\phi$$

As the phase difference is $90°$, so $P = 0$

(d) Average power transferred to the capacitor

$$P = I_{rms}.V_{rms}\cos\phi$$

As phase difference is $90°$, so $P = 0$.

(e) As there is no resistance in the circuit, so average power (total) is equal to sum of average power due to inductor and capacitor. That means the average power consumed is zero.

Question 19. Suppose the circuit in Q. 18 has a resistance of $15\,\Omega$. Obtain the average power transferred to each element of the circuit and the total power absorbed.

Solution   Given, the rms value of voltage $V_{rms} = 230$ V

$$\text{Resistance } R = 15\,\Omega$$

$$\text{Frequency } f = 50 \text{ Hz}$$

Average power across inductor and capacitor is zero as the phase difference between current and voltage is $90°$.

Total power absorbed = power absorbed in resistor, $P_{av} = V_{rms} \cdot I_{rms}$

So, $Z = \sqrt{R^2 + (X_L - X_C)^2}$

$$= \sqrt{15^2 + \left(2 \times 3.14 \times 50 \times 80 \times 10^{-3} - \frac{1}{2 \times 3.14 \times 50 \times 60 \times 10^{-6}}\right)^2}$$

$$= \sqrt{1002.85} = 31.67\,\Omega$$

$$I_{rms} = \frac{V_{rms}}{Z} = \frac{230}{31.67} = 7.26 \text{ A}$$

Total power absorbed $P_{av} = V_{rms} \cdot I_{rms}$

$$= I_{rms} \cdot R \cdot I_{rms}$$

$$= (7.26)^2 \times 15$$

$$= 790.6 \text{ W}$$

Thus, the total absorbed power is 790.6 W.

Question 20. A series LCR circuit with $L = 0.12$ H, $C = 480$ nF, $R = 23\ \Omega$ is connected to a 230 V variable frequency supply.

(a) What is the source frequency for which current amplitude is maximum. Obtain this maximum value.

(b) What is the source frequency for which average power absorbed by the circuit is maximum. Obtain the value of this maximum power.

(c) For which frequencies of the source is the power transferred to the circuit half the power at resonant frequency? What is the current amplitude at these frequencies?

(d) What is the Q-factor of the given circuit?

Solution   Inductance $L = 0.12$ H

Capacitance $C = 480$ nF $= 480 \times 10^{-9}$ F

Resistance $R = 23\,\Omega$

The rms value of voltage $V_{rms} = 230$ V

(a) Current is maximum at resonance.

At resonance impedance $Z = R = 23\,\Omega$

The rms value of current

$$I_{rms} = \frac{V_{rms}}{Z} = \frac{230}{23} = 10 \text{ A}$$

The maximum value of current

$$I_0 = \sqrt{2}I_{rms} = 1.414 \times 10 = 14.14 \text{ A}$$

At natural frequency, the current amplitude is maximum.

$$\omega = \frac{1}{\sqrt{LC}} = \frac{1}{2\pi\sqrt{0.12 \times 480 \times 10^{-9}}}$$

$$= 4166.6 = 4167 \text{ rad/s}$$

The source frequency

$$v_0 = \frac{\omega}{2\pi} = \frac{4167}{2\pi} = 663.48 \text{ Hz}$$

(b) Average power is maximum for resonance.

$$P_{av_{(max)}} = I_{rms}^2 \cdot R = 10 \times 10 \times 23 = 2300 \text{ W}$$

(c) Power transferred to the circuit is half the power at resonant frequency.

$$\Delta\omega = \frac{R}{2L} = \frac{23}{2 \times 0.12} = 95.83 \text{ rad/s}$$

$$\Delta v = \frac{\Delta\omega}{2\pi} = 15.2 \text{ Hz}$$

The frequencies at which power transferred is half

$$v = v_0 \pm \Delta v = 663.48 \pm 15.26$$

So, frequencies are 448.3 Hz and 678.2 Hz.

The maximum current

$$I = \frac{I_0}{\sqrt{2}} = \frac{14.14}{\sqrt{2}} = 10 \text{ A}$$

(d) Q-factor $= \dfrac{\omega_r L}{R} = \dfrac{4166.7 \times 0.12}{23} = 21.74$

Question 21. Obtain the resonant frequency and Q-factor of a series *LCR* circuit with $L = 3.0$ H, $C = 27\ \mu$F and $R = 7.4\ \Omega$. It is desired to improve the sharpness of the resonance of the circuit by reducing its 'full width at half maximum' by a factor of 2. Suggest a suitable way.

Solution   Given, inductance $L = 3$ H

Capacitance of capacitor $C = 27\ \mu$F $= 27 \times 10^{-6}$ F

Resistance $R = 7.4\ \Omega$

The resonant frequency of circuit,

$$\omega_r = \frac{1}{\sqrt{LC}} = \frac{1}{\sqrt{3 \times 27 \times 10^{-6}}} = \frac{1000}{9} = 111.1 \text{ rad/s}$$

Q-factor of a series LCR circuit,

$$Q\text{-factor} = \frac{\omega_r L}{R} = \frac{111.1 \times 3}{7.4} = 45.04$$

To reduce the full width at half by factor Q, we have to reduce the value of R as $\dfrac{R}{2}$.

$$\frac{R}{2} = \frac{7.4}{2} = 3.7 \,\Omega$$

Thus, we made the resistance as 3.7 Ω to made the sharpness of resonance reducing full width at half maximum.

Question 22. Answer the following questions:
   (a) In any AC circuit, is the applied instantaneous voltage equal to the algebraic sum of the instantaneous voltages across the series elements of the circuit? Is the same true for rms voltage?
   (b) A capacitor is used in the primary circuit of an induction coil.
   (c) An applied voltage signal consists of a superposition of a DC voltage and an AC voltage of high frequency. The circuit consists of an inductor and a capacitor in series. Show that the DC signal will appear across C and the AC signal across L.
   (d) A choke coil in series with a lamp is connected to a DC line. The lamp is seen to shine brightly. Insertion of an iron core in the choke causes no change in the lamp's brightness. Predict the corresponding observations, if the connection is to an AC line.
   (e) Why is choke coil needed in the use of fluorescent tubes with AC mains? Why can we not use an ordinary resistor instead of the choke coil?

Solution   (a) Yes, the applied voltage (instantaneous) equal to the algebraic sum of the instantaneous voltages across the series elements of the circuit.

No, it is not true for rms voltage because there is some phase differences across different elements of the circuit.

   (b) A capacitor is used in the primary circuit of an induction coil because when the circuit is broken, a large induced voltage is used up in charging the capacitor. So, the sparking or any damages are avoided.

   (c) As we know that

$$X_C = \frac{1}{2\pi f C}, \ X_L = 2\pi f L$$

For DC, $\qquad f = 0, X_C = \infty, X_L = 0$

Thus, the capacitor is blocked for DC and AC signal appears across C.
For AC of high frequency $X_L =$ very large, $X_C = 0$
Inductor blocked DC and AC signal appears across L.

(d) When the choke coil is connected to DC, there is no change in the brightness. Because $f = 0$, $X_L = 0$. So, no change in the brightness.
In AC, the choke offer impedance (X_L) so, it glows dim. As we insert an iron core the magnetic field increases and hence inductance increases.

$$BA = LI = \phi$$

$$L \propto B$$

So, X_L also increases and the brightness of bulb decreases.

(e) We use the choke coil instead of resistance because the power loss across resistor is maximum while the power loss across choke is zero.

For resistor, $$\phi = 0,$$

$$P = I_{rms}V_{rms} \cos 0° = I_{rms} \cdot V_{rms} = \text{maximum}$$

For inductor, $\quad \phi = 90°,\ P = I_{rms}V_{rms} \cos 90° = 0$

(choke coil)

Question 23. A power transmission line feeds input power at 2300 V to a step-down transformer with its primary windings having 4000 turns. What should be the number of turns in the secondary in order to get output power at 230 V?

Solution   Given, primary voltage $V_p = 2300$ V

$$N_p = 4000 \text{ turns}$$

Secondary voltage $V_S = 230$ V

Here, we assume that the transformer is ideal. No power loss in the form of heat etc.

Using the formula, $$\frac{V_S}{V_P} = \frac{N_S}{N_P}$$

$$\frac{230}{2300} = \frac{N_S}{4000}$$

$$N_S = 400$$

Thus, the number of turns in secondary are 400.

Question 24. At a hydroelectric power plant, the water pressure head is at a height of 300 m and the water flow available is $100 \text{ m}^3/\text{s}$. If the turbine generator efficiency is 60%, estimate the electric power available from the plant ($g = 9.8 \text{ m/s}^2$).

Solution   Given, height of water $h = 300$ m

Rate of flow of water $V = 100 \text{ m}^3/\text{s}$

Efficiency $\qquad\qquad\qquad\qquad \eta = 60\%$

$$g = 9.8 \text{ m/s}^2$$

As we know that input power is required to raise the water upto height $h = 300$ m.

$$\text{Power} = \frac{m \times g \times h}{t} = \frac{\text{Volume} \times \text{Density} \times g \times h}{t}$$

$$P_{\text{in}} = 100 \times 1000 \times 9.8 \times 300$$

$$= 2.94 \times 10^8 \text{ W}$$

$(\because$ volume/second $= 100$ m^3/s, density $= 1000$ kg/m$^3)$

Suppose, the power output is P_{out}, which is equal to the power available from the plant.

The efficiency of generator

$$\eta = \frac{P_{\text{out}}}{P_{\text{in}}}$$

$$\frac{60}{100} = \frac{P_{\text{out}}}{2.94 \times 10^8}$$

$$P_{\text{out}} = \frac{60}{100} \times 2.94 \times 10^8 = 1764 \times 10^5 \text{ W}$$

$$= 176.4 \text{ MW}$$

Question 25. A small town with a demand of 800 kW of electric power at 220 V is situated 15 km away from an electric plant generating power at 440 V. The resistance of the two wire line carrying power is 0.5 Ω per km. The town gets power from the line through a 4000-220 V step-down transformer at a sub-station in the town.

(a) Estimate the line power loss in the form of heat.

(b) How much power must the plant supply, assuming there is negligible power loss due to leakage?

(c) Characterise the step-up transformer at the plant.

Solution Generating power of electric plant $= 800$ kW at $V = 220$ V

Distance $= 15$ km

Generating voltage $= 440$ V

Resistance/ length $= 0.5$ Ω/km

Primary voltage, $V_p = 4000$ V

Secondary voltage $V_s = 220$ V

(a) $\qquad$ Power $= I_p . V_p$

$$800 \times 1000 = I_p \times 4000$$

$$I_p = 200 \text{ A}$$

Line power loss in form of heat $= (I_p)^2 \times$ Resistance of line (2 lines)

$$= (I_p)^2 \times 0.5 \times 15 \times 2$$
$$= (200)^2 \times 0.5 \times 15 \times 2$$
$$= 60 \times 10^4 \text{ W} = 600 \text{ kW}$$

(b) If there is no power loss due to leakage,

The plant supply should be $= 800 + 600$

$$= 1400 \text{ kW}$$

(c) Voltage drop across the line $= I_p \cdot R$ (2 lines)

$$= 200 \times 0.5 \times 15 \times 2$$
$$= 3000 \text{ V}$$

Voltage from transmission $= 3000 + 4000 = 7000$ V

As it is given that the power generated at 440 V. So, the step-up transformer needed at the plant is 440V-7000 V.

Question 26. Do the same question as above with the replacement of the earlier transformer by a 40000-220 V step-down transformer (neglect, as before, leakage losses though this may not be a good assumption any longer because of the very high voltage transmission involved). Hence, explain why high voltage transmission is preferred?

Solution   Given, primary voltage $V_P = 40000$ V

Let the current in primary is I_P. $\therefore$ $V_P . I_P = P$

$$800 \times 1000 = 40000 \times I_P$$
$$I_P = 20 \text{ A}$$

(a) Line power loss $= I_P^2 \times R$ (2 lines)

$$= (20)^2 \times 2 \times 0.5 \times 15 = 6000 \text{ W} = 6 \text{ kW}$$

(b) Power supply by plant $= 800 + 6 = 806$ kW

Voltage drop on line $= I_p . R$ (2 lines)

$$= 20 \times 2 \times 0.5 \times 15 = 300 \text{ V}$$

Voltage for transmission $= 40000 + 300 = 40300$ V

Step-up transformer needed at the plant $= 440$ V-40300 V

Power loss at higher voltage (Q. 25)

$$= \frac{6}{800} \times 100 = 0.74\%$$

Power loss at lower voltage (Q.25)

$$= \frac{600}{1400} \times 100 = 42.8\%$$

Hence, the power loss is minimum at higher voltage. So, the high voltage transmission is preferred.

Selected NCERT Exemplar Problems

Question 1. Draw the effective equivalent circuit of the circuit shown in figure at very high frequencies and find the effective impedance.

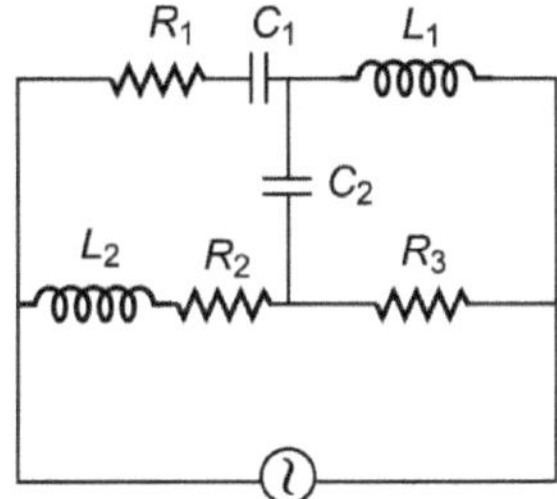

Solution As we know that

Inductive reactance $X_L = 2\pi f L$ and capacitative reactance $X_C = \dfrac{1}{2\pi f C}$

For very high frequencies, $X_L \approx$ infinity and $X_C \approx$ zero.
Both factor will remove from the circuit .
So, the equivalent circuits are

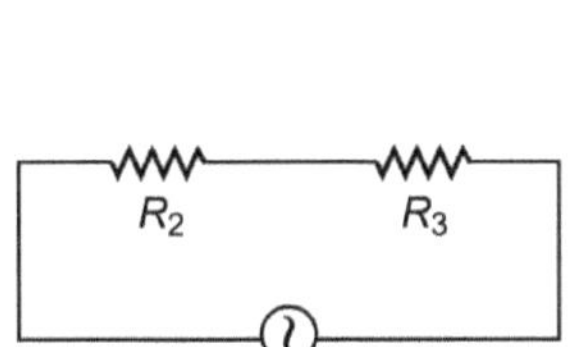

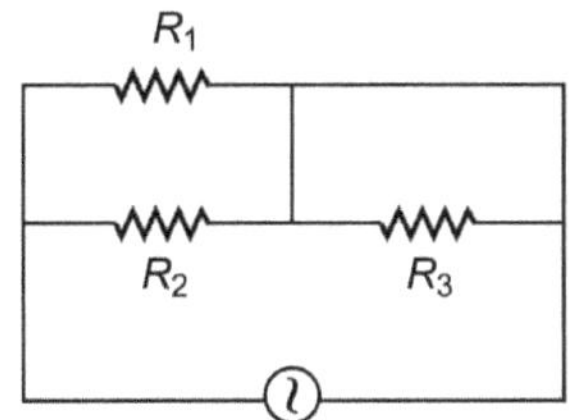

Question 2. Study the circuits (a) and (b) shown in figure and answer the following questions :

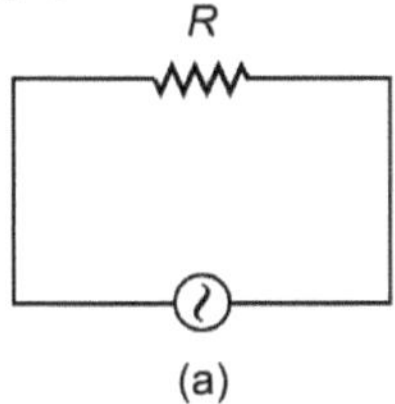

(a)

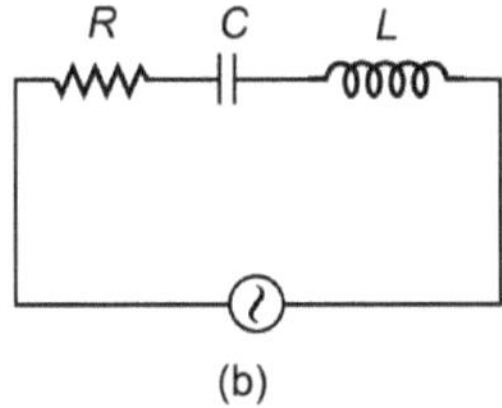

(b)

  (i) Under which conditions would the rms currents in the two circuits be the same?

  (ii) Can the rms current in circuit (b) be larger than that in (a)?

Solution (i) In the case of resonance in circuit (b) $= Z = R$, so the value of rms current in both the circuit is same.

(ii) In circuit (a), $\qquad I_{rms} = \dfrac{V}{R}$

In circuit (b), $\quad I_{rms} = -\dfrac{V}{\sqrt{R^2 + (X_L - X_C)^2}} = \dfrac{V}{Z}$

Here $Z > R$, so I_{rms} in circuit (a) is more than the I_{rms} in circuit (b).
Thus, the rms current in circuit (b) cannot be larger than that in (a).

Question 3. Can the instantaneous power output of an AC source ever be negative? Can the average power output be negative?

Solution   Yes, $P_{instantaneous} = I_{instantaneous} \times V_{instantaneous}$

No, because it is average so, it is positive.

Question 4. The alternating current in a circuit is described by the graph shown in figure. Show rms current in this graph.

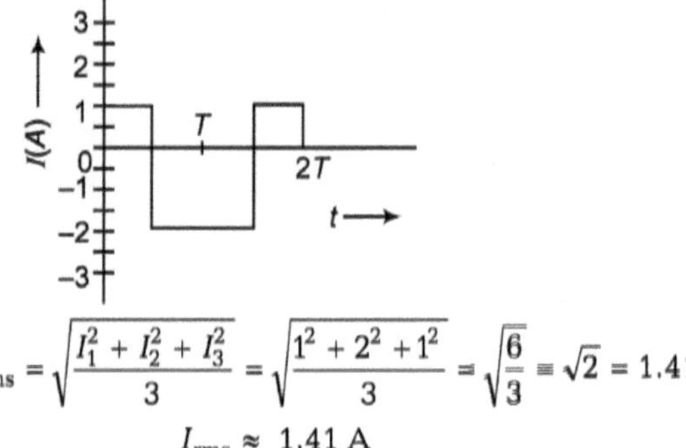

Solution $I_{rms} = \sqrt{\dfrac{I_1^2 + I_2^2 + I_3^2}{3}} = \sqrt{\dfrac{1^2 + 2^2 + 1^2}{3}} = \sqrt{\dfrac{6}{3}} = \sqrt{2} = 1.41$

$$I_{rms} \approx 1.41\ A$$

Question 5. Both alternating current and direct current are measured in amperes. But how is the ampere defined for an alternating current?

Solution   As we know that the AC current changes its direction with time. So, AC ampere must be defined in terms of some property which is independent of direction of current. This, Joule's heating effect is the property which defines rms value of AC.

Question 6. A coil of 0.01 H inductance and 1 Ω resistance is connected to 200 V, 50 Hz AC supply. Find the impedance of the circuit and time lag between maximum alternating voltage and current.

Solution   Given, inductance $L = 0.01$ H, resistance $R = 1\Omega$,

voltage $V = 200$ V and
Frequency $f = 50$ Hz
Impedance of the circuit

$$Z = \sqrt{R^2 + X_L^2} = \sqrt{R^2 + (2\pi f L)^2}$$
$$= \sqrt{1^2 + (2 \times 3.14 \times 50 \times 0.01)^2}$$

or $\qquad\qquad\qquad Z = \sqrt{10.86} = 3.3\ \Omega$

$$\tan\phi = \frac{\omega L}{R} = \frac{2\pi f L}{R} = \frac{2\times 3.14\times 50\times 0.01}{1} = 3.14$$

$$\phi = \tan^{-1}(3.14) = 72°$$

Phase difference $\phi = \dfrac{72\times\pi}{180}$ rad.

Time lag between alternating voltage and current

$$\Delta t = \frac{\phi}{\omega} = \frac{72\pi}{180\times 2\pi\times 50} = \frac{1}{250}\text{ s}$$

Question 7. A 60 W load is connected to the secondary of a transformer whose primary draws line voltage. If a current of 0.54 A flows in the load, what is the current in the primary coil? Comment on the type of transformer being used.

Solution Power $P_L = 60$ W, current $I_L = 0.54$ A

$$\text{Voltage } V_L = \frac{P_L}{I_L} = \frac{60}{0.54} = 110\text{ V}$$

On average, the input is half of load current

$$I_P = \frac{I_L}{2} = \frac{0.54}{2} = 0.27\text{ A}$$

The transformer is step-down.

Question 8. An electrical device draws 2 kW power from AC mains (voltage 223 V (rms) $= \sqrt{50000}$ V). The current differs (lags) in phase by $\phi\left(\tan\phi = \dfrac{-3}{4}\right)$ as compared to voltage. Find (a) R, (b) $X_C - X_L$ and (c) I_M.

Another device has twice the values for R, X_C and X_L. How are the answers affected?

Solution Power $P = 2$ kW, voltage $V_{\text{rms}} = 223$ V

$$\tan\phi = \frac{-3}{4}$$

$$\text{Power } P = \frac{V^2}{Z}$$

$$\Rightarrow \qquad Z = \frac{V^2}{P} = \frac{223\times 223}{2\times 10^3} = 25$$

$$\text{Impedance } Z = 25\ \Omega$$

$$\text{Impedance } Z = \sqrt{R^2 + (X_L - X_C)^2}$$

$$\Rightarrow \qquad 25 = \sqrt{R^2 + (X_L - X_C)^2}$$

$$\text{or} \qquad 625 = R^2 + (X_L - X_C)^2 \qquad\qquad \ldots(i)$$

Again,
$$\tan \phi = \frac{X_L - X_C}{R} = \frac{3}{4}$$

or
$$X_L - X_C = \frac{3R}{4} \qquad \qquad \dots\text{(ii)}$$

From Eq. (ii), we put $X_L - X_C = \dfrac{3R}{4}$ in Eq. (i), we get

$$625 = R^2 + \left(\frac{3R}{4}\right)^2 = R^2 + \frac{9R^2}{16}$$

or
$$625 = \frac{25R^2}{16}$$

(a) Resistance $R = \sqrt{\dfrac{25}{16}} = \dfrac{5}{4} = 1.25\ \Omega$

(b)
$$X_L - X_C = \frac{3R}{4} = \frac{3 \times 5}{4 \times 4} = \frac{15}{16}\ \Omega$$

(c) Main current $I_M = \sqrt{2}I = \sqrt{2}\,\dfrac{V}{Z}$

$$= \frac{223}{25} \times \sqrt{2} = 12.6\ \text{A}$$

As R, X_C, X_L are all doubled, $\tan \phi$ does not change. Z is doubled, current is halved. So, power is also halved.

Chapter **8**

Electromagnetic Waves

Important Results

1. Maxwell found an inconsistency in the Ampere's law and suggested the existence of an additional current called displacement current. This displacement current is due to time varying electric field and given by

$$I_d = \varepsilon_0 \frac{d\phi_E}{dt}$$

It acts as a source of magnetic field, as the same way as conduction current.

2. The ratio of amplitude of electric field to the amplitude of magnetic field gives the speed of light in vacuum.

i.e.,
$$\frac{E_0}{B_0} = c$$

3. The speed of light in vacuum $c = \dfrac{1}{\sqrt{\mu_0 \varepsilon_0}}$, where μ_0 is the absolute permeability of space and ε_0 be the absolute permittivity of space.

4. The speed of light or electromagnetic waves in a material medium is given by $v = \dfrac{1}{\sqrt{\mu\varepsilon}}$, where μ is the permeability of the medium and ε is its permittivity.

5. Electromagnetic waves carry energy as they travel through space and this energy is shared equally by the electric and magnetic fields.

6. The energy density of electric field is given by

$$u_E = \frac{1}{2}\varepsilon_0 E^2 = u_B$$

7. The energy density of magnetic field is given by

$$u_B = \frac{B^2}{2\mu_0} = u_E$$

8. Total average energy density $= u_E + u_B = 2u_E = 2u_B$

$$= \frac{1}{2}\varepsilon_0 E_0^2 = \frac{B_0^2}{2\mu_0}$$

9. Electric and magnetic fields oscillate sinusoidally in space and time in an electromagnetic wave. The oscillating electric and magnetic fields, **E** and **B** are perpendicular to each other as well as perpendicular to the direction of propagation of the electromagnetic wave.

10. The electromagnetic spectrum has infinite range of wavelengths, such as γ-rays, X-rays, UV rays, visible rays, infrared rays, micro and radio waves.

11. In electromagnetic wave, the variation of electric field vector can be given by the equation $E = E_0 \sin \omega \left(t - \dfrac{x}{c} \right)$ and of magnetic field vector by the equation

$$B = B_0 \sin \omega \left(t - \dfrac{x}{c} \right)$$

12. Maxwell's equations

   (i) $\oint E.\,dA = \dfrac{q}{\varepsilon_0}$ (Gauss's law for electricity)

   (ii) $\oint B.\,dA = 0$ (Gauss's law for magnetism)

   (iii) $\oint E.\,dl = -\dfrac{d\phi_E}{dt}$ (Faraday' law)

   (iv) $\oint B.\,dl = \mu_0 I_C + \mu_0 \varepsilon_0 \dfrac{d\phi_E}{dt}$ (Ampere-Maxwell law)

Exercises

Question 1.   Figure shows a capacitor made of two circular plates each of radius 12 cm and separated by 5.0 cm. The capacitor is being charged by an external source (not shown in the figure). The charging current is constant and equal to 0.15 A.

 (a) Calculate the capacitance and the rate of charge of potential difference between the plates.

 (b) Obtain the displacement current across the plates.

 (c) Is Kirchhoff's first rule (junction rule) valid at each plate of the capacitor? Explain.

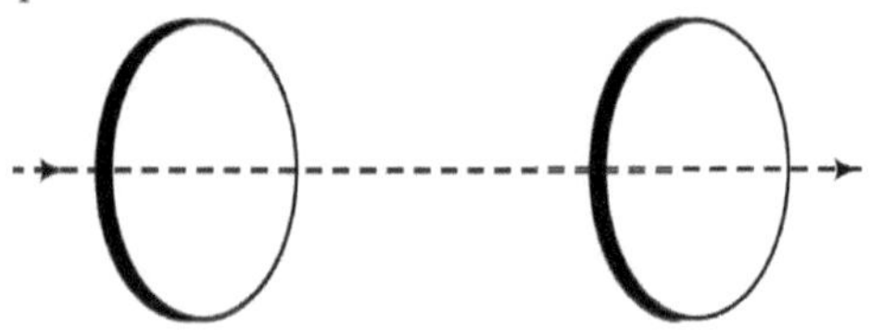

 Use the concept of parallel plate capacitor and capacitance of the capacitor $C = \dfrac{K A \varepsilon_0}{d}$.

Solution Given, radius of plates $r = 12$ cm $= 12 \times 10^{-2}$ m

Separation of two circular plates

$$d = 5 \text{ cm} = 5 \times 10^{-2} \text{ m}$$

$$\text{Current} \quad I = 0.15 \text{ A}$$

(a) Capacitance of parallel plate capacitor

$$C = \frac{\varepsilon_0 A}{d}$$

where, A is the area of plates.

$$C = \frac{8.854 \times 10^{-12} \times 3.14 \,(12 \times 10^{-2})^2}{5 \times 10^{-2}}$$

$$C = \frac{8.854 \times 3.14 \times 144 \times 10^{-12 \,-4 \,+2}}{5}$$

$$C = 8.01 \times 10^{-14} \text{ F} = 8.01 \text{ pF}$$

Charge on the plates of the capacitor

$$q = CV$$

$$\frac{dq}{dt} = C \cdot \frac{dV}{dt}$$

$$I = C \cdot \frac{dV}{dt} \qquad \left[\because \frac{dq}{dt} = I \right]$$

$$\frac{dV}{dt} = \frac{I}{C} = \frac{0.15}{8.01 \times 10^{-12}} = 18.7 \times 10^9 \text{ V/s}$$

Thus, the rate of change of potential is 18.7×10^9 V/s.

(b) The displacement current is equal to the conduction current $I_d = 0.15$ A.

(c) Yes, Kirchhoff's first rule is valid because we take the current to be the sum of conduction currents and the displacement currents.

Question 2. A parallel plate capacitor (shown in figure) made of circular plates each of radius $R = 6.0$ cm has a capacitance $C = 100$ pF. The capacitor is connected to a 230 V AC supply with a (angular) frequency of 300 rad/s.

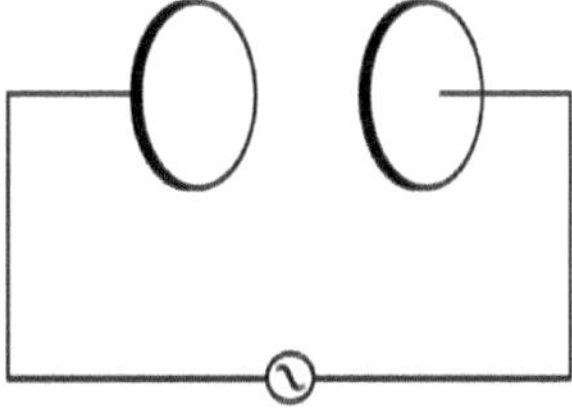

(a) What is the rms value of the conduction current?

(b) Is the conduction current equal to the displacement current?

(c) Determine the amplitude of **B** at a point 3.0 cm from the axis between the plates.

Solution   Given radius of plates $R = 6$ cm $= 6 \times 10^{-2}$ m

Capacitance of capacitor

$$C = 100 \text{ pF} = 100 \times 10^{-12} \text{ F} = 10^{-10} \text{ F}$$

Voltage of capacitor $V = 230$ V

Frequency of capacitance $\omega = 300$ rad/s

(a) The rms value of current $I_{rms} = \dfrac{V_{rms}}{X_C}$

$$\therefore \qquad X_C = \frac{1}{\omega C} = \frac{1}{300 \times 10^{-10}} = \frac{10^{10}}{300} \ \Omega$$

$$\therefore \qquad I_{rms} = \frac{230 \times 300}{10^{10}} = 3 \times 23 \times 1000 \times 10^{-10}$$

$$= 69 \times 10^{-7} = 6.9 \times 10^{-6} \text{ A}$$

$$I_{rms} = 6.9 \ \mu \text{ A}$$

(b) Yes, the conduction current is equal to displacement current

$$I_d = \varepsilon_0 \frac{d\phi_E}{dt} \quad \text{(By the definition of displacement current)}$$

$$I_d = \varepsilon_0 \frac{d}{dt}(EA) \qquad\qquad\qquad (\phi_E = EA)$$

$$I_d = \varepsilon_0 A \frac{dE}{dt} \qquad\qquad\qquad \left(E = \frac{\sigma}{\varepsilon_0} = \frac{Q}{\varepsilon_0 A}\right)$$

$$I_d = \varepsilon_0 A \frac{d}{dt}\left(\frac{Q}{\varepsilon_0 A}\right)$$

$$I_d = \varepsilon_0 A \cdot \frac{1}{\varepsilon_0 A} \cdot \frac{dQ}{dt} = \frac{dQ}{dt} = I$$

$$I_d = I$$

(c) Given, the distance of point from the axis between the plates

$$r = 3 \text{ cm} = 3 \times 10^{-2} \text{ m}$$

Radius of plates $R = 6$ cm $= 6 \times 10^{-2}$ m

The magnetic field at a point between the plates

$$B = \frac{\mu_0}{2\pi R^2} \cdot r \cdot I_d$$

$$B = \frac{\mu_0 r}{2\pi R^2} I \qquad\qquad\qquad (I_d = I)$$

If $I = I_0$, maximum value of current then $I = \sqrt{2} \ I_{rms}$

$$B = \frac{\mu_0 r}{2\pi R^2} \sqrt{2} I_{rms}$$

$$B = \frac{4\pi \times 10^{-7} \times 0.03 \times \sqrt{2} \times 6.9 \times 10^{-6}}{2\pi \times 0.06 \times 0.06}$$

$$B = 1.63 \times 10^{-11}\ \text{T}$$

Question 3. What physical quantity is the same for X-rays of wavelength 10^{-10} m, red light of wavelength 6800 Å and radiowaves of wavelength 500 m?

Solution Here, X-rays, red light and radiowaves all are the electromagnetic waves. As we know that all the electromagnetic waves travel with the same speed c that is speed of light. Thus, the speed is same for X-rays, red light and radiowaves.

Question 4. A plane electromagnetic wave travels in vacuum along Z-direction. What can you say about the directions of its electric and magnetic field vectors? If the frequency of the wave is 30 MHz, what is its wavelength?

Solution As we know that the direction of electromagnetic wave is perpendicular to both electric and magnetic fields. Here, electromagnetic wave is travelling in Z-direction, then electric and magnetic fields are in X-Y direction and are perpendicular to each other.

Frequency of waves $f = 30\ \text{MHz} = 30 \times 10^{6}\ \text{Hz}$

$$\text{Speed } c = 3 \times 10^{8}\ \text{m/s}$$

Using the formula, $\qquad\qquad c = f\lambda$

Wavelength of electromagnetic waves

$$\lambda = \frac{c}{f} = \frac{3 \times 10^{8}}{30 \times 10^{6}} = \frac{300}{30} = 10\ \text{m}$$

Thus, the wavelength of electromagnetic waves is 10 m.

Question 5. A radio can tune into any station in the 7.5 MHz to 12 MHz band. What is the corresponding wavelength band?

Solution Given, frequency $f_1 = 7.5\ \text{MHz}$

Frequency $f_2 = 12\ \text{MHz}$

Speed of EM wave $c = 3 \times 10^{8}\ \text{m/s}$

Wavelength corresponding to frequency f_1

$$\lambda_1 = \frac{c}{f_1} = \frac{3 \times 10^{8}}{7.5 \times 10^{6}} = \frac{3000}{7.5} = 40\ \text{m}$$

Wavelength corresponding to frequency f_2

$$\lambda_2 = \frac{c}{f_2} = \frac{3 \times 10^{8}}{12 \times 10^{6}} = \frac{300}{12} = 25\ \text{m}$$

Thus, the corresponding wavelength band is 25 m to 40 m.

Question 6. A charged particle oscillates about its mean equilibrium position with a frequency of 10^9 Hz. What is the frequency of the electromagnetic waves produced by the oscillator?

Solution According to the question,

Frequency of the electromagnetic waves $= 10^9$ Hz

The frequency of electromagnetic waves produced by the oscillator is same as that of the oscillating charged particle about its equilibrium position.

Question 7. The amplitude of the magnetic field part of a harmonic electromagnetic wave in vacuum is $B_0 = 510$ nT. What is the amplitude of the electric field part of the wave?

Solution Given, magnetic field part of harmonic electromagnetic wave

$$B_0 = 510 \text{ nT}$$

Speed of light in vacuum $\quad c = \dfrac{E_0}{B_0}$

where, E_0 is the electric part of the wave

$$3 \times 10^8 = \dfrac{E_0}{510 \times 10^{-9}}$$

or $\qquad\qquad\qquad\qquad E_0 = 153 \text{ N/C}$

Thus, the amplitude of the electric field part of wave is 153 N/C.

Question 8. Suppose that the electric field amplitude of an electromagnetic wave is $E_0 = 120$ N/C and that its frequency is $v = 50.0$ MHz. (a) Determine, B_0, ω, k and λ. (b) Find expressions for E and B.

Solution Given, amplitude of an electromagnetic wave, $E_0 = 120$ N/C

Frequency of wave $f = 50 \text{ MHz} = 50 \times 10^6$ Hz

(a) Speed of light in vacuum

$$c = \dfrac{E_0}{B_0}$$

$$B_0 = \dfrac{E_0}{c} = \dfrac{120}{3 \times 10^8} = 40 \times 10^{-8}$$

or $\qquad\qquad\qquad B_0 = 400 \times 10^{-9} \text{ T} = 400 \text{ nT}$

Angular frequency of wave,

$$\omega = 2\pi f = 2 \times 3.14 \times 50 \times 10^6$$

$$\omega = 3.14 \times 10^8 \text{ rad/s}$$

Wave number of electromagnetic waves

$$K = \dfrac{\omega}{c} = \dfrac{3.14 \times 10^8}{3 \times 10^8} = 1.05 \text{ rad/m}$$

Wavelength of electromagnetic wave

$$\lambda = \frac{c}{f} = \frac{3 \times 10^8}{50 \times 10^6} = 6.00 \text{ m}$$

(b) Expression of electric field $E = E_0 \sin (kx - \omega t)$

$$E = 120 \sin (1.05x - 3.14 \times 10^8 t)$$

Expression of magnetic field B

$$B = B_0 \sin (kx - \omega t)$$
$$B = 4 \times 10^{-7} \sin (1.05x - 3.14 \times 10^8 t)$$

Question 9. The terminology of different parts of the electromagnetic spectrum is given in the text. Use the formula $E = h\nu$ (for energy of a quantum of radiation : photon) and obtain the photon energy in units of eV for different parts of the electromagnetic spectrum. In what way are the different scales of photon energies that you obtain related to the sources of electromagnetic radiation?

Solution   Given, energy of photon $E = h\nu$

For γ-rays

Frequency of γ-rays $\nu = 3 \times 10^{20}$ Hz

Energy of γ-rays $E = h\nu = 6.6 \times 10^{-34} \times 3 \times 10^{20} = 19.8 \times 10^{-14}$ J

or $\qquad\qquad E = \dfrac{19.8 \times 10^{-14}}{1.6 \times 10^{-19}} = 1.24 \times 10^6$ eV

The source of γ-rays is nuclear origin.

For X-rays

Frequency of X-rays $\nu = 3 \times 10^{18}$ Hz

Energy of X-rays $E = h\nu = 6.6 \times 10^{-34} \times 3 \times 10^{18} = 19.8 \times 10^{-16}$ J

or $\qquad\qquad E = \dfrac{19.8 \times 10^{-16}}{1.6 \times 10^{-19}} = 1.24 \times 10^4$ eV

The retardation of high energy electron produces X-rays.

For ultraviolet rays

Frequency of rays $\nu = 10^{15}$ Hz

Energy of ultraviolet rays $E = h\nu = 6.6 \times 10^{-34} \times 10^{15} = 6.6 \times 10^{-19}$ J

or $\qquad\qquad E = \dfrac{6.6 \times 10^{-19}}{1.6 \times 10^{-19}} = 4.125$ eV

It originates by the excitation of atoms.

For visible rays

Frequency of visible rays $\nu = 6 \times 10^{14}$ Hz

Energy of visible rays $E = h\nu = 6.6 \times 10^{-34} \times 6 \times 10^{14} = 39.6 \times 10^{-20}$ J

or
$$E = \frac{39.6 \times 10^{-20}}{1.6 \times 10^{-19}} = 2.475 \text{ eV}$$

They produce by the excitation of valance electrons.

For infrared rays

Frequency of infrared rays $\nu = 10^{13}$ Hz

Energy of infrared rays $E = h\nu = 6.6 \times 10^{-34} \times 10^{13} = 6.6 \times 10^{-21}$ J

or
$$E = \frac{6.6 \times 10^{-21}}{1.6 \times 10^{-19}} = 4.125 \times 10^{-2} \text{ eV}$$

They originate by the excitation of atoms and molecules.

For microwaves

Frequency of microwaves $\nu = 10^{10}$ Hz

Energy of microwaves $E = h\nu = 6.6 \times 10^{-34} \times 10^{10} = 6.6 \times 10^{-24}$ J

or
$$E = \frac{6.6 \times 10^{-24}}{1.6 \times 10^{-19}} = 4.125 \times 10^{-5} \text{ eV}$$

They originate by the oscillating current in vacuum tubes.

For radiowaves

Frequency of radio waves $\nu = 3 \times 10^{8}$ Hz

Energy of radiowaves $E = h\nu = 6.6 \times 10^{-34} \times 3 \times 10^{8} = 19.8 \times 10^{-26}$ J

or
$$E = \frac{19.8 \times 10^{-26}}{1.6 \times 10^{-19}} = 1.24 \times 10^{-6} \text{ eV}$$

They originate by oscillating current.

Type of radiation	Photon energy
γ-rays	1.24×10^{6} eV
X-rays	1.24×10^{4} eV
Ultraviolet rays	4.12 eV
Visible waves	2.475 eV
Infrared waves	4.125×10^{-2} eV
Microwaves	4.125×10^{-5} eV
Radiowaves	1.24×10^{-6} eV

Question 10. In a plane electromagnetic wave, the electric field oscillates sinusoidally at a frequency of 2.0×10^{10} Hz and amplitude 48 V/m.

    (a) What is the wavelength of the wave?

    (b) What is the amplitude of the oscillating magnetic field?

    (c) Show that the average energy density of the E field equals the average energy density of the B field.
       $[c = 3 \times 10^{8}$ m/s.]

Solution Frequency of oscillation $= 2 \times 10^{10}$ Hz

Given, $\hspace{3cm} c = 3 \times 10^8$ m/s

Electric field amplitude $E_0 = 48$ V/m

(a) Wavelength of waves $\lambda = \dfrac{c}{f} = \dfrac{3 \times 10^8}{2 \times 10^{10}} = 1.5 \times 10^{-2}$ m

(b) Using the formula, $c = \dfrac{E_0}{B_0}$

The amplitude of the oscillating magnetic field
$$B_0 = \frac{E_0}{c} = \frac{48}{3 \times 10^8} = 1.6 \times 10^{-7} \text{ T}$$

(c) The average energy density of electric field
$$u_E = \frac{1}{4} \varepsilon_0 E_0^2 \hspace{3cm} \dots\text{(i)}$$

We know that $\dfrac{E_0}{B_0} = c$

Putting in Eq. (i),

$$\therefore \hspace{2cm} u_E = \frac{1}{4} \varepsilon_0 \cdot c^2 B_0^2 \hspace{3cm} \dots\text{(ii)}$$

Speed of electromagnetic waves, $c = \dfrac{1}{\sqrt{\mu_0 \varepsilon_0}}$

Putting in Eq. (ii), we get
$$u_E = \frac{1}{4} \varepsilon_0 B_0^2 \cdot \frac{1}{\mu_0 \varepsilon_0}$$
$$u_E = \frac{1}{4} \cdot \frac{B_0^2}{\mu_0} = \frac{B_0^2}{2\mu_0} = \mu_B.$$

Thus, the average energy density of the **E** field equals the average energy density of **B** field.

Additional Exercises

Question 11. Suppose that the electric field part of an electromagnetic wave in vacuum is

E = {(3.1 N/C) cos [(1.8 rad/m) y + (5.4 × 10^6 rad/s)t]} $\hat{\mathbf{i}}$.

(a) What is the direction of propagation?

(b) What is the wavelength λ?

(c) What is the frequency ν?

(d) What is the amplitude of the magnetic field part of the wave?

(e) Write an expression for the magnetic field part of the wave.

Solution (a) From the equation, it is moving in Y-axis and also in negative direction, so it moves in $-\hat{\jmath}$-direction.

(b) The electric part of electromagnetic wave in vacuum

$$E = 3.1\cos\,(1.8\,y + 5.4 \times 10^6 t)\,\hat{\imath}$$

Comparing with standard equation $E = E_0\cos\,(Ky + \omega t)$, we get
Angular frequency $\omega = 5.4 \times 10^6$ rad/s

Wave number $K = 1.8$ rad/m

The amplitude of the electric field part of the wave

$$E_0 = 3.1\,\text{N/C}$$

$$\lambda = \frac{2\pi}{K} = \frac{2\pi}{1.8} = 3.492\,\text{m}$$

$$\lambda = 3.5\,\text{m}$$

(c)
$$\omega = 2\pi v$$

$$v = \frac{\omega}{2\pi} = \frac{5.4 \times 10^6 \times 7}{2 \times 22} = 0.86 \times 10^6\,\text{Hz}$$

(d)
$$c = \frac{E_0}{B_0}$$

Amplitude of magnetic field

$$B_0 = \frac{E_0}{c} = \frac{3.1}{3 \times 10^8} = 1.03 \times 10^{-8}\,\text{T}$$

(e) Expression for the magnetic field part of wave

$$B = B_0\cos\,(Ky + \omega t)\,\hat{k}$$

$$B = 1.03 \times 10^{-8}\cos\,(1.8\,y + 5.4 \times 10^8\,t)\,\hat{k}$$

Question 12. About 5% of the power of a 100 W light bulb is converted to visible radiation. What is the average intensity of visible radiation?

(a) at a distance of 1m from the bulb?

(b) at a distance of 10 m?

Assume that the radiation is emitted isotropically and neglect reflection.

Solution Total power $= 100$ W

Visible radiation power $= 5\%$ of total power

$$= \frac{5}{100} \times 100 = 5\,\text{W}$$

(a) At a distance of 1m, the energy distributed in the form of sphere.

$$\text{Area of sphere} = 4\pi\,(\text{radius})^2$$

Intensity of visible radiation

$$= \frac{\text{Power}}{\text{Area}} = \frac{5}{4 \times 3.14 \times (1)^2} = 0.4\,\text{W/m}^2$$

Intensity of visible radiation at a distance of 10 m

$$= \frac{5}{4 \times 3.14 \,(10)^2} = 4 \times 10^{-3} \; \text{W/m}^2$$

Question 13. Use the formula $\lambda_m T = 0.29$ cm-K to obtain the characteristic temperature ranges for different parts of the electromagnetic spectrum. What do the numbers that you obtain tell you?

Solution
$$\lambda_m T = 0.29 \text{ cm-K}$$

$$\lambda_m = \frac{0.29}{T \times 100} \text{ m}$$

Let we take
$$\lambda_m = 10^{-6} \text{ m}$$

Required absolute temperature $T = \dfrac{0.29}{100 \times 10^{-6}} = 2900$ K

Let we take
$$\lambda_m = 5 \times 10^{-5} \text{ m}$$

Required absolute temperature $T = \dfrac{0.29}{100 \times 5 \times 10^{-5}} = 6000$ K

We can find the temperature for other parts of the electromagnetic spectrum. These number tell us about the temperature ranges for particular part of EM waves.

Question 14. Given below are some famous numbers associated with electromagnetic radiations in different contexts in physics. State the part of the electromagnetic spectrum to which each belongs.

  (a) 21 cm (wavelength emitted by atomic hydrogen in interstellar space).

  (b) 1057 MHz (frequency of radiation arising from two close energy levels in hydrogen; known as Lamb shift).

  (c) 2.7 K (temperature associated with the isotropic radiation filling all space-thought to be a relic of the 'big-bang' origin of the universe).

  (d) 5890 Å - 5896 Å (double lines of sodium).

  (e) 14.4 keV (energy of a particular transition in ^{57}Fe nucleus associated with a famous high resolution spectroscopic method (Mössbauer spectroscopy)).

Solution   (a) This wavelength (21 cm) corresponds to the radiowaves.

  (b) This frequency (1057 MHz) also corresponds to the radiowaves (short wavelength).

  (c)
$$T = 2.7 \text{ K}$$

Using the formula $\lambda_m T = b = 0.29$ cm-K

$$\lambda_m = \frac{0.29}{2.7} \text{ cm} = 0.11 \text{ cm}$$

This wavelength corresponds to the microwaves region of the electromagnetic waves.

(b) This wavelength lies in the visible region of the electromagnetic spectrum.

(c) Energy $E = 14.4$ keV $= 14.4 \times 10^3 \times 1.6 \times 10^{-19}$ J

Frequency of wave, $v = \dfrac{E}{h} = \dfrac{14.4 \times 1.6 \times 10^{-16}}{6.6 \times 10^{-34}} = 3 \times 10^{11}$ MHz

This frequency lies in the X-ray region of the electromagnetic spectrum.

Question 15.   Answer the following questions :

(a) Long distance radio broadcasts use short-wave bands. Why?

(b) It is necessary to use satellites for long distance TV transmission. Why?

(c) Optical and radiotelescopes are built on the ground but X-ray astronomy is possible only from satellites orbiting the earth. Why?

(d) The small ozone layer on top of the stratosphere is crucial for human survival. Why?

(e) If the earth did not have an atmosphere, would its average surface temperature be higher or lower than what it is now?

(f) Some scientists have predicted that a global nuclear war on the earth would be followed by a severe 'nuclear winter' with a devastating effect on life on earth. What might be the basis of this prediction?

Solution   (a) Long distance radio broadcasts use short waves because they are reflected by the ionosphere.

(b) It is necessary to use satellites for long distance TV transmission because the television signal are of high frequency and they are not reflected by the ionosphere. So, for the reflection of TV waves, satellites are needed.

(c) Optical and radio telescope uses optical and radiowaves which can penetrate the atmosphere whereas X-rays are of much smaller wavelengths and they are absorbed by the atmosphere. So, we can work with optical and radio telescopes on earth's surface but X-rays astronomical telescopes must be used on the satellite orbiting above the earth's atmosphere.

(d) The small ozone layer present on the top of the stratosphere absorbs most of the ultraviolet radiations from the sum which are dangerous and cause genetic damage to the living cells. Ozone layer prevent them from reaching the earth's surface and helps in the survival of the life.

(e) If the earth did not have atmosphere, its surface temperature would be lower because the green house effect of the atmosphere would be absent.

(f) The clouds produced by a global nuclear war would perhaps cover most parts of the sky preventing solar light from reaching many parts of the globe. This would cause a winter.

Selected NCERT Exemplar Problems

Question 1. Why is the orientation of the portable radio with respect to broadcasting station important?

Solution The orientation of the portable radio with respect to broadcasting station is important because the electromagnetic waves are plane polarized, so the receiving antenna should be parallel to the electric or magnetic vector part of the wave.

Question 2. Why does microwave oven heats up a food item containing water molecules most efficiently?

Solution Microwave oven heats up the food items containing water molecules most efficiently because the frequency of microwaves matches the resonant frequency of water molecules.

Question 3. The charge on a parallel plate capacitor varies as $q = q_0 \cos 2\pi v t$. The plates are very large and close together (area $= A$, separation $= d$). Neglecting the edges effects find the displacement current through the capacitor?

Solution The displacement current through the capacitor

$$I_d = I_c = \frac{dq}{dt} = \frac{d}{dt}(q_0 \cos 2\pi v t)$$

$$I_d = I_c = -q_0 \sin 2\pi v t \times 2\pi v$$

$$I_d = I_c = -2\pi v q_0 \sin 2\pi v t$$

Question 4. A variable frequency AC source is connected to a capacitor. How will the displacement current change with decrease in frequency?

Solution Capacitative reaction $X_C = \dfrac{1}{2\pi f C}$

$$\therefore \qquad X_C \propto \frac{1}{f}$$

As frequency decreases, X_C increases and current is inversely proportional to $X_C \left(\because I \propto \dfrac{1}{X_C} \right)$. So, displacement current decreases.

Question 5. The magnetic field of a beam emerging from a filter facing a floodlight is given by $B = 12 \times 10^8 \sin (1.20 \times 10^7 z - 3.60 \times 10^{15} t)$ T. What is the average intensity of the beam?

Solution Magnetic field $\mathbf{B} = B_0 \sin \omega t$

Given, equation $B = 12 \times 10^{-8} \sin (1.20 \times 10^7 z - 3.60 \times 10^{15} t)$ T

On comparing this equation with standard equation, we get

$$B_0 = 12 \times 10^{-8}$$

The average intensity of the beam

$$I_{avg} = \frac{1}{2}\frac{B_0^2}{\mu_0}\cdot c = \frac{1}{2}\times\frac{(12\times10^{-8})^2\times3\times10^8}{4\pi\times10^{-7}} = 1.71\ \text{W/m}^2$$

Question 6. You are given a $2\,\mu F$ parallel plate capacitor. How would you establish an instantaneous displacement current of 1 mA in the space between its plates?

Solution Given, capacitance of capacitor $C = 2\,\mu F$,

$$\text{Displacement current } I_d = 1\ \text{mA}$$

$$\text{Charge } q = CV$$

$$I_d dt = CdV \qquad\qquad [\because q = it]$$

or

$$I_d = C\frac{dV}{dt}$$

$$1\times10^{-3} = 2\times10^{-6}\times\frac{dV}{dt}$$

or

$$\frac{dV}{dt} = \frac{1}{2}\times10^{+3} = 500\ \text{V}$$

So, by applying a varying potential difference of 500 V/s we would produce a displacement current of desired value.

Question 7. Show that the radiation pressure exerted by an EM wave of intensity I on a surface kept in vacuum is I/C.

Solution $\text{Pressure} = \dfrac{\text{Force}}{\text{Area}} = \dfrac{F}{A}$

Force is the rate of change of momentum

i.e.,

$$F = \frac{dp}{dt}$$

Energy in time dt,

$$U = p\cdot C \ \text{ or } \ p = \frac{U}{C}$$

$\therefore$

$$\text{Pressure} = \frac{1}{A}\cdot\frac{U}{C\cdot dt}$$

$$\text{Pressure} = \frac{I}{C} \qquad \left[\because I = \text{Intensity} = \frac{U}{A\cdot dt}\right]$$

Question 8. What happens to the intensity of light from a bulb if the distance from the bulb is doubled? As a laser beam travels across the length of a room, its intensity essentially remains constant.

Solution As the distance is doubled, the area of spherical region $(4\pi r^2)$ will become four times, so the intensity becomes one fourth the initial value $\left(\because I\propto\dfrac{1}{r^2}\right)$ but in case of laser it does not spread so its intensity remains same.

Chapter **9**

Ray Optics and Optical Instruments

Important Results

1. According to laws of reflection, angle of incidence $\angle i$ is equal to angle of reflection $\angle r$.

2. Snell's law shows that, $\dfrac{\sin i}{\sin r} = \mu = \dfrac{\text{Velocity of light in vacuum}}{\text{Velocity of light in medium}}$

3. Refractive index of medium a w.r.t. medium b is given by ${}^{a}\mu_b = \dfrac{\mu_b}{\mu_a}$

4. $$ {}^{a}\mu_b = \dfrac{1}{{}^{b}\mu_a} $$

5. $$ {}^{a}\mu_b \times {}^{b}\mu_c \times {}^{c}\mu_a = 1 $$

6. $$ \mu = \dfrac{\text{Real depth}}{\text{Apparent depth}} $$

7. Lateral shift $= \dfrac{t\,[\sin(i-r)]}{\cos r}$

8. Normal shift $= t\left(1 - \dfrac{1}{{}^{a}\mu_n}\right)$

9. Critical angle $\sin i_C = \dfrac{1}{\mu}$

10. The necessary conditions for total internal reflection are
    (i) refraction takes place from denser medium to rarer medium.
    (ii) the angle of incidence must be greater than the critical angle for the pair of media in contact.

11. Mirror formula, $\dfrac{1}{f} = \dfrac{1}{v} + \dfrac{1}{u}$

12. For refraction through spherical surfaces
    (i) When refraction occurs from rarer to denser medium.
    $$ \dfrac{\mu_1}{-u} + \dfrac{\mu_2}{v} = \dfrac{\mu_2 - \mu_1}{R} $$

(ii) When refraction occurs from denser to rarer medium

$$-\frac{\mu_2}{u} + \frac{\mu_1}{v} = \frac{\mu_1 - \mu_2}{R}$$

13. The Lens formula, $\dfrac{1}{v} - \dfrac{1}{u} = \dfrac{1}{f}$

14. Lens makes formula for both convex and concave lenses

$$\frac{1}{f} = (\mu - 1)\left(\frac{1}{R_1} - \frac{1}{R_2}\right)$$

15. For combination of lenses $\dfrac{1}{f} = \dfrac{1}{f_1} + \dfrac{1}{f_2} + \ldots$

16. Power of lens $P = \dfrac{1}{f\,(m)} = \dfrac{100}{f\,(cm)}$ dioptre

For a converging lens or convex lens P is positive and for a diverging lens or concave lens P is negative.

17. For combination of lenses, the power is given by

$$P = P_1 + P_2 + P_3 + \ldots$$

18. For a fusion of angle A of refractive index μ is given by

$$\mu = \frac{\sin\left(\dfrac{A + \delta_m}{2}\right)}{\sin\dfrac{A}{2}}$$

19. In refraction through a prism

   (i) $A + \delta = i_1 + i_2$ (ii) $r_1 + r_2 = A$

  (iii) When $\delta = \delta_m \Rightarrow i_1 = i_2$ and $r_1 = r_2$

20. Magnifying power of simple microscope,

$$m = 1 + \frac{d}{f}$$

where, d is least distant of distinct vision.

21. Magnifying power of a compound microscope

$$m = \frac{L}{f_o}\left(1 + \frac{d}{f_e}\right) \quad \text{where, } L = \text{length of the tube}$$

22. Magnifying power of an astronomical telescope

  (i) In normal adjustment $m = -\dfrac{f_o}{f_e}$

  (ii) When image formed atleast distance of distinct vision

$$m = -\frac{f_o}{f_e}\left(1 + \frac{f_e}{d}\right)$$

where, d is the least distance of distinct vision.

23. (i) Length of astronomical telescope tube for normal adjustment is given by

$$L = f_o + f_e$$

(ii) Length of terrestrial telescope is given by

$$L = f_o + 4f + f_e$$

where, f is the focal length of the erecting lens.

24. Resolving power of telescope is given by

$$RP = \frac{d}{1.22\,\lambda}$$

25. Angular limit of resolution of a telescope is given by

$$d\theta = \frac{1.22\,\lambda}{d}$$

Exercises

Question 1. A small candle, 2.5 cm in size is placed at 27 cm in front of a concave mirror of radius of curvature 36 cm. At what distance from the mirror should a screen be placed in order to obtain a sharp image? Describe the nature and size of the image. If the candle is moved closer to the mirror, how would the screen have to be moved?

Solution　　Given, radius of curvature of concave mirror, $R = -36$ m

(For concave mirror radius of curvature is taken as negative)

$\therefore$　　Focal length $f = \dfrac{R}{2} = \dfrac{36}{2} = -18$ cm

Distance of object $u = -27$ cm

(Object distance is always taken as negative)

Height of object $O = 2.5$ cm

Use the mirror formula

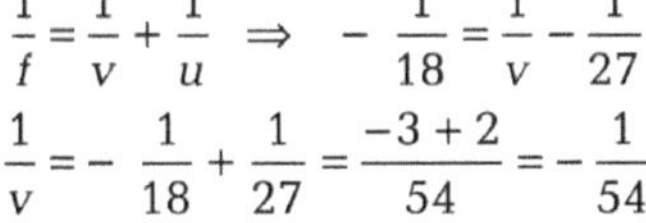

$$\frac{1}{f} = \frac{1}{v} + \frac{1}{u} \quad \Rightarrow \quad -\frac{1}{18} = \frac{1}{v} - \frac{1}{27}$$

$$\frac{1}{v} = -\frac{1}{18} + \frac{1}{27} = \frac{-3+2}{54} = -\frac{1}{54}$$

Distance of screen from mirror　$v = -54$ cm

Let the size of image be I. By using the formula of magnification for mirror

$$m = -\frac{v}{u} = \frac{I}{O}$$

$$\frac{-(-54)}{-27} = \frac{I}{2.5}$$

$$I = -5 \text{ cm}$$

The negative sign shows that the image is formed in front of the mirror and it is inverted. Thus, the screen should be placed at a distance 54 cm and the size of image is 5 cm, real, inverted and magnified in nature.

If we move the object near to the mirror (as $u \to f, v \to \infty$) the screen should be moved away from mirror. As the distance of object is less than focal length, $(u < f)$ no screen is required, because the image formed is virtual.

Question 2. A 4.5 cm needle is placed 12 cm away from a convex mirror of focal length 15 cm. Give the location of the image and the magnification. Describe what happens as the needle is moved farther from the mirror?

Solution Given, focal length of convex mirror $f = +15$ cm (Focal length of convex mirror is taken as positive)

Distance of object $\qquad u = -12$ cm

Size of object $\qquad O = 4.5$ cm

Using the mirror formula,

$$\frac{1}{f} = \frac{1}{v} + \frac{1}{u}$$

$$\frac{1}{15} = \frac{1}{v} - \frac{1}{12} \Rightarrow \frac{1}{v} = \frac{1}{15} + \frac{1}{12} = \frac{4+5}{60} = \frac{9}{60}$$

Distance of image from the mirror $v = 6.7$ cm

The positive sign shows that the image is formed behind the mirror. Using the formula of magnification,

$$m = -\frac{v}{u} = \frac{I}{O}$$

$$\frac{-6.7}{-12} = \frac{I}{4.5}$$

Size of image $\qquad I = 2.5$ cm

As I is positive, so image is erect and virtual.

Magnification m is given by

$$m = \frac{I}{O} = \frac{2.5}{4.5} = \frac{25}{45} = \frac{5}{9}$$

As the needle moves away from the mirror, the image also moves away from the mirror (as $u \to \infty, v \to f$) and the size of image goes on decreasing.

Question 3. A tank is filled with water to a height of 12.5 cm. The apparent depth of a needle lying at the bottom of the tank is measured by a microscope to be 9.4 cm. What is the refractive index of water? If water is replaced by a liquid of refractive index 1.63 up to the same height, by what distance would the microscope have to be moved to focus on the needle again?

Solution **Case I** When tank is filled with water

Given, the apparent depth $= 9.4$ cm

Height of water $t = 12.5$ cm

So, real depth $= 12.5$ cm

Refractive index of water

$$\mu_w = \frac{\text{Real depth}}{\text{Apparent depth}} = \frac{12.5}{9.4} = 1.33$$

Case II When tank is filled with the liquid

Refractive index of liquid $\qquad \mu = 1.63,$

$$\text{Again } \mu = \frac{\text{Real depth}}{\text{Apparent depth}}$$

$$\therefore \qquad 1.63 = \frac{12.5}{\text{Apparent depth}}$$

$$\text{Apparent depth} = \frac{12.5}{1.63} = 7.67 \text{ cm}$$

$\therefore$ The microscope is shifted by $= 9.4 - 7.67 = 1.73$ cm

Question 4. Figs. (a) and (b) show refraction of a ray in air incident at $60°$ with the normal to a glass-air and water-air interface, respectively. Predict the angle of refraction in glass when the angle of incidence in water is $45°$ with the normal to a water-glass interface [Fig. (c)].

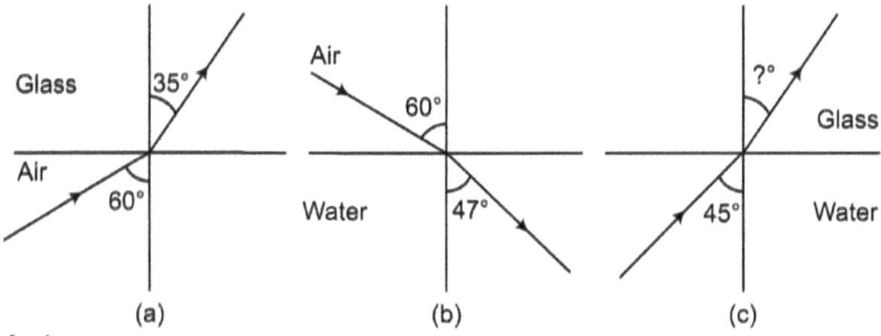

Solution Given, **from Fig. (a)**

Angle of incidence $\qquad\qquad i = 60°$

Angle of refraction $\qquad\qquad r = 35°$

Refractive index of glass w.r.t. air, $^a\mu_g = \dfrac{\sin 60°}{\sin 35°} = \dfrac{0.8660}{0.5736} = 1.51 \qquad$ ...(i)

From Fig. (b)

Angle of incidence $i = 60°$, angle of refraction $r = 47°$

Refractive index of water w.r.t. to air

$$^a\mu_w = \frac{\sin 60°}{\sin 47°} = \frac{0.8660}{0.7314} = 1.18 \qquad \text{...(ii)}$$

From Fig. (c)

Angle of incidence $i = 45°$, let r be the angle of refraction

Refractive index of glass w.r.t. to water

$$^w\mu_g = \frac{\sin 45°}{\sin r} \qquad \ldots(iii)$$

As, we know that

$$^w\mu_g = \frac{^a\mu_g}{^a\mu_w}$$

Putting the value of $^w\mu_g$ in Eq. (iii), we get

$$\frac{^a\mu_g}{^a\mu_w} = \frac{0.7071}{\sin r}$$

$$\frac{1.51}{1.32} = \frac{0.7071}{\sin r}$$

From Eqs. (i) and (ii), we get

$$\sin r = \frac{1.32 \times 0.7071}{1.51} = 0.6181$$

$$r = 38.2°$$

Question 5. A small bulb is placed at the bottom of a tank containing water to a depth of 80 cm. What is the area of the surface of water through which light from the bulb can emerge out? Refractive index of water is 1.33. (Consider the bulb to be a point source.)

 Use relation between critical angle and refractive index. When light is incident at an angle of incidence equal to the critical angle, the angle of refraction is 90° and light will pass through the interface of the two media.

Solution   Let the bulb is placed at point O

$$AB = AC = r$$

If the light falls at an angle of incidence equal to critical angle i_c, then only a circular area is formed because if angle of incidence is less than the critical angle it will refract into air and when angle of incidence is greater than critical angle then it will be reflected back in water)

The source of light is 80 cm below the surface of water *i.e.* $\qquad AO = 80$ cm, $\mu_w = 1.33$

Using the formula for critical angle,

$$\sin i_c = \frac{1}{\mu_w}$$

$$\sin i_c = \frac{1}{1.33} = 0.75$$

$$i_c = 48.6°$$

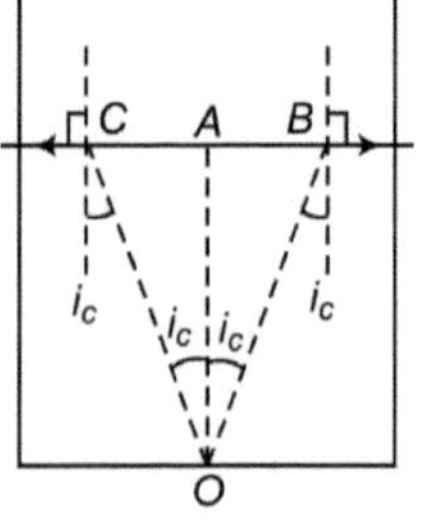

In $\triangle OAB$ $$\tan i_c = \frac{AB}{AO}$$

or $$\tan i_c = \frac{r}{l}$$

$$r = l \tan i_c = 80 \tan 48.6$$
$$r = 80 \times 1.1345 = 90.7 \text{ cm}$$

Area of circular surface of water, through which light will emerge
$$A = \pi r^2$$
$$A = 3.14 \times (90.7)^2 = 25865.36 \text{ cm}^2$$
$$A = 2.58 \text{ m}^2$$

Question 6. A prism is made of glass of unknown refractive index. A parallel beam of light is incident on a face of the prism. The angle of minimum deviation is measured to be 40°. What is the refractive index of the material of the prism? The refracting angle of the prism is 60°. If the prism is placed in water (refractive index 1.33), predict the new angle of minimum deviation of a parallel beam of light.

Solution Given, angle of minimum deviation $\delta_m = 40°$

The refracting angle of the prism $A = 60°$

Refractive index of glass w.r.t. air
$$^{a}\mu_g = \frac{\sin\left(\dfrac{A + \delta_m}{2}\right)}{\sin\dfrac{A}{2}} = \frac{\sin\left(\dfrac{60° + 40°}{2}\right)}{\sin 30°} = \frac{\sin 50°}{\sin 30°}$$

$$^{a}\mu_g = \frac{0.766}{0.5} = 1.532$$

When prism is placed in water

The refractive index of water w.r.t. air
$$^{a}\mu_w = 1.33$$

Refractive index of glass with respect to water
$$^{w}\mu_g = \frac{\sin\left(\dfrac{A + \delta'_m}{2}\right)}{\sin\dfrac{A}{2}}$$

(where the new angle of deviation is δ'_m)

$$\therefore \qquad \frac{^{a}\mu_g}{^{a}\mu_w} = \frac{\sin\left(\dfrac{A + \delta'_m}{2}\right)}{\sin 30°}$$

$$\sin\left(\frac{A + \delta'_m}{2}\right) = \frac{1.532 \times \sin 30°}{1.33}$$

or
$$\sin\left(\frac{A + \delta'_m}{2}\right) = \frac{0.5 \times 1.532}{1.33} = 0.5759$$

or
$$\sin\left(\frac{A + \delta'_m}{2}\right) = \sin 35° 10'$$

$$\delta'_m = 2\,(30° 10') - 60° = 70° 20' - 60°$$
$$\delta'_m = 10° 20'$$

Thus, the new angle of minimun deviation is $10° 20'$.

Question 7. Double-convex lenses are to be manufactured from a glass of refractive index **1.55**, with both faces of the same radius of curvature. What is the radius of curvature required if the focal length is to be **20 cm**?

Solution   Given, the refractive index of glass with respect to air
$$^a\mu_g = 1.55$$

($\because$ both faces have same redius of curvature)

For double convex lenses $R_1 = R,\ R_2 = -R$

(For double convex lens, one redius is taken positive and other negative)

Focal length of lens, $f = +20$ cm

Using the Lens maker's formula

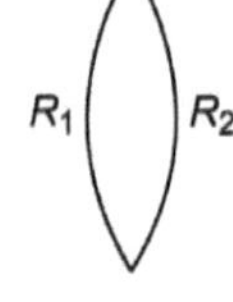

$$\frac{1}{f} = (^a\mu_g - 1)\left(\frac{1}{R_1} - \frac{1}{R_2}\right)$$

$$\frac{1}{20} = (1.55 - 1)\left(\frac{1}{R} + \frac{1}{R}\right)$$

$$\frac{1}{20} = 0.55 \times \frac{2}{R}$$

$$R = 0.55 \times 2 \times 20 = 22\ \text{cm}$$

Thus, the required radius of curvature is 22 cm.

Question 8. A beam of light converges at a point *P*. Now a lens is placed in the path of the convergent beam **12 cm** from *P*. At what point does the beam converge if the lens is (a) a convex lens of focal length **20 cm**, and (b) a concave lens of focal length **16 cm**?

Solution   Here, the point *P* is on the right side of lens acts as vertical object.

(a) Given, distance of object from the lens
$$u = 12\ \text{cm}$$

    Focal length of convex lens $f = +20$ cm

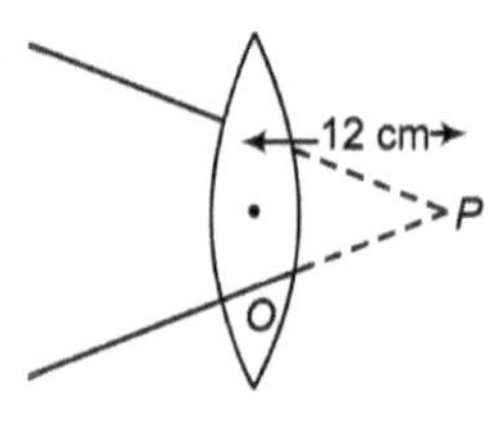

Using Lens formula, $\dfrac{1}{v} - \dfrac{1}{u} = \dfrac{1}{f}$

$$\dfrac{1}{v} - \dfrac{1}{12} = \dfrac{1}{20}$$

$$\dfrac{1}{v} = \dfrac{1}{20} + \dfrac{1}{12} = \dfrac{3+5}{60} = \dfrac{8}{60}$$

$$v = 7.5 \text{ cm}$$

Thus, the beam converges on the right side of lens at a distance of 7.5 cm.

(b) Distance of object from the lens $u = 12$ cm

Focal length of concave lens $\quad f = -16$ cm

Using Lens formula,

$$\dfrac{1}{v} - \dfrac{1}{u} = \dfrac{1}{f}$$

$$\dfrac{1}{v} - \dfrac{1}{12} = -\dfrac{1}{16}$$

$\Rightarrow \qquad \dfrac{1}{v} = \dfrac{1}{12} - \dfrac{1}{16} = \dfrac{4-3}{48}$

$$v = 48 \text{ cm}$$

Thus, the beam converges on the right side of lens at a distance of 48 cm.

Question 9. An object of size 3.0 cm is placed 14 cm in front of a concave lens of focal length 21 cm. Describe the image produced by the lens. What happens if the object is moved further away from the lens?

Solution Size of object, $O = 3$ cm

Focal length of lens $f = -21$ cm

(∵ Focal length of convex lens is taken as negative.)

Distance of object from the concave lens

$u = -14$ cm

(∵ Focal lenth of concave lens is taken as negative)

Using Lens formula,

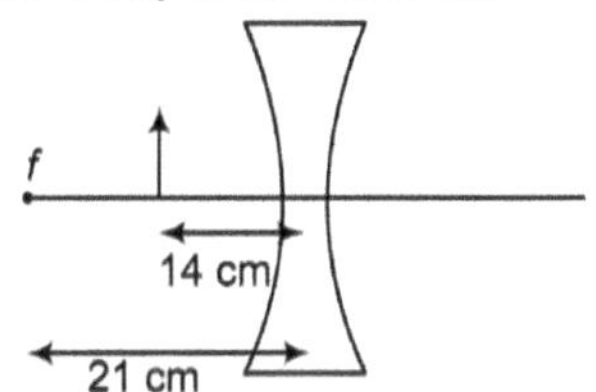

$$\dfrac{1}{v} - \dfrac{1}{u} = \dfrac{1}{f}$$

$$\dfrac{1}{v} + \dfrac{1}{14} = -\dfrac{1}{12}$$

$\Rightarrow \qquad \dfrac{1}{v} = -\dfrac{1}{21} - \dfrac{1}{14} = \dfrac{-2-3}{42} = -\dfrac{5}{42}$

$$v = -8.4 \text{ cm}$$

Using the formula of magnification

$$m = -\frac{v}{u} = \frac{I}{O} \qquad \text{where, } I = \text{height of image}$$

$$\frac{(-8.4)}{-14} = \frac{I}{3}$$

$$I = 1.8 \text{ cm}$$

I is positive, therefore the image formed is virtual and erect at a distance of 8.4 cm from the lens on the same side of object and height of image is 1.8 cm.

If the object moves further away from the lens, the image moves towards the lens (never beyond focus). The size of image decreases gradually.

Question 10. What is the focal length of a convex lens of focal length 30 cm in contact with a concave lens of focal length 20 cm? Is the system a converging or a diverging lens? Ignore thickness of the lenses.

Solution   Given, focal length of convex lens $f_1 = 30$ cm,

Focal lengh of concave lens $f_2 = -20$ cm

Using the formula of combination of lenses

$$\frac{1}{f} = \frac{1}{f_1} + \frac{1}{f_2} = \frac{1}{30} - \frac{1}{20} = \frac{2-3}{60} = -\frac{1}{60}$$

$$f = -60 \text{ cm}$$

Since, the focal length of combination is negative in nature. So the combination behaves like a diverging lens *i.e.* as a concave lens.

Question 11. A compound microscope consists of an objective lens of focal length 2.0 cm and an eye-piece of focal length 6.25 cm separated by a distance of 15 cm. How far from the objective should an object be placed in order to obtain the final image at (a) the least distance of distinct vision (25 cm), and (b) at infinity? What is the magnifying power of the microscope in each case?

Solution   Given, focal length of objective lens, $f_o = 2$ cm

Focal length of eye-piece $f_e = 6.25$ cm

Distance between both lenses $v = 15$ cm

 (a) Distance of final image from eye-piece

$$v_e = -25 \text{ cm}$$

    Using the Lens formula for eye-piece

$$\frac{1}{v_e} - \frac{1}{u_e} = \frac{1}{f_e}$$

$$\frac{1}{u_e} = \frac{1}{v_e} - \frac{1}{f_e}$$

$$= \frac{1}{-25} - \frac{1}{6.25} = \frac{-1-4}{25} = \frac{-5}{25}$$

$$u_e = -5 \text{ cm}$$

As the distance between objective and eye-piece $(v_o + u_e) = 15$ cm

$$L = v_o + u_e$$

Distance of image formed by object lens

$$v_o = L - |u_e| = 15 - 5 = 10 \text{ cm}$$

Using the lens equation for objective lens

$$\frac{1}{v_o} - \frac{1}{u_o} = \frac{1}{f_o}$$

$$\frac{1}{u_o} = \frac{1}{v_o} - \frac{1}{f_o} = \frac{1}{10} - \frac{1}{2} = \frac{1-5}{10} = -\frac{4}{10}$$

$$u_o = -2.5 \text{ cm}$$

So, the object should be 2.5 cm in front of convex lens.

Magnifying power of compound microscope

$$m = \frac{v_o}{u_o}\left(1 + \frac{d}{f_e}\right) = \frac{10}{2.5}\left(1 + \frac{25}{6.25}\right) \qquad (\because d = 25 \text{ cm})$$

$$m = 20$$

(b) The final image will be formed at infinity only if the image formed by the objective is in the focal plane of the eye-piece *i.e.,* at principal focus of the eye-piece.

Thus, here $v_e = -\infty, u_e = f_e = 6.25$ cm

Image distance of objective lens

$$v_o = L - f_e = -15 - 6.25 = 8.75 \text{ cm}$$

Using Lens formula,

$$\frac{1}{v_o} - \frac{1}{u_o} = \frac{1}{f_o}$$

$$\frac{1}{u_o} = \frac{1}{v_o} - \frac{1}{f_o} = \frac{1}{8.75} - \frac{1}{2} = \frac{2-8.75}{17.5}$$

$$u_o = -\frac{17.5}{6.75} = -2.59 \text{ cm}$$

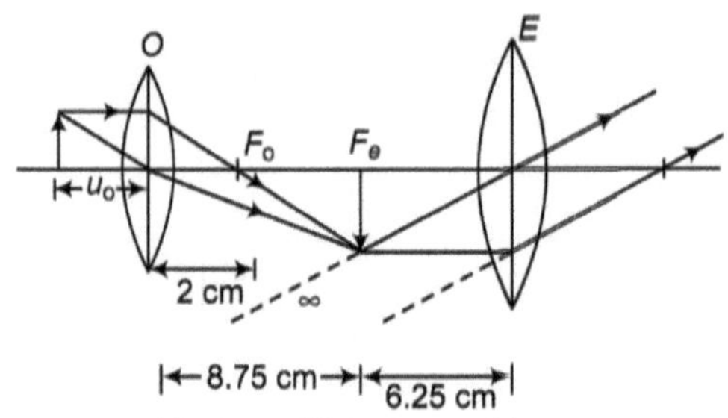

Magnifying power of the microscope

$$m = \frac{v_o}{u_o}\left(1 + \frac{d}{f_e}\right) = \frac{8.75}{2.59}\left(1 + \frac{25}{6.25}\right)$$

$$m = 13.51$$

Question 12. A person with a normal near point (25 cm) using a compound microscope with objective of focal length 8.0 mm and an eye-piece of focal length 2.5 cm can bring an object placed at 9.0 mm from the objective in sharp focus. What is the separation between the two lenses? Calculate the magnifying power of the microscope.

Solution   Given, focal length of objective $f_o = 8$ mm $= 0.8$ cm

Focal length of eye-piece $f_e = 2.5$ cm

Distance of object from objective $-u_o = -9$ mm $= -0.9$ cm

Distance of image from eye-piece

$$v_e = -d = -25 \text{ cm}$$

Using Lens equation for eye-piece

$$\frac{1}{v_e} - \frac{1}{u_e} = \frac{1}{f_e}$$

or

$$\frac{1}{u_e} = \frac{1}{v_e} - \frac{1}{f_e} = -\frac{1}{25} - \frac{1}{2.5} = \frac{-1-10}{25} = -\frac{11}{25}$$

$$u_e = -2.27 \text{ cm}$$

Using Lens equation for objective

$$\frac{1}{v_o} - \frac{1}{u_o} = \frac{1}{f_o}$$

or

$$\frac{1}{v_o} = \frac{1}{f_o} + \frac{1}{u_o} = \frac{1}{0.8} - \frac{1}{0.9} = \frac{0.9 - 0.8}{0.72} = \frac{0.1}{0.72}$$

Distance of image for objective lens

$$v_o = 7.2 \text{ cm}$$

Separation between two lenses

$$L = |u_e| + |v_o| = 2.27 + 7.2$$

$$L = 9.47 \text{ cm}$$

Magnifying power of compound microscope

$$m = \frac{v_o}{u_o}\left(1 + \frac{d}{f_e}\right) = \frac{7.2}{0.9}\left(1 + \frac{25}{2.5}\right)$$

$$m = 88$$

Question 13. A small telescope has an objective lens of focal length 144 cm and an eye-piece of focal length 6.0 cm. What is the magnifying power of the telescope? What is the separation between the objective and the eye-piece?

Solution   Given, focal length of objective lens $f_o = 144$ cm

Focal length of eye-piece $\qquad\qquad f_e = 6$ cm

Magnifying power of the telescope in normal adjustment

(*i.e.,* when the final image is formed at ∞)

$$m = -\frac{f_o}{f_e} = -\frac{144}{6} = -24$$

$\therefore$ Separation between lenses $L = f_o + f_e = 144 + 6 = 150$ cm

Question 14. (a)   A giant refracting telescope at an observatory has an objective lens of focal length 15 m. If an eye-piece of focal length 1.0 cm is used, what is the angular magnification of the telescope?

(b) If this telescope is used to view the moon, what is the diameter of the image of the moon formed by the objective lens? The diameter of the moon is 3.48×10^6 m, and the radius of lunar orbit is 3.8×10^8 m.

Solution   Given, focal length of objective lens, $f_o = 15$ m

Focal length of eye-piece $f_e = 1$ cm $= 0.01$ m

(a) Angular magnification by the telescope

$$m = \frac{f_o}{f_e} = \frac{15}{0.01} = 1500$$

Let d be the diameter of the image of the moon formed by the objective lens.

$\therefore$ Angle subtended by the image $= \dfrac{d}{f_o} = \dfrac{d}{15}$

(b) Diameter of object $\quad d_o = 3.48 \times 10^6$ m

$\qquad$ Radius of orbit $\qquad r = 3.8 \times 10^8$ m

$\qquad$ The angle subtended by the diameter of the moon

$$= \frac{\text{Diameter of moon}}{\text{Radius of lunar orbit}} = \frac{3.48 \times 10^6}{3.8 \times 10^8}$$

The angle subtended by the image is equal to the angle subtended by the object.

$$\therefore \qquad \frac{d_i}{15} = \frac{3.48 \times 10^6}{3.8 \times 10^8}$$

$$\text{or} \qquad d_i = \frac{3.48 \times 15 \times 10^{-2}}{3.8} = 13.73 \times 10^{-2} \text{ m}$$

$$\text{or} \qquad d_i = 13.73 \text{ cm}$$

Thus, the diameter of the image of moon is 13.73 cm.

Question 15. Use the mirror equation to deduce that

(a) an object placed between f and $2f$ of a concave mirror produces a real image beyond $2f$.

(b) a convex mirror always produces a virtual image independent of the location of the object.

(c) the virtual image produced by a convex mirror is always diminished in size and is located between the focus and the pole.

(d) an object placed between the pole and focus of a concave mirror produces a virtual and enlarged image.

[Note: This exercise helps you deduce algebraically properties of images that one obtains from explicit ray diagrams.]

Solution   (a) The mirror equation formula $\dfrac{1}{v} + \dfrac{1}{u} = \dfrac{1}{f}$

For concave mirror $f < 0$, as object always placed on the left side of mirror, so $u < 0$. According to question, $f < u < 2f$

(Object lies between f and $2f$)

$$\frac{1}{2f} > \frac{1}{u} > \frac{1}{f} \text{ or } -\frac{1}{2f} < -\frac{1}{u} < -\frac{1}{f}$$

Add $\dfrac{1}{f}$ on both sides, we get

$$\frac{1}{f} - \frac{1}{2f} < \frac{1}{f} - \frac{1}{u} < 0 \qquad \qquad \ldots(\text{i})$$

From Lens formula, $\dfrac{1}{f} - \dfrac{1}{u} = \dfrac{1}{v}$, so from Eq. (i), we get

$$\frac{1}{f} - \frac{1}{2f} < \frac{1}{v}$$

$$\frac{1}{2f} < \frac{1}{v} \text{ or } v > 2f$$

As, f is negative, $2f$ is also negative and hence v will be also negative. So, the image formed is real and image lies beyond $2f$.

(b) For convex mirror f is always positive $f > 0$. As object always placed on left side of mirror $u < 0$.

From Lens formula, $\dfrac{1}{v} = \dfrac{1}{f} - \dfrac{1}{u}$ as $f > 0$, and $u < 0$

The value of $\dfrac{1}{v} > 0$, or $v > 0$ or v is always positive. The image formed is virtual. It does not depends on the location of object.

(c) For convex mirror $f > 0, u < 0$

From Lens formula, $\dfrac{1}{v} = \dfrac{1}{f} - \dfrac{1}{u}$ so $\dfrac{1}{v} > \dfrac{1}{f}$ or $v < f$

Thus, image always located between pole and focus of the mirror, as $v < |u|$. So the image is always diminished in size.

(d) For concave mirror $f < 0$.

As object is placed between pole and focus.

$\therefore$ $$f < u < 0$$

$\therefore$ $$\dfrac{1}{f} - \dfrac{1}{u} > 0$$

From Lens formula, $\dfrac{1}{f} - \dfrac{1}{u} = \dfrac{1}{v} > 0 \Rightarrow v > 0$

It means that v is positive, image formed on right and virtual.

$$\dfrac{1}{v} < \dfrac{1}{u}$$

$v > |u|$ so image is enlarged.

Question 16. A small pin fixed on a table top is viewed from above from a distance of 50 cm. By what distance would the pin appear to be raised if it is viewed from the same point through a 15 cm thick glass slab held parallel to the table? Refractive index of glass = 1.5. Does the answer depend on the location of the slab?

Solution   Given, thickness of glass slab (real depth) $= 15$ cm

Refractive index of glass $^a\mu_g$ with respect to air $= 1.5$

Using the formula $\quad ^a\mu_g = \dfrac{\text{Real depth}}{\text{Apparent depth}} = \dfrac{15}{^a\mu_g}$

Apparent depth of pin $\quad y = 15 / 1.5 = 10$ cm

Distance by which the pin appears to be raised

$\quad\quad\quad\quad = \text{Real depth} - \text{Apparent depth} = 15 - 10 = 5$ cm

The answer does not depend on the location of the slab.

Alternate Method

Given thickness of glass slab $t = 15$ cm

Refractive index of glass $\mu = 1.5$

The normal shift in the position of the pin

$$d = t\left(1 - \dfrac{1}{\mu}\right) = 15\left(1 - \dfrac{2}{3}\right) = 15 \times \dfrac{1}{3} = 5 \text{ cm}$$

The pin appears raised by 5 cm.

Question 17. (a) Figure shows a cross-section of a 'light pipe' made of a glass fibre of refractive index 1.68. The outer covering of the pipe is made of a material of refractive index 1.44. What is the range of the angles of the incident rays with the axis of the pipe for which total reflections inside the pipe take place, as shown in the figure.

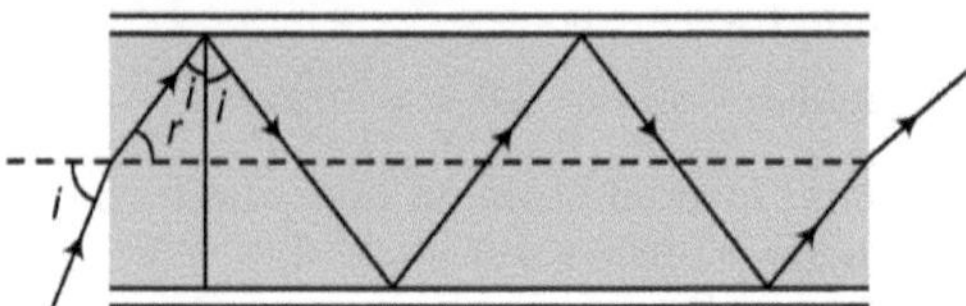

(b) What is the answer if there is no outer covering of the pipe?

The working of an optical fibre is based on the phenomena of total internal reflection. Therefore use condition for total internal reflection.

Solution

(a) Given, refractive index of the glass fibre with respect to air

$$\mu_2 = {}^a\mu_g = 1.68$$

Refractive index of the outer coating material with respect to air

$$\mu_1 = {}^a\mu_{outer} = 1.44$$

Let the critical angle be i_c.

$$\mu = \frac{\mu_2}{\mu_1} = \frac{1}{\sin i_c}$$

$$\sin i_c = \frac{\mu_1}{\mu_2} = \frac{1.44}{1.68} = 0.8571$$

$$i_c = 59°$$

The total internal reflection will take place when the angle of incidence i will be greater than the critical angle i_c
i.e., $i > 59°$ or when angle of refraction, $r < r_{max}$

where $$r_{max} = 90° - i_c = 90° - 59° = 31°$$

So, $${}^a\mu_g = \frac{\sin i_{max}}{\sin r_{max}} = 1.68$$

or $$\sin i_{max} = 1.68 \sin 31° = 1.68 \times 0.5156$$

$$i_{max} = \sin^{-1}(0.8662) = 60°$$

Thus, all the rays which are incident in the range $0 < i < 60°$, will suffer total internal reflection in the pipe (but $i \neq 0$).

(b) If there is no outer covering of the pipe then reflection inside the pipe shall take place from the glass to air

$$\sin i'_c = \frac{\mu_1}{\mu_2} = \frac{1}{1.68} = 0.5952 \quad [\because \mu_1 = 1 \text{ and } \mu_2 = 1.68]$$

Critical angle $\qquad i'_c = 36.5°$

Now, $i = 90°$, we have $r = 36.5°$, $r = 1.68 = \dfrac{\sin 90°}{\sin r}$

So, $i' = 90 - 36.5 = 53.5°$

Here, i' is greater than the critical angle. Thus all the rays incident at an angles in the range zero to $90°$ will suffer total internal reflection.

Question 18. Answer the following questions :

(a) You have learnt that plane and convex mirrors produce virtual images of objects. Can they produce real images under some circumstances? Explain.

(b) A virtual image, we always say, cannot be caught on a screen. Yet when we 'see' a virtual image, we are obviously bringing it on to the 'screen' (*i.e.*, the retina) of our eye. Is there a contradiction?

(c) A diver under water, looks obliquely at a fisherman standing on the bank of a lake. Would the fisherman look taller or shorter to the diver than what he actually is?

(d) Does the apparent depth of a tank of water change if viewed obliquely? If so, does the apparent depth increase or decrease?

(e) The refractive index of diamond is much greater than that of ordinary glass. Is this fact of some use to a diamond cutter?

Solution

(a) Yes, plane and convex mirrors produces the real image if the rays incident on the plane or convex mirror are converging to a point behind the mirror. Because they are reflected to a point on a screen in front of the mirror. In other words, a plane or convex mirror can produce a real image of the object is virtual.

(b) No, there is no contradiction because virtual image formed by the spherical mirror acts as virtual object for eye lens. Our eye lens is convergent and it forms a real image of virtual object on retina.

(c) As the fisherman in air, the rays of light travels from rarer to denser medium, they bends towards the normal. So, the fisherman appears taller.

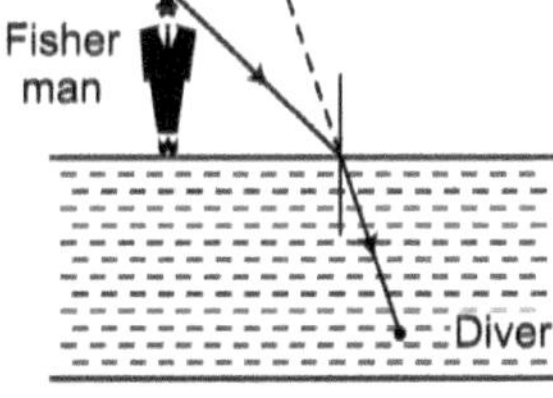

(d) Yes, the apparent depth decreases, further, when water tank is viewed obliquely as compared to the depth when seen near normally.

(e) Refractive index of diamond μ_{diamond} > Refractive index of glass μ_{glass}

Refractive index $\qquad\qquad \mu = \dfrac{1}{\sin i_c}$

where, i_c is the critical angle.

As, the refractive index of diamond is more than the refractive index of water, so the value of critical angle for glass is more than diamond. A diamond cutter, cuts the diamond at large range of angle of incidence to ensure that light entering in the diamond suffers multiple total external reflections. This gives the sparkling to diamond.

Question 19. The image of a small electric bulb fixed on the wall of a room is to be obtained on the opposite wall 3 m away by means of a large convex lens. What is the maximum possible focal length of the lens required for the purpose?

Solution   Suppose the object is placed at u metre in front of the lens and the distance of image from the lens is $(3 - u)$ m

i.e., $\qquad\qquad\qquad v = (3 - u)$ m

From Lens formula,

$$\frac{1}{v} - \frac{1}{u} = \frac{1}{f}$$

$$\frac{1}{(3 - u)} - \frac{1}{-u} = \frac{1}{f}$$

or $\qquad\qquad \dfrac{1}{(3 - u)} + \dfrac{1}{u} = \dfrac{1}{f}$

or $\qquad\qquad \dfrac{u + 3 - u}{u\,(3 - u)} = \dfrac{1}{f}$

$$3f = 3u - u^2$$

$$u^2 - 3u + 3f = 0$$

Now, $\qquad\qquad u = \dfrac{-(-3) \pm \sqrt{9 - 4 \times (3\,f)}}{2}$

$$u = \dfrac{+3 \pm \sqrt{9 - 2f}}{2}$$

Condition for image to be formed real on the screen.

$$9 - 12\,f \geq 0$$

or $\qquad\qquad 9 \geq 12f$ or $f \leq 0.75$ m

Thus, the maximum possible focal length of the lens required for this purpose is 0.75 m.

Question 20. A screen is placed 90 cm from an object. The image of the object on the screen is formed by a convex lens at two different locations separated by 20 cm. Determine the focal length of the lens.

Solution   Given, distance between screen and object $a = 90$ cm

Distance between two locations of the lens $d = 20$ cm

Using the displacement formula

$$f = \frac{a^2 - d^2}{4a} = \frac{(90)^2 - (20)^2}{4 \times 90} = \frac{7700}{360} = 21.4 \text{ cm}$$

Question 21. (a) Determine the 'effective focal length' of the combination of the two lenses in question 10, if they are placed 8.0 cm apart with their principal axes coincident. Does the answer depend on which side of the combination a beam of parallel light is incident? Is the notion of effective focal length of this system useful at all?

(b) An object 1.5 cm in size is placed on the side of the convex lens in the arrangement (a) above. The distance between the object and the convex lens is 40 cm. Determine the magnification produced by the two-lens system, and the size of the image.

Solution (a) Given, $f_1 = 30$ cm the focal length of convex lens.

The focal length of concave lens $f_2 = -20$ cm, $d = 8$ cm

Use the formula,

$$\frac{1}{f} = \frac{1}{f_1} + \frac{1}{f_2} - \frac{d}{f_1 f_2}$$

$$\frac{1}{f} = \frac{1}{30} - \frac{1}{20} - \frac{8}{30 \times (-20)} = \frac{20 - 30 + 8}{30 \times 20}$$

$$\frac{1}{f} = -\frac{2}{600}$$

$$f = -300 \text{ cm}$$

(i) Let us take that the incident beam falls on convex lens and assume that concave lens is absent.

$$u_1 = \infty, \ f_1 = 30 \text{ cm}$$

Using the Lens formula

$$\frac{1}{f_1} = \frac{1}{v_1} - \frac{1}{u_1}$$

$$\frac{1}{30} = \frac{1}{v_1} - \frac{1}{\infty}$$

Position of the image formed by convex lens

$$v_1 = 30 \text{ cm}$$

Now, this image acts as an object for concave lens.

Now, distance of object

$$u_2 = + (30 - 8) = 22 \text{ cm}$$

$$f_2 = -20 \text{ cm}$$

Using Lens formula

$$\frac{1}{f_2} = \frac{1}{v_2} - \frac{1}{u_2}$$

$$\frac{1}{v_2} = -\frac{1}{20} + \frac{1}{22} = -\frac{1}{220}$$

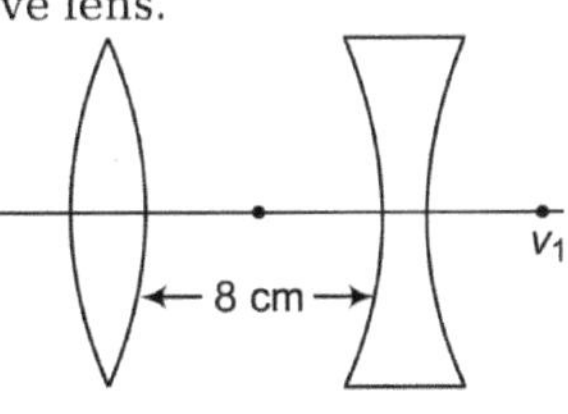

Distance of final image $v_2 = -220$ cm.

Thus, the parallel beam would appear to diverge from a point $220 - 4 = 216$ cm from the centre of two lens system.

(ii) Let us take that the parallel beam first falls on concave lens.

$u_1 = - \infty,\ f_1 = - 20$ cm, $v_1 = ?$

$$\frac{1}{v_1} + \frac{1}{\infty} = \frac{1}{-20}$$

$$v_1 = - 20 \text{ cm}$$

This acts as an object for convex lens.

$$u_2 = - (20 + 8) = - 28 \text{ cm},\ f_2 = 30 \text{ cm},\ v_2 = ?$$

$$\frac{1}{v_2} + \frac{1}{28} = \frac{1}{30}$$

$$\frac{1}{v_2} = \frac{1}{30} - \frac{1}{28} = \frac{14 - 15}{420} = - \frac{1}{420}$$

$$v_2 = - 420 \text{ cm}$$

The parallel beam appears to diverge from a point $420 - 4 = 416$ cm on the left of the centre of the two lens system. From the above two cases it concludes that the answer depends on which side of the lens system the parallel beam is incident. So, the notion of effective focal length does not seem to be useful here.

(b) Given, size of object $O_1 = 1.5$ cm

Distance from the convex lens $\quad u_1 = -40$ cm,

For the convex lens, $\quad \dfrac{1}{v_1} - \dfrac{1}{u_1} = \dfrac{1}{f_1}$

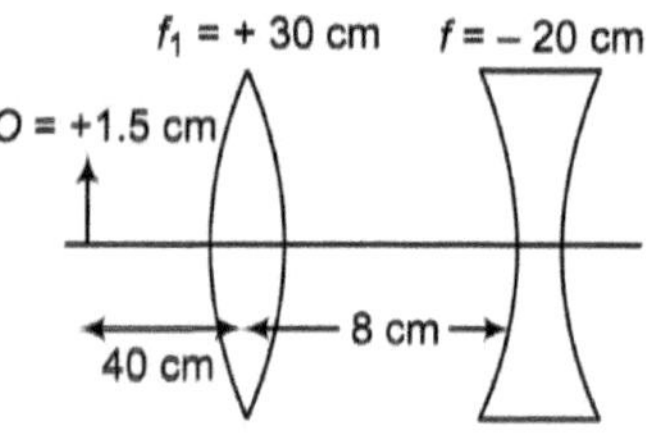

$$\frac{1}{v_1} = \frac{1}{30} + \frac{1}{(-40)}$$

$$= \frac{4 - 3}{120} = \frac{1}{120}$$

$$v_1 = 120 \text{ cm}$$

Magnification produced by convex lens

$$m_1 = \frac{v_1}{u_1} = \frac{120}{-40} = - 3$$

Now, this image acts as an object for concave lens.

∴ For concave lens $u_2 = 120 - 8 = 112$ cm, $f_2 = - 20$ cm

$$\frac{1}{v_2} = \frac{1}{-20} + \frac{1}{112} = \frac{-112 + 20}{112 \times 20} = \frac{-92}{112 \times 20}$$

$$v_2 = \frac{-112 \times 20}{92} \text{ cm}$$

Magnification produced by concave lens

$$m_2 = \frac{v_2}{u_2} = \frac{(-112 \times 20)}{92 \times 112} = \frac{20}{92}$$

Magnification produced by combination

$$m = m_1 \times m_2 = (-3) \times \left(-\frac{20}{90}\right) = \frac{60}{92}$$

$$m = 0.652$$

$$\text{Size of image} = m \times \text{size of objects}$$
$$= 0.652 \times 1.5 = 0.98 \text{ cm}$$

Thus, the magnification produced by the two lens system is 0.652 and size of image is 0.98 cm.

Question 22. At what angle should a ray of light be incident on the face of a prism of refracting angle 60° so that it just suffers total internal reflection at the other face? The refractive index of the material of the prism is 1.524.

Solution Angle of prism, $\qquad A = 60°$

Refractive index of prism $\mu = 1.524$

Let i be the angle of incidence. The critical angle is i_c because it just suffers total internal refraction, so we use critical angle.

$$\sin i_c = \frac{1}{\mu} = \frac{1}{1.524} = 0.6561$$

$$i_c = 41°$$

For a prism $r_1 + r_2 = A$ here $r_2 = i_c$

$$\therefore \qquad\qquad\qquad r_1 + i_c = A$$
$$r_1 + 41° = 60°$$
$$\Rightarrow \qquad\qquad\qquad r_1 = 19°$$

Using the formula, $\qquad\qquad \mu = \dfrac{\sin i_1}{\sin r_1}$

or $\qquad\qquad \sin i_1 = 1.524 \sin 19° = 1.524 \times 0.3256$

or $\qquad\qquad i_1 = \sin^{-1}(0.4962)$

$$i_1 = 29° \, 75'$$

Thus, the angle should be 29° 75'.

Question 23. You are given prisms made of crown glass and flint glass with a wide variety of angles. Suggest a combination of prisms which will

(a) deviate a pencil of white light without much dispersion.

(b) disperse (and displace) a pencil of white light without much deviation.

Solution (a) When a beam of white light is incident on a prism, the emergent beam is dispersed and is deviated from the original path. When two prisms of different material and angles are combined so as to produce dispersion without deviation then such a combination is called direct vision prism. If the two prisms combined produce deviation without dispersion, then such a combination is called a chromatic prism : For the deviation without dispersion, the angular dispersion produced by two prisms should be zero.

i.e., $$(\mu_b - \mu_r)\, A + (\mu'_b - \mu'_r)\, A' = 0$$

As $(\mu'_b - \mu'_r)$ for flint glass is more than that for crown glass. So, $A' < A$ *i.e.,* the prism of flint glass is suitable with crown glass prism of larger angle.

(b) For dispersion without deviation,

$$(\mu_y - 1)\, A + (\mu'_y - 1)\, A' = 0$$

As μ'_y for flint glass is more than μ_y for crown glass. So, $A' < A$, *i.e.,* we use a flint glass prism of smaller angle with crown glass prism of larger angle.

Question 24. For a normal eye, the far point is at infinity and the near point of distinct vision is about 25 cm in front of the eye. The cornea of the eye provides a converging power of about 40 D, and the least converging power of the eye lens behind the cornea is about 20 D. From this rough data estimate the range of accommodation (*i.e.,* the range of converging power of the eye lens) of a normal eye.

Solution Given, the power of cornea $= 40$ D and least converging power of eye lens $= 20$ D

To observe the objects at infinity, the eye uses its least converging power means power is maximum,

i.e., $$= 40 + 20 = 60\ \text{D}$$

The distance between cornea $=$ focal length of eye lens

$$f = \frac{100}{P} = \frac{100}{60} = \frac{5}{3}\ \text{cm}$$

To focus objects at the near point on the retina

$$u = -25\ \text{cm},\ v = \frac{5}{3}\ \text{cm}$$

Using Lens formula, $$\frac{1}{f} = \frac{1}{v} - \frac{1}{u} = \frac{1 \times 3}{5} + \frac{1}{25} = \frac{15 + 1}{25} = \frac{16}{25}$$

$$\Rightarrow \qquad f = \frac{25}{16}\ \text{cm}$$

$$\text{Power of lens} = \frac{1}{f} = \frac{100 \times 16}{25} = 64\ \text{D}$$

$$\therefore \qquad \text{Power of eye lens} = 64 - 40 = 24\ \text{D}$$

Thus, the range of accommodation of the eye lens is 20 D to 24 D.

Question 25. Does short-sightedness (myopia) or long-sightedness (hyper-metropia) imply necessarily that the eye has partially lost its ability of accommodation? If not, what might cause these defects of vision?

Solution No, short-sightedness or long-sightedness does not imply that the eye has partially lost its ability of accommodation. Short-sightedness (myopia) arises when the eye can see near by objects clearly but distant objects are not see clearly due to the shift of the farthest point towards the eye and thus it becomes difficult to see beyond certain limit. This defect (myopia) is due to the elongation of eye ball and in long sightedness (hyper-metropia) one cannot see near by objects clearly. This defect is due to the shortening of eye ball.

Question 26. A myopic person has been using spectacles of power – 1.0 D for distant vision. During old age he also needs to use separate reading glass of power + 2.0 D. Explain what may have happened?

Solution Initially power of spectacles $= -1\,D$, *i.e.*, focal length is (-100) cm. It means that far point of the person is 100 cm and near point is normal *i.e.*, 25 cm. Due to the old age the person use + 2D, spectacles *i.e.*, focal length $f = 50$ cm.

So, $$u = -25 \text{ cm}$$
and $$f = 50 \text{ cm}$$

From the Lens formula, $$\frac{1}{50} = \frac{1}{v} + \frac{1}{25}$$

$$\Rightarrow \quad \frac{1}{v} = \frac{1}{50} - \frac{1}{25} = \frac{1-2}{50} = -\frac{1}{50}$$

$$v = -50 \text{ cm}$$

The near point is a 50 cm.

Question 27. A person looking at a person wearing a shirt with a pattern comprising vertical and horizontal lines is able to see the vertical lines more distinctly than the horizontal ones. What is this defect due to? How is such a defect of vision corrected?

Solution When any person having problem is seeing the vertical and horizontal axes clearly, he/she is suffering from astigmatism. It arises due to non-spherical corneia. In this defect, the shape of eye ball is not perfect spherical. This defect is removed by using cylindrical lenses.

Question 28. A man with normal near point (25 cm) reads a book with small print using a magnifying glass: a thin convex lens of focal length 5 cm.

   (a) What is the closest and the farthest distance at which he should keep the lens from the page so that he can read the book when viewing through the magnifying glass?

(b) What is the maximum and the minimum angular magnification (magnifying power) possible using the above simple microscope?

Solution   Given, near point, $u = 25$ cm

(a) Focal length $f = + 5$ cm, $v = -25$ cm

It is for the closest distance

Using the Lens formula

$$\frac{1}{f} = \frac{1}{v} - \frac{1}{u}$$

$$\frac{1}{5} = \frac{1}{-25} - \frac{1}{u}$$

$$\Rightarrow \qquad \frac{1}{u} = -\frac{1}{25} - \frac{1}{5} = \frac{-1-5}{25} = -\frac{6}{25}$$

$$u = -4.2 \text{ cm}$$

For the farthest distance, $v' = \infty$ and $f = 5$ cm

$$\frac{1}{f} = \frac{1}{v'} - \frac{1}{u'}$$

$$\Rightarrow \qquad \frac{1}{5} = \frac{1}{\infty} - \frac{1}{u'}$$

$$u' = -5 \text{ cm}$$

Thus, the closest and the farthest distances are -4.2 cm and -5 cm, respectively.

(b) Maximum angular magnification

$$m_{\text{max}} = \frac{d}{u} = \frac{25}{\dfrac{25}{6}} = 6$$

Minimum angular magnification is at the farthest distance

$$m_{\text{min}} = \frac{d}{u'} = \frac{25}{5} = 5$$

Question 29. A card sheet divided into squares each of size 1 mm^2 is being viewed at a distance of 9 cm through a magnifying glass (a converging lens of focal length 10 cm) held close to the eye.

    (a) What is the magnification produced by the lens? How much is the area of each square in the virtual image?

    (b) What is the angular magnification (magnifying power) of the lens?

    (c) Is the magnification in (a) equal to the magnifying power in (b)? Explain.

Solution   (a) Given, focal length of converging lens $f = 10$ cm,

    Distance from lens $u = -9$ cm

    Size of object $= 1$ mm

Using Lens formula

$$\frac{1}{f} = \frac{1}{v} - \frac{1}{u}$$

$$\frac{1}{10} = \frac{1}{v} + \frac{1}{9}$$

$$\Rightarrow \qquad \frac{1}{v} = \frac{1}{10} - \frac{1}{9} = -\frac{1}{90}$$

or $$v = -90 \text{ cm}$$

The magnification produced by the lens

$$m = +\frac{v}{u} = -\frac{(+90)}{-9} = 10$$

$$m = \frac{v}{u} = \frac{I}{O}$$

$$I = O \times m = 1 \times 10 = 10 \text{ mm}$$

Area of each square in virtual image $= (10)^2 = 100 \text{ mm}^2$

Thus, the magnification is 10 and area of each square in the virtual image is 10 mm^2.

(b) Angular magnification, $m = \dfrac{d}{u} = \dfrac{25}{9} = 2.8$

$$(\because \text{ Least distance of distinct vision } D = 25 \text{ cm})$$

(c) No, they are equal if $v = d$ (least distance of distinct vision).

Question 30. (a) At what distance should the lens be held from the figure in question 29 in order to view the squares distinctly with the maximum possible magnifying power?

(b) What is the magnification in this case?

(c) Is the magnification equal to the magnifying power in this case? Explain.

Solution (a) Given, $v = -25$ cm and $f = 10$ cm.

For maximum possible magnifying power the image formed at least distant of distinct vision.

Using Lens formula

$$\frac{1}{f} = \frac{1}{v} - \frac{1}{u}$$

$$\Rightarrow \qquad \frac{1}{10} = \frac{1}{-25} - \frac{1}{u}$$

$$\frac{1}{u} = \frac{1}{-25} - \frac{1}{10} = \frac{-2-5}{50} = -\frac{7}{50}$$

$$u = -7.14 \text{ cm}$$

(b) Magnification in this case $m = \dfrac{v}{u} = \dfrac{-25}{-7.14} = 3.5$

(c) Magnifying power $= \dfrac{d}{u} = \dfrac{25}{7.14} = 3.5$

Yes the magnification equal to the magnifying power because, the image formed at least distance of distinct vision.

Question 31. What should be the distance between the object in question 30 and the magnifying glass if the virtual image of each square in the figure is to have an area of 6.25 mm^2. Would you be able to see the squares distinctly with your eyes very close to the magnifier?

Solution Given, area of image, $A_I = 6.25$ mm^2

Area of object, $\qquad\qquad A_O = 1$ mm^2

Focal length of lens, $\quad f = 10$ cm

Linear magnification, $m = \sqrt{\dfrac{A_I}{A_O}} = \sqrt{\dfrac{6.25}{1}} = 2.5$

Again, magnification, $m = \dfrac{v}{u}$

or $\qquad\qquad\qquad\qquad v = m \times v = 2.5 \times u \qquad\qquad\qquad\qquad$ ...(i)

From Lens formula,

$$\frac{1}{f} = \frac{1}{v} - \frac{1}{u}$$

$$\frac{1}{10} = \frac{1}{2.5\,u} - \frac{1}{u}$$

From Eq. (i),

or $\qquad\qquad\qquad\qquad \dfrac{1}{10} = \dfrac{1}{u}\left(\dfrac{1-2.5}{2.5}\right)$

or $\qquad\qquad\qquad\qquad u = \dfrac{-1.5 \times 10}{2.5} = -6$ cm

or $\qquad\qquad\qquad\qquad v = 2.5\,u = 2.5\,(-6) = -15$ cm

Thus, the virtual image is formed at a distance of 15 cm which is less than the near point (25 cm) of a normal human eye. So, it cannot be seen by the eyes distinctly.

Question 32. Answer the following questions :

(a) The angle subtended at the eye by an object is equal to the angle subtended at the eye by the virtual image produced by a magnifying glass. In what sense then does a magnifying glass provide angular magnification?

(b) In viewing through a magnifying glass, one usually positions one's eyes very close to the lens. Does angular magnification change if the eye is moved back?

(c) Magnifying power of a simple microscope is inversely proportional to the focal length of the lens. What then stops us from using a convex lens of smaller and smaller focal length and achieving greater and greater magnifying power?

(d) Why must both the objective and the eye-piece of a compound microscope have short focal lengths?

(e) When viewing through a compound microscope, our eyes should be positioned not on the eye-piece but a short distance away from it for best viewing. Why? How much should be that short distance between the eye and eye-piece?

Solution

(a) As the size of image is much bigger than the size of object and, angular size of image is equal to angular size of object. A magnifying glass helps to see the objects placed closer than the least distance of distinct vision (*i.e.* 25 cm). As closer the object larger be the angular size.

(b) Yes, the angular magnification changes. As the distance between eye and magnifying glass is increased, the angular magnification decreases.

(c) We cannot make the lenses having very small focal length very easily.

(d) As the angular magnification eye-piece produced by the eye-piece of a compound microscope is $\left(\dfrac{25}{f_e} + 1\right)$.

As f_e is small, the angular magnification will be large.

Further, magnification of objective lens is $\dfrac{v}{u}$. As object lies close to focus of objective lens $u \approx f_0$. To increase this magnification $\left(\dfrac{v}{f_0}\right)$,

f_0 should be smaller.

Thus, f_0 and f_e both are small.

(e) When we place our eyes too much close to the eye-piece of a compound microscope, we are unable to collect the refracted light in large amount because the field of view will be reduced. So, the clarity of image is blurred.

The best position of the eye for viewing through a compound microscope is at the eye ring attached to the eye-piece.

Question 33. An angular magnification (magnifying power) of 30 X is desired using an objective of focal length 1.25 cm and an eye-piece of focal length 5 cm. How will you set up the compound microscope?

Solution Given, focal length of objective, $f_0 = 1.25$ cm

Focal length of eye-piece, $\qquad f_e = 5$ cm

Least distance of distinct vision, $d = 25$ cm

Angular magnification of lens, $m_e = 30$

The magnification produced by eye-piece

$$m_e = 1 + \frac{d}{f_e} = 1 + \frac{25}{5} = 6$$

The magnification produced by microscope

$$m = m_o \times m_e$$
$$30 = m_o \times 6$$

where, m_o is the magnification produced by objective lens.

$$m_o = 5$$

Again, we know that magnification of objective lens

$$m_o = \frac{v_o}{u_o}$$

$$5 = \frac{-v_o}{u_o}$$

or $\qquad\qquad\qquad v_o = -5\,u_o \qquad\qquad\qquad\qquad$ ...(i)

Using Lens formula for objective lens,

$$\frac{1}{f_o} = \frac{1}{v_o} - \frac{1}{u_o}$$

$$\frac{1}{1.25} = \frac{1}{-5u_o} - \frac{1}{u_o} = -\frac{6}{5u_o}$$

From Eq. (i), we get

$$u_o = -\frac{6}{5} \times 1.25 = -1.5 \text{ cm}$$

$$v_o = -5u_o = -5\,(-1.5) = 7.5 \text{ cm}$$

Thus, the object should placed at a distance of 1.5 cm from the objective lens to get the desired magnification.

Now, using the Lens formula for eye-piece

$$\frac{1}{f_e} = \frac{1}{v_e} - \frac{1}{u_e}$$

$$\frac{1}{u_e} = \frac{1}{v_e} - \frac{1}{f_e}$$

$$= -\frac{1}{25} - \frac{1}{5} = -\frac{6}{25} \qquad (\because v_e = -25 \text{ cm})$$

$$u_e = -4.17 \text{ cm}$$

The separation between objective and eye-piece

$$|v_o| + |u_e| = 4.17 + 7.5$$
$$= 11.67 \text{ cm}$$

Thus, the microscope is settled as the distance between eye-piece and objective is 11.67 cm.

Question 34. A small telescope has an objective lens of focal length 140 cm and an eye-piece of focal length 5.0 cm. What is the magnifying power of the telescope for viewing distant objects when

    (a) the telescope is in normal adjustment (*i.e.*, when the final image is at infinity)?

    (b) the final image is formed at the least distance of distinct vision (25 cm)?

Solution Given, focal length of objective lens $f_o = 140$ cm and focal length of eye lens $f_e = 5$ cm

(a) For normal adjustment, the magnification

$$m = -\frac{f_o}{f_e} = -\frac{140}{5} = -28$$

(b) For least distance of distinct vision, the magnification

$$m = \frac{f_o}{f_e}\left(1 + \frac{f_e}{d}\right) = \frac{140}{5}\left(1 + \frac{5}{25}\right)$$

$$m = 28\,(1 + 0.2) = 33.6$$

Question 35. (a) For the telescope described in Q. 34 (a), what is the separation between the objective lens and the eye-piece?

    (b) If this telescope is used to view a 100 m tall tower 3 km away, what is the height of the image of the tower formed by the objective lens?

    (c) What is the height of the final image of the tower if it is formed at 25 m?

Solution Given, $f_o = 140$ cm, $f_e = 5$ cm and $d = 25$ cm

    (a) In normal adjustment, the separation between eye-piece and objective

$$= f_o + f_e = 140 + 5 = 145 \text{ cm}$$

    (b) Height of tower, $O_T = 100$ m

Distance of tower, $u = 3$ km $= 3000$ m

The angle subtended by the object.

$$\theta_O = \frac{O_T}{u} = \frac{100}{3000} = \frac{1}{30} \text{ rad} \qquad \ldots(i)$$

The angle subtended by the image.

$$\theta_I = \frac{I_T}{f_o} = \frac{I_T}{140} \qquad \ldots(ii)$$

$$(\because I_T = \text{height of image tower})$$

As

$$\theta_O = \theta_I$$

$$\frac{1}{30} = \frac{I_T}{140}$$

$$I_T = \frac{14}{3} = 4.7 \text{ cm}$$

Thus, the height of image tower is 4.7 cm.

(c) Image formed at distance, $d = 25$ cm, then magnification produced by eye-piece

$$m = 1 + \frac{d}{f_e} = 1 + \frac{25}{5} = 6$$

Let I be the height of the final image of the tower and size of the image formed by objective

$$O = \frac{14}{3} \text{ cm} = 4.7 \text{ cm} \quad \text{or} \quad m = \frac{I}{O}$$

$\therefore$ Height of final image $= m \times O = 6 \times 4.7 = 28.2$ cm

Thus, the height of final image of tower is 28.2 cm.

Question 36. A Cassegrain telescope uses two mirrors as shown in figure. Such a telescope is built with the mirrors 20 mm apart. If the radius of curvature of the large mirror is 220 mm and the small mirror is 140 mm, where will the final image of an object at infinity be?

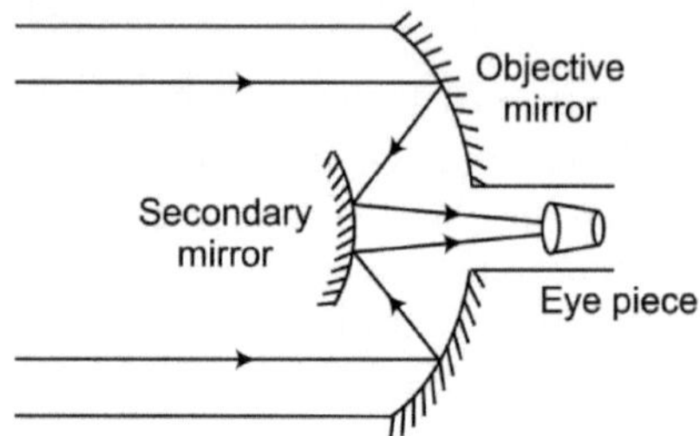

Solution   Given, distance between objective mirror and another mirror

$$d = 20 \text{ mm}$$

Radius of curvature of objective mirror $= R_1 = 220$ mm

$\therefore$ Focal length of objective mirror, $f_1 = \dfrac{220}{2} = 110$ mm

Radius of curvature of small mirror $= R_2 = 140$ mm

$\therefore$ Focal length of small mirror, $f_2 = \dfrac{140}{2} = 70$ mm

The image of an object placed at infinity, formed by the objective mirror, will act as a virtual object for small mirror.

So, the object distance for small mirror $u = f_1 - d$

i.e., $u = 110 - 20 = 90$ mm

Using mirror formula, $\dfrac{1}{v} + \dfrac{1}{u} = \dfrac{1}{f_2}$

$$\frac{1}{v} = \frac{1}{f_2} - \frac{1}{u} = \frac{1}{70} - \frac{1}{90} = \frac{9-7}{630} = \frac{2}{630}$$

$$v = 315 \text{ mm} \quad \text{or} \quad v = 31.5 \text{ cm}$$

Thus, the final image is formed at 315 mm away from small mirror.

Question 37. Light incident normally on a plane mirror attached to a galvanometer coil retraces backwards as shown in figure. A current in the coil produces a deflection of 3.5° of the mirror. What is the displacement of the reflected spot of light on a screen placed 1.5 m away?

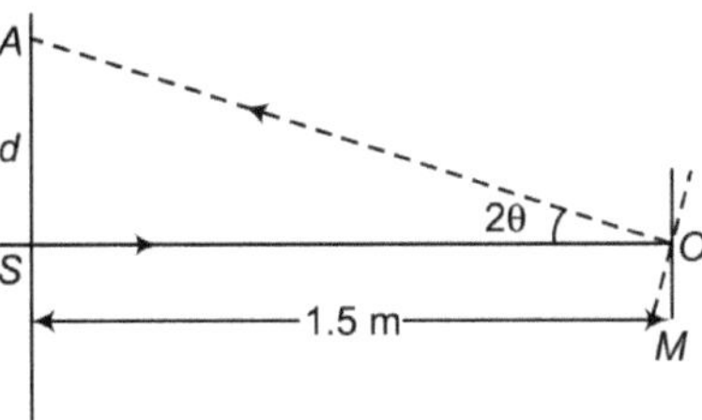

Solution   Given, deflection of the mirror, $\theta = 3.5°$

Distance between screen and mirror, $x = 1.5$ m

As, we know that when mirror turns by angle θ, the relfected ray turned by 2θ.

$$\therefore \qquad 2\theta = 3 \times 3.5 = 7° = \frac{7\pi}{180} \text{ rad}$$

Again, in $\triangle AOS$

$$\tan 2\theta = \frac{AS}{\sin \theta}$$

$$\tan \left(\frac{7\pi}{180}\right) = \frac{AS}{1.5} = \frac{d}{1.5}$$

or $$d = 1.5 \tan \left(\frac{7\pi}{180}\right)$$

For small angle, $$\tan \frac{7\pi}{180} \approx \frac{7\pi}{180}$$

$$d = 1.5 \times \frac{7\pi}{180} = 0.18 \text{ m}$$

Question 38. Figure shows an equiconvex lens (of refractive index 1.50) in contact with a liquid layer on top of a plane mirror. A small needle with its tip on the principal axis is moved along the axis until its inverted image is found at the position of the needle. The distance of the needle from the lens is measured to be 45.0 cm. The liquid is removed and the experiment is repeated. The new distance is measured to be 30.0 cm. What is the refractive index of the liquid?

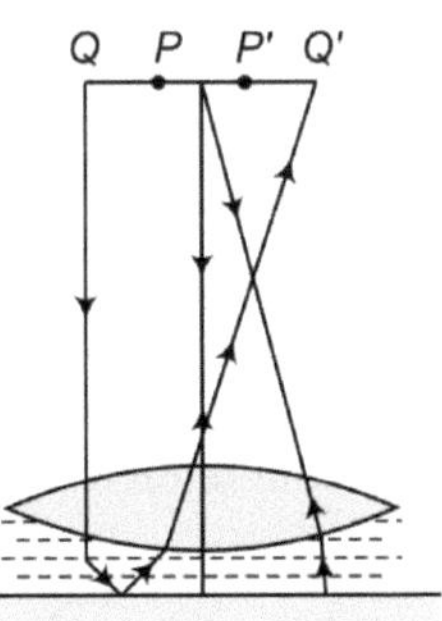

Solution   Given, focal length of double convex lens of glass, $f_1 = 30$ cm.

Focal length of combination of double convex lens and plano concave liquid lens $f = 45$ cm

Refractive index of lens, $\mu_g = 1.5$

Let f_2 be the focal length of the plano concave lens made of liquid between the convex lens and plane mirror.

For combination of lenses

$$\frac{1}{f_1} + \frac{1}{f_2} = \frac{1}{f}$$

$$\frac{1}{30} + \frac{1}{f_2} = \frac{1}{45}$$

$\Rightarrow$

$$\frac{1}{f_2} = \frac{1}{45} - \frac{1}{30} = -\frac{1}{90}$$

$$f_2 = -90 \text{ cm}$$

We know that radii of curvature of two surfaces of plano-concave lens of liquid formed between foci convex lens and plane mirror are $-R$ and ∞.

For the convex lens of glass, $R_1 = R, \ R_2 = -R$

Using Lens maker's formula

$$\frac{1}{f_1} = (\mu - 1)\left(\frac{1}{R_1} - \frac{1}{R_2}\right)$$

$$= \left(\frac{3}{2} - 1\right)\left(\frac{1}{R} + \frac{1}{R}\right)$$

$$\frac{1}{30} = \frac{1}{2} \times \frac{2}{R}$$

$\Rightarrow$

$$R = 30 \text{ cm}$$

Again, $R_1 = -R = -30$ cm, $R_2 = \infty$

Using the Lens maker's formula

$$\frac{1}{f_2} = (\mu_l - 1)\left(\frac{1}{R_1} - \frac{1}{R_2}\right)$$

$$-\frac{1}{90} = (\mu_l - 1)\left(\frac{1}{-30} - \frac{1}{\infty}\right)$$

$$\frac{1}{90} = \frac{1}{30}(\mu_l - 1)$$

$$\mu_l = 1 + \frac{1}{3} = \frac{4}{3} = 1.33$$

Thus, the refractive index of liquid is $\dfrac{4}{3}$ or 1.33.

Selected NCERT Exemplar Problems

Question 1. For a glass prims ($\mu = \sqrt{3}$) the angle of minimum deviation is equal to the angle of the prism. Find the angle of prism.

Solution For minimum deviation

Refractive index of the material of prism

$$\mu = \frac{\sin\left(\dfrac{A + \delta_m}{2}\right)}{\sin A/2} \qquad \begin{bmatrix} A \text{ be the angle of prism} \\ \text{and } \delta_m \text{ be the angle of} \\ \text{minimum deviation} \end{bmatrix}$$

Given, angle of deviation $\delta_m = A$

$$\mu = \frac{\sin (A)}{\sin A/2} = \frac{2\sin A/2 \cos A/2}{\sin A/2}$$

or

$$\frac{\mu}{2} = \cos(A/2)$$

or

$$A/2 = \cos^{-1}(\sqrt{3}/2) = 30°$$

or

$$A = 60°$$

Question 2. A short object of length L is placed along the principal axis of a concave mirror away from focus. The object distance is u. If the mirror has a focal length f . What will be the length of the image? You may take $L \ll (u - f)$.

Solution Length of object $= L$

Let O be the mid-point of the object O, u_1 and u_2 be the distances of both the ends from pole P

O_2 O O_1 P

u_1 u u_2

i.e.,

$$OP = u, O_1P = u_1, O_2P = u_2$$

$$(u_1 - u_2) = L = O_1O_2$$

$$OO_1 = OO_2 = \frac{L}{2}$$

$\therefore$

$$u_1 = u - \frac{L}{2} \quad \text{and} \quad u_2 = u + \frac{L}{2}$$

Let the image has ends at v_1 and v_2 and the length of image is $L' = (v_1 - v_2)$

Now using the mirror formula

$$\frac{1}{u} + \frac{1}{v} = \frac{1}{f} \quad \Rightarrow \quad v = \frac{fu}{u - f}$$

So,
$$v_1 = \frac{fu_1}{u_1 - f} = \frac{f(u - L/2)}{u - f - L/2}$$

and
$$v_2 = \frac{fu_2}{u_2 - f} = \frac{f(u + L/2)}{u - f + L/2}$$

$\therefore$
$$L' = (v_1 - v_2) = \left| \frac{f(u - L/2)}{-(u - f - L/2)} - \frac{f(u + L/2)}{(u - f + L/2)} \right|$$

or
$$L' = \frac{f^2 L \cdot u}{(u - f)^2 - L^2/4}$$

As the object is short and kept away from focus, we have $\dfrac{L^2}{4} << (u - f)^2$.

So, neglect $\dfrac{L^2}{4}$ as compared to $(u - f)^2$

$\therefore$
$$L' = \frac{f^2}{(u - f)^2} L$$

Question 3. A circular disc of radius R is placed co-axially and horizontally inside an opaque hemispherical bowl of radius a (figure). The far edge of the disc is just visible when viewed from the edge of the bowl. The bowl is filled with transparent liquid of refractive index μ and the near edge of the disc becomes just visible. How far below the top of the bowl is the disc placed?

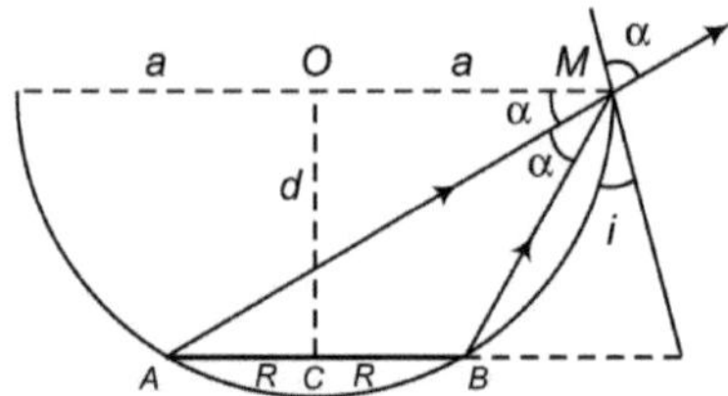

Solution Let the disc is placed at distance d from the top. Initially AM is the direction of incident ray before filling the liquid, as the liquid is filled the incident ray is BM.

Now
$$\frac{1}{\mu} = \frac{\sin i}{\sin r} = \frac{\sin i}{\sin \alpha} \qquad \ldots(i)$$

$$\sin i = \frac{a - R}{\sqrt{d^2 + (a - R)^2}} \qquad \text{and} \quad \sin \alpha = \cos(90 - \alpha)$$

$$\sin \alpha = \frac{a + R}{\sqrt{d^2 + (a + R)^2}}$$

Putting in Eq. (i), we get

$$\text{Distance, } d = \frac{(a-R)^2(a+R)^2[\mu^2-1]}{\sqrt{(a+R)^2-\mu(a-R)^2}} = \frac{(a^2-R^2)^2[\mu^2-1]}{\sqrt{(a+R)^2-\mu(a-R)^2}}$$

$$\frac{1}{\mu} = \frac{\dfrac{a-R}{\sqrt{d^2+(a-R)^2}}}{\dfrac{a+R}{\sqrt{d^2+(a+R)^2}}}$$

Question 4. A thin convex lens of focal length 25 cm is cut into two pieces 0.5 cm above the principal axis. The top part is placed at (0, 0) and an object placed at (– 50 cm, 0), Find the coordinates of the image.

Solution Focal length of convex lens $f = 25$ cm

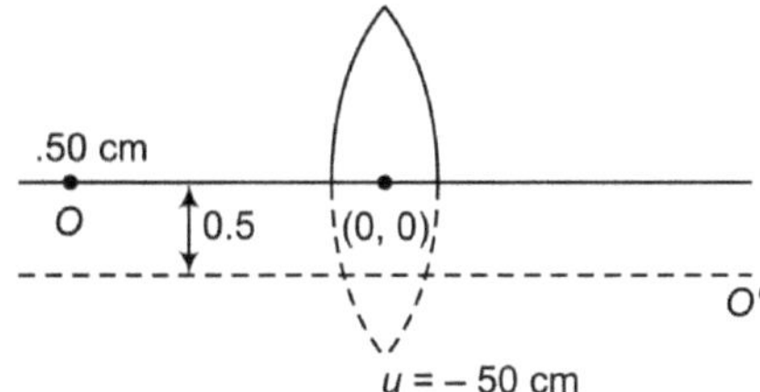

Let there is no cut, the object have been at a height of 0.5 cm from principal axis OO'.

Using Lens formula

$$\frac{1}{v} - \frac{1}{u} = \frac{1}{f}$$

$$\frac{1}{v} = \frac{1}{f} + \frac{1}{u} = -\frac{1}{50} + \frac{1}{25} = \frac{1}{50}$$

$$v = 50 \text{ cm}$$

$$\text{Magnification, } m = \frac{v}{u} = \frac{-50}{+50} = -1$$

Thus, the image would have been formed at 50 cm from lens and 0.5 cm below principal axis. Hence, the coordinates of image are (50 cm, – 1 cm).

Question 5. A jar of height h is filled with a transparent liquid of refractive index μ (figure). At the centre of the jar on the bottom surface is a dot. Find the minimum diameter of a disc, such that when placed on the top surface symmetrically about the centre the dot is invisible.

Solution From Snell's law,

$$\sin i = \frac{1}{\mu} \qquad \ldots(i)$$

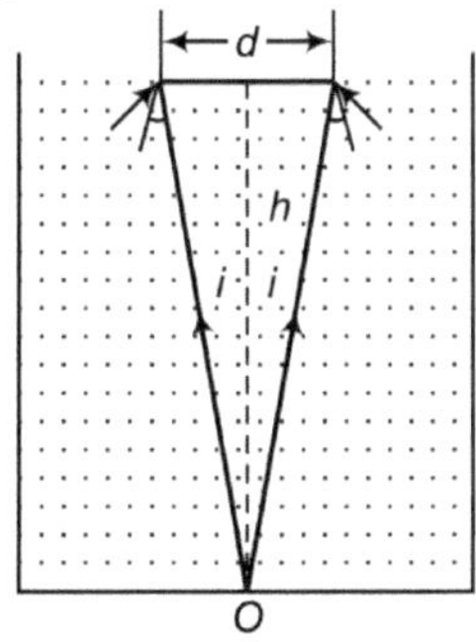

$$\tan i = \frac{d/2}{h} \qquad \text{[From Eq. (i)]}$$

or
$$d = 2h \tan i$$
$$d = \frac{2h}{\sqrt{(\mu^2 - 1)}}$$
$$\left[\because \tan i = \frac{1}{\sqrt{\mu^2 - 1}} \right]$$

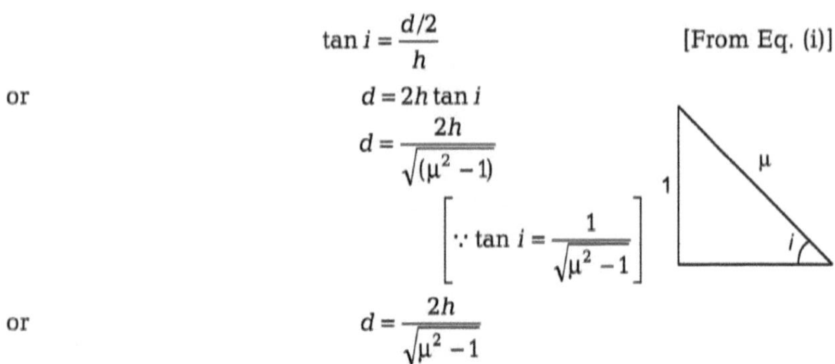

or
$$d = \frac{2h}{\sqrt{\mu^2 - 1}}$$

Question 6. Show that for a material with refractive index $\mu \geq \sqrt{2}$ light incident at any angle shall be guided along a length perpendicular to the incident face.

Solution Any ray which is entering at an angle of incidence i shall be guided along AC if the ray makes with the face $AC(\phi)$ is greater than the critical angle

$$\sin \phi \geq \frac{1}{\mu}$$

$$\cos r \geq \frac{1}{\mu}$$

or
$$1 - \cos^2 r \leq 1 - \frac{1}{\mu^2}$$

or
$$\sin^2 r \leq 1 - \frac{1}{\mu^2}$$

We know that
$$\sin i = \mu \sin r$$

$\therefore$
$$\frac{1}{\mu^2} \sin^2 i \leq 1 - \frac{1}{\mu^2}$$

or
$$\sin^2 i \leq \mu^2 - 1$$

The angle (smallest) ϕ shall be when $i = \pi/2$. If that is greater than the critical angle then all other angles of incidence shall be more than the critical angle.

If
$$i = \pi/2$$
$$\sin^2 \pi/2 \leq \mu^2 - 1$$
or
$$1 \leq \mu^2 - 1$$
or
$$\mu^2 \geq 2$$
or
$$\mu \geq \sqrt{2}$$

Question 7. An infinitely long cylinder of radius R is made of an unusual exotic material with refractive index-1 (figure). The cylinder is placed between two planes whose normals are along the Y-direction. The centre of the cylinder O lies along the Y-axis. A narrow laser beam is directed along the Y-direction from the lower plate. The laser source is at a horizontal distance x

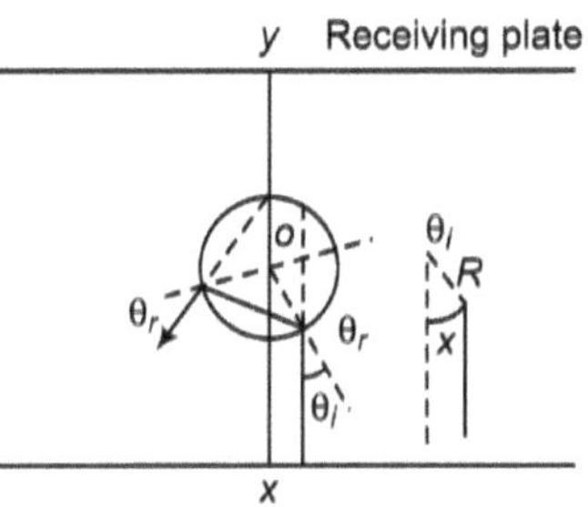

from the diameter in the Y-direction. Find the range of x such that light emitted from the lower plane does not reach the upper plane.

Solution The material of refractive index 1, θ_r is negative and θ'_r is positive.

Now
$$|\theta_i| = |\theta_r| = |\theta'_r|$$

For the total deviation of the outcoming ray from the incoming ray is $4\theta_i$. Rays shall not reach at receiving plate if

$$\frac{\pi}{2} \leq 4\theta_i \leq \frac{3\pi}{2}$$

$$\frac{\pi}{8} \leq \theta_i \leq \frac{3\pi}{8}$$

From the figure
$$\sin \theta_i = \frac{x}{R}$$

$\therefore$
$$\frac{\pi}{8} \leq \sin^{-1} \frac{x}{R} \leq \frac{3\pi}{8}$$

Thus, for $\dfrac{R\pi}{8} \leq x \leq \dfrac{R \cdot 3\pi}{8}$ light emitted from the source shall not reach the receiving plate.

Chapter **10**

Wave Optics

Important Results

1. $\dfrac{w_1}{w_2} = \dfrac{a^2}{b^2} = \dfrac{I_1}{I_2}$

   where, w_1, w_2 are the slit widths, a, b are the amplitudes of waves and I_1, I_2 are intensities.

2. When the two sources are coherent and there is interference

   $$\dfrac{I_{max}}{I_{min}} = \dfrac{(a+b)^2}{(a-b)^2}$$

3. The intensity at any point, where phase difference is ϕ.

   $$I = K[I_1 + I_2 + 2\sqrt{I_1 \cdot I_2}\, \cos \phi]$$

4. In the Young's double- slit experiment; the position

   (i) of bright fringes is given by $x = n\dfrac{D\lambda}{d}$,   where $n = 1, 2, 3, \ldots$

       D is distance between screen and slit,

       d is distance between two slits,

       λ is wavelength of light.

   (ii) of dark fringes is given by $x = (2n-1)\dfrac{D\lambda}{2d}$,   where $n = 1, 2, 3, \ldots$

5. Fringe width is given by $\beta = \dfrac{\lambda D}{d}$

6. When the apparatus is immersed in a transparent medium of refractive index, the fringe width will given by

   $$\beta' = \dfrac{\beta}{\mu} = \dfrac{\lambda D}{\mu d} \qquad\qquad (\lambda' = \lambda/\mu)$$

7. Angular fringe width is given by $\theta = \dfrac{\beta}{D} = \dfrac{\lambda}{d}$

8. Condition for diffraction

   (i) minima $a\sin\theta = n\lambda$,   where $n = 1, 2, 3, \ldots$

   (ii) maxima $a\sin\theta = (2n+1)\dfrac{\lambda}{2}$,   where $n = 1, 2, 3, \ldots$

9. Width of central maximum is given by $2x = \dfrac{2D\lambda}{d} = \dfrac{2f\,\lambda}{d}$

10. Angular width of central maxima is given by $2\theta = \dfrac{2\lambda}{a}$

11. According to the Brewster's law, refractive index is given by
$$\mu = \tan i_p,$$
where, i_p is polarising angle.

12. Fresnel's distance is given by $Z_f = \dfrac{a^2}{\lambda}$

where a is aperture and λ is wavelength.

Exercises

Question 1. Monochromatic light of wavelength 589 nm is incident from air on a water surface. What are the wavelength, frequency and speed of (a) reflected and (b) refracted light? Refractive index of water is 1.33.

Solution   Given, wavelength of light $\lambda = 589$ nm $= 589 \times 10^{-9}$ m

Refractive index of water $\mu_w = 1.33$

(a) **For reflected light**

 (i) Wavelength of reflected light $\lambda = 589 \times 10^{-9}$ m

 (ii) Frequency of reflected light $v = \dfrac{c}{\lambda} = \dfrac{3 \times 10^8}{589 \times 10^{-9}}$

 where c is velocity of light $(\because$ Speed of light $c = 3 \times 10^8$ m/s$)$
$$v = 5.09 \times 10^{14} \text{ Hz}$$

(iii) As the medium takes place in the same medium so
     Speed of reflected light $c = 3 \times 10^8$ m/s

(b) **For refracted light**   (In this process wavelength and speed changes but frequency remains the same)

Wavelength of refracted light $\lambda' = \dfrac{\lambda}{\mu} = \dfrac{589 \times 10^{-9}}{1.33} = 4.42 \times 10^{-7}$ m

Velocity of refracted light $v = \dfrac{c}{\mu} = \dfrac{3 \times 10^8}{1.33} = 2.25 \times 10^8$ m/s

Question 2. What is the shape of the wavefront in each of the following cases?

 (a) Light diverging from a point source.
 (b) Light emerging out of a convex lens when a point source is placed at its focus.

(c) The portion of the wavefront of light from a distant star intercepted by the earth.

Solution   (a) When the light diverging from a point source, then the shape of wavefront is diverging spherical as shown in diagram.

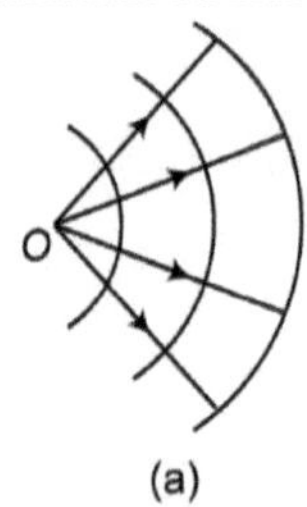

(a)

(b) As the rays of light becomes parallel after refraction from convex lens. So the wavefront is plane as shown in diagram.

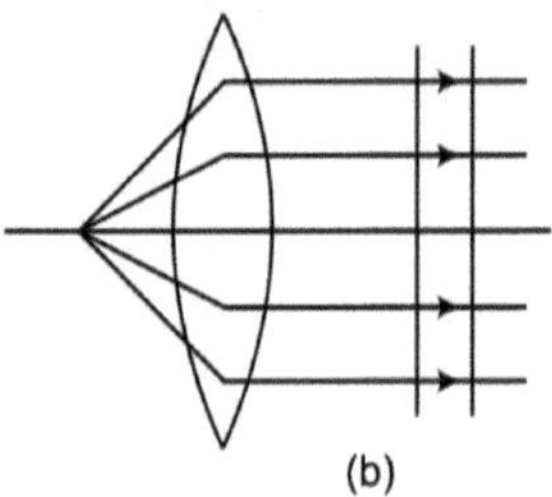

(b)

(c) The light rays which are coming from a distant star are almost parallel to each other. Thus, the wavefront is plane as shown in diagram.

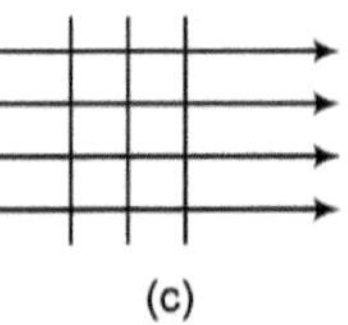

(c)

Question 3.   (a) The refractive index of glass is **1.5**. What is the speed of light in glass? (Speed of light in vacuum is 3.0×10^8 m/s)

(b) Is the speed of light in glass independent of the colour of light? If not, which of the two colours red and violet travels slower in a glass prism?

Solution   (a) Given, refractive index of glass $\mu_{glass} = 1.5$

Speed of light in vacuum $c = 3 \times 10^8$ m/s

Speed of light in glass $v = \dfrac{c}{\mu} = \dfrac{3 \times 10^8}{1.5}$

$$v = 2 \times 10^8 \text{ m/s}$$

(b) No, the speed of light is not independent of colour of light.

As we know that the refractive index of violet is greater than red,

$$\mu_V > \mu_R$$

So, velocity of violet is less than the velocity of red. Therefore, violet colour travels slower in glass, then the red colour

$$v_V < v_R$$

Question 4. In a Young's double-slit experiment, the slits are separated by 0.28 mm and the screen is placed 1.4 m away. The distance between the central bright fringe and the fourth bright fringe is measured to be 1.2 cm. Determine the wavelength of light used in the experiment.

Solution Given, separation between slits $d = 0.28$ mm $= 0.28 \times 10^{-3}$ m.

Distance between screen and slit $D = 1.4$ m,
Distance between central bright and fourth bright fringe
$$x = 1.2 \text{ cm} = 1.2 \times 10^{-2} \text{ m}$$

Number of fringes $n = 4$

For constructive interference $x = n\dfrac{D\lambda}{d}$

$$1.2 \times 10^{-2} = \frac{4 \times 1.4 \times \lambda}{0.28 \times 10^{-3}}$$

Wavelength,
$$\lambda = \frac{1.2 \times 10^{-2} \times 0.28 \times 10^{-3}}{4 \times 1.4}$$

$$\lambda = 6 \times 10^{-7} \text{ m}$$

or
$$\lambda = 600 \times 10^{-9} \text{ m}$$

$$= 600 \text{ nm} \qquad [\because 1 \text{ nm} = 10^{-9} \text{ m}]$$

The wavelength of light is 6×10^{-7} m.

Question 5. In Young's double-slit experiment using monochromatic light of wavelength λ, the intensity of light at a point on the screen where path difference is λ is K units. What is the intensity of light at a point where path difference is $\lambda/3$?

Solution Given, wavelength of light $= \lambda$

When the path difference is λ (x), the phase difference

$$\phi = \frac{2\pi}{\lambda} \cdot x = \frac{2\pi}{\lambda} \cdot \lambda = 2\pi$$

Resultant intensity $I_R = I_1 + I_2 + 2\sqrt{I_1 I_2} \cos \phi$

$$I_R = I + I + 2\sqrt{II} \cos 2\pi = 2I + 2I = 4I = K \qquad \text{(Given)} \qquad \ldots \text{(i)}$$

$$(\because I_1 = I_2 = I)$$

When path difference is $\lambda/3$, then

$$\text{Phase difference} = \frac{2\pi}{\lambda} \cdot \frac{\lambda}{3} = \frac{2\pi}{3}$$

In this condition, resultant intensity

$$I'_R = I + I + 2\sqrt{II}\ \cos\frac{2\pi}{3} = 2I + 2I\left(-\frac{1}{2}\right) \quad \left[\because \cos\frac{2\pi}{3} = -\frac{1}{2}\right]$$

$$I'_R = I = \frac{K}{4} \qquad\qquad\qquad\qquad \text{[From Eq. (i)]}$$

Thus, the intensity of light at a point of path difference $\dfrac{\lambda}{3}$ is $\dfrac{K}{4}$.

Question 6. A beam of light consisting of two wavelengths 650 nm and 520 nm is used to obtain interference fringes in a Young's double-slit experiment.

    (a) Find the distance of the third bright fringe on the screen from the central maximum for wavelength 650 nm.

    (b) What is the least distance from the central maximum where the bright fringes due to both the wavelengths coincide?

Solution   Given, wavelength $\lambda_1 = 650$ nm $= 650 \times 10^{-9}$ m

and $\qquad\qquad\qquad\qquad\qquad\qquad \lambda_2 = 520$ nm $= 520 \times 10^{-9}$ m

    (a) For third fringe bright, $n = 3$

        The distance of third bright fringe from central maximum.

$$x = \frac{n\lambda D}{d} = 3 \times 650 \times 10^{-9} \times \frac{D}{d}\ \text{m}$$

$$= \frac{3 \times 650 \times 10^{-9} \times 1.2}{2 \times 10^{-3}} = 1.17 \times 10^{-3}\ \text{m}$$

    (b) Let nth bright fringe due to wavelength $\lambda_2 = 520$ nm, coincide with $(n + 1)$th bright fringe due to wavelength $\lambda_1 = 650$ nm.

i.e., $\qquad\qquad\qquad\qquad n\lambda_2 \dfrac{D}{d} = (n - 1)\ \lambda_1 \dfrac{D}{d}$

$$n \times 520 \times 10^{-9} = (n - 1)\ 650 \times 10^{-9}$$

or $\qquad\qquad\qquad\qquad\qquad\qquad 4n = 5n - 5$

or $\qquad\qquad\qquad\qquad\qquad\qquad n = 5$

Thus, the least distance $\qquad\qquad\qquad x = n\lambda_2 \dfrac{D}{d} = 5 \times 520 \times 10^{-9}\ \dfrac{D}{d}$

$$x = 2600\ \frac{D}{d} \times 10^{-9}\ \text{m}$$

$$= 2600 \times \frac{1.2 \times 10^{-9}}{2 \times 10^{-3}}\ \text{m}$$

$$= 1.56 \times 10^{-3}\ \text{m} = 1.56\ \text{mm}$$

Question 7. In a double-slit experiment the angular width of a fringe is found to be 0.2° on a screen placed 1 m away. The wavelength of light used is 600 nm. What will be the angular width of the fringe if the entire experimental apparatus is immersed in water? Take refractive index of water to be 4/3.

Solution   Given, angular width $\theta = 0.2°$

Distance between screen and slit $D = 1\,\text{m}$

Wavelength of light $\lambda = 600\,\text{nm} = 600 \times 10^{-9}\,\text{m}$

Refractive index of water $\mu_w = \dfrac{4}{3}$

Using the formula of angular width

$$\theta = \frac{\lambda}{D} \qquad\qquad \dots(\text{i})$$

and

$$\theta' = \frac{\lambda'}{D} \qquad\qquad \dots(\text{ii})$$

where,

$$\lambda' = \frac{\lambda}{\mu}$$

Dividing Eq. (ii) from Eq. (i), we get

$$\frac{\theta'}{\theta} = \frac{\lambda'}{\lambda} = \frac{\lambda}{\mu\lambda}$$

or

$$\theta' = \frac{\theta}{\mu} = \frac{0.2 \times 3}{4} = 0.15 \qquad \left(\because \mu = \frac{4}{3}\right)$$

Thus, the angular fringe width is 0.15° as the apparatus is immersed in water.

Question 8.   What is the Brewster's angle for air to glass transition? (Refractive index of glass = 1.5)

Solution   Given, $\qquad\qquad \mu_g = 1.5$

Let i_p be the Brewster's angle.

From the Brewster's law,

Refractive index, $\qquad\qquad \mu = \tan i_p$

or $\qquad\qquad \tan i_p = 1.5$

$$i_p = \tan^{-1}(1.5)$$

$$i_p = 56°\,18'$$

Question 9.   Light of wavelength 5000 Å falls on a plane reflecting surface. What are the wavelength and frequency of the reflected light? For what angle of incidence is the reflected ray normal to the incident ray?

Solution   Given, wavelength of light $\lambda = 5000\,\text{Å} = 5000 \times 10^{-10}\,\text{m}$

On the reflection there is no change in wavelength and frequency. So, wavelength of reflected light will be 5000 Å.

Frequency of the incident light $v = \dfrac{c}{\lambda} = \dfrac{3 \times 10^{8}}{5 \times 10^{-7}} = 6 \times 10^{14}$ Hz

When reflected ray is normal to the incident ray
AO and BO are the incident and reflected rays.

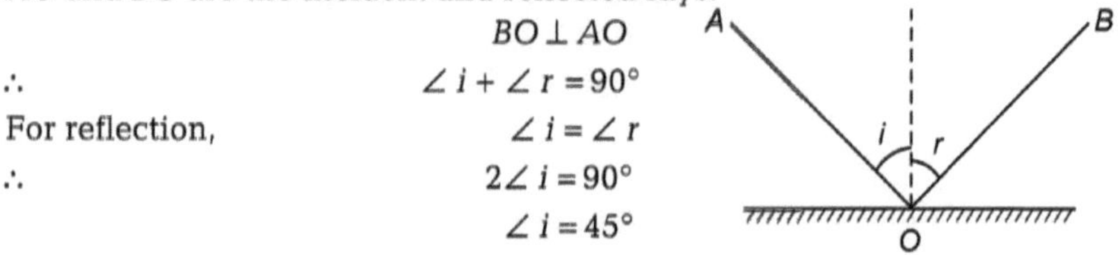

$$BO \perp AO$$
$\therefore$
$$\angle i + \angle r = 90°$$
For reflection,
$$\angle i = \angle r$$
$\therefore$
$$2\angle i = 90°$$
$$\angle i = 45°$$

Thus, the angle of incidence is 45°.

Question 10. Estimate the distance for which ray optics is good approximation for an aperture of 4 mm and wavelength 400 nm.

Solution   Given, aperture $a = 4$ mm $= 4 \times 10^{-3}$ m

Wavelength $\lambda = 400$ nm $= 400 \times 10^{-9}$ m

Ray optics is good approximation upto a distance equal to Fresnel's distance (Z_F).

$$Z_F = \dfrac{a^2}{\lambda} = \dfrac{4 \times 10^{-3} \times 4 \times 10^{-3}}{400 \times 10^{-9}}$$

$$Z_F = 40 \text{ m}$$

Additional Exercises

Question 11. The 6563 Å H_α sign line emitted by hydrogen in a star is found to be red-shifted by 15 Å. Estimate the speed with which the star is receding from the earth.

Solution   Given, wavelength of H_α, $\lambda = 6563$ Å $= 6563 \times 10^{-10}$ m

Red-shift $\Delta\lambda = 15$ Å

Since, the star is found to be red-shifted, hence star is receding away from earth and doppler's shift is negative.

$$\Delta\lambda = -v\dfrac{\lambda}{c}$$

$$v = -\dfrac{\Delta\lambda.c}{\lambda} = -\dfrac{15 \times 3 \times 10^{8}}{6563}$$

$$v = -6.86 \times 10^{5} \text{ m/s}$$

Negative sign shows that the star is receding away from earth.

Question 12. Explain, how Corpuscular theory predicts the speed of light in a medium, say, water, to be greater than the speed of light in vacuum. Is the prediction confirmed by experimental determination of the speed of light in water? If not, which alternative picture of light is consistent with experiment?

Solution   Suppose the speed of light in air is v_1 and the speed of light in water is v_2, $\angle i$ is the angle of incidence in air and $\angle r$ is the angle of refraction in water.

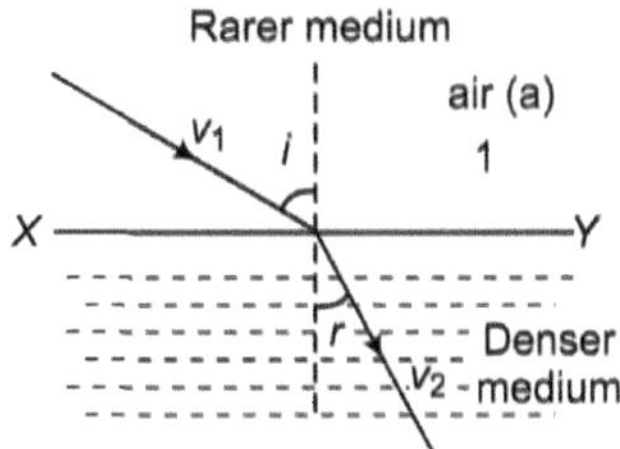

Now, according to Newton's Corpuscular theory of light, when the Corpuscular of light strike the interface XY, separating surface of denser and rarer mediums, the components of their velocities along XY remains the same.

The component of v_1 along $XY = v_1 \sin i$ ...(i)

The component of v_2 along $XY = v_2 \sin r$ ...(ii)

According to the Corpuscular theory

$$v_1 \sin i = v_2 \sin r$$

or $$\frac{v_2}{v_1} = \frac{\sin i}{\sin r}$$ ...(iii)

From Snell's law

$$\frac{\sin i}{\sin r} = {}^{air}\mu_{water}$$ ...(iv)

By Eq. (iii) and Eq. (iv), we get

$$\frac{v_2}{v_1} = {}^{air}\mu_{water}$$ $(\because {}^{a}\mu_w > 1)$

$\therefore$ $$\frac{v_2}{v_1} > 1$$

or $$v_2 > v_1$$

It means that the velocity of light in the denser medium is greater than the velocity of light in the rarer medium.

This prediction of Newton's theory is opposite to the experimental result.

Now, by the Huygen's wave theory predicts that $v_2 < v_1$ which is consistent with experiment.

Question 13. You have learnt in the text how Huygen's principle leads to the laws of reflection and refraction. Use the same principle to deduce directly that a point object placed in front of a plane mirror produces a virtual image whose distance from the mirror is equal to the object distance from the mirror.

Solution Let P be the point object placed at a distance r from a plane mirror M_1M_2. Now, take point P as a centre and $PO = r$ as radius, draw an arc XY. This is the spherical wavefront from the object, incident on M_1M_2. If mirrors were not present, the position of wavefront XY would be $X'Y'$ where $PP' = 2r$. In the presence of mirror, wavefront XY would appear as $X''PY''$, according to the Huygen's construction. As it is clear from the figure $X'Y'$ and

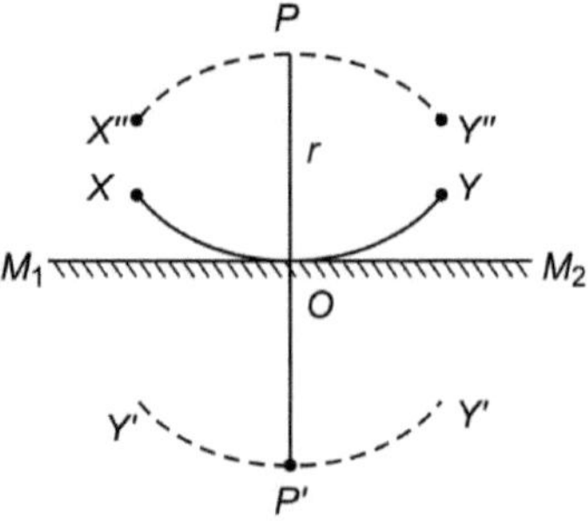

$X''Y''$ are two arcs located symmetrically on either side of M_1M_2. So, $X'PY'$ can be treated as reflected image of $X''PY''$ from geometry $OP = OP'$, which was to be proved.

Question 14. Let us list some of the factors which could possibly influence the speed of wave propagation

   (i) nature of the source.

  (ii) direction of propagation.

 (iii) motion of the source and/or observer.

  (iv) wavelength.

   (v) intensity of the wave.

On which of these factors, if any, does

  (a) the speed of light in vacuum,

  (b) the speed of light in a medium (say, glass or water), depend?

Solution (a) The speed of light in vacuum remains constant. According to Einstein's theory of relativity, the speed of light in vacuum does not depend upon any factor listed above.

  (b) The speed of light in medium say glass or water

  (i) does not depend on the nature of source.

 (ii) does not depend on the direction of propagation.

(iii) does not depend upon the motion of source but depends on the motion of observer as related to the Doppler's effect.

(iv) depends on the wavelength, as lesser be the wavelength lesser be the speed and *vice-versa*.

 (v) does not depend on the intensity of waves because intensity means energy falling per unit area in unit time.

Question 15. For sound waves, the Doppler formula for frequency shift differs slightly between the two situations: (i) source at rest; observer moving and (ii) source moving; observer at rest. The exact Doppler formulas for the case of light waves in vacuum are, however, strictly identical for these situations. Explain, why this should be so? Would you expect the formulas to be strictly identical for the two situations in case of light travelling in a medium?

Solution   The sound waves require a material medium for propagation. So, in the cases (i) and (ii), these are not identical physically through relative motion between the source and the observer is same in the two cases. Infact, relative motion of the observer relative to the medium is different in the two situations. So, the Doppler's effect formula for sound are different in the two cases. For light waves travelling in vacuum,there is nothing to distinguish between the two situations. So, the formulae are strictly identical. For the propagation in a medium, case (i) and case (ii) are not identical. The formulae governing the two situations would obviously be different.

Question 16. In double-slit experiment using light of wavelength 600 nm, the angular width of a fringe formed on a distant screen is 0.1°. What is the spacing between the two slits?

Solution   Given, wavelength of light $\lambda = 600$ nm $= 600 \times 10^{-9}$ m

Angular width of fringe $\theta = 0.1° = \dfrac{0.1\,\pi}{180}$ rad

Using the formula $\theta = \dfrac{\lambda}{d}$

Spacing between the slits $d = \dfrac{\lambda}{\theta} = \dfrac{600 \times 10^{-9} \times 180}{0.1 \times \pi}$

$$d = 3.44 \times 10^{-4} \text{ m}$$

Thus, the spacing between the two slits is 3.44×10^{-4} m.

Question 17. Answer the following questions:
   (a) In a single-slit diffraction experiment, the width of the slit is made double the original width. How does this affect the size and intensity of the central diffraction band?
   (b) In what way is diffraction from each slit related to the interference pattern in a double-slit experiment?
   (c) When a tiny circular obstacle is placed in the path of light from a distant source, *a* bright spot is seen at the centre of the shadow of the obstacle. Explain why?
   (d) Two students are separated by a 7 m partition wall in a room 10 m high. If both light and sound waves can bend around obstacles, how is it that the students are unable to see each other even though they can converse easily.

(e) Ray optics is based on the assumption that light travels in a straight line. Diffraction effects (observed when light propagates through small apertures/slits or around small obstacles) disprove this assumption. Yet the ray optics assumption is so commonly used in understanding location and several other properties of images in optical instruments. What is the justification?

Solution   (a) On doubling the slit width, $d' = 2d$

$$\text{Using formula } \theta' = \frac{\lambda}{d'} = \frac{\lambda}{2d} = \frac{\theta}{2}$$

The angular width of central maximum which is $\dfrac{\lambda}{2d}$ is halved. As the area

of central becomes $\dfrac{1}{4}$ times and the intensity is also one-fourth.

(b) If the width of each slit is of the order of λ, then interference pattern in the double-slit experiment is modified by the diffraction pattern from each of the two slits.

(c) As a tiny obstacle is placed in the path of light, a bright spot is seen because the waves diffracted from the edges of circular obstacle interfere constructively at the centre of shadow so a bright spot is formed.

(d) For the diffraction of waves by the aperture, the size of aperture should be of the order of wavelength of waves used.

For light waves, wavelength $\lambda = 10^{-7}$ m

and size of aperture $d = 3$ m

$$\sin \theta = \frac{\lambda}{d} = \frac{10^{-7}}{3} \simeq 10^{-8} \qquad\qquad \text{(order)}$$

$$\therefore \qquad\qquad \theta \approx 0$$

i.e., the bending in the light waves is almost zero.

So, the students are unable to see each other.

For sound wave, frequency $= 1000$ Hz

$$\text{Wavelength} \qquad\qquad \lambda = \frac{v}{f} = \frac{330}{1000} = 0.33 \text{ m}$$

where, v is the speed of sound

$$\sin \theta = \frac{\lambda}{d} = \frac{0.33}{3} = 0.11$$

It is clear that θ has a definite value *i.e.*, sound waves bends and the students can hear each other easily.

(e) The ray optics assumption is used to locate the images or formation of images by instruments. This is because typical size of apertures involved in ordinary, optical instruments are much larger than the wavelength of light. Thus, the bending of light (diffraction) has no significance.

Question 18. Two towers on top of two hills are 40 km apart. The line joining them passes 50 m above a hill halfway between the towers. What is the longest wavelength of radio waves which can be sent between the towers without appreciable diffraction effects?

Solution There is no obstruction by the hill to spreading the radio beams, the radial spread of the beam over the hill 20 km away must not exceed 50 m.

i.e. Z_F (Fresnel's distance) $= 20$ km $= 20 \times 10^3$ m

$$a = 50 \text{ m},$$

$$Z_F = \frac{a^2}{\lambda}$$

$$\lambda = \frac{a^2}{Z_F} = \frac{50 \times 50}{20 \times 10^3} = 1250 \times 10^{-4} \text{ m}$$

Thus, the longest wavelength of radio waves is 0.125 m.

Question 19. A parallel beam of light of wavelength 500 nm falls on a narrow slit and the resulting diffraction pattern is observed on a screen 1 m away. It is observed that the first minimum is at a distance of 2.5 mm from the centre of the screen. Find the width of the slit.

Solution Given, wavelength of light $\lambda = 500$ nm $= 500 \times 10^{-9}$ m

$D = 1$ m, $n = 1$, $x = 2.5$ mm $= 2.5 \times 10^{-3}$ m.

Distance of nth minimum from the centre $x = \dfrac{nD\lambda}{d}$

$$d = \frac{nD\lambda}{x} = \frac{1 \times 1 \times 500 \times 10^{-9}}{2.5 \times 10^{-3}} = 2 \times 10^{-4} \text{ m}$$

$$d = 0.2 \text{ mm}$$

Thus, the width of slit is 0.2 mm.

Question 20. Answer the following questions:

   (a) When a low flying aircraft passes overhead, we sometimes notice a slight shaking of the picture on our TV screen. Suggest a possible explanation.

   (b) As you have learnt in the text, the principle of linear superposition of wave displacement is basic to understanding intensity distributions in diffraction and interference patterns.

     What is the justification of this principle?

Solution (a) We notice a slight shaking of the picture on our TV screen because a low flying aircraft reflects the TV signal and there may be an interference between the direct signal and the reflected signal which results shaking.

   (b) The superposition principle follows the linear character of the differential equation governing wave motion. If y_1 and y_2 be the solution of wave equation, so there is any linear combination of y_1 and y_2. When the amplitudes are large and non-linear effects are important, then the situation is more complicated.

Question 21.   In deriving the single-slit diffraction pattern, it was stated that the intensity is zero at angles of $n\lambda/a$. Justify this by suitably dividing the slit to bring out the cancellation.

Solution   Let the slit be divided in n sections, so the width of each slit

$$d' = \frac{\lambda}{n}$$

The angular width, $\theta = \dfrac{n\lambda}{d} = \dfrac{n\lambda}{d'n} = \dfrac{\lambda}{d}$

Therefore, the each of the smaller slits would send zero intensity in the direction of θ. Thus, for the entire single slit, intensity at angle $\dfrac{n\lambda}{d}$ due to the combination would be zero.

Selected NCERT Exemplar Problems

Question 1.   Consider a point at the focal point of a convergent lens. Another convergent lens of short focal length is placed on the other side. What is the nature of the wavefronts emerging from the final image?

Solution   The final image wavefront is spherical in nature and converges at a point.

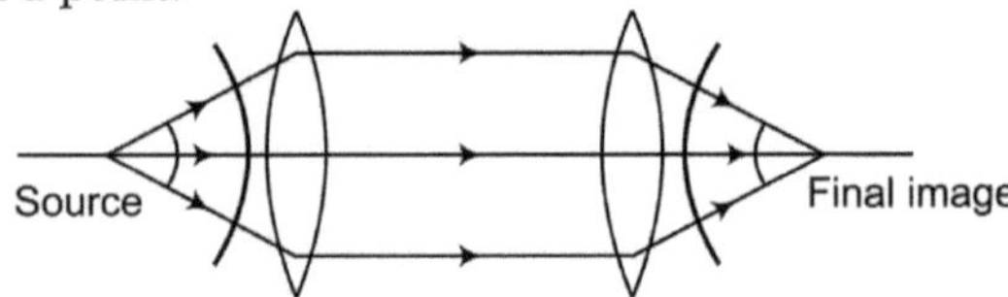

Question 2.   What is the shape of the wavefront on earth for sunlight?

Solution   It is basically spherical of very large radius so it looks almost plane.

Question 3.   Why is the diffraction of sound waves more evident in daily experience than that of light wave?

Solution   As we know that the frequencies of sound waves lie between 20 Hz to 20 kHz so that their wavelength ranges between 15 m to 15 mm. The diffraction occur if the wavelength of waves is nearly equal to still width.

As the wavelength of light waves is 7000×10^{-10} m to 4000×10^{-10} m.

The slit width is very near to the wavelength of sound waves as compared to light waves. Thus, the diffraction of sound waves is more evident in daily life than that of light waves.

Question 4. A polaroid (I) is placed in front of a monochromatic source. Another polaroid (II) is placed in front of this polaroid (I) and rotated till no light passes. A third polaroid (III) is now placed in between (I) and (II). In this case, will light emerge from (II). Explain.

Solution    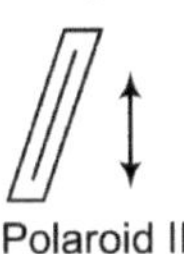

Monochromatic source   Polaroid I   Polaroid II

Now, polaroid II is rotated till no light passes, that means the axis of polaroid II is perpendicular to polaroid I.

  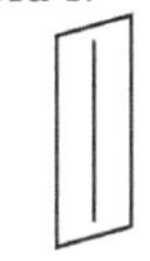 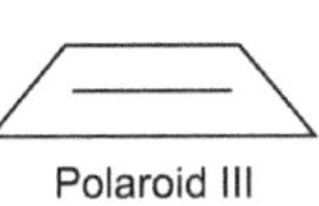

Monochromatic source   Polaroid I   Polaroid II   Polaroid III

Only when the axis of polaroid III is perpendicular to polaroid II, no light will pass. In other cases, there will be light because the axis of polaroid II is no longer perpendicular to polaroid III.

Question 5. Can reflection result in plane polarized light if the light is incident on the interface from the side with higher refractive index?

Solution Polarization by reflection occurs when the angle of incidence is the Brewster's angle

i.e., $$\tan i_p = {}^1\mu_2 = \frac{\mu_2}{\mu_1} \qquad \text{where, } \mu_2 < \mu_1$$

when the light rays travels in such a medium, the critical angle is

$$\sin i_c = \frac{\mu_2}{\mu_1}$$

where, $\mu_2 < \mu_1$

As $|\tan i_p| > |\sin i_c|$ for large angles

$$i_p < i_c$$

Thus, the polarization by reflection occurs definitely.

Question 6. For the same objective, find the ratio of the least separation between two points to be distinguished by a microscope for light of 5000 Å and electrons accelerated through 100 V used as the illuminating substance.

 Use the concept of resolving power of microscope $d = \dfrac{1.22\,\lambda}{2\sin\beta}$.

Solution $$d_{min} = \frac{1.22\lambda}{2\sin\beta}$$

where, λ is the wavelength of light and β is the angle subtended by the objective at the object.

For the light of wavelength 5500 Å

$$d_{min} = \frac{1.22 \times 5500 \times 10^{-10}}{2\sin\beta} \qquad \ldots(i)$$

For electrons accelerated through 100 V, the de-Broglie wavelength

$$\lambda = \frac{12.27}{\sqrt{V}} = \frac{12.27}{\sqrt{100}} = 0.12 \times 10^{-9} \text{ m}$$

$$d_{min} = \frac{1.22 \times 0.12 \times 10^{-9}}{2\sin\beta}$$

Ratio of the least separation

$$\therefore \qquad \frac{d'_{min}}{d_{min}} = \frac{0.12 \times 10^{-9}}{5500 \times 10^{-10}} = 0.2 \times 10^{-3}$$

Question 7.   Consider a two slit interference arrangements (see figure) such that the distance of the screen from the slits is half the distance between the slits. Obtain the value of D in terms of λ such that the first minima on the screen falls at a distance D from the centre O.

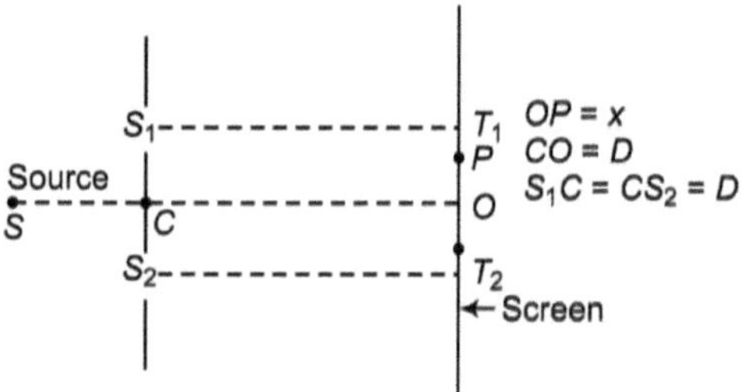

Solution   From the figure,

$$T_2 P = T_2 O + OP = D + x$$

and

$$T_1 P = T_1 O - OP = D - x$$

$$S_1 P = \sqrt{(S_1 T_1)^2 + (PT_1)^2} = \sqrt{D^2 + (D-x)^2}$$

and

$$S_2 P = \sqrt{(S_2 T_2)^2 + (T_2 P)^2} = \sqrt{D^2 + (D+x)^2}$$

The minima will occur when $S_2 P - S_1 P = \lambda/2$

i.e.,

$$[D^2 + (D+x)^2]^{1/2} - [D^2 + (D-x)^2]^{1/2} = \frac{\lambda}{2}$$

If $x = D$

Then,

$$[D^2 + 4D^2]^{1/2} = \frac{\lambda}{2}$$

$$\sqrt{5D^2} = \frac{\lambda}{2} \quad \text{or} \quad D = \frac{\lambda}{2\sqrt{5}}$$

Question 8.

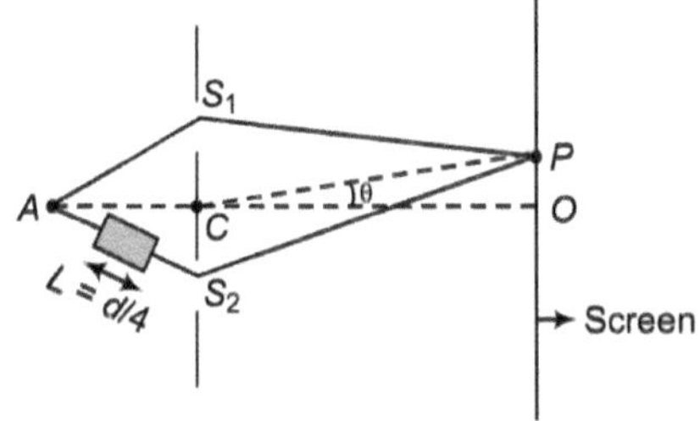

$$AC = CO = D, \ S_1C = S_2C = d \ll D$$

A small transparent slab containing material of $\mu = 1.5$ is placed along AS_2 (figure). What will be the distance from O of the principal maxima and of the first minima on either side of the principal maxima obtained in the absence of the glass slab.

Solution   In case of transparent glass slab of refractive index μ, the path difference $= 2d\sin\theta + (\mu - 1)L$

For the principal maxima, (path difference is zero)

i.e., $$2d\sin\theta_0 + (\mu - 1)L = 0$$

or $$\sin\theta_0 = -\frac{L(\mu - 1)}{2d} = \frac{-L(0.5)}{2d} \qquad [\because L = d/4]$$

or $$\sin\theta_0 = \frac{-1}{16}$$

$\therefore$ $$OP = D\tan\theta_0 = D\sin\theta_0 = \frac{-D}{16}$$

For the first minima, the path difference is $\pm\dfrac{\lambda}{2}$

$\therefore$ $$2d\sin\theta_1 + 0.5L = \pm\frac{\lambda}{2}$$

or $$\sin\theta_1 = \frac{\pm\lambda/2 - 0.5L}{2d} = \frac{\pm\lambda/2 - d/8}{2d} = \frac{\pm\lambda/2 - \lambda/8}{2\lambda} = \pm\frac{1}{4} - \frac{1}{16}$$

$[\because$ The diffraction occurs if the wavelength of waves in nearly equal to the slid width $(d)]$

On the positive side $$\sin\theta_1' = +\frac{1}{4} - \frac{1}{16} = \frac{3}{16}$$

On the negative side $$\sin\theta_1'' = -\frac{1}{4} - \frac{1}{16} = -\frac{5}{16}$$

The first principal maxima on the positive side is at distance

$$D\tan\theta_1' = D\frac{\sin\theta_1'}{\sqrt{1 - \sin^2\theta_1'}} = D\frac{3}{\sqrt{16^2 - 3^2}} = \frac{3D}{\sqrt{247}} \text{ above point } O$$

The first principal minima on the negative side is at distance

$$D\tan\theta_1'' = \frac{5}{\sqrt{16^2 - 5^2}} = \frac{5}{\sqrt{231}} \text{ below point } O.$$

Chapter 11

Dual Nature of Radiation and Matter

Important Results

1. Work function is given by $\phi_0 = h\nu_0 = \dfrac{hc}{\lambda_0}$, where ν_0 is the threshold frequency and λ_0 is the threshold wavelength. $h = 6.63 \times 10^{-34}$ is called Planck's constant.

2. Kinetic energy of emitted photoelectron
$$K_{\max} = \frac{1}{2} m v_{\max}^2 = h\nu - \phi_0 = \frac{hc}{\lambda} - \frac{hc}{\lambda_0} = eV_0$$
   where, V_0 is the stopping potential.

3. The photoelectric current depends on intensity of incident light, potential difference applied between the two electrodes and the nature of the emitter material.

4. Energy of each photon is given by $E = h\nu = \dfrac{hc}{\lambda}$

5. Momentum of each photon is given by $p = \dfrac{h}{\lambda} = \dfrac{h\nu}{c}$

6. Energy $E = mc^2 \Rightarrow m = \dfrac{E}{c^2} = \dfrac{h\nu}{c^2} = \dfrac{h}{c\lambda}$

7. de-Broglie wavelength is given by $\lambda = \dfrac{h}{mv}$

   where, $m = \dfrac{m_0}{\sqrt{1 - \dfrac{v^2}{c^2}}}$, m_0 being the rest mass of the particle and c is the speed of light.

   For an electron, $\lambda = \dfrac{12.27}{\sqrt{V}}$ Å

   where, V is potential difference.

8. de-Broglie wavelength of a particle is given by
$$\lambda = \frac{h}{\sqrt{2mE}} = \frac{h}{\sqrt{2meV}}$$

where, E is the kinetic energy.

9. Number of photons per sec per unit area $= \dfrac{\phi}{E}$

$$= \frac{\text{Energy flux}}{\text{Energy of photon per second per unit area}}$$

$$= \frac{\text{Energy radiated / second}}{\text{Energy of each photon}} = \frac{P}{E}$$

Exercises

Question 1.   Find the
(a) maximum frequency and
(b) minimum wavelength of X-rays produced by 30 kV electrons.

Solution   Given, voltage $V = 30\,\text{kV} = 30 \times 10^3$ V and $e = 1.6 \times 10^{-19}$ C

(a) Using formula for energy
$$E = eV = h\nu$$

or $$\nu = \frac{eV}{h} = \frac{1.6 \times 10^{-19} \times 30 \times 10^3}{6.63 \times 10^{-34}} = 7.24 \times 10^{18} \text{ Hz}$$

Maximum frequency $\nu = 7.24 \times 10^{18}$ Hz

(b) Minimum wavelength of X-ray,
$$\lambda = \frac{c}{\nu} = \frac{3 \times 10^8}{7.24 \times 10^{18}}$$

∴   where $c = 3 \times 10^8$ m/s (speed of light)

$$\lambda = 0.414 \times 10^{-10}$$

$$= 0.0414 \times 10^{-9} \text{ m}$$

$$= 0.0414 \text{ nm}$$

Question 2.   The work function of caesium metal is **2.14 eV**. When light of frequency 6×10^{14} Hz is incident on the metal surface, photoemission of electrons occurs. What is the
(a) maximum kinetic energy of the emitted electrons,
(b) stopping potential and
(c) maximum speed of the emitted photoelectrons?

Solution   Given, work function of caesium metal $\phi_0 = 2.14$ eV

Frequency of light $\nu = 6 \times 10^{14}$ Hz

(a) Maximum kinetic energy of emitted electrons (Einstein's photo electric equation)

$$KE_{max} = h\nu - \phi_0$$
$$= \frac{6.63 \times 10^{-34} \times 6 \times 10^{14}}{1.6 \times 10^{-19}} - 2.14$$
$$= 0.35 \text{ eV}$$

(b) Let stopping potential be V_0.

We know that

$$KE_{max} = eV_0$$
$$0.35 \text{ eV} = eV_0$$
$$V_0 = 0.35 \ \text{V}$$

(c) Maximum kinetic energy $KE_{max} = \dfrac{1}{2}mv_{max}^2$

$$0.35 \text{ eV} = \frac{1}{2}mv_{max}^2$$

(where, v_{max} is the maximum speed and m is the mass of electron)

or $\dfrac{0.35 \times 2 \times 1.6 \times 10^{-19}}{9.1 \times 10^{-31}} = v_{max}^2$ $(\because e = 1.6 \times 10^{-19})$

or $\qquad\qquad v_{max}^2 = 0.123 \times 10^{12}$

or $\qquad\qquad v_{max} = 350713.55 \text{ m/s}$

$$v_{max} = 350.7 \text{ km/s}$$

Question 3. The photoelectric cut-off voltage in a certain experiment is 1.5 V. What is the maximum kinetic energy of photoelectrons emitted?

Solution   Given, cut-off voltage $V_0 = 1.5$ V

Use the formula for maximum kinetic energy

$$KE_{max} = eV_0 = 1.5 \text{ eV}$$
$$= 1.5 \times 1.6 \times 10^{-19} = 2.4 \times 10^{-19} \text{ J}$$

Question 4. Monochromatic light of wavelength 632.8 nm is produced by a helium-neon laser. The power emitted is 9.42 mW.

(a) Find the energy and momentum of each photon in the light beam.

(b) How many photons per second, on the average, arrive at a target irradiated by this beam? (Assume the beam to have uniform cross-section, which is less than the target area.)

(c) How fast does a hydrogen atom have to travel in order to have the same momentum as that of the photon?

Solution Given, wavelength of monochromatic light, $\lambda = 632.8$ nm

$$= 632.8 \times 10^{-9} \text{ m}$$

$$\text{Power} = 9.42 \text{ mW} = 9.42 \times 10^{-3} \text{ W}$$

(a) Energy of each photon, $E = \dfrac{hc}{\lambda}$

$$= \frac{6.63 \times 10^{-34} \times 3 \times 10^{8}}{632.8 \times 10^{-9}} = 3.14 \times 10^{-19} \text{ J}$$

We know that momentum of each photon, $p = \dfrac{h}{\lambda}$

$$p = \frac{6.63 \times 10^{-34}}{632.8 \times 10^{-9}} = 1.05 \times 10^{-27} \text{ kg-m/s}$$

(b) Let n be the number of photons per second. So,

$$n = \frac{\text{Power}}{\text{Energy of each photon}} = \frac{9.42 \times 10^{-3}}{3.14 \times 10^{-19}}$$

$$= 3 \times 10^{16} \text{ photon/s}$$

(c) Momentum $p = mv$

Velocity of hydrogen atom, $v = \dfrac{p}{m} = \dfrac{1.05 \times 10^{-27}}{1.66 \times 10^{-27}} = 0.63 \text{ m/s}$

$$[\because m = 1.66 \times 10^{-27} \text{ kg (mass of electron)}]$$

Question 5.   The energy flux of sunlight reaching the surface of the earth is 1.388×10^{3} W/m^2. How many photons (nearly) per square metre are incident on the earth per second? Assume that the photons in the sunlight have an average wavelength of 550 nm.

Solution   Given, energy per unit area per second, $P = 1.388 \times 10^{3}$ W/m^2

Let n be the number of photons incident on the earth per square metre.
Wavelength of each photon $= 550$ nm $= 550 \times 10^{-9}$ m

Energy of each photon, $E = \dfrac{hc}{\lambda}$ (where h is the plant's constant)

$$= \frac{6.63 \times 10^{-34} \times 3 \times 10^{8}}{550 \times 10^{-9}} = 3.616 \times 10^{-19} \text{ J}$$

Number of photons incident on the earth's surface

$$n = \frac{P}{E} = \frac{1.388 \times 10^{3}}{3.616 \times 10^{-19}} = 3.838 \times 10^{21}$$

$$= 3.838 \times 10^{21} \text{ photon/m}^2\text{-s}$$

Question 6.   In an experiment on photoelectric effect, the slope of the cut-off voltage *versus* frequency of incident light is found to be 4.12×10^{-15} V-s. Calculate the value of Planck's constant.

Solution   Given, slope of graph $\tan \theta = 4.12 \times 10^{-15}$ V-s and charge on electron $e = 1.6 \times 10^{-19}$ C

For slope of graph $\tan\theta = \dfrac{V}{v}$

We know that $hv = eV$

$$\dfrac{V}{v} = \dfrac{h}{e}$$

$$\therefore \quad \dfrac{h}{e} = 4.12 \times 10^{-15}$$

$$h = 1.6 \times 10^{-19} \times 4.12 \times 10^{-15}$$

$$= 6.592 \times 10^{-34} \text{ J-s}$$

Question 7.   A 100 W sodium lamp radiates energy uniformly in all directions. The lamp is located at the centre of a large sphere that absorbs all the sodium light which is incident on it. The wavelength of the sodium light is 589 nm.

   (a) What is the energy per photon associated with the sodium light?

   (b) At what rate are the photons delivered to the sphere?

Solution   Given, power of lamp, $P = 100$ W

Wavelength of the sodium light, $\lambda = 589$ nm $= 589 \times 10^{-9}$ m

Planck constant $h = 6.63 \times 10^{-34}$ J-s

(a) Energy of each photon

$$E = \dfrac{hc}{\lambda} = \dfrac{6.63 \times 10^{-34} \times 3 \times 10^{8}}{589 \times 10^{-9}} \qquad (\because c = 3 \times 10^{8}\, \text{m/s})$$

$$= 3.38 \times 10^{-19} \text{ J}$$

$$= \dfrac{3.38 \times 10^{-19}}{1.6 \times 10^{-19}} \text{ eV}$$

$$= 2.11 \text{ eV}$$

(b) Let n photons are delivered per second.

$$\therefore \quad n = \dfrac{\text{Power}}{\text{Energy of each photon}} \qquad (\text{From } P = En)$$

$$= \dfrac{100}{3.38 \times 10^{-19}} = 3 \times 10^{20} \text{ photon/s}$$

$$= 3 \times 10^{20} \text{ photon/s are delivered}$$

Question 8.   The threshold frequency for a certain metal is 3.3×10^{14} Hz. If light of frequency 8.2×10^{14} Hz is incident on the metal, predict the cut-off voltage for the photoelectric emission.

Solution   Given, threshold frequency for a metal, $v_0 = 3.3 \times 10^{14}$ Hz

Frequency of light, $v = 8.2 \times 10^{14}$ Hz

Let V_0 be the cut-off voltage.

Using the formula for kinetic energy,

$$KE = eV_0 = h\nu - h\nu_0$$

$$V_0 = \frac{h(\nu - \nu_0)}{e} = \frac{6.63 \times 10^{-34}\,(8.2 \times 10^{14} - 3.3 \times 10^{14})}{1.6 \times 10^{-19}}$$

$$= \frac{6.63 \times 10^{-34} \times 10^{14} \times 4.9}{1.6 \times 10^{-19}}$$

$$= 2.03 \text{ V}$$

Question 9. The work function for a certain metal is **4.2 eV**. Will this metal give photoelectric emission for incident radiation of wavelength **330 nm**?

Solution Given, work function $\phi_0 = 4.2$ eV

$$= 4.2 \times 1.6 \times 10^{-19} \text{ J} = 6.72 \times 10^{-19} \text{ J}$$

Wavelength of radiation, $\lambda = 330$ nm $= 330 \times 10^{-9}$ m

If the energy of each photon is more than the work function, then only the photoelectirc emission takes place.
Energy of each photon,

$$E = \frac{hc}{\lambda} = \frac{6.63 \times 10^{-34} \times 3 \times 10^8}{330 \times 10^{-9}}$$

$$= 6.027 \times 10^{-19} \text{ J}$$

As the value of energy of each photon, $E = 6.027 \times 10^{-19}$ J is less than the work function, $\phi_0 = 6.72 \times 10^{-19}$ J. So, no photoelectric emission takes place.

Question 10. Light of frequency 7.21×10^{14} Hz is incident on a metal surface. Electrons with a maximum speed of 6.0×10^5 m/s are ejected from the surface. What is the threshold frequency for photoemission of electrons?

Solution Given, frequency of light, $\nu = 7.21 \times 10^{14}$ Hz
Mass of electron, $m = 9.1 \times 10^{-31}$ kg
Maximum speed of electrons, $v_{max} = 6 \times 10^5$ m/s
Let ν_0 be the threshold frequency.
Use the formula for kinetic energy

$$KE = \frac{1}{2} m v_{max}^2 = h\nu - h\nu_0$$

i.e., $\quad \frac{1}{2} \times 9.1 \times 10^{-31} \times 6 \times 10^5 \times 6 \times 10^5 = 6.63 \times 10^{-34}(\nu - \nu_0)$

or $\quad \nu - \nu_0 = \frac{36 \times 9.1 \times 10^{-21}}{2 \times 6.63 \times 10^{-34}} = 2.47 \times 10^{14}$

or $\qquad v_0 = 7.21 \times 10^{14} - 2.47 \times 10^{14}$ $\qquad (\because v = 7.21 \times 10^{14} \text{ Hz})$

$$= 4.74 \times 10^{14} \text{ Hz}$$

Question 11. Light of wavelength 488 nm is produced by an argon laser, which is used in the photoelectric effect. When light from this spectral line is incident on the emitter, the stopping (cut-off) potential of photoelectrons is 0.38 V. Find the work function of the material from which the emitter is made.

Solution   Given, wavelength of light, $\lambda = 488$ nm $= 488 \times 10^{-9}$ m

Cut-off potential $V_0 = 0.38$ V, $e = 1.6 \times 10^{-19}$ C

Planck constant $h = 6.62 \times 10^{-34}$ J-s

Velocity of light $c = 3 \times 10^8$ m/s

Let ϕ_0 be the work function.

Use the formula for kinetic energy,

$$\text{KE} = eV_0 = \frac{hc}{\lambda} - \phi_0$$

$$1.6 \times 10^{-19} \times 0.38 = \frac{6.63 \times 10^{-34} \times 3 \times 10^8}{488 \times 10^{-9}} - \phi_0$$

or $\qquad 6.08 \times 10^{-20} = 40.75 \times 10^{-20} - \phi_0$

or $\qquad \phi_0 = (40.75 - 6.08) \times 10^{-20} = 34.67 \times 10^{-20}$ J

or $\qquad\qquad = \dfrac{34.67 \times 10^{-20}}{1.6 \times 10^{-19}}$ eV

or $\qquad\qquad = 2.17$ eV

Question 12. Calculate the

  (a) momentum and

  (b) de-Broglie wavelength of the electrons accelerated through a potential difference of 56 V.

Solution   Given, potential difference, $V = 56$ V

 (a) Use the formula for kinetic energy

$$eV = \frac{1}{2} mv^2$$

$$\frac{2\,eV}{m} = v^2$$

$$v = \sqrt{\frac{2\,eV}{m}}$$

where, m is mass and v is velocity of electron.

Momentum associated with accelerated electron,

$$p = mv = m\sqrt{\frac{2eV}{m}} = \sqrt{2\,eVm}$$

$$= \sqrt{2 \times 1.6 \times 10^{-19} \times 56 \times 9 \times 10^{-31}}$$

$$= 4.02 \times 10^{-24} \text{ kg-m/s}$$

(b) de-Broglie wavelength of electron,

$$\lambda = \frac{12.27}{\sqrt{V}} \text{ Å}$$

$$= \frac{12.27}{\sqrt{56}} = 0.164 \times 10^{-9} \text{ m}$$

$$= 0.164 \text{ nm}$$

Question 13. What is the

(a) momentum,

(b) speed and

(c) de-Broglie wavelength of an electron with kinetic energy of 120 eV?

Solution   Given, kinetic energy $= KE = 120$ eV

(a) Momenum, $p = \sqrt{2\,eVm} = \sqrt{2\,KE \cdot m}$ and $e = 1.6 \times 10^{-19}$ $(\because KE = eV)$

$$= \sqrt{2 \times 120 \times 1.6 \times 10^{-19} \times 9.1 \times 10^{-31}}$$

$$= 5.91 \times 10^{-24} \text{ kg-m/s}$$

(b) We know that momentum $p = mv$

or $\qquad\qquad\qquad v = \dfrac{p}{m}$

$$= \frac{5.91 \times 10^{-24}}{9.1 \times 10^{-31}}$$

$$= 6.5 \times 10^6 \text{ m/s}$$

(c) de-Broglie wavelength associated with electron,

$$\lambda = \frac{12.27}{\sqrt{V}} \text{ Å} = \frac{12.27}{\sqrt{120}} \text{ Å}$$

$$= 0.112 \times 10^{-9} \text{ m}$$

$$= 0.112 \text{ nm}$$

Question 14. The wavelength of light from the spectral emission line of sodium is 589 nm. Find the kinetic energy at which

(a) an electron and

(b) a neutron would have the same de-Broglie wavelength.

Solution   Given, wavelength of light $= 589$ nm $= 589 \times 10^{-9}$ m

Mass of electron $m_e = 9.1 \times 10^{-31}$ kg

Mass of neutron $m_n = 1.67 \times 10^{-27}$ kg

Planck's constant $h = 6.62 \times 10^{-34}$ J-s

(a) Using of formula, $\lambda = \dfrac{h}{\sqrt{2KEm_e}}$

Kinetic energy of electron,

$$KE_e = \frac{h^2}{2\lambda^2 m_e} = \frac{(6.63 \times 10^{-34})^2}{2 \times (589 \times 10^{-9})^2 \times 9.1 \times 10^{-31}}$$

$$= 6.96 \times 10^{-25} \text{ J}$$

(b) Kinetic energy of neutron

$$KE_n = \frac{h^2}{2\lambda^2 m_n}$$

$$= \frac{(6.63 \times 10^{-34})^2}{2 \times (589 \times 10^{-9})^2 \times 1.66 \times 10^{-27}}$$

$$= 3.81 \times 10^{-28} \text{ J}$$

Question 15. What is the de-Broglie wavelength of

(a) a bullet of mass 0.040 kg travelling at the speed of 1.0 km/s,

(b) a ball of mass 0.060 kg moving at a speed of 1.0 m/s, and

(c) a dust particle of mass 1.0×10^{-9} kg drifting with a speed of 2.2 m/s?

Solution   Given, mass of bullet $m = 0.040$ kg

and speed of bullet $v = 1000$ m/s

(a) de-Broglie wavelength

$$\lambda = \frac{h}{mv} = \frac{6.63 \times 10^{-34}}{0.040 \times 1 \times 10^3} \qquad \left(\begin{array}{l} \because m = 0.040 \text{ kg} \\ v = 1 \text{ km/s} \\ = 1000 \text{ m/s} \end{array} \right)$$

$$= 1.66 \times 10^{-35} \text{ m}$$

(b) Mass of the ball, $m = 0.060$ kg and speed of the ball, $v = 1$ m/s

$$\lambda = \frac{h}{mv} = \frac{6.63 \times 10^{-34}}{0.060 \times 1}$$

$$= 1.1 \times 10^{-32} \text{ m}$$

(c) Mass of a dust particle, $m = 1 \times 10^{-9}$ kg and speed of the dust particle, $v = 2.2$ m/s

$$\lambda = \frac{h}{mv} = \frac{6.63 \times 10^{-34}}{1 \times 10^{-9} \times 2.2}$$

$$= 3.0 \times 10^{-25} \text{ m}$$

Question 16. An electron and a photon, each have a wavelength of 1.00 nm. Find

(a) their momenta,
(b) the energy of the photon and
(c) the kinetic energy of electron.

Solution Given, wavelength of electron and photon, $\lambda = 1\,\text{nm} = 10^{-9}$ m

(a) Momentum of electron,

$$p_e = \frac{h}{\lambda} = \frac{6.63 \times 10^{-34}}{10^{-9}} = 6.63 \times 10^{-25}\ \text{m}\,(\because h = 6.63 \times 10^{-34})$$

Momentum of photon,

$$p_{\text{ph}} = \frac{h}{\lambda} = \frac{6.63 \times 10^{-34}}{10^{-9}} = 6.63 \times 10^{-25}\ \text{m}$$

(b) Energy of photon,

$$E = \frac{hc}{\lambda} = \frac{6.63 \times 10^{-34} \times 3 \times 10^{8}}{10^{-9} \times 1.6 \times 10^{-19}}\ \text{eV}$$

$$= \frac{19.86 \times 10^{-17}}{1.6 \times 10^{-19}}\ \text{eV}$$

$$= 1243\ \text{eV or } E = 1.24\ \text{keV}$$

(c) Energy of electron,

$$E = \frac{p^2}{2m_e} = \frac{(6.63 \times 10^{-25})^2}{2 \times 9.1 \times 10^{-31} \times 1.6 \times 10^{-19}}\ \text{eV}$$

$$= 1.51\ \text{eV}$$

Question 17. (a) For what kinetic energy of a neutron will the associated de-Broglie wavelength be 1.40×10^{-10} m?

(b) Also find the de-Broglie wavelength of a neutron, in thermal equilibrium with matter, having an average kinetic energy of $(3/2)\,kT$ at 300 K.

Solution (a) de-Broglie wavelength $\lambda = 1.40 \times 10^{-10}$ m

Mass of neutron, $m_n = 1.675 \times 10^{-27}$ kg

Using the formula, wavelength associated with kinetic energy

$$\lambda = \frac{h}{\sqrt{2m\,\text{KE}}}$$

or

$$\text{KE} = \frac{h^2}{2\lambda^2 m_n} = \frac{(6.63 \times 10^{-34})^2}{2 \times (1.40 \times 10^{-10})^2 \times 1.675 \times 10^{-27}}$$

$$= 6.686 \times 10^{-21}\ \text{J}$$

(b) Kinetic energy associated with temperature

$$KE = \frac{3}{2} kT = \frac{3}{2} (1.38 \times 10^{-23}) \times 300 = 6.21 \times 10^{-21} \ J$$

($\because$ Absolute temperature $T = 300$ K and Boltzmann's constant $k = 1.38 \times 10^{-23}$ J/K)

$$KE = 6.21 \times 10^{-21} \ J$$

de-Broglie wavelength associated with kinetic energy

$$\lambda = \frac{h}{\sqrt{2m \cdot KE}}$$

$$\lambda = \frac{6.63 \times 10^{-34}}{\sqrt{2 \times 1.675 \times 10^{-27} \times 6.21 \times 10^{-21}}}$$

$$\lambda = 1.45 \times 10^{-10} \ m$$

$$\lambda = 1.45 \ \text{Å}$$

Question 18. Show that the wavelength of electromagnetic radiation is equal to the de-Broglie wavelength of its quantum (photon).

Solution The momentum of a photon of frequency ν, wavelength λ is given by

$$p = \frac{h\nu}{c} = \frac{h}{\lambda}$$

$$\lambda = \frac{h}{p}$$

de-Broglie wavelength of photon, $\lambda = \dfrac{h}{mv} \Rightarrow \dfrac{h}{p} = \dfrac{h}{h\nu/c} = \dfrac{c}{\nu}$

Thus, the wavelength of electromagnetic radiation is equal to the de-Broglie wavelength.

Question 19. What is the de-Broglie wavelength of a nitrogen molecule in air at 300 K? Assume that the molecule is moving with the root-mean-square speed of molecules at this temperature. (Atomic mass of nitrogen = 14.0076 u)

Solution Given, temperature $T = 300$ K

and Boltzmann's constant $= 1.38 \times 10^{-23}$ J/K

Molecular weight of nitrogen molecule $m = 28.0152$ u

$$= 28.0152 \times 1.67 \times 10^{-27} \ kg$$

Mean kinetic energy of molecules

$$\frac{1}{2} mv^2 = \frac{3}{2} kT$$

or $$v = \sqrt{\frac{3kT}{m}}$$

$$= \sqrt{\frac{3 \times 1.38 \times 10^{-23} \times 300}{28.0152 \times 1.66 \times 10^{-27}}}$$

$$= 516.78 \text{ m/s}$$

de-Broglie wavelength,

$$\lambda = \frac{h}{mv}$$

$$\lambda = \frac{6.63 \times 10^{-34}}{28.0152 \times 1.66 \times 10^{-27} \times 516.78}$$

$$(\because \text{ Planck's constant } h = 6.63 \times 10^{-34} \text{ J-s})$$

$$= 2.75 \times 10^{-11} \text{ m}$$

or $\qquad\qquad = 0.0275 \times 10^{-9} \text{ m} = 0.028 \text{ nm}$

Additional Exercises

Question 20. (a)   Estimate the speed with which electrons emitted from a heated emitter of an evacuated tube impinge on the collector maintained at a potential difference of 500 V with respect to the emitter. Ignore the small initial speeds of the electrons. The specific charge of the electron *i.e.*, its *e/m* is given to be 1.76×10^{11} C/kg.

(b) Use the same formula you employ in (a) to obtain electron speed for a collector potential of 10 MV. Do you see what is wrong ? In what way is the formula to be modified?

Solution   (a) Given, potential difference $V = 500$ V

Specific charge of the electron, $e/m = 1.76 \times 10^{11}$ C/kg

Kinetic energy of electron,

$$\text{KE} = \frac{1}{2} mv^2 = eV$$

$$v = \sqrt{\frac{e}{m} \times 2V}$$

$$= \sqrt{1.76 \times 10^{11} \times 2 \times 500}$$

$$= 1.326 \times 10^7 \text{ m/s}$$

(b) Potential, $V = 10 \text{ MV} = 10^7$ V

$$v = \sqrt{\frac{2e}{m} V} = \sqrt{2 \times 1.76 \times 10^{11}}$$

$$= 1.8762 \times 10^9 \text{ m/s}$$

This speed is greater than the speed of light, which is not possible. As v approaches to c, then mass

$$m = \frac{m_0}{\sqrt{1 - \dfrac{v^2}{c^2}}}$$

Question 21. (a) A monoenergetic electron beam with electron speed of 5.20×10^6 m/s is subject to a magnetic field of 1.30×10^{-4} T normal to the beam velocity. What is the radius of the circle traced by the beam, given e/m for electron equals 1.76×10^{11} C/kg?

(b) Is the formula you employ in (a) valid for calculating radius of the path of a 20 MeV electron beam? If not, in what way is it modified? [Note : Q. 20(b) and 21(b) take you to relativistic mechanics which is beyond the scope of this book. They have been inserted here simply to emphasise the point that the formulas you use in part (a) of the exercises are not valid at very high speeds or energies. See answers at the end to know what 'very high speed or energy' means.]

Solution   (a) Given, speed of electron $v = 5.20 \times 10^6$ m/s

Magnetic field $B = 1.30 \times 10^{-4}$ T

Specific charge $e/m = 1.76 \times 10^{11}$ C/kg

Let r be the radius of the circle traced by the beam force due to magnetic field is balanced by the centripetal force.

i.e., $$q(\mathbf{v} \times \mathbf{B}) = \frac{mv^2}{r} \quad \text{(Angle between } \mathbf{v} \text{ and } \mathbf{B} \text{ is } 90°)$$

or $$evB = \frac{mv^2}{r} \quad [\because \mathbf{v} \times \mathbf{B} = vB \sin 90°]$$

$$r = \frac{mv}{eB} = \frac{v}{\dfrac{e}{m} \cdot B}$$

$$= \frac{5.20 \times 10^6}{1.76 \times 10^{11} \times 1.30 \times 10^{-4}} = 0.227 \text{ m}$$

$$= 22.7 \text{ cm}$$

(b) Given, energy of electron, $E = 20$ MeV $= 20 \times 1.6 \times 10^{-13}$ J

Using energy formula, mass of electron, $m_e = 9.1 \times 10^{-31}$ kg

$$E = \frac{1}{2} mv^2$$

$$v = \sqrt{\frac{2E}{m}} = \sqrt{\frac{2 \times 20 \times 1.6 \times 10^{-13}}{9.1 \times 10^{-31}}} = 2.67 \times 10^9 \text{ m/s}$$

This speed is more than the speed of light, so the formula used in case (a) $r = \dfrac{mv}{eB}$ is not valid for calculating the radius of path of 20 MeV electron beam because electron with such a high energy has velocity in relatistic domain *i.e.*, comparable with the velocity of light and the mass varies with the increase in velocity but we have taken it as constant.

$\therefore\quad m = \dfrac{m_0}{1 - \dfrac{v^2}{c^2}}$ is to be considered.

Thus, the modified formula will be

$$r = \dfrac{mv}{qB} = \left(\dfrac{m_0}{\sqrt{1 - \dfrac{v^2}{c^2}}} \right) \dfrac{v}{eB}$$

Question 22. An electron gun with its collector at a potential of 100 V fires out electrons in a spherical bulb containing hydrogen gas at low pressure ($\sim 10^{-2}$ mm of Hg). A magnetic field of 2.83×10^{-4} T curves the path of the electrons in a circular orbit of radius 12.0 cm. (The path can be viewed because the gas ions in the path focus the beam by attracting electrons and emitting light by electron capture; this method is known as the 'fine beam tube' method.) Determine e/m from the data.

Solution Given, potential at a node $V = 100$ V

Magnetic field $B = 2.83 \times 10^{-4}$ T

Radius of circular path $r = 12$ cm $= 0.12$ m $\qquad \left(\begin{array}{l} m_e = 9.1 \times 10^{-31} \text{ kg} \\ \quad e = 1.6 \times 10^{-19} \text{C} \end{array} \right)$

Kinetic Energy (KE) $= \dfrac{1}{2} mv^2 = eV$

$$1.6 \times 10^{-19} \times 100 = \dfrac{1}{2} \times 9.1 \times 10^{-31} \times v^2$$

$$v^2 = \dfrac{2 \times 1.6 \times 10^{-17}}{9.1 \times 10^{-31}} = 3.516 \times 10^{13}$$

$$v = 5.93 \times 10^6 \text{ m/s}$$

As the angle between **v** and **B** is 90°.

The magnetic force ($F_m = evB$) is balanced by the centripetal force.

i.e., $\qquad evB = \dfrac{mv^2}{r} \quad$ or $\quad \dfrac{e}{m} = \dfrac{v}{Br} = \dfrac{5.93 \times 10^6}{2.83 \times 10^{-4} \times 0.12}$

Specific charge of electron $\qquad \dfrac{e}{m} = 1.74 \times 10^{11}$ C/kg

Question 23. (a) An X-ray tube produces a continuous spectrum of radiation with its short wavelength end at 0.45 Å. What is the maximum energy of a photon in the radiation?

(b) From your answer to (a), guess what order of accelerating voltage (for electrons) is required in such a tube?

Solution (a) Given, wavelength of radiation, $\lambda = 0.45 \text{ Å} = 0.45 \times 10^{-10}$ m

Energy of a photon
$$E = \frac{hc}{\lambda}$$

$$= \frac{6.63 \times 10^{-34} \times 3 \times 10^{8}}{0.45 \times 10^{-10} \times 1.6 \times 10^{-19}} \text{ eV}$$

$$= 27.6 \times 10^{3} \text{ eV}$$

$$= 27.6 \text{ keV}$$

(b) In X-ray tube, accelerating voltage provides the energy to the electrons which produce X-rays. For getting X-rays, photons of 27.51 keV is required that the incident electrons must process kinetic energy at length 27.61 keV.

Energy $= eV = E$

$$eV = 27.6 \text{ keV}$$

$$V = 27.6 \text{ kV}$$

So, the order of accelerating voltage is 30 kV.

Question 24. In an accelerator experiment on high-energy collisions of electrons with positrons, a certain event is interpreted as annihilation of an electron-positron pair of total energy 10.2 BeV into two γ-rays of equal energy. What is the wavelength associated with each γ-ray? $(1\text{BeV} = 10^{9} \text{ eV})$

Solution   Given, energy of γ-rays $= 10.2 \text{ BeV} = 10.2 \times 10^{9} \text{ eV}$ (2 γ-rays)

Energy of one γ-ray $= \dfrac{10.2 \times 10^{9}}{2} = 5.1 \times 10^{9} \text{ eV}$

$$= 5.1 \times 1.6 \times 10^{-19} \times 10^{9} \text{ J}$$

$$= 8.16 \times 10^{-10} \text{ J}$$

Let λ be the wavelength.

Energy of each ray

$$E = \frac{hc}{\lambda}$$

or
$$\lambda = \frac{hc}{E}$$

$$= \frac{6.63 \times 10^{-34} \times 3 \times 10^{8}}{8.16 \times 10^{-10}}$$

$$= 2.436 \times 10^{-16} \text{ m}$$

Question 25. Estimating the following two numbers should be interesting. The first number will tell you why radio engineers do not need to worry much about photons. The second number tells you why our eye can never 'count photons', even in barely detectable light?

(a) The number of photons emitted per second by a medium wave transmitter of 10 kW power, emitting radiowaves of wavelength 500 m.

(b) The number of photons entering the pupil of our eye per second corresponding to the minimum intensity of white light that we humans can perceive ($\sim 10^{-10}$ W/m^2). Take the area of the pupil to be about 0.4 cm^2 and the average frequency of white light to be about 6×10^{14} Hz.

Solution   (a) Given, $P = 10\ kW = 10 \times 10^3\ W$

Wavelength of radiowaves, $\lambda = 500\ m$

Energy of each photon, $E = \dfrac{hc}{\lambda} = \dfrac{6.63 \times 10^{-34} \times 3 \times 10^8}{500}$

$$E = 3.978 \times 10^{-28}\ J$$

The number of photons emitted per second $n = \dfrac{P}{E}$

$$n = \dfrac{10 \times 10^3}{3.978 \times 10^{-28}} = 2.51 \times 10^{31}$$

$$n = 2.51 \times 10^{31}\ photon/s$$

(b) Average frequency, $v = 6 \times 10^{14}\ Hz$

Energy/area-time $= 10^{-10}\ W/m^2$

Area of pupil $= 0.4\ cm^2 = 0.4 \times 10^{-4}\ m^2$

Total energy falling on pupil in unit time,
$$E' = 10^{-10} \times 0.4 \times 10^{-4} = 4 \times 10^{-15}\ J/s$$

Energy of each photon, $E'' = hv = 6.63 \times 10^{-34} \times 6 \times 10^{14} = 3.978 \times 10^{-19}\ J$

Number of photon/s, $n = \dfrac{E'}{E''} = \dfrac{4 \times 10^{-15}}{3.315 \times 10^{-19}}$

$$= 1.206 \times 10^4\ photon/s$$

As this number is not so large as in part (a), so it is large enough for us never to sense the individual photons by our eye.

Question 26. Ultraviolet light of wavelength 2271 Å from a 100 W mercury source irradiates a photo-cell made of molybdenum metal. If the stopping potential is –1.3 V, estimate the work function of the metal. How would the photo-cell respond to a high intensity ($\sim 10^5$ W m^2) red light of wavelength 6328 Å produced by a He-Ne laser?

Solution Given, wavelength of ultraviolet light, $\lambda = 2271$ Å

$$= 2271 \times 10^{-10} \text{ m}$$

Stopping potential, $V_0 = 1.3$ V;   Power $P = 100$ W
Planck's constant $h = 6.62 \times 10^{-34}$ J-s

Let ϕ_0 be the work function.
Using the formula for energy $E = h\nu - h\nu_0 = eV_0$

$$\frac{hc}{\lambda} - \phi_0 = eV_0$$

$$\phi_0 = \frac{hc}{\lambda} - eV_0 = \frac{6.63 \times 10^{-34} \times 3 \times 10^8}{2271 \times 10^{-10}} - 1.6 \times 10^{-19} \times 1.3$$

$$= 8.758 \times 10^{-19} - 2.08 \times 10^{-19}$$

$$\phi = \frac{6.678 \times 10^{-19}}{1.6 \times 10^{-19}} \text{ eV} = 4.17 \text{ eV}   \text{or}   \phi_0 = 4.2 \text{ eV}$$

Wavelength of red light, $\lambda = 6328$ Å $= 6328 \times 10^{-10}$ m

$$\text{Energy } E = \frac{hc}{\lambda} = \frac{6.63 \times 10^{-34} \times 3 \times 10^8}{6328 \times 10^{-10}} = \frac{3.143 \times 10^{-19}}{1.6 \times 10^{-19}} \text{ eV} = 1.96 \text{ eV}$$

Here, the energy $E = 1.96$ eV is less than the work function ϕ_0. So, the photocell will not respond to this red light. (It is independent of intensity.)

Question 27. Monochromatic radiation of wavelength 640.2 nm ($1 \text{nm} = 10^{-9}$ m) from a neon lamp irradiates photosensitive material made of caesium on tungsten. The stopping voltage is measured to be 0.54 V. The source is replaced by an iron source and its 427.2 nm line irradiates the same photo-cell. Predict the new stopping voltage.

Solution Given, for neon lamp wavelength of monochromatic radiation,

$$\lambda = 640.2 \text{ nm} = 640.2 \times 10^{-9} \text{ m}$$

Stopping voltage $V_0 = 0.54$ V
Let ϕ_0 be the work function.

$$\therefore \qquad eV_0 = \frac{hc}{\lambda} - \phi_0$$

Work function of photosensitive material,

$$\phi_0 = \frac{hc}{\lambda} - eV_0$$

$$= \frac{6.63 \times 10^{-34} \times 3 \times 10^8}{640.2 \times 10^{-9}} - 1.6 \times 10^{-19} \times 0.54$$

$$= 3.1 \times 10^{-19} - 0.864 \times 10^{-19} = 2.236 \times 10^{-19} \text{ J}$$

$$= \frac{2.236 \times 10^{-19}}{1.6 \times 10^{-19}} = 1.4 \text{ eV}$$

For iron ; given work function $\phi_0 = 1.4$ eV
Wavelength $\lambda = 427.2$ nm $= 427.2 \times 10^{-9}$ m

Let V_0' be the new stopping potential.

$$eV_0' = \frac{hc}{\lambda} - \phi_0$$

$$= \frac{6.63 \times 10^{-34} \times 10^8 \times 3}{427.2 \times 10^{-9} \times 1.6 \times 10^{-19}} - 1.4 = 1.51 \text{ eV}$$

Required stopping potential $V_0' = 1.51$ V

Question 28. A mercury lamp is a convenient source for studying frequency dependence of photoelectric emission, since it gives a number of spectral lines ranging from the UV to the red end of the visible spectrum. In our experiment with rubidium photo-cell, the following lines from a mercury source were used :

$\lambda_1 = 3650$ Å, $\lambda_2 = 4047$ Å, $\lambda_3 = 4358$ Å, $\lambda_4 = 5461$ Å, $\lambda_5 = 6907$ Å.

The stopping voltages respectively were measured to be

$V_{01} = 1.28$ V, $V_{02} = 0.95$ V, $V_{03} = 0.74$ V, $V_{04} = 0.16$ V, $V_{05} = 0$

Determine the value of Planck's constant h, the threshold frequency and work function for the material. [Note : You will notice that to get h from the data, you will need to know e (which you can take to be 1.6×10^{-19} C). Experiments of this kind on Na, Li, K, etc. were performed by Millikan, who using his own value of e (from the oil-drop experiment) confirmed Einstein's photoelectric equation and at the same time gave an independent estimate of the value of h.]

Solution   Given, the following wavelength from a mercury source were used

$$\lambda_1 = 3650 \text{ Å} = 3650 \times 10^{-10} \text{ m}$$
$$\lambda_2 = 4047 \text{ Å} = 4047 \times 10^{-10} \text{ m}$$
$$\lambda_3 = 4358 \text{ Å} = 4358 \times 10^{-10} \text{ m}$$
$$\lambda_4 = 5461 \text{ Å} = 5461 \times 10^{-10} \text{ m}$$
$$\lambda_5 = 6907 \text{ Å} = 6907 \times 10^{-10} \text{ m}$$

The stopping voltages are as follows :

$V_{01} = 1.28$ V, $V_{02} = 0.95$ V, $V_{03} = 0.74$ V, $V_{04} = 0.16$ V and $V_{05} = 0$

Frequencies to corresponding to wavelengths

(a) $$\nu_1 = \frac{c}{\lambda_1} = \frac{3 \times 10^8}{3650 \times 10^{-10}} = 8.219 \times 10^{14} \text{ Hz}$$

$$\nu_2 = \frac{c}{\lambda_2} = \frac{3 \times 10^8}{4047 \times 10^{-10}} = 7.412 \times 10^{14} \text{ Hz}$$

$$v_3 = \frac{c}{\lambda_3} = \frac{3 \times 10^8}{4358 \times 10^{-10}} = 6.884 \times 10^{14} \text{ Hz}$$

$$v_4 = \frac{c}{\lambda_4} = \frac{3 \times 10^8}{5461 \times 10^{-10}} = 5.493 \times 10^{14} \text{ Hz}$$

$$v_5 = \frac{c}{\lambda_5} = \frac{3 \times 10^8}{6907 \times 10^{-10}} = 4.343 \times 10^{14} \text{ Hz}$$

As we know that

$$eV_0 = hv - \phi_0$$
$$V_0 = \frac{hv}{e} - \frac{\phi_0}{e}$$

As the graph between V_0 and frequency v is a straight line.

The slope of this graph gives the values of $\frac{h}{e}$.

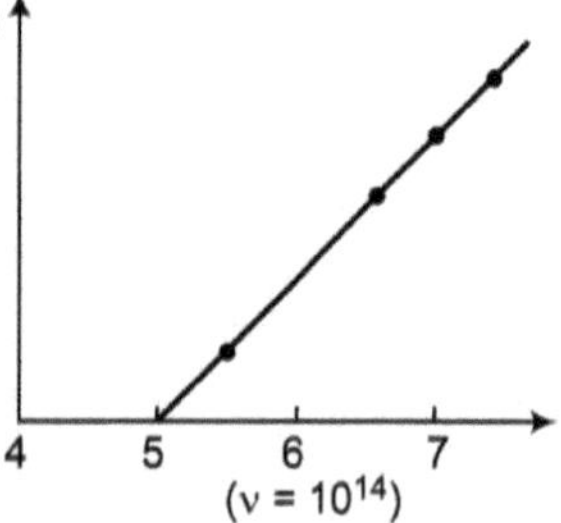

$$\therefore \quad \frac{h}{e} = \frac{V_{01} - V_{04}}{v_1 - v_4} = \frac{1.28 - 0.16}{(8.219 - 5.493) \times 10^{14}}$$

$$h = \frac{1.12 \times 1.6 \times 10^{-19}}{2.726 \times 10^{14}} = 6.674 \times 10^{-34} \text{ J-s}$$

(b) Work function $\phi_0 = hv_0$

$$= 6.574 \times 10^{-34} \times 5 \times 10^{14}$$

$$= 32.870 \times 10^{-20} \text{ J}$$

$$= 2.05 \text{ eV}$$

Question 29. The work function for the following metals is given :
Na : 2.75 eV; K : 2.30 eV; Mo : 4.17 eV; Ni : 5.15 eV. Which of these metals will not give photoelectric emission for a radiation of wavelength 3300 Å from a He-Cd laser placed 1 m away from the photocell? What happens, if the laser is brought nearer and placed 50 cm away?

Solution   Given, wavelength of radiation $= 3300 \text{ Å} = 3300 \times 10^{-10}$ m

Energy of incident radiation, $E = \dfrac{hc}{\lambda}$

$$= \frac{6.63 \times 10^{-34} \times 3 \times 10^8}{3300 \times 10^{-10} \times 1.6 \times 10^{-19}} = 3.75 \text{ eV}$$

The metals having work function less than 3.75 eV will give photoelectric emission. Here, Na, K has lesser work function than 3.75 eV. So, they produce photoelectric effect.

If the laser is bought nearer then only the intensity change or the number of photoelectrons change.

Question 30. Light of intensity 10^{-5} W/m^2 falls on a sodium photo-cell of surface area 2 cm^2. Assuming that the top 5 layers of sodium absorb the incident energy, estimate time required for photoelectric emission in the wave-picture of radiation. The work function for the metal is given to be about 2 eV. What is the implication of your answer?

Solution   Given, intensity of light $= 10^{-5}$ W/m^2

Area $= 2$ cm$^2 = 2 \times 10^{-4}$ m^2

Work function for the metal $\phi_0 = 2$ eV

Let t be the time.

The effective atomic area of Na $= 10^{-20}$ m^2 and it contains one conduction electron per atom.

$$\text{Number of conduction electrons in five layers} = \frac{5 \times \text{Area of one layer}}{\text{Effective atomic area}}$$

$$= \frac{5 \times 2 \times 10^{-4}}{10^{-20}} = 10^{17}$$

We know that sodium has one free electron (or conduction electron) per atom.

Incident power on the surface area of photo cell

$\quad = $ Incident intensity $\times$ Area on the surface area of photo cell

$\quad = 10^{-5} \times 2 \times 10^{-4}$

$\quad = 2 \times 10^{-9}$ W

The electron present in all the 5 layers of sodium will share the incident energy equally.

Energy absorbed per second per electron,

$$E = \frac{\text{Incident power}}{\text{Number of electrons in five layers}}$$

$$= \frac{2 \times 10^{-9}}{10^{17}} = 2 \times 10^{-26} \text{ W}$$

Time required for emission by each electron,

$$t = \frac{\text{Energy required per electron}}{\text{Energy absorbed per second}} = \frac{2 \times 1.6 \times 10^{-19}}{2 \times 10^{-26}}$$

$$= 1.6 \times 10^{7} \text{ s}$$

which is about 0.5 yr.

The answer obtained implies that the time of emission of electron is very large and is not agreement with the observed time of emission. There is no time lag between the incidence of light and the emission of photo electron.

Thus, it is implied that the wave theory cannot be applied in this experiment.

Question 31. Crystal diffraction experiments can be performed using X-rays or electrons accelerated through appropriate voltage. Which probe has greater energy? (For quantitative comparison, take the wavelength of the probe equal to 1 Å, which is of the order of inter-atomic spacing in the lattice.) ($m_e = 9.11 \times 10^{-31}$ kg)

Solution   Given, wavelength of X-rays, $\lambda = 1\,\text{Å} = 10^{-10}$ m

Mass of electron, $m_e = 9.11 \times 10^{-31}$ kg

The kinetic energy of electron, $\text{KE} = \dfrac{1}{2} mv^2$

or
$$mv = \sqrt{2m\,\text{KE}}$$

Wavelength associated with momentum, $\lambda = \dfrac{h}{mv}$

$\therefore$
$$\lambda = \dfrac{h}{\sqrt{2m\,\text{KE}}}$$

or
$$\text{KE} = \dfrac{h^2}{2\lambda^2 m} = \dfrac{(6.63 \times 10^{-34})^2}{2 \times (10^{-10})^2 \times 9.11 \times 10^{-31} \times 1.6 \times 10^{-19}}$$

$$= 150.78 \text{ eV}$$

Energy of photon $= \dfrac{hc}{\lambda}$

$$= \dfrac{6.63 \times 10^{-34} \times 3 \times 10^8}{1 \times 10^{-10} \times 1.6 \times 10^{-19}} = 12.4 \times 10^3 \text{ eV}$$

Thus, for the same wavelength a X-ray photon has much kinetic energy than an electron.

Question 32. (a)   Obtain the de-Broglie wavelength of a neutron of kinetic energy 150 eV. As you have seen in Q. 31, an electron beam of this energy is suitable for crystal diffraction experiments. Would a neutron beam of the same energy be equally suitable? Explain ($m_n = 1.675 \times 10^{-27}$ kg)

(b) Obtain the de-Broglie wavelength associated with thermal neutrons at room temperature (27 °C). Hence, explain why a fast neutron beam needs to be thermalised with the environment before it can be used for neutron diffraction experiments.

Solution   (a) Given, kinetic energy of neutron (KE) $= 150$ eV

Mass of neutron $m_n = 1.675 \times 10^{-27}$ kg

We know that $\text{KE} = \dfrac{1}{2} mv^2$

or
$$mv = \sqrt{2m \cdot \text{KE}}$$

Wavelength $\lambda = \dfrac{h}{mv}$

$$= \frac{h}{\sqrt{2m_n \cdot \text{KE}}} = \frac{6.63 \times 10^{-34}}{\sqrt{2 \times 1.675 \times 10^{-27} \times 150 \times 1.6 \times 10^{-19}}}$$

$$= 2.33 \times 10^{-12} \text{ m}$$

The interatomic spacing is 10^{-10} m, which is greater than this wavelength. So, neutron beam of 150 eV is not suitable for diffraction experiment.

(b) Temperature $T = 27 + 273 = 300$ K

Boltzmann's constant $k = 1.38 \times 10^{-23}$ J/mol/K

Energy of neutron, $E = \frac{3}{2} kT$

Wavelength of associated with energy

$$\lambda = \frac{h}{\sqrt{2mE}} = \frac{h}{\sqrt{2m \times \frac{3}{2} kT}} = \frac{h}{\sqrt{3mkT}}$$

$$= \frac{6.63 \times 10^{-34}}{\sqrt{3 \times 1.675 \times 10^{-27} \times 1.38 \times 10^{-23} \times 300}}$$

$$= 1.45 \times 10^{-10} \text{ m}$$

This wavelength is order of interatomic spacing. So, the neutron beam first thermalised and then use for diffraction.

Question 33. An electron microscope uses electrons accelerated by a voltage of 50 kV. Determine the de-Broglie wavelength associated with the electrons. If other factors (such as numerical aperture, etc.) are taken to be roughly the same, how does the resolving power of an electron microscope compare with that of an optical microscope which uses yellow light?

Solution Given, voltage of electron microscope $= 50$ kV $= 50000$ V

de-Broglie wavelength $\lambda = \dfrac{12.27}{\sqrt{V}} \text{ Å}$

$$= \frac{12.27}{\sqrt{50000}} = 0.055 \text{ Å}$$

$$= 5.5 \times 10^{-12} \text{ m}$$

For yellow light $(\lambda) = 5.9 \times 10^{-7}$ m

As the Resolving Power (RP) is inversely proportional to the wavelength.

i.e., $\text{RP} \propto \dfrac{1}{\lambda}$

$\therefore \quad \dfrac{\text{Resolving power of electron microscope}}{\text{Resolving power optical microscope}} = \dfrac{\lambda_y}{\lambda_e} = \dfrac{5.9 \times 10^{-7}}{5.5 \times 10^{12}} = 10^5$

Resolving power of electron microscope is 10^5 times than that of optical microscope.

Question 34. The wavelength of a probe is roughly a measure of the size of a structure that it can probe in some detail. The quark structure of protons and neutrons appears at the minute length-scale of 10^{-15} m or less. This structure was first probed in early 1970's using high energy electron beams produced by a linear accelerator at Stanford, USA. Guess what might have been the order of energy of these electron beams? (Rest mass energy of electron = 0.511 MeV.)

Solution   Given, wavelength $\lambda = 10^{-15}$ m, energy = 0.511 MeV

Momentum of particle, $p = \dfrac{h}{\lambda} = \dfrac{6.63 \times 10^{-34}}{10^{-15}} = 6.63 \times 10^{-19}$ kg-m/s

Rest mass energy $= m_0 c^2 = 0.511$ MeV

$$= 0.511 \times 1.6 \times 10^{-13} \text{ J}$$

Use the formula for energy for relativistic theory

$$E^2 = p^2 c^2 + m_0^2 c^4$$

$$= (3 \times 10^8 \times 6.63 \times 10^{-19})^2 + (0.511 \times 10^{-13} \times 1.6)^2$$

$$= 9 \times (6.63)^2 \times 10^{-22}$$

As the rest mass energy is negligible.

$\therefore$ $\quad$ Energy $E = \sqrt{p^2 c^2} = pc = 6.63 \times 10^{-19} \times 3 \times 10^8$

$$= \dfrac{1.989 \times 10^{-10}}{1.6 \times 10^{-19}} = 1.24 \times 10^9 \text{ eV}$$

$$= 1.24 \text{ BeV}$$

Thus, to energies the electron beam, the energy should be of the order of few BeV.

Question 35. Find the typical de-Broglie wavelength associated with a He atom in helium gas at room temperature (27 °C) and 1 atm pressure and compare it with the mean separation between two atoms under these conditions.

Solution   Given, temperature $T = 27°C + 273 = 300$ K

$k = 1.38 \times 10^{-23}$ J/mol/K

Pressure $p = 1$ atm $= 1.01 \times 10^5$ Pa

Mass of helium atom $= \dfrac{\text{Atomic weight}}{\text{Avagadro number}} = \dfrac{4}{6 \times 10^{23}}$ g $= \dfrac{4}{6 \times 10^{26}}$ kg

de-Broglie wavelength, $\lambda = \dfrac{h}{\sqrt{3mkT}} = \dfrac{6.63 \times 10^{-34}}{\sqrt{3 \times \dfrac{4}{6 \times 10^{26}} \times 1.38 \times 10^{-23} \times 300}}$

$$= 0.73 \times 10^{-10} \text{ m}$$

Now, $\quad\quad\quad\quad pV = RT = kNT$

$$\frac{V}{N} = \frac{kT}{p}$$

Mean separation $r = \left(\dfrac{V}{N}\right)^{1/3} = \left(\dfrac{kT}{p}\right)^{1/3} = \left(\dfrac{1.38 \times 10^{-23} \times 300}{1.01 \times 10^5}\right)^{1/3}$

$$r = 3.4 \times 10^{-9} \text{ m}$$

$$\therefore \qquad \frac{\lambda}{r} = \frac{0.73 \times 10^{-10}}{3.4 \times 10^{-9}} = 0.021$$

We can see that the wavelength λ with mean separation r, it can be observed ($r \gg \lambda$) that separation is larger than wevelength.

Question 36. Compute the typical de-Broglie wavelength of an electron in a metal at 27°C and compare it with the mean separation between two electrons in a metal which is given to be about 2×10^{-10} m.
[Note: Q. 35 and 36 reveal that while the wave-packets associated with gaseous molecules under ordinary conditions are non-overlapping, the electron wave-packets in a metal strongly overlap with one another. This suggests that whereas molecules in an ordinary gas can be distinguished apart, electrons in a metal cannot be distinguished apart from one another. This indistinguishibility has many fundamental implications which you will explore in more advanced physics courses.]

Solution   Given, temperature $T = 27°C + 273 = 300$ K

Separation $r = 2 \times 10^{-10}$ m

Momentum $p = \sqrt{3m\,kT}$

$$= \sqrt{3 \times 9.11 \times 10^{-31} \times 1.38 \times 10^{-23} \times 300} = 1.06 \times 10^{-25} \text{ kg-m/s}$$

de-Broglie wavelength $\lambda = \dfrac{h}{p} = \dfrac{6.63 \times 10^{-34}}{1.06 \times 10^{-25}} = 62.6 \times 10^{-10}$ m

Mean separation $r = 2 \times 10^{-10}$ m

$$\therefore \qquad \frac{\lambda}{r} = \frac{62.6 \times 10^{-10}}{2 \times 10^{-10}} = 31.3$$

We can see that de-Broglie wavelength is much greater than the electron separation.

Question 37. Answer the following questions :
   (a) Quarks inside protons and neutrons are thought to carry fractional charges [$(+2/3)e$: $(-1/3)e$]. Why do they not show up in Millikan's oil-drop experiment?
   (b) What is so special about the combination e/m? Why do we not simply talk of e and m separately?

(c) Why should gases be insulators at ordinary pressures and start conducting at very low pressures?

(d) Every metal has a definite work function. Why do all photoelectrons not come out with the same energy if incident radiation is monochromatic? Why is there an energy distribution of photoelectrons?

(e) The energy and momentum of an electron are related to the frequency and wavelength of the associated matter wave by the relations:

$$E = h\,\nu,\, p = \frac{h}{\lambda}$$

But while the value of λ is physically significant, the value of ν (and therefore, the value of the phase speed ν) has no physical significance. Why?

Solution (a) The quarks have fractional charges. These quarks are bound by forces. These forces become stronger when the quarks are tried to be pulled apart. That is why, the quarks always remain together. It is due to this reason that tough fractional charges exists in nature but the observable charges are always integral multiple of charge of electron.

(b) The motion of electron in electric and magnetic fields are governed by these two equations,

$$\frac{1}{2}mv^2 = eV \quad \text{or} \quad BeV = \frac{mv^2}{r}$$

In these equation, e and m both are together *i.e.,* there is no equation in which e or m are alone. So, we always take e/m.

(c) At ordinary pressure, only very few positive ions and electrons are produced by the ionisation of gas molecules. They are not able to reach the respective electrodes and becomes insulators. At low pressure, density decreases and the mean free path becomes large. So, at high voltage, they acquire sufficient amount of energy and they collide with molecules for further ionisation. Due to this, the number of ions in a gas increases and it becomes a conductor.

(d) Because all the electrons in the metal do not belong to same level but they occupy a continuous band of levels, therefore for the given incident radiation, electrons comes out from different levels with different energies.

(e) de-Broglie wavelength $\lambda = \dfrac{h}{p}$ or $p = \dfrac{h}{\lambda}$

Energy of the wave $E = h\nu = \dfrac{hc}{\lambda}$

Energy of moving particle $E' = \dfrac{1}{2}\dfrac{p^2}{m} = \dfrac{1}{2}\dfrac{(h/\lambda)^2}{m} = \dfrac{1}{2}\dfrac{h^2}{\lambda^2 m}$

For the relation of E and p, we note that there is a physical significance of λ but not for frequency ν.

Selected NCERT Exemplar Problems

Question 1. There are two sources of light, each emitting with a power of 100 W. One emits X-rays of wavelength 1 nm and the other visible light at 500 nm. Find the ratio of number of photons of X-rays to the photons of visible light of the given wavelength.

Solution Power $= 100$ W

Wavelength of X-rays $\lambda_1 = 1\,\text{nm} = 10^{-9}$ m

Wavelength of visible light $\lambda_2 = 500\,\text{nm} = 500 \times 10^{-9}$ m

Let n_1 and n_2 be the number of X-rays and visible light respectively. Since, power is same that means energy is same.

$\therefore$
$$n_1 E_1 = n_2 E_2$$

or
$$\frac{n_1}{n_2} = \frac{E_2}{E_1} = \frac{(hc/\lambda_2)}{(hc/\lambda_1)} = \frac{\lambda_1}{\lambda_2} = \frac{10^{-9}}{500 \times 10^{-9}}$$

or
$$\frac{n_1}{n_2} = \frac{1}{500}$$

Question 2. Consider a metal exposed to light of wavelength 600 nm. The maximum energy of the electron doubles when light of wavelength 400 nm is used. Find the work function in eV.

Solution Given, wavelength $\lambda_1 = 600\,\text{nm} = 600 \times 10^{-9}$ m

Energy correspond to $\lambda_1 = E_1$
Again, wavelength $\lambda_2 = 400\,\text{nm} = 400 \times 10^{-9}$ m

Energy correspond to $\lambda_2 = E_2$
Let the work function of metal is ϕ.
According to question $2E_1 = E_2$

i.e.,
$$2\left(\frac{hc}{\lambda_1} - \phi_0\right) = \frac{hc}{\lambda_2} - \phi_0$$

or
$$\frac{2hc}{\lambda_1} - \frac{hc}{\lambda_2} = 2\phi_0 - \phi_0$$

or
$$hc\left[\frac{2}{\lambda_1} - \frac{1}{\lambda_2}\right] = \phi_0$$

$$\phi_0 = 6.63 \times 10^{-34} \times 3 \times 10^8 \left[\frac{2}{600 \times 10^{-9}} - \frac{1}{400 \times 10^{-9}}\right]$$

or
$$= \frac{6.63 \times 10^{-34} \times 3 \times 10^8}{10^{-7}}\left[\frac{1}{3} - \frac{1}{4}\right]$$

or
$$= 6.63 \times 3 \times 10^{-9}\left[\frac{4-3}{12}\right]\,\text{J}$$

or $\qquad = \dfrac{6.63 \times 3 \times 10^{-19} \times 1}{1.6 \times 10^{-19} \times 12} \text{ eV}$

or $\qquad = 1.02 \text{ eV}$

Question 3.   Two monochromatic beams A and B of equal intensity I, hit a screen. The number of photons hitting the screen by beam A is twice that by beam B. Then, what inference can you make about their frequencies?

Solution   Intensity$_A$ = Intensity$_B$

The number of photons of beam $A = n_A$

The number of photons of beam $B = n_B$

According to question, $\qquad n_A = 2n_B$

Let ν_A be the frequency of beam A and ν_B be the frequency of beam B.

$\therefore \qquad\qquad\qquad$ Intensity $\propto$ Energy of photons

$$I \propto (h\nu) \times \text{Number of photons}$$

$\therefore \qquad\qquad\qquad \dfrac{I_A}{I_B} = \dfrac{n_A \nu_A}{n_B \nu_B}$

According to question, $\qquad I_A = I_B$

$\therefore \qquad\qquad\qquad n_A \nu_A = n_B \nu_B$

$$\dfrac{\nu_A}{\nu_B} = \dfrac{n_B}{n_A} = \dfrac{1}{2}$$

So, $\qquad\qquad\qquad \nu_B = 2\nu_A$

Question 4.   Two particles A and B of de-Broglie wavelengths λ_1 and λ_2 combine to form a particle C. The process conserves momentum. Find the de-Broglie wavelength of the particle C. (The motion is one-dimensional).

Solution   de-Broglie wavelength of particle $A = \lambda_1$

de-Broglie wavelength of particle $B = \lambda_2$

Let the de-Broglie wavelength of particle $C = \lambda_3$

According to the question, momentum is conserved.

$$p_C = p_A + p_B \quad \Rightarrow \quad \dfrac{h}{\lambda_A} + \dfrac{h}{\lambda_B} = \dfrac{h}{\lambda_C} \quad \text{or} \quad \lambda_C = \dfrac{\lambda_A \lambda_B}{\lambda_A + \lambda_B}$$

(If $p_A, p_B > 0$ or $p_A, p_B < 0$)

Then, momentum $p_C = \dfrac{h(\lambda_A + \lambda_B)}{\lambda_A \lambda_B}$

If $p_A > 0, p_B < 0$ or $p_A < 0, p_B > 0$; then

$$\text{Momentum } p_C = \dfrac{h(\lambda_B - \lambda_A)}{\lambda_A \cdot \lambda_B} = \dfrac{h}{\lambda_C}$$

de-Broglie wavelength of the particle C, $\lambda_C = \dfrac{\lambda_B \cdot \lambda_A}{\lambda_A - \lambda_B}$

Question 5. A neutron beam of energy E scatters from atoms on a surface with a spacing $d = 0.1$ nm. The first maximum of intensity in the reflected beam occurs at $\theta = 30$. What is the kinetic energy E of the beam in eV?

Solution Given, distance $d = 0.1$ nm $= 10^{-10}$ m, angle $\theta = 30°$

By Bragg's equation, $n\lambda = 2d\sin\theta$

Here $n = 1$, first maximum

$$\lambda = 2d\sin\theta = 2 \times 10^{-10} \times \sin 30° = 10^{-10} \text{ m}$$

$$\text{Momentum } p = \frac{h}{\lambda} = \frac{6.6 \times 10^{-34}}{10^{-10}} = 6.6 \times 10^{-24}$$

$$\text{Kinetic energy of the beam (KE)} = \frac{p^2}{2m} = \frac{(6.6 \times 10^{-24})^2}{2 \times 1.67 \times 10^{-27}}$$

$$(\because m_n = 1.67 \times 10^{-27} \text{ kg})$$

$$= 1.3 \times 10^{-20} \text{ J}$$

Question 6. Consider a thin target $(10^{-4}$ m^2, 10^{-3} m thickness) of sodium, which produces a photocurrent of 100 µA when a light of intensity 100 W/m^2 ($\lambda = 660$ nm) falls on it. Find the probability that a photoelectron is produced when a photons strikes a sodium atom. (Take density of Na $= 0.97$ kg/m^3)

Solution Given, area $= 10^{-4}$ m^2, thickness $= 10^{-3}$ m^3

Photocurrent $I = 100 \times 10^{-6}$ A

Intensity of light $= 100$ W/m^2

Wavelength of light $\lambda = 660$ nm $= 660 \times 10^{-9}$ m

Density of sodium $= 0.97$ kg$/$m^3

Volume of target $=$ area $\times$ thickness $= 10^{-4} \times 10^{-3} = 10^{-7}$ m^3

Mass of target $=$ volume $\times$ density $= 10^{-7} \times 0.97$ kg

23 g Na contains atom $= 6.023 \times 10^{23}$

$$0.97 \times 10^{-7} \text{ kg Na coutains atom} = \frac{6.023 \times 10^{23} \times 0.97 \times 10^{-7} \times 10^{3}}{23}$$

$$= 2.54 \times 10^{18} \text{ atoms}$$

Total energy per second $=$ Intensity $\times$ area of tangent

$$= 100 \times 10^{-6} \times 10^{-4} = 10^{-2} \text{ W}$$

$$\text{Energy of each photon} = \frac{hc}{\lambda} = \frac{6.63 \times 10^{-34} \times 3 \times 10^{8}}{660 \times 10^{-9}} = 3.01 \times 10^{-19} \text{ J}$$

$$\text{Number of photons} = \frac{\text{Total energy}}{\text{Energy of one photon}} = \frac{10^{-2}}{3.28 \times 10^{-19}}$$

$$= 3.05 \times 10^{16} \text{ per s}$$

If P is the probability of emission per atom for photons.
The number of photoelectrons emitted per second

$$= P \times 3.05 \times 10^{16} \times 2.54 \times 10^{18}$$

$$\text{Current} = P \times 3.05 \times 10^{16} \times 2.54 \times 10^{18} \times 1.6 \times 10^{-19} \text{ A}$$

$$= P \times 1.25 \times 10^{16} \text{ A}$$

In this question, produced photocurrent is equal to $100\,\mu\text{A}$

i.e., $$100 \times 10^{-6} = P \times 1.25 \times 10^{16}$$

$$P = 8 \times 10^{-21}$$

Thus, the probability is very less.

Question 7. Consider an electron in front of metallic surface at a distance of (treated as an infinite plane surface). Assume the force of attraction by the plate is given as $\dfrac{1}{4}\dfrac{q^2}{4\pi\varepsilon_0 d^2}$.

Calculate work in taking the charge to an infinite distance from the plate. Taking $d = 0.1$ nm, find the work done in electron volt. (Such a force law is not valid for $d < 0.1$ nm).

Solution   Force of attraction $F = \dfrac{1}{4}\cdot\dfrac{q^2}{4\pi\varepsilon_0 d^2}$

Work done by external energy, $W = Fdx$

$$W = \frac{1}{4\pi\varepsilon_0}\frac{q^2}{4}\cdot\int_d^\infty \frac{1}{x^2}\,dx$$

$$W = \frac{1}{4}\cdot\frac{q^2}{4\pi\varepsilon_0}\cdot\left[\frac{1}{x}\right]_d^\infty = \frac{q^2}{4.4\pi\varepsilon_0 \cdot d}$$

According to question, $d = 0.1$ nm

Energy (work done) $W = \dfrac{(1.6 \times 10^{-19})^2 \times 9 \times 10^9}{4 \times 0.1 \times 10^{-9} \times 1.6 \times 10^{-19}}$ eV

Work done in electron volt $W = 3.6$ eV

Chapter **12**

Atoms

Important Results

1. The distance of closest approach (r_0) is calculated by the formula of kinetic energy of α-particle is given by

$$KE = \frac{1}{2} mv^2 = \frac{1}{4\pi\varepsilon_0} \cdot \frac{Ze\,(Ze)}{r_0}$$

2. Impact parameter is given by $b = \dfrac{Ze^2 \cot \dfrac{\theta}{2}}{4\pi\varepsilon_0 \left(\dfrac{1}{2} mv^2\right)}$

3. For Bohr's atomic model

(a) $\dfrac{K \cdot Ze^2}{r^2} = \dfrac{mv^2}{r}$

(b) Angular momentum of the electron $\quad mvr = \dfrac{nh}{2\pi}$

where $n = 1, 2, 3, 4, \ldots$

(c) $h\nu = E_2 - E_1$

(d) Radius of stationary orbit, $\quad r = \dfrac{n^2 h^2}{4\pi^2\, mKZe^2}$

(e) Velocity of electron, $v = \dfrac{2\pi Ke^2}{nh} = \dfrac{c}{n}\left(\dfrac{2\pi Ke^2}{ch}\right)$

(f) Total energy of electron in an orbit, $\quad E = -\dfrac{2\pi^2\, mK^2 e^4}{n^2 h^2}$

(g) $KE = \dfrac{KZe^2}{2r}, \qquad PE = -\dfrac{KZe^2}{r}$

(h) Total energy of electron in an orbit is calculated as $E = -\dfrac{13.6}{n^2}$ eV

(i) The origin of spectral lines

$$\bar{\nu} = \frac{1}{\lambda} = R\left[\frac{1}{n_1^2} - \frac{1}{n_2^2}\right]$$

where, $R = 1.0973 \times 10^7$ m^{-1} is the Rydberg's constant.

Exercises

Question 1.   Choose the correct alternative from the clues given at the end of the each statement:

(a) The size of the atom in Thomson's model is .... the atomic size in Rutherford's model. (much greater than/no different from/much less than)

(b) In the ground state of .... electrons are in stable equilibrium, while in .... electrons always experience a net force. (Thomson's model/ Rutherford's model)

(c) A classical atom based on .... is doomed to collapse. (Thomson's model/ Rutherford's model)

(d) An atom has a nearly continuous mass distribution in a .... but has a highly non-uniform mass distribution in .... (Thomson's model/ Rutherford's model)

(e) The positively charged part of the atom possesses most of the mass in .... (Rutherford's model/both the models)

Solution   (a) No different from

(b) Thomson's model, Rutherford's model

(c) Rutherford's model

(d) Thomson's model, Rutherford's model

(e) Both the models

Question 2.   Suppose you are given a chance to repeat the alpha particle scattering experiment using a thin sheet of solid hydrogen in place of the gold foil. (Hydrogen is a solid at temperatures below 14 K.) What results do you expect?

Solution   The basic purpose of scattering experiment is not completed because solid hydrogen will be a much lighter target as compared to the alpha particle acting as a projectile. By using the conditions of elastic collisions, the hydrogen will move much faster as compared to alpha after the collision. We cannot determine the size of hydrogen nucleus.

Question 3.   What is the shortest wavelength present in the Paschen series of spectral lines?

Solution   For Paschen series, $n_1 = 3$ and $n_2 = \infty$ for shortest wavelength

Using the formula,

$$\frac{hc}{\lambda} = R\left[\frac{1}{n_1^2} - \frac{1}{n_2^2}\right] \quad \text{[where } R \text{ is the Rydberg constant]}$$

$$\frac{hc}{\lambda} = 13.6 \times 1.6 \times 10^{-19}\left[\frac{1}{3^2} - \frac{1}{\infty^2}\right]$$

or $$\frac{hc}{\lambda} = \frac{21.76 \times 10^{-19}}{9}$$

or
$$\lambda = \frac{9 \times 6.63 \times 10^{-34} \times 3 \times 10^8}{21.76 \times 10^{-19}} = 8.2265 \times 10^{-7} \text{ m}$$

$$= 822.65 \text{ nm}$$

Thus, the shortest wavelength present is 822.65 nm.

Question 4. A difference of 2.3 eV separates two energy levels in an atom. What is the frequency of radiation emitted when the atom makes a transition from the upper level to the lower level?

Solution Given, difference in energy level $E = 2.3$ eV
$$= 2.3 \times 1.6 \times 10^{-19} \text{ J}$$

Planck's constant $h = 6.63 \times 10^{-34}$ J-s

Let v be the frequency, then $E = hv$

or
$$v = \frac{E}{h} = \frac{2.3 \times 1.6 \times 10^{-19}}{6.63 \times 10^{-34}}$$

$$= 5.6 \times 10^{14} \text{ Hz}$$

Question 5. The ground state energy of hydrogen atom is −13.6 eV. What are the kinetic and potential energies of the electron in this state?

Solution Given, the ground state energy of hydrogen atom
$$E = -13.6 \text{ eV}$$

We know that
$$\text{Kinetic Energy (KE)} = -E = 3.6 \text{ eV}$$
$$\text{Potential Energy (PE)} = -2\text{KE} = -2 \times 13.6 = -27.2 \text{ eV}$$

Question 6. A hydrogen atom initially in the ground level absorbs a photon, which excites it to the $n = 4$ level. Determine the wavelength and frequency of photon.

 To find the wavelength and frequency of photon, use the relation of energy of electron in hydrogen atom $E_n = -\dfrac{13.6}{n^2}$ eV.

Solution For ground state $n_1 = 1$ to $n_2 = 4$

Energy absorbed by photon, $E = E_2 - E_1$

$$= +13.6 \left(\frac{1}{n_1^2} - \frac{1}{n_2^2} \right) \times 1.6 \times 10^{-19} \text{ J}$$

$$= 13.6 \left(\frac{1}{1} - \frac{1}{4^2} \right) \times 1.6 \times 10^{-19}$$

$$= 13.6 \times 1.6 \times 10^{-19} \left(\frac{15}{16} \right)$$

$$= 20.4 \times 10^{-19}$$

or
$$E = h\nu = 20.4 \times 10^{-19}$$

$$\text{Frequency } \nu = \frac{20.4 \times 10^{-19}}{h}$$

$$= \frac{20.4 \times 10^{-19}}{6.63 \times 10^{-34}}$$

$$= 3.076 \times 10^{15}$$

$$= 3.1 \times 10^{15} \text{ Hz}$$

$$\text{Wavelength of photon } \lambda = \frac{c}{\nu}$$

$$= \frac{3 \times 10^8}{3.076 \times 10^{15}}$$

$$= 9.74 \times 10^{-8} \text{ m}$$

Thus, the wavelength is 9.7×10^{-8} m and frequency is 3.1×10^{15} Hz.

Question 7. (a) Using the Bohr's model calculate the speed of the electron in a hydrogen atom in the $n = 1, 2,$ and 3 levels.
  (b) Calculate the orbital period in each of these levels.

Solution   (a) Speed of the electron in Bohr's nth orbit $v = \dfrac{c}{n}\alpha$

$$\text{where, } \alpha = \frac{2\pi K e^2}{ch}$$

$$\alpha = 0.0073$$

$$\therefore \qquad v = \frac{c}{n} \times 0.0073$$

For $n = 1,$
$$v_1 = \frac{c}{1} \times 0.0073 = 3 \times 10^8 \times 0.0073$$

$$= 2.19 \times 10^6 \text{ m/s}$$

For $n = 2,$
$$v_2 = \frac{c}{2} \times 0.0073 = \frac{3 \times 10^8 \times 0.0073}{2}$$

$$= 1.095 \times 10^6 \text{ m/s}$$

For $n = 3,$
$$v_3 = \frac{c}{3} \times 0.0073 = \frac{3 \times 10^8 \times 0.0073}{3}$$

$$= 7.3 \times 10^5 \text{ m/s}$$

(b) Orbital period of electron is given by
$$T = \frac{2\pi r}{v}$$

Radius of nth orbit
$$r_n = \frac{n^2 h^2}{4\pi^2 K m e^2}$$

$$\therefore \qquad r_1 = \frac{(1)^2 \times (6.63 \times 10^{-34})^2}{4 \times 9.87 \times (9 \times 10^9) \times 9 \times 10^{-31} \times (1.6 \times 10^{-19})}$$

$$= 0.53 \times 10^{-10} \text{ m}$$

For $n = 1$, $\qquad T_1 = \frac{2\pi r_1}{v_1}$

$$= \frac{2 \times 3.14 \; 0.53 \times 10^{-10}}{2.19 \times 10^6} = 1.52 \times 10^{-16} \text{ s}$$

For $n = 2$, radius $r_n = n^2 r_1$

$$\therefore \qquad r_2 = 2^2 . r_1 = 4 \times 0.53 \times 10^{-10}$$

and $\quad$ velocity $v_n = \dfrac{v_1}{n}$

$$\therefore \qquad v_2 = \frac{v_1}{2} = \frac{2.19 \times 10^6}{2}$$

Time period $\quad T_2 = \dfrac{2 \times 3.14 \times 4 \times 0.53 \times 10^{-10} \times 2}{2.19 \times 10^6}$

$$= 1.216 \times 10^{-15} \text{ s}$$

For $n = 3$, radius $r_3 = 3^2 r_1 = 9 r_1 \doteq 9 \times 0.53 \times 10^{-10}$ m

and $\quad$ velocity $v_3 = \dfrac{v_1}{3} = \dfrac{2.19 \times 10^6}{3}$ m/s

Time period $T_3 = \dfrac{2\pi r_3}{v_3} = \dfrac{2 \times 3.14 \times 9 \times 0.53 \times 10^{-10} \times 3}{2.19 \times 10^6}$

$$= 4.1 \times 10^{-15} \text{ s}$$

Question 8. The radius of the innermost electron orbit of a hydrogen atom is 5.3×10^{-11} m. What are the radii of the $n = 2$ and $n = 3$ orbits?

Solution Given, the radius of the innermost electron orbit of a hydrogen $r_1 = 5.3 \times 10^{-11}$ m

As we know that $\qquad r_n = n^2 r_1$

For $n = 2$, $\quad$ radius $r_2 = 2^2 r_1 = 4 \times 5.3 \times 10^{-11} = 2.12 \times 10^{-10}$ m

For $n = 3$, $\quad$ radius $r_3 = 3^2 r_1 = 9 \times 5.3 \times 10^{-11} = 4.77 \times 10^{-10}$ m

Question 9. A 12.5 eV electron beam is used to bombard gaseous hydrogen at room temperature. What series of wavelengths will be emitted?

Solution Energy of electron beam $E = 12.5$ eV $= 12.5 \times 1.6 \times 10^{-19}$ J

Planck's constant $h = 6.63 \times 10^{-34}$ J-s

Velocity of light $c = 3 \times 10^8$ m/s

Using the relation $\quad E = \dfrac{hc}{\lambda} = \dfrac{6.62 \times 10^{-34} \times 3 \times 10^{8}}{12.5 \times 1.6 \times 10^{-19}}$

$$= 0.993 \times 10^{-7} \text{ m} = 993 \times 10^{-10} \text{ m}$$

$$= 993 \text{ Å}$$

This wavelength falls in the range of Lyman series (912 Å to 1216 Å) thus, we conclude that Lyman series of wavelength 993 Å is emitted.

Question 10. In accordance with the Bohr's model, find the quantum number that characterises the earth's revolution around the sun in an orbit of radius 1.5×10^{11} m with orbital speed 3×10^{4} m/s. (Mass of earth $= 6.0 \times 10^{24}$ kg.)

Solution   Given, radius of orbit $r = 1.5 \times 10^{11}$ m

Orbital speed $v = 3 \times 10^{4}$ m/s;   Mass of earth $M = 6 \times 10^{24}$ kg

Angular momentum, $mvr = \dfrac{nh}{2\pi}$

or $\quad\quad\quad\quad\quad\quad\quad n = \dfrac{2\pi vrm}{h}$

[where, n is the quantum number of the orbit]

$$= \dfrac{2 \times 3.14 \times 3 \times 10^{4} \times 1.5 \times 10^{11} \times 6 \times 10^{24}}{6.63 \times 10^{-34}}$$

$$= 2.57 \times 10^{74}$$

or $\quad\quad\quad\quad\quad\quad n = 2.6 \times 10^{74}$

Thus, the quantum number is 2.6×10^{74} which is too large.

The electron would jump from $n = 1$ to $n = 3$.

$$E_3 = \dfrac{-13.6}{3^2} = -1.5 \text{ eV}$$

So, they belong to Lyman series.

Additional Exercises

Question 11. Answer the following questions, which help you to understand the difference between Thomson's model and Rutherford's model better.

    (a) Is the average angle of deflection of α-particles by a thin gold foil predicted by Thomson's model much less, about the same, or much greater than that predicted by Rutherford's model?

    (b) Is the probability of backward scattering (*i.e.*, scattering of α-particles at angles greater than 90°) predicted by Thomson's model much less, about the same, or much greater than that predicted by Rutherford's model?

(c) Keeping other factors fixed, it is found experimentally that for small thickness t, the number of α-particles scattered at moderate angles is proportional to t. What clue does this linear dependence on t provide?

(d) In which model is it completely wrong to ignore multiple scattering for the calculation of average angle of scattering of α-particles by a thin foil?

Solution

(a) The average angle of deflection is almost same, because we are taking almost average value.

(b) The probability of backward scattering is much less because in Thomson's model, there is no such massive central core called the nucleus in Rutherford's model.

(c) It suggests that the scattering is predominantly due to a single collision because chance of a single collision increases with the number of target atoms which increases linearly with the thickness of foil.

(d) In the Thomson's model, positive charge is uniformly distributed in the spherical atom. Therefore, a single collision causes very small deflection. Therefore, average scattering angle can be explained only by considering multiple scattering. So, it is wrong to ignore multiple scattering in Thomson's model.

In Rutherford's model, most of the scattering comes through a single collision and multiple scattering effects can be ignored as a first approximation.

Question 12. The gravitational attraction between electron and proton in a hydrogen atom is weaker than the Coulomb attraction by a factor of about 10^{-40}. An alternative way of looking at this fact is to estimate the radius of the first Bohr orbit of a hydrogen atom, if the electron and proton were bound by gravitational attraction. You will find the answer interesting.

Solution As we know that the radius of first Bohr orbit of hydrogen atom is

$$r_0 = \frac{4\pi\varepsilon_0 \left(\dfrac{h}{2\pi}\right)^2}{m_e e^2}$$

Let we consider that the atom is bound by the gravitational force

$$= \frac{Gm_p m_e}{r^2}$$

We replace $\dfrac{e^2}{4\pi\varepsilon_0}$ by $Gm_p m_e$. In that case, radius of first orbit (Bohr) of hydrogen atom would be

$$r_0 = \frac{\left(\dfrac{h}{2\pi}\right)^2}{G m_p \cdot m_e^2}$$

By substituting the standard values, we get

$$r_0 = \frac{\left(\dfrac{6.6 \times 10^{-34}}{2 \times 3.14}\right)^2}{6.67 \times 10^{-11} \times 1.67 \times 10^{-27} \times (9.1 \times 10^{-31})^2}$$

$$= 1.2 \times 10^{29} \text{ m}$$

This is much greater than the estimated size of the whole universe.

Question 13. Obtain an expression for the frequency of radiation emitted when a hydrogen atom de-excites from level n to level $(n-1)$. For large n, show that this frequency equals the classical frequency of revolution of the electron in the orbit.

Solution   Let v be the frequency when a hydrogen atom jumps from level n to $(n-1)$.

i.e., $$n_1 = (n-1), \, n_2 = n$$

Energy $E = hv = E_2 - E_1$

or $$v = \frac{1}{2} \frac{mc^2 \alpha^2}{h} \times \left[\frac{1}{(n-1)^2} - \frac{1}{n^2}\right] = \frac{mc^2 \alpha^2}{2h} \left[\frac{n^2 - (n-1)^2}{n^2 (n-1)^2}\right]$$

or $$v = \frac{mc^2 \alpha^2 \left[(n+n-1)(n-n+1)\right]}{2hn^2 (n-1)^2} = \frac{mc^2 \alpha^2 (2n-1)}{2hn^2 (n-1)^2}$$

For large values of n, $(2n-1 \approx 2n)$, $(n-1 \approx n)$.

$$v = \frac{mc^2 \alpha^2 \, 2n}{2h \, n^2 n^2} = \frac{mc^2 \alpha^2}{hn^3} \qquad \left(\because \alpha = \frac{2\pi Ke^2}{ch}\right)$$

or $$v = \frac{mc^2}{hn^3} \frac{4\pi^2 K^2 e^4}{c^2 n^2}$$

or $$v = \frac{4\pi^2 K^2 m e^4}{h^3 n^3} \qquad \qquad \ldots\text{(i)}$$

In Bohr's atomic model, velocity of nth orbit $v = \dfrac{hn}{2\pi mr}$ and radius

$$r = \frac{n^2 h^2}{4\pi^2 mKe^2}$$

Thus, frequency of oscillation

$$v = \frac{v}{2\pi r} = \frac{nh}{2\pi mr}\left(\frac{4\pi^2 mKe^2}{2\pi n^2 h^2}\right)$$

$$= \frac{Ke^2}{nhr} = \frac{Ke^2}{nh}\left(\frac{4\pi^2 mKe^2}{n^2 h^2}\right) = \frac{4\pi^2 mK^2 e^4}{n^3 h^3}$$

It is same as Eq. (i).

So, we can say that for large values of n, the classical frequency of revolution of electron in nth orbit is same as the frequency of radiation emitted when hydrogen atom de-excites from level n to level $(n-1)$.

Question 14. Classically, an electron can be in any orbit around the nucleus of an atom. Then what determines the typical atomic size? Why is an atom not, say, thousand times bigger than its typical size? The question had greatly puzzled Bohr before he arrived at his famous model of the atom that you have learnt in the text. To simulate what he might well have done before his discovery, let us play as follows with the basic constants of nature and see if we can get a quantity with the dimensions of length that is roughly equal to the known size of an atom ($- 10^{-10}$ m).

(a) Construct a quantity with the dimensions of length from the fundamental constants e, m_e, and c. Determine its numerical value.

(b) You will find that the length obtained in (a) is many orders of magnitude smaller than the atomic dimensions. Further, it involves c. But energies of atoms are mostly in non-relativistic domain where c is not expected to play any role. This is what may have suggested Bohr to discard c and look for 'something else' to get the right atomic size. Now, the Planck's constant h had already made its appearance elsewhere. Bohr's great insight lay in recognising that h, m_e and e will yield the right atomic size. Construct a quantity with the dimension of length from h, m_e and e and confirm that its numerical value has indeed the correct order of magnitude.

Solution

(a) Using the constants e, m_e and c, we construct a quantity which has the dimensions of length.

i.e.,
$$\frac{e^2}{4\pi\varepsilon_0 m_e c^2}$$

Now,
$$\frac{e^2}{4\pi\varepsilon_0 m_e c^2} = \frac{(1.6 \times 10^{-19})^2}{4 \times 3.14 \times 8.85 \times 10^{-12} \times 9.1 \times 10^{-31} \times (3 \times 10^8)^2}$$

$$= 2.82 \times 10^{-15} \text{ m}$$

This is much smaller as compared to atomic size.

(b) Using h, m_e and e, the quantity having dimensions of length is

$$\frac{4\pi\varepsilon_0 \left(\dfrac{h}{2\pi}\right)^2}{m_e \cdot e^2}$$

Now,
$$\frac{4\pi\varepsilon_0\left(\dfrac{h}{2\pi}\right)^2}{m_e e^2} = \frac{\left(\dfrac{6.6\times 10^{-34}}{2\times 3.14}\right)^2}{9\times 10^9 \times 9.1\times 10^{-31}\times (1.6\times 10^{-19})^2}$$

$$= 0.53\times 10^{-10} \text{ m}$$

This is of the order of atomic sizes.

Question 15. The total energy of an electron in the first excited state of the hydrogen atom is about -3.4 eV.

   (a) What is the kinetic energy of the electron in this state?

   (b) What is the potential energy of the electron in this state?

   (c) Which of the answers above would change if the choice of the zero of potential energy is changed?

Solution   The kinetic energy of electron $(KE) = \dfrac{KZe^2}{2r}$

Potential energy of electron $(PE) = \dfrac{-KZe^2}{r} \quad \Rightarrow \quad PE = -2\,KE$

In this calculation, the electric potential and potential energy are zero at infinity.

$$\text{Total energy} = PE + KE = -2KE + KE = -KE$$

   (a) In the first excited state, total energy $= -3.4$ eV

$$KE = -(-3.4) = 3.4 \text{ eV}$$

   (b) PE of electron in this first excited state

$$= -2\,KE = -2\,(3.4) = -6.8 \text{ eV.}$$

   (c) If zero of potential energy is changed, kinetic energy does not change and continue to be $+3.4$ eV. So, the potential energy and total energy of the state would change with the choice of zero of potential energy.

Question 16. If Bohr's quantization postulate (angular momentum $nh/2\pi$) is a basic law of nature, it should be equally valid for the case of planetary motion also. Why then do, we never speak its quantization of orbits of planets around the sun?

Solution   Applying Bohr's quantization postulate

$$mvr = \frac{nh}{2\pi}$$

$$n = mv \times \frac{2\pi r}{n}$$

$$n = \frac{6\times 10^{24}\times 3000\times 1.49\times 10^{11}\times 2\times 3.14}{6.626\times 10^{-14}}$$

$$= 0.10^{72}$$

We can see that the Bohr's quantisation postulate is in terms of Planck's constant (h). But angular momenta associated with plantary motion are $\approx 10^{72}$ h (for earth). In term of Bohr's quantization postulate, this corresponds to $n = 10^{72}$, for such large value of n, the differences in the successive energies and angular momenta of the quantized levels are so small compared to the energies and angular momentum respectively of the levels can be considered as continuous.

Question 17. Obtain the first Bohr's radius and the ground state energy of a muonic hydrogen atom (*i.e.*, an atom in which a negatively charged muon ($\bar{\mu}$) of mass about 207 m_e orbits around a proton).

Solution Muonic hydrogen is the atom in which a negatively charged muon of mass about 207 m_e revolves around a proton.

In Bohr's atom model, $\qquad r \propto \dfrac{1}{m}$

$$\because \qquad \frac{r_{\text{muon}}}{r_{\text{electron}}} = \frac{m_e}{m_\mu} = \frac{m_e}{207\, m_e} = \frac{1}{207} \qquad (\because m_\mu = 207\, m_e)$$

Here, r_e is radius of orbit of electron in hydrogen atom = 0.53 Å

$$r_\mu = \frac{r_e}{207} = \frac{0.53 \times 10^{-10}}{207} = 2.56 \times 10^{-13} \text{ m}$$

Again in Bohr's atom model.

$$\because \qquad E \propto m$$

$$\therefore \qquad \frac{E_\mu}{E_e} = \frac{m_\mu}{m_e} = \frac{207\, m_e}{m_e}$$

$$\Rightarrow \qquad E_\mu = 207\, E_e$$

For ground state, energy of electron in hydrogen atom

$$E_e = -\,13.6 \text{ eV}$$

$$\therefore \qquad E_\mu = 207\,(-\,13.6) = -\,2815.2 \text{ eV}$$

$$= -\,2.8152 \text{ keV}$$

Selected NCERT Exemplar Problems

Question 1. The mass of an H-atom is less than the sum of the masses of a proton and electron. Why is this?

Solution According to Einstein's mass energy equation, $E = mc^2$

The mass of H-atom is $m_p + m_e - \dfrac{E}{c^2}$.

where, energy $E = 13.6$ eV, which is binding energy.

Question 2. Would the Bohr formula for the H-atom remain unchanged, if proton had a charge $(+4/3)e$ and electron had a charge $(-3/4)e$, where $e = 1.6 \times 10^{-19}$ C. Give reasons for your answer.

Solution According to Bohr's theory, centripetal force required by the electron for their motion around the nucleus = Electric force between the protons and electrons.

$$\frac{mv^2}{r} = \frac{1}{4\pi\varepsilon_0} \frac{(q_p)\,(q_e)}{r^2} \qquad \text{(From Coulomb's law)}$$

where r = atomic radius, q_p = charge of proton = $+e$

q_e = charge of electron = $-e$

$$= \frac{1}{4\pi\varepsilon_0} \frac{(e)\,(-e)}{r^2} = \frac{1}{4\pi\varepsilon_0} \frac{-e^2}{r^2}$$

Now, given charge on proton $q_p = +\dfrac{4}{3} e$

Charge on electron $q_e = -\dfrac{3}{4} e$

Putting the new value (keeping after factors unchanged)

$$\frac{mv^2}{r} = \frac{1}{4\pi\varepsilon_0} \frac{\left(\dfrac{4}{3} e\right)\left(-\dfrac{3}{4} e\right)}{r^2}$$

$$= \frac{1}{4\pi\varepsilon_0} \frac{-e^2}{r^2}$$

i.e., Bohr's formula remain unchanged.

Question 3. Consider two different hydrogen atoms. The electron in each atom is in an excited state. Is it possible for the electrons to have different energies but the same orbital angular momentum according to the Bohr's model?

Solution No, it is not possible for the electron to have different energies because according to Bohr's model,

$$E_n = \frac{-13.6}{n^2}$$

The electrons which are in different energies, they have different values of n.

Angular momentum, $mvr = \dfrac{nh}{2\pi}$, so as n changes angular momentum changes.

Question 4. Positronium is just like an H-atom with the proton replaced by the positively charged anti-particle of the electron (called the positron which is as massive as the electron). What would be the ground state energy of positronium?

Solution The Bohr's formula, $E_n = \dfrac{-me^4}{8\varepsilon_0 n^2 h^2}$

For H-atom $m \approx m_e$ (mass of electron) and mas of positronium, $m = \dfrac{m_e}{2}$

So, the energy, $E'_n = \dfrac{E_n}{2} = \dfrac{-13.6}{2} = -6.8$ eV

Question 5. Using Bohr's model, calculate the electric current created by the electron when the H-atom is in the ground state.

Solution Let v be the velocity of electron and a_0 be Bohr's radius.

$$\text{Number of revolutions/time} = \frac{\text{Revolution}}{\text{Time}} = \frac{\text{Distance}}{\text{Speed}}$$

$$n = \frac{2\pi a_0}{v}$$

$$\text{Current } I = ne$$

$$I = \frac{2\pi a_0}{v} e$$

Question 6. What is the minimum energy that must be given to an H-atom in ground state so that it can emit an H_γ line in Balmer series. If the angular momentum of the system is conserved, what would be the angular momentum of such H_γ photons?

Solution H_γ line in Balmer series corresponds to transition $n = 5$ to $n = 2$.

Since, the electron is in ground state $n = 1$.

So, energy required $= E_1 - E_5 = 13.6 - 0.54 = 13.06$ eV $\qquad \left[\because E_n = -\dfrac{13.6}{n^2} \right]$

As given in the question, the angular momentum is conserved.

The angular momentum of photon

$$= \text{Change in angular momentum of electron}$$
$$= L_5 - L_2 = 5\hbar - 2\hbar$$
$$= 3\hbar = 3 \times 1.06 \times 10^{-34}$$
$$= 3.18 \times 10^{-34} \text{ kg-m}^2/\text{s}$$

Chapter 13

Nuclei

Important Results

1. The radius of nucleus is given by $R = R_0 A^{1/3}$

   where, R_0 = emperical constant = 1.1 fm

2. Density of nucleus is given by $\rho = \dfrac{3m}{4\pi R_0^3}$

3. 1 amu = 1.66×10^{-27} kg, m = mass of neucleon = 1.66×10^{-27} kg

4. 1 MeV = 1.6×10^{-13} J

5. 1 amu = 931 MeV

6. Mass defect is given by $\Delta m = Z[m_p] + (A - Z)\, m_n - m_N$

7. Total binding energy = $\Delta m \cdot c^2$

8. Average binding energy per nucleon = $\dfrac{\Delta m \cdot c^2}{A}$

   where, $c = 3 \times 10^8$ m/s

9. Packing fraction = $\dfrac{M - A}{A}$

   where, A is the mass number.

10. According to radioactive decay law, $\dfrac{dN}{dt} = \lambda N$ or $N = N_0 e^{-\lambda t}$

    where, λ is disintegration constant.

11. Half life of a radioactive element is given by $T_{1/2} = \dfrac{0.6931}{\lambda}$

12. Average life or mean life of radioactive element is given by

$$\tau = \frac{1}{\lambda} = 1.44\, T_{1/2}$$

13. $\dfrac{N}{N_0} = \left(\dfrac{1}{2}\right)^n$ where, n is number of half lives.

14. Activity $A = \dfrac{dN}{dt} = \lambda N$

15. $A = A_0 e^{-\lambda t}$

16. $\dfrac{A}{A_0} = \dfrac{N}{N_0} = \left(\dfrac{1}{2}\right)^n$ where, n is number of half lives.

17. In alpha decay, mass number decreases by 4 and charge number decreases by 2. In beta decay, mass number remain unaffected and charge number increases by one. In gamma decay, the mass number and charge number both remain unaffected. Only the energy changes.

18. Units of radioactivity —

1 Curie $= 3.7 \times 10^{10}$ disintegration/s

1 Rutherford $= 10^6$ disintegration/s

19. $m_H = 1.007825,\ m_n = 1.008665$ u, $m_e = 0.000548$ u

$m\left({}^{4}_{2}\text{He}\right) = 4.002603,\ N = 6.023 \times 10^{23}$ per mol

$N = 6.023 \times 10^{23}$ per mole

$k = 1.381 \times 10^{-23}$ J/K

$1\mu = 931.5$ MeV/C^2

Exercises

Question 1. (a) Two stable isotopes of lithium, ${}^{6}_{3}\text{Li}$ and ${}^{7}_{3}\text{Li}$ have respective abundance of 7.5% and 92.5%. These isotopes have masses 6.01512 u and 7.01600 u, respectively. Find the atomic mass of lithium.

(b) Boron has two stable isotopes, ${}^{10}_{5}\text{B}$ and ${}^{11}_{5}\text{B}$. Their respective masses are 10.01294 u and 11.00931 u and the atomic mass of boron is 10.811 u. Find the abundances of ${}^{10}_{5}\text{B}$ and ${}^{11}_{5}\text{B}$.

Solution

(a) Given, abundance per cent of ${}^{6}\text{Li} = 7.5\%$

Abundance per cent of ${}^{7}\text{Li} = 92.5\%$

Atomic mass of ${}^{6}\text{Li} = 6.01512$ u

Atomic mass of ${}^{7}\text{Li} = 7.01600$ u

Atomic mass = Weighed average of the isotopes

$$= \frac{6.01512 \times 7.5 + 7.01600 \times 92.5}{7.5 + 92.5}$$

$$= \frac{45.1134 + 648.98}{100} = 6.941 \text{ u}$$

(b) Given, mass of ^{10}B = 10.01294 u

Mass of ^{11}B = 11.00931 u

Atomic mass of boron = 10.811 u

Let the abundance of ^{10}B be x%.

So, the abundance of ^{11}B be (100 − x)%.

Atomic mass = Weighted average of the isotopes

$$10.811 = \frac{x \times 10.01294 + (100 - x) \times 11.00931}{(x + 100 - x)}$$

Abundance of $^{10}B, x$ = 19.9%

Abundance of $^{11}B, (100 - x)$ = 100 − 19.9 = 80.1%

Thus, the abundance of ^{10}B is 19.9% and the abundance of ^{11}B is 80.1%.

Question 2. The three stable isotopes of neon, $^{20}_{10}Ne$, $^{21}_{10}Ne$ and $^{22}_{10}Ne$ have respective abundances of **90.51%, 0.27%** and **9.22%**. The atomic masses of the three isotopes are **19.99 u, 20.99 u** and **21.99 u**, respectively. Obtain the average atomic mass of neon.

Solution Given, abundance per cent of Ne^{20} = 90.51%

Abundance per cent of ^{21}Ne = 0.27%

Abundance per cent of ^{22}Ne = 9.22%

Mass of ^{20}Ne = 19.99 u

Mass of ^{21}Ne = 20.99 u

Mass of ^{22}Ne = 21.99 u

Average atomic mass (m) = Weighted average of all isotopes

$$= \frac{90.51 \times 19.99 + 0.27 \times 20.99 + 9.22 \times 21.99}{90.51 + 0.27 + 9.22}$$

$$= \frac{1809.29 + 5.67 + 202.75}{100} = \frac{2017.7}{100}$$

$$= 20.18 \text{ u}$$

Thus, the average atomic mass of neon is 20.18 u.

Question 3. Obtain the binding energy (in MeV) of a nitrogen nucleus ($^{14}_{7}N$), given $m(^{14}_{7}N)$ = 14.00307 u.

Solution Given, mass of proton, m_p = 1.007834,

Mass of neutron, m_n = 1.00867 u

$^{14}_{7}N$ nucleus contains 7 protons and 7 neutrons.

Mass defect (Δm) = mass of nucleons − mass of nucleus

$$= 7m_p + 7m_n - m_N$$

$$= 7 \times 1.00783 + 7 \times 1.00867 - 14.00307$$

$$= 7.05481 + 7.06069 - 14.00307 = 0.11243 \text{ u}$$

Binding energy of nitrogen nucleus $= \Delta m \times 931$ MeV
$$= 0.11243 \times 931 \text{ MeV}$$
$$= 104.67 \text{ MeV}$$

Thus, the binding energy is 104.67 MeV.

Question 4. Obtain the binding energy of the nuclei $^{56}_{26}$Fe and $^{209}_{83}$Bi in units of MeV from the following data :
$$m\,(^{56}_{26}\text{Fe}) = 55.934939 \text{ u}, \; m\,(^{209}_{83}\text{Bi}) = 208.980388 \text{ u}.$$

Solution   Given, mass of proton $m_p = 1.00783$ u

Mass of neutron, $m_n = 1.00867$ u

(i) For $^{56}_{26}$Fe

$^{56}_{26}$Fe contains 26 protons and $(56 - 26) = 30$ neutrons

Mass defect $(\Delta m) =$ mass of nucleons $-$ mass of nucleus of $^{56}_{26}$Fe

$$\begin{aligned}
\text{Mass defect } (\Delta m) &= 26 \times m_p + 30 \times m_n - m_N \\
&= 26 \times 1.00783 + 30 \times 1.00867 - 55.934939 \\
&= 26.20345 + 30.25995 - 55.934939 \\
&= 0.528461 \text{ u}
\end{aligned}$$

$$\begin{aligned}
\text{Total binding energy} &= \Delta m \times 931 \text{ MeV} \\
&= 0.528461 \times 931.5 \\
&= 492.26 \text{ MeV}
\end{aligned}$$

Average binding energy per nucleon of $^{56}_{26}$Fe

$$= \frac{\text{Binding energy}}{\text{Total number of nucleons}}$$

$$= \frac{492.26}{56}$$

$$= 8.790 \text{ MeV}$$

(ii) For $_{83}$Bi^{209}

It contains 83 protons and $(209 - 83) = 126$ neutrons

Mass defect $(\Delta m) =$ mass of nucleons $-$ mass of nucleus of $^{209}_{83}$Bi

$$\begin{aligned}
&= 83 \times m_p + 126 \times m_n - m_N \\
&= 83 \times 1.007825 + 126 \times 1.008665 - 208.980388 \\
&= 83.649475 + 127.091790 - 208.980388 \\
&= 1.760877 \text{ u}
\end{aligned}$$

Binding Energy $= \Delta m \times 931$ MeV $= 1.760877 \times 931.5 = 1640.26$ MeV

Average binding energy per nucleon of $^{209}_{83}$Bi

$$= \frac{\text{Binding energy}}{\text{Total number of nucleon}} = \frac{1640.26}{209} = 7.848 \text{ MeV}$$

Thus, the binding energy per nucleon of Fe is more than Bi.

Question 5.   A given coin has a mass of 3.0 g. Calculate the nuclear energy that would be required to separate all the neutrons and protons from each other. For simplicity, assume that the coin is entirely made of $^{63}_{29}$Cu atoms (of mass 62.92960 u).

Solution   Given, mass of coin $= 3$ g

$$\text{Number of atoms in 1 g of Cu} = \frac{6.023 \times 10^{23}}{63}$$

$$\text{Number of atoms in 3 g of Cu} = \frac{6.023 \times 10^{23}}{63} \times 3 = 2.868 \times 10^{22}$$

Number of protons in Cu atom, $= 29$

Number of neutrons in Cu atom $= 63 - 29 = 34$

mass defect in each atom, $\Delta m = 29 \times m_p + 34 \times m_n - m_{Cu}$

$$= 29 \times 1.00783 + 34 \times 1.00867 - 62.9260$$

$$= 0.59225 \text{ u}$$

$\therefore$ Total mass defect in all atoms $= 0.59225 \times 2.868 \times 10^{22}$

$$= 1.6985 \times 10^{22} \text{ u}$$

Binding energy $=$ Mass defect $\times 931$ MeV

$$= 1.6985 \times 10^{22} \times 931 = 1.58 \times 10^{25} \text{ MeV}$$

Thus, the energy required to separate all the neutrons and protons is 1.58×10^{25} MeV *i.e.*, equal to binding energy.

Question 6.   Write nuclear reaction equations for

    (a) α-decay of $^{226}_{88}$Ra,   (b) α-decay of $^{242}_{94}$Pu,

    (c) β^--decay of $^{32}_{15}$P,   (d) β^--decay of $^{210}_{83}$Bi,

    (e) β^+-decay of $^{11}_{6}$C,   (f) β^+-decay of $^{97}_{43}$Tc,

    (g) electron capture of $^{120}_{54}$Xe.

Solution   As we know that

1. in α-decay, the mass number is reduced by 4 and atomic number is reduced by 2.
2. in β-decay, the mass number remains constant and atomic number is increased by 1.
3. in a γ-decay, the mass number and atomic number remains same.

    The following equations are given :

(a) $^{226}_{88}\text{Ra} \xrightarrow{\;-\alpha\;} {}^{222}_{88}\text{Rn} + {}^{4}_{2}\text{He}$

(b) $^{242}_{94}\text{Pu} \xrightarrow{\;-\alpha\;} {}^{238}_{92}\text{U} + {}^{4}_{2}\text{He}$

(c) $^{32}_{15}\text{P} \xrightarrow{\;-(-\beta)\;} {}^{32}_{16}\text{S} + {}^{0}_{-1}\text{e} + \bar{\nu}$

    i.e., β^--decay is accompanied by release of antineutrino.

(d) $^{210}_{83}\text{Bi} \xrightarrow{-(-\beta)} {}^{210}_{84}\text{X} + {}^{0}_{-1}e + \bar{\nu}$

(e) $^{11}_{6}\text{C} \xrightarrow{-(+\beta)} {}^{11}_{5}\text{B} + e^{+} + \nu$

β^{+} decay of $^{11}\text{C}_6$ is accompanied by the release neutrino.

(f) $^{97}_{43}\text{TC} \xrightarrow{-(+\beta)} {}^{97}_{42}\text{X} \times e^{+} + \nu$

(g) $^{120}_{54}\text{Xe} + {}^{0}_{-1}e \longrightarrow {}^{120}_{53}\text{X}$

Question 7. A radioactive isotope has a half-life of T years. How long will it take the activity to reduce to
(a) **3.125%** and
(b) **1% of its original value?**

Solution Given, half-life $T_{1/2} = T$ yr

(a) $N = 3.125\%$ of N_0

$\therefore \qquad \dfrac{N}{N_0} = \dfrac{3.125}{100} = \dfrac{1}{32}$

We know that

$$\dfrac{N}{N_0} = \left(\dfrac{1}{2}\right)^n$$

$\therefore$

$$\dfrac{1}{32} = \left(\dfrac{1}{2}\right)^n$$

$\Rightarrow$

$$\left(\dfrac{1}{2}\right)^5 = \left(\dfrac{1}{2}\right)^n$$

or $\qquad n = 5$

So, $\qquad$ time $t = n \times T_{1/2} = 5\,T$

After 5 half-time periods activity reduces to 3.125% of initial activity.

(b) Given, $N = 1\%$ of N_0

$\therefore \qquad \dfrac{N}{N_0} = \dfrac{1}{100}$

We know that

$$\dfrac{N}{N_0} = e^{-\lambda t}$$

$\therefore$

$$\dfrac{1}{100} = e^{-\lambda t}$$

Taking log on both the sides, we get

$$\log_e 1 - \log_e 100 = -\lambda t \log_e e$$

$$-2.303 \times 2 = -\lambda t$$

or $\qquad t = \dfrac{4.606}{\lambda}$

Also, we know that $\lambda = \dfrac{0.693}{T_{1/2}}$

$$\therefore \qquad t = \dfrac{4.606 \cdot T_{1/2}}{0.693} = 6.65\, T$$

Question 8. The normal activity of living carbon containing matter is found to be about 15 decays per minute for every gram of carbon. This activity arises from the small proportion of radioactive $^{14}_{6}C$ present with the stable carbon isotope $^{12}_{6}C$. When the organism is dead, its interaction with the atmosphere (which maintains the above equilibrium activity) ceases and its activity begins to drop. From the known half-life (5730 yr) of $^{14}_{6}C$ and the measured activity, the age of the specimen can be approximately estimated. This is the principle of $^{14}_{6}C$ dating used in archaeology. Suppose a specimen from Mohenjodaro gives an activity of 9 decays per minute per gram of carbon. Estimate the approximate age of the Indus-Valley civilization.

Solution Given, normal activity, $A_0 = 15$ decay/min

Present activity, $A = 9$ decay/min

$T_{1/2} = 5730$ yr

Using the formula,

$$\frac{A}{A_0} = e^{-\lambda t}$$

$$\frac{9}{15} = e^{-\lambda t}$$

or

$$\frac{3}{5} = e^{-\lambda t}$$

or

$$e^{\lambda t} = \frac{5}{3}$$

Taking log on both the sides, we get

$$\lambda t \log_e e = \log_e 5 - \log_e 3$$

or

$$\lambda t = 2.303\,(0.69 - 0.47)$$

$$\lambda t = 0.5109 \qquad \left(\because \lambda = \frac{0.693}{T_{1/2}} \right)$$

$$\therefore \qquad t = \frac{0.5066 \times T_{1/2}}{0.693}$$

$$= \frac{0.5066 \times 5730}{0.693}$$

$$= 4224.47 \text{ yr}$$

Thus, the approximate age of Indus-Valley civilization is 4224 yr.

Question 9. Obtain the amount of $_{27}^{60}\text{Co}$ necessary to provide a radioactive source of 8.0 mCi strength. The half-life of $_{27}^{60}\text{Co}$ is **5.3 yr.**

Solution   Activity, $\dfrac{dN}{dt} = 8 \text{ mCi} = 8 \times 10^{-3} \times 3.7 \times 10^{10} = 8 \times 3.7 \times 10^{7}$

$$\text{disintegration/s}$$
$$(\because 1 \text{ Ci} = 3.7 \times 10^{10} \text{ disintegration/s})$$

Half-life of $_{27}^{60}\text{Co}$, $T_{1/2} = 5.3 \text{ yr} = 5.3 \times 365 \times 24 \times 60 \times 60$

$$= 1.67 \times 10^{8} \text{ s}$$

We know that

$$\lambda = \frac{0.693}{T_{1/2}} = \frac{0.693}{1.67 \times 10^{8}} = 4.14 \times 10^{-9}/\text{s}$$

Activity, $\dfrac{dN}{dt} = \lambda N$

or $N = \dfrac{dN/dt}{\lambda} = \dfrac{8 \times 3.7 \times 10^{7}}{4.14 \times 10^{-9}} = 7.133 \times 10^{16}$

By using the concept of Avogadro number —

Mass of 6.023×10^{23} atoms of $_{27}^{60}\text{Co} = 60 \text{ g}$

Mass of 7.133×10^{16} atoms of $_{27}^{60}\text{Co} = \dfrac{60 \times 7.133 \times 10^{16}}{6.023 \times 10^{23}}$

Mass $m = 7.12 \times 10^{-6} \text{ g}$

Thus, the required mass of $_{27}^{60}\text{Co}$ is 7.12×10^{-6} g.

Question 10. The half-life of $_{38}^{90}\text{Sr}$ is 28 yr. What is the disintegration rate of 15 mg of this isotope?

Solution   Given, half life of $_{38}^{90}\text{Sr}$, $T_{1/2} = 28 \text{ yr}$

$$= 28 \times 365 \times 24 \times 60 \times 60 \text{ s}$$

According to Avogadro number concept—

90 g of Sr contains $= 6.023 \times 10^{23}$ atom

15 mg of Sr contains $= \dfrac{6.023 \times 10^{23} \times 15 \times 10^{-3}}{90}$

Number of atoms, $N = 1.0038 \times 10^{20}$

Activity, $\dfrac{dN}{dt} = \lambda N$

or $\dfrac{dN}{dt} = \dfrac{0.6931}{T_{1/2}} \cdot N = \dfrac{0.6931 \times 1.0038 \times 10^{20}}{28 \times 365 \times 24 \times 60 \times 60}$ $\left(\because \lambda = \dfrac{0.693}{T_{1/2}} \right)$

$$\dfrac{dN}{dt} = 7.877 \times 10^{10} \text{ disintegration/s}$$

$$= 7.877 \times 10^{10} \text{ Bq}$$

Question 11. Obtain approximately the ratio of the nuclear radii of the gold isotope $^{197}_{79}$Au and the silver isotope $^{107}_{47}$Ag.

Solution   Radius of nuclei, $R = R_0\, A^{1/3}$

where A is the mass number of nucleus and R_0 is an empirical constant.

$\therefore$ $$R \propto A^{1/3}$$

$\therefore$ $$\frac{R_{\text{gold}}}{R_{\text{silver}}} = \left(\frac{A_{\text{gold}}}{A_{\text{silver}}}\right)^{1/3} = \left(\frac{197}{107}\right)^{13} = 1.225$$

$$= 1.23$$

Question 12. Find the Q-value and the kinetic energy of the emitted α-particle in the α-decay of (a) $^{226}_{88}$Ra and (b) $^{220}_{86}$Rn.

Given, $m(^{226}_{88}$Ra$) = 226.02540$ u, $m(^{222}_{86}$Rn$) = 222.01750$ u,

$m_\alpha = 4.00260$ u, $m(^{220}_{86}$Rn$) = 220.01137$ u,

$m(^{216}_{84}$Po$) = 216.00189$ u

Solution   (a) The process of α -decay of $^{226}_{88}$Ra can be expressed as

$$^{226}_{88}\text{Ra} \longrightarrow {}^{222}_{86}\text{Rn} + {}^{4}_{2}\text{He} + Q$$

Q-value of the reaction is given by

$$Q\text{-value} = [m\,(^{226}_{88}\text{Ra}) - m\,(^{222}_{86}\text{Rn}) - m_\alpha] \times 931.5 \text{ MeV}$$

$$= (226.02540 - 222.01750 - 4.00260) \times 931.5$$

$$= 0.0053 \times 931.5 = 4.94 \text{ MeV}$$

Kinetic energy of emitted α-particle $= \left(\dfrac{A-4}{A}\right)\cdot Q = \dfrac{226-4}{226} \times 4.94$

$$= 4.85 \text{ MeV}$$

(b) The process of α-decay of $^{220}_{86}$Rn can be expressed as

$$^{220}_{86}\text{Rn} \longrightarrow {}^{216}_{84}\text{Po} + {}^{4}_{2}\text{He}$$

Q-value of the reaction—

$$Q\text{-value} = [m(^{220}_{86}\text{Rn}) - m(^{216}_{84}\text{Po}) - m_\alpha] \times 931.5 \text{ MeV}$$

$$= [220.01137 - 216.00189 - 4.00260] \times 931.5$$

$$= 6.41 \text{ MeV}$$

Kinetic energy of emitted α-particle $= \dfrac{(A-4)Q}{A} = \dfrac{220-4}{220} \times 6.41$

$$= 6.29 \text{ MeV}$$

Question 13. The radionuclide ^{11}C decays according to

$$^{11}_{6}\text{C} \longrightarrow {}^{11}_{5}\text{B} + e^+ + \nu : T_{1/2} = 20.3 \text{ min}$$

The maximum enregy of the emitted positron is 0.960 MeV.

Given, the mass values

$$m(_{6}^{11}\text{C}) = 11.011434 \text{ u and } m(_{6}^{11}\text{B}) = 11.009305 \text{ u}$$

Calculate Q and compare it with the maximum energy of the positron emitted.

Solution Mass of $e = 0.000548$ u

The mass defect, $\Delta m = [m(_{6}^{11}\text{C}) - m(_{5}^{11}\text{B}) - m_e]$

where, the masses used are those of nuclei and not of atoms. If we use atomic masses, we have to add 6 m_e in case of ^{11}C and 5 m_e in case of ^{11}B.

As $_{6}^{11}$C atom is made up of $_{6}^{11}$C nucleus and 6 protons.

$\therefore$ Mass of $_{6}^{11}$C nucleus

$$= \text{Mass of } _{6}^{11}\text{C atom} - \text{mass of 6 electrons}$$

$$= 11.011434 \text{ u} - 6\ m_e$$

Similarly mass of $_{5}^{11}$B nucleus

$$= \text{Mass of } _{5}^{11}\text{B atom} - \text{mass of 5 electrons}$$

$$= 11.00930 - 5\ m_e$$

$\therefore$

$$Q = [(11.011434 - 6m_e) - (11.009305 - 5m_e) - m_e]$$

$$\Delta m = [m(_{6}^{11}\text{C}) - m(_{5}^{11}\text{B}) - 2m_e]$$

$$= 11.011434 - 11.009305 - 2 \times 0.000548$$

$$= 0.001033$$

$$Q = \text{Binding energy} = \Delta m \times 931$$

$$= 0.001033 \times 931$$

$$= 0.9617 \text{ MeV}$$

The daughter nucleus is too heavy compared to e^+ and V. So it carries neglible energy $(E_d = 0)$. It the kinetic energy (E_V) carried by the neutrino is minimum (*i.e.* zero, the positron carries maximum energy and this is practically all energy Q; hence maximum $E_e \approx Q$.)

Question 14. The nucleus $_{10}^{23}$Ne decays by β^- emission. Write down the β-decay equation and determine the maximum kinetic energy of the electrons emitted. Given that

$$m(_{10}^{23}\text{Ne}) = 22.994466 \text{ u}$$

$$m(_{11}^{23}\text{Na}) = 22.989770 \text{ u}.$$

Solution The β-decay equation of $_{10}^{23}$Ne is given by

$$_{10}^{23}\text{Ne} \xrightarrow{\ -\beta\ } {}_{11}^{23}\text{Na} + {}_{-1}e^0 + \bar{v} + Q$$

Similar to Q. 13 the mass defect can be given as

Mass defect $\Delta m = m(^{23}_{10}\text{Ne}) - m(^{23}_{11}\text{Na})$

$$= 22.994466 - 22.989770$$

$$= 0.004696 \text{ u}$$

$$Q = \Delta m \times 931 = 0.004696 \times 931 = 4.372 \text{ MeV}$$

The maximum kinetic energy of the electron of the emitted β-particle is equal to the Q-value.

$$E_e = Q = 4.37 \text{ MeV}$$

$^{23}_{10}\text{Na}$ nucleus is much heavier than electron-neutron, practically whole of the energy released is carried by electron-neutrino pair. When neutrino gets zero energy, the electron will carry the maximum energy. So the maximum KE of the electron is 4.374 MeV.

Question 15. The Q-value of a nuclear reaction $A + b \to C + d$ is defined by $Q = [m_A + m_b - m_C - m_d]c^2$, where the masses refer to the respective nuclei. Determine from the given data, the Q-value of the following reactions and state whether the reactions are exothermic or endothermic.

(a) $^1_1\text{H} + ^3_1\text{H} \longrightarrow ^2_1\text{H} + ^2_1\text{H}$

(b) $^{12}_6\text{C} + ^{12}_6\text{C} \longrightarrow ^{20}_{10}\text{Ne} + ^4_2\text{He}$

Atomic masses are given to be

$m(_1\text{H}^1) = 1.007825 \text{ u},$ $\qquad m(^2_1\text{H}) = 2.014102 \text{ u},$ $\qquad m(^3_1\text{H}) = 3.016049 \text{ u},$

$m(^{12}_6\text{C}) = 12.000000 \text{ u},$ $\qquad m(^{20}_{10}\text{Ne}) = 19.992439 \text{ u}.$

Solution The given reaction

(a) $^1_1\text{H} + ^3_1\text{H} \longrightarrow ^2_1\text{H} + ^2_1\text{H}$

Mass defect $\Delta m = m(^1_1\text{H}) + m(^3_1\text{H}) - 2m(^2_1\text{H})$

$$= 1.007825 + 3.016049 - 2\,(2.014102)$$

$$= -0.00433 \text{ u}$$

Q-value of the reaction

$$Q = \Delta m \times 931 = -0.00433 \times 931 = -4.031 \text{ MeV}$$

As the energy is negative so, the reaction is endothermic.

(b) The given reaction $^{12}_6\text{C} + ^{12}_6\text{C} \longrightarrow ^{20}_{10}\text{Ne} + ^4_2\text{He}$

$$\Delta m = 2m(^{12}_6\text{C}) - m(^{20}_{10}\text{Ne}) - m(^4_2\text{He})$$

$$= 2 \times 12 - 19.992439 - 4.002603$$

$$= 0.00495 \text{ u}$$

$$Q = \Delta m \times 931 = 0.00495 \times 931 = 4.62 \text{ MeV}$$

Since, the energy is positive thus, the reaction is exothermic.

Question 16. Suppose, we think of fission of a $^{56}_{26}\text{Fe}$ nucleus into two equal fragments, $^{28}_{13}\text{Al}$. Is the fission energetically possible? Argue by working out Q of the process. Given $m(^{56}_{26}\text{Fe}) = 55.93494$ u and $m(^{28}_{13}\text{Al}) = 27.98191$ u.

Solution The given reaction for the decay process

$$^{56}_{26}\text{Fe} \longrightarrow 2\,^{28}_{13}\text{Al}$$

Mass defect $\Delta m = m\left(^{56}_{26}\text{Fe}\right) - 2m\left(^{28}_{13}\text{Al}\right)$

$$= 55.93494 - 2(27.98191)$$

$$= -0.02888 \text{ u}$$

$$Q = \Delta m \times 931 = -26.88728 \text{ MeV}$$

Because the energy is negative so, the fission is not possible energetically.

Question 17. The fission properties of $^{239}_{94}\text{Pu}$ are very similar to those of $^{235}_{92}\text{U}$. The average energy released per fission is 180 MeV. How much energy, in MeV, is released if all the atoms in 1 kg of pure $^{239}_{94}\text{Pu}$ undergo fission?

Solution According to the concept of Avogadro number

The number of atoms in 239 g of $^{239}_{94}\text{Pu} = 6.023 \times 10^{23}$

$$\text{Number of atoms in 1 kg of } ^{239}_{94}\text{Pu} = \frac{6.023 \times 10^{23} \times 1000}{239}$$

$$= 2.52 \times 10^{24}$$

The average energy released in one fission $= 180$ MeV

So, total energy released in fission of 1 kg of $^{239}_{94}\text{Pu} = 180 \times 2.52 \times 10^{24}$

$$= 4.53 \times 10^{26} \text{ MW}$$

Question 18. A 1000 MW fission reactor consumes half of its fuel in 5 yr. How much $^{235}_{92}\text{U}$ did it contain initially? Assume that the reactor operates 80% of the time that all the energy generated arises from the fission of $^{235}_{92}\text{U}$ and that this nuclide is consumed only by the fission process.

Given power of reactor $P = 1000$ MW

Solution Use the concept that the energy generated in one fission of $^{235}_{92}\text{U}$ is 200 MeV.

Let x kg of ^{235}U is used.

According to Avogadro number concept

235 g of ^{235}U contains $= 6.023 \times 10^{23}$ atoms

$\therefore$ x kg of ^{235}U contains $= \dfrac{6.023 \times 10^{23}}{235 \times 10^{-3}} \times x$ atoms

As half fuel is used in 5 yr and each atoms gives energy of 200 MeV, so energy given by fuel is

$$= \frac{6.023 \times 10^{23} \times x \times 200 \times 1.6 \times 10^{-13}}{235 \times 2 \times 10^{-3}} \, \text{J} \qquad \ldots(i)$$

Energy produced in reactor in 5 yr as 80%

$$= 1000 \times 10^6 \times 5 \times 365 \times 24 \times 60 \times 60 \times \frac{80}{100}$$

$$\text{(From formula } E = Pt) \qquad \ldots(ii)$$

Equate Eqs. (i) and (ii), we get

$$\frac{6.023 \times 10^{23} \times 200 \times 1.6 \times 10^{-13} \, x}{235 \times 2 \times 10^{-3}} = \frac{10^9 \times 5 \times 365 \times 24 \times 3600 \times 80}{100}$$

$$\Rightarrow \qquad x = \frac{5 \times 365 \times 24 \times 36 \times 80 \times 235 \times 2 \times 10^{-3} \times 10^9}{6.023 \times 10^{10} \times 200 \times 1.6}$$

$$= 3071.5 \, \text{kg}$$

The initial amount of $^{235}_{92}$U is 3071.5 kg.

Question 19. How long can an electric lamp of 100 W be kept glowing by fusion of 2.0 kg of deuterium? Take the fusion reaction as
$$^2_1\text{H} + \, ^2_1\text{H} \longrightarrow \, ^3_1\text{He} + n + 3.27 \text{ MeV}$$

Solution   Let t be the time.

According to the Avogadro number concept

Number of atoms in 2 g of deuterium $= 6.023 \times 10^{23}$

Number of atoms in 2 kg of deuterium $= \dfrac{6.023 \times 10^{23} \times 2 \times 10^3}{2}$

$$= 6.023 \times 10^{26} \text{ nuclei}$$

From given equation, energy released during fusion of two deuterium
$$= 3.27 \text{ MeV}$$

$\therefore$ Energy released by one deuterium $= \dfrac{3.27}{2} = 1.635$ MeV

Energy relesed in 6.023×10^{26} deuterium atoms

$$= 1.635 \times 6.023 \times 10^{26} = 9.848 \times 10^{26} \text{ MeV}$$

$$= 9.848 \times 10^{26} \times 1.6 \times 10^{-13} = 15.75 \times 10^{13} \text{ J}$$

Energy used by bulb in 1s $= 100$ J

100 J energy used in time $= 1$ s

15.75×10^{13} J energy used in time $= \dfrac{1 \times 15.75 \times 10^{13}}{100} = 15.75 \times 10^{11}$ s

$(\because$ We know that 1 yr $= 60 \times 24 \times 60 \times 365$ s$)$

$$= \dfrac{15.75 \times 10^{11}}{60 \times 24 \times 60 \times 365} \text{ yr} = 4.99 \times 10^4 \text{ yr}$$

Thus, the bulbs glow for 4.99×10^4 yr.

Question 20. Calculate the height of the potential barrier for a head on collision of two deuterons. [Hint : The height of the potential barrier is given by the Coulomb repulsion between the two deuterons when they just touch each other. Assume that they can be taken as hard spheres of radius 2.0 fm.]

Solution Given, radius $r = 2$ fm $= 2 \times 10^{-15}$ m

For head on collision, the distance between the centres of two deuterons

$$d = r$$
$$d = 2 \times 10^{-15} = 2 \times 10^{-15} \text{ m}$$

Charge on each deuteron, $e = 1.6 \times 10^{-19}$ C

$$\text{Potential energy} = \dfrac{1}{4\pi\varepsilon_0} \cdot \dfrac{q_1 q_2}{d} = \dfrac{9 \times 10^9 \times 1.6 \times 10^{-19} \times 1.6 \times 10^{-19}}{2 \times 10^{-15}}$$

$$\left(\because \dfrac{1}{4\pi\varepsilon_0} = 9 \times 10^9 \right)$$

$$= \dfrac{5.76 \times 10^{-14}}{1.6 \times 10^{-19}} = 720000 \text{ eV}$$

According to the law of conservation of energy.This potential energy will be equal to kinetic energy of both deuteron.

$\therefore$ Potential energy $= 2 \times$ Kinetic energy of each deuteron

Kinetic energy of each deuteron $= \dfrac{720000}{2} = 360000$ eV $= 360$ keV

Thus, the potential barrier is 360 keV.

Question 21. From the relation $R = R_0 A^{1/3}$, where R_0 is a constant and A is the mass number of a nucleus, show that the nuclear matter density is nearly constant (*i.e.*, independent of A).

Solution Given, the expression of the radius of nucleus is given by $R = R_0 A^{1/3}$ where R_0 is a constant and A is the mass number of nucleus.

$$\text{Density of nucleus} = \dfrac{\text{Mass}}{\text{Volume}}$$

$$\rho = \dfrac{\text{Mass of each neucleon} \times \text{Number of neucleons}}{\dfrac{4}{3}\pi R^3}$$

$$= \frac{m \times A \times 3}{4\pi R^3}$$

$$= \frac{Am\,3}{4\pi R_0^3\,A} = \frac{3m}{4\pi R_0^3} = \frac{3 \times 1.66 \times 10^{-27}}{4 \times 3.14 \times (1.1 \times 10^{-15})^3}$$

$$= 2.97 \times 10^{17} \text{ kg/m}^3$$

As R_0 is a constant so, density is constant or independent of A.

Question 22. For the β^+ (positron) emission from a nucleus, there is another competing process known as electron capture (electron from an inner orbit say, the K-shell is captured by the nucleus and a neutrino is emitted).

$$e^+ + {}_Z^A X \rightarrow {}_{Z-1}^A Y + \nu$$

Show that if β^+ emission is energetically allowed, electron capture is necessarily allowed but not *vice-versa*.

Solution   Let us first consider positron emission

$$_Z X^A \rightarrow {}_{Z-1}Y^A + {}_1 e^0 + Q_1 \qquad \ldots\text{(i)}$$

Let us now consider electron capture

$$_Z X^A + {}_{-1}e^0 \longrightarrow {}_{Z-1}Y^A + \nu + Q_2 \qquad \ldots\text{(ii)}$$

The energy released in Eq. (i),

$$Q_1 = [m_N({}_Z X^A) - m_N({}_{Z-1}Y^A) - m_e]\,c^2$$
$$= [m_N({}_Z X^A) + Zm_e - m_N({}_{Z-1}Y^A) - (Z-1)\,m_e - m_e]\,c^2$$
$$= [m_N({}_Z X^A) - m_N({}_{Z-1}Y^A) - 2m_e]c^2 \qquad \ldots\text{(iii)}$$

where, m_e = mass of electron

Energy released in Eq. (ii),

$$Q_2 = [m_N({}_Z X^A) + m_e - m_N({}_{Z-1}Y^A)]\,c^2$$
$$= [m_N({}_Z X^A) + Zm_e + m_e - m_N({}_{Z-1}Y^A) - (Z-1)\,m_e - m_e]c^2$$
$$= [m_N({}_Z X^A) - m_{N(Z-1)}Y^A]\,c^2 \qquad \ldots\text{(iv)}$$

Here, if $Q_1 > 0$ then $Q_2 > 0$.

i.e., if positron emission is energitically allowed electron capture is necessarily allowed.

But if $Q_2 > 0$ does not necessarily mean that $Q_1 > 0$. Hence, converse is not true.

Question 23. In a periodic table, the average atomic mass of magnesium is given as 24.312 u. The average value is based on their relative natural abundance on earth. The three isotopes and their masses are

$^{24}_{12}$Mg (23.98504 u), $^{25}_{12}$Mg (24.98584 u) and $^{26}_{12}$Mg (25.98259 u). The natural abundance of $^{24}_{12}$Mg is 78.99% by mass. Calculate the abundances of other two isotopes.

Solution Given, atomic mass of Mg = 24.312 u

Mass of $^{24}_{12}$Mg = 23.98504 u

Mass of $^{25}_{12}$mg = 24.98584 u

Mass of $^{26}_{12}$Mg = 25.98259 u

Abundance of $^{24}_{12}$Mg = 78.99%

Let the abundance of $^{25}_{12}$Mg be x%.

The abundance of $^{26}_{12}$Mg $= 100 - 78.99 - x$

$$= (21.01 - x)\%$$

Atomic mass = Weighted average of masses

$$= \frac{\text{Abundance of the isotopes}}{\text{Total abundance}}$$

$$24.312 = \frac{78.99 \times 23.98504 + x \times 24.98584 + (21.01 - x) \times 25.98259}{100}$$

$\Rightarrow \qquad\qquad\qquad\qquad x = 9.303\%$

So, the abundance of $_{12}$Mg^{25} is 9.303% and the abundance of $_{12}$Mg^{26} is 11.71%.

Question 24. The neutron separation energy is defined as the energy required to remove a neutron from the nucleus. Obtain the neutron separation energies of the nuclei $^{41}_{20}$Ca and $^{27}_{13}$Al from the following data :

$m(^{40}_{20}\text{Ca}) = 39.962591$ u

$m(^{41}_{20}\text{Ca}) = 40.962278$ u

$m(^{26}_{13}\text{Al}) = 25.986895$ u

$m(^{27}_{13}\text{Al}) = 26.981541$ u

Solution (i) When a neutron is separated, from $^{41}_{20}$Ca, we are left with $^{40}_{20}$Ca and the reaction becomes

$$^{41}_{20}\text{Ca} \longrightarrow\ ^{40}_{20}\text{Ca} +\ _0n^1$$

Mass defect $\Delta m = m\left(^{40}_{20}\text{Ca}\right) + m(_0n^1) - m(^{41}\text{Ca})$

$$= 39.962591 + 1.008665 - 40.962278$$

$$= 0.008978 \text{ u}$$

Energy for separation of neutron $= \Delta m \times 931 = 0.008978 \times 931 = 8.362$ MeV

(ii) When a neutron is separated from $^{27}_{13}\text{Al}$, we are left with $^{28}_{13}\text{Al}$. Thus the reaction

$$^{27}_{13}\text{Al} \longrightarrow {}^{26}_{13}\text{Al} + {}^{1}_{0}n$$

Mass defect $\Delta m = m\left(^{26}_{13}\text{Al}\right) + m(_0 n^1) - m(^{27}_{13}\text{Al})$

$$= 25.986895 + 1.008665 - 26.981541$$
$$= 0.014019$$

Energy for separation of neutron $= \Delta m \times 931 = 0.014019 \times 931$
$$= 13.06 \text{ MeV}$$

Question 25. A source contains two phosphorous radio nuclides $^{32}_{15}\text{P}$ $(T_{1/2} = 14.3 \text{ day})$ and $^{33}_{15}\text{P}(T_{1/2} = 25.3 \text{ day})$. Initially, 10% of the decay come from $^{33}_{15}\text{P}$. How long one must wait until 90% do so?

Solution   Initially, the source have 90% of $^{32}_{15}\text{P}$ and 10% of $^{33}_{15}\text{P}$. Let x g be initial number of ^{32}P nuclides and 9x g be initial number of ^{33}P.
After t days, the source has 90% of ^{33}P and 10% of ^{32}P *i.e.*, y g of ^{33}P and 9y g of ^{32}P.

Using the equation,

$$\frac{N}{N_0} = e^{-\lambda t} = \left(\frac{1}{2}\right)^{t/T_{1/2}}$$

$$N = N_0 \left(\frac{1}{2}\right)^{t/T_{1/2}}$$

For P^{33}, $y = 9x \cdot 2^{-t/14.3}$ ...(i)

For P^{32}, $9y = x2^{-t/25.3}$ ...(ii)

Dividing Eq (i) by Eq. (ii),

$$\frac{y}{9y} = \frac{9x}{x} \cdot \frac{2^{-t/14.3}}{2^{-t/25.3}}$$

or

$$\frac{1}{9} = 9 \times 2^{(t/25.3 - t/14.3)}$$

or

$$\frac{1}{81} = 2^{-11t/25.3 \times 14.3}$$

Taking log on both the sides,

$$\log 1 - \log 81 = -\frac{11t}{25.3 \times 14.3} \log 2$$

or

$$-1.9085 = \frac{-11 \times t}{25.3 \times 14.3} \times 0.3010$$

or

$$t = \frac{25.3 \times 14.3 \times 1.9085}{11 \times 0.3010}$$

$$= 208.5 \text{ days}$$

So, we must wait for 208.5 days to do so.

Question 26. Under certain circumstances, a nucleon can decay by emitting a particle more massive than an α-particle. Consider the following decay processes :

$$^{223}_{88}\text{Ra} \longrightarrow {}^{209}_{82}\text{Pb} + {}^{14}_{6}\text{C}$$

$$^{223}_{88}\text{Ra} \longrightarrow {}^{219}_{86}\text{Rn} + {}^{4}_{2}\text{He}$$

Calculate, the Q-values for these decays and determine that both are energetically allowed.

Solution   (a) The given reaction

$$^{223}_{88}\text{Ra} \longrightarrow {}^{209}_{82}\text{Pb} + {}^{14}_{6}\text{C}$$

Mass defect $\Delta m = m({}^{223}_{88}\text{Ra}) - m({}^{209}_{82}\text{Pb}) - m({}^{14}_{6}\text{C})$

$$\Delta m = 223.01850 - 208.98107 - 14.00324 = 0.03419 \text{ u}$$

Q-value for the given decay process

$$Q = \Delta m \times 931.5 = 0.03419 \times 931.5 = 31.83 \text{ MeV}$$

(b) The given reaction

$$^{223}_{88}\text{Ra} \longrightarrow {}^{219}_{86}\text{Rn} + {}^{4}_{2}\text{He}$$

Mass defect $\Delta m = m\left({}^{223}_{88}\text{Ra}\right) - m\left({}^{219}_{86}\text{Rn}\right) - m\left({}^{4}_{2}\text{He}\right)$

$$= 223.01850 - 219.00948 - 4.00260 = 0.00642 \text{ u}$$

Q-value for the given decay process,

$$Q = \Delta m \times 931.5 = 0.00642 \times 931.5 = 5.98 \text{ MeV}$$

Here, in both the case, value of Q is positive so, the decays are energetically possible.

Question 27. Consider the fission of $^{238}_{92}\text{U}$ by fast neutrons. In one fission event, no neutrons are emitted and the final end products, after the beta decay of the primary fragments, are $^{140}_{58}\text{Ce}$ and $^{99}_{44}\text{Ru}$. Calculate Q for this fission process. The relevant atomic and particle masses are

$m({}^{238}_{92}\text{U}) = 238.05079 \text{ u}$

$m({}^{140}_{58}\text{Ce}) = 139.90543 \text{ u}$

$m({}^{99}_{44}\text{Ru}) = 98.90594 \text{ u}$

Solution   The fission reaction is given by

$$^{238}_{92}\text{U} + {}_{0}n^{1} \longrightarrow {}^{140}_{58}\text{Ce} + {}^{99}_{44}\text{Ru} + Q$$

Mass defect $\Delta m = m({}^{238}_{92}\text{U}) + m({}_{0}n^{1}) - m({}^{140}_{58}\text{Ce}) - m({}^{99}_{44}\text{Ru})$

$$= 238.05079 + 1.00867 - 139.90543 - 98.90594$$

$$= 0.24809 \text{ u}$$

Q-value for the given decay process,

$$Q = \Delta m \times 931.5 = 0.24809 \times 931.5 = 231.1 \text{ MeV}$$

Question 28. Consider the D-T reaction (deuterium-tritium fusion)
$$^2_1H + {}^3_1H \longrightarrow {}^4_2He + n$$

   (a) Calcualte the energy released in MeV in this reaction from the data
$$m(^2_1H) = 2.014120 \text{ u}$$
$$m(^3_1H) = 3.016049 \text{ u}$$

   (b) Consider the radius of both deuterium and tritium to be approximately 2.0 fm. What is the kinetic energy needed to overcome the coulomb repulsion between two nuclei? To what temperature must the gas be heated to initiate the reaction?
(Hint : Kinetic energy required for one fusion event = Average thermal kinetic energy available with the interacting particles $= 2(3kT/2); k = $ Boltzmann's constant, $T = $ absolute temperature)

Solution   (a) The D-T reaction is given by
$$^2_1H + {}^3_1H \longrightarrow {}^4_2He + {}_0n^1 + Q$$

Mass defect $\Delta m = m(^2_1H) + m(^3_1H) - m(^4_2He) - m(_0 n^1)$

$$= 2.014102 + 3.016049 - 4.002603 - 1.00867$$
$$= 0.018878 \text{ u}$$

Q-value for the given decay process
$$Q = \Delta m \times 931 = 0.018878 \times 931 = 17.58 \text{ MeV}$$

  (b) Repulsive potential energy of two nuclei when they almost touch each other
$$U = \frac{1}{4\pi\varepsilon_0} \cdot \frac{q^2}{2r} = \frac{9 \times 10^9 \, (1.6 \times 10^{-19})^2}{2 \times 2 \times 10^{-15}}$$
$$= 5.76 \times 10^{-14} \text{ J}$$

Also we know that kinetic energy required for one fusion event = average thermal kinetic energy available with the interacting particles.

$$\text{Kinetic energy} = \frac{3}{2} \times kT \times 2 \qquad \text{(Two nuclei)}$$
$$= 3kT$$
$$T = \frac{\text{Kinetic energy}}{3k} = \frac{5.76 \times 10^{-14}}{3 \times 1.38 \times 10^{-23}}$$
$$= 1.39 \times 10^9 \text{ K}$$

This temperature cannot be achieved in actual behaviour.

Question 29. Obtain the maximum kinetic energy of β-particles, and the radiation frequencies of γ decays in the decay scheme shown. You are given that

$m(^{198}\text{Au}) = 197.968233$ u

$m(^{198}\text{Hg}) = 197.966760$ u

Solution   The energy corresponding to γ_1,

$$E_1 = 1.088 - 0 = 1.088 \text{ MeV}$$
$$= 1.088 \times 1.6 \times 10^{-13} \text{ J}$$

Frequency for γ_1,

$$\nu_1 = \frac{E_1}{h} = \frac{1.088 \times 1.6 \times 10^{-13}}{6.63 \times 10^{-34}}$$
$$= 2.63 \times 10^{20} \text{ Hz}$$

The energy corresponding to γ_2,

$$E_2 = 0.412 - 0 = 0.412 \text{ MeV}$$
$$= 0.412 \times 1.6 \times 10^{-13} \text{ J}$$

Frequency for γ_2,

$$\nu_2 = \frac{E_2}{h} = \frac{0.412 \times 1.6 \times 10^{-13}}{6.63 \times 10^{-34}}$$
$$= 9.98 \times 10^{19} \text{ Hz}$$

The energy corresponding to γ_3,

$$E_3 = 1.088 - 0.412 = 0.676 \text{ MeV}$$
$$= 0.676 \times 1.6 \times 10^{-13} \text{ J}$$

Frequency for γ_3,

$$\nu_3 = \frac{E_3}{h} = \frac{0.676 \times 1.6 \times 10^{-13}}{6.63 \times 10^{-34}}$$
$$\nu_3 = 1.64 \times 10^{20} \text{ Hz}$$

Maximum KE of β_1,

$$K_{\text{max}} (\beta_1) = [m(^{198}_{79}\text{Au}) - \text{mass of second excited state of } ^{198}_{80}\text{Hg}] \times 931 \text{ MeV}$$
$$= 931 [197.968233 - 197.66760] - 1.088$$
$$= 1.371 - 1.088 = 0.283 \text{ MeV}$$

Maximum KE of β_2,

$$K_{\text{max}} (\beta_2) = [m(^{198}_{79}\text{Au}) - \text{mass of third excited state of } ^{198}\text{Hg}] \times 931 \text{ MeV}$$
$$= 931 [197.968233 - 197.66760] - 0.412$$
$$= 0.957 \text{ MeV}$$

Question 30. Calculate and compare the energy released by (a) fusion of 1.0 kg of hydrogen deep within sun and (b) the fission of 1.0 kg of ^{235}U in a fission reactor.

Solution   (a) In sun, four hydrogen nuclei fuse to form a helium nucleus with release of 26 MeV energy.

$\because$ 1 g of hydrogen contains 6.023×10^{23} nuclei.

$\therefore$ Energy released by fusion of 1 kg ($=1000$ g) of hydrogen

$$E_1 = \frac{6.023 \times 10^{23} \times 26 \times 10^3}{4} = 39 \times 10^{26} \text{ MeV}$$

(b) Energy released in one fission of $^{235}_{92}$U nucleus = 200 MeV.

Mass of uranium = 1 kg = 1000 g
We know that 235 g of ^{235}U has 6.023×10^{23} atoms or nuclei.

$\therefore$ Energy released in fission of 1 kg of U^{235},

$$E_2 = \frac{6.023 \times 10^{23} \times 1000 \times 200}{235}$$

$$E_2 = 5.1 \times 10^{26} \text{ MeV}$$

$$\therefore \quad \frac{E_1}{E_2} = \frac{39 \times 10^{26}}{5.1 \times 10^{26}} = 7.65 \approx 8$$

Thus, the energy released in fusion is 8 times the energy released in fission.

Question 31. Suppose India had a target of producing by 2020 AD, 200000 MW of electric power, ten percent of which was to be obtained from nuclear power plants. Suppose we are given that, on an average, the efficiency of utilization (*i.e.*, conversion to electric energy) of thermal energy produced in a reactor was 25%. How much amount of fissionable uranium would our country need per year by 2020? Take the heat energy per fission of ^{235}U to be about 200 MeV.

Solution   Total target power = 200000 = 2×10^5 MW

Total nuclear power = 10% of total

$$= \frac{10}{100} \times 2 \times 10^5 = 2 \times 10^4 \text{ MW}$$

Energy produced/fission = 200 MeV

Efficiency of power plant = 25%

Energy converted into electrical energy per fission

$$= \frac{25}{100} \times 200 = 50 \text{ MeV}$$

$$= 50 \times 1.6 \times 10^{-13} \text{ J}$$

Total electrical energy to be produced in per year

$$= 2 \times 10^4 \text{ MW} = 2 \times 10^4 \times 10^6 \text{ W}$$

$$= 2 \times 10^{10} \text{ W} = 2 \times 10^{10} \text{ J/s}$$

$$= 2 \times 10^{10} \times 60 \times 60 \times 24 \times 365 \text{ J/yr.}$$

Number of fission in one year, $n = \dfrac{2 \times 10^{10} \times 60 \times 60 \times 24 \times 365}{50 \times 1.6 \times 10^{-13}}$

$$n = \frac{2 \times 36 \times 24 \times 365}{8} \times 10^{24}$$

Mass of 6.023×10^{23} atoms of $^{235}\text{U} = 235 \text{ g} = 235 \times 10^{-3}$ kg

Mass of $^{235}_{92}\text{U}$ required to produce $\dfrac{2 \times 36 \times 24 \times 365}{8} \times 10^{24}$ atom

$$= \frac{235 \times 10^{-3} \times 2 \times 36 \times 24 \times 365 \times 10^{24}}{6.023 \times 10^{23} \times 8}$$

$$= 3.08 \times 10^{4} \text{ kg}$$

Thus, the mass of uranium needed per year is 3.08×10^{4} kg.

Selected NCERT Exemplar Problems

Question 1.   Why do stable nuclei never have more protons than neutrons?

Solution   Because the protons are positively charged and repel each other. This repulsion force is more, so that an excess of neutrons are required to reduce this repulsion.

Question 2.   Consider a radioactive nucleus A, which decays to a stable nucleus C through the following sequence

$$A \to B \to C$$

Here, B is an intermediate nuclei, which is also radioactive. Considering that there are N_0 atoms of A initially, plot the graph showing the variation of number of atoms of A and B *versus* time.

Solution   At $t = 0, N_A = N_0$ (maximum) while $N_B = 0$. As time increases, N_A decreases exponentially and the number of atoms of B increases. They becomes (N_B) maximum and finally drop to zero exponentially by radioactive decay law.

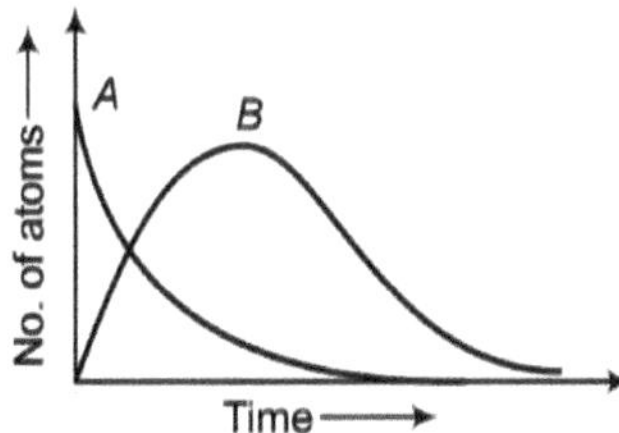

Question 3.   A piece of wood from the ruins of an ancient building was found to have a ^{14}C activity of 12 disintegrations per minute per gram of its carbon content. The ^{14}C activity of the living wood is 16 disintegrations per minute per gram. How

lond ago did the tree, from which the wooden sample came, die? Given half-life of ^{14}C is 5760 yr.

Solution   Given, $R = 12$ dis/min per g

$R_0 = 16$ dis/min per g

$T_{1/2} = 5760$ yr

Let t be the time span of the tree.

According to radioactive decay law,

$$R = R_0 e^{-\lambda t}$$

or
$$\frac{R}{R_0} = e^{-\lambda t}$$

or
$$e^{\lambda t} = \frac{R_0}{R}$$

Taking log on both the sides

$$\lambda t \log_e e = \log_e \frac{R_0}{R}$$

$$\lambda t = \left(\log_{10} \frac{16}{12}\right) \times 2.303$$

$$t = \frac{2.303 \,(\log 4 - \log 3)}{\lambda}$$

$$= \frac{2.303 \,(0.6020 - 4.771) \times 5760}{0.6931} \quad \left(\because \lambda = \frac{0.6931}{T_{1/2}}\right)$$

$$= 2391.20 \text{ yr}$$

Question 4.   Are the nucleons fundamental particles or do they consist of still smaller parts? One way to find out is to probe a nucleon just as Rutherford probed an atom. What should be the kinetic energy of an electron for it to be able to probe a nucleon? Assume the diameter of a nucleon to be approximately 10^{-15} m.

Solution   Each particle (neutron and proton) present inside the nucleus is called a nucleon.

Let λ be the wavelength $\lambda = 10^{-15}$ m

To detect separate parts inside a nucleon, the electron must have wavelength less than 10^{-15} m.

We know that

$$\lambda = \frac{h}{p} \quad \text{and} \quad \text{KE} = \text{PE} \qquad \qquad \text{...(i)}$$

$$\text{Energy} = \frac{hc}{\lambda} \qquad \qquad \text{...(ii)}$$

From Eq. (i) and Eq. (ii)

$$\text{kinetic energy of electron} = PE = \frac{hc}{\lambda} = \frac{6.6 \times 10^{-34} \times 3 \times 10^8}{10^{-15} \times 1.6 \times 10^{-19}}\ eV$$

$$KE = 10^9\ eV$$

Question 5. Sometimes a radioactive nucleus decays into a nucleus which itself is radioactive. An example is

$$^{38}\text{Sulphur} \xrightarrow[= 2.48\,h]{\text{half-life}}\ ^{38}\text{Cl} \xrightarrow[= 0.62\,h]{\text{half-life}}\ ^{38}\text{Ar} \qquad \text{(stable)}$$

Assume that we start with 1000 ^{38}S nuclei at time $t = 0$. The number of ^{38}Cl is of count zero at $t = 0$ and will again be zero at $t = \infty$. At what value of t, would the number of counts be a maximum?

Solution Let at any time t, ^{38}S have N_1 active nuclei and ^{38}Cl have N_2 active nuclei.

We know that $\dfrac{dN_1}{dt} = -\lambda_1 N_1 = $ Rate of formation of Cl^{38}

$$\frac{dN_2}{dt} = -\lambda_1 N_1 - \lambda_2 N_2$$

But $\qquad\qquad N_1 = N_0 e^{-\lambda_1 t}$

$\therefore \qquad\qquad \dfrac{dN_2}{dt} = -\lambda_1 N_0 e^{-\lambda_1 t} - \lambda_2 N_2 \qquad\qquad\qquad \ldots(i)$

$$dN_2 = -\lambda_1 N_0 e^{-\lambda_1 t} dt - \lambda_2 N_2 dt$$

Multiplying both sides by $e^{\lambda_2 t}$,

$$e^{\lambda_2 t}\, dN_2 + \lambda_2 N_2 e^{\lambda_2 t} \cdot dt + \lambda_1 \cdot N_0 e^{(\lambda_2 - \lambda_1)t} = 0$$

Integrating, $\qquad \displaystyle\int \lambda_1 N_0 e^{(\lambda_2 - \lambda_1)t} dt + \int d(N_2 e^{\lambda_2 t}) = 0$

$$N_2 e^{\lambda_2 t} + \frac{\lambda_1 N_0 e^{(\lambda_2 - \lambda_1)t}}{(\lambda_2 - \lambda_1)} = C$$

At $t = 0$, $N_2 = 0$ $\qquad\qquad\qquad 0 + \dfrac{\lambda_1 N_0}{\lambda_2 - \lambda_1} = C$

$\therefore \qquad\qquad N_2 e^{\lambda_2 t} + \dfrac{\lambda_1 N_0}{(\lambda_2 - \lambda_1)}[e^{(\lambda_2 - \lambda_1)t} - 1] = 0$

$$e^{\lambda_2 t} + \left(\frac{N_0}{N_2}\right) \frac{\lambda_1}{(\lambda_2 - \lambda_1)}[e^{(\lambda_2 - \lambda_1)t} - 1] = 0 \qquad\qquad \ldots(ii)$$

For maximum count, $\qquad\qquad \dfrac{dN_2}{dt} = 0$

$\therefore \qquad\qquad \lambda_1 N_0 e^{-\lambda_1 t} - \lambda_2 N_2 = 0 \qquad\qquad\qquad \text{[From Eq. (i)]}$

$$\frac{N_0}{N_2} = -\frac{\lambda_2}{\lambda_1}\, e^{\lambda_1 t}$$

From Eq. (ii),

$$e^{\lambda_2 t} - \frac{\lambda_2}{\lambda_1} \cdot \frac{\lambda_1}{(\lambda_1 - \lambda_1)}\, e^{\lambda_1 t}\,[e^{(\lambda_2 - \lambda_1)t} - 1] = 0$$

or

$$e^{\lambda_2 t} - \frac{\lambda_2}{(\lambda_2 - \lambda_1)}\, e^{\lambda_2 t} + \frac{\lambda_2}{\lambda_2 - \lambda_1}\, e^{\lambda_1 t} = 0$$

$$1 - \frac{\lambda_2}{(\lambda_2 - \lambda_1)} + \frac{\lambda_2}{(\lambda_2 - \lambda_1)}\, e^{(\lambda_1 - \lambda_2)t} = 0$$

$$\frac{\lambda_2}{(\lambda_2 - \lambda_1)}\, e^{(\lambda_1 - \lambda_2)t} = \frac{\lambda_2}{(\lambda_2 - \lambda_1)} - 1$$

$$e^{(\lambda_1 - \lambda_2)t} = \frac{\lambda_1}{\lambda_2}$$

$$t = \left(\log \frac{\lambda_1}{\lambda_2} \right) \Big/ (\lambda_1 - \lambda_2)$$

$$= \frac{\log_e\left(\dfrac{2.48}{0.62}\right)}{2.48 - 0.62} \qquad \left(\lambda = \frac{0.693}{T_{1/2}} \right)$$

$$= \frac{\log_e 4}{1.86} = \frac{2.303 \times 2 \times 0.3010}{1.86}$$

$$= 0.745 \text{ s}$$

Question 6.   Deuteron is a bound state of a neutron and a proton with a binding energy $B = 2.2$ MeV. A γ-ray of energy E is aimed at a deuteron nucleus to try to break it into a (neutron + proton) such that the n and p move in the direction of the incident γ-ray. If $E = B$, show that this cannot happen. Hence, calculate how much bigger than B must E be for such a process to happen?

Solution   Binding energy $B = 2.2$ MeV

From the energy conservation law,

$$E - B = K_n + K_p = \frac{p_n^2}{2m} + \frac{p_p^2}{2m} \qquad \dots\text{(i)}$$

From conservation of momentum

$$p_n + p_p = \frac{E}{c} \qquad \dots\text{(ii)}$$

As $E = B$, Eq. (i) $\qquad p_n^2 + p_p^2 = 0$

It only happen if $\qquad p_n = p_p = 0$

So, the Eq. (ii) cannot satisfied and the process cannot take place.

Let $E = B + X$, where $X \ll B$ for the process to take place

Put value of p_n from Eq. (ii) in Eq. (i), we get

$$X = \frac{\left(\dfrac{E}{c} - p_p\right)^2}{2m} + \frac{p_p^2}{2m}$$

or $\quad 2p_p^2 - \dfrac{2Ep_p}{c} + \dfrac{E^2}{c^2} - 2mX = 0$

Using the formula of quadratic equation, we get

$$p_P = \frac{\dfrac{2E}{c} \pm \sqrt{\dfrac{4E^2}{c^2} - 8\left(\dfrac{E^2}{c^2} - 2mX\right)}}{4}$$

For the real value P_p, the discriminant is positive

$$\frac{4E^2}{c^2} = 8\left(\frac{E_2}{c_2} - 2mX\right)$$

$$16mX = \frac{4E^2}{c^2}$$

$$X = \frac{E^2}{4mc^2} \simeq \frac{B^2}{4mc^2}$$

Chapter **14**

Semiconductor Electronics

Important Results

1. For a *p-n* junction diode—

    (a) Dynamic resistance $R_d = \dfrac{\Delta V}{\Delta I}$

    (b) Wattage of diode = Voltage drop × Current

2. In a *p-n* junction diode as a half-wave rectifier—

    (a) $I_{DC} = \dfrac{I_0}{\pi}$, $I_{rms} = \dfrac{I_0}{2}$

    (b) Output rms voltage = $V_0 / 2$

3. In a *p-n* junction diode as a full-wave rectifier—

    (a) $I_{DC} = \dfrac{2I_0}{\pi}$, $I_{rms} = \dfrac{I_0}{\sqrt{2}}$

    (b) Output DC voltage = $I_{DC} \times R_L = \dfrac{2I_0}{\pi} \times R_L$

4. In a transistor

    (a) $I_E = I_B + I_C$

    (b) $\alpha = \dfrac{I_C}{I_E}$ and $\alpha_{AC} = \dfrac{\Delta I_C}{\Delta I_E}$

     where , α = current gain in common-base amplifier

    (c) $\beta = \dfrac{I_C}{I_B}$ and $\beta_{AC} = \dfrac{\Delta I_C}{\Delta I_B}$

     where, β = current gain in common-emitter amplifier

    (d) For common-base amplifier—

     Voltage gain $A_V = \dfrac{\Delta V_C}{\Delta V_i} = \alpha_{AC} \times \dfrac{R_o}{R_i}$

    (e) For common emitter amplifier—

     Voltage gain $A_V = \dfrac{\Delta V_C}{\Delta V_B} = \beta_{AC} \times \dfrac{R_o}{R_i}$

(f) Power gain $=$ Voltage gain $\times$ Current gain

where I_C = collector current

$\quad\quad I_E$ = emitter current,

$\quad\quad I_B$ = base current

$\quad\quad \Delta V_C$ = change in collector voltage

$\quad\quad \Delta V_i$ = change in input voltage

$\quad\quad \Delta V_B$ = change in base voltage

$\quad\quad R_o$ = output resistance

$\quad\quad R_i$ = input resistance

5. When the transistor is used in the cut-off or saturation state, it acts as a switch.

6. There are some special circuits which handle the digital data consisting of 0 and 1 levels. This forms the subject of digital electronics.

7. The important digital circuits performing special logic operations are called logic gates. These are OR, AND, NOT, NAND and NOR gates.

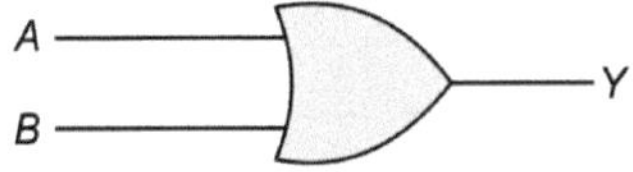

(i) Symbol of OR gate

Truth table of OR gate

A	B	Y
0	0	0
0	1	1
1	0	1
1	1	1

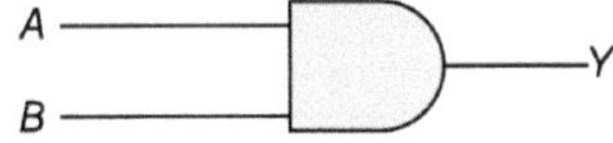

(ii) Symbol of AND gate

Truth table of AND gate

A	B	Y
0	0	0
0	1	0
1	0	0
1	1	1

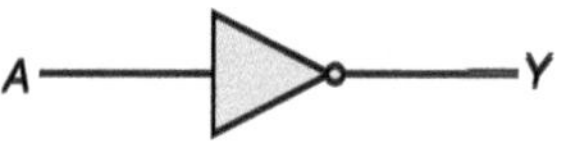

(iii) Symbol of NOT gate

Truth table of NOT gate	
A	B
0	1
1	0

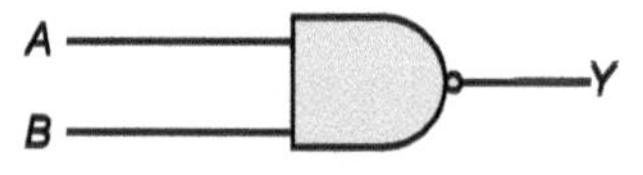

(iv) Symbol of NAND gate

Truth table of NAND gate		
A	B	Y
0	0	1
1	0	1
0	1	1
1	1	0

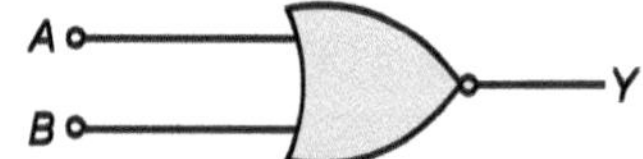

(v) Symbol of NOR gate

Truth table of NOR gate		
A	B	Y
0	0	1
1	0	0
0	1	0
1	1	0

8. In modern days, the circuit contains integrated in one single chip. These are known as Integrated Circuit (IC).

Exercises

Question 1.   In an n-type silicon, which of the following statements is true?

   (a) Electrons are majority carriers and trivalent atoms are the dopants.

   (b) Electrons are minority carriers and pentavalent atoms are the dopants.

   (c) Holes are minority carriers and pentavalent atoms are the dopants.

   (d) Holes are majority carriers and trivalent atoms are the dopants.

Solution   (c) In an n-type semiconductor, it is obtained by doping the Ge or Si with pentavalent atoms. In n-type semiconductor, electrons are majority carriers and holes are minority carriers.

Question 2.   Which of the statements given in Q. 1 is true for p-type semiconductors?

Solution   A p-type semiconductor is obtained by doping Ge or Si with trivalent atoms. In p-type semiconductor holes are majority carriers and electrons are minority carriers.

Question 3.   Carbon, silicon and germanium have four valence electrons each. These are characteried by valence and conduction bands separated by energy band-gap respectively equal to $(E_g)_C, (E_g)_{Si}$ and $(E_g)_{Ge}$. Which of the following statements is true?

   (a) $(E_g)_{Si} < (E_g)_{Ge} < (E_g)_C$ (b) $(E_g)_C < (E_g)_{Ge} > (E_g)_{Si}$

   (c) $(E_g)_C > (E_g)_{Si} > (E_g)_{Ge}$ (d) $(E_g)_C = (E_g)_{Si} = (E_g)_{Ge}$

Solution   (c) The energy band-gap is largest for carbon, less for silicon and least for germanium.

Question 4.   In an unbiased p-n junction, holes diffuse from the p-region to n-region because

   (a) free electrons in the n-region attract them

   (b) they move across the junction by the potential difference

   (c) hole concentration in p-region is more as compared to n-region

   (d) All of the above

Solution   (c) In an unbiased p-n junction, the diffusion of charge carriers across the junction takes place from higher concentration to lower concentration. Therefore, hole concentration in P-region is more as compared to n-region.

Question 5.   When a forward bias is applied to a p-n junction. It

   (a) raises the potential barrier

   (b) reduces the majority carrier current to zero

   (c) lowers the potential barrier

   (d) None of the above

Solution   (c) When a forward bias is applied across the *p-n* junction, the applied voltage opposes the barrier voltage. Due to this, the potential barrier across the junction is lowered.

Question 6.   For transistor action, which of the following statements are correct?

  (a) Base, emitter and collector regions should have similar size and doping concentrations
  (b) The base region must be very thin and lightly doped
  (c) The emitter junction is forward biased and collector junction is reverse biased
  (d) Both the emitter junction as well as the collector junction are forward biased

Solution   (b), (c)

$$\text{For a transistor } \beta = \frac{I_C}{I_B}$$

or

$$I_B = \frac{I_C}{\beta}$$

$$R_{\text{input}} = \frac{V_{\text{input}}}{I_B}$$

$$= \frac{V_{\text{input}}}{I_C} \cdot \beta$$

i.e.,

$$R_{\text{input}} \propto \frac{1}{I_C}$$

Therefore R_{input} is inversely proportional to the collector current. For high collector current, the R_{input} should be small for which the base region must be very thin and lightly doped for a transistor action, the emitter junction is forward biased and collector junction is reverse biased.

Question 7.   For a transistor amplifier, the voltage gain

  (a) remains constant for all frequencies
  (b) is high at high and low frequencies and constant in the middle frequency range
  (c) is low at high and low frequencies and constant at mid frequencies
  (d) None of the above

Solution   (c) The voltage gain is low at high and low frequencies and constant at mid frequency.

Question 8.   In half-wave rectification, what is the output frequency, if the input frequency is 50 Hz. What is the output frequency of a full-wave rectifier for the same input frequency?

Solution   A half wave rectifier rectifies only the half of AC input *i.e.*, it conducts once during an AC input cycle while a full-wave rectifior rectifies both the half cycles of the AC input *i.e.*, it conducts twice during a cycle.

$\therefore$ The output frequency for half-wave is 50 Hz.

The output frequency of a full-wave rectifier is $2 \times 50 = 100$ Hz.

Question 9.   For a CE-transistor amplifier, the audio signal voltage across the collector resistance of 2 kΩ is 2 V. Suppose the current amplification factor of the transistor is 100. Find the input signal voltage and base current, if the base resistance is 1 kΩ.

Solution   Given, collector resistance $R_{output} = 2$ k$\Omega = 2000\ \Omega$

Current amplication factor of the transistor $\beta_{AC} = 100$

Audio signal voltage $V_{output} = 2$ V

Input (base) resistance $R_{input} = 1$ k$\Omega = 1000\ \Omega$

$\because$ Voltage gain $A_V = \dfrac{V_{output}}{V_{input}} = \beta_{AC}\dfrac{R_{output}}{R_{input}}$

$\therefore$ Input signal voltage $V_{input} = \dfrac{V_{output}}{\beta_{AC}(R_{output}/R_{input})}$

$$= \dfrac{2}{100\,(2000/1000)}$$

$$= 0.01\ \text{V}$$

Base (input) current $I_B = \dfrac{V_{input}}{R_{input}}$

$$= \dfrac{0.01}{1000} = 10 \times 10^{-6}\ \text{A} = 10\ \mu\text{A}$$

Question 10.   Two amplifier are connected one after the other in series (cascaded). The first amplifier has a voltage gain of 10 and the second has a voltage gain of 20. If the input signal is 0.01 V, calculate the output AC signal.

Solution   Given, voltage gain of first amplifier, $A_{V_1} = 10$

Voltage gain of second amplifier, $A_{V_2} = 20$

Input voltage $V_i = 0.01$ V

$$\text{Total voltage gain } A_V = \frac{V_o}{V_i} = A_{V_1} \times A_{V_2}$$

$$\therefore \qquad \frac{V_o}{0.01} = 10 \times 20$$

$$V_o = 2 \text{ V}$$

Question 11. A *p-n* photodiode is fabricated from a semiconductor with band-gap of 2.8 eV. Can it detect a wavelength of 6000 nm?

Solution   Energy $E = \dfrac{hc}{\lambda} = \dfrac{6.6 \times 10^{-34} \times 3 \times 10^8}{6000 \times 10^{-9} \times 1.6 \times 10^{-19}}$ eV

$$= 2.06 \text{ eV}$$

The band-gap is 2.8 eV and energy E is less than the band-gap $(E < E_g)$, so *p-n* junction cannot detect the radiation of given wavelength 6000 nm.

Additional Exercises

Question 12. The number of silicon atoms per m^3 is 5×10^{28}. This is doped simultaneously with 5×10^{22} atoms per m^3 of arsenic and 5×10^{20} per m^3 atoms of indium. Calculate the number of electrons and holes. Given that $n_i = 1.5 \times 10^{16} / m^3$. Is the material *n*-type or *p*-type.

Solution   We know that for each atom doped of arsenic one free electron is received. Similarly, for each atom doped of indium a vacancy is created. So, the number of free electrons introduced by pentavalent impurity added,

$$n_e = N_{As} = 5 \times 10^{22} \text{ m}^3 \qquad \qquad \text{...(i)}$$

The number of holes introduced by trivalent impurity added.

Now, $\qquad \qquad n_e - n_h = 5 \times 10^{22} - 5 \times 10^{20}$

$$= 4.95 \times 10^{20} \qquad \qquad \text{...(ii)}$$

So, $\qquad \qquad (n_e + n_h)^2 = (n_e - n_h)^2 + 4 n_e n_h$

$$n_e + n_h = \sqrt{(4.95 \times 10^{22})^2 + 4(1.5 \times 10^{16})^2} \qquad \text{...(iii)}$$

Adding Eqs. (iii) and (ii),

$$2n_e = 4.95 \times 10^{22} + \sqrt{(4.95 \times 10^{22})^2 + 4(1.5 \times 10^{16})^2}$$

$$n_e = \frac{1}{2} [4.95 \times 10^{22} + \sqrt{(4.95 \times 10^{22})^2}]$$

$$= 4.95 \times 10^{22} / m^3$$

Now
$$n_i^2 = n_h \times n_e$$

or
$$n_h = \frac{n_i^2}{n_e} = \frac{(1.5 \times 10^{16})^2}{4.95 \times 10^{22}}$$

$$= 4.54 \times 10^9 \,/\text{m}^3$$

As number of electrons $n_e (= 4.95 \times 10^{22})$ is greater than number of holes $n_h (= 4.5 \times 10^9)$.

So, the material is n-type semiconductor.

Question 13. In an intrinsic semiconductor, the energy-gap E_g is 1.2 eV. Its hole mobility is much smaller than electron mobility and independent of temperature. What is the ratio between conductivity at 600 K and that at 300 K? Assume that the temperature dependence of intrinsic carrier concentration n_i is given by

$$n_i = n_o \, \exp - \left(\frac{E_g}{2k_B T} \right)$$

where n_o is a constant.

Solution Given, intrinsic carrier concentration $n_i = n_o e^{-E_g/2k_B T}$ and energy gap $E_g = 1.2$ eV

$$k_B = 8.62 \times 10^{-5} \text{ eV/K}$$

For $T = 600$ K,

$$n_{600} = n_o e^{-E_g/2k_B \times 600} \qquad \qquad \ldots\text{(i)}$$

For $T = 300$ K

$$n_{300} = n_o e^{-E_g/2k_B \times 300} \qquad \qquad \ldots\text{(ii)}$$

Dividing Eq. (i) by Eq. (ii), we get

$$\frac{n_{600}}{n_{300}} = e^{\left[-\frac{E_g}{2k_B} \left(\frac{1}{600} - \frac{1}{300} \right) \right]}$$

$$= e^{\frac{E_g}{2k_B} \left(\frac{1}{300} - \frac{1}{600} \right)}$$

$$= e^{\frac{1.2}{2 \times 8.62 \times 10^{-5}} \left(\frac{1}{600} \right)}$$

$$= e^{11.6} = (2.718)^{11.6} \qquad \qquad (\because e = 2.718)$$

$$= 1.1 \times 10^5$$

Let the conductivities are σ_{600} and σ_{300}.

$$\frac{\sigma_{600}}{\sigma_{300}} = \frac{n_{600}}{n_{300}} = 1.1 \times 10^5 \qquad \qquad (\because \sigma = en\mu_e)$$

Question 14. In a *p-n* junction diode, the current I can be expressed as

$$I = I_0 \exp \frac{eV}{k_BT} - 1$$

where, I_0 is called the reverse saturation current. V is the voltage across the diode and is positive for forward bias and negative for reverse bias and I is the current through the diode, k_B is the Boltzmann constant $(8.6 \times 10^{-5}$ eV/K) and T is the absolute temperature. If for a given diode $I_0 = 5 \times 10^{-12}$ A and $T = 300$ K, then

(a) what will be the forward current at a forward voltage of 0.6 V?

(b) what will be the increase in the current, if the voltage across the diode is increased to 0.7 V?

(c) what is the dynamic resistance?

(d) what will be the current, if reverse bias voltage changes from 1 V to 2 V?

Solution   Given, $I_0 = 5 \times 10^{-12}$ A, $T = 300$ K

$$k_B = 8.6 \times 10^{-5} \text{ eV/K}$$

$$= 8.6 \times 10^{-5} \times 1.6 \times 10^{-19} \text{ J/K}$$

(a) Given, voltage $V = 0.6$ V

$$\therefore \qquad \frac{eV}{k_BT} = \frac{1.6 \times 10^{-19} \times 0.6}{8.6 \times 10^{-5} \times 1.6 \times 10^{-19} \times 300} = 23.26$$

The current I through a junction diode is given by

$$I = I_0 e^{\left[\frac{eV}{2k_BT} - 1\right]}$$

$$= 5 \times 10^{-12} (e^{23.26} - 1)$$

$$= 5 \times 10^{-12} (1.259 \times 10^{10} - 1)$$

$$= 5 \times 10^{-12} \times 1.259 \times 10^{10} = 0.063 \text{ A}$$

(b) Given, voltage $V = 0.7$ V

$$\therefore \qquad \frac{eV}{k_BT} = \frac{1.6 \times 10^{-19} \times 0.7}{8.6 \times 10^{-5} \times 1.6 \times 10^{-19} \times 300} = 27.14$$

Now, $\qquad I = I_0 e^{\frac{eV}{k_BT} - 1}$

$$= 5 \times 10^{-12} (e^{27.14} - 1)$$

$$= 5 \times 10^{-12} (6.07 \times 10^{11} - 1)$$

$$= 5 \times 10^{-12} \times 6.07 \times 10^{11} = 3.035 \text{ A}$$

Change in current $\Delta I = 3.035 - 0.063 = 2.9$ A

(c) $\Delta I = 2.9$ A, voltage $\Delta V = 0.7 - 0.6 = 0.1$ V

Dynamic resistance $R_d = \dfrac{\Delta V}{\Delta I}$

$$= \dfrac{0.1}{2.9} = 0.0336\ \Omega$$

(d) As the voltage changes from 1 V to 2 V, the current I will be almost equal to $I_0 = 5 \times 10^{-12}$ A.

It is due to that the diode possesses practically infinite resistance in the reverse bias.

Question 15. Show that given circuit (a) acts as OR gate while the given circuit (b) acts as AND gate.

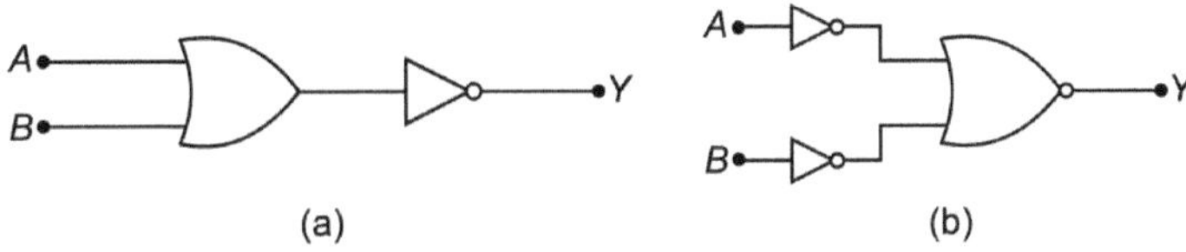

(a)   (b)

Solution   (a) Split the gate,

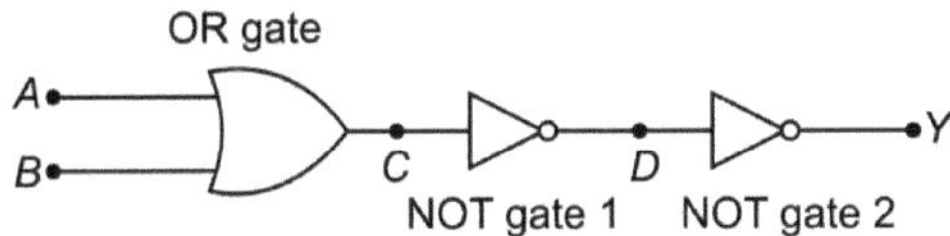

The truth table

A	B	C	D	Y
0	0	0	1	0
0	1	1	0	1
1	0	1	0	1
1	1	1	0	1

Here, for given A and B as inputs, C is the output of OR gate and input of NOT gate 1, D is the output of NOT gate 1 and input of NOT gate 2, Then Y is finally output.

A	B	Y
0	0	0
0	1	1
1	0	1
1	1	1

This is same as OR gate. So, this circuit acts as OR gate.

(b) Split the gate,

Truth table

A	B	C	D	E	Y
0	0	1	1	1	0
1	0	0	1	1	0
0	1	1	0	1	0
1	1	0	0	0	1

Here, for given A and B as inputs, C is the output of A and D is the output of B, E is the output of OR gate and input of NOT gate 3, then Y is finally output.

A	B	Y
0	0	0
1	0	0
0	1	0
1	1	1

This is same as AND gate, so the given circuit acts as an AND gate.

Question 16. Write the truth table for a NAND gate connected as shown in figure. Hence, identify the exact logic operation carried out by this circuit.

Solution   Split the gate

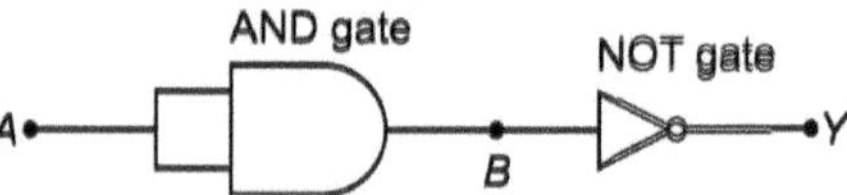

Draw the truth table

A	B	Y
0	0	1
1	1	0

B is the output of AND gate and input of NOT gate.

So, for input A and output Y, the table is

A	Y
0	1
1	0

Here, it is same as NOT gate, so the logic operation is carried by this circuit as NOT gate.

Question 17. Which of the following circuits consists of **NAND** gate? Identify the logic operations carried out by the two circuits.

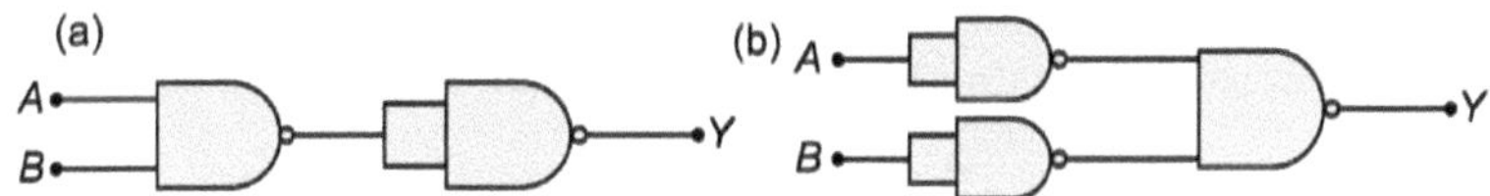

Solution (a) Split the gate

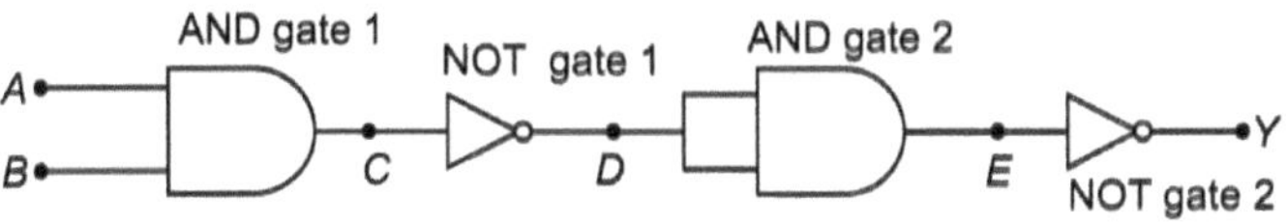

A	B	C	D	E	Y
0	0	0	1	1	0
0	1	0	1	1	0
1	0	0	1	1	0
1	1	1	0	0	1

C is the ouput of AND gate 1 and input of NOT gate 1, D is output of NOT gate 1 and input of the AND gate 2, E is the output of AND gate 2 and input of NOT gate 2, Y is final output.

Truth table

A	B	Y
0	0	0
0	1	0
1	0	0
1	1	1

So, this logic operation as AND gate.

(b) Split the gate

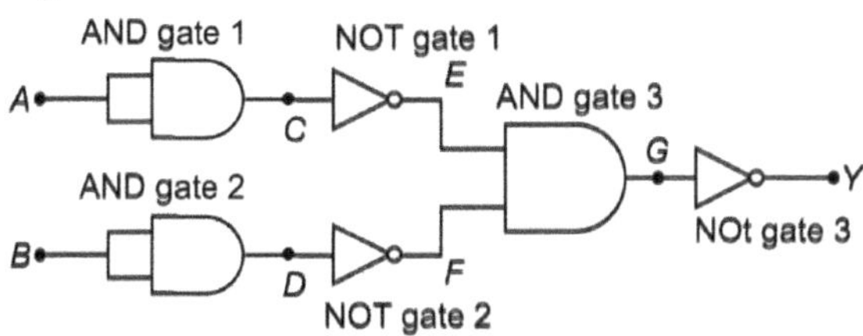

A	B	C	D	E	F	G	Y
0	0	0	0	1	1	1	0
1	0	1	0	0	1	0	1
0	1	0	1	1	0	0	1
1	1	1	1	0	0	0	1

C is the output of AND gate 1

D is the output of AND gate 2

E is the output of NOT gate 1

F is the output of NOT gate 2

G is the output of AND gate 3 and input NOT gate 3

Here, it is same as OR gate. A and B are inputs and Y is output.

A	B	Y
0	0	0
1	0	1
0	1	1
1	1	1

So, this logic operation resembles to OR gate.

Question 18. Write the truth table circuit given in figure below consisting of **NOR** gates and identify the logic operations (OR, AND, NOT). Which this circuit is performing?

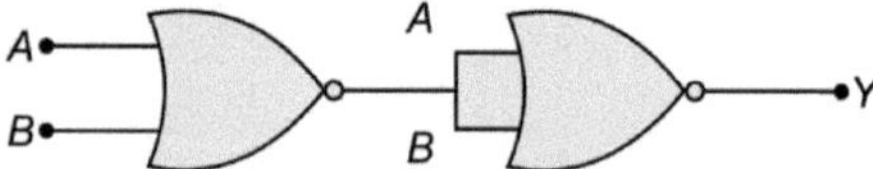

[Hint : $A = 0$, $B = 1$, then A and B inputs of second NOR gate will be 0 and hence $Y = 1$. Similarly, work out the values of Y for other combinations of A and B. Compare with the truth table of OR, AND, NOT gates and find the correct one.]

Solution   Split the gate

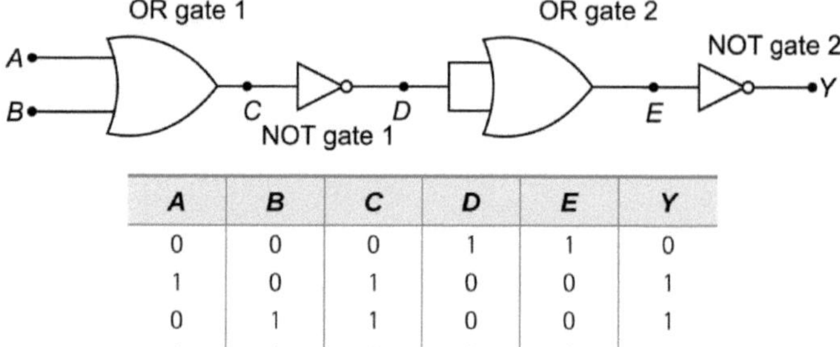

A	B	C	D	E	Y
0	0	0	1	1	0
1	0	1	0	0	1
0	1	1	0	0	1
1	1	1	0	0	1

C is the output of OR gate 1 and D is the output of NOT gate 1 and input of the NOT gate 2. E is the output of OR gate 2 and input of the NOT gate 2.

Here, it is same as OR gate. A and B are inputs and Y is output.

A	B	Y
0	0	0
1	0	1
0	1	1
1	1	1

So, this logic operation resembles to OR gate.

Question 19. Write the truth table for the circuits given in figure consisting of **NOR** gates identify the logic operations (**OR, AND, NOT**) performed by the two circuits.

(a)   (b)

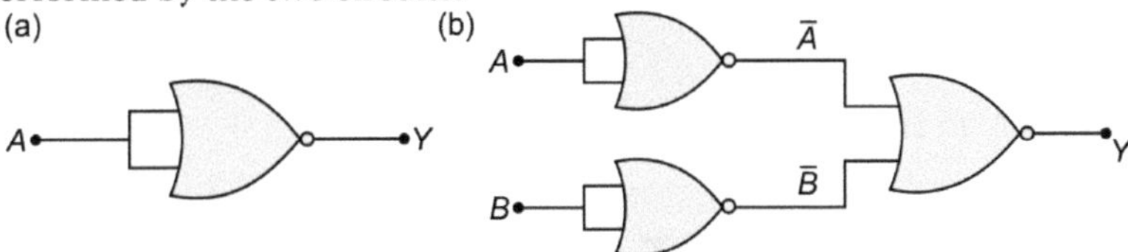

Solution   (a) Split the gate

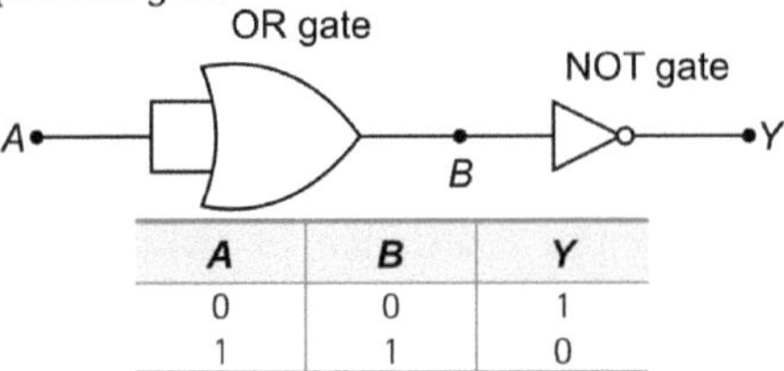

A	B	Y
0	0	1
1	1	0

B is the output of OR gate and input of NOT gate.

So, the gate resembles to NOT gate as A is input and Y is output.

A	Y
0	1
1	0

(b) Split the gate

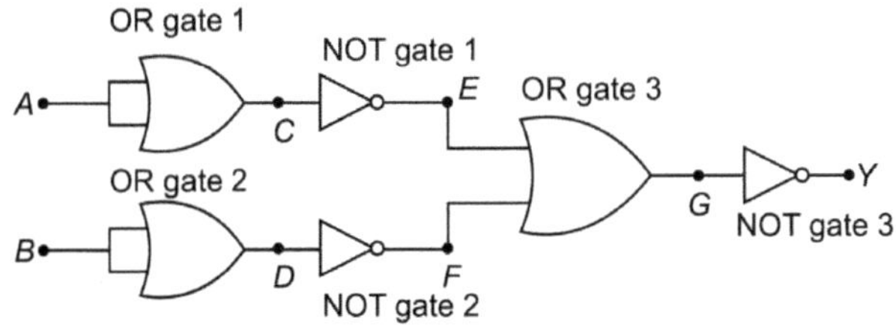

A	B	C	D	E	F	G	Y
0	0	0	0	1	1	1	0
1	0	1	0	0	1	1	0
0	1	0	1	1	0	1	0
1	1	1	1	0	0	0	1

C is the output of OR gate 1 and input of NOT gate 1
D is the output of OR gate 2 and input of NOT gate 2
E is the output of NOT gate 1; F is the output of NOT gate 2
G is the output of OR gate 3 and input of the NOT gate 3
The truth table resembles to AND gate as A and B inputs and Y is output.

A	B	Y
0	0	0
1	0	0
0	1	0
1	1	1

This operation is AND gate.

Selected NCERT Exemplar Problems

Question 1. Can the potential barrier across a *p-n* junction be measured by simply connecting a voltmeter across the junction.

Solution We cannot measure the potential barrier across a *p-n* junction by a voltmeter because the resistance of voltmeter is very high as compared to the junction resistance.

Question 2. Draw the output waveform across the resistor.

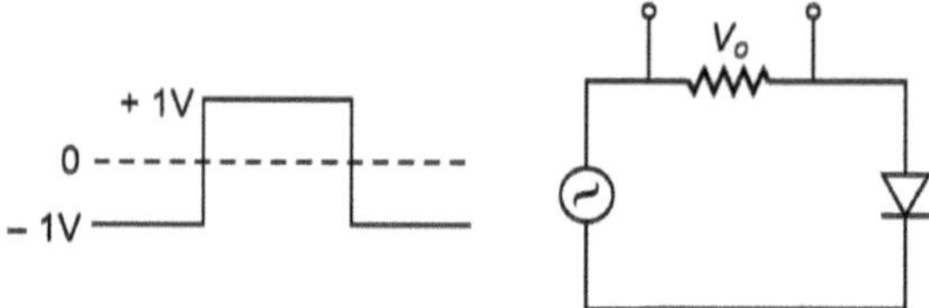

Solution As we know that the diode only works in forward biased, so the output is obtained only when positive input is given, so the output waveform is

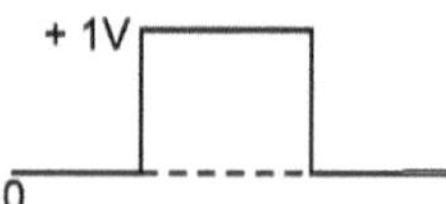

Question 3. Three photodiodes D_1, D_2 and D_3 are made of semiconductors having band-gaps of 2.5 eV, 2 eV and 3 eV respectively. Which one will be able to detect light of wavelength 6000 Å?

Solution Given, wavelength of light $\lambda = 6000\ \text{Å} = 6000 \times 10^{-10}$ m

Energy of the light photon

$$E = \frac{hc}{\lambda} = \frac{6.6 \times 10^{-34} \times 3 \times 10^{8}}{6000 \times 10^{-10} \times 1.6 \times 10^{-19}} \text{ eV} = 2.06 \text{ eV}$$

The incident radiation which is detected by the photodiode having energy should be greater than the band-gap. So, it is only valid for diode D_2. Then, diode D_2 will detect this radiation.

Question 4. If the resistance R_l is increased (see figure.), how will the readings of the ammeter and voltmeter change?

Solution As we know the formula for base current, $I_B = \dfrac{V_{BB} - V_{BE}}{R_l}$

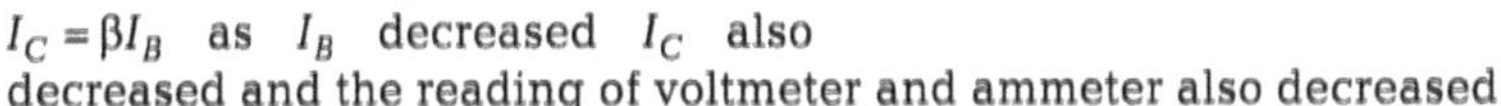

As R_l is increased, I_B is decreased. Now, the current in ammeter is collector current I_C.

$I_C = \beta I_B$ as I_B decreased I_C also decreased and the reading of voltmeter and ammeter also decreased.

Question 5. Two car garages have a common gate which needs to open automatically when a car enters either of the garages or cars enter in both. Devise a circuit that resembles this situation using diodes for this situation.

Solution As car enters in the gate, any one or both are opened. The device is shown.

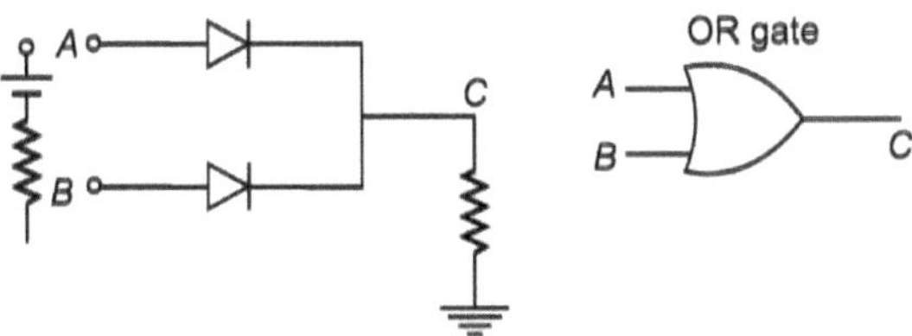

So, OR gate gives the desired output.

A	B	C
0	0	0
0	1	1
1	0	1
1	1	1

Question 6.　A zener of power rating 1 W is to be used as a voltage regulator. If zener has a breakdown of 5 V and it has to regulate voltage which fluctuated between 3 V and 7 V, what should be the value of R_s for safe operation Z (see figure) ?

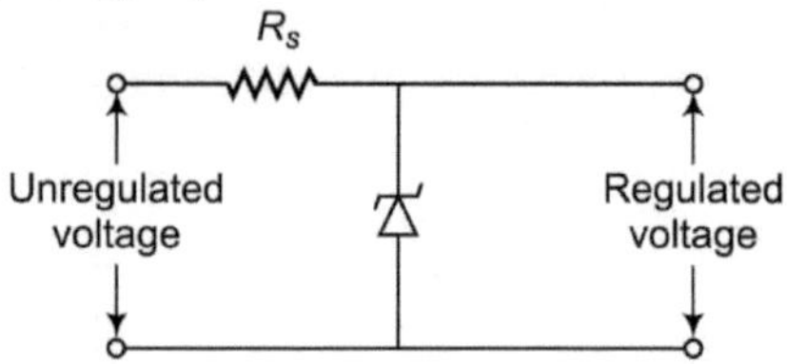

Solution　Given, power $= 1\,\text{W}$

Zener breakdown $V_z = 5\,\text{V}$

Minimum voltage $V_{\min} = 3\,\text{V}$

Maximum voltage $V_{\max} = 7\,\text{V}$

Current $I_{Z_{\max}} = \dfrac{P}{V_Z} = \dfrac{1}{5} = 0.2\,\text{A}$

The value of R_s for safe operation $R_s = \dfrac{V_{\max} - V_Z}{I_{Z_{\max}}} = \dfrac{7-5}{0.2} = \dfrac{2}{0.2} = 10\,\Omega$

Question 7.　If each diode in figure has a forward bias resistance of $25\,\Omega$ and infinite resistance in reverse bias. What will be the values of the currents I_1, I_2, I_3 and I_4?

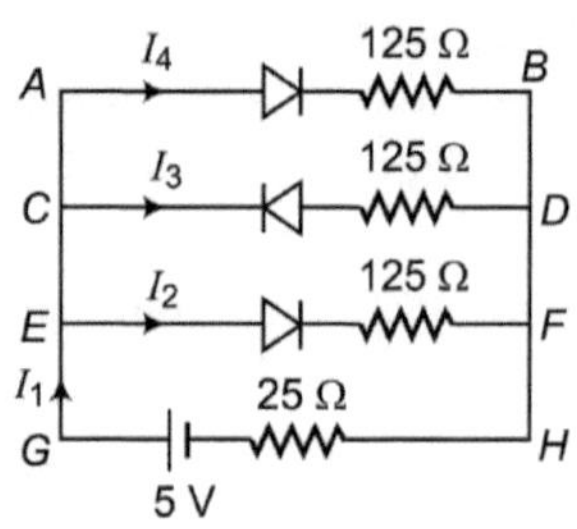

Solution　Given, forward biased resistance $= 25\,\Omega$

Reverse biased resistance $= \infty$

As the diode in branch CD is in reverse biased which having resistance infinite, so $I_3 = 0$

Resistance in branch $AB = 25 + 125 = 150\,\Omega$ say R_1

Resistance in branch $EF = 25 + 125 = 150\,\Omega$ say R_2

AB is parallel to EF.

So, resultant resistance $\dfrac{1}{R'} = \dfrac{1}{R_1} + \dfrac{1}{R_2} = \dfrac{1}{150} + \dfrac{1}{150} = \dfrac{2}{150}$

or $\qquad\qquad\qquad\qquad\qquad R' = 75\,\Omega$

Total resistance $R = R' + 25 = 75 + 25 = 100\,\Omega$

$$\text{Current } I_1 = \dfrac{V}{R} = \dfrac{5}{100} = 0.05\,\text{A}$$

$$I_1 = I_4 + I_2 + I_3 \qquad\qquad \text{(Here } I_3 = 0)$$

So, $\qquad I_1 = I_4 + I_2$

Here, the resistances R_1 and R_2 is same.

i.e., $\qquad I_4 = I_2$

$\therefore \qquad I_1 = 2I_2$

or $\qquad I_2 = \dfrac{I_1}{2} = \dfrac{0.05}{2} = 0.025$ A

and $\qquad I_4 = 0.025$ A

Thus, $I_1 = 0.05$ A, $I_2 = 0.025$ A, $I_3 = 0$ and $I_4 = 0.025$ A

Question 8. In the circuit shown in figure. when the input voltage of the base resistance is 10 V, V_{BE} is zero and V_{CE} is also zero. Find the values of I_B, I_C and β.

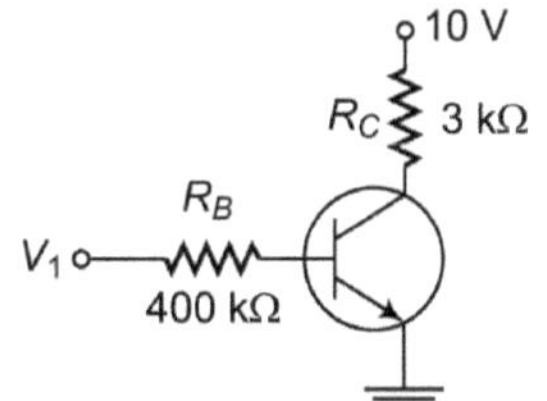

Solution Given, voltage across $R_B = 10$ V

Resistance $R_B = 400$ kΩ

$$V_{BE} = 0,\ V_{CE} = 0\ \ R_C = 3\ \text{k}\Omega$$

$$I_B = \frac{\text{Voltage across } R_B}{R_B} = \frac{10}{400 \times 10^3} = 25 \times 10^{-6}\ \text{A}$$

$$= 25\ \mu\text{A}$$

Voltage across $R_C = 10$ V

$$I_C = \frac{\text{Voltage across } R_C}{R_C} = \frac{10}{3 \times 10^3} = 3.33 \times 10^{-3}\ \text{A}$$

$$= 3.33\ \text{mA}$$

$$\beta = \frac{I_C}{I_B} = \frac{3.33 \times 10^{-3}}{25 \times 10^{-6}} = 1.33 \times 10^2$$

$$= 133$$

Question 9. Draw the output signals C_1 and C_2 in the given combination of gates.

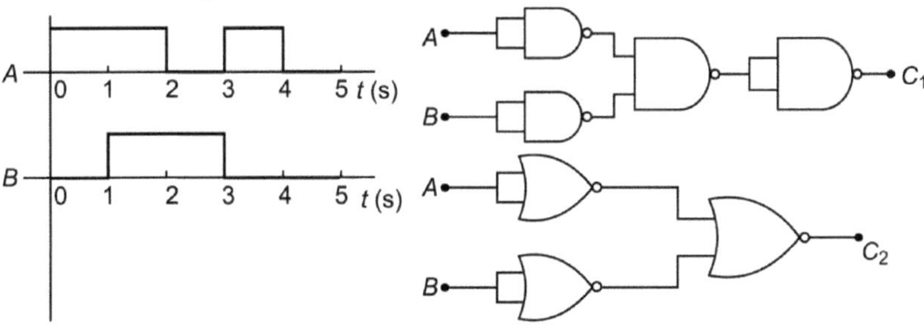

Solution First draw the truth table of C_1 and C_2.

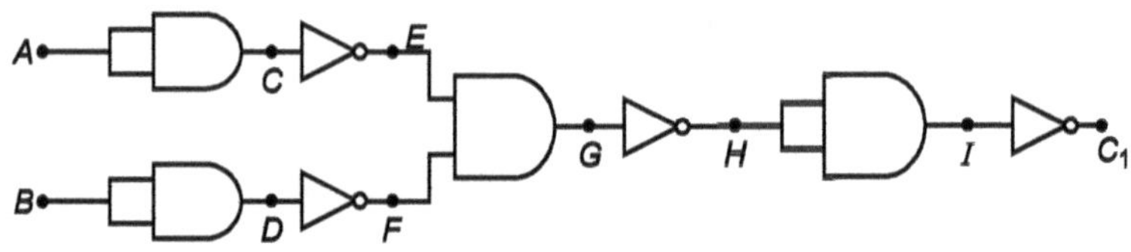

A	B	C	D	E	F	G	H	I	C_1
0	0	0	0	1	1	1	0	0	1
1	0	1	0	0	1	0	1	1	0
0	1	0	1	1	0	0	1	1	0
1	1	1	1	0	0	0	1	1	0

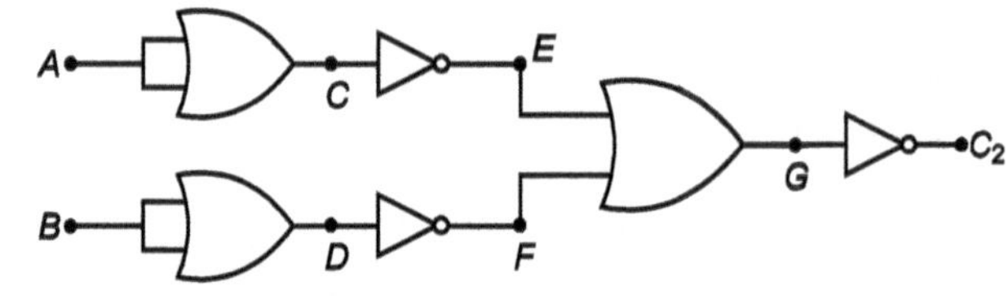

A	B	C	D	E	F	G	C_2
0	0	0	0	1	1	1	0
1	0	1	0	0	1	1	0
0	1	0	1	1	0	1	0
1	1	1	1	0	0	0	1

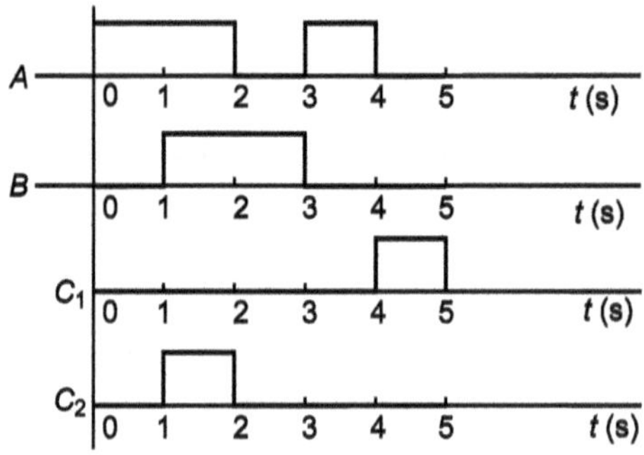

Question 10. Consider the circuit arrangement shown in figure for studying input and output characteristics of *n-p-n* transistor in CE configuration.

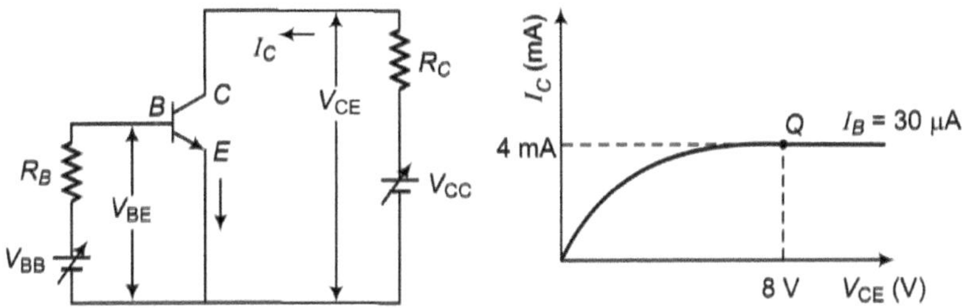

Select the values of R_B and R_C for a transistor whose $V_{BE} = 0.7$ V, so that the transistor is operating at point Q as shown in the characteristics (see figure).

Given that the input impedance of the transistor is very small and $V_{CC} = V_{BB} = 16$ V, also find the voltage gain and power gain of circuit making appropriate assumptions.

Solution Given, $V_{BE} = 0.7$ V, $V_{CC} = V_{BB} = 16$ V

$$V_{CE} = 8 \text{ V} \qquad \text{(from graph)}$$

$$I_C = 4 \text{ mA} = 4 \times 10^{-3} \text{ A}$$

$$I_B = 30 \ \mu\text{A} = 30 \times 10^{-6} \text{ A}$$

For the output characteristic at θ, $V_{CC} = I_C R_C + V_{CE}$

$$R_C = \frac{V_{CC} - V_{CE}}{I_C}$$

$$= \frac{16 - 8}{4 \times 10^{-3}} = \frac{8 \times 1000}{4} = 2 \text{ k}\Omega$$

Using the relation, $V_{BB} = I_B R_B + V_{BE}$

$$R_B = \frac{V_{BB} - V_{BE}}{I_B} = \frac{16 - 0.7}{30 \times 10^{-6}}$$

$$= 510 \times 10^3 \ \Omega = 510 \text{ k}\Omega$$

$$\beta = \frac{I_C}{I_B} = \frac{4 \times 10^{-3}}{30 \times 10^{-6}} = 133$$

$$\text{Voltage gain} = \beta \frac{R_C}{R_B} = \frac{133 \times 2 \times 10^3}{510 \times 10^3} = 0.52$$

Power gain = $\beta \times$ Voltage gain = $133 \times 0.52 = 69$

Question 11. For the transistor circuit shown in figure, evaluate V_E, R_B, R_E. Given $I_C = 1$ mA, $V_{CE} = 3$ V, $V_{BE} = 0.5$ V and $V_{CC} = 12$ V, $\beta = 100$.

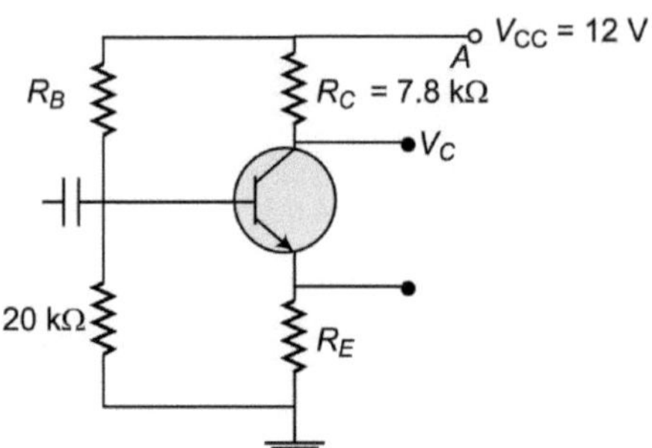

Solution $I_C \approx I_E$ (As base current is very small)

$$R_C = 7.8 \text{ k}\Omega$$

From the figure,

$$I_C(R_C + R_E) + V_{CE} = 12$$

$$(R_E + R_C) \times 1 \times 10^{-3} + 3 = 12$$

$$R_E + R_C = 9 \times 10^3 = 9 \text{ k}\Omega$$

$$R_E = 9 - 7.8 = 1.2 \text{ k}\Omega$$

$$V_E = I_E \times R_E$$

$$= 1 \times 10^{-3} \times 1.2 \times 10^3$$

$$= 1.2 \text{ V}$$

$$\text{Voltage } V_B = V_E + V_{BE} = 1.2 + 0.5 = 1.7 \text{ V}$$

$$\text{Current } I = \frac{V_B}{20 \times 10^3} = \frac{1.7}{20 \times 10^3} = 0.085 \text{ mA}$$

$$\text{Resistance } R_B = \frac{12 - 1.7}{\dfrac{I_C}{\beta} + 0.085} = \frac{10.3}{0.01 + 0.085} \qquad \text{(Given } \beta = 100)$$

$$= 108 \text{ k}\Omega$$

Question 12. In the circuit shown in figure, find the value of R_C.

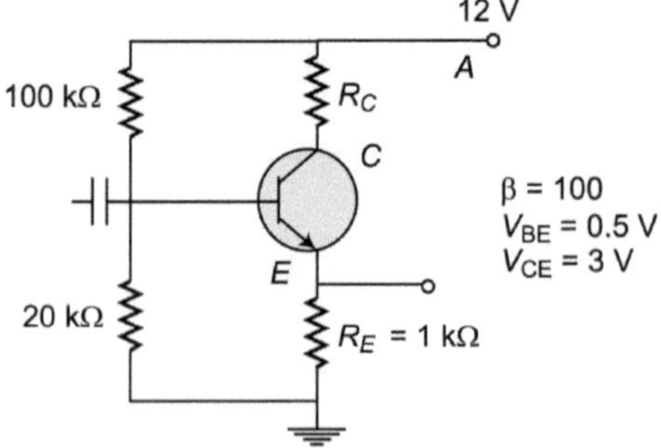

Solution

$$I_E = I_C + I_B \quad \text{and} \quad I_C = \beta I_B \qquad \qquad \text{...(i)}$$

$$I_C R_C + V_{CE} + I_E R_E = V_{CC} \qquad \qquad \text{...(ii)}$$

$$R I_B + V_{BE} + I_E R_E = V_{CC} \qquad \qquad \text{...(iii)}$$

$$\because \qquad I_E \approx I_C = \beta I_B$$

From Eq. (iii),

$$(R + \beta R_E) I_B = V_{CC} - V_{BE}$$

or

$$I_B = \frac{V_{CC} - V_{BE}}{R + \beta \cdot R_E}$$

$$= \frac{12 - 0.5}{80 + 1.2 \times 100} = \frac{11.5}{200} \text{ mA}$$

From Eq. (ii),

$$(R_C + R_E) = \frac{V_{CC} - V_{BE}}{I_C} = \frac{V_{CC} - V_{CE}}{\beta I_B} \qquad \qquad (\because I_C = \beta I_B)$$

$$(R_C + R_E) = \frac{2}{11.5}(12 - 3) \text{ k}\Omega = 1.56 \text{ k}\Omega$$

$$R_C + R_E = 1.56$$

$$R_C = 1.56 - 1 = 0.56 \text{ k}\Omega$$

Chapter **15**

Communication System

Important Results

1. **Marconi antenna** It is grounded and its length = $\lambda/4$, where λ is a wavelength of waves transmitted. It is called quarter wave antenna.

2. **Hertz antenna** It is not grounded and its length = $\lambda/2$. It is also called half wave antenna.

3. $\lambda = \dfrac{c}{\nu}$, where ν is the frequency of waves.

4. If an antenna radiates electromagnetic waves from a height h_T, then the range d_T is given by $\sqrt{2Rh_T}$, where R is the radius of earth.

5. Low frequencies cannot be transmitted to long distances. Therefore, they are superimposed on a high frequency carries signal by a process called modulation.

6. In modulation, some characteristic of the carrier signal like amplitude, frequency or phase varies in accordance with the modulating or message signal. They are called Amplitude Modulated (AM), Frequency Modulated (FM) or Phase Modulated (PM) waves.

7. Amplitude modulated signal contains frequencies $(\omega_c - \omega_m)$, ω_c and $(\omega_c + \omega_m)$.

8. Pulse modulation could be classified as, Pulse Amplitude Modulation (PAM), Pulse Duration Modulation (PDM) or Pulse Width Modulation (PWM) and Pulse Position Modulation (PPM).

9. The electromagnetic waves of frequency ranging from a few kilo hertz to about a few hundred mega hertz are called radio waves.

   The radiowaves emitted from a transmitter antenna can reach the receiver antenna by any of the following modes of propagation :
   (a) Ground wave or surface wave propagation
   (b) Sky wave propagation
   (c) Space wave propagation
   (d) Satellite communication

10. The radio waves are the electromagnetic waves of frequency ranging from 500 kHz to about 1000 MHz.

11. The ground wave propagation is useful for low frequency signal waves (530 kHz to 1710 kHz).

12. In skywave propagation, we use radio waves of frequency range 1710 kHz to 40 MHz.

13. The space waves are the radiowaves of frequency range from 54 MHz to 4.2 GHz.

Exercises

Question 1. Which of the following frequencies will be suitable for beyond the horizon communication using sky waves?

  (a) 10 kHz   (b) 10 MHz

  (c) 1 GHz   (d) 1000 GHz

Solution (b) 10 kHz frequencies cannot be radiated due to large antenna size, 1 GHz and 1000 GHz will be penetrated. So, option (b) is correct.

Question 2. Frequencies in the UHF range normally propagate by means of

  (a) ground waves   (b) sky waves

  (c) surface waves   (d) space waves

Solution (d) The frequencies in UHF range normally propagate by means of space waves. The high frequency space does not bend with ground but are ideal for frequency modulation.

Question 3. Digital signals

  (i) do not provide a continuous set of values

  (ii) represent values as discrete steps

  (iii) can utilize binary system and

  (iv) can utilize decimal as well as binary systems

Which of the above statements are true?

  (a) (i) and (ii)

  (b) (ii) and (iii)

  (c) (i), (ii) and (iii)

  (d) All of (i), (ii), (iii) and (iv)

Solution (c) A digital signal is a discontinuous function of time in contrast to an analog signal. The digital signals can be stored as digital data and cannot be transmitted along the telephone lines. Digital signal cannot utilize decimal signals.

Question 4. Is it necessary for a transmitting antenna to be at the same height as that of the receiving antenna for line of sight communication? A TV transmitting antenna is 81 m tall. How much service area can it cover, if the receiving antenna is at the ground level?

Solution   Given, height of antenna $h = 81$ m

$$\text{Radius of earth } R = 6.4 \times 10^6 \text{ m}$$

No, it is not necessary for line of sight communication, the two antennas may not be at the same height.

$$\text{Area} = \pi d^2$$

$\because$ Range $d = \sqrt{2hR}$

$$\therefore \quad \text{Service Area} = \pi \times 2hR = \frac{22}{7} \times 2 \times 81 \times 6.4 \times 10^6$$

$$= 3258.5 \times 10^6 \text{ m}^2 = 3258.5 \text{ km}^2$$

Question 5. A carrier wave of peak voltage 12 V is used to transmit a message signal. What should be the peak voltage of the modulating signal in order to have a modulation index of 75%?

Solution   Given, peak voltage $V_0 = 12$ V

$$\text{Modulation index } \mu = 75\% = \frac{75}{100}$$

We know that

$$\text{Modulation index } (\mu) = \frac{\text{Peak voltage of modulating signal}(V_m)}{\text{Peak voltage } (V_0)}$$

So, peak voltage of modulating signal,

$$V_m = \mu \times \text{Peak voltage}$$

$$= \frac{75}{100} \times 12 = 9 \text{ V}$$

Question 6. A modulating signal is a square wave as shown in figure. The carrier wave is given by $c(t) = 2\sin(8\pi t)$ volt.

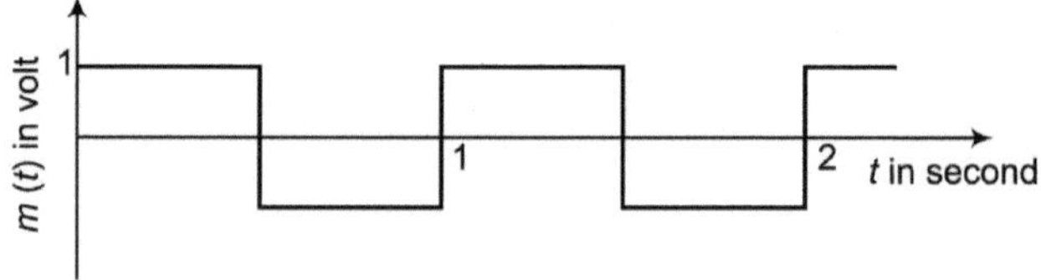

(a) Sketch the amplitude modulated waveform.
(b) What is the modulation index?

Solution   Given, the equation of carrier wave

$$c(t) = 2\sin(8\pi t) \qquad \qquad \ldots(i)$$

(a) According to the diagram,

Amplitude of modulating signal
$$A_m = 1\,\text{V}$$

Amplitude of carrier wave $A_c = 2$ V [By Eq. (i)]

$$T_m = 1\,\text{s} \qquad \text{(From diagram)}$$

$$\omega_m = \frac{2\pi}{T_m} = \frac{2\pi}{1} = 2\pi\,\text{rad/s} \qquad \ldots(\text{ii})$$

From Eq. (i),

$$c(t) = 2\sin 8\pi t$$

$$= A_c \sin \omega_c t$$

So, $\qquad \omega_c = 8\pi$

From Eq. (ii),

So, $\qquad \omega_c = 4\omega_m$

Amplitude of modulated wave $A = A_m + A_c = 2 + 1 = 3$ V

The sketch of the amplitude modulated waveform is shown below.

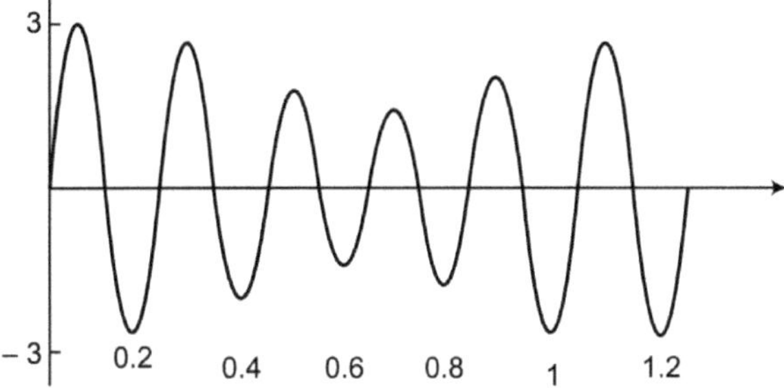

(b) Modulation index $\mu = \dfrac{A_m}{A_c} = \dfrac{1}{2} = 0.5$

Question 7. For an amplitude modulated wave, the maximum amplitude is found to be **10 V** while the minimum amplitude is found to be **2 V**. Determine the modulation index μ.

What would be the value of μ, if the minimum amplitude is 0 V?

Solution Given, maximum amplitude $A_{\max} = 10$ V

Minimum amplitude $A_{\min} = 2$ V

Let A_c and A_m be the amplitudes of carrier wave and signal wave.

$\therefore \qquad A_{\max} = A_c + A_m = 10 \qquad \ldots(\text{i})$

and $\qquad A_{\min} = A_c - A_m = 2 \qquad \ldots(\text{ii})$

Adding the Eqs. (i) and (ii), we get

$$2A_c = 12$$

or $\qquad A_c = 6$ V

and $\qquad A_m = 10 - 6 = 4$ V

Modulation index $\mu = \dfrac{A_m}{A_c} = \dfrac{4}{6} = \dfrac{2}{3}$

When the minimum amplitude is zero, then $i.e., A_{min} = 0$

$$A_c + A_m = 10 \qquad \qquad \ldots\text{(iii)}$$
$$A_c - A_m = 0 \qquad \qquad \ldots\text{(iv)}$$

By solving Eqs. (iii) and (iv), we get

$$2A_m = 10$$

or
$$A_m = 5$$

and
$$A_c = 5$$

Modulation index $\mu = \dfrac{A_m}{A_c} = \dfrac{5}{5} = 1$

Question 8. Due to economic reasons, only the upper sideband of an AM wave is transmitted but at the receiving station, there is a facility for generating the carrier. Show that if a device is available which can multiply two signals, then it is possible to recover the modulating signal at the receiver station.

Solution Let ω_c be the angular frequency of carrier waves and ω_m be the angular frequency of signal waves.

Let the signal received at the receiving station be

$$e = E_1 \cos(\omega_c + \omega_m)t$$

Let the instantaneous voltage of carrier wave

$$e_c = E_c \cos \omega_c t$$

is available at receiving station.

Multiplying these two signals, we get

$$e \times e_c = E_1 E_c \cos \omega_c t \cos(\omega_c + \omega_m)t$$

$$E = \frac{E_1 E_c}{2} \cdot 2 \cos \omega_c t \cdot \cos(\omega_c + \omega_m)t \qquad (\text{Let } e \times e_c = E)$$

$$= \frac{E_1 E_c}{2}[\cos(\omega_c + \omega_c + \omega_m)t + \cos(\omega_c + \omega_m - \omega_c)t]$$

$$\left[\because 2\cos A \cos B = \cos(A+B) + \cos(A-B)\right]$$

$$= \frac{E_1 E_c}{2}[\cos(2\omega_c + \omega_m)t + \cos \omega_m t]$$

Now, at the receiving end as the signal passes through filter, it will pass the high frequency $(2\omega_c + \omega_m)$ but obstruct the frequency ω_m. So, we can record the modulating signal $\dfrac{E_1 E_c}{2} \cos \omega_m t$

which is a signal of angular frequency ω_m .

Selected NCERT Exemplar Problems

Question 1. Two waves A and B of frequencies 2 MHz and 3 MHz, respectively are beamed in the same direction for communication *via* sky wave. Which one of these is likely to travel longer distance in the ionosphere before suffering total internal reflection?

Solution As the frequency of wave B is more than wave A, it means the refractive index of wave B is more than refractive index of wave A (as refractive index increases with frequency increases). For higher frequency waves (*i.e.*, higher refractive index) the angle of refraction is less *i.e.*, bending is less. So, waves B travel longer distance in the ionosphere before suffering total internal reflection.

Question 2. The maximum amplitude of an AM wave is found to be 15 V while its minimum amplitude is found to be 3 V. What is the modulation index?

Solution Let A_c and A_m be the amplitudes of carrier wave and modulating wave respectively. So,

Maximum amplitude $\qquad A_{\max} = A_c + A_m = 15\,V$ $\qquad\qquad$ ...(i)

Minimum amplitude $\qquad A_{\min} = A_c - A_m = 3\,V$ $\qquad\qquad$ ...(ii)

Adding Eqs. (i) and (ii), we get

$$2A_c = 18$$

or $$A_c = 9\,V$$

and $$A_m = 15 - 9 = 6\,V$$

Modulating index of wave $\mu = \dfrac{A_m}{A_c} = \dfrac{6}{9} = \dfrac{2}{3}$

Question 3. Compute the LC product of a tuned amplifier circuit required to generate a carrier wave of 1 MHz for amplitude modulation?

Solution Given, the frequency of carrier wave is 1 MHz.
Formula for the frequency of tuned amplifier,

$$\frac{1}{2\pi\sqrt{LC}} = 1\,\text{MHz}$$

$$\sqrt{LC} = \frac{1}{2\pi \times 10^6}$$

$$LC = \frac{1}{(2\pi \times 10^6)^2} = 2.54 \times 10^{-14}\,s$$

Thus, the product of LC is $2.54 \times 10^{-14}\,s$.

Question 4. Why is an AM signal likely to be more noisy than a FM signal upon transmission through a channel?

Solution   In case of AM, the instantaneous voltage of carrier waves is varied by the modulating wave voltage. So, during the transmission, noise signals can also be added and receiver assumes noise a part of the modulating signal. In case of FM, the frequency of carrier waves is changed as the change in the instantaneous voltage of modulating waves. This can be done by mixing and not while the signal is transmitting in channel. So, noise does not affect FM signal.

Question 5.   Figure shows a communication system. What is the output power when input signal is of **1.01 mW**? (Gain in dB $= 10 \log_{10} \dfrac{P_o}{P_i}$).

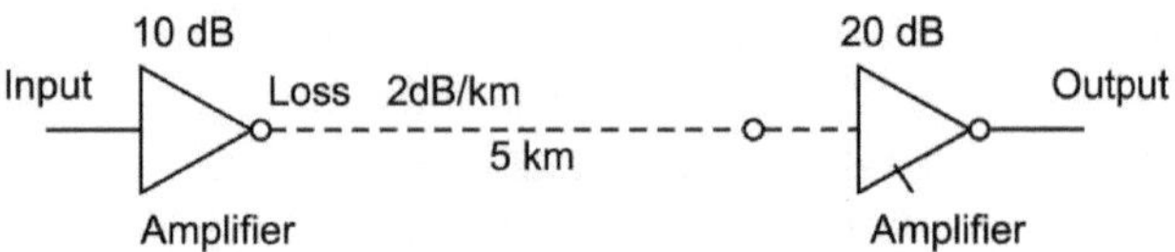

Solution   The distance travelled by the signal is 5 km.

Loss suffered in path of transmission $= 2$ dB/km

So, total loss suffered in 5 km $= -2 \times 5 = -10$ dB

Total amplifier gain $= 10$ dB $+ 20$ dB $= 30$ dB

Overall gain in signal $= 30 - 10 = 20$ dB

According to the question, gain in dB $= 10 \log_{10} \dfrac{P_o}{P_i}$

$$\therefore \qquad 20 = 10 \log_{10} \frac{P_o}{P_i} \quad \text{or} \quad \log_{10} \frac{P_o}{P_i} = 2$$

Here $P_i = 1.01$ mW and P_o is the output power.

$$\therefore \qquad \frac{P_o}{P_i} = 10^2 = 100 \Rightarrow P_o = P_i \times 100 = 1.01 \times 100$$

or $\qquad P_o = 101\,\text{mW}$

Thus, the output power is 101 mW.

Question 6.   A TV transmission tower antenna is at a height of **20 m**. How much service area can it cover, if the receiving antenna is (a) at ground level, (b) at a height of **25 m**? Calculate the percentage increase in area covered in case (b) relative to case (a).

Solution   Given, height of antenna $h = 20$ m

Radius of earth $= 6.4 \times 10^6$ m

At the ground level—

(a) Range $= \sqrt{2hR} = \sqrt{2 \times 20 \times 6.4 \times 10^6} = 16000$ m $= 16$ km

   Area covered $A = \pi \,(\text{range})^2 = 3.14 \times 16 \times 16 = 803.84$ km^2

(b) At a height of $H = 25$ m from ground level

   Range $= \sqrt{2hR} + \sqrt{2HR}$

$$= \sqrt{2 \times 20 \times 6.4 \times 10^6} + \sqrt{2 \times 25 \times 6.4 \times 10^6}$$

$$= 16 \times 10^3 + 17.9 \times 10^3 = 33.9 \times 10^3 \text{ m} = 33.9 \text{ km}$$

$$\text{Area covered} = \pi \, (\text{Range})^2 = 3.14 \times 33.9 \times 33.9 = 3608.52 \text{ km}^2$$

$$\text{Percentage increase in area} = \frac{\text{Difference in area}}{\text{Initial area}} \times 100$$

$$= \frac{(3608.52 - 803.84)}{803.84} \times 100$$

$$= 348.9\%$$

Thus, the percentage increase in area covered is 348.9%

Question 7. The maximum frequency for reflection of sky waves from a certain layer of the ionosphere is found to be $f_{max} = 9 \, (N_{max})^{1/2}$, where N_{max} is the maximum electron density at that layer of the ionosphere. On a certain day, it is observed that signals of frequencies higher than 5 MHz are not received by reflection from the F_1 layer of the ionosphere while signals of frequencies higher than 8 MHz are not received by reflection from the F_2 layer of the ionosphere. Estimate the maximum electron densitities of the F_1 and F_2 layers on that day.

Solution The maximum frequency for reflection of sky waves

$$f_{max} = 9 \, (N_{max})^{1/2}$$

where, N_{max} is a maximum electron density.

For F_1 layer, $\qquad\qquad\qquad f_{max} = 5 \text{ MHz}$

So, $\qquad\qquad\qquad\qquad 5 \times 10^6 = 9 \, (N_{max})^{1/2}$

$$\text{Maximum electron density } N_{max} = \left(\frac{5}{9} \times 10^6\right)^2 = 3.086 \times 10^{11} / \text{m}^3$$

For F_2 layer, $\qquad\qquad\qquad f_{max} = 8 \text{ MHz}$

So, $\qquad\qquad\qquad\qquad 8 \times 10^6 = 9 \, (N_{max})^{1/2}$

$$\text{Maximum electron density } N_{max} = \left(\frac{8 \times 10^6}{9}\right)^2 = 7.9 \times 10^{11} / \text{m}^3$$

Question 8. (a) The intensity of a light pulse travelling along a communication channel decreases exponentially with distance x according to the relation, $I = I_0 e^{-\alpha x}$, where I_0 is the intensity at $x = 0$ and α is the attenuation constant.

Show that the intensity reduces by 75 % after a distance of $\left(\dfrac{\ln 4}{\alpha}\right)$.

(b) Attenuation of a signal can be expressed in decibel (dB) according to the relation $\mathrm{dB} = 10 \log_{10}\left(\dfrac{I}{I_0}\right)$. What is the attenuation in dB/km for an optical fibre in which the intensity falls by 50 % over a distance of 50 km?

Solution　(a) Given, the intensity of a light pulse $I = I_0 e^{-\alpha x}$

where, I_0 is the intensity at $x = 0$ and α is constant.

According to the question, $I = 25\%$ of $I_0 = \dfrac{25}{100} \cdot I_0 = \dfrac{I_0}{4}$

Using the formula mentioned in the question.

$$I = I_0 e^{-\alpha x}$$

$$\frac{I_0}{4} = I_0 e^{-\alpha x}$$

or

$$\frac{1}{4} = e^{-\alpha x}$$

Taking log on both sides, we get

$$\ln 1 - \ln 4 = -\alpha x \ln e \qquad\qquad (\because \ln e = 1)$$

$$-\ln 4 = -\alpha x$$

$$x = \frac{\ln 4}{\alpha}$$

Therefore, at distance $x = \dfrac{\ln 4}{\alpha}$, the intensity is reduced to 75% of initial intensity.

(b) Let α be the attenuation in dB/km. If x is the distance travelled by signal, then $10 \log_{10}\left(\dfrac{I}{I_0}\right) = -\alpha x$ 　　　　　　...(i)

where, I_0 is the intensity initially.

According to the question, $I = 50\%$ of $I_0 = \dfrac{I_0}{2}$

and 　　　　　　　　　　　　　　$x = 50 \text{ km}$

Putting the value of x in Eq. (i), we get

$$10 \log_{10} \frac{I_0}{2 I_0} = -\alpha \times 50$$

$$10 \left[\log 1 - \log 2\right] = -50\alpha$$

$$\frac{10 \times 0.3010}{50} = \alpha$$

$\therefore$ The attenuation for an optical fibre

$$\alpha = 0.0602 \text{ dB/km}$$

Question 9. A 50 MHz sky wave takes 4.04 ms to reach a receiver *via* retransmission from a satellite 600 km above earth's surface. Assuming retransmission time by satellite negligible, find the distance between source and receiver. If communication between the two was to be done by Line of Sight (LOS) method, what should size and placement of receiving and transmitting antennas be?

Solution Let the receiver is at point A and source is at B.

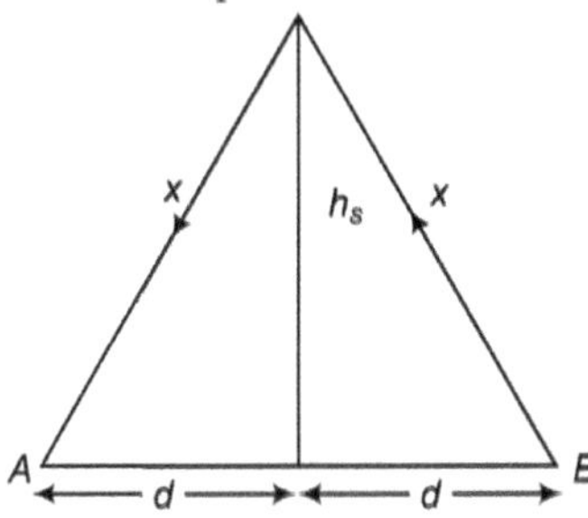

Velocity of waves $= 3 \times 10^8$ m/s

Time to reach a receiver $= 4.04$ ms $= 4.04 \times 10^{-3}$ s

Let the height of satellite is $h_s = 600$ km

Radius of earth $= 6400$ km

Size of transmitting antenna $= h_T$

We know that

$$\frac{\text{Distance travelled by wave}}{\text{Time}} = \text{Velocity of waves}$$

$$\frac{2x}{4.04 \times 10^{-3}} = 3 \times 10^8$$

or $$x = \frac{3 \times 10^8 \times 4.04 \times 10^{-3}}{2} = 6.06 \times 10^5 = 606 \text{ km}$$

Using Phythagoras theorem,

$$d^2 = x^2 - h_s^2 = (606)^2 - (600)^2 = 7236$$

or $$d = 85.06 \text{ km}$$

So, the distance between source and receiver $= 2d$

$$= 2 \times 85.06 = 170 \text{ km}$$

The maximum distance covered on ground from the transmitter by emitted EM waves $d = \sqrt{2Rh_T}$

or $$\frac{d^2}{2R} = h_T$$

or size of antenna $$h_T = \frac{7236}{2 \times 6400} = 0.565 \text{ km} = 565 \text{ m}$$

Question 10. An amplitude modulated wave is as shown in figure. Calculate (a) the percentage modulation, (b) peak carrier voltage and (c) peak value of information voltage.

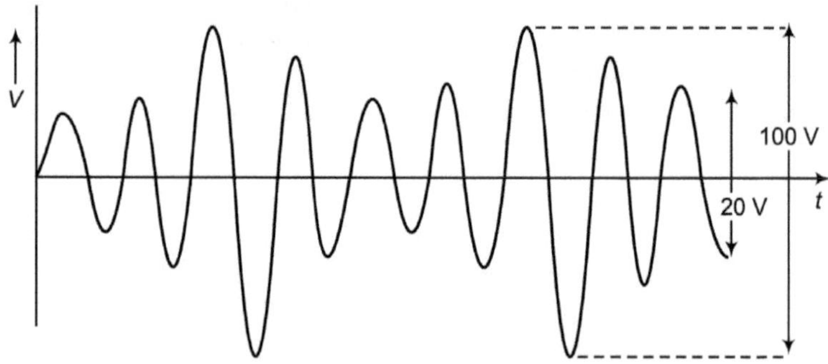

Solution From the diagram,

$$\text{Maximum voltage } V_{max} = \frac{100}{2} = 50 \text{ V}$$

$$\text{Minimum voltage } V_{min} = \frac{20}{2} = 10 \text{ V}$$

(a) Percentage modulation,

$$\mu = \frac{V_{max} - V_{min}}{V_{max} + V_{min}} \times 100$$

$$= \frac{50 - 10}{50 + 10} \times 100$$

$$= \frac{40}{60} \times 100 = 66.67\%$$

(b) Peak carrier voltage,

$$V_c = \frac{V_{max} + V_{min}}{2} = \frac{50 + 10}{2} = 30 \text{ V}$$

(c) Peak value of information voltage,

$$V_m = \mu V_c = \frac{66.67}{100} \times 30 = 20 \text{ V}$$

Printed by Libri Plureos GmbH in Hamburg, Germany